SQL Server 6.5 SECRETS®

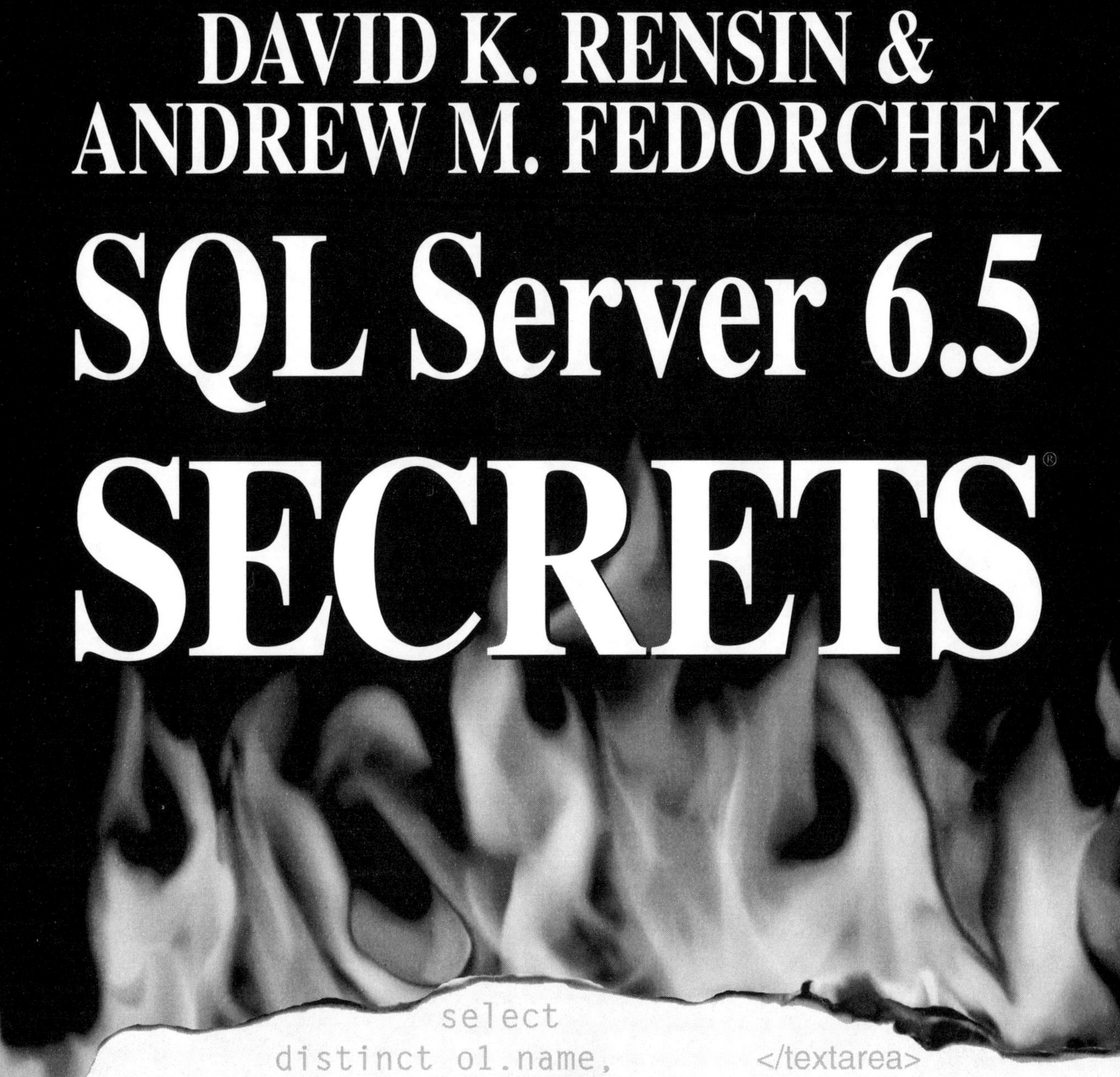

A Division of IDG Books Worldwide, Inc., An International Data Group Company

Foster City, CA • Chicago, IL • Indianapolis, IN • Southlake, TX

THE IDG BOOKS *SECRETS*® ADVANTAGE

SQL Server 6.5 SECRETS® is part of the SECRETS series of books brought to you by IDG Books Worldwide. We designed the SECRETS series because we know how much you appreciate insightful and comprehensive works from computer experts. Authorities in their respective areas, the authors of the SECRETS books have been selected for their ability to enrich your daily computing tasks.

The formula for a book in the SECRETS series is simple: Give an expert a forum to pass on his or her knowledge to readers. A SECRETS author, rather than the publishing company, directs the organization, pace, and treatment of the subject matter. SECRETS authors maintain close contact with end-users through feedback from articles, training sessions, e-mail exchanges, user group participation, and consulting work. Because our authors know the realities of daily computer use and are directly tied to the reader, our SECRETS books have a strategic advantage.

SECRETS authors have the experience to approach a topic in the most efficient manner, and we know that you, the reader, will benefit from a "one-on-one" relationship with the author. Our research shows that readers make computer book purchases because they want expert advice on a product. Readers want to benefit from the author's experience, so the author's voice is always present in a SECRETS series book.

In addition, the author is free to include or recommend useful software in a SECRETS book. The software that accompanies a SECRETS book is not intended to be casual filler but is linked to the content, theme, or procedures of the book. We know that you will benefit from the included software.

You will find what you need in this book whether you read it from cover to cover, section by section, or simply one topic at a time. As a computer user, you deserve a comprehensive resource of answers. We at IDG Books Worldwide are proud to deliver that resource with *SQL Server 6.5 SECRETS*.

Brenda McLaughlin
Senior Vice President and Group Publisher
Internet: YouTellUs@idgbooks.com

SQL Server 6.5 SECRETS®
Published by
IDG Books Worldwide, Inc.
An International Data Group Company
919 E. Hillsdale Blvd., Suite 400
Foster City, CA 94404
http://www.idgbooks.com (IDG Books Worldwide Web Site)

Library of Congress Catalog Card No.: 96-76833
ISBN: 1-56884-698-3

Printed in the United States of America
10 9 8 7 6 5 4 3 2
1B/SR/RR/ZW/FC-IN

Distributed in the United States by IDG Books Worldwide, Inc.

Distributed by Macmillan Canada for Canada; by Contemporanea de Ediciones for Venezuela; by Distribuidora Cuspide for Argentina; by CITEC for Brazil; by Ediciones ZETA S.C.R. Ltda. for Peru; by Editorial Limusa SA for Mexico; by Transworld Publishers Limited in the United Kingdom and Europe; by Academic Bookshop for Egypt; by Levant Distributors S.A.R.L. for Lebanon; by Al Jassim for Saudi Arabia; by Simron Pty. Ltd. for South Africa; by Pustak Mahal for India; by The Computer Bookshop for India; by Toppan Company Ltd. for Japan; by Addison Wesley Publishing Company for Korea; by Longman Singapore Publishers Ltd. for Singapore, Malaysia, Thailand, and Indonesia; by Unalis Corporation for Taiwan; by WS Computer Publishing Company, Inc. for the Philippines; by WoodsLane Pty. Ltd. for Australia; by WoodsLane Enterprises Ltd. for New Zealand. Authorized Sales Agent: Anthony Rudkin Associates for the Middle East and North Africa.

For general information on IDG Books Worldwide's books in the U.S., please call our Consumer Customer Service department at 800-762-2974. For reseller information, including discounts and premium sales, please call our Reseller Customer Service department at 800-434-3422.

For information on where to purchase IDG Books Worldwide's books outside the U.S., please contact our International Sales department at 415-655-3172 or fax 415-655-3295.

For information on foreign language translations, please contact our Foreign & Subsidiary Rights department at 415-655-3021 or fax 415-655-3281.

For sales inquiries and special prices for bulk quantities, please contact our Sales department at 415-655-3200 or write to the address above.

For information on using IDG Books Worldwide's books in the classroom or for ordering examination copies, please contact our Educational Sales department at 800-434-2086 or fax 817-251-8174.

For press review copies, author interviews, or other publicity information, please contact our Public Relations department at 415-655-3000 or fax 415-655-3299.

ABOUT IDG BOOKS WORLDWIDE

Welcome to the world of IDG Books Worldwide.

IDG Books Worldwide, Inc., is a subsidiary of International Data Group, the world's largest publisher of computer-related information and the leading global provider of information services on information technology. IDG was founded more than 25 years ago and now employs more than 8,500 people worldwide. IDG publishes more than 275 computer publications in over 75 countries (see listing below). More than 60 million people read one or more IDG publications each month.

Launched in 1990, IDG Books Worldwide is today the #1 publisher of best-selling computer books in the United States. We are proud to have received eight awards from the Computer Press Association in recognition of editorial excellence and three from *Computer Currents*' First Annual Readers' Choice Awards. Our best-selling *...For Dummies®* series has more than 30 million copies in print with translations in 30 languages. IDG Books Worldwide, through a joint venture with IDG's Hi-Tech Beijing, became the first U.S. publisher to publish a computer book in the People's Republic of China. In record time, IDG Books Worldwide has become the first choice for millions of readers around the world who want to learn how to better manage their businesses.

Our mission is simple: Every one of our books is designed to bring extra value and skill-building instructions to the reader. Our books are written by experts who understand and care about our readers. The knowledge base of our editorial staff comes from years of experience in publishing, education, and journalism — experience we use to produce books for the '90s. In short, we care about books, so we attract the best people. We devote special attention to details such as audience, interior design, use of icons, and illustrations. And because we use an efficient process of authoring, editing, and desktop publishing our books electronically, we can spend more time ensuring superior content and spend less time on the technicalities of making books.

You can count on our commitment to deliver high-quality books at competitive prices on topics you want to read about. At IDG Books Worldwide, we continue in the IDG tradition of delivering quality for more than 25 years. You'll find no better book on a subject than one from IDG Books Worldwide.

John Kilcullen
President and CEO
IDG Books Worldwide, Inc.

Eighth Annual Computer Press Awards 1992

Ninth Annual Computer Press Awards 1993

Tenth Annual Computer Press Awards 1994

Eleventh Annual Computer Press Awards 1995

IDG Books Worldwide, Inc., is a subsidiary of International Data Group, the world's largest publisher of computer-related information and the leading global provider of information services on information technology. International Data Group publishes over 275 computer publications in over 75 countries. Sixty million people read one or more International Data Group publications each month. International Data Group's publications include: **ARGENTINA:** Buyer's Guide, Computerworld Argentina, PC World Argentina; **AUSTRALIA:** Australian Macworld, Australian PC World, Australian Reseller News, Computerworld, IT Casebook, Network World, Publish, Webmaster; **AUSTRIA:** Computerwelt Osterreich, Networks Austria, PC Tip Austria; **BANGLADESH:** PC World Bangladesh; **BELARUS:** PC World Belarus; **BELGIUM:** Data News; **BRAZIL:** Annuário de Informática, Computerworld, Connections, Macworld, PC Player, PC World, Publish, Reseller News, Supergamepower; **BULGARIA:** Computerworld Bulgaria, Network World Bulgaria, PC & MacWorld Bulgaria; **CANADA:** CIO Canada, Client/Server World, ComputerWorld Canada, InfoWorld Canada, NetworkWorld Canada, WebWorld; **CHILE:** Computerworld Chile, PC World Chile; **COLOMBIA:** Computerworld Colombia, PC World Colombia; **COSTA RICA:** PC World Centro America; **THE CZECH AND SLOVAK REPUBLICS:** Computerworld Czechoslovakia, Macworld Czech Republic, PC World Czechoslovakia; **DENMARK:** Communications World Danmark, Computerworld Danmark, Macworld Danmark, PC World Danmark, Techworld Denmark; **DOMINICAN REPUBLIC:** PC World Republica Dominicana; **ECUADOR:** PC World Ecuador; **EGYPT:** Computerworld Middle East, PC World Middle East; **EL SALVADOR:** PC World Centro America; **FINLAND:** MikroPC, Tietoverkko, Tietoviikko; **FRANCE:** Distributique, Hebdo, Info PC, Le Monde Informatique, Macworld, Reseaux & Telecoms, WebMaster France; **GERMANY:** Computer Partner, Computerwoche, Computerwoche Extra, Computerwoche FOCUS, Global Online, Macwelt, PC Welt; **GREECE:** Amiga Computing, GamePro Greece, Multimedia World; **GUATEMALA:** PC World Centro America; **HONDURAS:** PC World Centro America; **HONG KONG:** Computerworld Hong Kong, PC World Hong Kong, Publish in Asia; **HUNGARY:** ABCD CD-ROM, Computerworld Szamitastechnika, Internetto online Magazine, PC World Hungary, PC-X Magazin Hungary; **ICELAND:** Tolvuheimur PC World Island; **INDIA:** Information Communications World, Information Systems Computerworld, PC World India, Publish in Asia; **INDONESIA:** InfoKomputer PC World, Komputek Computerworld, Publish in Asia; **IRELAND:** ComputerScope, PC Live!; **ISRAEL:** Macworld Israel, People & Computers/Computerworld; **ITALY:** Computerworld Italia, Macworld Italia, Networking Italia, PC World Italia; **JAPAN:** DTP World, Macworld Japan, Nikkei Personal Computing, OS/2 World Japan, SunWorld Japan, Windows NT World, Windows World Japan; **KENYA:** PC World East African; **KOREA:** Hi-Tech Information, Macworld Korea, PC World Korea; **MACEDONIA:** PC World Macedonia; **MALAYSIA:** Computerworld Malaysia, PC World Malaysia, Publish in Asia; **MALTA:** PC World Malta; **MEXICO:** Computerworld Mexico, PC World Mexico; **MYANMAR:** PC World Myanmar; **NETHERLANDS:** Computer! Totaal, LAN Internetworking Magazine, LAN World Buyers Guide, Macworld Netherlands, Net, WebWereld; **NEW ZEALAND:** Absolute Beginners Guide and Plain & Simple Series, Computer Buyer, Computer Industry Directory, Computerworld New Zealand, MTB, Network World, PC World New Zealand; **NICARAGUA:** PC World Centro America; **NORWAY:** Computerworld Norge, CW Rapport, Datamagasinet, Financial Rapport, Kursguide Norge, Macworld Norge, Multimediaworld Norge, PC World Ekspress Norge, PC World Nettverk, PC World Norge, PC World ProduktGuide Norge; **PAKISTAN:** Computerworld Pakistan; **PANAMA:** PC World Panama; **PEOPLE'S REPUBLIC OF CHINA:** China Computer Users, China Computerworld, China InfoWorld, China Telecom World Weekly, Computer & Communication, Electronic Design China, Electronics Today, Electronics Weekly, Game Software, PC World China, Popular Computer Week, Software Weekly, Software World, Telecom World; **PERU:** Computerworld Peru, PC World Profesional Peru, PC World SoHo Peru; **PHILIPPINES:** Click!, Computerworld Philippines, PC World Philippines, Publish in Asia; **POLAND:** Computerworld Poland, Computerworld Special Report Poland, Cyber, Macworld Poland, Networld Poland, PC World Komputer; **PORTUGAL:** Cerebro/PC World, Computerworld/Correio Informático, Dealer World Portugal, Mac*In/PC*In Portugal, Multimedia World; **PUERTO RICO:** PC World Puerto Rico; **ROMANIA:** Computerworld Romania, PC World Romania, Telecom Romania; **RUSSIA:** Computerworld Russia, Mir PK, Publish, Seti; **SINGAPORE:** Computerworld Singapore, PC World Singapore, Publish in Asia; **SLOVENIA:** Monitor; **SOUTH AFRICA:** Computing SA, Network World SA, Software World SA; **SPAIN:** Communicaciones World España, Computerworld España, Dealer World España, Macworld España, PC World España; **SRI LANKA:** Infolink PC World; **SWEDEN:** CAP&Design, Computer Sweden, Corporate Computing Sweden, Internetworld Sweden, it.branschen, Macworld Sweden, MaxiData Sweden, MikroDatorn, Nätverk & Kommunikation, PC World Sweden, PCaktiv, Windows World Sweden; **SWITZERLAND:** Computerworld Schweiz, Macworld Schweiz, PCtip; **TAIWAN:** Computerworld Taiwan, Macworld Taiwan, NEW ViSiON/Publish, PC World Taiwan, Windows World Taiwan; **THAILAND:** Publish in Asia, Thai Computerworld; **TURKEY:** Computerworld Turkiye, Macworld Turkiye, Network World Turkiye, PC World Turkiye; **UKRAINE:** Computerworld Kiev, Multimedia World Ukraine, PC World Ukraine; **UNITED KINGDOM:** Acorn User UK, Amiga Action UK, Amiga Computing UK, Apple Talk UK, Computing, Macworld, Parents and Computers UK, PC Advisor, PC Home, PSX Pro, The WEB; **UNITED STATES:** Cable in the Classroom, CIO Magazine, Computerworld, DOS World, Federal Computer Week, GamePro Magazine, InfoWorld, I-Way, Macworld, Network World, PC Games, PC World, Publish, Video Event, THE WEB Magazine, and WebMaster; online webzines: JavaWorld, NetscapeWorld, and SunWorld Online; **URUGUAY:** InfoWorld Uruguay; **VENEZUELA:** Computerworld Venezuela, PC World Venezuela; and **VIETNAM:** PC World Vietnam. 10/22/96

Credits

This book was produced electronically using Adobe Illustrator 6.0, Adobe Photoshop 3.0.5. QuarkXPress 3.32, and Microsoft Word 6, The typefaces used are Berkeley, Futura, Sabon, Souvenir, Times, and Trump Mediaeval.

Senior Vice President & Group Publisher
Brenda McLaughlin

Publishing Director
John Osborn

Editorial Director
Anne Marie Walker

Marketing Manager
Jill Reinemann

Managing Editors
Andy Cummings, Kim Field

Administrative Assistant
Laura J. Moss

Editorial Assistant
Timothy J. Borek

Production Director
Andrew Walker

Supervisor of Page Layout
Craig A. Harrison

Development Editors
Susan Pines, Clare A. Mansfield

Editor
Hugh Vandivier

Copy Editors
Deb Kaufmann, Gregory R. Robertson

Technical Reviewers
Michael Shulman, Sam Hakim

CD-ROM Technical Reviewer
Tom C. Reyes,
Software Engineer, UniSQL, Inc.

Project Coordinator
Phyllis Beaty

Graphics & Production Specialists
Vincent F. Burns, Renée Dunn,
Mary Ellen Moran, Stephen Noetzel,
Christopher Pimentel, and Elsie Yim

Quality Control Specialist
Mick Arellano

Proofreader
Carrie O'Neill

Indexer
Ty Koontz

Cover Design
Liew Design

About the Authors

David K. Rensin is Consulting Manager for Noblestar Systems Corp. He has been a contributing book author and has written for PowerSource, a PowerBuilder newsletter. In 1995 and 1996, Dave was a featured presenter at the Mid-Atlantic PowerBuilder User Conferences.

Dave's hobbies include computers, music, and reading. His goals in life are to be obscenely rich, wildly happy, and have a big family. He and his wife, Lia, live with their cats Ginny and Ashley in Centreville, Virginia.

Andrew M. Fedorchek is a database administrator for the U.S. Army in the Pentagon, where he has managed several production SQL Server databases since 1993. He supervised the successful migration of the databases from DB2 to SQL Server. He currently administers an enterprise of SQL Servers that use replication and publish data on an Intranet.

Andrew's interests include cycling, GO (a famous Oriental board game), Star Trek, and computers. He lives with his wife of over three years, Andrea Fedorchek.

Dedication

To my wife, Lia. I dedicate this labor of love to you, the love of my life.
David Rensin

To my father, who has always been an unending source of love, strength, and inspiration for me.
Andrew Fedorchek

Acknowledgments

Writing a book takes more than just committed authors. It requires the involvement of a whole host of characters, all of whom play a critical role.

First and foremost, we would like to thank IDG Books for giving us the opportunity to write this text. Specifically, we want to mention the following folks.

In the beginning...there was John Osborn (our acquisitions manager), and John said, "Let there be a proposal," and he saw that the proposal was good. Seriously, John had a great amount of faith in us from day one. He signed us, sight unseen, and made sure we had all the software and support we needed. We owe him a lot. Thanks, John.

Next, there was Clare Mansfield. Clare was our original project editor and is the person who gave us stylistic help while we were putting together the original material. Her comments were very helpful and, no doubt, made this book much easier to read.

After Clare moved on to an assignment at Network World, we got a new project editor, Sue Pines. Sue has steadily shepherded us through the technical review and copyediting phases of this book. Her help and comments have been absolutely invaluable to us, and we are thankful to have worked with her.

Finally, we would like to thank our copy editors, Deb Kaufmann, Greg Robertson, and Hugh Vandivier, who worked on the book through production. Their diligence and nit-picking helped make sense out of even the most jumbled sentences. Thanks guys, you've been great.

David Rensin:
Five years ago, something extraordinary happened. I fell in love. Actually the extraordinary part about it wasn't the fact that I fell for my wife (she's really cute!). The truly odd thing was that she fell in love with me, too. To truly appreciate the enormity of this fact, you have to understand that I am a computer geek. No bones about it, I am a bona fide computer nerd. When my wife and I built our house, I had it wired with 10baseT. I write computer programs in my sleep. If scientists could find a way to hard-wire a CPU into a human brain, I'd be the first in line. I think in C!

Despite my obvious lack of social conformity (not to mention my odd collection of T-shirts), my wife still fell in love with me.

When Andrew and I started this book eight months ago, I had no idea how many long nights or lost weekends would be devoted to this task.

Throughout it all, my wife, Lia, has been enormously supportive. Between my full-time job and this book, she hasn't seen me much for the last several months. I can't imagine how I could exist without her, and quite frankly, I'm glad I'll never have to find out. Thank you, sweetie. I love you!

Finally, I would like to extend a very special thanks and acknowledgment to my partner, Andrew Fedorchek. In my wildest dreams I couldn't have imagined a more skilled person to work with or a better friend to have. There were many times over the last year when this project could have died. It didn't, and much of that has to do with Andrew's optimism, enthusiasm, patience, and dedication. He has truly been an inspiration. Thank you, Andrew. You have no idea what this experience has meant to me. I will never truly be able to adequately express my gratitude to you for the last several months.

Andrew Fedorchek:
It is a pleasure to acknowledge the people whose support was indispensable in writing this book. First I would like to thank my wife, Andrea Fedorchek, for all her patience, encouragement, and hard work. Next I would like to thank Dave Rensin; I could not ask for a better partner or friend. Finally, I wish to thank Scott Morris, Ralph Liberati, Christine Flanagan, Fred Rosen, Lorraine Saatman, Addison Woods, and Gene Ramsey for their support and encouragement.

The publisher would like to give special thanks to Patrick J. McGovern, without whom this book would not have been possible.

Contents

INTRODUCTION

So you want to be a SQL Server guru, do you? You realize, of course, that to master this most useful software, you must spend years fiddling, tinkering, and otherwise cajoling your server to perform seemingly impossible feats of computational strength. You must throw yourself with wild abandon into the internal workings of this most complicated and elegant system. In short, in order to master SQL Server, you must surrender every last semblance of an outside life to the study and practice of good DBMS management. Or, if all of that is too much, you could always simply read this book. *grin*

WHY THIS BOOK?

We were in a meeting not very long ago, during which a senior manager asked us what we thought of SQL Server. In general, we gave a cautious but glowing report. After we were finished, another person chortled, "Yeah... you're only saying that because you're writing a book on it!" One of us — we won't say who — had to be restrained from hitting the loudmouth. The truth of the matter is that we have written this book because we like the product so much, not the other way around. It's a common — and really annoying — misconception.

More to the point, we wrote this book to enhance the overall usability of SQL Server. So much of what a skilled DBA or programmer can do with SQL Server is subtle and hidden, not because Microsoft wrote an obfuscated product, but because SQL Server is very rich and deep.

It is certainly true that you will find features in competing DBMSs (like Oracle, Sybase, Informix) that SQL Server does not have. For example, the dialect of SQL implemented in Oracle 7 allows something called a row value constructor (it's not important that you know what that is now; we'll teach you about it later), which is a really handy thing to have. (There have been numerous times that we have cursed Microsoft for this omission.) Nonetheless, we like SQL Server better than Oracle — or any other DBMS, for that matter. Why, you may ask? It's simple. In our opinion, SQL Server is the friendliest and most flexible DBMS available.

It is our hope that after you have read this book you will view SQL Server like a big database "Swiss Army knife": applicable in almost any situation, even those for which it was not intended.

In this book, we talk about SQL Server for Windows NT only. We don't address SQL Workstation at all. The reason for this is that SQL Workstation is the same product as SQL Server, except that it only allows a few simultaneous connections. It was created by Microsoft so that developers could create applications that would run against SQL Server without having to spend the money for a full SQL Server installation.

WHO WE ARE

The back cover of the book gives the usual list of credentials, so we don't need to stuff that in here. Rather we want to give you a feeling of who we are and what we bring to this book.

This is what Andrew has to say about Dave:

> Dave is without reservation the most brilliant programmer I have ever met. He has years of experience writing database applications, and so he is uniquely qualified to write this book. He has taught himself everything he needs to know about SQL Server because that's just the way he is. If he needs to use something even tangentially related to his work, he still learns everything about it. Dave makes sure that this book goes into the technical depth he loves, but he also makes sure it is clear to someone who isn't Andrew. Which leads us to our next author...

This is what Dave says about Andrew:

> I am amazed that Andrew isn't working for Microsoft because I have no doubt that he knows more about SQL Server than they do. He is so much a DBA that I think he should start using those initials instead of "AMF." Andrew also has the habit of making SQL Server perform feats of utter magic and of solving a problem with SQL Server ten times faster than anyone else. I have seen very experienced developers claim that a given task was absolutely impossible and nearly faint when Andrew performed it with six lines of SQL. His skill and good nature illicit a kind of respect and admiration from his peers that make him one of the most respected and admired people in any organization to which he happens to belong. He provides a depth of knowledge to this book that will rocket you to the top of any SQL Server project on which you work. It has truly been an honor to work with him.

Who We Think You Are

There are really only two things we think you ought to have in order to get the most out of this book. First, you will need at least a basic understanding of relational database principles. This does not mean that you should be able to recite all the normal forms from memory, just that you understand the basics of how any two tables of data might relate. The second thing that would be nice to have is at least a basic understanding of SQL. It is true that the chapter in this book (Chapter 8) devoted to beginning Transact-SQL — the SQL dialect of SQL Server — does, by necessity, cover certain basic principles of SQL in general. We recommend, however, that you have been exposed to a non-dialect–specific treatment of the language. We think it will help you understand many of these concepts better. Other than that, your background is not important.

The Reality of It All

In truth, you can read this book without any SQL or relational database experience at all. You just won't get all you can from it.

Other than that, your background is not important. The only other caveat we have is this: this is a technical book. The secrets, shortcuts, and experiences related in these pages are specifically technical in nature. We have made every effort to transform the complex into the simple without sacrificing the subtleties that come with the in-depth treatment of a subject.

What You Can Expect

The truth. We are neither Microsoft cronies, nor are we persistent Microsoft bashers. The zeal with which we advocate the use of this product is a direct result of our several years of experience with it. If we think the product has a shortcoming in a particular area, we will tell you.

You can also expect to learn things that only come from experience. If there's a mistake to be made with this tool, we've made it! As a result, we hope to steer you clear of the many pitfalls we have encountered over time and direct you to many of the hidden gems we have discovered.

How This Book Is Organized

When we first sat down to outline this book, we decided that it must have two critical qualities. First, each chapter must flow smoothly into the next so that you can read the text from beginning to end. Second, each chapter must be as self-contained and as modular as possible so that you can use this book as a reference. To this end, we have worked very hard to meet these requirements. There will be, however, some cases in which we deviate from some of these principles for the sake of clarity or technical correctness. When such a thing is a about to occur, we will let you know.

At the beginning of each chapter is a "What's in This Chapter" section that will give you a brief idea of the subject matter. At the end of each chapter are two things. First, the material, which is different from the synopsis outline at the beginning of the chapter. Finally, questions and answers are designed to test your understanding of the material presented. We highly recommend that you attempt to answer all of these questions and look up, in the chapter, those answers which you cannot readily discern.

Distinguishing Features

This book is a member of IDG's SECRETS series. As such, it has two conventions of which you ought to be aware.

Icons and sidebars

Throughout this book you will see icons positioned beside certain paragraphs. They include notes, tips, warnings, secrets, cross-references, and CD-ROM references.

- A note icon means that the following text is an aside to the main point. It just wasn't long enough to justify a sidebar.◀

- This icon indicates cool things that we have picked up along the way that we want to share with you.◀

- This icon alerts you to things you need to be aware of as potential problem areas.◀

- The secret icon marks information that isn't readily available through normal means. In many cases, you won't find it anywhere else but here.◀

- This icon indicates that you can look up further information on a particular topic in another section of the book.◀

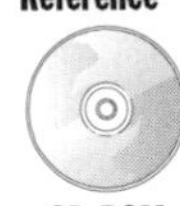

- This icon indicates that the item in the text references something on the companion CD-ROM.◀

Sidebars

In other places, you will see a sidebar. Typically, these are interesting facts or stories related to the text. They are physically removed from the main text so as not to impede the intended flow.

Depth

It is not possible for us to cover absolutely every possible feature about SQL Server. We do, however, cover a lot. Because this is a SECRETS book (and because we're neurotic about completeness), you are guaranteed that any topic we cover will be explained in great depth. For example, SQL Server's Bulk Copy Program (BCP) utility has an entire chapter. Most texts only give it a page or two. This, we reason, is why you bought this book!

Parting Thoughts

Over the years, we have found SQL Server to be an absolutely indispensable tool for many computing tasks that you may not normally think of for using a DBMS. For this reason, we have developed a great affinity for SQL Server. This leads us to write constant e-mail to Microsoft reporting problems and suggesting enhancements. With respect to this book, we expect the same from you. Please feel free to contact us as the occasion warrants. If you have a question, disagree with a point, find what you think is an error, or just want to say hi, please send us e-mail. We'll try very hard to answer it promptly. Here's our contact information:


```
Andrew Fedorchek: fedorche@pentagon-asafm.army.mil
Dave Rensin: drensin@noblestar.com
```


You also may want to check out the USENET news group *comp.databases.ms-sqlserver*. We are constant participants there.

This brings us to our final point. We have made every effort to make sure that the information contained in these pages is absolutely accurate. The problem is that large sections of the text have been written while using various beta versions of the software. We reread all sections of this book each time a new release candidate of the software came out so that we could make sure that the text remained pristine in its technical accuracy. We do not doubt, however, that some very small things may have fallen through the cracks. To this end, it is critical that we hear from you. Any feedback that we get from you will help make us better authors and subsequent books more useful. Please accept, in advance, our thanks for reading this book. We hope that you get as much from reading it as we did from writing it.

Part I

GETTING STARTED

Like us, you are probably eager to discuss the cool new features of SQL Server 6.5, such as what new Transact-SQL commands you can use, what is new in replication, and so on. However, setting all this up assumes that you actually have installed SQL Server 6.5, that you know your way around the SQL Enterprise Manager, that you have configured SQL Server properly, and that you have set up all the client software for SQL Server 6.5. If indeed this is the case, by all means, please jump to Part II.

If not, welcome to Part I. Chapter 1 is all about installing SQL Server. The good news is that installing SQL Server isn't hard: the product practically sets up itself. However, you should put some serious thought into a few decisions, especially hardware procurement, disk array configuration, sort order, and character set. Chapter 2 discusses upgrading. Despite what you might think, upgrading is *harder* than installing because you have to be thoroughly prepared for any problems. We will cover at length all the troubles we have had upgrading in hopes that you can avoid the same pitfalls.

Once you get the product up and running, you have basically one application to use called the SQL Enterprise Manager. Microsoft upgraded this tool with SQL Server 6.5, but SQL Server 6.0 users will find much that is familiar. For everyone else, Chapter 3 explains the SQL Enterprise Manager. We intentionally cover this tool immediately after the installation discussion because the rest of the advice in the book assumes you can use the SQL Enterprise Manager to interact with your servers and databases. Here we also discuss in detail the Query Analyzer, a powerful little tool for executing Transact-SQL, Microsoft's implementation of SQL. As you will see in this book *everything* has a Transact-SQL equivalent, so having a robust knowledge of your query tool is critical.

Chapter 4 gives you your first chance to use the SQL Enterprise Manager, in this case to configure your SQL Server. Even if you have had SQL Server up and running for some time, this chapter is worth reading. Some of the default parameters are not so good, and it would be a shame to suffer with bad performance because you didn't change one little configuration number. Chapter 5 winds up with configuration of client software.

Chapter 1

Installing SQL Server 6.5

If you have listened to Microsoft's sales pitches, you have heard the company brag about how easy its network software is to install. In the case of SQL Server, this claim is certainly justified. The installation consists basically of dialog boxes asking you to make decisions; the setup program does everything else. This chapter provides a detailed explanation of what you are deciding during the setup process and what factors weigh on each decision.

What's in This Chapter

Our tour of your installation decisions includes the following:

- What kind of hardware you should buy to run SQL Server
- How to configure your drive array
- How to set up Windows NT for SQL Server use
- What the installation options are and which ones to pick

Only a few of the decisions that you make during installation are not easy to change later, and we highlight what they are. You can change the rest of the options later if you decide you don't like your original choices. Even so, we recommend you read through this chapter once before you install so that you can get an overview of what to expect. If you have already installed SQL Server and you want to change your options, you are in the right place; this chapter covers that, too.

Upgrading to a new version of SQL Server is a lot messier. Plenty of potential pitfalls exist, and because your production system probably hangs in the balance, you have to get it right the first time. Therefore, we devote Chapter 2 to guiding you through that.◀

For many of you, this is the beginning of your SQL Server 6.5 journey, but some of you will be using an already installed SQL Server. If you are in the latter category, you can certainly skip this chapter, but you may want to read it anyway. This chapter shows you the kinds of decisions someone else made for you, decisions that affect your database design and performance.

The installation of SQL Server Workstation runs the same as the installation of SQL Server, so we do not distinguish between the two in this chapter except when we talk about server requirements.◀

Server Requirements

We assume you have already bought SQL Server 6.5 or you are planning to buy a copy. If you have not yet chosen the machine on which to put it, read this section to gather the information you need to make that choice. For the rest of this chapter, we refer to the machine on which you install SQL Server as simply *the server*. We give our analysis of the requirements, but of course hardware technology advances so rapidly that it is impossible for any printed book to be current for more than a few months. Therefore, you should always refer to Microsoft's SQL Server requirements documentation before you make a purchase.

Operating system

You have no choice of an operating system: you have to install SQL Server on Windows NT version 3.51 or later. Even Windows NT 3.5 isn't supported. A long time ago, Microsoft had a version of SQL Server for OS/2, but that's gone. You can't get by with Windows 95 either; you have to have Windows NT.

Microsoft tells you that you must install SQL Server on Windows NT Server, which isn't true. If you have Windows NT Server, that is certainly preferred, but the software installs and runs on Windows NT Workstation. This is a real plus for developers. The disadvantages to running the software on NT Workstation are as follows:

- Microsoft doesn't support it, so if it breaks, you may be on your own.
- NT Workstation isn't going to take advantage of multiprocessor machines properly.
- NT Workstation has other limitations that may indirectly affect SQL Server, such as the limit of ten Remote Access (RAS) connections.

You can install SQL Server Workstation on either Windows NT Server or Windows NT Workstation.◀

Microprocessors

In this section, we cover the choices you have regarding microprocessors: which to choose, how many to buy, and the elements that will weigh in these decisions.

Which one to choose

You can install Microsoft SQL Server 6.5 on the big four that Windows NT supports: Alpha AXP microprocessors, Intel 32-bit x86-based microprocessors (486, Pentium, Pentium-Pro), MIPS microprocessors, and PowerPC. The big question you have to ask yourself is not if you can install SQL Server, but if you can get Windows NT to run on your machine. If Windows NT runs, you can feel pretty confident that SQL Server will, too. The Windows NT software comes with an exhaustive list of what it supports. This isn't something to fool around with; if you have an unusual machine, make sure it is compatible.

If you want our opinion on which chip to buy, we think the Alpha is a far superior chip. We have had the pleasure of running Windows NT 4.0 on an Alpha machine, and it is really hot stuff. If the prices of Alpha processors come down a little more, one of us (Dave) is considering buying one for home use. Having said that, let's be realistic for a minute. Intel has cornered the market on processors, and most of you will be installing on an *x*86 machine. If you plan to get an Intel chip, we have three words for you: get a Pentium. Both Windows NT and Microsoft SQL Server 6.5 are robust, complex systems that are very demanding for microprocessors. We know people who run SQL Server on a 486 processor, and the performance is not very good.◀

How many to buy

SQL Server is designed to take advantage of *symmetric multiprocessing (SMP)*, which means that if something takes a certain amount of time with one processor, it takes roughly half as long on a machine with two processors, roughly one fourth as long with four processors, and so on. How closely SMP adheres to these rules of thumb is called *scalability*. Your anticipated use of SQL Server determines how many processors you want to buy. Ask yourself these questions:

- Will you be using the server for Online Transaction Processing (OLTP) or Decision Support System (DSS) applications?
- How many concurrent users will be actively attempting to use the server?
- How computationally complex will the use be?
- What is the server going to be doing besides hosting the SQL Server service?
- How fast does the response time need to be?

Will you be using the server for OLTP or DSS applications?

The answer to this question helps you answer the subsequent questions. Database use has developed sufficient sophistication that most folks devote a server to a specific type of database application. An OLTP system, as the name implies, processes transactions interactively to update a database. A good example is an airline reservation system. In an OLTP system, you expect a lot of random reads and writes. This often means a heavy stream of disk I/O. However, the queries will probably have been written by developers and are hopefully optimized.

On the other hand, you have DSS, which supports analysis of the database. For the purposes of hardware purchase we can safely lump Online Analytic Processing (OLAP) and Data Warehousing in the DSS category. DSS usually has a lot of complex queries, both in terms of joins and in terms of aggregating data. In a DSS system, you expect almost no transaction type updating, but you will have big bulk data loads.

If you have a small organization, be careful about casting yourself in one of these two categories. We have a server devoted to DSS, but our other server is used for both DSS and OLTP. This isn't optimal, but at least we recognize what we have and we have purchased our hardware accordingly.

How many concurrent connections will be actively attempting to use the server?

This question and the next one are hard to answer. First, you have to guess how many people will actively use the server at the same time. You may have 100 people in your organization but find that on average only ten are logged in at a given moment. Furthermore, having ten people logged in doesn't mean ten people are tying up processor resources all day long. SQL Server generally responds faster than a user can issue demands, so most user connections are characterized by idle time punctuated by brief spurts of activity. Thus, your hundred-person organization may average only two or three people actually hitting a processor at the same time.

You also have to consider how many connections each of these users is likely to have. One power user has easily two or three active connections. Regrettably, we don't have a magic equation for how many processors you need for a certain number of concurrent connections. One of our offices has about 15 people with all of them usually logged in, but which averages about two to four active connections at an instant in time. We use a dual Pentium machine and generally have few complaints. We would advise you to have at least two processors if you are doing even small-scale client server work. With just a single processor, Window NT imposes a slight delay on the execution of a thread that demands processor time the instant after another thread has just started. With just two processors, this delay disappears. If you can't afford two processors, at least buy a machine that allows you to upgrade to two processors.

Don't forget to consider the requirements of the database owners and system administrators who will always be doing very resource-intensive tasks. Organizations generally try to schedule administrative and maintenance functions at night, and SQL Server gives you many features to allow that work to go on unattended. However, sometimes these operations are done during the workday. For example, a company developing client-server software may have its database owners tinkering with the databases all day long as other people work. That is worth another processor in and of itself.

How computationally complex will the use be?

How complex the use of the server will be is as important as the number of users. One person can kick off a process that keeps two Pentiums busy for

15 minutes, and everyone else will see his or her performance drag. You have to guess at this too, but consider these points as you guess:

- A DSS tends to be more demanding on processors than an OLTP system. People running queries in a DSS will kick off complex joins, and they will run queries requiring a lot of vector aggregates and temporary tables. DSS queries often return more rows, too. OLTP tends to run highly optimized queries with short transactions:

Cross-Reference

- An application that shifts the business logic back to the server in stored procedures requires a lot more server processor time than an application that does this work on the client side. We go into this a lot more in Chapter 14, but you have a great opportunity with SQL Server to make applications that take business logic out of the desktop machine and shift it back to the server. You will expect to save in application development and in client workstation hardware, you will reduce network reads and writes, but you will probably need more processors for the server.◀
- Applications using server-side cursors will put a heavier load on your processors. We don't like cursors, either on the server or the client. The row-by-row manipulation of a cursor runs counter to the whole set manipulation paradigm of a relation database, and no relational database management systems (RDBMSs), including SQL Server, executes cursors quickly. If your applications are built on cursors, buy the processors to support it.

If any of these points leads you to conclude that your system will be more demanding than most, you might consider simply buying the fastest processors you can (see our Tip earlier on the Alpha chip). If you are already buying the fastest stuff, you might consider getting another chip for good measure.

What is the server going to be doing besides hosting SQL Server?

Ideally, nothing. If at all possible you should dedicate a machine exclusively to SQL Server. Your SQL Server machine should not be a file server, a print server, or a mail server. Make sure it isn't a backup domain controller (BDC) either because that takes up extra resources you don't have. Don't even do your server administration at the server machine if you can help it; the administrative tools for SQL Server don't ever require you to go to the machine itself to do any SQL Server related task. Having said this, if you decide that the server will be doing other tasks, you may need more processors to handle the load.

If you have a machine that is already a backup domain controller and you want to discontinue that function, you have to *reinstall the operating system*. You can't even upgrade, you have to reinstall. You will not want to do this once you have set up SQL Server 6.5. Take the time *now* to change your server.◀

How fast does the response time need to be?

Perhaps a better way to phrase this is "How much are you willing to pay for optimum response time?" The questions just listed may lead you to conclude that you need four processors when you can only afford two. If you have any indications that you could use more than one processor, at least try to buy a machine that lets you expand, even if you only buy one processor to start. At the time of this writing, there seems to be a serious difference in the price of motherboards that allow two processors and those that allow four processors. This is certainly an important consideration when purchasing the machine.

Disk space

According to Microsoft, the minimum space you need for SQL Server is 81MB for a new installation, 22MB for an upgrade from SQL Server 6.0, 74MB for an upgrade from SQL Server 4.2*x*, and 1 to 15MB for the SQL Server Books Online. However, that is a bare-bones minimum with no room left for the databases you intend to have SQL Server manage. Add to the 81MB whatever amount of space your databases are going to take. If you have no idea how much space you need, you are not alone. Few people do, especially if they are new to the client-server environment. If you are reading this chapter to decide what to buy, we have some thoughts for you:

- Don't cut corners in hardware to save a few hundred or even a few thousand dollars. SQL Server is a lot cheaper than many of its competitors. Roll some of that savings into good hardware.
- Buy a Redundant Array of Inexpensive Drives (RAID). They let you add more hard drives as you need more space, and they are more reliable. We use them and have not had a single problem in years. When we had simple mirroring, we suffered a number of annoying hard drive crashes in our production environment. Depending on how you choose to configure RAID, you may see faster disk I/O as well.

The acronym *RAID* is often quoted (incorrectly) as *Redundant Array of Independent Drives*. The *I* stands for inexpensive. Ironically, for most users a RAID is among the most expensive hardware purchases. Call a vendor for prices on the smallest mainframe they sell, and you will begin to see why inexpensive is the appropriate word to use.◀

- In the scheme of things, disk space is cheap. Buy a lot. How much is a lot? Even home computers these days have gigabytes of space. That's a start. We have a machine that has 10GB for a database that supports a couple hundred folks. Buy SCSI-II, not IDE. SCSI drives are easier to chain and are typically a lot faster. Also, if you are going to have a large drive that will be FAT, be sure to use several partitions. FAT fails miserably at managing large file spaces. (We go into greater depth on that later.)
- If you know the size of your data, you can do some computations to estimate your requirements. An appendix in the SQL Server *Administrator's Companion* guides you through this. The main thing to know is that the space you need in SQL Server will be several times the actual data size, at least. You need space for indexes, free space for each of your data pages, and so on. Don't forget that you need space for transaction logs and space for SQL Server's own databases (master, tempdb, model, msdb, and pubs). Err on the side of too much space. (We discuss transaction logs and SQL Server's databases later.)
- Beware of using your legacy system as a guide. Few people migrate to the client-server environment simply by transferring a database table by table exactly as they were on the mainframe. Most organizations take advantage of the opportunity to redesign their systems at the same time. You may develop a better data model so that you can store things more compactly on your SQL Server, but you may get roped into supporting all kinds of new user requirements that significantly expand your databases. Treat the legacy system as an order-of-magnitude guide.

Microsoft SQL Server comes with all reference books online, and if you install the books on a hard drive, they consume 15MB of space, but we don't count that as part of the server space requirement unless you're setting up a *standalone* (i.e., non-network) system. If you are on a network, you shouldn't need to worry about space for books on the server because the SQL Server machine should be dedicated exclusively to SQL Server. Put the books on a file server or on your workstation.

Memory

Windows NT needs 16MB of memory, and that is the minimum that SQL Server requires. As you can imagine, more is better, up to certain limits. Microsoft says you must have 32MB of memory to set up a server for distribution, a replication feature of SQL Server. We have found that you can do distribution with 16MB, but we wouldn't recommend it. If your network is going to have multiple SQL Servers and they are going to share data, you need the 32MB of RAM.

In any production environment, however, you will want more RAM — probably a lot more. There are two big reasons for buying a lot more RAM:

- SQL Server can use extra RAM as a data cache. SQL Server will keep the most recently referenced database data pages in RAM, which saves disk I/O. Because disk I/O is often the biggest performance limitation, a large data cache is essential to any serious production system.
- SQL Server will let you put its temporary database, tempdb, in RAM. If you perform a lot of complex queries, SQL Server uses tempdb a lot, so keeping it in RAM will dramatically boost your performance.

As we said, our network has a couple hundred clients (not all connecting to the database at once, of course), and the servers have 128MB of RAM. For the applications we run, this is overkill. The good news is that SQL Server gives you ways to see if more memory would improve performance. Our recommendation is to buy 32MB of RAM to start, and make sure you can easily expand to more. Based on what you read in this book, you will be able to use SQL Server's memory management features to decide if you need more RAM.

Tape backup

SQL Server does not require a tape backup drive, but it does provide extensive utilities for using tape backups, so you should have one. Having some other machine on your network with a tape backup drive isn't sufficient: the tape backup must be in the SQL Server machine itself for SQL Server to use it. As with disk space, bigger is better when it comes to tape drives. When you have high-capacity tape drives, you can store multiple backups on the same tape, which reduces the number of times a human being has to swap tapes. Another selling point is that you will be able to use the tape backup drive with Windows NT to backup files.

Network software

Between SQL Server and NT, you should have all that you need to run on a Windows NT or a Novell NetWare LAN. If you plan to use Banyan Vines or DEC PATHWORKS, check with Microsoft or your SQL Server salesman about additional network software you may need.

SMS software

If you are planning to use Microsoft's Systems Management Server (SMS) with SQL Server, you need version 1.0A. SQL Server 6.5 doesn't work with SMS 1.0.

How to prioritize

So far we have listed the dream system requirements, but if you are seeking to minimize your costs for whatever reasons, you may be worrying about tradeoffs such as whether to get more memory or more disk space. The needs of your specific operation should be your guide, but here are some general priorities:

- Buy a machine that you can expand or upgrade. If you don't have the money now for all the bells and whistles, you can use SQL Server's diagnostic features to find out what extra hardware you need most. Most machines allow you to add more memory, more disk space, and more tape drives. Adding a different processor is another story. If you think you might want this, try to stretch your budget to get a machine that allows you to add processors. Ask what the price for extra processors is, too. We were taken for a ride on our purchase.
- Make sure you get enough disk space. Especially when you have a machine with one disk, it is cheaper to get the size you need up front rather than to buy another disk later. A slow processor or a limited amount of memory drags your performance down, but if you run out of disk space, your operations come to a halt.
- You have to buy 16MB of memory. Try for 32MB if you can. There is a noticeable boost in the jump from 16MB to 32MB because in the first case, you allocate 8MB to SQL Server, and in the second, you can give SQL Server up to 24MB. Thus, you are effectively *tripling* what SQL Server gets. We place this higher on the list than getting a faster processor

because it has been our experience that a big application runs significantly better on a 486 DX2/66 with 32MB of RAM than on a Pentium 90 with 16MB. Furthermore, most single chip Pentium motherboards support 75, 90, 100, and 133MHz processors, so you aren't locked into one chip for all time. Ask about this when you buy. In many cases, upgrading the processor is easier than installing the memory.

Warning

One thing you can't do is symmetric multiprocessing (SMP) for two chips of different speeds. For example, if you have a Pentium 90 in an SMP machine, you can't later buy a Pentium 166 to put alongside the Pentium 90. Either you will have to buy another Pentium 90 (if you can still find one), or you will have to buy two Pentium 166 and forget about using the Pentium 90. This argues for buying the faster chip available for an SMP machine if you think you will have to buy more chips down the road.◀

- Finally, the better your processor is, the more performance you can squeeze out of SQL Server. Your first decision is whether to buy a Reduced Instruction Set Chip (RISC), such as the Alpha, or a Complex Instruction Set Chip (CISC), such as the Pentium. We have expressed our bias for RISC chips. Within a given type of chip, go for the fastest clock speed you can find.

Buying and Configuring a Drive Array

If you are purchasing more that a couple gigabytes of disk space, you should seriously consider getting a drive array. If you really need a lot of space you will have no choice.

With a drive array you have a myriad of configuration options. Do you let the hardware controller stripe the data or the NT operating system? Do you use SQL Server mirroring, or do you use SQL Server segments? Do you set up the drives in one big array, or do you keep one or two drives out of the array for operations you expect will have a lot of sequential I/O? Do you put the drive array in RAID 0 (no fault tolerance) because you want the speed and extra space, and rely on the database backups and network backup for recovery, or do you use RAID 5 to get fault tolerance and keep a hot-swappable drive handy? Do you mirror the disk(s) that are not in the array? How best to configure a drive array is a subject of a lot of debate. The only safe answer is "it depends." The problem is, you have to decide this *before* you install the operating system, let alone SQL Server. This is why we put a quick RAID discussion in the installation chapter.

RAID levels at a glance

Before we throw around a lot of recommendations about RAID levels, let's pause briefly to define the important ones. RAID levels are different ways of storing data across an array of drives. There are six levels, numbered 0 through 5.

RAID 0 is a simple striping strategy. The hardware or software implementing the RAID, usually the hardware controller card, presents all the drives to the operating system as one logical unit so that you can't access the individual drives anymore. When you want to write data to the disk, the controller breaks your data into a convenient size called a *block* and stores the first block on the first disk, the second block on the second disk, and so on. (The size of the block depends on your controller — it is 16K on our system.) The advantage of RAID 0 is that the read/write load is distributed across multiple disks. For example, if you have RAID 0 running on five drives and you need to write 1GB of data, each disk has to write only 200MB of data. This makes RAID 0 a great performer in disk I/O. The major disadvantage to RAID 0 is that if one disk fails, everything is lost. The other disks do not contain complete files or complete databases, just blocks of data that mean nothing without the missing blocks on the failed drive.

RAID 1 is your basic mirroring. When two disks mirror each other, everything written to disk A is also written to disk B. Writing to a mirrored pair should take no longer that writing to a single disk, but with a good controller you can read twice as fast by reading half the data from A and half the data from B. RAID 1 extends to multiple disks: if you have four disks holding data, you need four more to serve as the mirrors. The major advantage to RAID 1 is that you have excellent fault tolerance; the major disadvantage is the cost of buying twice as much disk space as you need. Furthermore, there is a limit to how many disks a controller can handle (usually less than a dozen), so using RAID 1 with a lot of disks will force you to buy another controller card, too.

We skip now to RAID 4 because RAID 2 and RAID 3 add little to the picture and are never used. Actually RAID 4 is never used either, but you need to understand it to understand RAID 5. RAID 0 is nice because it is fast, RAID 1 is nice because it protects your data. RAID 4 is a first attempt at compromise. Rather than mirroring each and every disk, RAID 4 uses a parity disk, which contains the bitwise Exclusive OR (XOR) of the blocks written to the other disks. If one of the non-parity disks fails, the controller can reconstruct what was on it by reading the remaining good disks and figuring out what the failed disk must have contained to produce what is on the parity disk. This is a great way to obtain fault tolerance on all your drives by purchasing just one more drive. The total usable space in the drive array is (n – 1)/n × *total array space*. Therefore, if you have three 1GB disks, you have 2GB of space (66 percent of what you purchased). If you have seven 2 GB disks, you have 12 GB of space (86 percent). The only flaw in RAID 4 is that the parity disk becomes the bottleneck on all writes, which brings us to RAID 5.

RAID 5, by far the most commonly used RAID level, extends the idea of RAID 4 by distributing the parity blocks throughout the drives. Therefore, each drive contains data and some parity information. There is no parity drive bottleneck. The advantage of RAID 5 is that you have distributed the read/write load of your system across all the drives, and you still won't lose any data if a drive fails. The major disadvantage of RAID 5 is that it is slower than either RAID 0 or RAID 1 when it comes to writing data. To write a block of data, RAID 5 first must know what must be written to the parity block, which necessitates a *read* of the original block and the parity block. Then RAID 5 can write the block and write the parity block. Another possible disadvantage of RAID 5 is that if *two* disks fail, you are toasted, but if that happens you made a pretty pathetic choice in your hardware components.

If you are interested, Appendix D of the *SQL Server Administrators Companion* reprints a whole white paper on the factors you need to consider in using RAID, but our guess is that you don't have the luxury of curling up in bed to pore over a white paper on the intricacies of database I/O before you do this installation. We give you some general recommendations that are good choices for many production systems. However, we freely admit that for any drive array configuration, including the configurations that we recommend, there are applications whose individual quirks make them run better in a different configuration.

Recommendation 1: Isolate your sequential I/O

The biggest delay in reading or writing data to a disk is seek time: waiting for the head of the hard drive to reach the place where your data is stored. If you can keep the head from bouncing all over the disk, your performance will improve dramatically. Regrettably, a relational database involves random access, so you are stuck with the seek time performance penalty, except for a few select areas:

- Reading or writing transaction logs
- Creating database backups to operating system files

- Operating system files being read by SQL Server for loading tables
- Table scans by SQL Server

Of these, the first is most important. An OLTP database has a lot of users changing data in it. It this case, there are bursts of heavy write activity for the data storage area, but a steady stream of writes to the transaction logs. Therefore, we recommend that you *put the data of an OLTP database on RAID 5, but put the transaction log on a RAID 1 pair*. The reason for leaving the transaction log disks out of the RAID 5 is that SQL Server writes to them sequentially, so the head movement on those drives is minimized. If you put the transaction log disks in RAID 5 with everything else, the heads are forced to do all kinds of random seeks to support the rest of the OLTP. With a DSS server you will be primarily querying data, not updating, so you can just set up the whole array in RAID 5.

You notice that we recommend RAID 5 for the data, not RAID 0, even though RAID 5 doesn't write as quickly as RAID 0. You could argue that if only the database data is on the group of drives in RAID, you might as well put them in RAID 0 for maximum performance. If a drive fails, you would just restore from tape backups. Our answer to this is that after you experience your first drive failure, you will regret your decision. Restoring all master and *all* your other databases is a lot of work and a lot of down time.

If you have a server dedicated to one primary database, you are in great shape. When you have more than one high activity database on the same server, the isolation of the transaction logs is harder. To do this correctly, you should devote a separate disk to each database transaction log; otherwise, you get back to the same seek problems. When two high activity transaction logs are on the same disk, you will have the head for that drive constantly moving back and forth between the locations of the two different logs.

What about the other sequential I/O, such as the backups and table loads? If you are just swimming in disk space, you could devote a drive to serving as a staging area. This drive would be the place to load and unload your data. If there are times when you know your transaction log is not being used, you could use the transaction log drive for this purpose, too.

An interesting question is where should you install Windows NT? On the RAID 5 or on the mirrored pair? This isn't what you usually hear, but we recommend you put Windows NT on the RAID for two reasons:

- The reason for leaving the mirrored drives out of the RAID was the sequential I/O of transaction log writes. The reads and writes associated with NT are going to be more random.
- You may decide to use a FAT on the mirrored drives, but you want Windows NT itself to be stored on an NTFS volume.

Recommendation 2: Let the hardware drive controller handle the RAID if you have that option

You have three choices here for controlling how data is written to the disks:

1. The hardware drive controller
2. Windows NT
3. SQL Server features, such as segments and device mirroring

We recommend you use the hardware to set up RAID, if your machine supports that. Lots of vendors sell drive arrays with "hot swappable" drives. You can rig these things to kick in automatically. That way, when a drive fails on the weekend, you won't be getting frantic phone calls.

You could let Windows NT control the RAID instead, but presumably you bought a quality computer with a good controller card. This card can probably do the job better, and it frees up your computer's processors for other stuff. If you balked at the cost of a good controller and you have a bunch of drives, then by all means, let Windows NT do RAID for you. The load on your processors isn't enough for you to worry about, and Windows NT will distribute your data much better than you can within SQL Server. Which brings us to the option you don't want.

The third option is not to use RAID on the drive array at all, and instead devise your own scheme of distributing data on the drives using SQL Server segments. This will take a lot of time and effort on your part, and to do it right you need to consider every variable: every table, every index, and how each will be updated. When you are done, there is no guarantee that what you come up with will perform better than either RAID done by the controller card or by Windows NT. In fact, your solution could easily run slower. Furthermore, because your fault tolerance will not be as efficient as the RAID and because you can't do striping within SQL Server, we advise against this option.

Making do with fewer disks

So far, we have implicitly assumed that you have at least five disks in your array because it takes three to set up RAID 5 and two to mirror. What if you have fewer? The flippant answer is "buy more," but seriously, that is your best solution. Tell your boss we said it was worth the money. If you really can't swing it, here's what to do:

Four drives

This is a tough call. We would be tempted to set up the first three in RAID 5 and just leave the logs on an unmirrored device. If you have four 1-gigabyte drives, this would mean 3 – 1 = 2 gigabytes for your data and 1 gigabyte for transaction logs. For a lot of folks this might mean not enough data space and too much log space. If you think you will be in that category, just put all four disks in RAID 5. What you do *not* want to do is have some of your database data in RAID 5 and some on the lone drive with no fault tolerance. Not only does this raise your risk for data loss, it screws up your I/O performance.

Three drives

With three drives, something has to give. You can't have good fault tolerance and good performance. Assuming that you want some protection against disk failure, we recommend you just set up all three disks in RAID 5. Your logs will have to go on the RAID 5 with the data, so you lose the potential performance gain from writing them sequentially, but this isn't the end of the world. We used to have a machine set up like this, and it worked just fine.

If you have a lot of confidence in your hardware, you could just do without any fault tolerance whatsoever. RAID 0 would be the best choice unless you expect a *large* transaction log. If you reserve a disk for a database transaction log, remember that nothing else, especially not database data, should go on the transaction log disk. Otherwise, the random access to this other data ruins the isolation of your sequential I/O.

Two drives

Presumably this isn't a drive array (no vendor should sell an array without at least three drives), so we are talking about a file server that you are going to put SQL Server on. If you are not concerned about losing half the space, mirror the drives. Otherwise, just leave them as they are, and you can use SQL Server to mirror key pieces of your data.

Configuring Windows NT

Following are some important things in the Windows NT operating system that you want to decide and set up before you install SQL Server.

What file system to use

You have three choices for your file system in holding SQL Server data:

- NTFS
- FAT
- Raw partition (no file system)

We recommend using NTFS. Microsoft says SQL Server performance isn't affected by choosing NFTS over FAT, but you may gain a small performance boost by using a raw partition. Rare are the shops that need the small performance gain of using a raw partition. For the rest of us, why saddle yourself with a disk that can do *nothing* but hold SQL Server data? (Remember, if no file system exists, you can't put any files on the drive.) Besides, we spent a lot of time convincing you to use RAID, which means you have rolled all your disk space into one logical drive and you will put a file system on this drive.

As far as we are concerned, FAT is slightly faster that NTFS, despite what Microsoft says, but not enough to make you want to use it. A key exception, however, is creating SQL Server devices (operating system files for databases to use). NTFS runs a lot faster than a FAT for this operation, but it isn't something you do very often, so don't base your decision on that.◀

For most folks the decision is NTFS or FAT. The reasons to use NTFS are

- You get the full space of your drives. With a FAT you lose space. This sounds hard to believe, but ask anyone who is familiar with operating systems. A 1GB drive running under a FAT doesn't really give you a full gigabyte of space. Worse yet, a little bit bigger drive loses a lot more space.
- NTFS provides all kinds of security features you don't have in FAT.

The reason you would choose FAT is if you need to dual boot to MS-DOS or Windows 95. Windows 95 doesn't recognize NTFS, even though NTFS was released with Windows NT a full two years earlier. Go figure. However, there shouldn't be any reason to dual boot your SQL Server machine if it is dedicated to SQL Server. If you need to dual boot, consider setting up an NTFS partition and a FAT, rather than one big FAT.

What about using NTFS compression?

We recommend against using NTFS compression for your SQL Server machine for these reasons:

- It hurts your performance.
- You never know how much space you have, which creates headaches for you and for SQL Server. We are getting ahead of ourselves here, but SQL Server stores your databases in operating system files that you create up front. Suppose that you go to allocate a 500 megabyte file for database use on a compressed drive that reports 1 gigabyte free. This file may suck up almost all of your free space because Windows NT doesn't know what the compression ratio of the file will be as it changes, so it plans for the worst.

Buy the amount of disk space you need up front; don't be cheap and try to cut corners by having the operating system compress your drive.

Tip

When you install SQL Server, it is going to take the computer's name as its SQL Server name. In SQL Server 6.0, the computer name had to be a valid SQL Server identifier. This isn't true any more in SQL Server 6.5, but you will have to go through some extra headaches if you break the rules. We recommend sticking to computer names that are valid SQL Server identifiers: the first character should be a letter or an underscore (_); the remaining characters can be letters, numbers, or the symbols #, $, or _.◀

Don't use a screen saver

This may sound trivial, but it isn't. If you are familiar with computer graphics, you know that all those fancy screen savers that come with Windows NT use a lot of processor power. Even the "Beziers," which look like a simple bunch of curves, require a lot of math. Set the screen saver to "None" and turn the monitor of the server off.

Installing SQL Server

You can install or upgrade SQL Server directly from the SQL Server CD-ROM, or you can copy the contents of the CD-ROM to a network directory and run it from there. The CD-ROM isn't as large as you would think: it is only about 80 to 90MB. There are six directories on the CD-ROM: \I386 for Intel-based computers; \MIPS for MIPS-based computers; \ALPHA for AXP-based computers; \PPC for PowerPCs \CLIENT, which contains 16-bit client software; and \SQLBK565, which contains the SQL Server Books Online. Run SETUP.EXE in the directory for your processor. You get the familiar blue background for Microsoft installations and the Welcome dialog box shown in Figure 1-1.

Cross-Reference

Note

This chapter assumes that you are installing SQL Server on a machine where no version of SQL Server exists. If you are planning to install SQL Server 6.5 on a machine with an older version, refer to Chapter 2.◀

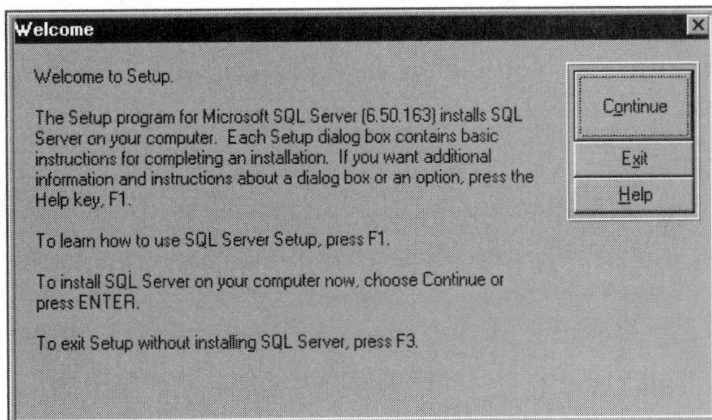

Figure 1-1:
This is the first screen you see when you run SETUP.EXE.

Click Continue or press Enter. If you have installed SQL Server once already, you see a SQL Server Already Installed dialog box letting you know that. If not, you see the usual dialog box in Figure 1-2 for supplying your name and organization.

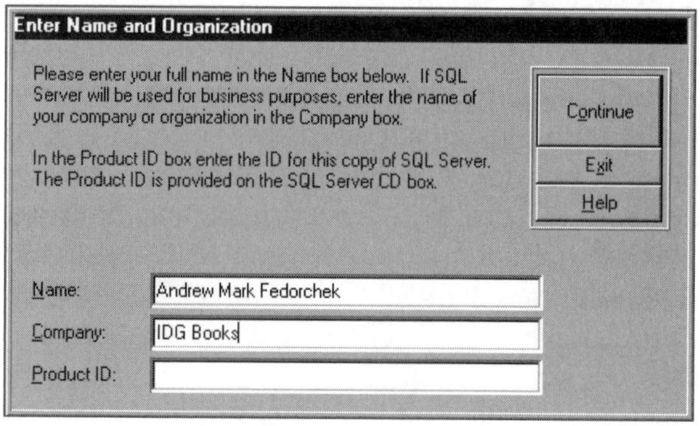

Figure 1-2:
As usual, you have to supply your name, company, and so on.

As with all other such registrations, the Name is mandatory, and the other two are optional. The product ID should be on your CD-ROM box. Click Continue after you've filled in this screen. The Verify Name and Organization dialog box appears. Continue or press Enter if everything is correct. Now you should see the Microsoft SQL Server 6.5 Options dialog box (Figure 1-3).

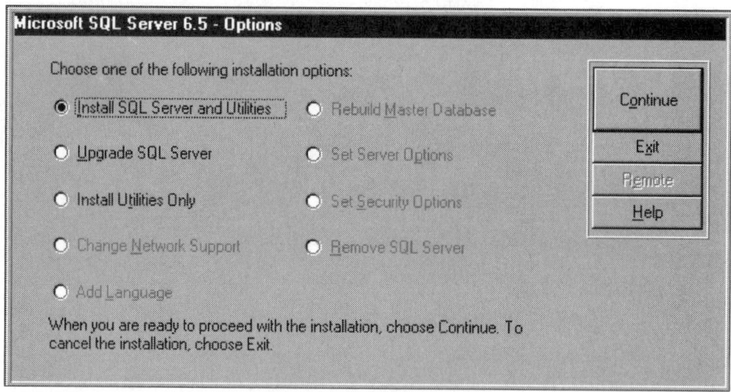

Figure 1-3:
Choose Install SQL Server and Utilities from the Options window.

Check Install SQL Server and Utilities (if you are upgrading, check that option) and click Continue or press Enter. Now you are at the Choose Licensing Mode dialog box (Figure 1-4).

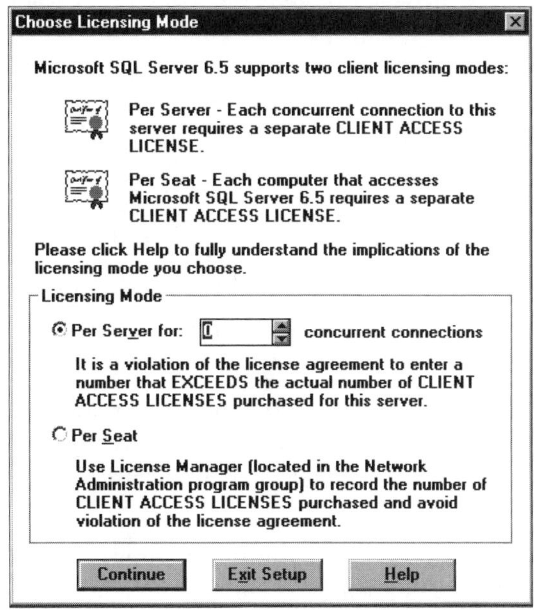

Figure 1-4:
Choose the licensing method in this dialog box best suited to your needs.

In your SQL Server box should be a folded card that says MICROSOFT LICENSE AGREEMENT. The number of licenses you have purchased should be above that. The question you must now answer is how you want to use those licenses. This idea of how to "use" licenses is intended to give you more flexibility in using SQL Server. The first option, Per Server, specifies the number of connections SQL Server should allow. The second option, Per Seat, limits the number of computers or workstations that can connect to SQL Server. Here are some points to keep in mind about the license use options:

- If you don't know which one you want, take the first one, Per Server. You can change from Per Server to Per Seat at no charge. If you do change, it is a one-time, one-way change.
- It is illegal for you to type in a number of licenses higher than the number you purchased. The software lets you type in whatever number you want because there is nothing on the CD-ROM indicating how many licenses you have.
- Both options try to use node-based client access. This means that SQL Server 6.5 tries to identify the originating workstation for each connection and counts all connections from the same workstation as one client.

For example, if you have the SQL Enterprise Manager, MS Access, and MS Query all open and all connected to SQL Server, it is still one client, both in Per Server and Per Seat mode. Previous versions of client software don't support node-based access, so every connection you make with them counts as a separate client. Other vendors' software may or may not support node-based licensing. Check with the vendor.

- Microsoft's SQL Server tools register as clients, too. This may seem obvious, but we didn't want you to think that maybe you could have an unlimited number of SQL Enterprise Manager clients.
- Per Server mode is particularly useful for a server that won't have many connections, but is always being accessed from different locations.
- Per Seat mode gets a workstation into all SQL Servers on the network. This is what starts making Per Seat really pay off. This is also why you don't type the number of client licenses in for that mode; it is controlled by the network.
- When you reach the connection limit in Per Server licensing, SQL Server gives you an error message and won't allow a new connection until at least one existing connection closes.

Once you have selected the licensing mode you want, click Continue. You get a confirmation dialog box, and you must check "I agree that..." to continue. Now you get to the SQL Server Installation Path dialog box shown in Figure 1-5.

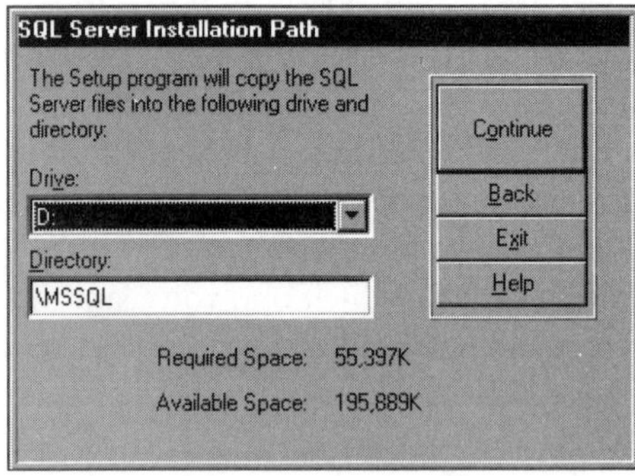

Figure 1-5:
Type a valid FAT 8.3 path in the SQL Server Installation Path dialog box.

The directory and filenames must conform to the FAT 8.3 naming convention, even if installed on an NTFS volume. Be particularly careful not to put spaces in the name. The Setup program does not give you an error if you type in a long filename. It chugs along and lets you pick all your other options and then aborts later on.◀

If you change the default directory, reading the SQL Server manuals and reading this book will be confusing for you, because you have to remember that your files are in a different location than the one you see in the text.◀

Remember the long discussion about drive arrays earlier in this chapter? If you do have your server set up with both a RAID 5 and a mirrored pair, make sure you pick the RAID 5 drive for your installation directory. You are reserving the mirrored pair for the transaction log. Click Continue or press Enter when you are ready. Now we get to the Master Device Creation dialog box (Figure 1-6).

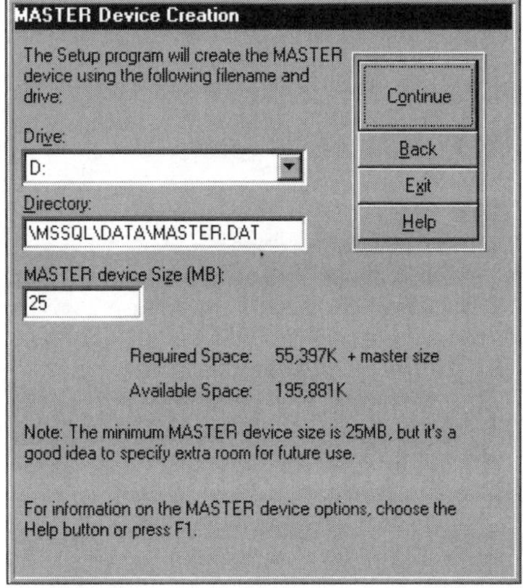

Figure 1-6:
Choose a location for the master device with good fault tolerance in this dialog box.

You do not have to put the master device in the same drive or directory as SQL Server. The master database does not have a separate device for the log; the data and log are together. Your two decision criteria for where to put the master device are as follows:

- Put the master device wherever you have the most fault tolerance. Hopefully, you have either a RAID 5 or a mirror pair of drives on which to put the master. If not, make a note that you need to set up mirroring in SQL Server for the master device.
- This is a less important consideration, but ideally you would put the master device wherever you plan to put the rest of the data devices. For I/O optimization, you expect more random than sequential access to the master database.

For example, suppose your server has a mirrored pair labeled as C: where you have installed Windows NT, and a RAID 5 labeled as drive D:. You may have chosen C: and \SQL60 in the SQL Server Installation Path dialog box, but you ought to put D: for the drive in the master device dialog box.

Click Continue and you see the SQL Server Books Online dialog box (Figure 1-7).

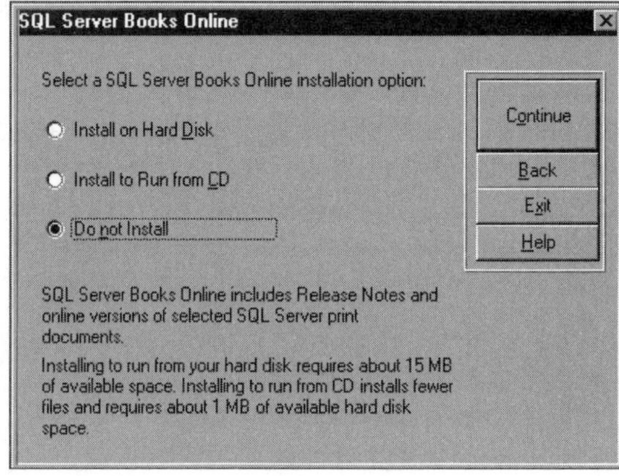

Figure 1-7:
Don't install books on the Server; install them on some other file server.

You can always install these later if you aren't sure what you want to do right now. If you are planning to put the books on a hard disk on a file server of the network, choose Do not Install because right now Setup isn't going to let you decide what drive to put the books on. Go back later and use Setup to put the books on some other server. Don't let your SQL Server machine become a file server. If you do want to put the books on this hard drive, you need another 15MB of space. Click Continue or press Enter, and we get to the good stuff: Installation Options.

If you are upgrading, Setup asks you to specify the master device to upgrade. You can't change the location. Here the installation and upgrade part ways. In upgrade you do not get to specify options: SQL Server 6.5 inherits the options you set in SQL Server 4.21 or SQL Server 6.0.◀

Choosing your installation options

If you have been following along you are now at the *Installation Options* dialog box (Figure 1-8). You can also get here by choosing Set Server Options in the Microsoft SQL Server 6.5 Options dialog box. Slow down because this is the important stuff.

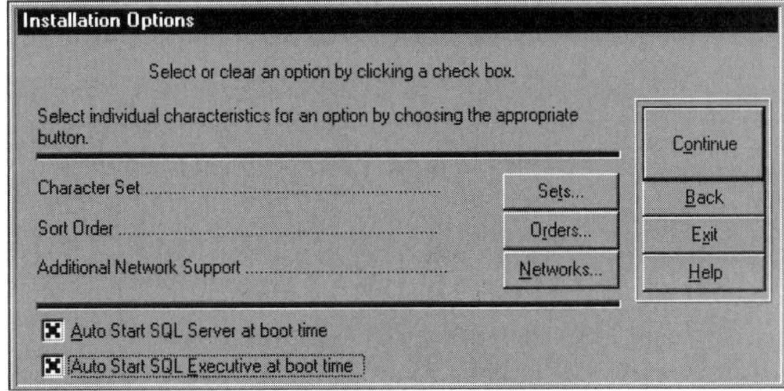

Figure 1-8:
You probably want to have SQL Server and SQL Executive start at boot time.

Character set

A character set is a set of 256 uppercase and lowercase letters, numbers, and symbols. The printable characters of the first 128 values are the same for all character set choices; it is the remaining 128 that vary. The default is ISO 8859-1 (Latin 1 or ANSI). Accept the default unless you have a good reason not to.

All the servers in your network should have the same character set, if at all possible. Otherwise, you cannot restore a backup from one server into another, and replication might give you misleading results.

If you are planning to load backups from an older version of SQL Server, you must choose the same character set that database had.

This is one of the options you can't easily change if you later decide you want something different. To change it, you would have to rebuild the master database and reload your data. *Reload* does not mean something simple like restoring from a backup because, as we have said, a backup from one character set does not work in another. You would have to do something more complex, like bulk copy all your data in.

Sort order

The sort order of your server provides the rules for collating data. Thus, not only does this affect the order in which SQL Server sorts your data, but also the sort order affects comparisons in WHERE clauses and DISTINCT queries. Unless you have some special requirements, your decision boils down to this: Do you accept the default (Dictionary order, case insensitive), or do you go for Binary? In any case-insensitive order a query like:

```
SELECT name, suid
   FROM sysusers
   WHERE name = 'DBO'
```

will return a result even though the name will be stored as 'dbo'. But in a binary sort order, 'DBO' is not the same as 'dbo', so the query above would return no rows. This can be maddening if you aren't used to it. The trouble is, Microsoft's testing shows that "Dictionary order, case-insensitive" sorts are 20 percent slower than Binary sorts. This doesn't mean your whole SQL Server will be 20 percent slower, of course, just your sorting operations.

It's up to you. When we first started with SQL Server years ago, we chose Binary. It took all of one week for our users, who were coming from a case-insensitive mainframe environment, to demand that we convert to case-insensitive.

This is the other option you can't easily change if you later decide you want something different. To change it, you would again have to rebuild the master database and reload your data, and as we said before, *reload* does not mean something simple like restoring databases from a backup.

Additional network support

Cross-Reference

You can add more network support easily after installation. By default, SQL Server sets up Named Pipes, but you can add others. Refer to Chapter 4 for more information.◀

Auto start options

These options specify whether you want SQL Server and the SQL Executive to start at boot time. These options are cleared by default, which puzzles us. That means you have to start these services manually. We recommend that you check these two boxes, unless you are running in a development environment where you will only occasionally use SQL Server. You will be able to change these options after you install SQL Server.

SQL executive log on account

Click Continue and you see the SQL Executive Log On Account dialog box (Figure 1-9).

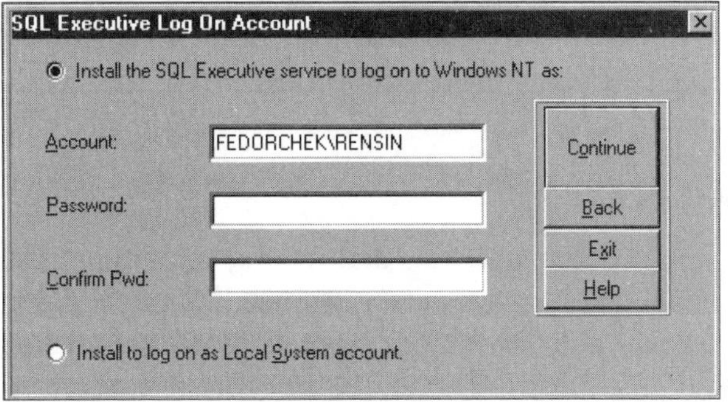

Figure 1-9:
Enter a valid password in the SQL Executive Log On Account dialog box.

Supplying an account here lets SQL Server go out and do things on the network, like performing replication. You can give SQL Server its own login or just put in the login of someone who is in the Administrators group of the network. If you click Local System account, you can change it later. This is the last option. After you click Continue here, you can go for a cup of coffee; Setup takes several minutes at least.

Two services need a login and password: SQL Executive and MS SQL Server. The latter gets the local system account by default in the installation, and you can only change it from the Control Panel.◀

When you are finished

When the setup is completed, you should see the Microsoft SQL Server 6.5 - Completed dialog box (Figure 1-10).

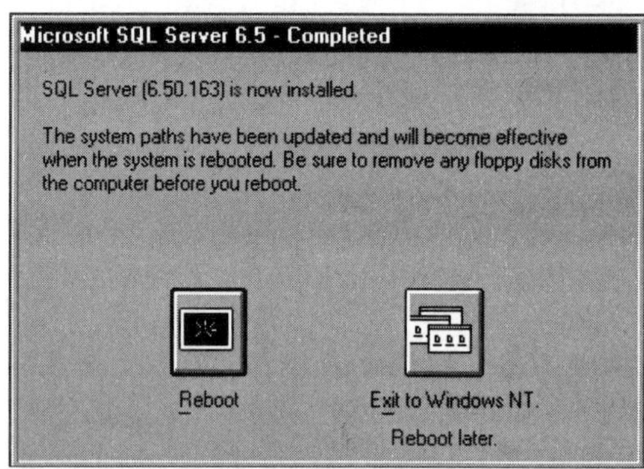

Figure 1-10:
If you don't see this at the end, something went wrong.

If you do not see this dialog box, something is seriously wrong, and you probably will have to rerun the installation program. If you do get this far, you need to do two things *immediately*. First, make sure SQL Server installed correctly. From the Microsoft SQL Server 6.5 program group, double-click the ISQL/w icon. Without changing any of the text boxes or radio buttons, click connect. If a query window opens, your installation was successful. Type these two lines:

```
select @@servername
select @@version
```

Click the green arrow. You should get back your server name and the SQL Server version number.

The second thing you need to do is change the sa password. Right now it is null. Click the Query tab, press Ctrl-Shift-Del to clear the text, and type the following:

```
sp_password null, 'your_new_password', sa
```

Then, click the green arrow. You should get this message:

```
Password changed.
```

Close this application. If you try to use it again, you have to supply the new password in the password box.

If you forget the password, you do *not* have to reinstall SQL Server, but you do have to have an administrator of the network bail you out. More on that in Chapter 7.◀

SUMMARY

SQL Server setup is pretty easy, provided you give it some thought before you dive in. The hardware requirements are about what you would expect for a high-end server machine. If you have a drive array, there are a bunch of ways to set it up, but usually you want to use RAID 5 for your data and mirrored drives for the logs. Make sure you take care of Windows NT-related issues before running Setup, such as making sure your computer is not a BDC, choosing your file system, and deciding whether to use disk compression. When you run Setup, you have to choose either Per Server or Per Seat client licenses. You set several options. The most critical and hardest to change are Character Set and Sort Order. When you have finished, you should test your installation and change the sa password.

REVIEW QUESTIONS

Q: How much RAM does a SQL Server machine require?

A: 16MB, but 32MB is better.

Q: What are two reasons for buying much more that 32MB of RAM?

A: SQL Server can use the extra RAM as a data cache, and you can put tempdb in RAM.

Q: Which operating systems does SQL Server run on?

A: Windows NT, Server or Workstation. That's all. Not Windows 95, not OS/2, not UNIX.

Q: Which RAID level gives you the most disk space? The least?

A: RAID 0 gives you the most, 100 percent of the space you purchased space. RAID 1 gives you the least, only 50 percent of what you purchased. RAID 5 gives you one disk less of space than you purchased.

Q: Which RAID level writes data the fastest? The slowest?

A: RAID 0 writes the fastest, because it has no fault tolerance. (Fault tolerance, by definition, involves some level of duplication, and will therefore write more slowly than RAID 0.) RAID 5 writes data the slowest because each write involves reading two blocks and writing two blocks.

Q: What is the rationale for leaving a disk or mirrored pair out of RAID 5 just for the transaction log?

A: SQL Server writes to a transaction log sequentially, which means you can minimize seek time by putting the log on its own disk.

Q: Which file system gives better performance, NTFS or FAT?

A: They are about the same performance-wise, but NTFS is preferable for other reasons.

Q: What mode of client licensing should you pick if you aren't sure which will be best for you?

A: Per Server because you can switch from Per Server to Per Seat. You can't switch the other way.

Q: What special rules are there for naming the installation path and the path for the master device?

A: You must use 8.3 names, even if you choose NTFS.

Q: What are the two Setup options that are hardest to change later?

A: Character Set and Sort Order.

Q: What happens if you want to change them later?

A: You have to rebuild the master device and reload your data.

Q: What is the most important thing to do when the installation is finished, other than testing the installation and changing the system administrator password?

A: Reading the next chapter of this book!

Chapter

UPGRADING SQL SERVER

2

*T*he fact that we decided to devote a whole chapter to how to upgrade SQL Server should tell you something: the upgrade isn't like falling off a log, in our opinion. If you skipped the first chapter, please go back and read it. When you upgrade, you shut down operations anyway, so why not take this opportunity to review all your hardware and operating system choices. We address both upgrading from SQL Server 4.2 and SQL Server 6.0 in this chapter.

WHAT'S IN THIS CHAPTER

This chapter discusses upgrading to SQL Server 6.5 from all aspects, including the following:

- Why you should upgrade at all
- Problems to look for in upgrading
- Strategies to protect yourself in upgrading
- How actually to do the upgrade
- Things to do after you upgrade

Why Bother to Upgrade?

You may be wondering if you should bother upgrading. As the saying goes, "If it ain't broke, don't fix it." If you are using SQL Server 4.21, we strongly recommend that you upgrade. Here are two reasons:

- If you are still using SQL Server 4.21, you'd better upgrade while you still can. Who knows how long Microsoft is planning to support SQL Server 4.21? You can upgrade from SQL Server 4.21 to SQL Server 6.5, but there is no guarantee that the next version of SQL Server will allow you to upgrade from SQL Server 4.21.
- SQL Server 6.5 contains several new features compared with SQL Server 4.21: Declarative Referential Integrity (DRI), replication, better query optimization, and Transact-SQL cursors, to name only a few. We can't possibly overstate the difference between these products.

If you are using SQL Server 6.0 and wondering if you should upgrade to SQL Server 6.5, our answer again is an unqualified "Yes," though we have to admit this upgrade isn't as urgent. The reasons for upgrading include

- SQL Server 6.5 fixes "undocumented features" (a.k.a. bugs) of SQL Server 6.0. Microsoft isn't going to distribute any more patches for SQL Server 6.0, so you need to upgrade to have the best code.
- SQL Server 6.5 includes a lot of Transact-SQL enhancements, including ANSI-Standard joins, CUBE and ROLLUP, and more.
- SQL Server 6.5 gives you the SQL Trace utility to trap all SQL going to a server.
- Replication works better in SQL Server 6.5.
- All the documentation you will find, including this book, focuses on SQL Server 6.5 (although we tried hard to include sidebars on relevant SQL Server 6.0 and 4.2 topics, where appropriate).

You may not use the new features right away, but it won't hurt to have them. Your databases and application should run just fine. The CD-ROMs for both SQL Server 6.0 and SQL Server 6.5 contain extensive lists of what's new in each version.

Some Words of Warning

You have probably done more upgrades than you can count: Windows 3.1 to Windows for Workgroups to Windows 95; Windows NT 3.1 to 3.5 to 3.51 to 4.0; various versions of Word, Excel, MS-DOS, and so on. Most people have few, if any problems with upgrading. *This is different.* We don't know of anyone who *didn't* have a problem in upgrading from one version of SQL Server to another. Read this section carefully, please.

Consider installing instead of upgrading

We are jumping ahead of ourselves because we know some of you may be actually planning to do the upgrade as you read this chapter. The rest of this section will explain in detail why we make the warning statement above. Before you upgrade to SQL Server 6.5, you should consider whether it is feasible for you just to install SQL Server 6.5 on the same computer and either transfer your data or restore it from a backup into SQL Server 6.5.

SQL Server 4.x and SQL Server 6.5 can run at the same time on the same machine, which means you can transfer databases from one to the other. SQL Server 6.0 and SQL Server 6.5 can't do this because they share the same Registry Key. If you want to use the Transfer Manager, you would have to install SQL Server 6.0 on another machine, restore a backup into that machine, and then transfer it over.◀

Alternatively, you could make the scripts for your databases, bulk copy all the data out, and then run the scripts and bulk copy into SQL Server 6.5. Chapter 11 shows you a quick and easy way to bulk copy out or in *all* your tables in one shot. What you aren't going to get out of a transfer or a script is the configuration settings of your existing SQL Server installation, such as how much RAM SQL Server gets, the maximum number of user connections, and so on. These you must remember to transfer by hand.◀

The advantages of doing a fresh installation are the following:

- If something goes wrong, you haven't lost what you had before. One of the things we like about Windows NT upgrades is that if something goes wrong, the upgrade program is usually pretty good about leaving the previous operating system and all your files intact. You won't have any such luck with SQL Server upgrades. A failed SQL Server upgrade usually destroys all existing data, forcing you to reinstall the old version of SQL Server and restore all databases from tape. No kidding. It has happened to us several times.◀

- When you try to run your database scripts in SQL Server 6.5, you get to preview *everything* that SQL Server 6.5 doesn't like. The utility for checking your databases before you upgrade, CHKUPG.EXE, which we discuss later, is woefully inadequate. It doesn't check a lot of problem areas, and what it does check, it doesn't always report accurately. Running scripts to create a copy of a database identifies all bad data definition language (DDL).
- It lets you do all the housecleaning you need to do anyway, like reestablishing the correct fill factors on your tables (when you transfer data in).
- You have the comfort of knowing that your old version is there sleeping, waiting for you to fall back to it if you hit a wall with SQL Server 6.5.

The only real disadvantage to doing the fresh installation is that you obviously need as much free disk space as your current production SQL Server environment occupies (yet another reason to buy a lot of hard drive space). Even if you don't have enough space for all your data, you really should find some machine with the 81MB of free space you need for an installation and run just the scripts for your databases. Ninety-five percent of the problems show up in this exercise.

Cross-Reference

Be sure to skip to Chapter 18 for tips on how to cope with the SQL Server Script Generator.◀

Warning

If you choose a fresh installation instead of an upgrade, don't transfer a 6.0 database with the Transfer Manager. In case you haven't already noticed, the SQL Server 6.0 Transfer Manager application does *not* transfer any of your DRI. (This major shortcoming is corrected in SQL Server 6.5, yet another reason to upgrade.) Therefore, you shouldn't transfer a 6.0 database into 6.5 with the Transfer Manager. You should use scripts to build the database, and then you can either transfer or bulk copy it.◀

Before you install SQL Server 6.5 on a machine that has SQL Server 6.0, you have to use either the 6.0 or the 6.5 SETUP.EXE program to "Remove" SQL Server. Be very, very careful that you do not delete the contents of the \SQL60 directory. By default, the program plays it safe and doesn't wipe out this directory, so you would have to go out of your way to do this. Export the SQL Server 6.0 Registry Key to a file before you do this.

No turning back

You can't "un-upgrade" SQL Server. Once you upgrade, that's it. However, all the applications that worked with an older version of SQL Server should work with a newer version, provided the applications don't depend on some feature (or bug) that is no longer supported. For example, a query like the following was legal in 4.2*x* (but is illegal in ANSI-SQL, which is why SQL Server no longer supports it):

```
SELECT user_name(uid), o.name, sysindexes.name, i.indid
   FROM sysobjects o, sysindexes i
   WHERE o.id = i.id
```

We have tried as much as possible in this book not to use a particular topic, such as SQL, until we reach the chapter that explains it. This chapter is the one exception. If you are reading this chapter, you are already using a previous version of SQL Server and will be familiar with all its features.◀

Try this in 6.*x* and you get

```
Msg 107, Level 15, State 1
The column prefix 'sysindexes' does not match with a table name or alias name used
in the query.
```

The correct query uses i.name instead of sysindexes.name. Another trick you could pull in SQL Server 4.2*x* is this:

```
SELECT *
   FROM sysobjects
   GROUP BY name
   HAVING COUNT(*) > 1
```

This isn't ANSI standard (either SQL89 or SQL92), and Microsoft eliminated it in SQL Server 6.0. These are the kinds of things that will cause your application trouble. What's worse is if you have used them in views or stored procedures in the database. The upgrade *should* be able to be handle it, but you'd better make database backups just in case.

There are workarounds for these and all other problems, of course. The cheap solution is to use trace flag 204 to invoke SQL Server 4.2 behavior on this query. See Chapter 26 for more details. Another idea is to see if you can get by with just the name and count in the SELECT list:

```
SELECT name, COUNT(*) row_count
   FROM sysobjects
   GROUP BY name
   HAVING COUNT(*) > 1
```

Finally, if you must see all the rows of sysobjects, you can write

```
SELECT *
   FROM sysobjects
   WHERE name IN ( SELECT name
      FROM sysobjects
      GROUP BY name
      HAVING COUNT(*) > 1 )
```

Another problem is how well the upgrade copes with the aftermath of bugs in earlier versions. For example, the first release of SQL Server 6.0 allowed you to use the ALTER TABLE command to establish a primary key on columns that allow nulls. SQL Server 6.5 doesn't allow this. What is the upgrade supposed to do? Drop your offending primary key and all foreign keys that reference it? Alert you to the problem and cancel the upgrade? Or will it just hang, taking your production environment down with it?

To weed out all these problems in SQL Server databases themselves, create the script for your current version and try to run it in a fresh 6.5 installation. As for your applications, you may not find out that you are using unsupported SQL features until you test the applications with the upgraded server.

By the way, the SQL Server 4.21 client tools will in fact work after you upgrade, but you have to run two scripts from the server's INSTALL directory. They are \MSSQL\INSTALL\ADMIN60.SQL and \MSSQL\INSTALL \OBJECT60.SQL. (They are named *60.SQL because they haven't changed between SQL Server 6.0 and SQL Server 6.5.)

In SQL Server 4.*x*, by default your server software was installed in \SQL. In SQL Server 6.0 the default installation put the SQL Server application in \SQL60. Now with SQL Server 6.5 the stuff goes in \MSSQL. We will always refer to \MSSQL, unless we are explicitly asking you to get a program from a previous version.

Before You Even Start to Upgrade

Here is list of things you must do before you upgrade. As far as we are concerned, these steps aren't optional if you are upgrading anything other than a test environment.

Back up your databases

Before you start, make a full backup of all your databases, including the master database. Test one of the backups to make sure all your hardware is still working. Go find the CD from your existing version of SQL Server and make sure you still have it. Don't just rely on your last scheduled backup. We aren't kidding here. One of us had an upgrade bomb in a production environment and spent the rest of the night restoring everything from tape.

You can restore the backups of an older version into a newer version, provided you use the same sort order and character set when you install the new version. Note that the default character set changed from SQL Server 4.21 to SQL Server 6.0, so if you just accept the installation defaults you will *not* be able to use your old backups. This is another reason for making the scripts and doing bulk copies, which is our next point.

Make scripts for your databases

At the risk of beating a dead horse, we have found that scripts are an invaluable upgrade tool. They document your meta-data, your data definition language. It wouldn't hurt to make scripts for your databases, including some of the options you may not usually check, like "all logins." You can use the SQL Server 6.0 Transfer Manager to bulkcopy the data out and make the script at the same time if you aren't worried about capturing the DRI. Otherwise you need to use the SQL Server 6.0 Script Generator.

Do a Windows NT backup

The main thing here is to use Windows NT to back up the SQL Server directories — all directories that contain SQL Server devices or SQL Server installation files. If there is any doubt about just where all the files are for your SQL Server devices, run this query:

```
SELECT phyname
   FROM master..sysdevices
```

You must back up each of these files. Remember when we told you that an aborted upgrade can sometimes destroy your existing SQL Server installation? That is why you are doing this backup. You might find it a lot easier to restore the SQL Server device files than to restore all the databases from backups.

Make sure no databases are read only

The upgrade is going to have to change things in every database (like the system tables), so you cannot have any database in read-only mode. You can easily find your read only databases with this query:

```
SELECT name
   FROM master..sysdatabases
   WHERE POWER( 2, 10 ) & status != 0
```

Run CHKUPG.EXE

This is a program that checks for three things:

- All database statuses are acceptable (what we just checked above).
- All necessary comments exist in all syscomments system tables. Each CHECK constraint, default, DEFAULT constraint, rule, stored procedure, trigger, and view in a database should have at least one row of text in syscomments to define it. If you or an application deleted the text, the upgrade program can't upgrade that database.
- You have no keyword conflicts. With each release of SQL Server there are reserved words, which you shouldn't use, and keywords, which you can't use. Typically, the reserved words of one release become keywords in the next release. You may have tables, columns, and so on named with a word that SQL Server 6.5 needs to use. For example, if you have table with columns named "left" and "right", CHKUPG will flag that table because these words are used in the new ANSI style joins.

  The syntax for CHKUPG.EXE is

```
chkupg /Usa /Ppassword [/Sservername] /ofilename
```

filename is the name of the output file that chkupg will create as it runs. If you run it at the server machine, you can leave /S off. The rest of the parameters are required. After you run it, you get

```
SQL Server message 5701, state 2, severity 0:
Changed database context to 'master'.
DB with Status problems: 0, DB with Syscomments problems: 0, DB with Keyword
problems: 0
```

You are looking for 0, 0, 0 problems. If you have problems, open the output file you specified to see what you need to correct.

Make sure you have enough free disk space

An upgrade from SQL Server 6.0 needs 20MB of free space, plus 2MB in the master database. An upgrade from SQL Server 4.2*x* needs 65MB of free space, plus 9MB of free space in the master database. Don't risk cutting it close. Take this opportunity to do some housekeeping on your drive.

Backup the Windows NT Registry

You should be really interested in the SQL Server key of the Windows NT Registry for the local machine, which you can simply export to file, but backing up the whole Registry is the safest approach. By the way, if you don't have a Windows NT Emergency disk, now would be a good time to make one. Just in case.

Backup the passwords separately

In SQL Server 6.0, the passwords are already encrypted, so if you're upgrading from 6.0, you can ignore this section. If you are using SQL Server 4.*x* and have become addicted to the fact that you as the system administrator can see everyone's passwords in syslogins, know that you are about to lose that convenience. Copy the names and passwords into another table or a file if that data is important to you.

Upgrading to SQL Server 6.5

Once you have done all the preparatory work, the upgrade itself is quite simple. The procedure is virtually identical to the installation, except you get fewer options. Therefore, we are only going to highlight the extra steps of an upgrade:

1. Log on to the server with administrator privileges. We forgot this step once and got into trouble. SQL Server upgrade needs the Administrator's privileges.

2. Close all applications on the server, including SQL Server itself. You can shut SQL Server down either from the SQL Enterprise Manager (SQL Server 6.0) or from the SQL Service Manager (SQL Server 6.0 or SQL Server 4.2). Technically you only need to make sure that no application is open that might be using SQL Server DLLs, but the safest bet is to close all applications. Don't forget the Performance Monitor, and don't forget to stop the existing SQL Server service.

Cross-Reference

3. Proceed by running SETUP.EXE. You will, of course, select Upgrade SQL Server. From that point on, the upgrade is just like an installation but with a few less options. Refer to Chapter 1 for help.◀

After You Upgrade from SQL Server 4.x - DRI

One of the major reasons we rushed to upgrade from SQL Server 4.2 to SQL Server 6.*x* was to take advantage of DRI. We were really hoping for some kind of utility to help us with this specific conversion. There isn't one. Here we cover what we did; we hope you can make use of it, too.

Warning

We cover SQL later in this book, the system tables later still. This section unashamedly assumes you are an experienced SQL Server database owner and well-versed in all the intricacies of SQL and the system tables. If the information below looks like Greek, don't worry. We explain how to do this kind of stuff later in the book.◀

Converting your unique clustered indexes to primary keys

Our approach to upgrading to DRI starts with converting the unique indexes to primary keys. If you've been a good database owner and put a unique index on all tables, or even better a clustered unique index, you can convert these indexes to primary keys. But before we begin, let's see what *won't* be converted.

Tables with no unique index

If a table has no unique index, you can't even guess what its primary key should be. See if you can get some kind of unique index on them. The way to identify such rogue tables is to look for table entries in sysobjects without a corresponding unique index entry in sysindexes. Unique indexes have the second bit of the status field turned on.

```
SELECT USER_NAME(uid), name
   FROM sysobjects o
   WHERE type = 'u'
      AND NOT EXISTS (SELECT *
         FROM sysindexes i
         WHERE o.id = i.id
            AND power(2,1) & status != 0)
ORDER BY 1, 2
```

This returns a list of tables without unique indexes. They will not get any DRI from the methods that follow.

Tables with no clustered index

Whether a table has a clustered index isn't necessarily relevant from a DRI perspective, but you should check for this at this time. If you later put on a clustered index, SQL Server will rebuild all your non-clustered indexes, including the primary key, if it is not clustered. Identifying a table without a clustered index is simple because they all have indid = 0 in the sysindexes table.

```
SELECT USER_NAME(uid), o.name
   FROM sysindexes i, sysobjects o
   WHERE indid = 0
      AND i.id = o.id
      AND type = 'u'
   ORDER BY 1, 2
```

This returns a list of tables without clustered indexes. You may want to examine why this is so. We go into great detail on this in Chapter 28.◀

Establishing primary keys

We want to drop the unique, clustered indexes and replace them with primary keys. Here's how: the results of this query do the conversion for you. Run the query, make sure you are happy with the SQL it produces, and then copy and paste the results window back into the query window. Run it if you are satisfied with the primary keys it wants to set up.

```
SELECT "DROP INDEX "+o.name+"."+i.name
      +char(13)+"GO"+char(13)
      +"ALTER TABLE "+o.name+" ADD CONSTRAINT PK_"+ltrim(str(o.id,12))
+" PRIMARY KEY ("
      +INDEX_COL(o.name,1,1)
      +CASE INDEX_COL(o.name,1,2) WHEN null THEN ""
         ELSE ","+INDEX_COL(o.name,1,2) END
      +CASE INDEX_COL(o.name,1,3) WHEN null THEN ""
         ELSE ","+INDEX_COL(o.name,1,3) END
      +CASE INDEX_COL(o.name,1,4) WHEN null THEN ""
         ELSE ","+INDEX_COL(o.name,1,4) END
      +CASE INDEX_COL(o.name,1,5) WHEN null THEN ""
         ELSE ","+INDEX_COL(o.name,1,5) END
      +CASE INDEX_COL(o.name,1,6) WHEN null THEN ""
         ELSE ","+INDEX_COL(o.name,1,6) END
      +CASE INDEX_COL(o.name,1,7) WHEN null THEN ""
         ELSE ","+INDEX_COL(o.name,1,7) END
      +CASE INDEX_COL(o.name,1,8) WHEN null THEN ""
         ELSE ","+INDEX_COL(o.name,1,8) END
      +CASE INDEX_COL(o.name,1,9) WHEN null THEN ""
         ELSE ","+INDEX_COL(o.name,1,9) END
      +CASE INDEX_COL(o.name,1,10) WHEN null THEN ""
         ELSE ","+INDEX_COL(o.name,1,10) END
      +CASE INDEX_COL(o.name,1,11) WHEN null THEN ""
         ELSE ","+INDEX_COL(o.name,1,11) END
      +CASE INDEX_COL(o.name,1,12) WHEN null THEN ""
         ELSE ","+INDEX_COL(o.name,1,12) END
      +CASE INDEX_COL(o.name,1,13) WHEN null THEN ""
         ELSE ","+INDEX_COL(o.name,1,13) END
      +CASE INDEX_COL(o.name,1,14) WHEN null THEN ""
         ELSE ","+INDEX_COL(o.name,1,14) END
      +CASE INDEX_COL(o.name,1,15) WHEN null THEN ""
         ELSE ","+INDEX_COL(o.name,1,15) END
      +CASE INDEX_COL(o.name,1,16) WHEN null THEN ""
         ELSE ","+INDEX_COL(o.name,1,16) END
      +")"
      +char(13)+"GO"
   FROM sysindexes i, sysobjects o
   WHERE i.id = o.id
      AND indid = 1
      AND type = 'u'
      AND power(2,1) & status != 0
```

When you run this in pubs (the example database that comes with SQL Server), you see the following:

```
DROP INDEX authors.UPKCL_auidind
GO
ALTER TABLE authors ADD CONSTRAINT PK_16003088 PRIMARK KEY (au_id)
GO
DROP INDEX publishers.UPKCL_pubind
GO
ALTER TABLE publishers ADD CONSTRAINT PK_112003430 PRIMARK KEY (pub_id)
GO
DROP INDEX titles.UPKCL_titleidind
GO
ALTER TABLE titles ADD CONSTRAINT PK_192003715 PRIMARK KEY (title_id)
GO
DROP INDEX titleauthor.UPKCL_taind
GO
ALTER TABLE titleauthor ADD CONSTRAINT PK_288004057 PRIMARK KEY (au_id, title_id)
GO
DROP INDEX stores.UPK_storeid
GO
ALTER TABLE stores ADD CONSTRAINT PK_368004342 PRIMARK KEY (stor_id)
GO
DROP INDEX sales.UPKCL_sales
GO
ALTER TABLE sales ADD CONSTRAINT PK_416004513 PRIMARK KEY (stor_id, ord_num,
title_id)
GO
DROP INDEX jobs.PK__jobs__job_id__243D6C4D
GO
ALTER TABLE jobs ADD CONSTRAINT PK_592005140 PRIMARK KEY (job_id)
GO
DROP INDEX pub_info.UPKCL_pubinfo
GO
ALTER TABLE pub_info ADD CONSTRAINT PK_688005482 PRIMARK KEY (pub_id)
GO
```

Converting your foreign keys

This is a mess. You could write similar SQL for reading syskeys, *provided* you made sure your SQL Server 4.2 syskeys entries matched your unique, clustered indexes. However, even if you do that, you will still have the triggers enforcing your foreign keys, which sticks you with double checking. If you have nonreferential integrity logic in your triggers, the only safe way to upgrade them to DRI is one by one in an editor.

SUMMARY

SQL Server upgrades aren't to be taken lightly. We have found them to be more likely to fail than any other kind of upgrade. Consider installing and transferring your data instead of upgrading. If you do upgrade, back up everything seven ways from Sunday, including SQL Server backups, scripts and bulk copies, and Windows NT backups. Shut everything down before you upgrade.

REVIEW QUESTIONS

Q: Why would an upgrade bomb?

A: For any number of reasons. Insufficient drive space, failure to stop the old version of SQL Server, failure to run CHKUPG.EXE, failure to log on as the Administrator, to name just a few.

Q: How many kinds of backups should you do?

A: As many as you can think of. You must absolutely back up master and all your SQL Server databases. Back up the SQL Server directories with Windows NT utilities. Back up the Windows NT Registry. Make scripts for your databases just in case, and bulkcopy out the data and stick that on another tape.

Q: Which versions of SQL Server can run simultaneously?

A: SQL Server 4.21 and SQL Server 6.x can run at the same time. SQL Server 6.0 and SQL Server 6.5 can't run at the same time on the same box.

Q: What is a good alternative to upgrading?

A: Just installing fresh and transferring your data to the new installation.

Chapter 3

The SQL Enterprise Manager

The SQL Enterprise Manager is one of the things that puts SQL Server out in front of its competition. It virtually *is* SQL Server, at least from the perspective of a database owner or a system administrator. Add it to your StartUp folder because you will use it all the time. Microsoft intended it to be the one tool that you would need to administer everything from individual objects to whole databases, from one server to large groups of servers. Consequently, much of this book is about using the SQL Enterprise Manager. This chapter focuses on the basic elements and functions of the SQL Enterprise Manager so that you'll be comfortable using it to perform the tasks described in other chapters.

What's in This Chapter

The generic SQL Enterprise Manager concepts that we cover in this chapter are the following:

- Learning what you need to know before you start SQL Enterprise Manager
- Getting started with the SQL Enterprise Manager
- Using the Server Manager window

- Getting acquainted with the SQL Enterprise Manager menus and toolbar buttons
- Understanding how to use the Query Analyzer

The SQL Enterprise Manager runs only in Windows NT and Windows 95. There are some minor SQL Enterprise Manager features that do not work if you are using Windows 95; we cover those in this chapter. The SQL Enterprise Manager is installed by SETUP.EXE on the server. We discuss installing it on a client machine in Chapter 5.◀

Before You Start

Before we get into the nitty-gritty of the SQL Enterprise Manager, it is important to understand some background about SQL Server applications.

How the SQL Enterprise Manager is built

Microsoft's SQL Server applications are constructed according to an important hierarchy called the SQL Distributed Management Framework (SQL-DMF). At the bottom level are Transact-SQL commands. Transact-SQL is Microsoft's version of the SQL standard. Everything in SQL Server can be done from simple text commands if you know what you are doing. The next level up is a set of distributed management objects that invoke the Transact-SQL commands. These objects provide programmers with an object-oriented interface to SQL Server, and they are what you should use in your Visual Basic or Visual C++ applications to communicate with SQL Server. At the top of the hierarchy are graphical tools like the SQL Enterprise Manager.

If you already have some experience with SQL Server, you might think there are some tasks that you just can't do with Transact-SQL, such as managing the login security of your server or sending email messages. Microsoft gets around this by including in Transact-SQL extended stored procedures, which make function calls to Dynamic Link Libraries (DLLs).◀

What the SQL Enterprise Manager does (and doesn't do)

Tip

The SQL Enterprise Manager is a graphical tool for managing your SQL Server universe. This is true whether you are an end-user, an object owner, a database owner, or a system administrator. It is a 32-bit application, which is why you can't use it with Windows 3.1 or Windows for Workgroups. With the advent of Windows 95, you can't turn around without hearing the buzzwords *32-bit application*. If you want some entertainment, ask the next people who use this phrase what it means. After they finish tap dancing, impress them with this: A 32-bit application is a program that makes better use of memory. A 32-bit application can address (request) memory linearly, which makes it faster and more stable.◀

With the SQL Enterprise Manager you can do the following:

- Configure servers
- Create and manage devices
- Create and administer databases
- Backup and restore databases
- Create, modify, and drop user objects
- Manage logins and database users
- Run queries
- Set up and modify automated tasks
- Control replication between servers
- Do just about anything else you can think of in SQL Server

There are a limited number of things that you can't do from the SQL Enterprise Manager directly. For these tasks you either have to switch to the tools indicated in parentheses or use the workarounds we discuss. With the SQL Enterprise Manager you can't do the following:

- Map NT groups to SQL Server groups (Use the SQL Security Manager). For some odd reason, security functions are in a separate application. There is a bunch of extended stored procedures (Transact-SQL calls to DLLs) that you can use if you want to do this without leaving the SQL Enterprise Manager.

- Bulk copy data in or out (Use the BCP utility). There is no graphical interface to loading or unloading data from tables, just a program you run from the command prompt. Supposedly this boosts performance on the resource intensive task of moving data around quickly, but when dealing with small tables it is pretty annoying to switch to a command prompt. We just use the extended stored procedure xp_cmdshell to run the BCP program from a Query Window, but some folks still use the SQL Server 4.2 tools, which did have a graphical interface to bulk copy.
- Graphically transfer objects, both data and schema (the structure of your data) into a SQL Server 6.0 Server (Use the SQL Server 6.0 Transfer Manager). In an obnoxious attempt to pressure everyone into upgrading, Microsoft has given us a feature in the SQL Enterprise Manager for transferring objects that doesn't work with SQL Server 6.0.
- Monitor the SQL being sent to SQL Server (Use the SQL Trace utility). There is an extended stored procedure for this, but the raw output is not fun to deal with. You really want to use the SQL Trace program.
- Configure your connection to SQL Server (Use the Client Configuration Utility).

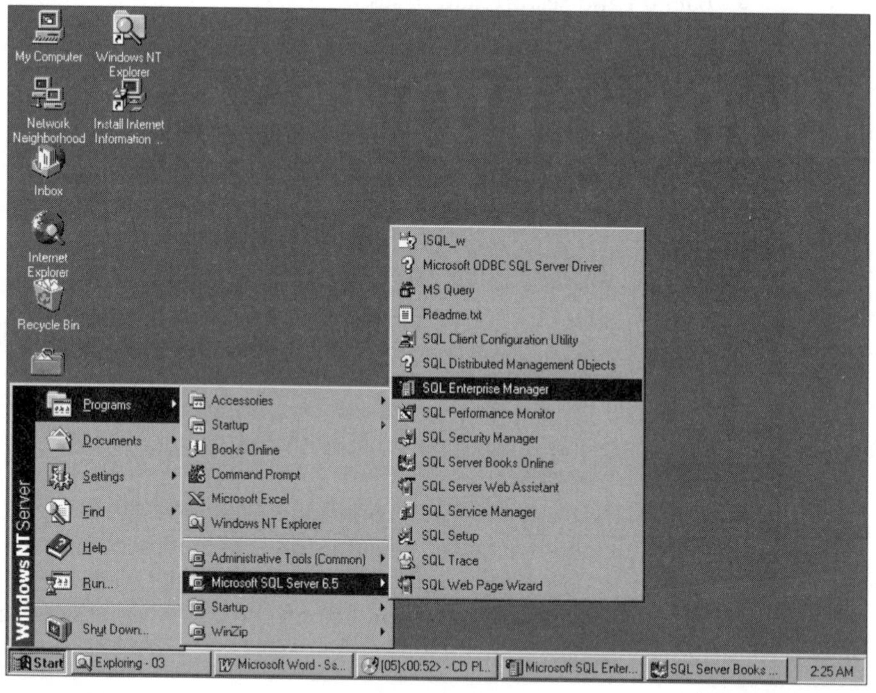

Figure 3-1:
Start the SQL Enterprise Manager by choosing it from the SQL Server 6.5 [Utilities] folder.

Who can use the SQL Enterprise Manager?

Any login can and should use the SQL Enterprise Manager for SQL Server work. The SQL Enterprise Manager simply restricts a login to menu items for which it has the appropriate underlying database permissions.

GETTING STARTED WITH THE SQL ENTERPRISE MANAGER

The SQL Enterprise Manager is in the Microsoft SQL Server 6.5 folder of the server machine, and the Microsoft SQL Server 6.5 Utilities folders are in the clients. (See Figure 3-1.) The actual executable is SQLEW.EXE; you can just run that directly if you want to.

The first time you start the SQL Enterprise Manager, it looks like Figure 3-2. All the buttons are grayed out, as are most of the menu items, and the SQL Enterprise Manager has opened a dialog box for you. Let's talk about what you are going to do in this dialog box.

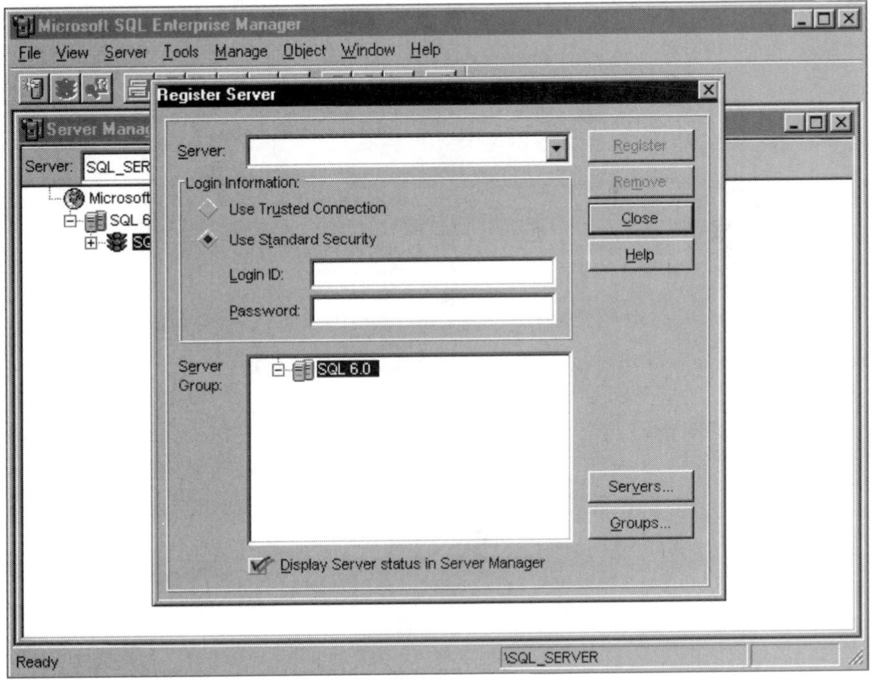

Figure 3-2:
This is what you see the first time you start the SQL Enterprise Manager.

Registering a server

The SQL Enterprise Manager isn't much good if it doesn't have one or more servers to manage, so any time you start it with no servers registered (which will be the case the very first time you start it after installation), it prompts you to register a server. Registering a server simply means providing a server name, a login, and a password.

Where your configuration Information is stored

The SQL Enterprise Manager stores your configuration information, and any other information that customizes the SQL Enterprise Manager, in your Registry. If you are using Windows 95 without personalized profiles, go turn them on. Otherwise, anyone can go into the Registry (Figure 3-3) and see your SQL Server password, if you have to supply it (more on that later).

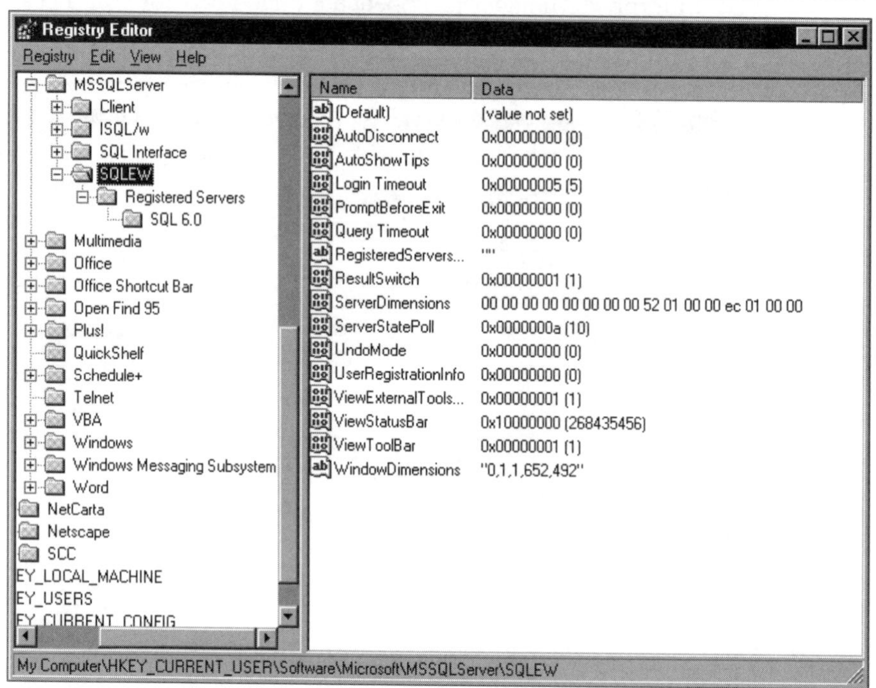

Figure 3-3:
The SQL Enterprise Manager stores configuration data in the Registry.

If you are using SQL Server 6.0, the information is in your workstation's SQL60\BINN\ directory in a file called SERVERS.BIN. When you upgrade to SQL Server 6.5, the data in this file is automatically moved to the Registry.

Choosing how to supply login information

The SQL Enterprise Manager handles logins a little differently than other applications that you may be used to, and differently than the other SQL Server applications such as ISQL/w, the SQL Security Manager, SQL Trace, and so on. You are probably used to having an application prompt you for a server, login, and password when the application opens. The SQL Enterprise Manager can't really do that because you may be managing one, ten, or even a hundred servers from within the SQL Enterprise Manager. Clearly, it can't have you enter, or even review, all that connection information each time you use it. Hence the idea of registering.

The preferred way to register is via a trusted connection, which is an authenticated connection between the client and the server. When you log into the network via a trusted path and your network login is mapped to a SQL Server login, the SQL Enterprise Manager can force a trusted connection no matter what your server security mode is. If you are unsure whether you have a trusted connection to the network, try the Trusted Connection option when you register your first server and see if it works. If it does work, the big advantage for you is that if other people log into the network from your PC, they can't use the database with your login and privileges. We cover the pros and cons of trusted connections in great detail in Chapter 7.◀

If you usually use SQL Server as the system administrator, you may find that you didn't get connected that way with the trusted connection. Chapter 7 discusses how to fix this.◀

With standard security the SQL Enterprise Manager stores your password locally on your PC, in the Registry, which is obviously not good. First of all, you have to reregister whenever you change your password. Second, although Microsoft has made a reasonable attempt to secure the Registry such that one user can't see another's Registry keys, the data is still on the PC. That makes us uncomfortable, especially in Windows 95.

If you are using standard security and you are still using the SQL Server 6.0 version of the SQL Enterprise Manager, you are a lot worse off. If you have Windows 95, people can always make up a new username and password to log into your PC, and then they can connect to SQL Server with your SQL Server login, thus getting whatever privileges you have. You have more protection in NT because in order to use your computer to begin with, a user needs a valid login to either your NT Workstation or a domain on the network. However, almost everyone in your company presumably has a login to a domain on the network.◀

Note

Already you can see how messy this is getting. However, it gets worse. When you register a server with standard security using the SQL Server 6.0 Enterprise Manager, it stores your password unencrypted in the SERVERS.BIN file of your PC! Anyone with a text editor who can access that file has your password. Therefore, in Windows 95 you are totally vulnerable, whereas in NT you have to remember to restrict read access to this file. This makes two points:

- Even if you are waiting to upgrade your server to 6.5, upgrade all your client tools now!
- Don't register with standard security if you can get a trusted connection to the server machine. ◀

The registration steps

Here are the basic steps to register a SQL Server.

Step 1: Open the Register Server dialog box

If you have just started the SQL Enterprise Manager for the first time or if you have just started the SQL Enterprise Manager with no servers registered, the Register Server dialog box (Figure 3-4) is already open. Otherwise, you can choose Server⇨Register Server, or you can right-click on any group or server already in the Server Manager window and choose Register Server in the pop-up menu. You can also choose the leftmost button on the toolbar.

Step 2: In the Server drop-down list box, either type the name of a server or pick a name from the list.

The drop-down list contains the names of the last five servers to which you connected. If you are sitting at a SQL Server machine, you can also type **(local)** to connect to that local SQL Server instead of its name.

Cross-Reference

Let's talk about what this "name" means. When you attempt to connect, the SQL Enterprise Manager looks for the Server name in the list of connection strings that you define with the Client Configuration Utility (we do this in Chapter 5). If it finds the name there, it uses that information to connect. If the SQL Enterprise Manager does not find the name there, it looks for a machine on the network with that name listening on the default Named Pipe. This can be confusing because most people assume that the Server name is the actual network name of the server machine. ◀

If you are unsure what servers are available, you can click the List Servers button. Unfortunately, this list can come up empty if you do not have browsing set up correctly on your network. If the list is empty, you must type in a server name. You can't have a server registered twice with the same name, so if you type in or select the name of a server that is already registered, the Register Server dialog box immediately switches to Edit mode.

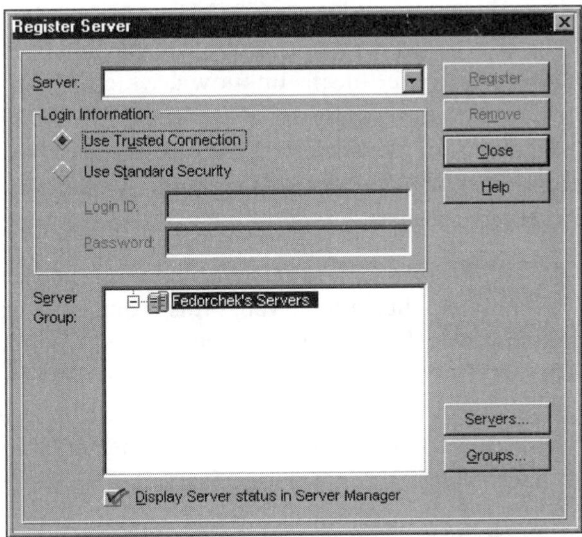

Figure 3-4:
Use the Register Server dialog box to connect to a server.

Step 3: In the Login Information area, select either Use Trusted Connection or Use Standard Security

Refer to "Choosing how to supply login information" earlier in this chapter if you are not sure which to use. If you selected Use Standard Security, you must type in a valid login ID and password. The confusing thing here is that leaving the login and password blank is the way to request a trusted connection in other applications, and you can do that here as well. Thus, you have a trusted connection even though you selected standard security. You will learn all about how to force trusted connections in Chapter 7.◀

Step 4: Choose a group in which to put the server

By default, the server is always added to the first group listed, even if you launched the Register Server dialog box by right-clicking on a specific group. If you have no groups (you would have to delete the SQL 6.5 group that the SQL Enterprise Manager already has for this to be true), the Register Server dialog box re-creates the SQL 6.5 group for you. You can easily change which group a server is in later. The Server Groups button opens the Manage Server Groups dialog box which we discuss in "Managing groups," later in this chapter.

Step 5: If you do not want to see the status (Stopped/Paused/Started) of the server displayed in the SQL Enterprise Manager, clear the "Display Server status in Server Manager" check box

You will find that servers get registered with a little traffic light icon that monitors their status. Choose File⇨Toggle Legend to see the valid server states. Green means running, yellow means paused, and red means stopped. No color whatsoever means unknown, which might mean the network connection to that server is down. If you check this box, the SQL Enterprise Manager will poll the servers at the interval specified in Tools⇨Perferences Configure, which is ten seconds by default. This way you can always see when servers are going up and down.

Warning

If you have Windows 95, you can't see the status even if you have this box checked because checking server status requires using the Windows NT Service Control APIs, which are unavailable in Windows 95. If you have Windows NT, we recommend that you leave this box checked. Whatever you do, don't try to poll server status yourself by trying to connect to a server to see if it is up. If the server is on the fritz, your attempt to connect to it can hang your SQL Enterprise Manager. ◀

Step 6: Click Register

The microhelp changes to "Validating Registration Information..." and if the SQL Enterprise Manager finds the server, an icon for the server appears in the Server Manager window. The Register Server dialog box stays open so that you can register other servers, but it clears the server, login, and password boxes. (The group you selected remains selected.) If you are using Windows NT, you will notice that the traffic light of this newly registered server isn't on. It comes on once you close the Register Server dialog box.

What to do when a server doesn't register properly

If the SQL Enterprise Manager can't register a server, you get an error saying

```
Unable to Connect to Server (reason: <Whatever the SQL Enterprise Manager perceives
is wrong>) Register anyway?
```

This message may give several reasons for the problem. These are the ones we have often encountered and what to do about them:

Unable to Connect: SQL Server is unavailable or does not exist. Specified SQL Server not found.

This means the SQL Enterprise Manager could not reach the server on the network. Make sure you spelled the server name correctly. Make sure the SQL Server is up and running. If you are connecting on Named Pipes, is there any chance either you or the server is not using the default Named Pipe? If so, change your connection string to match the pipe (see Chapter 5).◀

If the SQL Server is simply down, you can register anyway, and when it comes up, you will be able to use it. When you are getting the "unavailable" message, you can at least rule out problems in the login or password. That produces one of the two messages below.

Login failed - User: <Domain_NetworkLogin> Reason: Not defined as a valid user of a trusted SQL Server Connection.

You tried to use a trusted connection, and your network login is not mapped to a valid SQL Server login. If you have a SQL Server login separate from your network login and your SQL Server is running in either mixed or standard security, you can simply say No to "Register anyway?", select Use Standard Security, type in your login and password, and click Register again. If you want to use a trusted connection or if you have to use a trusted connection, someone with system administrator privileges must use the SQL Security Manager to map your network login to a SQL Server login. Refer to Chapter 7.◀

Login failed.

You attempted a standard security connection and either you misspelled your login or your password.

SQL Server has been paused; No new connections will be allowed.

A system administrator has paused the server. To pause a server simply means to tell the SQL Server to deny all new connections. Usually one does this in preparation for a shutdown; you don't want new people logging in while you are trying to get the current users to log off. At this point, you could go ahead and register the server, but we recommend that you wait. While the server is paused, it does not verify your login or password, so you don't know if you typed them in correctly.

Editing a server's registration

Once a server is registered, you can change the registration information and what group it is in.

To change a server's registration information, right-click the server's name in the Server Manager window. In the pop-up menu, select Edit. This opens the Register Server dialog box again, but the Register button says Modify instead. Change the Login information as desired. When you are done, click Modify. If there are any problems, you get the same errors we described earlier in this chapter in "What to do when a server doesn't register properly."

However, the SQL Enterprise Manager is just testing the connection to the server, it isn't reestablishing the connection. For example, if you are connected to the SQL Server with a login of "Adams" and you modify your registration to connect as "sa," when you close the Register Server dialog box, you are still connected as "Adams." The next time you start the SQL Enterprise Manager you will be connected as "sa." If you want to reconnect now, right-click the server's name in the Server Manager window, choose Disconnect, and then click the plus sign on the Server to reconnect.

Changing a server's group is as simple as dragging it from its current group to a different group. You can also drag the server up to the Microsoft SQL Servers icon and release it. Then it is not in any group. If all your groups are empty at this point, you can delete them all, if you so choose. The SQL Enterprise Manager will not create the default SQL Server 6.5 group until the next time you try to register something.

Deleting a server's registration

Deleting a server's registration simply means you do not want it displayed in the SQL Enterprise Manager. You are not uninstalling the software or in any way affecting the server itself. There are three ways you can delete a server's registration:

- Right-click on the server in the Server Manager window and choose UnRegister.
- Click on a Server's name and press Del.
- Edit a Server and choose the Remove button.

In all three cases, SQL Server asks you if you are sure and then deletes the registration. There is no undo.

Tip

If you simply want to break your connection to the server don't UnRegister it. That's what the Disconnect option is for. Just right-click on the server's traffic light to get the menu you need.◀

Saving a server's registration

You don't have to worry about saving your server registrations; that happens automatically as you create them.

Note

The SQL Enterprise Manager 6.0 saves all the registration information to SERVERS.BIN when it exists, so if you want to save your work early, you have to quit the SQL Enterprise Manager.◀

USING THE SERVER MANAGER WINDOW

There is always one window open in the SQL Enterprise Manager, the Server Manager window, shown in Figure 3-5. You can't close this window.

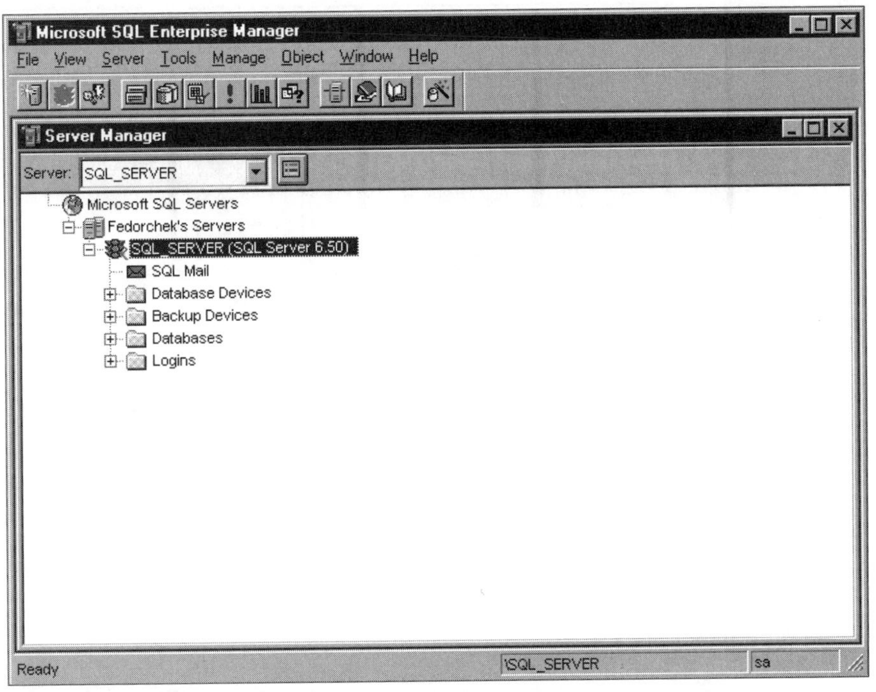

Figure 3-5:
The Server Manager window will always be open in the SQL Enterprise Manager.

The Server Manager window presents all your servers to you with a tree control; you can drill down into them. A good percentage of the menu items in the SQL Enterprise Managers is also available from pop-up menus in the Server Manager window. This window is also useful for obtaining lists of objects simply by expanding a tree branch.

In the Server Manager window you organize your servers into groups. These are just like folders or directories, but they have no meaning beyond that: that is, you can't stop a group of servers or show the current activity on a group of servers or do any other management task on groups.

Opening more Server Manager windows

You can open additional Server Manager windows for individual servers. This can be a great convenience when you work with two or more servers at the same time or when you drill down into two or more areas of one server. With additional Server Manager Windows, you can tile windows to make such work easier (see Figure 3-6). Unlike the master Server Manager window, you can close these windows at will. You can't open a group of servers in another window.

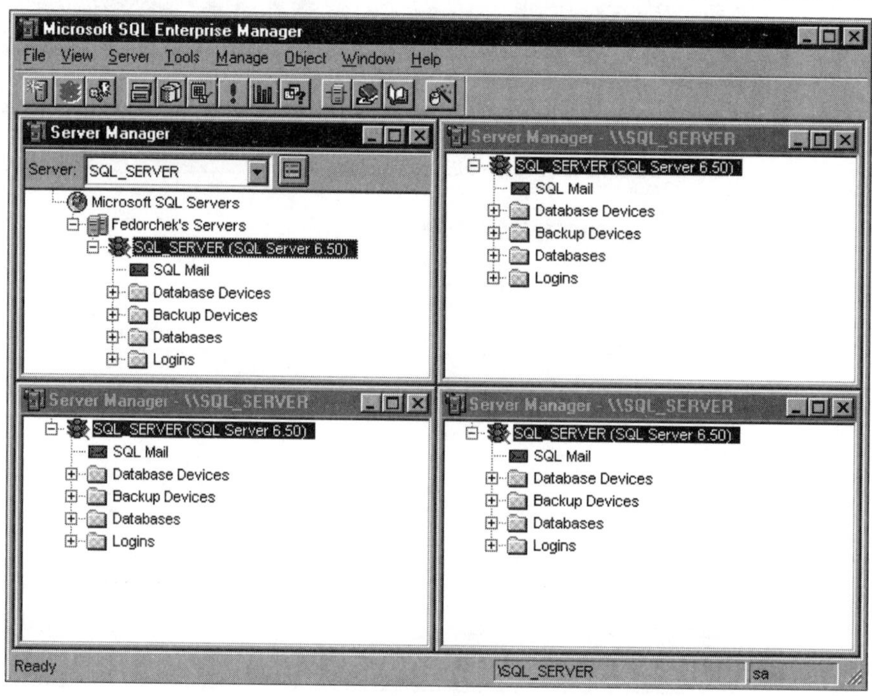

Figure 3-6:
Open additional Server Manager windows as you need to when you work.

To open additional Server Manager windows for individual servers, simply drag a server's icon into some blank space in the client area of the SQL Enterprise Manager and drop it. If you have no blank space because you have other windows tiled or maximized, you have to work a bit harder. Notice that when you start dragging the server you have the outline of a traffic light with a big X through it. As you get into the border of the Server Manager, the X disappears. Drop the icon while the X is gone, and you get a new window.

Managing groups

You can create, rename, move, and delete groups in the Server Manager window. Most of these actions come from pop-up menus or from drag and drop operations. Let's quickly cover the steps involved in group management.

Creating a server group

To create a server group from the Server Manager window:

1. Select Server⇨Server Groups from the main menu or right-click any existing group and select New Server Groups from the pop-up menu. The Manage Server Groups dialog box (Figure 3-7) appears.

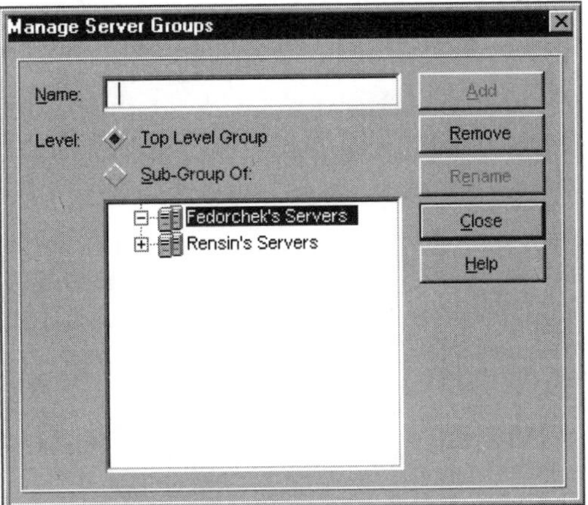

Figure 3-7:
Use the Manage Server Groups window to create a group.

2. Type in the name you want to use. These are not SQL Server identifiers, so you can use any characters you want, such as spaces, apostrophes, periods, and so on. You are limited to 30 characters, though. Individual group names do not have to be unique. This has the advantage that you could have two top-level groups called Europe and Asia, with a subgroup under each called Sales. It has the disadvantage that you can create groups on the same level with the same name. For example, there is nothing to stop you from having three top-level groups all called SQL 6.5.
3. If you want this group to be created as a subgroup of another group, check "Sub-Group of:" and select the group under which you want your new group to be. Even if you entered the Manage Server Groups dialog box by right-clicking the group under which you wanted your new one, you still have to select it again here.
4. Click Add Group. The group appears both in the Server Manager window and in the Manage Server Groups dialog box. The Manage Server Groups dialog box stays open.
5. When you are finished adding groups, choose Close.

Renaming a server group

Renaming a group requires you to use the same Manage Server Groups dialog box shown in Figure 3-6. You would think that the pop-up menu you get when you right-click a group would include a Rename menu item, but no, the same Manage Server Groups dialog box is the only way to do it.

To rename a server group:

1. Select Server⇨Server Groups from the main menu or right-click any existing group and select Edit from the pop-up menu. The Manage Server Groups dialog box appears.
2. Type in the new name you want to use.
3. Select the group you want to rename from the servers displayed in this dialog box. Whatever group you have selected in the Server Manager window doesn't matter. The group you choose here in the Manage Server Groups dialog box is the group that will get renamed. By default the group you originally highlighted is selected, so you should be safe.
4. Click Change Name. The name changes both in the Server Manager window and in the Manage Server Groups dialog box. The Manage Server Groups dialog box stays open. Be careful not to press Enter by mistake because that will select Add Group instead.

Tip

Notice that the SQL Enterprise Manager does not automatically resort the groups, so the group you just changed is right where it was before. To resort a renamed group, drag and drop it onto the higher-level group of which it is a member. For a top-level group, drop it on the Microsoft SQL Servers globe icon.◀

5. When you are finished renaming groups, choose Close.

Removing a server group

You can delete a group provided it has no servers or subgroups. Two easy ways to remove a single server are

- Right-click on a group and choose Delete.
- Choose a group and hit the Del key.

Either way you get a confirmation dialog box and then the group is gone. There is no undo.

Tip

If you are planning to do a whole bunch of changes, you might want to make a copy of your Registry Key (version 6.5) or SERVERS.BIN file (version 6.0) before you start. If you want to undo all your changes, restore the Registry Key or replace SERVERS.BIN with the copy you made.◀

Another way to remove servers is to use the Manage Server Groups dialog box. This will prove faster for getting rid of a bunch of groups. Here is the procedure:

1. Select Server⇨Server Groups from the main menu or right-click any existing group and select New Server Groups from the pop-up menu. The Manage Server Groups dialog box appears, shown in Figure 3-7.
2. Select the group you want to remove from the servers displayed in this dialog box. Whatever group you have selected in the Server Manager window doesn't matter. The group you choose here is the group that is removed. By default the group you right clicked on is selected.
3. Click Remove Group or press Enter. The group disappears from both the Server Manager window and the Manage Server Groups dialog box. For some reason, the Server Manager window insists on now jumping to the very last group, which is really distracting if you have more than a page of groups. The Manage Server Groups dialog box stays open, so you can delete more groups if you want to.
4. When you are finished deleting groups, choose Close.

Moving a server group

To move a SQL Server group, in the Server Manager window simply drag and drop it onto the group of which you want it to be a subgroup. If you want it to be a top-level group, drop it on the Microsoft SQL Servers globe.

Navigating in the Server Manager window

The great thing about graphical tools like SQL Enterprise Manager is that you can usually figure out how they work by just playing, but here is a list of what you should discover as you play with the Server Manager:

- You expand a branch (a group or a server or a folder within the server) by clicking the plus sign. The first time you expand a server, it takes a few seconds because the SQL Enterprise Manager has to establish a connection. Windows 95 users may be used to using the right arrow key to expand a branch; that doesn't work here.
- You collapse a branch by clicking the minus sign.
- The Server folders don't always refresh automatically. If you make a change from their menus they refresh themselves, but if a change comes from elsewhere, such as something you do with the Query Analyzer, you have to select the last item of the pop-up menu, Refresh. For example, if you expand the Databases folder while a database is still recovering, the cylinder for that database will be gray. After the database finishes recovering, the cylinder will stay gray, even if you collapse the database or even the whole server branch. You must specifically choose Database⇨Refresh or Refresh from the pop-up menu to get the SQL Enterprise Manager to display the database as online.
- Virtually everything has a pop-up menu that you can access with a right mouse click.
- You can make another window out of any branch (except groups) by dragging it outside the Server Manager window. For example, if you wanted to get the Logins folder into its own window away from the clutter of everything else, you would just drag it and drop it outside the Server Manager window.
- The Page Up and Page Down keys do exactly what you would expect: they move you up or down a page in the Server Manager window, with a page being the viewable space of window in its current size.

- The Home and End keys don't do what you would expect. Home moves you one level higher in a branch. For example, if you are looking at the list of stored procedures in master, with any procedure selected, pressing Home takes you to the Stored Procedures folder. If you keep pressing Home, you go to Objects, then master, then Databases, and so on. End moves you to the last item one level down of the folder you are on, if it is expanded. For example, if you have Stored Procedures of master highlighted and the folder is expanded to show all procedures, End takes you to "sp_who" (which is the last procedure).
- The icon brings up a legend of the symbols the Server Manager Window uses (Figure 3-8).

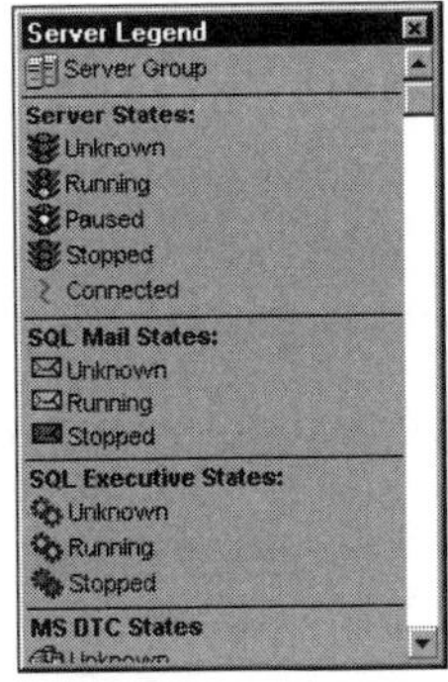

Figure 3-8:
Check the Server Manager legend for an explanation of the SQL Enterprise Manager symbols.

SQL Enterprise Manager Orientation

As you read the rest of this book, you will become intimately familiar with each SQL Enterprise Manager menu item and toolbar button. Because you'll be using the SQL Enterprise Manager in virtually every chapter, we give a general orientation here to avoid repeating ourselves.

The toolbar

The SQL Enterprise Manager has a floating, dockable toolbar, with icons for these common tasks:

- Register Server

- Stop/Pause/Start Server

- Configure SQL Server

- Configure SQL Mail

- Configure SQL Executive

- Manage Logins

- Manage Database Devices

- Manage Databases

- Manage Scheduled Tasks

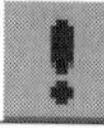

- Manage Alerts and Operators

- Current Activity

- Query Analyzer

- Replication Topology

- Replication — Manage Publications

- Replication — Manage Subscriptions

- Database Maintenance Wizard

When menu items are available

Many of the menu items and all but the leftmost toolbar button relate to actions you can take on a specific server. Consequently, they are grayed out until you select a server. You can select a server by single-clicking it or by choosing Tools⇨Set Server/Database from the main menu and picking a server.

All the Object menu items and all but the first four Manage menu items are things you do within a specific database. They will be grayed out until you pick a database in which to work. You can select a database by expanding a server, then expanding the database folder, and then clicking a database. You can also choose Tools⇨Set Server/Database from the main menu, pick a server, and pick a database. There is even a third way to pick a database, but this one is less obvious. Once a server is open, you can start the Query Analyzer from Tools⇨SQL Query Tool, which connects you to your default database. Thus, you have, in effect, selected a database, so the Object and Manage menu items come to life.

Finally, the last two menu items of the Object menu, Drop and Rename, are only active if you have selected a specific object.

How focus changes

At any given time, one server and one database at most can be in focus. These will always be the server and, if applicable, the database selected in the active window. When you choose a menu item, the SQL Enterprise Manager always executes the action for the server and database in focus. For example, let's say you have three windows open:

- The Server Manager, with the (LOCAL) SQL Server and no database selected
- Manage Stored Procedures for SomeOtherServer\master
- Query for (LOCAL)\tempdb

If you try to select Manage⇨Tables, what happens? Well, it depends. If you are in the Server Manager window, you can't even select this item because the SQL Enterprise Manager doesn't know what database you want to manage tables in. If you are in the Manage Stored Procedures window, you will be managing the user tables in master for the SomeOtherServer server. If you are in the Query window, you open Manage Tables for tempdb.

Manipulating multiple databases in the same server

You can have multiple windows open at the same time for different databases. For example, you might have two different Manage Stored Procedures windows open side by side for different databases. What you can't do is have two instances of the same window, unless they are Manage Server windows, but you need to understand what the SQL Enterprise Manager considers to be the same. Managing any object (Tables, Views, Stored Procedures, Rules, Defaults, User Defined Datatypes) is specific to a database.

Thus, you can't have two Manage Views windows open for the same database. All other windows, except Manage Server windows, are specific to a server. For example you can only have one Query window open for a server. This isn't really a limitation, though, because you can have multiple queries in one Query window, each going to different databases.

How the SQL Enterprise Manager executes commands

The Query Analyzer runs queries asynchronously. This means you can fire off your first query, and while it is running also send a second, a third, as many as you like. You can deal with the results as they come back. This is multitasking at its finest. If you've ever worked on mainframe RDBMSs, this is heaven.

The bad news is that except for the Query Analyzer, all SQL Enterprise Manager commands execute synchronously. This means that if you use the SQL Enterprise Manager to set up a big index, to create a foreign key between large tables, or to perform any other demanding task, or if someone else is doing one of these things, you get to stare at an hourglass for as long as it takes. So much for the great multitasking environment of Windows 95 and Windows NT. Sure, you can open another instance of the SQL Enterprise Manager, but that isn't a very good solution. Even if you have lots of asynchronous queries running, you won't be able to get to them. And you can't see any changes you might have made that haven't been executed in a Manage Stored Procedures window.

This means you really have to save your queries often. You never know when you are going to get stuck running a second instance of the SQL Enterprise Manager and calling up your queries from disk.

The SQL Enterprise Manager executes all tasks serially because the SQL-DMO model isn't designed to be threadsafe. Therefore, the SQL Enterprise Manager, and all other applications that use the SQL-DMO, must serialize their access to avoid reentrancy.◀

SQL Enterprise Manager preferences

If you select Tools⇨Preferences/Configure from the SQL Enterprise Manager menu, you get a Configure box of important options. It contains three tabs, each with important little details.

Application

The application tab, shown in Figure 3-9, controls how you register servers and poll server status.

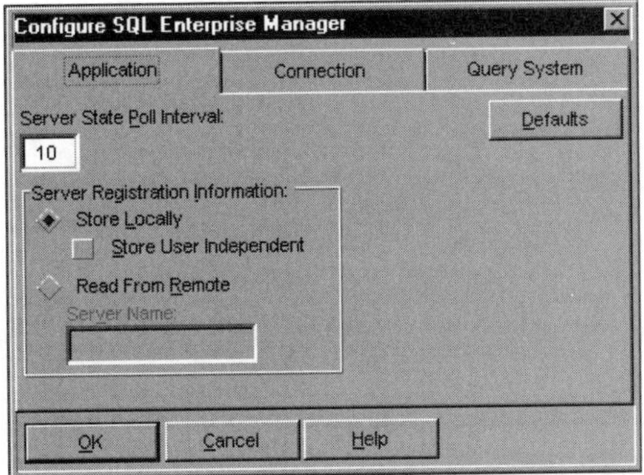

Figure 3-9:
Control how you define registrations and poll server status with the Application tab.

Server State Poll Interval

This is how often your NT Workstation polls the network to update server statuses in the traffic lights. It has no effect for Windows 95 clients. We use the default of 10 seconds, and it works just fine. We certainly would not recommend setting it any lower because it just increases network traffic without providing any real benefit to you.

Server Registration Information

Here you can choose to have the information stored either locally or remotely. If you choose locally, you can further choose Store User Independent. This determines whether the Registration Information is stored under HKEY_LOCAL_MACHINE or HKEY_CURRENT_USER in the Registry. User Independent would store under HKEY_LOCAL_MACHINE. Clearing that box would mean that under standard security, everyone who uses your machine can access SQL Server as if they were you. We don't recommend this.

Defaults

Press this button, and everything else goes back to the defaults. All three tabs of the Configure SQL Enterprise Manager dialog box have this feature.

Connection

The connection tab, shown in Figure 3-10, controls how you connect to SQL Server. The key parameters are Login timeout and Query timeout.

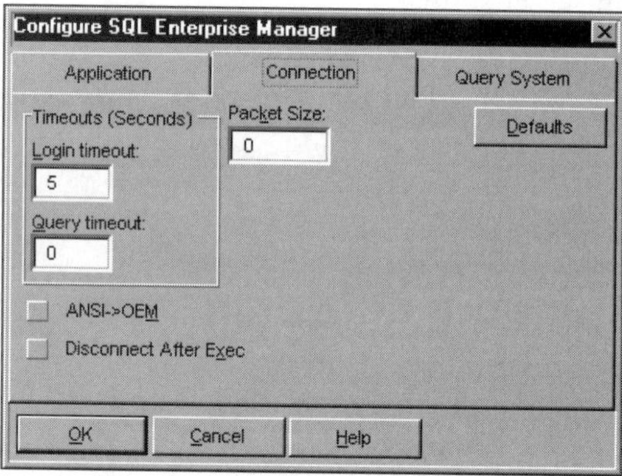

Figure 3-10:
Set your connection parameters with the Connection tab.

Login timeout

This is how long the SQL Enterprise Manager waits before giving up on a login attempt. Remember that the SQL Enterprise Manager is actually logging in and out all the time while you work, so this value should be small. The default of 5 works just fine.

Query timeout

This is the number of seconds SQL Enterprise Manager will let one of its processes (not just queries) run before giving you a dialog box asking you if you really want to keep waiting. The default is zero, which means there is no limit to how long something can run. Setting the timeout to zero is not a wise thing to do if you are not the system administrator, and a questionable idea even if you are the system administrator. A bad query can really hose your SQL Enterprise Manager. Try this one out when no one needs to use your server:

```
use master
go
```

```
select *
   from syscomments a, syscomments b, syscomments c
   where substring(a.text,100,3) = substring(b.text,200,3)
      and substring(a.text,200,3) = substring(c.text,100,3)
      and substring(b.text,100,3) = substring(c.text,200,3)
```

If you don't have the Query timeout set to a nonzero value, you don't have any way to pull the plug on this except by using the kill command from another application, and only the system administrator can use that command. You may not be able to get to the Cancel button of the Query window. We have never waited for this query to return, so we can't tell you how long it would take. If you do decide to run it, make sure you are logged in as the sa login, and click the Current Activity button to monitor your connection. You can kill the query from there.

Query System

The query system tab, shown in Figure 3-11, controls a lot of nifty features relating to text display and files.

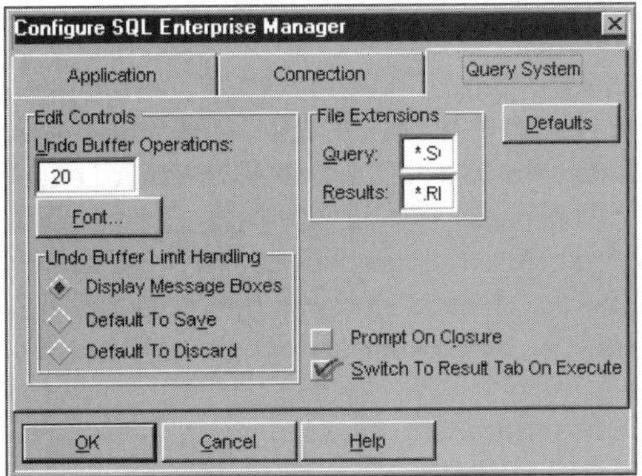

Figure 3-11:
Set Query parameters with the Query System tab.

Undo Buffer operations

This is the number of times you can undo typing in Query or Manage <Object> windows. The default is 20, which might seem like a lot, but it isn't. If you select a word, start typing over it, and then change your mind, each keystroke counts as an operation. For example, if you highlight a big, long select statement and start to type instead:

```
SELECT * FROM sysobjects
```

That is 24 operations, so you can only undo it back 20 operations, or to:

```
sele
```

You can't get your original query back. However, a more likely scenario is that you highlight something, accidentally delete it, cuss loudly, and then want it back. This is just one operation, and the undo works fine. It is our experience that 20 is more than enough. You can set it as high as 32,000, but then you have lots of garbage sucking up memory.

Font

This brings up the usual Windows font selection box, where you can pick the font, font style, and size. The font you pick will be used in the Query, Manage Tables, Manage Stored Procedures, and Manage Views windows. The default font is Courier 10 point. Because the SQL Enterprise Manager is what-you-see-is-what-you-get (WYSIWYG), this is the only way to change what comes out of the printer.

Undo Buffer Limit Handing

We recommend changing this one. The default is Display Message Boxes, which means every time you cut and paste more than 20 lines or so, this dialog box gets in your way. Decide whether you prefer to have your pastes and deletes saved in the buffer, and pick either Default to Save or Default to Discard. The latter is a bit sneaky because if you do a big cut and paste, the SQL Enterprise Manager will not put it in the undo buffer, and it will discard all other changes in the buffer. But this option is the best way to make sure your machine's memory does not get filled with junk.

File Extensions

You can change the default extensions of query and results files here. For example, if you are often opening results in Excel you could set the default report extension to .XLS.

Prompt On Closure

As we will discuss soon, this feature isn't worth much. Either you always get a confirmation box when you close the Query Analyzer, even if you saved everything 0.2 seconds ago, or you never get any confirmation, no matter how much work you are about to lose.

Switch to Result Tab On Execute

This one is nice to leave checked. It shows your results automatically when you run a query.

THE QUERY ANALYZER WINDOW

The Query Analyzer is going to be your friend for the rest of this book. Every text command we discuss can be run from here, including all SQL, so let's pause to cover its features. Open it now by choosing a server in the SQL Enterprise Manager and selecting Tools⇨Query Analyzer. You see a screen like Figure 3-12.

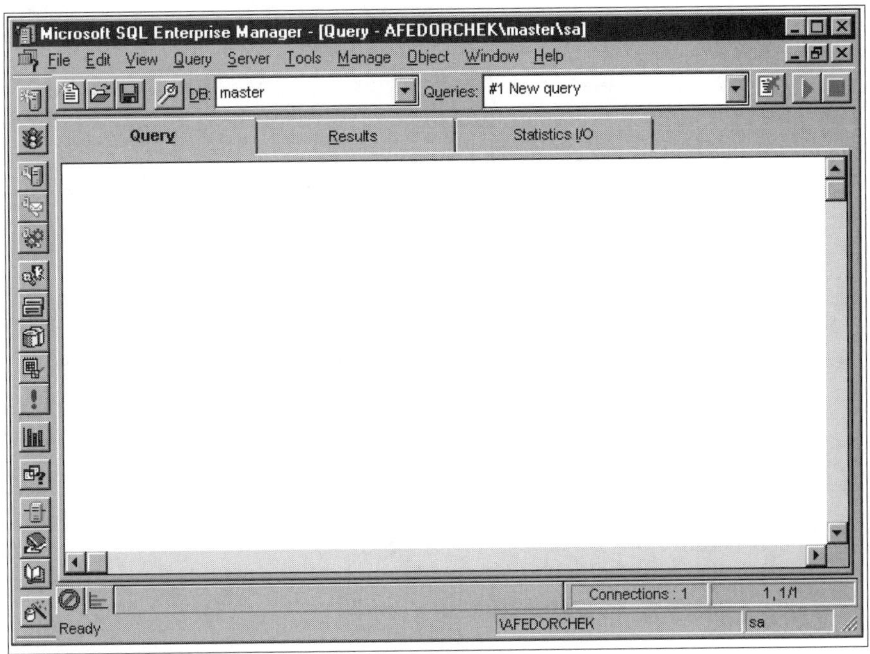

Figure 3-12:
Run all your text commands and SQL from the Query Analyzer.

The Query Analyzer is a windowed ASCII text editor connected to the SQL Server Transact-SQL compiler. It offers roughly the same features as the Windows Notepad, with the notable enhancement that the Query Analyzer can open a file of arbitrarily large size.

When you first open the Query Analyzer window, a counter in the lower right displays 1, 1/1. This is the current character number that the cursor is on, a comma, the current line the cursor is on, a slash, and the total number of lines in the file. The "current character number" is not the same as the current column of the cursor. Press Tab about five times. The cursor looks like it is in column 41, but the counter says 5, 1/1.

The File menu has all the usual stuff: New, Open, Close, Save, Save As, Print, Print Setup, and so on. The Edit menu also has what you would expect including Undo, Find, Replace. Bear in mind that the Undo is an undo of your text editing. It doesn't roll back any commands you sent to the database. The only surprise command might be Edit⇨Goto, which command prompts you for a line number and jumps to that location.

You can highlight text by double clicking it, but you won't get the same kind of behavior you do in other Windows applications, such as Microsoft Word. In the Query Analyzer, double clicking an item highlights everything to the left and right up to the first space. This makes sense in database work because if you write 'master.dbo.syslocks', you will want to cut and paste that string all at once. (Word stops at the periods on a highlight from a double click.) If you highlight some text, that text is automatically displayed in the Find and Replace dialog boxes.

The Window menu of the SQL Enterprise Manager lets you tile your Query Analyzer horizontally or vertically with other open windows, but it won't let you cascade windows. (The Window menu of ISQL/w lets you cascade but doesn't give you a choice of how to Tile. Go figure.)

There is an annoying omission in the Help menu of the SQL Enterprise Manager: it doesn't include the Keyboard menu item that ISQL/w has. (This option is in the Help menu of the SQL Security Manager, which needs it a lot less than the SQL Enterprise Manager.) Even if you have never used the ISQL/w application and never plan to, open it now to look at this menu item. You will find it in your SQL Server 6.5 folder, and the icon should be simply labeled "ISQL_w." Just click Cancel on the Connect dialog box and go straight to Help⇨Keyboard. Pick the last item, ISQL/w keys. You get a list of cool shortcuts, shown in Table 3-1.

Query Window Tabs

There are three tabs in the Query window of the Query Analyzer:

- **Query.** Your Transact-SQL commands go here.
- **Results.** Shows the text output from your commands.
- **Statistics I/O.** When the Display Statistics I/O button is pressed, this tab graphs the I/O of the most recently run set of commands. If the button isn't pressed, this tab just shows an empty gray background.

Table 3-1
Cool Keyboard Shortcuts

Key(s)	Function
Ctrl-N	Opens a new query window.
Ctrl-O	Displays the Connect Server dialog box.
Ctrl-E or Alt-X	Executes a query.
Ctrl-Z	Reverses the last action. (You can reverse up to 20 actions by default. You can change this number in the Configure ISQL/w dialog box.)
Ctrl-C	Cancels the query.
F1	Displays Transact-SQL Help information for the selected syntax.
Alt-F1	Displays Help (sp_help) information for the selected object.
F6	Moves right between the tabs.
SHIFT-F6	Moves left between the tabs.
Ctrl-Up Arrow and Ctrl-Down Arrow	Toggles between result sets.
Ctrl-Del	Clears the Query window.
Alt-Del	Removes the current query/result set.

SQL Server connections

The Query Analyzer provides you one or more connections to a specific SQL Server, numbered sequentially. Each connection is a separate text document — a separate query — and has a separate set of four tabs. We follow Microsoft's convention of referring to each connection as a Query window. All the queries run asynchronously, which gives you the flexibility to run many queries at once. The Query Analyzer shows the number of connections you have open in the lower right corner.

You cannot connect to more than one SQL Server in the same Query Analyzer window in the SQL Enterprise Manager, but you can have multiple Query Analyzer windows open in the SQL Enterprise Manager, each pointing to a separate SQL Server. If you try to open a second Query Analyzer for a specific server, the SQL Enterprise Manager simply switches focus back to the first Query Analyzer.

Cross-Reference

If it's really important to you to have two Query Analyzer windows open on the same server, you can trick the SQL Enterprise Manager by registering a server twice with two different connection strings (Chapter 5). This is one area where ISQL/w is different: you can directly open as many Query windows as you want simply by choosing File⇨Connect. Remember, though, that one Query Analyzer window can have any number of simultaneous connections to a server. The only reason for needing another Query Analyzer is to compare two queries side by side on your screen.◀

What follows are the other features available to you in the Query Analyzer.

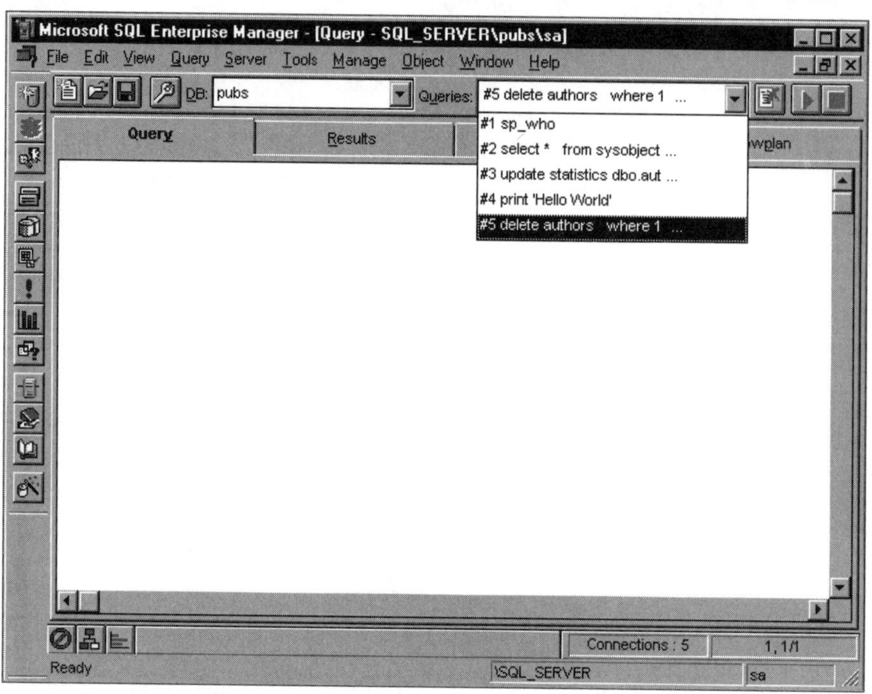

Figure 3-13:
Make multiple connections to one server in the Query Analyzer.

New Query Button/Ctrl-N/File⇨New

Executing this command opens a new connection to SQL Server in a new Query window. The new window gets the next unused connection number and will not reuse numbers from closed Query windows. The new window will be pointing to the same database as the last window you were using. The window does not open its connection until you try to execute something. Notice that the number of connections in the lower right does not increase just because you clicked New Query. Once you try to execute something you will have an open connection until you close that particular Query window. This is important to understand when you have a database in single user mode.

Because this is a new window, whatever you were working on before is still there, in another window.

Load SQL Script Button/File⇨Open

This item brings up the standard Open File dialog box. When you open a file, the Query window contents are replaced, and you lose unsaved text without warning. Be careful!

You don't have to load just .SQL files; the Query window will attempt to open any file you select as a text document. This can be handy when you are running bulk copies because you can open your input or output files in the Query window to see what is going on.

Warning

Opening a file with the Query window doesn't put a lock on the file the way more sophisticated applications like Microsoft Word do. There is nothing to stop you from messing with the file with another application while it is open in the Query window. For that matter, you can have the same file open in two Query windows; you won't get any warnings. Be aware, though, that when you save, you will completely replace the file; any changes made by other applications or other Query windows will be lost without warning.◀

The size of the document you can open is limited only by the size of the virtual memory of your machine. The SQL Script for one of our production databases is over 1MB, so we appreciate this feature. Be careful, however, because there is no explicit cancel feature to abort opening an extremely large file. If you try to open something larger that what your machine's physical memory can hold, you may get error messages from Windows NT about being low on virtual memory, but the file open will chug along, filling up your PAGEFILE.SYS file. If you want to bail out, you have to use the Windows NT Task Manager to end the SQL Enterprise Manager task.

The Load SQL Script button and the File⇨Open menu item are grayed out if you are on any tab other than the Query tab.

Save Query/Result Button/File⇨Save

This item saves your Query or your Result to a text file, depending on which tab you have selected. The File⇨Save menu items are grayed out when you are on the Statistics I/O tab, but for some unknown reason the button stays active: clicking it here saves your Query, not your Result.

Query Options Button/Query➪Set Options

Click this button or select the menu choice and you get the Query Options dialog box (Figure 3-14), with the Query Flags tab selected. These Query Options are stored in your Registry, and so they apply to all instances of the SQL Enterprise Manager and ISQL/w that you open on your PC after you change an option.

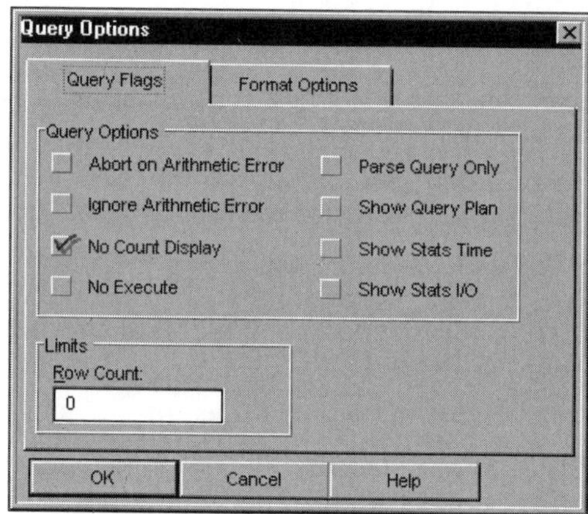

Figure 3-14:
Use Query Flags to control what the server does as it processes your query.

Here are some key points about the option flags:

- **No Count Display.** Turns off the row count messages of the output. Turning off the row counts is helpful when you execute a number of separate Transact-SQL commands at once, each of which affects only one or two rows.
- **No Execute.** Compiles a query but does not execute it. This option is the same as the No Execute button in the lower lefthand corner of the Query Analyzer. However, the two don't play nicely with each other; see the sidebar No Execute button bug.
- **Parse Query Only.** Checks the syntax of each query and returns any error messages without executing the query. There is a subtle difference between this option and the previous one. Conceptually there are three steps in the execution of a query. First there is parsing, where the compiler makes sure what you have written is syntactically correct. If you check the Parse Query Only option the process stops here. The second

step is compilation, where the compiler figures out what indexes and working tables to use. The No Execute option stops the process there. Because of this difference Showplan works with No Execute, but not with Parse Query Only.

- **Show Query Plan.** Generates a text description of how your Transact-SQL will be executed. We have a lot to say about this in Chapter 29. Here, we simply note that this will give you a lot of extra output, especially if you run a stored procedure.◀
- **Show Stats Time.** Gives you text output telling you how long it took to parse, compile, and execute each of your Transact-SQL statements. This is not the same as the Display Statistics I/O button; it turns on the graphics.
- **Row Count.** Limits how many rows you want returned. A value of zero, the default, means no limit.

Click the Format Option tab and you see the screen shown in Figure 3-15. There are several unexpected behaviors with these options:

- **Result Output Format.** Here you choose either column-aligned (the default), comma, tab, or custom delimiter. The tab-delimited option is especially helpful when you plan to import a result file into a word processor or a spreadsheet. Watch out with pasting results in directly, though. If you paste a zip code of '06432' into Excel, it might treat it as the number 6,432. If you select anything other than column-aligned, No Count Display is turned on, but you can turn it back off if you wish. If you switch back to column aligned while No Count Display was checked, it is not cleared automatically: you have to clear it explicitly.

No Execute Button Bug

If you press the No Execute button, the No Execute option gets checked in the Query Options. This is as it should be. Unfortunately the reverse is not true. Checking the No Execute option won't make the button look pressed. This is a bug. It really looks weird if you press the button, clear the No Execute option flag, and run a query. The query runs just fine and returns results, even though No Execute appears to be pressed.

This bug also causes the strange behavior that you can click the No Execute button in some Query window, which changes the Registry, and then you can open either the SQL Enterprise Manager or ISQL/w later and find No Execute on, even though the button is not pressed. Just click the button twice to set things right.

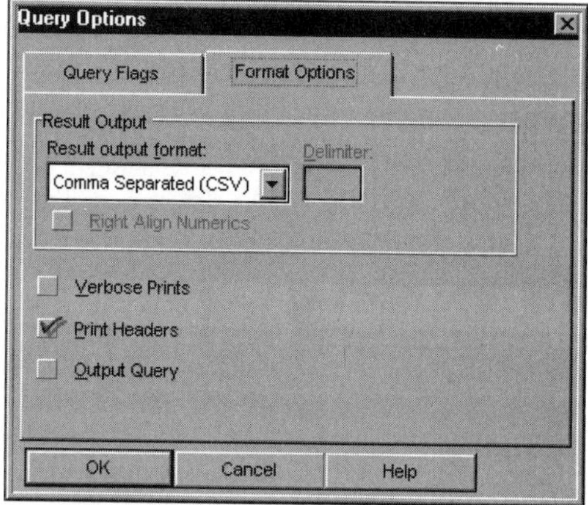

Figure 3-15:
Use Format Options to control how your query results are displayed.

- **Verbose Prints.** This is a mixed blessing. As you will learn later, there is a PRINT command in Transact-SQL. When you use the graphical statistics or Showplan, all your print statements are suppressed, which is annoying when you aren't expecting it. This option turns your PRINT statements back on. Unfortunately, it turns on the Show Stats Time text if you have the Display Statistics I/O button depressed. There is no way to see (a) a graphic of your stats, (b) text for the plan or stats, and (c) the output of your PRINT commands. What a pain!
- **Print Headers.** This just controls whether or not you get the column headings. Turning them off is helpful when you are trying to make a raw data file for importing into SQL Server or any other application.
- **Output Query.** This is supposed to echo your query back, but it is pretty worthless because it echoes only the first three lines of your query file, not the first three lines of each command. But even worse is that if you have chosen a Result output format other than column aligned, all you ever see echoed is this:

```
set nocount on

go
```

SQL Server is inserting these three lines (including the middle blank line) behind the scenes at the beginning of your file before execution.

Select Database Drop-down list box/Alt-D

Here you choose a database with which to work. If you have just created a database and it is not listed, choose the <Refresh> entry in the drop-down list box. You can switch what database you are in at any time, not just when you first connect.

Select Query Set Drop-down list box/Alt-U

You can click this text field to get a drop-down list of your connections. This is helpful because occasionally your windows will be sized in such a way that you cannot get to the actual arrow for the drop-down list. When you are in a Query window, Ctrl-PgUp and Ctrl-PgDn move you forward and backward through your queries from the keyboard. Both of these commands wrap, so if your last query is #5 and you press CNTL+PGDN, you will go to Query #1. Be careful about selecting a query with the mouse and then immediately using arrow keys to navigate the text of the query. Until you click in the text area of the query the Select Query Set box has focus; an up and down arrow will step you through your open windows.

Remove Current Query/Result Set Button/ Alt-Del/File⇨Close

This item deletes the Query and Result Set. You always get a warning, whether you have saved one or both of them.

Execute Query Button/Ctrl-E or Alt-X/ Query⇨Execute

This executes any highlighted text; if no text is highlighted, it executes the whole query. The capability to run just highlighted text is an enormous convenience; otherwise, you would be forever commenting out what you didn't want and uncommenting what you did. The keyboard shortcuts are worth memorizing because your hands are obviously on the keyboard as you finish typing your query. When you run a query, you immediately switch to the Results tab. You can change that under Tools⇨Preferences/Configure if you wish.

Cancel Executing Query Button/Ctrl-C/ Query⇨Cancel

This item should cancel your query. Don't be surprised when it doesn't always work or if it takes a long time between when you press this button and when a query really stops. SQL Server doesn't have the best facilities for unconditionally interrupting a query. If the Cancel button doesn't seem to be working, try to kill the process if you can. The best things you can do for yourself are to save your queries often and tie critical units of work together as transactions. (More on that in Chapter 21.)◀

Summary

The SQL Enterprise Manager is the graphical tool for almost all SQL Server work. When you first start it, you have to register the servers you want to use by supplying a login and password. If you have a lot of servers, you can organize them into groups. The Server Manager window lets you expand and collapse branches to see as much detail as you want in a server or an individual database. You can create additional Server Manager windows by dragging and dropping folders outside of the Server Manager window. When you select menu items, they apply to the most recently referenced server or database. There are a number of configuration options you can set.

Review Questions

Q: What are the three layers to the SQL-DMF?

A: Transact-SQL commands, SQL distributed management objects, and graphical tools like the SQL Server Enterprise Manager.

Q: Can you register a server using standard security with a trusted connection?

A: Yes. The SQL Enterprise Manager can force a trusted connection.

Q: What kind of management functions can you do on groups?

A: None. Groups simply let you organize your servers for easier viewing.

Q: If you are registering a server in the SQL Enterprise Manager on the server machine itself, what can you put in the server box instead of the server name?

A: (**local**).

Q: If the SQL Enterprise Manager tells you "Login failed" when you try to register a server, could it mean the server is down?

A: No. That would give you a different message.

Q: How can the information in the server's branches get out of date?

A: When you change something outside the menu system, such as via SQL.

Chapter

Basic Server Setup

4

Top database performance has as much to do with good server configuration as it has to do with good database design. This fact has led database vendors to build systems that allow great latitude in their configuration options. This kind of flexibility affords users the opportunity to tune their databases to their specific needs. This process of tweaking for maximum performance is often referred to as "tuning for maximum smoke." As you may expect, however, the more freedom users have in the configuration of their systems, the more potential there is for bad results. SQL Server is no exception in this regard.

A properly configured SQL Server system responds with the agility and speed of a cheetah, while a poorly configured system more resembles a wounded turtle. Scared? Don't be. In this chapter, you learn the basic server configuration options and how each can potentially affect your environment. By the time you are through here, you will be comfortable enough with your server setup to experiment with confidence. Feel better? Good.

What's in This Chapter

By the time you finish this chapter, you will learn the following:

- Which default options to change immediately
- Which are the most important SQL Server options
- How to determine when your configuration needs adjusting
- How to squeeze every last ounce of performance from your configuration settings

The easiest way to get at your server's configuration settings is through the SQL Enterprise Manager. As you probably remember from our discussion in Chapter 3, the SQL Enterprise Manager only runs under Windows NT 3.5*x* and Windows 95. Because we discuss most material in this chapter from the point of view of this utility, you should have ready access to one of those operating systems.◀

Server configuration options are accessed in the SQL Enterprise Manager from the Server➪Configurations menu option. When you select this option, you are met with the screen shown in Figure 4-1.

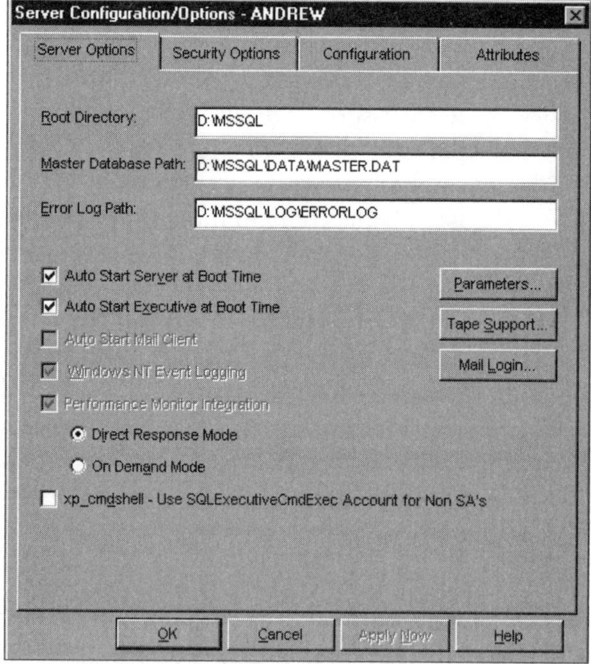

Figure 4-1:
Accessing your server settings.

This screen allows you to access the three major areas of your server configuration: general server options, general security options, and other server-specific configuration items. The Attributes tab is actually a read-only display of server statistics.

Server Options

The items in the Server Options tab should already be familiar to you if you originally installed your server. If not, don't worry, we review them here.

The first thing you probably notice is that some presented options are grayed out. This is because they can only be set by running the SQL Server Setup Utility. Since you can't change these options, we won't discuss them here. These are the options you have here:

- **Auto Start Server at Boot Time.** This option determines whether SQL Server is started when NT starts. This option is handy if you are concerned about things like power outages and remote server restarts.
- **Auto Start Executive At Boot Time.** This option determines whether the SQL Server Executive is started automatically each time NT restarts. This option has the same advantage as the previous option.
- **Auto Start License Logging.** This option determines whether SQL Server will automatically log certain events for the purpose of keeping track of licenses.
- **Performance Monitor Integration.** Your choices here are either Direct Response Mode or On Demand Mode. This option affects how the SQL Server Performance Monitor gathers statistics. In direct response mode, statistics are updated immediately. The problem is that the results are always one period behind. This "phase delay" is a problem if you need to have the very latest information. In on demand mode, server statistics are gathered during every refresh period. Obviously, the former gives quicker results and as such is the preferred option if you can do with slightly older results.
- **xp_cmdshell - Impersonates Client.** SQL Server has an extended stored procedure named xp_cmdshell that executes valid Windows NT commands on the server and displays any results. If this option is selected, only users who have Administrator privileges can execute this stored procedure. You still have to GRANT execute authority for this procedure to explicit users in order for them to use it.

Server startup parameters

Clicking the Parameters button on the Server Options tab opens a dialog box in which you can edit the SQL Server startup parameters. Your choices are as follows:

- **-c.** This option starts SQL Server independent of the Windows NT Service Control Manager. Starting the server from the command line with this option will reduce its startup time. There are a few things to be aware of, though. If you do start SQL Server with this option you will not be able to stop the server by using the SQL Service Manager or the net stop command. The other thing to be aware of is that if you log off of your Windows NT session after having started the server with this command, SQL Server will be terminated.
- **-dmaster_device_ path.** This option indicates the *fully qualified* path for the master database device. This is usually c:\sql\data\master.dat.
- **-eerror_log_path.** This option indicates the *fully qualified* path for the server error log. If you do not use this option, no error log is kept. This option is typically not used because NT keeps an event log that captures SQL Server errors.

You can't actually update either the master device path or the error log path unless you go to the text boxes.◀

- **-f.** This option starts SQL Server in minimal configuration mode. This option is most useful if you have inadvertently set a server option that has prevented it from starting normally. Think of this as starting the server in safe mode.
- **-m.** This option starts SQL Server in single-user mode. When you use this option only a single user can connect at a time. This option is helpful if you want to change server options that require that no other users are logged on.
- **-n.** This option prevents the Windows NT event log from keeping track of SQL Server events. If you elect to use this option, it is advisable to use the -e option also, or there will be no record of your server errors.
- **-rmaster_mirror.** This option indicates the *fully qualified* path for the device used to mirror the master database. In the event that your master database is damaged, SQL Server uses the device found at this path to start your system. Not to worry, though, SQL Server always tries to use the device specified with the -d option first.

- **-sregistry_key.** SQL Server startup parameters are stored in the Windows NT Registry. This option allows you to start your server with an alternate Registry key. This means that you could keep several sets of parameters in the system registry and use this option to start your server in a specific mode. We cover setting registry keys a little later.
- **-x.** This option prevents SQL Server from keeping CPU time and cache-hit ratio statistics. Using this option boosts performance but greatly reduces your ability to monitor your system's performance.

Tape support

You can change how long your server waits for a ready tape device before aborting a tape dump or backup. After clicking the Tape Support button on the Server Options tab, you are presented with the following options:

- **Wait Indefinitely.** This causes your server to wait as long as needed for a ready tape device.
- **Try Once and Quit.** This option tells your server to try the tape device only once. If it is not ready, the server should abort the process.
- **Try for *N* Minutes.** This instructs the server to try the tape device for *N* minutes before aborting the procedure.

Mail Login

SQL Server has the capability to send mail using Microsoft Mail and other compatible systems. In order to do so, however, it must first know the user ID and password of a valid mail account. You can set these options by pressing the Mail Login button on the Server Options tab and filling in the appropriate information.

Be sure to create a new mail ID for the Mail Login. Don't use a preexisting user ID because MS Mail does not support two people logged in with the same ID.◀

Security Options

Clicking on the Security Options tab displays the dialog box shown in Figure 4-2.

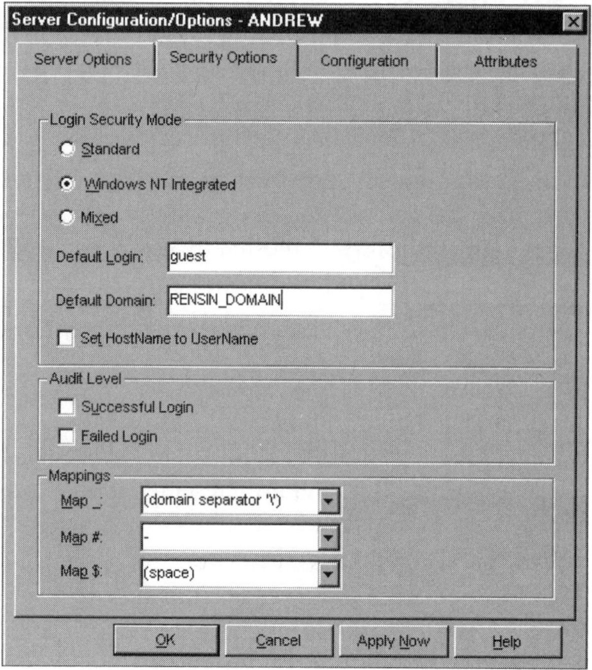

Figure 4-2:
SQL server security options.

The options on this screen control how SQL Server handles user logins. You have three choices here: Standard, Windows NT Integrated, and Mixed.

Standard security means that SQL Server handles all user logins and authentication. This is a good option if you don't want to have to create a separate user account on your NT server for each client logging into the database.

Windows NT integrated security, however, means that SQL Server uses the built-in authentication scheme of Windows NT to validate connections. The advantage of this option is that Windows NT has a far more robust and secure user validation mechanism than SQL Server. The problem with this method is that every user who wants to connect to your database must have a valid Windows NT account on your NT domain server. Users connecting in this fashion are said to have a *trusted login*.

The last security method is a mixed mode. In this mode SQL Server will accept connections from both NT-authenticated and non-NT-authenticated users. Use this option if you only want to give access to certain server functions to people who have been authenticated by Windows NT. We will cover this topic in *much* greater detail in Chapter 7.◀

The Security Options tab also helps define how SQL Server differentiates between users with the same username. Assume that there are two users. One is named Joe Schmoe and the other is named John Schmoe. Joe has the user ID of jschmoe in the NT1 domain, while his brother John has the name jschmoe in the NT2 domain. What if you want to give both John and Joe access to your database and you are using integrated security? How will the server distinguish between the two users?

The answer lies with the Default Domain option. This field holds the name of the default domain to check for user IDs. Those users attempting to login to the database from another domain will be given a unique name that contains their domain and user ID. For example, let's say that the default domain is NT1. When Joe tries to log in to the server, he will be reported as jschmoe because he is from the default domain. John, on the other hand, will be reported as something like NT2_jschmoe.

The Security Options screen also controls how SQL Server records logins. The Set Hostname To Username option determines how SQL Server reports users who have trusted connections. Normally, when you run the sp_who stored procedure, it shows the hostname of those users logged in via trusted connections and the SQL Server username of those users authenticated by SQL Server. If this option is selected, however, SQL Server will, for trusted connections, replace the hostname with the user's network username.

No system is really secure without some sort of audit trail, either the Windows NT event log or SQL Server error log. Which one you use depends on how you have started your server. From the Security Options screen you can choose whether to log successful logins, unsuccessful logins, or both.

As you may expect, there are differences between the security schemes of Windows NT and SQL Server. One of the biggest distinctions is the naming rules for valid usernames. Windows NT accepts characters in usernames that SQL Server will not. This is what the Map_, Map#, and Map$ options are for. The first of the three determines which characters from a Windows NT username are mapped to an underscore (_). The second determines which characters are mapped to a number sign (#), and the third determines which are mapped to a dollar sign ($).

This means that a valid Windows NT username of \\dave-rensin+ may be reported by SQL Server as __dave#rensin$. This mapping helps ensure that SQL Server doesn't choke on an invalid username introduced via an NT username.

CONFIGURATION

Clicking on the Configuration tab brings up the screen shown in Figure 4-3. You must first make sure that the Show Advanced Options setting is set to 1, or you will not see all of these options.

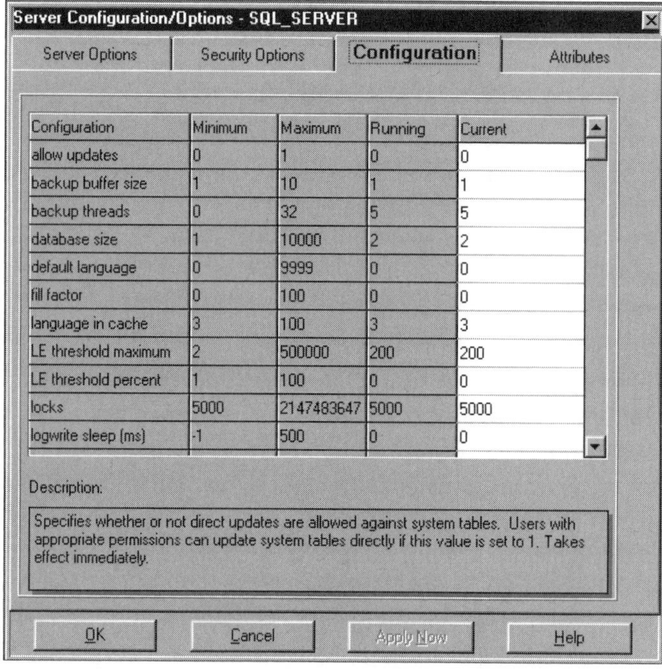

Server Configuration/Options - SQL_SERVER
Server Options
Security Options
Configuration
Attributes
Configuration Minimum Maximum Running Current
allow updates 0 1 0 0
backup buffer size 1 10 1 1
backup threads 0 32 5 5
database size 1 10000 2 2
default language 0 9999 0 0
fill factor 0 100 0 0
language in cache 3 100 3 3
LE threshold maximum 2 500000 200 200
LE threshold percent 1 100 0 0
locks 5000 2147483647 5000 5000
logwrite sleep (ms) -1 500 0 0
Description:
Specifies whether or not direct updates are allowed against system tables. Users with appropriate permissions can update system tables directly if this value is set to 1. Takes effect immediately.
OK
Cancel
Apply Now
Help

Figure 4-3:
SQL Server performance configuration options.

From this window, you can change almost every conceivable option relevant to your server.

Please be sure to take care when adjusting the items on the Configuration tab as they can cause SQL Server not to restart. In the following pages, we will explain what each option is and how it can affect your server.

Allow updates

The allow updates option determines whether users with appropriate access levels can alter the system tables directly. When this option is set to false (0), system tables can only be updated via system stored procedures. Changing the value to true (1) allows users to change critical systems settings with ad-hoc queries. Our advice is to leave this choice set to false. Should you choose, however, to enable this item, there is something you need to know. All stored procedures that you or your users create while this option is set to true will *always* be able to modify the system tables even if you later set this option to false. If you want to disable one of these procedures from doing so, you must drop it and recreate it with this flag set to false.

If you want to let some users update the system tables, turn the allow updates option on, create a stored procedure, and then disable this option. You can then GRANT specific users the right to execute the stored procedure.◀

There are some options that require you to stop and restart SQL Server. They are indicated in the configuration window. The allow updates option takes effect immediately (is dynamic), so you don't have to restart SQL Server to see the change.

Backup buffer size

The backup buffer size option sets the size of the dump and load buffer. This value reflects the size of this buffer in 32-page increments. In other words, if the value here is 3, the size of the dump and load buffer will be 96 pages (32 × 3). The larger you set this value, the faster your backups should run. The tradeoff is, of course, the increased use of memory.

Backup threads

This setting determines the number of system threads reserved for striped dump and load operations. If the backup threads value is set to zero, disk striping is turned off.

Some servers are set up to write to a series of disks in parallel. In this scenario, parts of a disk write are spread across several physical disks. Some of these writes are also redundant. This technique is used to minimize the effects of a disk failure. This method is called *disk striping*. If you have hardware RAID support, you do not need to worry about this.◀

Cursor threshold

SQL Server can create a cursor either synchronously or asynchronously. For cursors with large result sets, asynchronous generation will be faster, while small result set cursors may perform better with synchronous generation. When SQL Server creates a cursor, it estimates the number of rows that will eventually be returned. If that number is greater than the value in this field, the cursor will be generated asynchronously.

Essentially, cursor threshold defines the point at which the SQL Server optimizer considers a cursor to be large. If this value is set to –1, all cursors will be generated synchronously. If, however, this field is set to zero, all cursors will be generated asynchronously. Because smaller result set cursors are faster to build synchronously, it is wise not to set this value too low.

Database size

The database size attribute sets the default size, in megabytes, for each new user database. This value can be set as low as 1. This field, of course, can be overridden by specifying a database size with a CREATE DATABASE statement. When an explicit value is not supplied, SQL Server will use the larger value between the size of the model database or this option. For example, if database size is configured to 2 (the default) and the model database has been altered to 3MB, the database will be 3MB.

Default language

This field holds the ID of the language used by SQL Server to display system messages. By default, this value is set to zero (us_english).

Default sort order

This attribute is the number of the sort order currently installed for the server. SQL Server supports the following sort orders:

- Dictionary Order, Case-insensitive
- Binary Order
- Dictionary Order, Case-sensitive
- Dictionary Order, Case-insensitive, Uppercase Preference

- Dictionary Order, Case-insensitive, Accent-insensitive
- Additional Sort Orders for Code Page 850
- Version 1.*x*-compatible Sort Order
- Alternate Sort Orders
- Scandinavian Dictionary Order, Case-sensitive
- Sort Order IDS
- Performance Comparisons
- Custom

Warning

Do not change your default sort order! Changing your server's default sort order has enormous effects on your database. If you do decide that you want to alter this value, you will have to rebuild your master database completely. The default value is Dictionary Order, Case-insensitive. We *strongly* recommend that you leave it that way even though this setting is not typically your fastest option. Setting your sorts to binary order will usually boost sort performance by about 20 percent. The important thing to remember, though, is that binary order is not the same as dictionary order. You will not see rows returned to you in the order you expect, and you will see different results returned by queries with string comparisons. If you do decide that you must change your default sort order, do so in the SQL Server Setup Utility, not here.◀

Fill factor

The fill factor attribute tells SQL Server how full to make each data page when creating an index on existing data. This value is a percentage. In other words, a value of 70 means that the server attempts to make each data page 70 percent full when it first creates a new index.

Note

Technically, you only have 2,016 of 2,048 bytes available for actual data on each page, so a fill factor of 100 means you get 98 percent full, and a fill factor of 70 means you actually get 69 percent full.◀

In a practical sense, you can think of a data page as a bucket of memory. Each time SQL Server has to search across pages, it takes a small performance hit. The more full you make each page, the less pages SQL Server will potentially have to search through.

At this point, you are probably wondering why, if having fewer pages is better, the system doesn't automatically minimize the number of needed data pages by setting the fill factor to 100. It's a tradeoff. Values in an index are maintained in a certain order. That is, after all, the purpose of having an index. If you initially make your data pages very full, the server will have to do more work to insert new values in the middle of the index. This is because SQL Server takes a performance hit each time it has to split data across a page. Tables that will have a lot of inserting and updating activity should have a smaller fill factor to leave room on a page for new index values.

There is, however, a memory concern with small fill factors. Again, it is useful to think of data pages as buckets because the two share an important characteristic. Even if a bucket is only 1 percent full, it still occupies the same amount of space as if it were completely full. A data page is the same way. The smaller you make your fill factor, the more pages you will need for each index. More pages mean more memory.

Because this particular configuration item is the *default* fill factor for each new index, it's probably best if you leave it alone. You can always assign a fill factor to a specific index when you create it with the CREATE INDEX command.

Tip

The rule of thumb is this: Use larger fill factors for tables that have data that are not likely to change and smaller fill factors for tables that have only a small amount of the data they will eventually hold.◀

Free buffers

This attribute sets the minimum number of free buffers available to the system. This value may be as low as 20 and as high as one-half the number of buffers available when the server is started. One of SQL Server's system processes, known as the *Lazy Writer* process, makes sure that the number of free buffers never falls below this minimum.

Hash buckets

Hash buckets, like data pages, are finite amounts of memory used to hold information temporarily. Hash buckets, in particular, shuttle information to and from SQL Server's data cache. The data cache is where SQL Server holds the most recently accessed table data. The greater the number of hash buckets you have, the faster you can retrieve data from the data cache.

Why Prime?

You may wonder why the hash buckets value has to be prime. Technically, the number of hash buckets only has to be relatively prime to the size of your data cache, which means that the hash bucket number and the data cache size share no common divisors.

If these two numbers were not relatively prime, you wouldn't utilize your entire data cache. The hashing algorithm would cycle through a subset of the memory values. SQL Server requires the number of hash buckets to be prime to guarantee that it will always be relatively prime to your data cache size, even if you change the data cache size.

The number of server hash buckets is always specified as a prime number. If you enter a value that is not a prime number, SQL Server chooses the closest prime number. The default value for this attribute is 7,993. If your system has a large amount of memory (greater than 160 megabytes), you might want to increase this value.

Language in cache

You have already learned that SQL Server supports many different languages for system messages. The language in cache option specifies how many different languages SQL Server will hold in memory at a time. The default value is 3.

LE (Lock Escalation) threshold maximum

This attribute determines how many page locks SQL Server will hold before escalating to a table lock. When you issue a query that returns a large number of rows, SQL Server uses a scheme called *page locking*. All page locking really means is that a database table is divided into logical units called *pages*. Each page contains a certain number of rows, depending on the row size. If SQL Server needs to lock any rows from a given page, it will lock all the rows on that page. If SQL Server locks more pages than the number specified by this attribute, SQL Server will promote the individual row locks to a table lock. This is because it is more efficient to check a single table lock than many individual page locks. This configuration option trumps all others. In other words, if you exceed this value, you get a table lock, no matter what the other lock escalation values are in place. The default for this item is 200.

LE (Lock Escalation) threshold percent

This configuration item specifies the percentage of pages in the table that must be locked before SQL Server escalates the lock to a table lock. If, for example, this value is 50, after 50 percent of a table's pages are locked, SQL Server requests a table lock. If this attribute is set to zero, a table lock is only requested after the LE threshold maximum has been exceeded. The default for this item is zero.

LE (Lock Escalation) threshold minimum

The LE threshold percentage attribute can cause problems for small tables. Because it is easier to get a high percentage of page locks on a table with little data, smaller tables are more prone to have their locks promoted to table locks. The LE threshold minimum helps relieve this problem by specifying the minimum number of page locks, above the LE threshold percent value, that a user must have before being promoted to a full table lock. For example, assume the LE threshold percent is 50 and the LE threshold minimum is 30. For a table with 40 pages, SQL Server won't promote page locks to table locks at 20 page locks; rather, it will escalate to a page lock only when 30 pages have been locked.

Locks

The locks value sets the total number of available locks on the server. If your database server is going to have a lot of simultaneous users, you may want to increase this value. Like most other options, however, this will take memory. Each lock requires 32 bytes of system memory. The default value here is 5,000, or a little over 152K.

Having a lot of users is not the only thing that can push the default limit. We have hit the 5,000 ceiling with *one* procedure. But when you hit it, you know because your process will bomb and tell you so. Then, you raise the limit, stop and start the server, and drive on. How will you know you have bombed? Easy, SQL Server will tell you explicitly with an error message on you screen (if you are using an interactive query tool) or with a return code.◀

Logwrite sleep

SQL Server first writes all database log entries to a buffer and then flushes the buffer to disk when the buffer is full. The logwrite sleep option specifies, in milliseconds, the amount of time SQL Server should wait before writing the log to disk if the buffer is not full. Because two users can issue statements that logically negate one another, delaying the writing of the log file can reduce the number of physical writes actually needed. In practical terms, the larger you make this value, the greater the possible reduction in physical log writes to disk. There is a risk, though. If your server experiences a fatal error before the log buffer has been flushed, you will lose those transactions.

The values for this attribute can range from –1 to 500. Both –1 and 0 hold special meanings. If you specify a value of –1, log writes will not be delayed. If, however, you specify a value of 0, SQL Server will wait until all users are ready before it writes to the log file. The default value is 0.

Max async IO

This option specifies the maximum number of total simultaneous input/output (IO) operations SQL Server can perform. The default value of 8 is more than sufficient for most systems. Users who are using more than one physical device or taking advantage of disk striping can increase this number.

Max lazywrite IO

The max lazywrite IO option specifies how many of the total simultaneous IO processes (specified by the max async IO option) can be used by SQL Server's Lazy Writer system process.

Max worker threads

Windows NT is a multithreaded operating system. You can think of a thread as an independent process, without most of the expense of starting a new process. This means that Windows NT can execute multiple independent processes at a time. SQL Server uses separate threads for various system processes. It also uses a pool of threads for user connections. The number of threads in this pool depends on the max worker threads attribute. If the number of user connections is less than the number of pool threads, each connection will get a dedicated thread. If, however, the number of connections exceeds the number of threads in the pool, each subsequent user request is handled by the next available thread. The default value for this option is 255.

Media retention

One of the most important functions any database administrator (DBA) performs is backing up the system data. One of the most troublesome problems in this operation occurs when a DBA accidentally overwrites one backup with another backup. SQL Server has a built-in guard against this occurrence. The media retention attribute specifies the number of days you expect you will retain each backup before you reuse the media. If, for example, this value is set to 7, any time you attempt to backup data to media that was last used less than 7 days ago, SQL Server will generate a warning. If this value is set to zero, SQL Server disables all warnings.

Memory

The memory setting is the single most important configuration change you can make to your SQL Server system. This attribute specifies, in 2K blocks, the amount of total memory allocated to SQL Server. Obviously, the more memory you can give to the database, the better it performs.

The way to compute the correct value for this setting is relatively simple:

1. You have to figure out how much your Windows NT system needs in order to perform its normal functions without paging to disk. This value will depend on the number of other programs and services your system has been configured to run.
2. After you have determined this value, subtract it from the total system memory on your server. The remaining amount should go to SQL Server.

There are two things to keep in mind when changing the memory value. First, if you change this option, SQL Server may adjust the free buffers option accordingly. Second, the value you give this parameter *does not* include any memory you may specify in the tempdb in ram option. (We cover that item a little later.) The maximum value for this parameter is 2GB.

Nested triggers

The nested triggers setting specifies whether triggers cascade in your system. A value of 1 allows cascading triggers and a value of zero disallows them.

Network packet size

SQL Server exchanges data with clients in bursts of information called *packets*. The network packet size setting controls the size of each packet. Some network protocols only support packets of a given size. In this case, it is useless to set this value any higher. In the case of a multiprotocol installation, you should set this value to the packet size of your most commonly used protocol. The default for this setting is 4,096 (4KB).

Open databases

This configuration item sets the maximum number of databases that can be open at any one time. The default is 20.

Open objects

This option sets the maximum number of database objects that can be open at any one time. If you have a lot of concurrent users or processes, you might want to increase this value from the default of 500. Of course, each new object requires memory. This means that you may also have to increase the value of the memory option. If you think that your users are waiting to open objects, even though they have free memory, you might consider upping this option. In most cases, though, the default is fine.

Priority boost

This item determines whether SQL Server gets to run at higher priority than other tasks on the same server. If it is set to 1, the Windows NT scheduler gives SQL Server the highest weighting. The default is zero. Our advice is to leave this at zero. We have tried this and found that setting this option to 1 locked our machine too much.

Procedure cache

This option specifies what percentage of memory is devoted to the procedure cache. The procedure cache is an area of memory devoted to holding commonly used stored procedures. This boosts performance because SQL Server can read the code from memory, rather than from disk.

After SQL Server allocates any memory it needs for system code, base processes, and user connections, it allocates the remaining memory between the procedure cache and the data cache depending on the value of this setting. A setting of 20, for example, means that SQL Server gives 20 percent of all available memory, after critical functions, to the procedure cache and 80 percent to the data cache. The default value for this item is 30. If, however, your system will routinely have to process a wide range of different stored procedures or queries, you may want to increase this value.

RA (Read-Ahead) cache hit limit

When SQL Server determines that it is reading data sequentially, it starts threads to read different parts of the intended result set in parallel. This boosts the overall retrieval performance of the query. This process of determination and action is called *read ahead*.

The RA cache hit limit option sets the number of allowable cache hits a read-ahead (RA) request can have before it is canceled. If a particular RA request can get a lot of its data from the data cache, it is of minimal use to the system. This option sets the threshold at which that determination is made. The default value for this option is 4.

Warning

Changing any of SQL Server's default RA values can severely degrade performance. We don't recommend that you change this, but if you do, tread with care!

RA (Read-Ahead) cache miss limit

This option sets the number of cache misses any particular data request can have before an RA request is initiated. Setting this value too low will cause an RA request to be generated every time data is read from disk. This will bring performance to a virtual standstill. This is probably a good thing to leave alone.

RA (Read-Ahead) delay

When the RA Manager receives a data request, it must find the required information before it can begin servicing the request. The RA delay setting determines how long, in milliseconds, the RA Manager process waits before beginning service of a request. The default value is 15.

If your server is using symmetric multiprocessing (running more than one processor), this value should *always* be set to 15.◀

RA (Read-Ahead) pre-fetches

SQL Server allocates space for database objects in 16K units called *extents*. The value specified in the RA pre-fetches attribute determines how many extents ahead of the current scan position the RA Manager resides. For example, a value of 6 means that the RA Manager will always read 6 extents, (96K) ahead of the current scan position.

RA (Read-Ahead) slots per thread

The RA Manager has a certain number of process threads at its disposal. The value in the RA slots per thread attribute specifies how many simultaneous requests each RA thread can handle. This means that the total number of concurrent requests the RA Manager can handle is the number of allocated RA threads times the number of RA slots per thread.

RA (Read-Ahead) worker threads

The RA worker threads option sets the number of system threads available to the RA Manager. Use this value in conjunction with the RA slots per thread attribute to determine the total number of concurrent requests the RA Manager can handle. This setting should be set to the maximum number of concurrent users defined for your system. In other words, if your server is set to allow a maximum of 15 simultaneous connections, you should allocate 15 threads to the RA Manager.

Recovery flags

When SQL Server has to recover from a database error, it writes certain information to the error log. The amount of information written depends on this attribute. If the recovery flags option is set to zero, SQL Server writes only the database name and the fact that a recovery is in process. If, however, this flag is set to 1, SQL Server writes information about each transaction. This information includes what the transaction is and whether the transaction was successfully committed.

Recovery interval

This flag specifies the maximum time, in minutes, allotted to SQL Server for the recovery of each database in the event of a system failure. Changing the recovery interval setting affects how often SQL Server writes dirty data pages to disk. If, for example, this value is set to 3, SQL Server knows that it needs to write dirty data pages to disk frequently enough so that if the system has to recover, it only takes 3 minutes to recover each database. Obviously, the lower you set this value, the more often SQL Server writes to disk. If, however, you set this value too high, your recovery process will be unacceptably long. The default value is 5.

This is not bullet-proof. If you send a super-long single transaction to the server and the power fails, your recovery time can still be long.◀

Remote access

This item determines whether your SQL Server will allow remote logins from other SQL Servers. A value of 1, the default, allows remote access while a value of zero prevents it.

Remote login timeout

If SQL Server attempts to establish a remote connection to a machine that is particularly busy, it can take a while to return. The value in the remote login timeout attribute sets the maximum number of seconds SQL Server can use to try to connect to a remote server. If this period is exceeded before the connection is made, SQL Server aborts the attempt. The default value of zero means that SQL Server has an infinite time limit, and that it doesn't have a timeout.

Remote query timeout

This settings determines the maximum number of seconds in which to process a remote query. If the query cannot be finished in this time frame, it is aborted. A value of zero means that SQL Server has no time limit for this process.

Remote sites

This option sets the maximum number of OS/2-based servers allowed to connect at any one time.

Set working set size

This flag tells SQL Server to reserve physical memory equal to the amount specified in the memory setting plus the amount specified in the tempdb in ram setting. The default for this option, zero, disables this option.

Show advanced options

This item determines whether the SQL Enterprise Manager and sp_configure should display advanced configuration options. If this item is not set to 1, you will not able to change some of the options listed here. The default is zero.

SMP concurrency

SQL Server can utilize more than one processor on a machine through a process called *symmetric multiprocessing (SMP)*. The SMP concurrency option governs the number of processors SQL Server can use on a given machine.

Each SQL Server machine will operate in one of three distinct modes. These modes depend on the number of installed processors and whether or not the machine is a dedicated SQL Server machine. These modes are

- Single-processor (SP)
- Multi-processor/dedicated server (MP/DS)
- Multi-processor/non-dedicated server (MP/NDS)

When SQL Server is running on an SP machine, the SMP concurrency setting should be 1. When the server is an MP/DS machine, this setting should be –1. This means that SQL Server takes advantage of as many processors as possible. Finally, when the server is an MP/NDS machine, this setting varies depending on how much CPU you want to dedicate to SQL Server. The larger you make this value, the poorer other non-SQL Server applications run on the server.

Sort pages

This option specifies the number of memory pages that will be allocated to each user for the purpose of sorting. If your users will be performing large sorts on a frequent basis, increasing this value helps improve performance. Keep in mind, though, that more pages means more memory. This means that you may have to increase the amount in the memory setting as well.

Spin counter

This configuration setting specifies the maximum number of times a process can attempt to gain the use of a system resource. On SP machines, this value is set to 10, while on MP/DS and MP/NDS machines, this value is set to 10,000.

Tempdb in ram

SQL Server will sometimes create temporary objects in a database called tempdb. The tempdb in ram option sets, in megabytes, the size of tempdb and places it in RAM, rather than on disk. If this item is set to zero, tempdb will reside on disk.

Like many other SQL Server configuration options, Tempdb in ram can be a double-edged sword. On machines that have a lot of physical ram (64MB+), putting tempdb in RAM can help performance considerably. The less memory a machine has, however, the less worthwhile this option becomes. SQL Server will perform best on machines with limited physical memory by setting the memory option as high as possible and keeping tempdb on disk. If you do decide to keep tempdb in RAM, remember two important points:

- Always keep at least 2MB free on your default database device. We recommend you do this because when you attempt to upgrade SQL Server, it will move tempdb to disk. If you do not have at least 2MB free on your default device, SQL Server fails to start.
- When tempdb resides in RAM, it can only be altered ten times before the server must be restarted. This has to do with the way SQL Server allocates memory for tempdb when the ALTER statement is used.

Time slice

This setting specifies the number of times a user process can ignore a yield command before processing it. If this option is set too low, users will experience long delays in server response times. If, however, this item is set too high, SQL Server switches tasks too often and overall system performance will fall. The default value is 100. Our advice is to leave it at that setting. There are too many other things you can change about the server to help performance without having to worry about the time slice each process gets.

User connections

This setting determines the maximum number of allowable user connections your specific SQL Server installation currently supports. For SQL Workstation, this value has a maximum of 15 while SQL Server will support up to 32,767 connections.

In practical terms, however, the number of actual user connections your server can support may be less than this value. This will depend on your hardware and the kind of usage your database experiences. Unfortunately, there is no formula to compute what this setting should be. We recommend that you set this number up to 50 right away. We have found that 20 is very often not enough. If you do decide to increase this number, there is a way to help you estimate what its value should be.

Choose a time when your server is being worked its hardest and run the following query:

```
SELECT @@max_connections
```

This query returns to you the maximum number of user connections your system can currently support. This will give you an idea of what the worst-case scenario will be for your server. You can use this number in conjunction with the number of current connections to determine an appropriate setting for user connections.

Windows NT Configuration for SQL Server

Earlier in this chapter, we alluded to a few things you could do to your Windows NT system settings to boost your SQL Server performance. This section attempts to cover these areas briefly. It is, however, important to note that this is not an exhaustive list of things you can do. SQL Server and Windows NT are very closely integrated. There is almost an infinite number of configuration changes you can make to improve the performance of SQL Server. As a result, we cover only those things we feel have the greatest value to you.

Balancing network throughput versus file server throughput

Most installations will use SQL Server on a dedicated machine. If you have the choice, this is the configuration we recommend. If, however, your SQL Server computer must also act as a file server, you will have to do some load balancing. How you decide to resolve this problem depends entirely on your environment. If your database is used very little and your network files are used a lot, you will obviously want to give file sharing services the highest priority.

The easiest way to do load balancing on a Windows NT machine is to edit its network settings. To do this, follow these steps:

1. Open the Control Panel applet from the main program group.
2. Double-click the Network icon and choose the Services tab. Select the Server icon and press Properties. The Server dialog shown in Figure 4-4 appears.

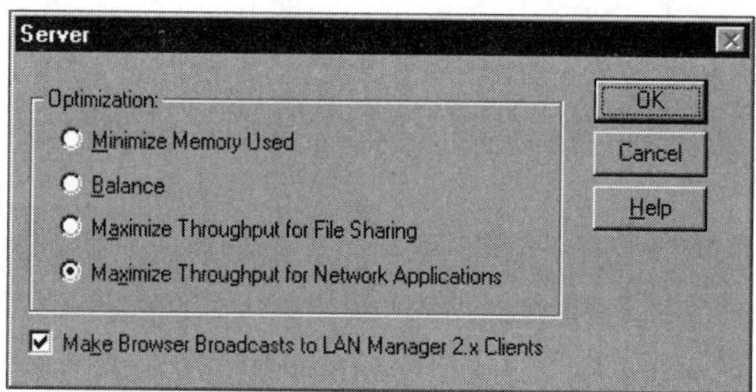

Figure 4-4:
NT Server load balancing options.

3. At this point, you need to choose the best option for your particular configuration. If you are running a dedicated SQL Server machine, choose Maximize Throughput for Network Applications. If, however, you are running a mixed environment, you may wish to choose either the Balance or Maximize Throughput for File Sharing options.

Creating registry keys for alternate startup modes

Earlier in the chapter we briefly talk about SQL Server's capability to determine its startup parameters by reading the Windows NT Registry. This section teaches you how to create new Registry keys for this purpose.

When SQL Server is first installed, it creates a set of keys in the system Registry in which to store startup configuration information. You can add your own keys and then use the "-s" startup option to start SQL Server with an alternate configuration. One use for this would be if you commonly start your server in single-user mode. In the following example, we take you through the steps of adding a new key for starting SQL Server in single-user mode. You can use this process to add other keys as you need them.

Warning

A person can break *a lot* of things by editing the Registry incorrectly. *Please* be careful. If you accidentally erase or otherwise mangle the basic SQL Server keys, you will not be able to restart your server. You may not even be able to boot NT. Remember, we warned you.◀

The Windows NT System Registry

The Windows NT System Registry is comprised of items called *keys*. A key is just a label that can hold some value. For example, *MyKey* might be a string key that holds the value *"this is a test"*. Keys can also have subkeys. Think of this as a tree where *MyKey* is a branch and its subkeys are leaves. In fact, the Windows NT Registry is just a big tree of keys where information about various applications is stored in different branches and leaves. For example, Figure 4-5 shows what a basic registry key looks like when it is expanded.

The topmost key in the System Registry, also known as the *root* key, is HKEY_LOCAL_MACHINE. This root key has many subkeys that describe various things about the server. SQL Server sets up its configuration options from the HKEY_LOCAL_MACHINE⇨SOFTWARE⇨Microsoft⇨ MSSQLServer branch. Figure 4-6 shows these specific branches.

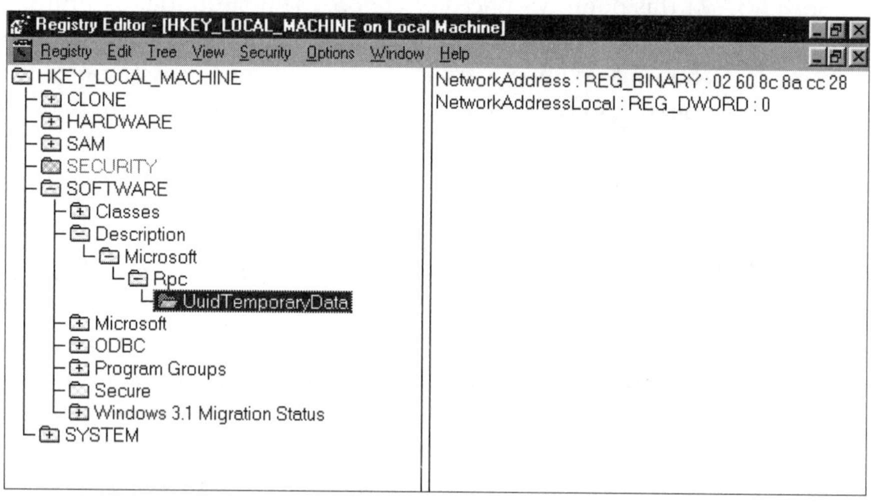

Figure 4-5:
A Basic registry branch.

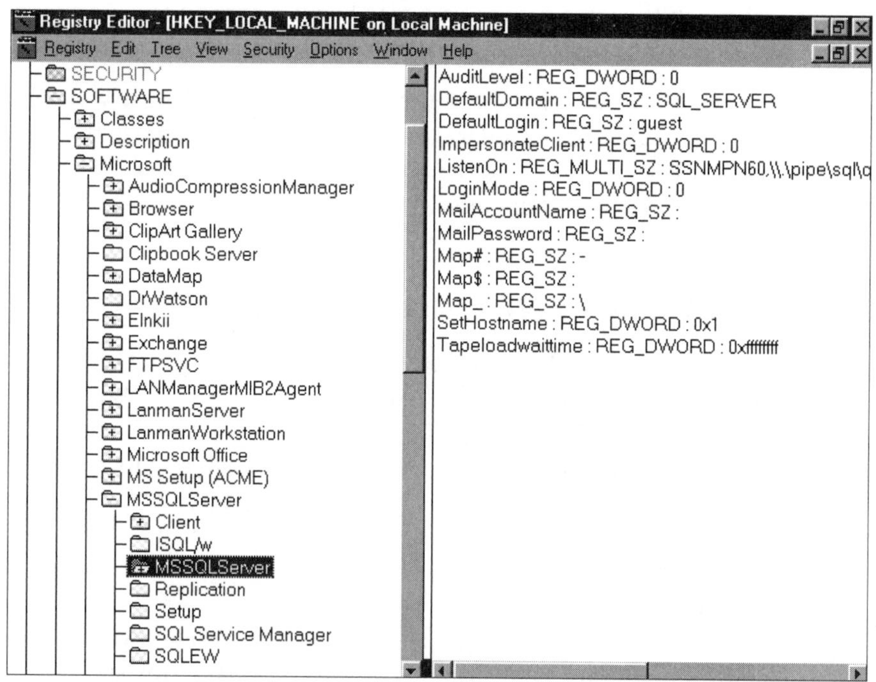

Figure 4-6:
The SQL Server registry branches.

The Windows NT System Registry can be a confusing place. It is, after all, the central repository for application-specific configurations on your server. If, however, you follow our instructions, you will be able to greatly customize your SQL Server environment. Ready? Good, because here we go.

Adding a new key for single-user mode

Run the program regedt32.exe. You can find this in your c:\winnt35\system32 directory, or you can run it from a command (C:\>) prompt. Find the HKEY_LOCAL_MACHINE⇨SOFTWARE⇨Microsoft⇨MSSQLServer branch and double-click on the MSSQLServer node. The items that appear on the right pane of the window are the things you will want to copy to a new key. To do this, perform the following steps:

1. Click the MSSQLServer entry.
2. Select the Edit⇨Add Key menu option.
3. Enter the name of your new key (something like *SingleUser*)in the dialog box and click OK.
4. Click the MSSQLServer key and choose Registry⇨Save Key from the menu.
5. Enter a temporary filename in the dialog box and click OK.
6. Click the new key you created in Step 3 (*SingleUser* or whatever) and choose Registry⇨Restore.
7. Enter the temporary filename from Step 5 in the dialog box and click OK.
8. When prompted about overwriting the current key, click Yes.

You have copied the values in the MSSQLServer key to your new key. You can edit any of the values in the new key by double-clicking them. You can also add new values to your key by choosing the Edit⇨Add Value from the menu. When prompted for the type of value, use REG_SZ, which is a string value.

When you are finished, you can restart SQL Server by running

```
sqlservr -c -sYour_New_Key_Here
```

For example, if your new key was called *SingleUser*, you would type

```
sqlservr -c -sSingleUser
```

Once again, however, we must caution you about editing the SQL Server Registry keys. You can get into big trouble if you are not careful.

Summary

The easiest way to configure your SQL Server setup is through the SQL Enterprise Manager. In this utility, you can configure basic access and security options, backup options, startup parameters, and more advanced memory and thread management items. Keep in mind that most configuration items require you to stop and restart SQL Server before they take effect.

This chapter also introduces you to ways you can configure your Windows NT environment to optimize your database output. These include throughput tuning, load balancing, and registry editing.

SQL Server affords its administrators a wide variety of configuration and tuning options. Giving preferences to certain server functions or increasing certain memory spaces may improve your overall database performance considerably. These actions, however, have risks. It is always wise to keep careful track of how your system was configured before you make a change. This will help you undo it later. In this chapter, we introduced you to all of SQL Server's configuration options and familiarized you with their implications on your system. We encourage you to experiment with your configuration, but always do so safely. If you can afford to have a test machine handy, that would be optimal. You may be surprised how upset your users can get if you start experimenting with a production machine!

Review Questions

Please take a few moments to answer the following review questions. If you can answer these without going back through the chapter, you have probably learned what you need to thus far.

Q: Why is it a bad idea to run SQL Server with the "-n" option and not include the "-e" option?

A: No error logging will be performed.

Q: Which of the following modes gives the fastest response to the Performance Monitor: Direct Response Mode or On Demand Mode?

A: Direct Response Mode.

Q: What startup option do you use to start SQL Server in "safe" mode?

A: -f

Q: What is a trusted connection?

A: It's a connection where the user has been authenticated by Windows NT, rather than by SQL Server.

Q: What Registry key branch contains the SQL Server configuration options?

A: HKEY_LOCAL_MACHINE⇨SOFTWARE⇨Microsoft⇨MSSQLServer.

Q: How much RAM should you have before you consider putting your tempdb in RAM?

A: 64MB or more.

Chapter 5

Basic Client Configuration

Now that we've covered basic server setup, we turn to configuring the various client utilities that come with SQL Server 6.5. By the time you finish here, you will understand the different protocols by which SQL Server communicates and how to configure your programs for them.

What's in This Chapter

In this chapter, you learn the answers to such interesting questions as the following:

- What are Named Pipes?
- Is one protocol faster than another?
- Is using TCP/IP ever a good idea?
- Can I query my SQL Server machine from DOS?

Who Can Talk to the Database?

Microsoft SQL Server 6.5 ships with client programs for the following platforms:

- Windows NT
- Windows 95
- Windows 3.1*x*
- MS-DOS

This list is also in order of flexibility. In other words, the client programs for Windows NT provide the most power to the user while the Windows 95 files provide a little less. The Windows 3.1*x* files are even less flexible and so on. Our advice is to use either Windows NT or Windows 95. Server administration is much more difficult from the Windows 3.1*x* clients and almost impossible from MS-DOS programs. If you're wondering why OS/2 isn't on the list, see the sidebar, "OS/2 Who?"

When we talk about the SQL Server 6.5 client programs we are speaking of eight specific applications. They are

- **ISQL/W — Interactive SQL / Windows.** This program lets you run adhoc queries as well as all other Transact-SQL statements.
- **SQL Security Manager.** This program lets you manage the logins and security of your SQL Server for Mixed and Integrity security.

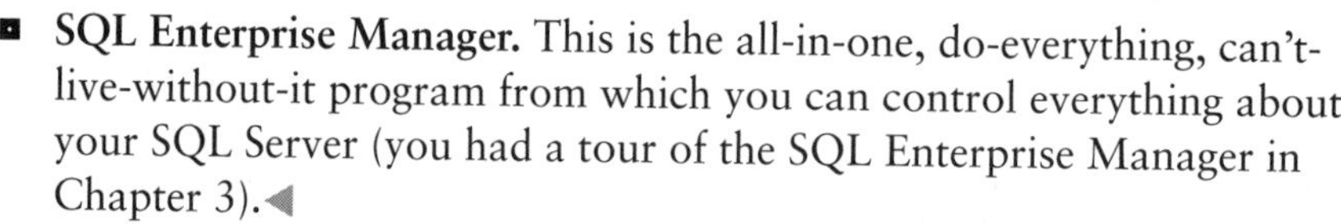

- **SQL Enterprise Manager.** This is the all-in-one, do-everything, can't-live-without-it program from which you can control everything about your SQL Server (you had a tour of the SQL Enterprise Manager in Chapter 3).◀

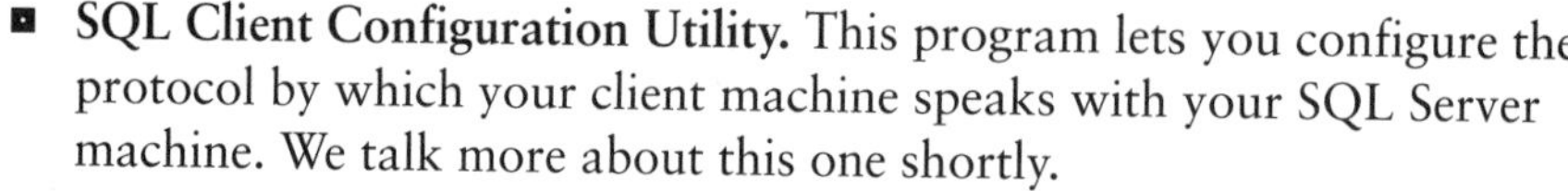

- **SQL Client Configuration Utility.** This program lets you configure the protocol by which your client machine speaks with your SQL Server machine. We talk more about this one shortly.

OS/2 Who?

SQL Server 4.2 shipped with a client program for OS/2. As you may have heard, Microsoft and IBM are not as friendly as they once were. Therefore, SQL Server release 6.5 does not come with an OS/2 client.

If you have an urgent need to access your SQL Server from OS/2, you can probably run the Windows 3.1*x* utilities under the Windows subsystem in OS/2. To be perfectly honest, though, neither one of us has access to an OS/2 system, so we haven't tried it.

- **SQL Transfer Manager.** This utility lets you move data from one server to another without having to set up replication.

Note

For some reason, Microsoft chose not to include the Transfer Manager utility in the Windows 95 client programs. You can, however, copy it from an NT machine or the SQL Server CD-ROM.◀

- **SQL Trace.** This handy little tool lets you see all the SQL calls made to a particular SQL Server machine by a given login. This is particularly useful when you want to see what SQL the SQL Enterprise Manager is actually performing.
- **SQL Web Page Wizard.** This program lets you create an HTML document from an SQL query or stored procedure. This is useful if you periodically want to post certain information contained in your databases to a World Wide Web site.

Cross-Reference

- **BCP.** This program allows the user to copy data *en masse* in and out of database tables. This program is so complex that we devote Chapter 16 to it.◀

The only one of these applications that requires any configuration beyond the initial installation is the SQL Client Configuration Utility.

The SQL Client Configuration Utility

The SQL Client Configuration Utility allows your clients to talk to a SQL Server machine through a variety of languages called *protocols*. In the following sections, we discuss each and how to use it.

Supported protocols

SQL Server clients and servers talk to one another through a set of defined languages. Each protocol specifies how much data is carried in each packet and how each packet is transmitted. Protocols can also specify if any error-correction measures need to be taken. SQL Server can use four distinct protocols:

- Named Pipes
- TCP/IP

- NWLink IPX/SPX
- Banyan Vines

Named Pipes

The easiest way for two processes to share information is to read and write to a common resource. When a program or programmer specifically allocates a shared resource for two processes to communicate through, that resource is often called a *pipe*. Pipes come in two flavors: unidirectional and bidirectional. The pipes used by SQL Server are bidirectional.

When the two processes are running on the same machine they are said to be using a *Local Pipe*. When, however, they are running on different machines, they are said to be using a *Network Pipe* or *Named Pipe*.

The default Named Pipe for a SQL Server machine is *computername* \pipe\sql\query. If, for example, the name of your SQL Server machine is *my_sql_machine*, the default pipe for that server would be \\my_sql_machine\pipe\sql\query. If you can use this protocol it will be the fastest for you. This protocol is implemented on top of NetBEUI, the low-level LAN Manager and NT networking protocol.

TCP/IP

TCP/IP stands for *Transmission Control Protocol / Internet Protocol*. As you probably already know, TCP/IP is the protocol on which the Internet is based and is supported on just about every major platform and network in existence. SQL Server allows clients to connect via TCP/IP. This means that any client (with appropriate permissions, of course) can connect to any server that is on the Internet. If you are trying to connect to a server that is very far removed from you geographically, this protocol is probably your best bet.

NWLink IPX/SPX

The IPX/SPX protocol was developed by Novell for its NetWare family of network operating systems. It is, in fact, an extension to the TCP/IP protocol. NWLink is a Microsoft compatibility add-on for NT to allow it to speak IPX/SPX. If your network is primarily comprised of NetWare servers, this protocol may suit you well.

Banyan Vines

If you are an OS/2 user, you have probably heard of Banyan Vines. It is a networking system that is very popular among OS/2 users. SQL Server allows connections via the Banyan Vines IP protocol. If your clients are running in a Banyan Vines environment, you probably have to use this protocol.

Configuring your clients

Now that you have a basic understanding of the protocols that SQL Server supports, we show you how to configure your clients to use each one.

When discussing the SQL Client Configuration Utility, we talk about the Windows NT and Windows 95 programs. Windows 3.1*x* users have a slightly different interface. The information still applies, but some of the GUI references are different. *MS-DOS users: Don't despair!* The information you need follows in the "MS-DOS Client Configuration" section.◀

When you run the SQL Client Configuration Utility, you are greeted with the screen shown in Figure 5-1.

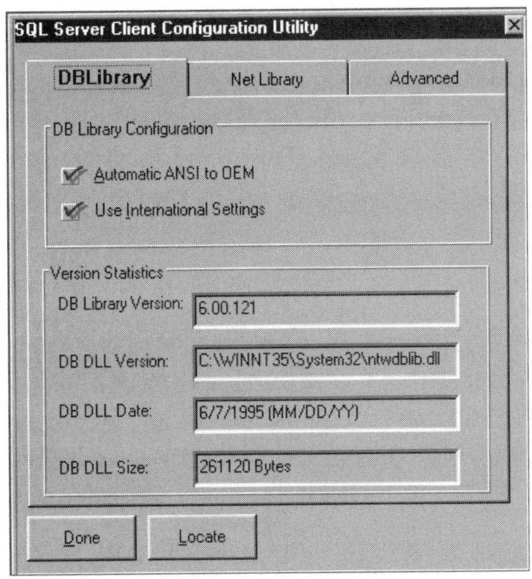

Figure 5-1:
The SQL Client Configuration Utility Main Screen.

DBLibrary tab

The DBLibrary tab contains information and options relating to the specific DLL (dynamic-link library) being used to connect to SQL Server. This information is located in the Version Statistics box and includes

- Net Library Version. This is the release number for the DBLibrary code contained in the DLL specified in the DB DLL Version box.
- **DB DLL Version.** This is the specific DLL and path used to connect to SQL Server.
- **DB DLL Date.** This is the creation date of the DLL.
- **DB DLL Size.** This is the size of the specified DLL.

The DBLibrary tab also lets you configure two DBLibrary configuration options:

- **Automatic ANSI to OEM.** If this option is selected, data being transferred to SQL Server from a client machine will be converted from OEM text to ANSI text. When the data is going the opposite way, the reverse conversion is performed. This option is set on by default.
- **Use International Settings.** If this option is selected, the client utilities obtain all currency, date, and time formatting information from the SQL Server machine to which they connect. If this option is set to off, this information is read from either hard-coded parameters or the SQLCOMMN.LOC file. This item is also set on by default.

Net Library tab

When you click on the Net Library tab, the screen illustrated in Figure 5-2 appears.

This screen allows you to choose what protocol you usually want to use for your SQL Server connections. You can change this option by selecting a different protocol from the Default Network list box. If you drop down the list box, you should notice an extra option in this list that we didn't discuss previously, marked Multi-Protocol.

The Multi-Protocol library option allows a client machine to connect to a SQL Server machine via any protocol that Windows NT supports. In other words, by selecting this option, you could connect to one server via Named Pipes and another server via TCP/IP *at the same time*. This can have some very practical applications. Let's say you want to connect to a database server that is on your local network but you also want to connect to a database server that is 3,000 miles away. If you didn't have the multi-protocol option, you would have to reconfigure your machine to use Named Pipes each time you wanted to connect to your local server and to use TCP/IP each time you wanted to connect to your remote server.

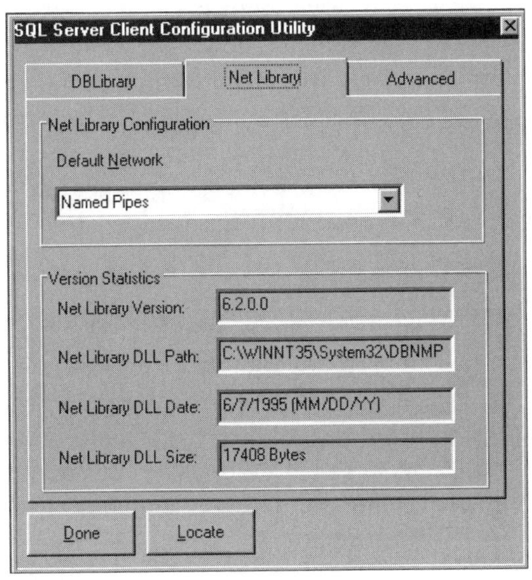

Figure 5-2:
The Net Library Configuration Window.

Warning

Not all protocols are created equal. In theory, every time you install a new protocol on a Windows NT machine that is also running SQL Server, any client machine should be able to connect using that new protocol by selecting the multi-protocol option. Microsoft has made it very clear, though, that the *only* protocols they consider "tested and supported" are Named Pipes, NWLink IPX/SPX, and TCP/IP. That means that if you elect to use a protocol other than those three, you will not get technical support from Microsoft because it will not be "supported." Please note, however, that simply installing a new protocol on your NT server machine will not magically make your clients able to use it. You will also have to install software on the client machine that allows it to use the new protocol.◀

The next thing you are probably wondering is this: Why would anyone use anything other than the multi-protocol option? After all, it gives the best of all worlds, right? Actually, you can get into a little trouble using this option. The are two reasons. First, Named Pipes connects *a lot* faster than all the other protocols. In order to understand the second reason, we need to talk a bit about how each protocol does name resolution.

What's in a name?

When you specify a server name to connect to, your client application has to figure out what the network address of that server is. This process of mapping each name to a network address is called *name resolution*. Each protocol uses a different mechanism for name resolution. Named Pipes uses NetBIOS calls to resolve server name, IPX/SPX uses SAP broadcasts, and TCP/IP uses WINS. We are not going to get into what each of these resolution methods is, but suffice it to say, they are not the same.

A machine could have one NetBIOS name and another WINS name. For example, machine A could have the NetBIOS name *Dave* and the WINS name *David* while machine B could have the NetBIOS name *David* and the WINS name *Davey*. (Note that we're not recommending that you set up your server names this way!) If your client program is using the multi-protocol option and you try to connect to the machine named *David*, are you going to connect to machine A or B? When you use the multi-protocol option you run the risk of connecting to a machine you didn't want. This dilemma leads nicely into the next topic.

Advanced tab

When you click on the Advanced tab you see the screen shown in Figure 5-3.

The Advanced tab lets you specify how you want certain machine names resolved. In other words, you could specify that you want to connect to machine A via Named Pipes and machine B via TCP/IP. This is accomplished by setting up *connection strings*. As you might expect, connection strings are just strings that supply certain connection information.

If you are not using the multi-protocol option, connection strings will be of little value to you unless you are using both SQL Server version 4.21 and version 6.5 on same server.◀

Three pieces of information are needed to build a connection string. They are the name of the server to map, the type of connection to make, and any other vital connection information. The connection string formats for each protocol type are listed in Table 5-1.

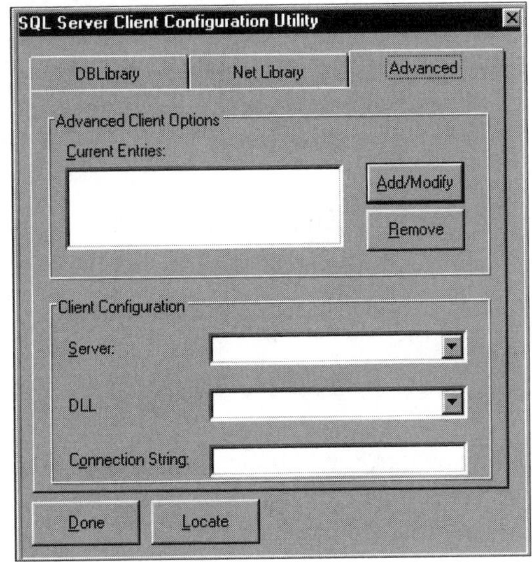

Figure 5-3:
Advanced Configuration Options.

Table 5-1
Server Protocols and Connection Strings

Protocol	*Connection String*
TCP/IP	WINS_machine_name[,port] or ip_address[,port]
NWLink IPX/SPX	network_address,port,network_number
Banyan Vines	servicename@group@org
Named Pipes	\\server_name\pipe

If, for instance, there existed a machine named *foo* that had an IP address of 10.0.3.2 and you wanted to specify that all connections to *foo* should be made through TCP/IP, you would do the following in the Advanced tab:

1. Enter **foo** in the Server field.
2. Select **TCP/IP** from the DLL Name field.
3. Enter **10.0.3.2** in the Connection String box.
4. Press Enter.

From then on, when you tried to connect to server foo, your program would try to connect via TCP/IP to the machine at address 10.0.3.2. As another example, if you wanted to connect to a machine named bar via Named Pipes, you would would put **bar** in the Server field, select Named Pipes in DLL Name, and enter **\\bar\pipe\sql\query** as the Connection String.

Remember that the default Named Pipe for a server is \\servername\pipe\sql \query.◀

MS-DOS Client Configuration

As you may expect, the SQL Server 6.5 character mode client utilities for MS-DOS are just a little bit more complicated to use than other client utilities. They are really divided into two distinct classes: the library transport programs and the actual utilities.

Library transport programs

The library transport programs load the necessary routines in memory for the client applications to communicate with a SQL Server machine. They are all TSRs (Terminate and Stay Resident programs) and can be removed from memory by running ENDDBLIB.EXE. The basic sequence of events for using one of the MS-DOS utilities is as follows:

1. Load a transport TSR.
2. Use the desired program.
3. Run ENDDBLIB.EXE.

You select your protocol by loading the transport TSR for that protocol. The transport TSRs all have names like DB*.EXE.

DBMSSPX.EXE

This TSR initializes the client machine to communicate with SQL Server via the IPX/SPX protocol. The *MS* in the name indicates that this is a Microsoft implementation of the Novell protocol.

DBMSVINE.EXE

This TSR initializes the client machine to communicate with SQL Server via Banyan Vines IP packets. Again, the *MS* indicates that this implementation is by Microsoft.

DBNMPIPE.EXE

This TSR initializes the client machine to communicate with SQL Server via Named Pipes.

ENDDBLIB.EXE

This TSR unloads the previously loaded transport TSR from memory. As the message points out, make sure not to load any other TSRs between loading the SQL Server TSR and trying to unload it. Running ENDDBLIB.EXE should give you the following response:

```
DB-Library TSR Unloader Utility. Version 4.21.00.
Copyright (c) 1989-1995, Microsoft Corp., All rights reserved.

This utility will safely unload the Resident Network
Interface only if it was the last memory resident (TSR) utility
loaded. If other memory resident utilities were loaded later,
removing this TSR may cause unpredictable results.

Do you wish to continue (Y/N): y

DB-Library TSR Removed.
```

MS-DOS client utility programs

The MS-DOS character mode client utility programs consist of three utilities:

Cross-Reference

- **bcp.** This program copies data in and out of tables. See Chapter 16 for more specific information.◀
- **isql.** This is a character-mode interactive SQL executer.
- **readpipe.** This utility tests the validity of a given Named Pipe. You use this when you are having problems connecting to your SQL Server machine. You will want to refer to your SQL Server companion documentation for more information on how to use this utility.

Summary

Oh sure, this chapter was a little shorter than some of the others. Would you rather we put in extraneous screen shots and useless information? We didn't think so. OK then, let's review what we've covered so far.

In this chapter, you learned about the various protocols SQL Server uses to communicate with other programs. You also learned how to configure you client machines to use multiple protocols and how to fix name resolution problems.

Review Questions

Q: What protocol do you use for the fastest server connections, if your network supports it?

A: Named Pipes.

Q: Is using TCP/IP ever a good idea?

A: Absolutely. TCP/IP is supported on many more networks than either IPX/SPX or Named Pipes. It may be your only choice for connections over great distances.

Q: When do you use IPX/SPX?

A: When you are running in a predominantly NetWare environment.

Q: How can you fix name resolution conflicts that arise from using multiple protocols?

A: Enter specific server resolution information in connection strings.

Q: What are the basic steps to run an MS-DOS based client program?

A: Follow these steps:

(1) Load a transport TSR.
(2) Use the desired program.
(3) Run ENDDBLIB.EXE.

Part

II

Server Administration

All complex systems (whether they be an automobile, a corporation, a toaster, and so on) require some level of routine maintenance and care. Your database systems are no different.

In this part of the book, we will cover the basics of creating and administering the basic objects in your system and keeping unwanted guests out.

Chapter 6

Devices, Databases, and Logs

Administering a database server doesn't make much sense unless you have some data. This statement may seem obvious, but the truth of the matter is that it has many more implications than you think. Before you can write a single line of SQL or do a data diagram, you have to have the basic physical and logical data topology of your system in place. When we say *data topology*, we mean how and where your data resides on disk. The kinds of things we discuss here are independent of table design. This chapter covers the three basic elements of data topology in SQL Server: *devices*, *databases*, and *logs*. By the time you finish this chapter, you will understand the difference between each and how they relate. You will also understand key performance and maintenance issues associated with all three.

What's in This Chapter

In this chapter you will learn

- How to create and maintain databases
- Proven strategies of device administration that both increase performance and help preserve your data

- Helpful hints for choosing the best logging options for your particular needs

Note

Before we continue, we need to clear something up. The term *database* is often misused. From this point on, in this book, the term *database* refers to a very specific definition. We appreciate that other texts may have a slightly different view of what a database is, but this is the definition we are going to use:

> A *database* is a logical unit that holds related SQL Server items such as tables, views, indexes, stored procedures, and user lists.◄

This definition is a lot stricter than the general use of the term and a lot simpler than some other usages. In this book, however, when we refer to a database, we are using this definition.

Devices

A *device* is the storage file used by SQL Server to hold databases or parts of databases. Devices come in two flavors: database devices and dump devices.

Database devices

A *database device* is used to store a database or a part of a database. Any time you retrieve data from your server, you are getting it from a database that resides on one or more database devices.

The term *device* is also a bit misleading in this context. Usually in the computer world, when we talk about a device it refers to a piece of hardware such as a hard disk or tape drive. In SQL Server terms, however, a device is actually a file that resides on a disk or tape. This means that each physical disk can have multiple devices which in turn can have multiple databases. This is actually a pretty handy idea. If the concept of a device is separated from the physical medium on which it resides, SQL Server can leave the details of dealing with a particular type of media to the operating system. This is a good thing because it makes the job of porting SQL Server to other operating systems a lot easier. (We know, we know, Microsoft isn't interested in supporting any operating system they don't own, but devices are still a good idea.)

Dump devices

A *dump device*, like a database device, is a storage file, except that it holds database *dumps*. A *dump* is an operation that stores a complete database or transaction log as compressed data. These operations are typically performed in order to back up and restore a database. You cannot run any SQL commands against the data on a dump device, nor can you create a standard database on it. The sole purpose of a dump device is to archive and load entire databases or logs quickly.

Managing database and dump devices

The easiest way to manage a database or dump device is through the SQL Enterprise Manager. This is accomplished by opening either the Database Devices or Backup Devices folders under any server. The following sections will explain what you can do to manage these devices.

Please be aware that the operations to manage a database device and the operations to manage a dump device are identical. To this end, we will only show you how to perform these things on database devices.◀

When you open the Database Devices folder in the SQL Enterprise Manager, you see a tree of all the defined database devices on a particular server. In Figure 6-1, there are three database devices: master, MSDBData, and MSDBLog.

You can do four basic things with a database device. You can create a device, edit a device, delete a device, or mirror a device.

Creating a device

To create a new database device, highlight the Database Devices folder, click the right mouse button to display a pop-up menu, and select New Device. The screen shown in Figure 6-2 appears.

The graph on the bottom of the window shows the space in use for all available media. Red indicates free space and cyan indicates space used.

The first thing you should do is decide on a name for your new device.

We strongly recommend that you use descriptive names. It makes your system more manageable as it begins to grow. For example, if the device will hold databases pertaining to your tax records, you would probably want to name it something like *tax_records_device*. Once you have settled on a name, enter it in the Name box.◀

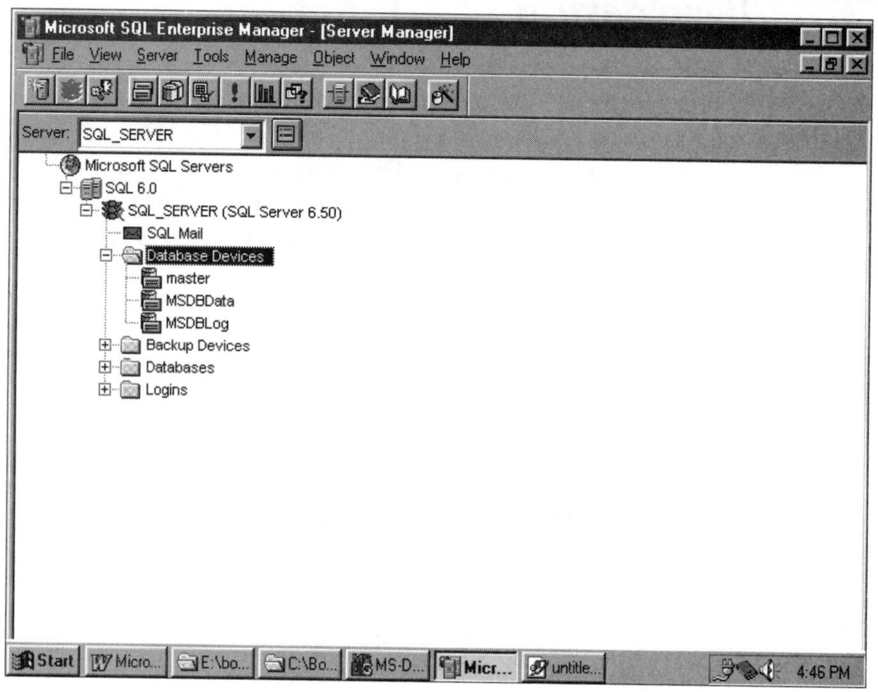

Figure 6-1:
Here are the default devices that ship with SQL Server.

Please remember that you must name your files in accordance with the rules of the file system you are using. For example, you cannot use long filenames in a FAT file system.◀

The next thing you need to do is select the path in which you want your new device to reside. Do this by selecting a drive and directory from the Location drop-down list box.

Now, you need to assign a filename to your device. You will notice that SQL Server has already suggested a choice. It arrived at this suggestion by concatenating the default data path with the name you entered earlier. We *very strongly* recommend that you give your .DAT file the same name as the value you put in the Name field. This will help you figure out which .DAT file is which when looking at a directory listing. This is most helpful when you are patrolling your disk looking for a dead device. A dead device occurs when you drop a device (covered later) and don't delete the associated .DAT file.

The last thing you need to do is decide how large you want your new device. This depends on two things:

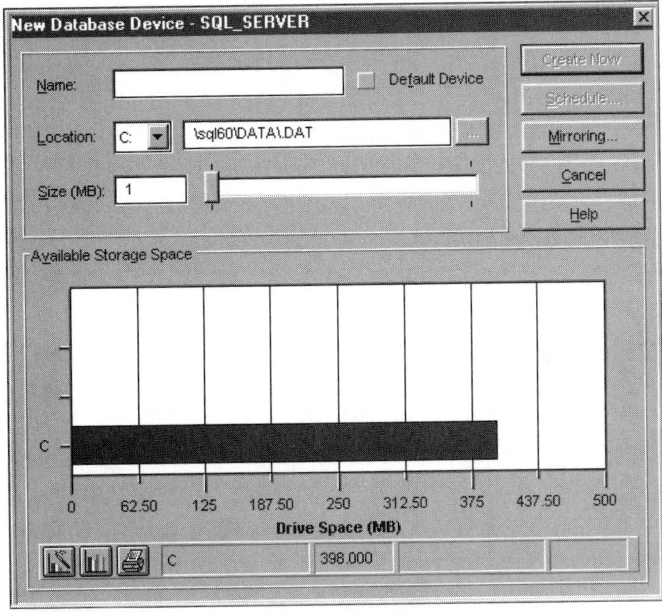

Figure 6-2:
When you select New Device, this screen appears.

- How much free space is on the target drive
- How much data you think you will store on the device

Chances are you will not easily be able to predict the amount of data you are going to store on the device. Don't worry. You can always expand the device size later. For now, a size of 20 megabytes is probably large enough.

When you are satisfied with your settings, click the OK button.

There is also a Mirroring button on the New Database Device dialog; we're going to cover mirroring a little later. For now, skip it. You can also ignore the Schedule button. We cover the scheduler in greater detail in Chapter 17 when we cover backing up and restoring your data.

Editing a device

The time will eventually come when the databases on a particular device become too large for the device to handle. When that happens, you have three choices: trim the databases, increase the size of the device, or create a new device. You can easily increase the device size by editing its definition.

To edit a particular device highlight it, right-click on it, and select Edit from the pop-up menu that appears. The screen that appears should look very familiar to you because it's the same as the New Database window. The first thing you probably notice is that you cannot change many of the settings. Fortunately, one of things you can change is the device size. You can increase it, but not decrease it. Obviously, you cannot increase the device size beyond the available space of your drive.

Deleting a device

Deleting (also known as *dropping*) a database device is the simplest operation of all. Just highlight the doomed item, right-click it, and select Delete from the pop-up menu. You see the Delete Non-Empty Device window shown in Figure 6-3.

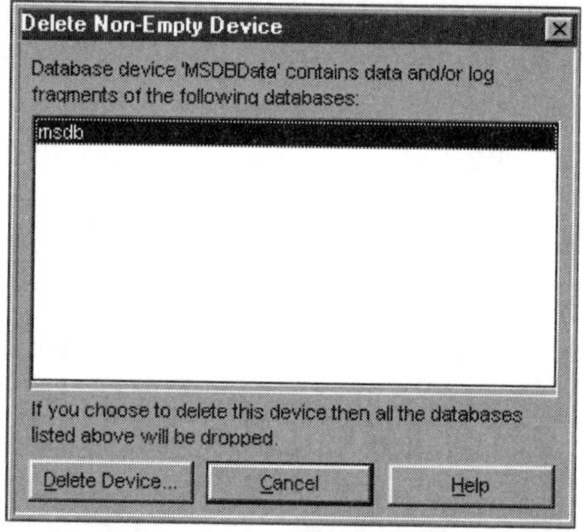

Figure 6-3:
Here is where you delete (drop) a database device.

This is a list of databases that will also be dropped if you continue. If you are satisfied that you still want to perform this operation, click the Drop button.

Usually, when you drop an object in SQL Server, it's gone. There's no Undrop command. This is not the case, however, with a database device. When you delete a database device, the associated .DAT file is still around. You can re-mount the device by using the sp_dbinstall stored procedure.◄

Don't worry that you don't know what the sp_dbinstall stored procedure is. After you read the sections on Transact SQL and Stored Procedures, you will be able to run this command with confidence.◀

Mirroring a device

It's an irrefutable fact of computing life that no system is crash-proof. That is, after all, why we perform routine backups of our data. Most relational database management systems (RDBMSs) have a facility where data is simultaneously written to two different files. The second file acts as a backup if the primary file should ever be corrupted. This process is called *mirroring*.

Like anything else, though, mirroring has both good points and bad points:

- Pro: Unlike standard backups, there is no concern about losing data entered after the last backup.
- Con: Mirroring means your system will use DOUBLE the disk space.
- Pro: Mirrored data can be used in a matter of seconds.
- Con: That's right, we said DOUBLE the disk space.
- Pro: Mirroring is instantaneous, automatic, and hidden.
- Con: DOUBLE!

Mirroring also has some performance implications. Please see the following sidebar.

A Serious Performance Concern

One of the great design benefits of log devices — a database device dedicated to holding transaction logs — is that they are written to disk in a linear fashion. This increases performance because the disk head doesn't have to move around a lot. If you choose to create a log mirror on the same physical device as the log, you lose this benefit because the disk heads will have to bounce around a lot for each operation. There's also a integrity concern here. In general, having the mirror on the same disk as the original is pretty short sighted. If you have a disk crash or controller failure, you'll lose both copies. Trust us, that's not a good thing!

You get the point. Mirroring is very cool if you have the spare drive space. But before you throw out all your tapes, consider one final point. Between transaction logs and mirroring, you could need 4 megabytes for every 1 megabyte of data. That's right, *quadruple* the disk space.

Many people make their log devices the same size as their data devices. Log devices need to be mirrored, too. That means that 1 gigabyte of data will need 4 gigabytes of disk space: 1 gig for the database device, 1 gig for the log device, 1 gig for the database device mirror, and 1 gig for the log device mirror. Tape is looking a little more attractive, isn't it?

Assuming that you have decided that mirroring is a worthwhile endeavor (and it is), here's how to do it. Right-click on the database device you want to mirror and select Mirror from the pop-up menu. The screen shown in Figure 6-4 will appear.

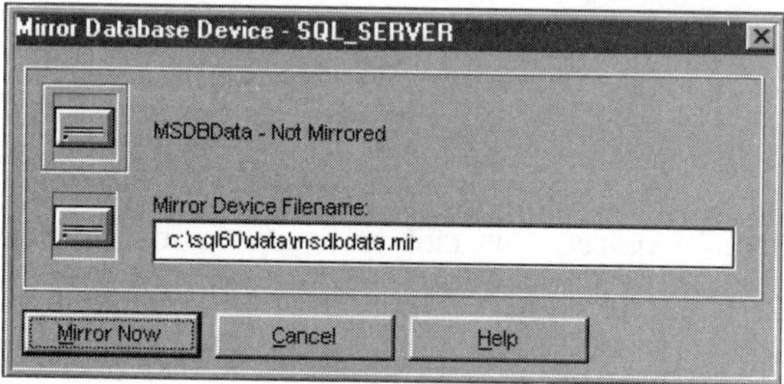

Figure 6-4:
This screen allows you to set the mirroring options for your device.

Edit the name in the Mirror Device Filename field and click the Mirror Now button. That's all there is to it. From now on all transactions performed on databases on that database device will be simultaneously mirrored to the mirror device.

Warning

Keep your database devices and your mirror devices on separate drives. Your mirror does you no good if both it and the device it was supporting are on a drive that crashes. Do yourself a favor and keep a separate data drive and mirror drive. You'll thank us the next time one crashes.◀

Using a mirror

Picture this. It's a cold, blustery day as you make your way into work. You click on the lights in your office, only to notice that your SQL Server machine has rebooted sometime during the evening. You log in and restart your database. To your horror, you find that the *if_This_Goes_Down_Im_Dead* database device is toast. This is a bad thing. Calmly, you click your mouse three times and think "There's no place like home. There's no place like home." Seconds later your data is restored. Good work!

So what were those three magic mouse clicks? Easy:

1. Right-click on the affected database device and select Mirror.
2. Select Switch to Mirror Device - Retain.
3. Click OK.

Actually, you had a choice of four actions when you right-clicked the database device:

- **Switch to Mirror Device - Retain.** This option will switch over to the mirror device but retain the old data device.
- **Switch to Mirror Device - Replace.** This option will switch to the mirror device and replace the old device with the mirrored device.
- **Turn Off Mirroring - Retain Mirror Device.** This option suspends data mirroring but allows you to re-mirror the device later.
- **Turn Off Mirroring - Remove Mirror Device.** This option permanently removes the mirror device.

Also, once you switch over to a mirrored device, you need to re-enable mirroring. You do this by right-clicking on the device, selecting Mirror and clicking the Re-Mirror button.

Databases

Earlier in this chapter, we defined a database as a logical unit that holds related items such as tables, views, indexes, and stored procedures.

In SQL Server, however, a database can hold many more types of things.

You can browse these items in the SQL Enterprise Manager by opening the Databases folder and double-clicking a database, as shown in Figure 6-5.

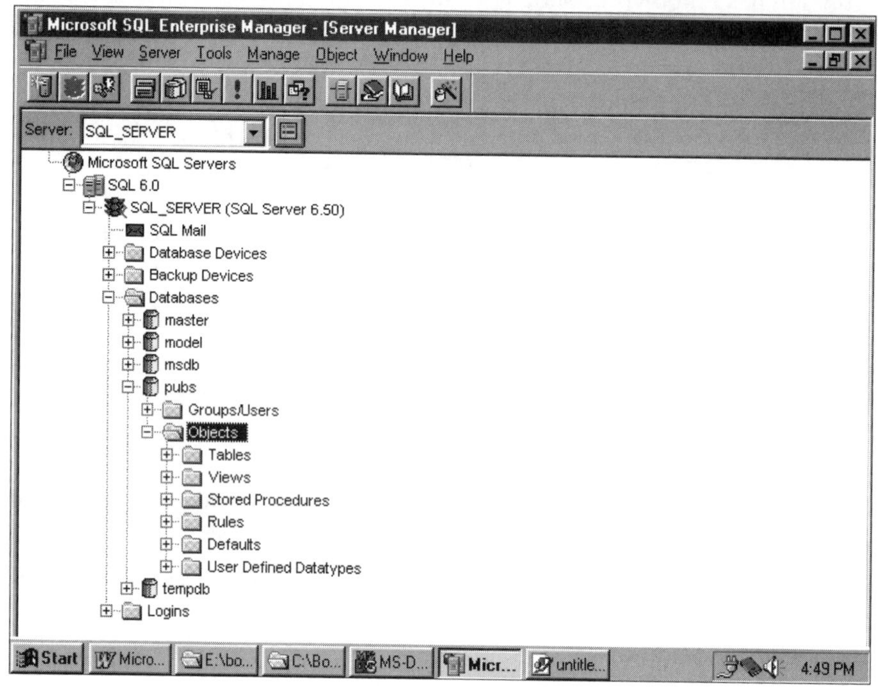

Figure 6-5:
This is an example of an expanded database tree.

There are three categories of things you can store in a database. They are the following:

- Publications
- Users or groups of users
- Objects

In the following sections, we will discuss each of these items.

Publications

One of the new features introduced in SQL Server 6.0 is the capability of one server to allow other servers to get copies of its data periodically. When a server allows this kind of access, it is said to be *publishing* or *replicating* its data. The Publications folder of a database shows information about any objects in the database that are being published. The details of SQL Server's replication scheme can get pretty complicated. As such, we cover this topic in much more detail in Part VII.◀

Groups and Users

The second general type of thing a database holds is information regarding users or groups of users. A *group* is a related set of users with common permissions. Groups are a convenient way of assigning system rights to similar users. Once again, the concept of group rights versus user rights can get a little tricky. As a result, this topic has its own chapter: Chapter 7.◀

Objects

The last kind of item found in a database is called an *object*. An object can be one of six different things:

- **Table.** An object that contains rows of data
- **View.** A virtual table whose contents are defined by an SQL statement
- **Stored Procedure.** A compiled set of SQL statements that runs on a server
- **Rule.** An object that defines acceptable values for a particular column in a table
- **Default.** The value SQL Server places in a column when the user does not enter any data
- **User Defined Datatype.** A datatype defined by the user in terms of existing system datatypes

Managing databases

When you open the Databases folder in the SQL Enterprise Manager, you will see a tree of all the defined databases on a particular server. Figure 6-6 shows the pubs database selected.

There are four basic things you can do to a database: create, edit, delete, and backup/restore.

Creating a database

To create a new database, right-click on Databases folder, and select New Database from the pop-up menu. You'll see the Create Database screen shown in Figure 6-7.

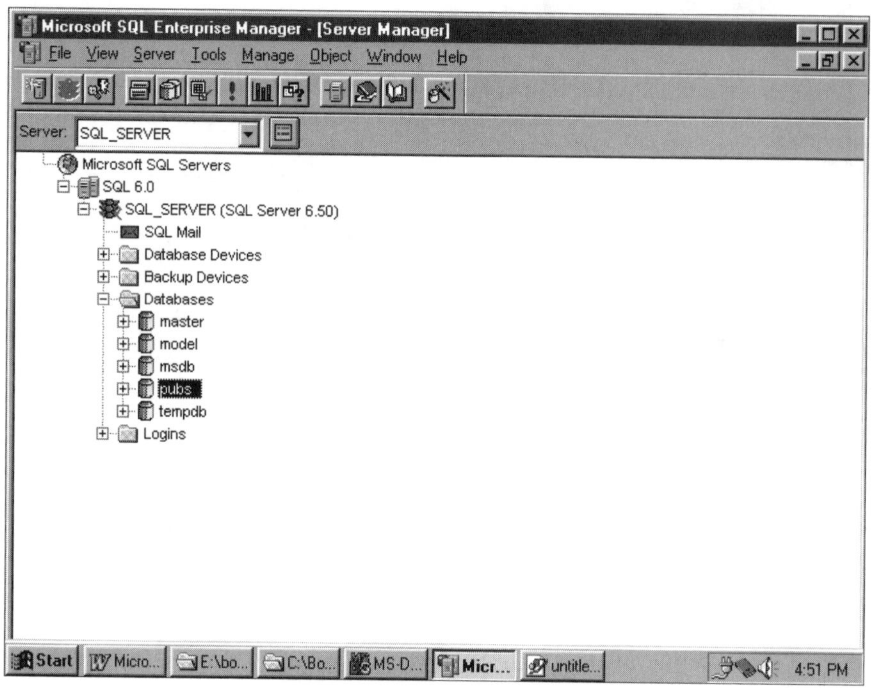

Figure 6-6:
This is the object tree for the pubs database.

The graph on the bottom of the window in Figure 6-7 shows the space usage for all available media. Yellow indicates free space and blue indicates space used.

The first thing you should do is decide on a name for your new database. Once again, we cannot emphasize enough the value of descriptive names. Once you have settled on a name, enter it in the Name box.

The next thing to do is enter the information about the location of your data and log devices. If you do not put in a device name in the Log Device field, the log for your new database will go on the same device as the data. (You don't want to do that; see the next paragraph.)

Warning

Never, ever put your log on the same device as your data. This is one of the biggest mistakes you can make. If you do, you will *never* be able to do incremental backups. Don't believe us? Consider this real-world scenario. You and your users are clicking along one day when your transaction log fills up. If your log and data are on different devices, you can just dump the log to the old bit bucket (planning to do a complete backup that evening, of course). If, however, the two are on the same device, you have a problem. You need to stop what you're doing and back up the entire database so the log gets flushed. Trust us, you would rather have a ten inch spike driven through your head than go through this!◀

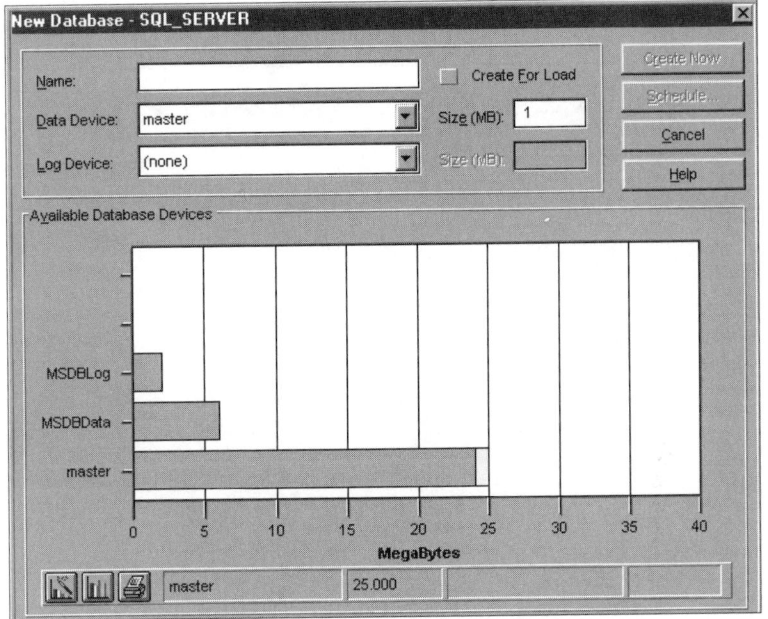

Figure 6-7:
This screen appears when you create a new database.

Then, you enter information on how large (in megabytes) you want your data and logs in the Size fields. What you enter here will depend on how much available space you have on your data and log devices.

The final option in the Create New Database dialog is something called Create For Load. If you check this box, SQL Server will not zero-initialize data pages when your database is being created. This will speed up the creation process; you should use this option immediately when you intend to load from a backup directly into the new database. Be aware, though, that users other than the database owner (DBO) will not be able to use the new database because the Create For Load. option also enables the DBO Use Only option. You will have to turn the DBO Use Only option, (covered later), off before others can use your data.

When you are satisfied with your new database settings, press OK.

Editing a database

Once you create your new database, you probably want to set some database-specific options and permissions. This is accomplished by editing the database definition. To do this, right-click on the desired database and select the Edit option. The Edit Database window (Figure 6-8) appears.

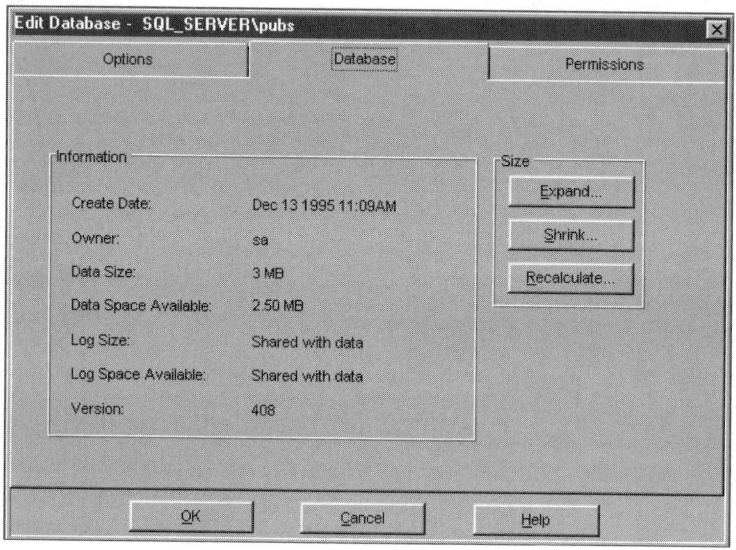

Figure 6-8:
The database settings for the pubs *database.*

The three tabs, Options, Database, and Permissions, control general database options, database size and information, and database permissions, respectively.

Click the Options tab to bring up the set of general database options.

- **Select Into/Bulk Copy.** Certain database procedures, like bulk copy, do not write to the transaction log when they are performed. Enabling this option will allow non-logged operations to occur on this database. The drawback is that you can no longer do incremental backups of your database; you have to do full backups. If you turn this on, you might as well turn on Truncate Log on Checkpoint too because the log is now worthless for backups.
- **DBO Use Only.** This option allows only the database owner (DBO) to access the database.
- **No Checkpoint On Recovery.** You have already learned that SQL Server keeps some data in a memory cache. When this data is finally written to the database, SQL Server writes a *checkpoint* to the transaction log. All transactions in the log before the checkpoint have been committed to the database. This option will prevent SQL Server from writing a checkpoint to the log after it finishes a recovery process. We don't think it's a good idea for you to use this option.
- **Read Only.** This option will allow users to read, but not alter, the table data. With this option set to 1, not even the database owner can change any data in any table in the database. This prevents you from adding users, creating views, and so on.
- **Single User.** This option prevents multiple users from accessing the table simultaneously.
- **Columns Null by Default.** When a new table is defined, its columns can either be set to allow NULL values or not. If this option is checked, SQL Server will create all new columns as allowing NULLs. You can override this default when you create your tables. We recommend that you leave this option off, which means that columns are created with the NOT NULL attribute by default, so users will not be able to insert ROWS with NULL data.
- **Truncate Log on Checkpoint.** If this option is enabled, the transaction log will be truncated after every checkpoint. We recommend that you turn this option on because it will avoid filling up your transaction log. A checkpoint, after all, means that the transaction has been successfully committed to the database. There's no real need to keep it around. The drawback is that you can no longer do incremental backups of your database; you have to do full backups.

Clicking on the next tab of the Edit Database window, Database, brings up a screen where you can adjust the size of your database. This tab is shown in Figure 6-8. Here, you can expand, shrink, and recalculate the size of your database.

Expanding a database

The time eventually comes when you run out of room in your database. When this happens, you will want to expand it. You can do this by clicking on the Expand button in the Database tab to display the Expand Database dialog shown in Figure 6-9.

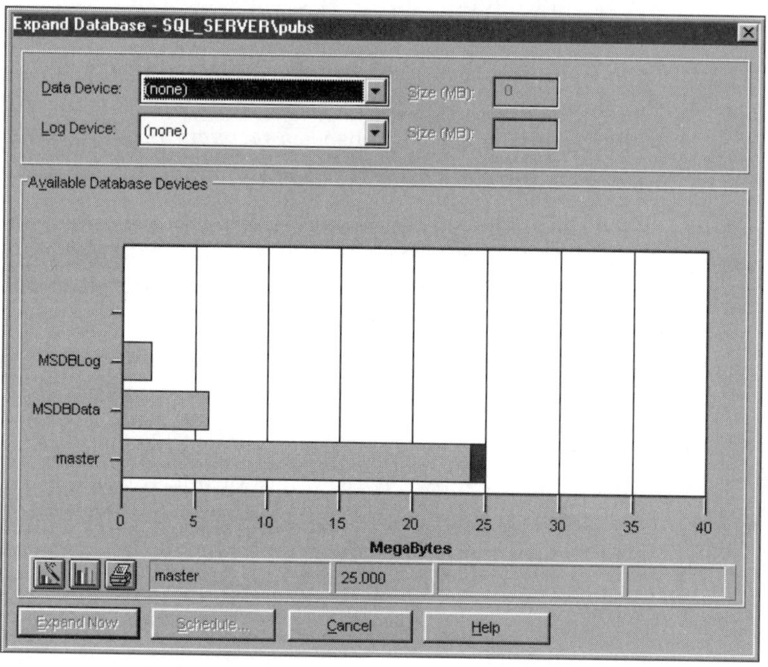

Figure 6-9:
This screen allows you to expand your database.

The graph at the bottom of the screen shows all the database devices on the server and their current space utilization. You can increase the size of your database by selecting a device from the Data Device drop-down list. When you do, the available space on that device will appear in the Size field. Edit this value for your needs. Repeat this operation for the log.

This interface has some interesting implications. You can expand your database onto a second or third device.Our advice, however, is to keep each database on a single device. Splitting a database onto multiple devices can mean that it is split across multiple physical drives. This can be a big problem if a disk crashes.

Shrinking a database

Over a period of time, you may decide to archive some of your data. This may mean that you can reclaim some device space by shrinking your databases. You accomplish this by clicking on the Shrink button in the Database tab in the Edit Database window, entering the new size, and pressing OK. There are, however, two important things to keep in mind:

- While your database is being resized, it is unavailable to all other users.
- You cannot shrink any database below the minimum database size set in your server configurations.

Deleting a database

If you *really* want to reclaim device space, though, there's no substitute for deleting a database. You perform this operation by right-clicking on the intended victim in the list of databases and selecting Delete from the pop-up menu.

Backing up/restoring a database

The last option you have in managing a particular database is to backup/restore it. We discuss the whole process in detail in Chapter 17.◀

Logs

Every time an SQL Server table is modified, a record of that action is kept. This ongoing record is called a *transaction log*. Transaction logs are listed in the system table syslogs.

Why keep a transaction log?

Don't laugh, it's a good question. Transaction logs are kept for two major reasons. The first reason is that they can aid greatly in the recovery of a database. The second reason is that they can speed up the process of backing up your database.

Recovery

To understand fully how a transaction log helps with a database recovery, it is first important to understand how and when entries are written to the log. When you issue a SQL statement against one of your tables, SQL Server follows these steps, shown in Figure 6-10:

1. Writes a copy of your statement to the transaction log, preceded by a BEGIN TRANSACTION statement
2. Executes your statement
3. If your statement is successful (i.e. It had a logical conclusion that did not generate a SQL error), writes a COMMIT to the log; otherwise, writes a ROLLBACK to the log
4. Writes an END TRANSACTION statement to the log

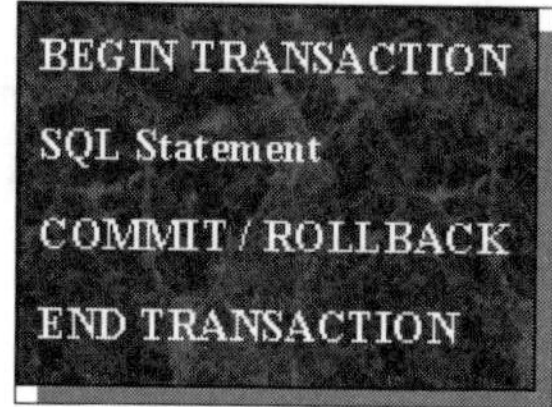

Figure 6-10:
This is an overview of the log process.

The interesting thing about this sequence is that SQL Server records the action you are attempting *before* it actually attempts the process, so it can easily tell which operations were completed by looking for either a COMMIT or a ROLLBACK in the log. This is how a log file aids in the recovery process. SQL Server will assume that all transactions that have either a COMMIT or a ROLLBACK completed without a catastrophic problem (i.e. the server lost power during the middle of the operation).

The other way a log file helps is in the event of a media failure. If, for some horrible reason, the disk containing your data devices goes bad, you can apply the most recent log against an older backup and have a near-perfect copy of your tables at the time you lost your disk. (The copy is only *near* perfect because any uncommitted changes will be lost.) This process leads us nicely into our next topic: backups.

Backing up

When backing up a database, you typically have two options: backing up the entire database or backing up the log. If you have a very large database, backing up the log can be a lot more appealing than backing up the entire database. In this case you can perform an *incremental backup* of the log.

In an incremental backup, you would back up your entire 2-gigabyte database, *BigDB*, only periodically, let's say every Monday. On Tuesday through Friday, however, you would just back up *BigDB*'s log. This is going to be *a lot* less data. If you need to restore *BigDB* for any reason, you just restore the last full backup and apply each subsequent log. You will get the exact same data as if you had backed up the entire database every night.

Cross-Reference

However, choosing a backup scheme can be a lot more complex than these last few paragraphs might lead you to believe. That's why we devote Chapter 17 to *Backing Up and Restoring.*◄

Managing logs

Just as with databases, transaction logs reside on a data device. In fact, you create a device for a log the same way you create a device for a database. This is because they are the same kind of device.

Tip

Create your log devices on a separate physical disk from your database devices. If you don't, in the event of a disk crash, you will lose any changes you make to your databases between backups. This also does good things for performance.◄

Don't believe us? Look under the Database Devices folder in the SQL Enterprise Manager, and you will see the MSDBLog device. This is the log device for the MSDBData device.

You must specify that a particular database will use a specific log device when you create the database. You cannot change a log device after you have created the database!

How big?

This is a good question. Estimating log device sizes is even harder than estimating database sizes. Microsoft recommends that your log device be 20 percent of the size of your database device. We think it should be more like

50 percent. One of the most frustrating things is to have a large transaction roll back because you ran out of log space. Disk space is pretty cheap, time is not!

Controlling the log size

Periodically, SQL Server issues a statement called a CHECKPOINT to itself. This statement tells the system that all transactions up to this point were resolved. In other words, each transaction either succeeded or failed. What this means is that the appropriate change has been made to the affected database. One of the ways you can keep your log from growing too large is to have SQL Server truncate it every time it issues a checkpoint. You can edit this setting when you click on the Options tab of the Edit Database window while editing a specific database.

There are, of course, a few disadvantages to truncating the log. First, if a disk fails, you will only be able to recover as far as the last backup. Second, you will have to perform a complete database backup every time you back up rather than an incremental backup. After all, what use is backing up a log if only contains a few of the completed transactions? Our advice is not to use this option on your production databases precisely because of these problems. We feel that is simply safer to have a large log device.

Please don't misunderstand what we are saying here. It is a necessary administrative task to truncate your log files periodically. It is, however, not necessary to do it at every checkpoint. In fact, we think the appropriate time to perform this operation is after a successful backup of the log. After all, once you have preserved a copy of the transactions, there is no reason to keep them around.

Cross-Reference

You can truncate a log file by executing a DUMP TRANSACTION <DBNAME> WITH TRUNCATE_ONLY. This operation truncates the transaction log associated with the database <DBNAME>. We cover the *DUMP* SQL statement when we cover backup and restore procedures in Chapter 17. For now, though, this is all you need to know about it. If you are backing up your database/logs nightly (which you should), the odds of your ever filling up your transaction log are very small. This is, of course, predicated on the notion that you will truncate your logs every time you do a backup.◀

SUMMARY

In this chapter, you learned the essentials of SQL Server's data topology. You learned the difference between a device, database, and a log, and you learned how to manage each. You also learned various configuration options you can use to ensure the safety and soundness of your data.

Sound database administration begins with the intelligent design of your server's data topology. You can greatly minimize your risk of data loss by separating your databases, logs, and mirrors. We understand that this means multiple physical disks, but drive space is *a lot* cheaper than lost time and data. Your clients and company will be happy to spend the extra $1,000 to know that they are not going to lose production data in the event of a media failure. This is not a lesson you need to learn firsthand!

REVIEW QUESTIONS

Q: What is a database?

A: A database is a logical unit that holds related SQL Server items, such as tables, views, indexes, and stored procedures.

Q: What factors constrain the size of a database device?

A: There are two factors:

1. How much free space is on the target drive
2. How much data you think you will store on the device

Q: What do you do if you accidentally drop a device or database?

A: Use the sp_dbinstall stored procedure to reinstall it.

Q: What are the three types of items a database can hold?

A: Publications, groups/users, and objects

Q: What are the six things that are defined as database objects?

A: Tables, Views, Stored Procedures, Rules, Defaults, and User Defined Datatypes

Q: Is it ever a good idea to put your log on the same device as your data?

A: No! (We realize that the pubs database violates this rule. In our opinion, this was a very poor design choice by Microsoft and sets a bad example.)

Q: What system table is the transaction log list kept in?

A: syslogs

Chapter

Security and Logins

7

SQL Server provides robust features for controlling *security*, the authority to view and update data. In our experience, these are some of the most underutilized features of SQL Server. In large part this is because folks just don't know what's available or how to use it. In this chapter, we clearly explain SQL Server's security features. We also discuss *logins*, the names people use to identify themselves to SQL Server. The whole point of having logins is security, so it doesn't make much sense to talk about one without the other. We cover user-level security in this chapter; we postpone discussing object-level security until after we have covered the objects themselves.

What's in This Chapter

In this chapter, we:

- Start with some security definitions to lay the foundation for our discussion
- Examine the security modes of SQL Server in great detail, with emphasis on the pros and cons of each one

- Tell you about using the SQL Security Manager with mixed or integrated security modes
- Discuss logins and users of SQL Server itself

Controlling Access to SQL Server

Because Microsoft developed both SQL Server and Windows NT, some SQL Server features *integrate* the security procedures of the two systems. The integration is optional: you can choose to allow it, choose to disallow it, or decide not to decide, deferring the decision to developers and users. The way you specify how much integration you want is to pick one of three separate mechanisms for validating logins, called *security modes*. We touched upon the security modes very briefly in Chapter 4. Here, we go into the details.◀

Windows NT security overview

Because you are being asked to choose whether to integrate SQL Server's security features with those of Windows NT, it would be nice to understand some of the basics of security in Windows NT. We will cover how Windows NT controls access and how that relates to SQL Server. First we start with domains; then, we discuss what it means for domains to trust one another.

Domains

The primary organizational unit of security in Windows NT is a *domain*. A domain is a group of computers that are all sharing a common security accounts database. (Here we mean a database maintained by the Windows NT operating system, *not* a SQL Server database.) This database contains such information as the Windows NT logins of the domain, the groups of the domain, and all kinds of properties of the logins and groups. Most importantly, it contains the information needed to validate the passwords of the logins. There are four kinds of computers in this group:

- **Primary Domain Controller (PDC).** The PDC maintains the security accounts database for the group. There must be one and only one PDC for a domain. The PDC runs the Windows NT Server operating system.

- **Backup Domain Controllers (BDCs).** BDCs assist the PDC by maintaining copies of the security accounts database and by sharing the load of managing it. They also run the Windows NT Server operating system. A domain can have zero, one, or many BDCs.
- **Servers.** These are computers in the domain that are running the Windows NT Server operating system. This set can include File Servers and SQL Servers.
- **Workstations.** Workstations are computers in the domain that are running the Windows NT Workstation operating system .

The servers and workstations have their own security accounts database, and they can validate their own local logins, but they can also accept the login validations of the PDC and the BDC. You will notice we said nothing about other computer operating systems, such as Windows 95 or Window for Workgroups. These operating systems do not share the security accounts database, so they are not considered members of the domain.

This can be a bit confusing, so let's consider an example. You have a Windows NT Workstation machine that is a member of the domain PEOPLE. Among the logins in this domain are FEDORCHE and RENSIN. As it happens, your workstation has these logins: Administrator, FEDORCHE, and ANDREW. Here's what happens when you try the logins ANDREW, FEDORCHE, and RENSIN:

- **ANDREW.** You have logged into the workstation only. You have not gained access to the domain because ANDREW is not a valid login of the PEOPLE domain.
- **FEDORCHE.** You have logged into the workstation and the domain.
- **RENSIN.** You have still logged into both the workstation and the domain, even though RENSIN is not a valid login on the workstation. This is because the workstation accepts login validation from the PDC and BDCs.

When users log into a domain, their access to the shared resources depends on their privileges. In the above example, FEDORCHE or RENSIN could use the resources of the domain to which they have been granted access. ANDREW could not use any resources of the domain, even resources open to "Everyone" because the login ANDREW is not in the domain PEOPLE.

Your SQL Server machine should be either a server in the domain or just a workstation in the domain. It should *not* be a PDC or a BDC because those machines do resource-intensive tasks that will drag down the performance of your SQL Server.

When you boot your SQL Server machine, it becomes an active member of the domain, even if you have not yet logged in to the domain. If you set the SQL Server service to start on startup, it is already available to users of the domain. In the example we used, FEDORCHE and RENSIN can use the SQL Server if they have privileges on it; ANDREW cannot use it even though the owner of that login holds a valid SQL Server account.

What about computers using Windows 95, Windows for Workgroups, MS-DOS, or — heaven forbid — *non-Microsoft operating systems*? None of these computers are members of the domain in the sense outlined here because they do not share the security accounts database of the domain. To continue our example, FEDORCHE, RENSIN, *and* ANDREW can get to the shared directories and other resources of the non-Windows NT computers on the network. There may be passwords protecting these resources, and you can limit access to members of the domain, but non-Windows NT computers are not sharing the security accounts database.

What happens when your SQL Server machine is on some non-Windows NT network, such as Novell? Then it is not in a domain, and it behaves like the Windows 95 and other machines described previously. Anyone on the network can get to the server, though you may have set privileges on the server restricting who can do what once they connect.

Trust

In Windows NT, larger networks will comprise of multiple domains. Needing to use services from two different domains would appear to be a problem because no machine can simultaneously be a member of two domains at the same time. The solution is for one domain to *trust* another. For our purposes, we will define trust to mean that one domain accepts the login validation of another. Trust can be set up independently in each direction. For example, you might have a domain called HEADQUARTERS and one called FIELDOFFICE. You could set things up so that FIELDOFFICE trusts HEADQUARTERS, but HEADQUARTERS doesn't trust FIELDOFFICE. This means the folks logged into the HEADQUARTERS domain can access the resources of the FIELDOFFICE domain, but not vice versa.

Now we have the background we need to understand SQL Server's three security modes because they revolve around using or not using domains.

The security modes

The three security modes for validating logins are *standard*, *Windows NT integrated*, and *mixed.*

- Standard security means that SQL Server maintains its own list of SQL Server logins and passwords, and it does all the login validation itself. SQL Server pays no attention to what domain, if any, the network logins are using.
- Integrated security uses the domain features of Windows NT for validation of logins. All users are being allowed or denied access to SQL Server based on the SQL Server privileges attached to their Windows NT domain logins.
- Mixed security is what the name implies. Each login attempt sent to SQL Server requests one of the two validation methods above. At any given time you might have a mixture of connections to SQL Server, and any given login is able to use either method.

Some of the pros and cons of these modes are obvious; some aren't. Let's look at the issues involved.

Standard security

Standard security is a very straightforward validation method, and it is automatically set up by the SQL Server installation program. In the syslogins table of the master database, SQL Server stores the name and encrypted password of each valid user of the server. SQL Server does all its own login validation. Anyone can access SQL Server from any client PC on the network (or the Internet, if you are using TCP/IP and your firewall allows it) by supplying a valid login and password. The advantages of using standard security are as follows:

- It is simple to set up and manage.
- You don't have to have access to, or understand anything about, Windows NT security.
- You don't have to create Windows NT logins for your SQL Server users.
- People can log in to your SQL Server over the Internet. (Provided you are running TCP/IP and there's no firewall in the way, of course.)
- Your Windows NT login and SQL Server login can be totally different. For example, you could be logged into Windows NT as "FEDORCHE," but connected to SQL Server as "*sa*." This is particularly useful if you are helping an end user. You can do a small task as the system administrator or as a database owner, without forcing that user to log off the workstation.

- You can log in to SQL Server with different logins at the same time on one workstation. This is useful if you are a developer trying to test an application with a user's privileges, while still being connected to SQL Server in another window with your own login.
- The system administrator can allow other users to create logins (with a modification that we will show you).
- The system administrator can change any users' passwords. (You cannot lock your Windows NT LAN administrators out of SQL Server, however, even if you change the sa password. More on that later.)
- Any login can be simultaneously logged from multiple workstations. This might be a disadvantage, too, depending on your perspective.

Some of the disadvantages of using standard security are

- It isn't secure enough for the requirements of some organizations. The Windows NT domain is an added security control for Windows NT networks, and standard security doesn't recognize or use Windows NT domains. Standard security doesn't do any sophisticated login or password management, such as forcing users to change their passwords at certain times or limiting a user to logging in from only one workstation at a time.
- You have to remember more passwords. Maybe *you* have a photographic memory, but certainly some of your users don't. Now they can add their SQL Server password to the long list of codes the modern world tells them to memorize and never write down.
- You have to keep typing your login and password. If you are at a WfW (Windows for Workgroups) client you might type in your password once for ISQL/w, once when you connect via Microsoft Access, then again for some other database application. Eventually, you will close some of these because you want to free up RAM for something else, and then when you reopen them, you have to type the login and password again. Database administrators (DBAs) will find themselves typing their password each time they use the Transfer Manager (for 6.0 and lower databases) and each time they use BCP. It gets old. Some applications may let the user store the password with the application to get around this problem, and that can lead to more security risks.
- You have to set up separate logins in SQL Server for each user: another administrative detail for you to forget.

- There is nothing stopping you from annoying your users by assigning a user named Rachel Jackson a Windows NT login of *jacksonr* but a SQL Server login of *rjackson*. If the Windows NT administrator is a different person than the SQL Server system administrator, the chances of this happening are even greater.
- If you have multiple SQL Servers on your network and you want to let all your users have access to each of them, *you* constantly have to keep the logins and passwords on each of them synchronized. This a *major* headache. We haven't covered replication yet, but if you were thinking it might support this, it doesn't. We will show you a way to jury-rig it, but that means you don't get to manage things with the nifty graphical interface tools that are supposed to be SQL Server's strength.

Basically, standard security is easy to set up and flexible in the access it allows. However, its security isn't as rigorous or as elegant as it could be. There is a lot to consider, but before you make a decision about which security mode to use, you need to know more about the other two modes.

Integrated security

Integrated security means that SQL Server login validation is *integrated* with Windows NT login validation. Therefore, users don't have to be listed in the syslogins table, and their encrypted passwords won't be stored there. Users can connect to SQL Server without supplying a login or a password because SQL Server is going to rely on the Windows NT login. In fact, SQL Server will *ignore* any login or password you supply. Some of the advantages of integrated security are as follows:

- You get to use the robust security features of Windows NT, which include such things as forcing users to change their passwords when they first log in, making passwords expire after a certain amount of time, restricting users to being logged in at only one workstation at a time, remembering old passwords, preventing users from changing their own passwords, and more. (See your Windows NT documentation for full details on all its security features.) Because Windows NT is handling the logins and passwords, the SQL Server system administrator will not be able to change a users password; the network administrator will have to do it.
- You can control which domains can access your SQL Server. Suppose your network has two Windows NT domains called Development and Production. These domains have a trusted relationship to share files and

printers and so on, but you don't want users logged into the Production domain to be able to access a SQL Server in Development. With integrated security, you can enforce this.

- Once your users log into their Windows NT domain, they can use all applications that connect to SQL Server without ever having to supply another login or password.
- You don't have to set up separate SQL Server logins for each user. However, all users without a login get the same privileges, namely the privileges of the Default Login, usually *guest.* Note that you *will* have to set up Windows NT logins for each user who needs access to SQL Server.
- You can sort of map Windows NT Groups and users to SQL Server groups and users. We say *sort of* because Windows NT groups and SQL Server groups operate under different rules, but this is a nice feature nonetheless. It does do a good job of keeping the user list between Windows NT and SQL Server synchronized.
- When you have multiple SQL Servers, you have no worries about the synchronization of logins and passwords among them because they can all be using Windows NT's security.

The many advantages boil down to convenience for the users and tight security. There are some drawbacks to integrated security, of course. By now, many of these disadvantages should be obvious: many of the advantages of standard security don't apply with integrated security precisely because SQL Server's login validation is integrated with Windows NT's. The drawbacks of integrated security can be summarized in three basic questions, which are detailed in the following sections.

Do you need to access your server over a non-trusted connection?

If yes, you can't use integrated security on your server. Trusted connections include Named Pipes and multi-protocol sessions running from Windows NT, Windows 95, or Windows for Workgroups clients, as well as Microsoft LAN Manager sessions running from Windows or MS-DOS clients. Notice that TCP/IP sessions are *not* trusted connections. Therefore, if you want to support Internet access to your SQL Server, you can't use integrated security. SQL Server hammers this point home by not even letting you set up integrated security if you have already installed any other Net-Libraries besides Named Pipes and Multi-Protocol. You have to remove these Net-Libraries first. (A *Net-Library* is a library of functions for managing network connections and routing. Each Net-Library you installed when you set up SQL Server allows SQL Server to use a particular network protocol.)

Can you live with your Windows NT login dictating your SQL Server connection?

This is a concern particularly for developers and administrators. Consider these two examples:

- Suppose you are a developer of an application that runs in a database for which you are not the database owner. Your Windows NT login is FEDORCHE, which is mapped to the SQL Server login FEDORCHE. When you want to test your application, you usually connect to the server with the login ANYUSER, an account set up with the same privileges as your end-users. With standard security you can test your application any time you want by typing ANYUSER in the login text box. However, with integrated security this doesn't work. SQL Server will ignore the fact that you typed in ANYUSER and log you in as FEDORCHE anyway. You can't use the setuser command (See "Impersonating other users", later in this chapter) to assume the identity of ANYUSER because FEDORCHE is not the database owner. What can you do? You have to get a new account created on the network called ANYUSER, and you have to log off the domain and re-login as ANYUSER, thus disconnecting yourself from all network resources in the process, which will include anything on your desktop connected to SQL Server. This gets tedious quickly.
- One security strategy sometimes used in application development is to create a login for use exclusively by an application. The developers grant insert, update, and delete privileges on database objects to this login alone. When users run the application, they are logged in to the database as themselves, but when they change data in tables, the application logs in behind the scenes with its own login (the password is stored in the application). This doesn't work in integrated security because, again, SQL Server ignores the login and password the application tries to supply.

We don't think these are valid excuses for eschewing integrated security, but you have to plan for these kinds of events. We do log off our domain and log back in as another user to test applications. We don't design our applications to work like the one described in the second case; there are better ways to approach security.

Do you trust your LAN users with integrated security?

It sounds like a silly question, but integrated security requires everyone to do some thinking. You probably have some sensitive data in your SQL Server: salaries, restricted client information, and so on. If someone with read access — or worse yet, write access — to a database logs into the network and then leaves — for the restroom, for a meeting, for whatever reason — that unattended machine can be used to see and change SQL Server data. The same thing can happen in standard security, but *only if you leave a database application open.* With integrated security, it doesn't matter if the user closed all applications; anyone can reopen the application without supplying a user name or password. You can deal with this problem in integrated security in three ways:

- Train your users to log off the domain when they leave their desks. This isn't going to be a popular solution because it's annoying.
- Train your users to lock their workstations when they leave their desks. This only really works with Windows NT Workstation, where you have a true "lock workstation" command.
- Have all your users use password-protected screen savers. You would have to trust your users not to set their screen saver delay times to be too large.

The first two options require you to trust your users to do something, the last requires you to trust them not to alter something you set up. Remember that you have similar problems in standard security mode, but at least with standard security all you have to do is get people to close any applications connected to SQL Server. For applications that you develop, you can log people off after a certain amount of idle time. You don't have that luxury for applications you purchase.

If you've seen some things you liked in each of these security modes but can't quite commit to either, you are in luck. Read on!

Mixed security

Mixed security mode lets SQL Server validate clients using either of the two previous methods. Any login attempt over a non-trusted connection will be handled with standard security validation. Users coming in over trusted connections tell SQL Server how to verify them by the login string they pass. When the login is either the same as the Windows NT login, blank, or spaces, SQL Server ignores the supplied password and validates the login with integrated security. If the login is anything else, SQL Server uses standard security validation.

Clearly, the advantage of this option is that you have maximum flexibility. You can use some of the conveniences of integrated security when you want them but fall back to some of the advantages of standard security when you want. The key disadvantages of mixed security are the following:

- You lose out on the airtight access control of integrated security because the Standard Security door is always open.

- You can get in trouble quickly if you are not careful. With integrated security, it doesn't matter what passwords SQL Server has encrypted in the syslogins table. You can let all the passwords be null or have SQL Server pick random passwords. In mixed security, you are probably going to have certain logins, maybe most logins, that you know will always use trusted connections. But don't let these logins have null passwords because then someone unwanted could get in via standard security: because the userids have no password, someone can gain access by knowing only the login.

Tip

Even if you plan to go with standard security, we recommend that you start with mixed security just to take advantage of the capability to set up SQL Server logins automatically for Windows NT logins. Then, you can switch back to standard security with just a couple of mouse clicks. (See Chapter 4 for complete instructions on changing security modes.)◀

Cross-Reference

Client-requested trusted connections

Just when you thought you were getting all these security modes clear in your mind, here is another curve ball: even standard security is in some sense mixed because a client application can be set up to request integrated security login validation from SQL Server no matter which of the three security modes the server is using. This why you can choose to register a standard security mode SQL Server in the SQL Enterprise Manager with a trusted connection. It is also what the SQL Executive (the local administrative agent responsible for scheduling tasks, implementing replication, handling alerts, and monitoring SQL Server) uses to connect to remote servers. If you find it necessary, you can stop this by changing the Windows NT user group that has system administrator privileges. We cover how to do that later in this chapter.

The fact that you can force a trusted connection regardless of server security mode is the reason you can never truly be locked out of SQL Server, even if you have forgotten the system administrator password. Simply log in to the domain as a member of the group mapped to system administrator from a machine that supports a trusted connection. From there, you can change the system administrator password. There is always one such machine: the server itself.

Note

Though it should be obvious, we feel it is important to note that the SQL Enterprise Manager isn't affected by the security modes of the various servers. You can have servers registered running all different kinds of security modes in the same instance of the SQL Enterprise Manager. Furthermore, there is no such thing as a command that can only be executed over a trusted connection.◀

Impersonating other users

Before you make your final decision on security modes, you should know that as a system administrator or database owner you can impersonate other users with the SETUSER command. This command lets you fully assume the identity of another user. You will have the exact same privileges and permissions as that user: you can create, alter, and drop objects belonging to the user you impersonate. The SETUSER capability virtually eliminates the need for a database owner to log out of the Windows NT domain to assume the identity of a database user. The syntax is

```
SETUSER ['username' [WITH NORESET]]
```

The "WITH NORESET" means you can't go back to your identity as the sa or dbo for the duration of the session. Otherwise, you can always switch back to being the sa or dbo by typing simply SETUSER with no parameters.

Security mode recommendations

We recommend using integrated security unless you know you will have users who need non-trusted connections, such as connections over the Internet. In that case, we recommend using mixed security. Once you get used to integrated security, you won't want to use anything else.

Setting up a security mode

When you installed SQL Server, it didn't give you a security mode choice; it just set up standard security. In Chapter 4, we cover how to change to a different a security mode. Refer to that chapter if you want to change your security mode.◀

Giving Windows NT groups and users access to SQL Server

If you are using standard security, you can skip this section and go on to "Managing SQL Server Logins and Database Users."◀

Most networks have lots of users, often hundreds or even thousands. Specifying a detailed set of privileges for each individual user would be time-consuming to say the least. The good news is that Windows NT and SQL Server each provide a way to handle privileges for collections of users: groups.

Want to join a group?

Using user groups will simplify your job in controlling who logs in to SQL Server. The bad news is that Windows NT groups behave differently than SQL Server groups. A Windows NT user can be a member of any number of groups. A SQL Server user can be a member of only one user-defined group, which is a serious drawback, in our opinion. (There is one system-defined group in SQL Server called *public*, which by definition contains all logins; you can't remove a user from this group.) Another difference is that in Windows NT groups can be members of other groups. SQL Server doesn't support this.

Microsoft recommends that you implement your integrated or mixed security with just two local Windows NT groups, one called SQLAdmins (or your existing Windows NT administrator group, if appropriate) for those users who will need system administrator privileges, and one called SQLUsers for everyone else. Given how the SQL Security Manager does group mappings (more about that soon), we have to concur.

Suppose you wanted to use several smaller Windows NT groups instead of the catch-all SQLUsers category. You might have a Sales group, a Developers group, and so on for each of your company's divisions. Then, you might have a Managers group so that if Warren is a sales manager, he would be a member of both the Sales group and the Managers group. No matter which group you map first, you will have a problem setting up the other. Say you do Sales first so that Warren is now a member of the group Sales in SQL Server. When you map Managers, you get an error on Warren: he is already a member of Sales and cannot be added to Managers.

Undaunted, you forge ahead by parceling out your users so that no user is a member of more than one Windows NT group. You have groups such as Sales, Developers, Accounting, and VicePresidents. (In this company VPs are not considered members of specific divisions.) Warren gets a long overdue promotion to VP, so you remove him from the Windows NT Sales group and add him to the Windows NT VicePresidents group. What happens in SQL Server? Nothing. Warren will stay in the SQL Server Sales group until you move him. Worse yet, the SQL Security Manager gives you no hint that this discontinuity exists.

Which brings us back to the idea of a simple SQLUsers group in Windows NT. Because you have to manage your own SQL Server groups anyway, why bother mapping them to an elaborate set of Windows NT groups to begin with?

The SQL Security Manager

The graphical tool for administering mixed and integrated security is the SQL Security Manager, which is in your the Microsoft SQL Server 6.5 folder. It creates SQL Server groups that mirror your Windows NT groups, and it can make SQL Server logins if you want. It lets you resynchronize groups that are already created. The SQL Security Manager can revoke the privileges of Windows NT groups, and it can show you what privileges a Windows NT user has in SQL Server.

If you are wondering why SQL Security Manager is a separate application, so are we. Microsoft worked very hard to integrate everything else under the sun into the SQL Enterprise Manager. Maybe in the next release SQL Security Manager, too, will be part of one big management tool.

Starting the SQL Security Manager

Here are the basic steps for starting the SQL Security Manager and logging in to a server:

1. Start the SQL Security Manager by choosing "SQL Security Manager" from the Microsoft SQL Server 6.5 Utilities folder. The Connect Server dialog box appears (Figure 7-1).

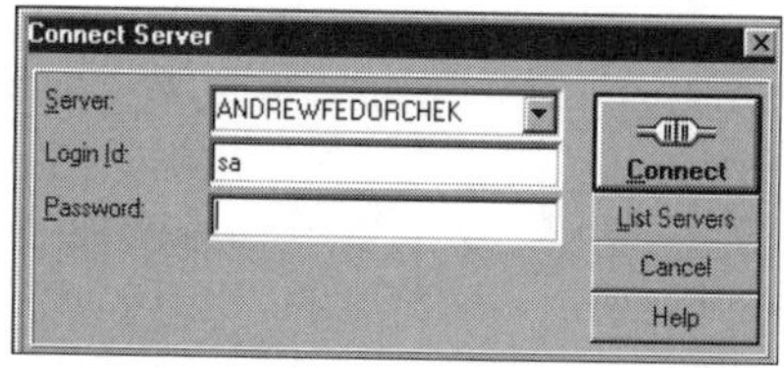

Figure 7-1:
Log in to a server with the Connect Server dialog box.

2. In the Server drop-down list box, select or type the name of the server you want. This list contains only the last five servers you logged in to with this tool. You can see a list of servers on the network by choosing the List Servers button.

3. If this is the first time you are using this tool or if you last logged in as the system adminstrator (sa), the Login ID box says *sa*. If you are going to make a trusted connection and your Windows NT login maps to sa, just choose the Connect button. (If you aren't sure, choose Connect any- way. The worst that can happen is that you get an error and you type in

the sa password.) If you know you are not going to make a trusted connection, enter the sa password before connecting. You must login as the sa to use the SQL Security Manager.◀

4. Once you have chosen to Connect, you should see the SQL Security Manager window shown in Figure 7-2. If no logins are mapped to SQLUsers, as will be the case when you first start, you see a message saying so.

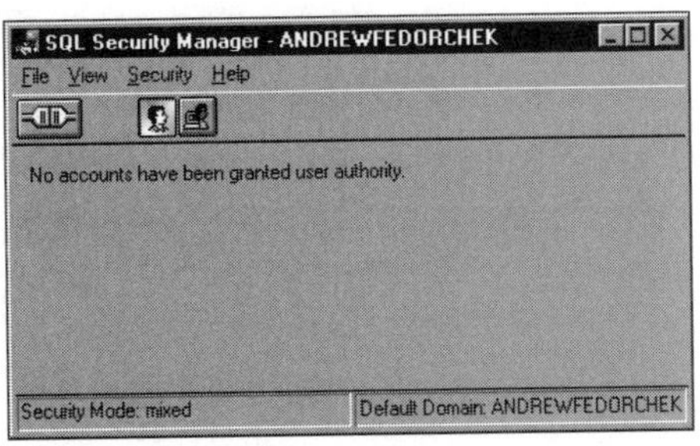

Figure 7-2:
The SQL Security Manager when you first open it.

Familiarizing yourself with the SQL Security Manager

You are now in the SQL Security Manager. In the title bar you see which SQL Server you are connected to (in Figure 7-2, the server is called ANDREWFEDORCHEK); in the status bar you see the security mode of that server and its default domain, which may or may not be your domain. One of the first things you will notice is that this isn't a Multiple Document Interface (MDI) application. There are no child windows, and you cannot connect to more than one server. To manage another server you would have to open another instance of the application.

Mapping Windows NT groups to SQL Server groups

First, we would like to grant access for some of our Windows NT users to SQL Server and optionally add logins for them. Remember that SQL Server doesn't allow users to be in more than one group; Windows NT does. SQL Server uses the following rules in mapping Windows NT group users to SQL Server group users:

1. If the user is not a SQL Server login, SQL Server creates the login, creates the group in the selected database, and adds the user to the database and the group.

2. If the user already has a SQL Server login but is not in the selected database, SQL Server just adds the user to the database and group.
3. If the user is already in the database, SQL Server does nothing for that user.

To grant users access to SQL Server, Select View⇨User privilege or press the User toolbar button, shown at left. Now select Security⇨Grant New. The Grant User Privilege window (Figure 7-3) appears.

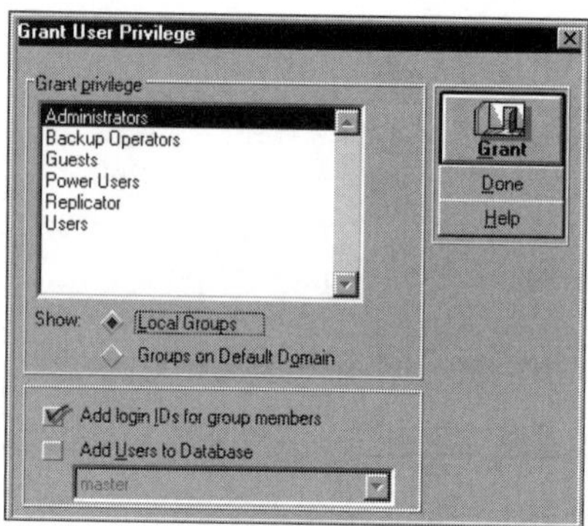

Figure 7-3:
Use the Grant User Privilege window to map Windows NT groups to SQL Server groups.

Mapping a group is very easy. To map a group:

1. Pick the group you want.
2. If you want to create individual logins in SQL Server for the members of the group, check Add login IDs for group members.
3. If you want to add the users to a specific database, check Add users to database. Select a database.
4. Click Grant.

The window stays open for you to map more groups. When you are finished, click Done.

Mapping Windows NT groups to the SQL Server sa login

This is even easier than mapping groups. Select View⇨sa privilege or press the SA toolbar button, shown at left. Now, select Security⇨Grant New. The Grant User Privilege window appears again, but the *Add login IDs for group members* and *Add users to database* options are grayed out. To map a group to sa, do the following:

1. Pick the group you want.
2. Click Grant.

The window stays open for you to map more groups to the sa privilege. When you are finished, click Done. Really difficult, huh? You just gave a Windows NT group sa privileges on the server. This means that anyone in that group can do anything to the server, so don't grant this privilege lightly.◀

Forcing your way into SQL Server

The SQL Server documentation tells you that if you forget the sa password you must reinstall SQL Server. Not true. If you have a Windows NT in a group mapped to the sa privilege, you can access SQL Server via a trusted connection and change the sa password. This works no matter what the security mode of the server is.◀

The real fun begins if someone has revoked access to the sa privilege from all Windows NT groups. You can still access SQL Server as the sa, but you need a Windows NT login in the Administrators group for the domain. Below we tell you what to do, but first a word of warning. Be very careful with the Registry Editor. Do not deviate from the steps below, or you risk trashing not only your entire SQL Server installation but the rest of the computer, too.◀

1. Log into the Windows NT domain of the SQL Server as a member of the domain's Administrators group.
2. Choose Start⇨Run.
3. Type REGEDT32 and press Enter. You are now in the Registry Editor (Figure 7-4).
4. Choose Registry⇨Select Computer to open the registry for your SQL Server machine. If you are sitting at the SQL Server machine, skip this step.
5. Switch to the HKEY_LOCAL_MACHINE on SERVER_NAME window, where SERVER_NAME is the name of your SQL Server. This is the window we have open in Figure 7-4.
6. Select the SOFTWARE/Microsoft/MSSQLServer/MSSQLServer key. It will be grayed out.
7. Select Security⇨Permissions. The Registry Key Permissions window opens, Figure 7-5.

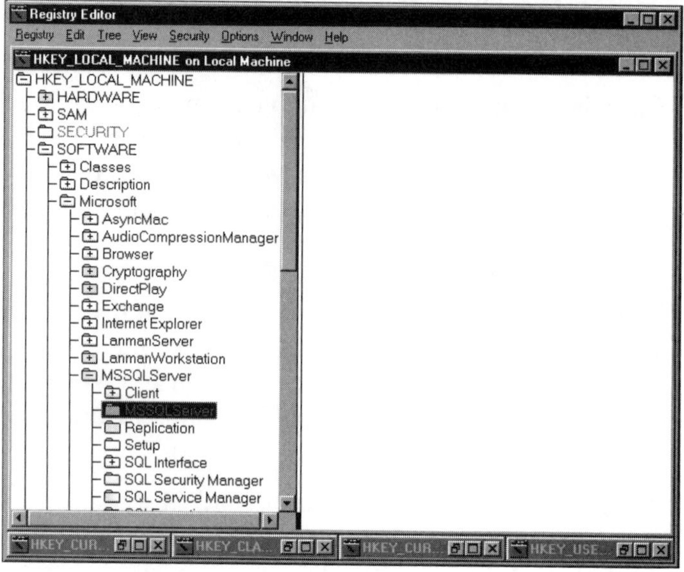

Figure 7-4:
Use the Registry Editor to force your way into SQL Server.

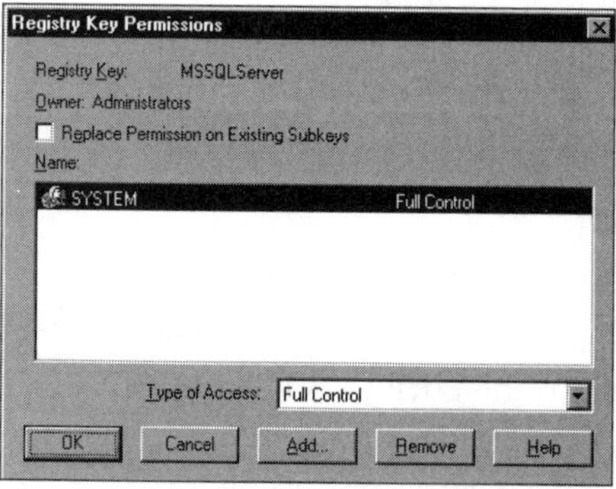

Figure 7-5:
Use the Registry Key Permissions to grant yourself access to the MSSQLServer key.

8. Click Add. The Add Users and Groups window opens, Figure 7-6.

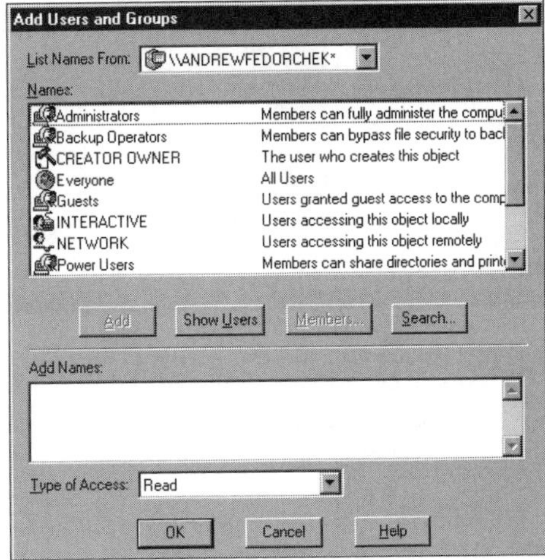

Figure 7-6:
Use Add Users and Groups to grant Administators Full Control.

9. Highlight Administrators and Click Add. In the Type of Access drop-down list box, choose Full Control. Click OK twice. The right side of the HKEY_LOCAL_MACHINE window fills with information (Figure 7-7).

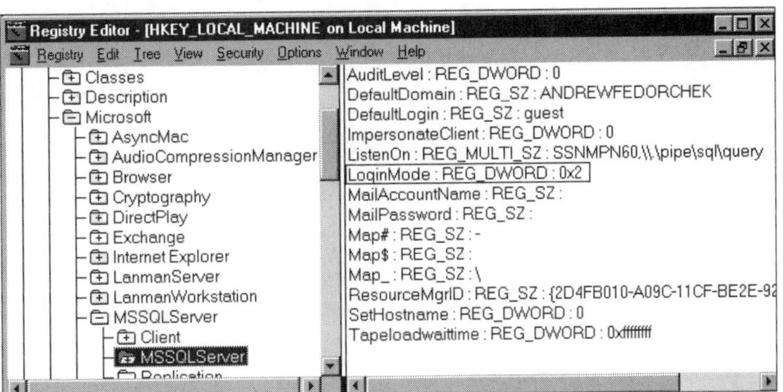

Figure 7-7:
You can see the MSSQLServer key after you grant yourself access.

10. Double click the key labeled Login Mode. This brings up the DWORD Editor (Figure 7-8). The values for this key are 0, 1, and 2 for standard, integrated, and mixed, respectively. Change the value to 0 and click OK.

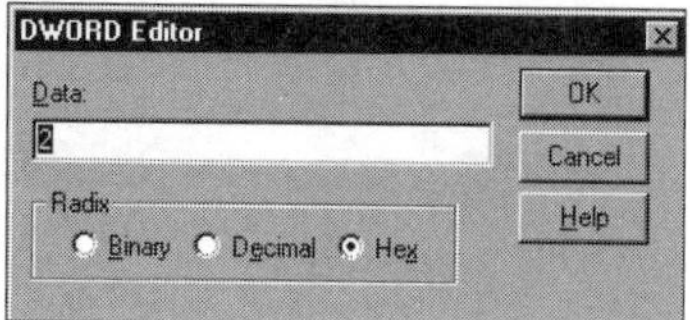

Figure 7-8:
Change the MSSQLServer key to a 0 with the DWORD editor.

11. Exit the Registry Editor. You can now get a trusted connection to SQL Server because by default Standard Security allows access to Administrators.

Viewing your mappings

The SQL Security Manager shows you a tree structure (Figure 7-9) somewhat like the SQL Enterprise Manager. Click the icon for either User or SA, and double-click the group you want to see.

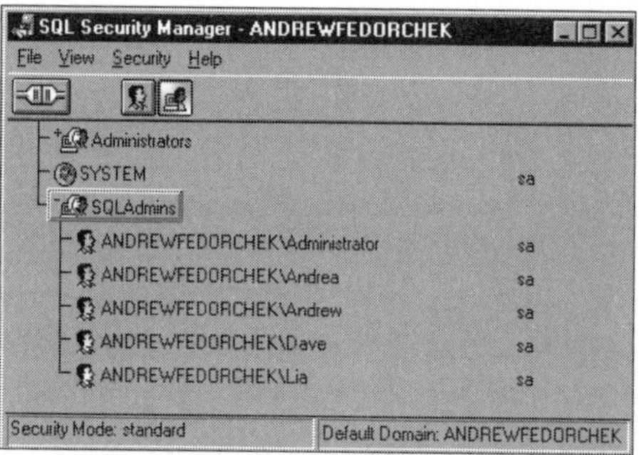

Figure 7-9:
Expand the SQL Security Manager tree to see who is in a group.

Revoking privileges

Taking away privileges is much easier than granting them. Simply select a group, and choose Security⇨Revoke. SQL Server asks you if you are sure you know what you are doing, and then, zap, the privileges are revoked.

Extended stored procedures for security

The SQL Security Manager is a nice little application in that it provides a graphical interface to security, but if you know the Transact-SQL commands, you can manage security a lot more easily that way. All you need to grant access to SQL Server is xp_grantlogin. The syntax is

```
xp_grantlogin 'account_name' [, {'admin' | 'repl' | 'user'}]
```

It is best to qualify account_name fully in the form 'domain/user_name' or 'domain/group_name'. If you just provide a user or group name, SQL Server looks for the account first on the local computer, then the primary domain controller, and finally on trusted domains. Notice that with this command you can map individual users. With the SQL Security Manager, you are restricted to group management.◀

If you do not supply the second parameter, the account is mapped as a user, 'admin' denotes sa privileges, and 'repl' maps an account to the repl_publisher login. For example, to give the sa privilege to a user named 'Rensin' on a domain named 'HEADQUARTERS', you would execute this command:

```
xp_grantlogin 'HEADQUARTERS/Rensin', 'admin'
```

You can revoke privileges with xp_revokelogin, which takes only 'acount_name' as a parameter.

Managing SQL Server Logins and Database Users

Here, we cross the conceptual boundary between letting users into your SQL Server and letting them into your databases. You can see that the SQL Security Manager already muddies the waters by adding users to a default database and setting up groups in that database, but it doesn't finish the job. If you want the same groups and users in another database, you have to go back to the SQL Enterprise Manager. If you are setting up standard security access, SQL Enterprise Manager and this section are your starting points. From here on, we just talk about managing your logins, and we won't need to differentiate among security modes.

SQL Server Login Basics

One of the jobs the system administrator is stuck with is administering logins: adding them, dropping them, and changing their various attributes, both global and within specific databases. The system administrator isn't supposed to delegate adding and dropping, but the rest of the stuff can be changed by the owner of the login, the database owner, or both. Before we discuss the graphical tools for managing logins, it is important to understand the underlying objects. We are tracking several pieces of information:

- The *suid* (unique identifier for a login)
- The *dbname* (a login's default database)
- The *name* (the actual "everyday" name of the login)
- The *password* (SQL server's encrypted password string)

suid

SQL Server tracks logins throughout the entire system, not by their name, but by their *suid*, which is a unique integer assigned to each login. *suids* start at 1, which is the system administrator. The only other entries in the syslogins table when you first install SQL Server are probe (see "Existing Logins and Users"), which has a *suid* of 10, and repl_publisher (16382) and repl_subscripber (16383). All the logins that you add get the next available integer, starting with 11.

dbname

The *dbname* is the default database. This must be a valid database name in the sysdatabases table when you add a login, but there is nothing to stop you from later dropping a database while some users still have it as a default. In that case when such users log in, they will get an error and SQL Server will connect them to master by default.

The default database controls such things as what database ISQL/w will initially connect you to and what database bcp assumes you are using when you don't specify a database. The default database does not imply any special privileges for the login in that database, nor limit the login's access to other databases.

name

This is the actual "friendly" name of the login, like "SmithB."

password

SQL Server stores an encrypted password string. By default, only the system administrator can see it. Don't get too excited about being able to see this string if you are the system administrator; the password system is still pretty secure. The virtue of letting you see it is that if you need to, you can call on the pwdencrypt and pwdcompare functions. The former encrypts a password; the latter compares a password and an encrypted string and lets you know if the password encrypts to the string.

Notice there is no "unencrypt" function. If Microsoft did its job right, it is logically impossible to construct a function that reverses the encryption. If you have a lot of time on your hands, play with trying to find a pattern that would let you decode any random encrypted string. Eventually, you will conclude that only a professional would have a chance at it. If you have access to the password column and to the pwdcompare function, you can test a word list, like the English dictionary, for password matches. This is why it's a bad idea to pick an English word as your password. This is also why only the system administrator can see the encrypted password or use pwdencrypt or pwdcompare.

If the encrypted password is null, then the real password is in fact null. If you are in either mixed or standard security mode, this is a major problem. Your security has holes.

The encrypted string for a password is dependent on the password string and the time offset from when SQL Server started. For example, suppose you stop and start SQL Server and then immediately set the password for the user 'fedorche' to 'pass.test0', and you find that the encrypted string is '!1!J!,TWE*9J8/+8'. If you later set the password for 'fedorche' or any other user to 'pass.test0', you will get a different encrypted string. However, if you stop and start SQL Server again and immediately set the password for *any login* to 'pass.test0', the encrypted string will again be '!1!J!,TWE*9J8/+8'.◄

The fact that the password encryption depends solely on the password string and a time offset lets you transfer passwords from one server to another. We shall refer to the server you are transferring from as the first server and the server you are transferring to as the second server. Here's what you want to do:

1. On the second server, enable updates to the system catalog:

```
sp_configure 'allow updates', 1
  RECONFIGURE WITH OVERRIDE
```

2. Construct the update statement(s) from the first server. They will be of the form:

```
UPDATE syslogins
    SET password = encryted_string
    WHERE name = login_name
```

Where encryted_string is the encrypted string from the first server. Remember that if the string contains a single quote ('), you must write that as two quotes in the UDPATE statement. For example, if the string for fedorche is !1!D3'$E:L/F"&0!, you would write

```
UPDATE syslogins
   SET password = '!1!D3''$E:L/F"&0!'
   WHERE name = 'fedorche'
```

3. If you have a lot of logins for which you are transfering passwords, you can generate most of the SQL you need this way:

```
SELECT 'UPDATE syslogins SET password = '''+password+'''',
          'WHERE name = '''+name+''''
   FROM syslogins
   WHERE password NOT LIKE '%['']%'
UNION
SELECT 'UPDATE syslogins SET password = "'+password+'"',
          'WHERE name = '''+name+''''
   FROM syslogins
   WHERE password LIKE '%['']%'
      AND password NOT LIKE '%"%'
   ORDER BY 2
```

We exclude passwords that contain both the characters (') and (") because these require special handling.◀

Warning

4. Run the UPDATE statements on the second server. Be very careful that you include the WHERE clause; you don't want to change the password column for all logins.◀
5. Disable updates to the system catalog on the second server.

This procedure works even when the first Server is a 6.0 server and the second server is a 6.5 server. Notice, however, that the two servers *must have the same character set and sort order.*

Database users

Within each database, we have login and group information stored again. Just because users have SQL Server logins, they do not automatically have rights to use each database on that SQL Server. A user must be explicitly added to each database, unless the database has a guest account (see the next section). When you add a user to a database, SQL Server needs a local name of the user inside the database. This must be unique within the database.

Tip

A word on the local names of users inside databases. You can play tricks like this: one of your users is Rachel Jackson, and her Windows NT and SQL Server logins are both *jacksonr*, to differentiate her from the other Jacksons in the company. If she is the only Jackson in the Projects database, however, you could rename her "*jackson*" in this particular database. We don't recommend this; we find it just adds confusion to have Rachel be *jacksonr*, *rjackson*, *jackson*, ... depending on which database you are in. Now, everyone in the company has to remember which permutation of his or her last name is active in a given context. It's a lot easier for her just to be *jacksonr*.◀

Just as with logins, there are a couple of key pieces of information to track:

- The *uid*, a unique integer id that SQL Server uses to track a user within a database.
- The *name*, which is the local name of the user within the database.
- The *guid*, which is the integer identifier for the group to which a user belongs.

Existing logins and database users

Cross-Reference

There are four special logins that SQL Server sets up for you: sa, probe, repl_publisher, and repl_subscriber. We will defer discussion of the replication logins to Part VII. SQL Server also makes two or three user entries in each database: *public*, *dbo*, and sometimes *guest*.◀

sa

Cross-Reference

The sa login is the key to the SQL Server universe. It can do everything. The default database for the sa login is master, but if you change that, it won't hurt anything. *When SQL Server is first installed, the password for sa is null*, which you will want to change immediately (see Chapter 1).◀

probe

SQL Server uses the probe login for two-phase commits (a process that ensures that transactions that apply to more than one server are completed on all servers or on none) and in standard security for certain applications like the Performance Monitor. The password for probe is null, and you are supposed to leave it that way. We feel this is a serious loose end in SQL Server's security because anyone familiar with SQL Server can get into a mixed or standard security system with it. Worse yet, having gained access, someone can then use any databases that have the guest user ID, which includes master! This means that the lists of login names are visible to anyone, because anyone can log in as probe and type

```
SELECT name FROM syslogins
```

So we tried changing the password of probe, and then, of course, the Performance Monitor didn't work properly. We called Microsoft for help, and the company told us not to change the password of probe. Thanks, guys. This is yet another selling point for integrated security. In that security mode, the Performance Monitor uses the sa login and the backdoor is closed. You could even drop the probe login (sp_droplogin probe) if you use integrated security.

public

The group public is the one group every database has. Its uid and gid (uid = gid for a group) are zero in all databases. The suid for public is -2, which isn't really a valid suid. Negative suids usually indicate groups.

dbo

The suid of the database owner (DBO) is mapped to a uid of 1 and the name *dbo* inside the database. The owner cannot also be a separately listed user in the database. The system administrator can change the owner of any database except master or tempdb (the system administrator must be the owner of these). The system administrator assumes the identity of "dbo" when using a database, so you can never explicitly add sa as a user in a database.

guest

The guest user ID is special. There is no such login in syslogins, the list of valid logins. If a database has a guest account, and by default only master and pubs do, anyone with a valid SQL Server login can access that database. Just like all other users, guest is a member of public, so if you add this user to a database, you are by default giving every SQL Server login the privileges of public. If you don't want to be quite so free-wheeling but do want to have guest in your database, you can revoke specific privileges from guest.

Using the SQL Enterprise Manager to manage logins

You can use the SQL Enterprise Manager to add a new login, add a new user, or change a group or user name. Here we outline these procedures.

Adding a new login

Right-click the Logins folder of the SQL Server in the Server Manager Window. Select New Login. The Manage Logins window (Figure 7-10) appears.

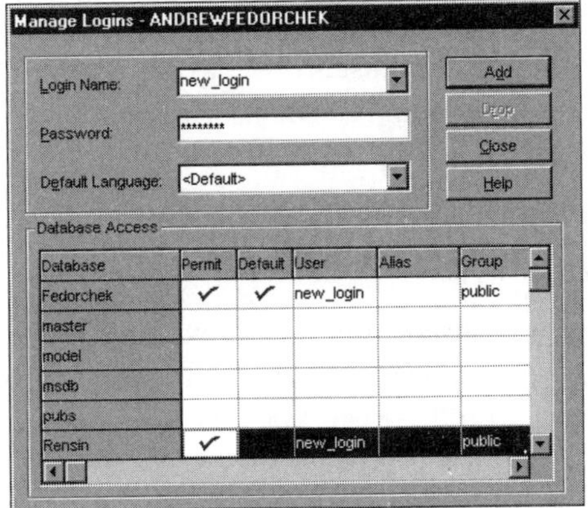

Figure 7-10:
Use the Manage Logins Window to create and edit logins.

To add a new login, simply type in a login name and password in the appropriate fields. The login name must be a valid SQL Server identifier. The password can be anything up to 30 characters long. If you are modifying an existing login, you can select a login from the drop-down list.

If you selected a case-*in*sensitive sort order when installing SQL Server, that setting affects passwords, too. For example, if you give a login a password of "RememberThis," the user can login with "rememberthis," "REMEMBERTHIS," "reMeMbERThiS," and so on. SQL Server converts it to all uppercase before it encrypts it.◀

You should add the user to at least one database by checking the Permit column of the Database Access section of the Manage Logins window. The first database you check automatically becomes the default . You can move that check to any other database that you later permit the user to access. When you are done, click the Add button.

Tip

A confirmation box for the password appears. Here, the case does matter, even on a server with a case-insensitive sort order. The SQL Enterprise Manager isn't smart enough to differentiate between server sort orders and react accordingly.◀

Adding a new database user

To add a new database user, expand the Logins folder, right-click the login you want to add to a database, and select Edit from the pop-up menu, which displays the Manage Logins window. Check the Permit column for the appropriate database and then click Modify.

You can also add a user to a database by selecting the Groups/Users folder of a database, right-clicking it, and selecting New, but we don't like that method. In that case, the Manage Users window forces you to type in the login all over again in the user name box. There is no way to indicate that they are to be the same.

Changing a group or user name

To change a group or user name, expand the Groups/Users folder of the database you are interested in, expand a group, pick a login, right-click it, and choose Edit. You'll see the Manage Users window shown in Figure 7–11.

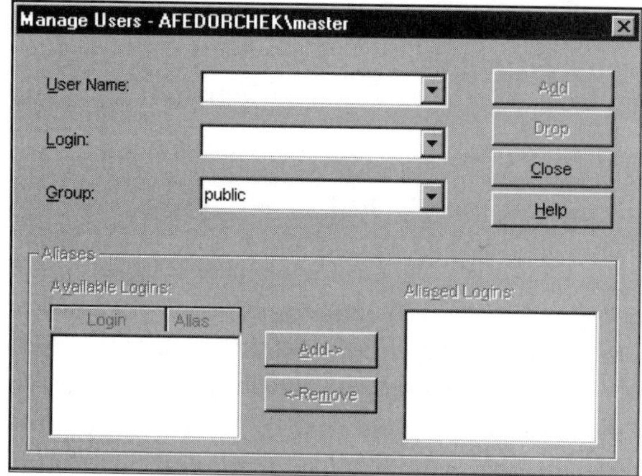

Figure 7-11:
Change a login's name or group with the Manage Users window.

Type in a new name or pick a group. Don't pick a name from the list, though, because that just switches you to the login attached to that name.

Login management via SQL

The previous steps are great for manipulating one or two logins, but what happens when someone tells you that everyone in the Sales database needs to be added to the Marketing database, and Sales has 125 users? Like it or not, the command line still has its place, and in SQL Server the "command line" is Transact-SQL. (We cover Transact-SQL in more detail in Part III.)

Here is the command to add a login in Transact-SQL:

```
exec sp_addlogin login_id [, passwd [, defdb [, deflanguage]]]
```

where login_id is the name for the user and is a valid SQL Server identifier. The rest of the parameters are optional. Passwd will default to NULL, defdb defaults to master, and deflanguage defaults to the server's default language, for example:

```
exec sp_addlogin 'fedorche', 'waxca.42', 'pubs'
```

adds a login with a login ID of fedorche, a password of waxca.42, and a default database of pubs. The user's default language will be the server's default language.

To add a user with Transact-SQL, you should be in the database where you want to add the user, and give the command

```
sp_adduser login_id [, username [, grpname]]
```

where login_id is the same name as above, username defaults to login_id, and grpname defaults to public. The procedure sp_addlogin does not add the user to the default database; you must do that explicitly with sp_adduser.◀

Statement Permissions

There are three good security reasons for setting up individual user ids within a database. With user ids you can

- Control who has access to a database.
- Control what powers users have within each database.
- Limit access to resources within a database by user.

So far we have discussed only limiting access to a database; now we delve into the other two.

In the next several parts of the book, we will discuss all kinds of work that you can do in a database, including the following:

- Creating tables (the objects that store your data)
- Creating views (virtual tables)
- Creating stored procedures (compiled SQL)
- Creating defaults (automatically supplied values)
- Creating rules (constraints on columns)
- Backing up the database
- Backing up the transaction log

The owner of the database can automatically do all of these. The system administrator always assumes the identity of the database owner, and, therefore, can do all the actions listed above. Everyone else, by default, cannot perform any of these actions. As the database owner, you must explicitly grant permission to other users to create objects or perform backups.

Graphical interface to statement permissions

To edit the permissions of your users, right-click on a database in the Server Manager window and choose Edit from the pop-up menu. When the Edit Database window appears, choose the Permissions tab (Figure 7-12).

The first column of the Edit Database window is Group\User. You can grant permissions to entire groups, to individual users, or to both. Granting permission to a group means everyone in the group has that authority. Granting permission to an individual user naturally means that just that user has the permission. The tricky question is what happens when you manage both ways. For example, suppose you grant CREATE TABLE to public, but you revoke CREATE TABLE from rensin, who is a member of public (all users are always members of public)? Can rensin create tables or not?

The answer is that the last editing session takes precedence; within an editing session, the user-level grant takes precedence. An editing session is closed by clicking OK. For example, if you grant CREATE TABLE to public, click OK, and revoke CREATE TABLE from rensin; the user rensin can't create tables. On the other hand, if you revoke CREATE TABLE from rensin, click OK, and then grant CREATE TABLE to public; rensin can create tables. Finally, if you do either of the above all in one session (you haven't clicked OK yet), rensin has whatever privileges you specifically specified for rensin, regardless of what the group has.

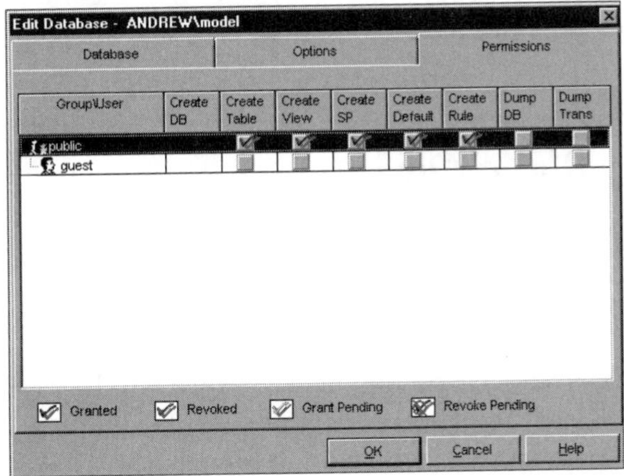

Figure 7-12:
Use the Edit Database window to change statement permissions.

Transact-SQL for statement permissions

The two commands you need to know are simply GRANT and REVOKE. The syntax is

```
GRANT | REVOKE {ALL | statement_list} TO { PUBLIC | name_list} [WITH GRANT OPTION]
```

The options for the statement list are the same as you saw in the Edit Database window: CREATE DATABASE, CREATE TABLE, CREATE VIEW, CREATE PROCEDURE, CREATE DEFAULT, CREATE RULE, DUMP DATABASE, and DUMP TRANSACTION. The name list can be groups or users, for example:

```
GRANT CREATE TABLE, CREATE VIEW TO Dave, Andrew
```

This is what the SQL Enterprise Manager is calling for you when you use the Edit Database window. The order in which you execute the commands is important. For example, this sequence leaves Andrew without CREATE TABLE authority:

```
GRANT CREATE TABLE TO Andrew
REVOKE CREATE TABLE TO public
```

However, in the reverse order, the commands would make it so that Andrew did have CREATE TABLE permission.

WITH GRANT OPTION means that the user can, in turn, give the permission to someone else.

Object Permissions

We haven't yet discussed tables and views (Chapter 12) nor stored procedures (Chapter 13), but the best time for us to talk about the permissions is now, while we are on the subject of permissions and security.◀

Tables and views contain data. As a user in the database, you can take the following actions on the data of a whole table or view: look at, add to it, change it, or delete some (or all) of it. These actions correspond to SELECT, INSERT, UPDATE, and DELETE permission in SQL Server. Data in tables and views are arrayed in rows and columns. You can look at or change data in specific columns; therefore, SELECT and UPDATE permissions apply at the column level. Because you must INSERT or DELETE an entire row at a time, INSERT and DELETE are meaningless at the column level. Finally, you can use the data in a table (but not a view) to validate the integrity of data in another table; this corresponds to REFERENCES permission, which we discuss in great detail in Chapter 11. In addition to the five actions that you can take on the data of a table or view, there is one more permission that you can have: the permission to grant permission to others. This is called "WITH GRANT OPTION".◀

Stored procedures are simpler. The only thing you can grant to users is EXECUTE, which means they can run the procedure.◀

The Object Permissions Window

The rather cluttered user interface for object permissions comes from selecting Object⇨Permissions (Figure 7-13). By default, the By Object tab is selected, so the screen displays the permissions of the table or view in the drop-down list box. You can also click on the By User tab (Figure 7-14) to see all the permissions a specific user has. Let's start with the By Object tab, which is simpler. On the left, you see the same type of group/user interface that you saw for statement permissions: groups and users are listed together, with users indented. There are check boxes for each of the permissions, but REFERENCES is labeled DRI. If you want to go to the column level, you can check the Column Level Permissions box, and the columns of the table or view appear with SELECT and UPDATE check boxes. The most common action you will take on an object is to grant everything, so the Object

Permissions window conveniently has Grant All and Revoke All buttons; use these when you want to check or clear all the permission boxes.

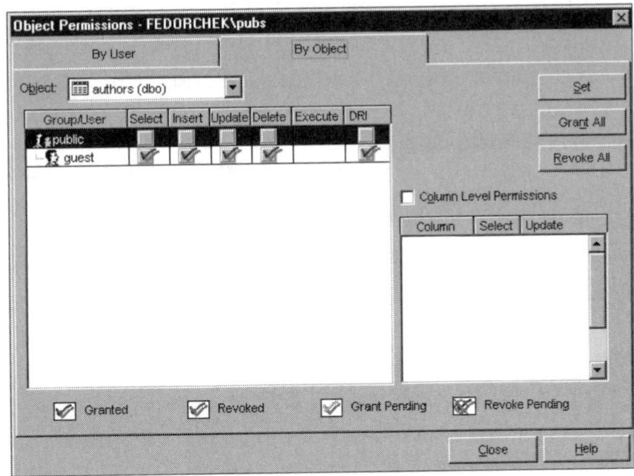

Figure 7-13:
Use the By Object tab of the Object Permissions window to see GRANTs by object.

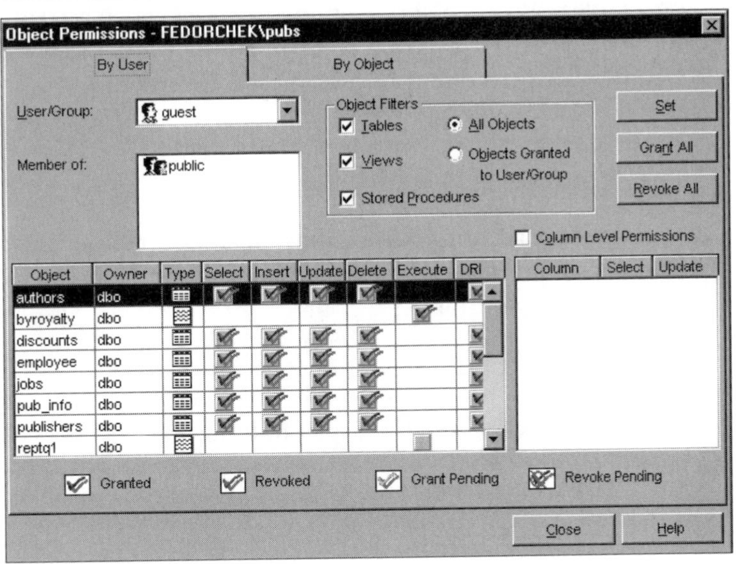

Figure 7-14:
Use the By User tab of the Object Permissions window to see GRANTs by user.

If you study the Object Permissions window carefully, you will notice something is missing. Where can you specify that you want to delegate grant authority? You can't. Microsoft stuffed the WITH GRANT OPTION capability into SQL Server for ANSI SQL-92 compatibility, but the feature didn't make it into the SQL Enterprise Manager. You must give WITH GRANT OPTION permission from Transact-SQL, which brings us to our next topic.

Object permission management from SQL

Object permissions are controlled by the GRANT and REVOKE commands, just like statement permissions. This time the syntax for GRANT is

```
GRANT {ALL [PRIVILEGES][column_list]
   | permission_list [column_list]}
ON {table_name [(column_list)]
   | view_name [(column_list)]
   | stored_procedure_name}
TO {PUBLIC | name_list }
[WITH GRANT OPTION]
```

The permission list can be any combination of SELECT, INSERT, UPDATE, DELELE, and REFERENCES when you are granting permissions on a tables. When you are granting permissions on a view, you can't use REFERENCES. If you want to grant all the permissions that apply, simply specify ALL instead of a permission list, for example:

```
GRANT ALL ON authors TO Dave, Lia WITH GRANT OPTION
GRANT INSERT, UPDATE ON employees TO PUBLIC
```

If you are granting permissions on specific columns, you can only use SELECT and UPDATE. For stored procedures the permission list must be EXECUTE, for example:

```
GRANT SELECT(password) ON syslogins TO Andrew
```

The syntax for REVOKE is as follows:

```
REVOKE [GRANT OPTION FOR]
   {ALL [PRIVILEGES] | permission_list } [(column_list)]
   ON { table_name [(column_list)]
   | view_name [(column_list)]
   | stored_procedure_name | extended_stored_procedure_name}
   FROM {PUBLIC | name_list}
   [CASCADE]
```

This is similar to the GRANT statement, with two key exceptions:

- In GRANT, you give the permission to grant by appending WITH GRANT OPTION to the GRANT statement. In REVOKE, you precede the permission list with GRANT OPTION FOR to revoke the authority to grant.
- REVOKE includes the CASCADE option, which allows you to revoke not only the privileges you granted but also the privileges that others GRANTED because you gave them WITH GRANT OPTION authority.

Here's an example. Suppose that Lia and Mark are users in pubs, and suppose neither currently has SELECT authority on authors.

```
GRANT SELECT ON authors TO Lia WITH GRANT OPTION
```

Lia can now SELECT from authors and give others the authority to do so.

```
GRANT SELECT ON authors TO Mark /* Lia is running this command */
```

If the dbo now runs this command:

```
REVOKE SELECT ON authors FROM Lia
```

Mark can still SELECT from authors. When the dbo uses the CASCADE option on the command above, Mark loses his SELECT authority.

Permission Chains

The last thing you need to know about object security is how permission chains work. Suppose you own object X, and you only want Sue to use that object. You GRANT her the permissions that you want her to have, and you do not use the WITH GRANT OPTION because you don't want her to delegate her authority. Sue might get tricky and realize that she can either create a view on your table or view or create a procedure that calls your procedure. Sue now owns her view or procedure, so she can grant permissions to others on her object, right? For example, Sue runs this SQL:

```
CREATE VIEW Sue.X AS SELECT * FROM dbo.X
GRANT SELECT ON Sue.X TO PUBLIC WITH GRANT OPTION
```

If this worked, object security would be a joke: anyone with CREATE VIEW or CREATE PROCEDURE statement permissions could delegate his or her object permissions to the world. Fortunately, SQL Server doesn't allow the security violation, *but it does let you run the SQL above.* The catch is when someone tries to access Sue.X. At run time, SQL Server checks the object permission chain: the sequence of objects being referenced and who owns them. SQL Server only allows the SQL to run if the owner granted access to each object to the executor of the query, either explicitly or implicitly. An object owner grants explicit permission with the GRANT statement. An owner grants implicit permission in a object chain if a sequence of objects referenced by the query is all owned by the same user. In that case, the user need only grant permissions on the object at the top of the chain. For example, suppose you own object Z, which depends on Y, which depends on X:

```
CREATE VIEW Y AS SELECT * FROM X
CREATE VIEW Z AS SELECT * FROM Y
GRANT SELECT ON Z TO PUBLIC
```

If someone queries Z they are really getting data from X, so the chain is Z-Y-X. Even though you granted no permissions on X or Y to anyone, queries against Z will work.

Summary

Security is controlling access to SQL Server and the databases inside it. You have three choices of modes for managing security in SQL Server: integrated, standard, and mixed. Integrated security ties you tightly to Windows NT and is the most rigorous. Standard security trades some rigor for more flexibility, and mixed security tries to offer the best of both worlds. The SQL Security Manager lets you map Windows NT groups and users to SQL Server groups and users. You can also add logins directly from the SQL Enterprise Manager or with Transact-SQL commands. Within databases you can give users statement and object-level permissions.

Review Questions

Q: What are the three security modes of SQL Server?

A: Integrated, standard, and mixed.

Q: Which one is put on your server during SQL Server setup?

A: Standard.

Q: How many groups can a SQL Server user be in? A Windows NT user?

A: A SQL Server user can be in one group per database. A Windows NT user can be in any number of groups.

Q: When you first install Windows NT, who on the network has system administrator access?

A: Everyone in the Administrators group of the domain.

Q: How many times can a user (not the system administrator) log in to SQL Server under standard security?

A: An unlimited number of times for all users.

Q: If you don't specify a default database, what is a user's default database?

A: Master.

Q: If a login isn't a user in master, why can the login see and use procedures in master?

A: Because master has a guest account.

Q: Can you remove guest from master?

A: No.

Part

III

TRANSACT-SQL

Throughout this book, we show you SQL Server's many wondrous capabilities. At each turn, however, we allude to the dialect of SQL that SQL Server supports — Transact-SQL (T-SQL). In this part, we cover the more interesting points of the language in great depth.

In Chapter 8, we introduce you to this powerful programming dialect. If you are familiar with T-SQL, you may want to skip this chapter.

In Chapter 9, we take you through the more advanced and useful features of T-SQL. We think that this chapter will be useful to even the most seasoned SQL Server user.

Chapter 10 gives you a perspective on where T-SQL fits with the rest of the SQL world. This chapter also attempts to glimpse into the likely future of the SQL language in general and T-SQL in particular.

We conclude this part with a chapter on the SQL Server system tables and procedures (Chapter 11). It is within these objects that the true power of SQL Server lies. This chapter is a must-read.

It is our hope that after this section of the book, you will possess enough knowledge to write some truly nifty SQL code.

Chapter

Getting Started with Transact-SQL

8

Transact-SQL is Microsoft's version of Structured Query Language (SQL). Because it's a programming language, it involves a command-line interface, some commands, and some syntax. And because it's a query language, it's primarily used for retrieving data from databases. The SQL Enterprise Manager is actually based on SQL commands, and you can run SQL from the Enterprise Manager, among other places. In this chapter, we get you started with the basics of using Transact-SQL.

What's in This Chapter

In this chapter we tell you:

- Where to edit and run your Transact-SQL
- How Transact-SQL is structured
- How to get started with querying

About SQL

SQL is all about working at a command prompt. The hard-core programmers among you, no doubt, are justifiably excited at this. We can promise that you will enjoy all the benefits you expect from a command-line interface, such as more control, faster execution, more flexibility, and so on. Nonprogrammers should not recoil, however. Although SQL is a programming language, it isn't nearly as difficult to learn as most others. It only takes a couple of commands to get a lot of information out of your database. Basic SQL is about as basic as using the DIR command in MS-DOS.

Although the original intent of SQL was for retrieving information from databases, it has gone beyond that. Now SQL is used to administer all facets of an RDBMS. Later in this book, we go into great detail about how to retrieve all kinds of data with SQL, but we leave the administration parts of SQL for the appropriate chapters in the rest of the book. Virtually everything that you do with the SQL Enterprise Manager has an equivalent in Transact-SQL. There are at least two reasons for this:

- The SQL Enterprise Manager is actually based on SQL commands. Microsoft uses their SQL Distributed Management Framework (SQL-DMF) to build applications, which means the SQL Enterprise Manager is based on Distributed Management Objects, which are in turn based on Transact-SQL.
- It would be a nightmare for application developers if SQL Server, Sybase, Oracle, and so on, each had its own syntax for common database tasks, such as creating and altering tables. It is in everyone's interest to have standards for these things, so some database administration commands were added to the SQL standard.

SQL isn't perfect of course — no language is. The original idea was that there would be a structure for nesting queries within queries, and the database would be smart enough to find the shortest path to your answer no matter how you wrote your query. That turned out to be quite a challenge for the software vendors, and they are still struggling with it. There are a number of limitations to SQL, and we will tell you what they are in the next few chapters.

By the way, SQL got started in 1972 and came from — you guessed it — IBM. Interestingly enough, according to E. F. Codd (the inventor of the relational database model) the language does not come from his work. He considers SQL inferior to some other relational languages that have been proposed.◀

Where to Edit and Run Transact-SQL

As every good author will tell you, the best way to learn is by doing, so before we launch into a Transact-SQL discussion, we'd better tell you where you can test the commands. Here are the places you can edit and run Transact-SQL:

- The Query Analyzer of the SQL Enterprise Manager, a text editor customized to make writing and executing Transact-SQL easy. This is the preferred place to run Transact-SQL commands because it offers the most flexibility.
- The ISQL/w standalone application. With minor differences that we will highlight, this is the same as the Query Analyzer window of the SQL Enterprise Manager. The only problem the ISQL/w is you don't have the rest of the SQL Enterprise Manager graphical tools available to you. The main reason to use this would be if you are working on a 16-bit client because in that case you cannot run the SQL Enterprise Manager. If you are reading this chapter and working with ISQL/w on a 16-bit client, you will have no trouble running any of the commands.◀

Cross-Reference

There are both 16-bit and 32-bit versions of ISQL/w. Refer to Chapter 5 for installation instructions.◀

- The ISQL.EXE command-prompt application. If you have to run SQL from this MS-DOS application and forgo all the benefits of graphical tools, we're sorry. The only good reason for using ISQL.EXE to process SQL is for batch files being run from the command, but with all the task scheduling of SQL Server 6.*x*, even that should not be necessary. Again, this tool has both 16-bit and 32-bit versions.
- The Manage Procedures, Manage Triggers, and Manage Views windows of the SQL Enterprise Manager. These windows are primarily for running the Transact-SQL commands associated with their objects and give some nice conveniences. However, they can actually be used to run most Transact-SQL commands (you could create a view in the Manage Triggers window, for example). The drawbacks of these windows are that they provide no output (which makes them useless for queries), and for some unknown reason, they lack such basic text editor features as Print, Find, and Replace.
- Any other tool that connects to SQL Server. (For example, MS-Query in the Microsoft Office Professional software set, or a programming language that makes calls to ODBC or DB-Library.) Some tools impose

restrictions on what you can do with Transact-SQL, such as limiting you to using only queries or to using only one command at a time. Give SQL Server's tools a try before you sink money into a third-party package. We have found that the SQL Server applications alone meet all our needs.

How Transact-SQL is Structured

We mentioned that Transact-SQL is a programming language. Why do we say this? Because in Transact-SQL you can

- Perform input and output functions
- Declare variables
- Control the flow of your program
- Modularize your program with functions (stored procedures in Transact-SQL)

These are all substantial improvements over the basic SQL-92 standard. With these features you can take chunks of business logic out of your program and run them solely in SQL.

Having said this, SQL is primarily for retrieving and manipulating data, and it is very powerful at that. The rest of this chapter is about unleashing that basic power. The biggest leap in using SQL is to think solely in terms of *tables*. Most SQL commands manipulate one or more tables to present a virtual table to the user.

Getting Started with Querying

A large part of SQL is about retrieving information from a database. The command for retrieving data is SELECT, and one complete SELECT command is called a SELECT statement. The SELECT statement has the following general structure:

```
SELECT parameters
   SUBCOMMAND parameters
   SUBCOMMAND parameters
   .
   .
   .
   SUBCOMMAND parameters
```

We start with the most critical subcommands and their essential parameters so that you can write queries after reading the next few paragraphs. Then, we expand into less used subcommands and more esoteric options and parameters.

Remember that when we query we are at a minimum demanding output from the database and optionally manipulating the data. In this vein, we cover the following:

- Bare-bones SELECT statements: requests for output
- WHERE clauses, which restrict the data
- Options for refining the format of the output
- GROUP BY and HAVING clauses, which further restrict the data

The simplest possible request for information is to ask for a complete listing of what is in a single table. This is sinfully easy in SQL, as it should be. You can follow along and do the examples with us, if you like.

Running a Query: The SELECT Statement

The syntax of the simplest possible SELECT statement, and the minimum number of subcommands you can use, is

```
SELECT * FROM table_name
```

The * means retrieve all columns. You execute this from the Query Analyzer window as follows:

1. Open the SQL Enterprise Manager.
2. In the Server Manager window, choose a server. Optionally, you can choose the database you want to run your query in.
3. Open the Query window (Figure 8-1) either by clicking the Query Analyzer toolbar button (shown here) or by selecting Tools⇨Query Analyzer.

4. Select the database you want from the DB drop-down list box. If you selected a database in step 2, it should already be selected in the list box.
5. Type in your query (for an example, see the next paragraph).

6. Click the Execute Query toolbar button (the green arrow) or press Ctrl-E or Alt-X (they all do the same thing). The Query window switches to the Results tab and displays your output.

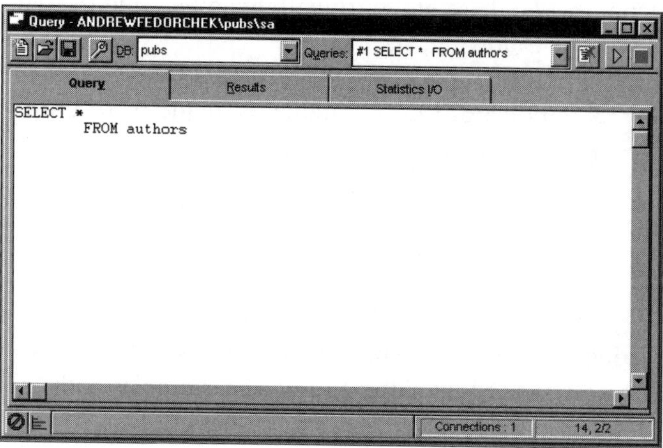

Figure 8-1:
Use the Query Analyzer to run all your Transact-SQL.

For example, to see what is in the authors table of the pubs database, you would open the Query Analyzer, choose pubs from the drop-down list box, and type

```
SELECT * FROM authors
```

Then, click the Execute Query toolbar button or press Ctrl+E.
Your output will be something like this:

```
au_id       au_lname
------------------------
172-32-1176 White
213-46-8915 Green
238-95-7766 Carson
267-41-2394 O'Leary
274-80-9391 Straight
341-22-1782 Smith
409-56-7008 Bennet
427-17-2319 Dull
472-27-2349 Gringlesby
486-29-1786 Locksley
527-72-3246 Greene
648-92-1872 Blotchet-Halls
```

```
672-71-3249 Yokomoto
712-45-1867 del Castillo
722-51-5454 DeFrance
724-08-9931 Stringer
724-80-9391 MacFeather
756-30-7391 Karsen
807-91-6654 Panteley
846-92-7186 Hunter
893-72-1158 McBadden
899-46-2035 Ringer
998-72-3567 Ringer

(23 row(s) affected)
```

(You'll have a bunch more columns off to the right that we don't have room for on this page.) Notice that the result of the SELECT looks like a table. This will be true of most SELECT statements. Whether the data gets printed in your Results tab or attached to a grid object of some programming language, the SELECT statement returns rows and columns.

Playing with queries

If you want to poke around, you can see the lists of available tables for you to query by expanding Objects⇨Tables under a given database in the Server Manager window.

Controlling the output of SELECT

When you run "SELECT * FROM table_name", you don't have any control over the output of the results at all. The data is in rows and columns, but you have no say over the order of your rows, nor the question of which rows and columns you want to see. Let's remedy some of that. We expand the basic syntax of a SELECT statement to look like this:

```
SELECT [column_name [, column_name2 [..., column_nameN]]]|*
   FROM table_name
   [ORDER BY column_nameA [, column_nameB [..., column_nameC]]]
```

The keyword SELECT identifies that what follows is a SELECT statement. The column names are whatever columns you want to see, in the order you want them. When you choose a subset of the total set of available columns, you create a *vertical partition*. You have no more control than that; you choose to see or not to see a column. It cannot be dynamically determined as the SELECT statement runs.

With rows, however, you have a lot more control — so much control that we save the discussion of what you can do with rows for the "WHERE CLAUSE".

The keyword FROM tells SQL Server from what table or view (a virtual table) the data originates. Finally, the keywords ORDER BY, followed by one or more columns, tell SQL Server which columns, in order, to use to sort the rows it returns. The rows will be sorted based on these columns using the installed sort order of your SQL Server. Therefore, case-sensitivity will be dependent on your server and is not something you can change or override with any SQL command. (We covered case-sensitivity in Chapter 1.)◀

If you wanted to see the last name and first names of all the authors in the *authors* table of the pubs databases, sorted by last name and first name, you would write:

```
SELECT au_lname, au_fname
   FROM authors
   ORDER BY au_lname, au_fname
```

This refines our main point that all you are doing is manipulating one table to make it look like another table. You now know how to manipulate a table such that you specify which columns you want, in what order the columns will be, and in what order the rows are listed.

General observations about SQL syntax

You may have typed the above example query exactly as you saw it here, but you actually have a lot of freedom in how you write your SQL commands. Here are a few points to keep in mind.

SQL commands are case-insensitive

This is true whether you choose a case-sensitive sort order for your SQL Server or not. We follow the Microsoft convention of putting the SQL commands in CAPITAL LETTERS in the text, but the authors query will work just fine as

```
select au_lname, au_fname
   from authors
   order by au_lname, au_fname
```

Note that if you choose a case-sensitive sort order, the case of the column and table names *does* matter. The following command will not work on a case-sensitive server:

```
SELECT AU_LNAME, AU_FNAME
   FROM AUTHORS
   ORDER BY AU_LNAME, AU_FNAME
```

If you run this query the result will be

```
Msg 208, Level 16, State 1
Invalid object name 'AUTHORS'.
```

because there is no such table in pubs named *AUTHORS*. The table is called *authors* if your server is case-sensitive.

SQL Server ignores white space

Keywords such as SELECT and FROM must be separated from one another and from other parts of the query by white space, which means one or more spaces '', tabs '\t', or new-line characters '\n'. We could write the authors query as

```
SELECT au_lname, au_fname FROM authors ORDER BY au_lname, au_fname
```

or we could write

```
SELECT
au_lname,
au_fname
FROM
authors          ORDER BY          au_lname,
au_fname
```

We format all the queries in this book for easy readability, but it makes no difference to SQL Server.

White space around commas is optional

In Transact-SQL, this is legal:

```
SELECT au_lname    ,    au_fname
   FROM authors
   ORDER BY au_lname    ,    au_fname
```

And so is this:

```
SELECT au_lname,au_fname
   FROM authors
   ORDER BY au_lname,au_fname
```

We usually put no space before a comma, and one space after, as in ordinary English usage.

The ORDER BY shortcut

Transact-SQL accepts the syntax

```
SELECT [column_name [[, column_name2 [..., column_nameN]]]|*
   FROM table_name
   [ORDER BY column_nameA|numA [, column_nameB|numB [..., column_nameC|numC]]]
```

Where *numX* is an integer referencing either the SELECT list column number when you list columns or the table column number when you use "“*”". Therefore we could write

```
SELECT au_lname, au_fname
   FROM authors
   ORDER BY 1, 2
```

To get the same ordering from a "‘SELECT *’", we need to know the au_lname and au_fname are the second and third columns of *authors*:

```
SELECT *
   FROM authors
   ORDER BY 2, 3
```

You don't have to use all numbers, you don't have to put them in order, and you can mix them with real column names. We could write

```
SELECT au_lname, au_fname
   FROM authors
   ORDER BY 2, 1
```

or

```
SELECT au_lname, au_fname
   FROM authors
   ORDER BY 2, au_lname
```

or just:

```
SELECT au_lname, au_fname
   FROM authors
   ORDER BY 2
```

However, the following will give you an error:

```
SELECT au_lname, au_fname
   FROM authors
   ORDER BY 3
```

There is no third column in the SELECT list, even though there is a third column in the *authors* table. Though using ORDER BY with numbers is a nice typing convenience, it is a bad programming practice. Someone can change the order of the columns in a view or even a table (by dropping and re-creating it), and your query will no longer do what it used to. Furthermore, it is easier to read and understand the code if you use names instead of numbers.

Descending sort order

All sorts are ascending (smallest to largest, A to Z), which is the default. You can reverse the sort order of any column by writing DESC after its name in the ORDER BY clause. For example:

```
SELECT au_lname, au_fname
   FROM authors
   ORDER BY au_fname DESC, au_lname
```

will order this list by the authors' first names in descending order.

You must specify DESC after each column name that you want to sort in descending order. You can have some columns sorted in ascending order and some in descending order. If you want to specify ascending order explicitly, use ASC, though we can't imagine a situation where you would use this.

Not all SELECT statements are equal

If you don't already know SQL, and even if you do, we encourage you to adhere to two rules in all SELECT statements you write, especially statements you put in anything that gets compiled (procedures, triggers, and views) and in application code.

1. Explicitly list the column names instead of using SELECT *.
2. Use ORDER BY columnNameA, ... columnNameN on all queries that will return more than one row, or enforce sorting in your application.

   We know it is a real nuisance to write

```
SELECT au_id, au_lname, au_fname, phone, address, city, state, zip, contract
   FROM authors
   ORDER BY au_lname, au_fname
```

when you can just write

```
SELECT *
   FROM authors
   ORDER BY au_lname, au_fname
```

This is a great convenience when you are typing in the SQL Enterprise Manager. It is *lousy* for use in any stored procedure, trigger, view, or application you might create.

The reason that "SELECT *" is dangerous is that you will be in trouble if anyone changes the structure of a table. The table owner might add new columns that you neither want nor need. This generally causes significant, if not fatal, errors. With views you have the opposite problem: the view doesn't include the new column unless you drop and re-create the view. This can lead to some hard-to-find bugs. Stored procedures also will not include the new columns — until they are recompiled. This recompilation can happen without warning, and SQL Server itself may trigger it; you don't have to be the one requesting a recompile. Thus, a procedure may quit working days after you changed a table. Triggers are a special kind of stored procedure, so they behave exactly the same way. At any rate, we'll say it again: Explicitly list the column names instead of using SELECT *.

Cross-Reference

We talk about tables, views, stored procedures, and triggers in Part IV.◀

Tip

The real trouble with typing out all the column names, of course, is doing all that darn typing! For a table with more than a few columns, you can save yourself a lot of work by first typing "SELECT * FROM table_name," switching to comma-separated output with headers, running and quickly canceling the query, and finally pasting the header list into the SELECT statement instead of the "*".◀

Now, onto that second rule (always using an ORDER BY statement on queries that will return more than one row). You always want to include an ORDER BY statement because even when a table doesn't change its structure, the default order in which rows return can change. For example, this query

```
SELECT au_lname, au_fname
   FROM authors
```

returns authors in what appears to be a random order. (They are actually coming back in the order in which they are physically stored on the disk, which is by au_id.) However, a smart database owner can and will sometimes rearrange the ordering on the disk to improve performance. Tomorrow, the table might be stored on disk sorted by name or by phone number. Always use the ORDER BY clause to protect yourself against changes like this.

The DISTINCT keyword: preserving uniqueness

In this book, we will work hard to convince you that the rows of your tables should be unique (meaning there are no duplicate rows). The same goes for the results of your SELECT statements. Ensuring that you return unique results forces you into the good habit of viewing all SELECT statements as new tables. In fact, you will see later how easy it is to put the results of a SELECT statement into a table.

The way to return a unique result set is to put the word DISTINCT before the column names in the SELECT list. For example, to see which states are represented by the authors in pubs, you would query

```
SELECT DISTINCT state
   FROM authors
   ORDER BY state
```

This query will list each state in authors only once, even when a state has several authors. Without the keyword distinct you would see the same states listed over and over again.

The WHERE Clause: Limiting Your Results

Let's switch now to the master database and run a slightly different query:

```
SELECT *
   FROM sysprocedures
```

You can switch databases simply by choosing another database in the DB drop-down list box (See Figure 8-1). When you run the query against the master..sysprocedures table, notice the row counter in the lower right-hand corner. It keeps going, and going, and going... . Press the Cancel Executing Query button (the red square to the right of the green arrow) or Alt-Break when you get bored. Notice that switching back to the Query tab does *not* stop the query execution. The spinning globe next to the query name in the Queries drop-down list box tells you it is still running.

This table is too large for you to retrieve all its data to your Query window and search through that window for the information you need. What you need is a way to limit the scope of the result set. This brings us to the next part of the SELECT statement, the WHERE clause.

The WHERE clause: basic syntax

Restricting the size of your result set, often called filtering, is done with a WHERE clause. This is yet another way of converting one table into another, but now we are creating what is called a horizontal partition. The basic syntax of a SELECT statement with a WHERE clause is

```
SELECT column_name [, column_name2 [..., column_nameN]]
   FROM table_name
   WHERE search_conditions
   [ORDER BY column_nameA [, column_nameB [..., column_nameC]]]
```

The search_conditions specify a test to be applied to each row of the new table. If the search_conditions are true for a given row, then SQL Server will include that row in what the SELECT statement returns. The search_conditions are always of the form:

```
[NOT] Boolean_expression1
[AND/OR [NOT] Boolean_expression2
[AND/OR [NOT] Boolean_expression3
.
.
.
[AND/OR [NOT] Boolean_expressionN
```

"Boolean_expression" can be any of a long and intimidating laundry list that we are going to cover piece by piece. Before we do that, however, let's start with the most common Boolean expression:

```
column_name = value
```

WHERE clause with a single condition

Suppose that the authors table actually had thousands and thousands of authors. If you are looking for a list of authors in Virginia, you could write

```
SELECT au_lname, au_fname
   FROM authors
   WHERE state = 'VA'
   ORDER BY au_lname, au_fname
```

This returns a more manageable set of data. Here are some key points about this simple WHERE clause:

For the sake of brevity, in this section we will often write the WHERE clause only. The rest of the query is understood to be the usual:

```
SELECT au_lname, au_fname
   FROM authors
   ORDER BY au_lname, au_fname
```

- The columns in your WHERE clause don't have to be in your SELECT list. Notice that in our example we filtered on state, even though we did not display state.
- It doesn't matter which expression is on the left side of the equality. You could run the query with:

  ```
  WHERE ''VA'' = state
  ```

  and get the same result.

- If you compare a column of a character datatype (Chapter 13) to a value, the value must be in quotes. It doesn't matter if you use single (") or double ("") quotes. However, later we are going to cover something called quoted identifiers, which will assign another meaning to the double quote (""). For this reason, you might want to stick to single quotes (").
- In a character value string, leading spaces are important; trailing spaces are not. If you are looking for authors whose last name is "Miller,"

```
WHERE au_lname = '  Miller'
```

returns nothing, whereas

```
WHERE au_lname = 'Miller  '
```

works. SQL Server automatically ignores trailing blanks in all string comparisons. This is not ANSI Standard behavior. If you want to make trailing blanks significant, use this command:

```
SET ANSI_PADDING ON
```

WHERE clause with multiple conditions

In the syntax of the WHERE clause, you can string together as many conditions as you need using AND and OR, like this (we've capitalized AND and OR in text for clarity, but not in our code because as you know, SQL is not case-sensitive):

```
WHERE state = 'VA'
      AND city = 'Arlington'
      AND zip = '22201'
```

or:

```
WHERE city = 'Fairfield'
      OR au_lname  = 'Hamilton'
      OR zip = '02021'
```

The AND and OR operators are used differently than they are in English when the same column is used twice. For example, if we want to find the authors who live in VA and the authors who live in NY, we would say

```
WHERE state = 'VA'
OR state = 'NY'
```

We wouldn't get any authors back if we said

```
WHERE state = 'VA'
AND state = 'NY'
```

because there aren't authors who live in both states.

Using parentheses to control order of evaluation

The fun begins when you have to mix AND, OR, and NOT. Suppose you are looking for an author and you know the following:

- The last name is Johnson or Jones or James (not much help there), and...
- The state *isn't* NY or CT, and...
- The city is Bridgeport.

If we look at the key words in these criteria, we have "Johnson or Jones or James and not NY or CT and Bridgeport." Suppose that there is only one name in authors that fits these criteria. When we naively write the query below that way and run it, we would probably get over a hundred names out of our imaginary authors table that has many thousands of rows. What is wrong?

```
SELECT au_lname, au_fname, city, state
   FROM authors
   WHERE au_lname = 'Johnson'
      OR au_lname = 'Jones'
      OR au_lname = 'James'
      AND NOT state = 'NY'
      OR state = 'CT'
      AND city = 'Bridgeport'
```

The problem is that AND and OR have equal precedence, and SQL Server evaluates them from left to right. Thus, the query above says in English "I want any rows where the last name is 'Johnson' *or* <some other stuff>." A row where the last name is Johnson *will* be in the result set no matter what else happens. What we needed here were some parentheses, as in

```
WHERE (au_lname = 'Johnson' OR au_lname = 'Jones' OR au_lname = 'James') AND …
```

Another problem is that the English phrase "not NY or CT" does not translate to:

```
WHERE NOT state = 'NY' OR state = 'CT'
```

When you say that aloud, there are implied parentheses around NY and CT. Thus, we should have written

```
WHERE NOT (state = 'NY' OR state = 'CT')
```

There are often times when you need to "distribute" the NOT and get rid of the parentheses. The rules to remember here are

```
NOT (expression1 AND expression2) = (NOT expression1 OR NOT expression2)
```

and

```
NOT (expression1 OR expression2) = (NOT expression1 AND NOT expression2)
```

With these considerations in mind, the correct query is

```
SELECT au_lname, au_fname, city, state
   FROM authors
   WHERE (au_lname = 'Johnson'
         OR au_lname = 'Jones'
         OR au_lname = 'James')
      AND NOT (state = 'NY'
         OR state = 'CT')
      AND city = 'Bridgeport'
```

Computed and Renamed Columns

Up until now, our result sets have always been subsets of columns in the original table. The select list (what comes between the keywords SELECT and FROM) can actually contain all of the following:

- The '*', which means all columns
- A list of columns (what we have been using so far)
- New headings (names) for your columns
- Expressions, which include concatenations of strings, functions, and subqueries (Chapter 9)◀

Giving new names to your columns

There are two ways SQL Server can rename the column you retrieve in a SELECT list. You can precede a column name with a string in quotes followed by '=':

```
'This is the new name' = column_name
```

or you can follow the column name with a string. When the string is not a valid SQL Server identifier it must be in quotes. You can optionally include the keyword AS between the column name and the new heading, but this is like the ASC option of ORDER BY: it is assumed if you leave it out, so there is no reason to include it.

```
column_name [AS] 'This is the new name'
column_name [AS] ThisIsTheNewName
```

For example, here is a query of authors that renames columns:

```
SELECT 'Social Security #' = au_id, au_lname 'Last Name',
      au_fname First, phone
   FROM authors
   WHERE au_lname > 'M'
   ORDER BY 'Last Name', First
```

Note

You'll notice three key things about this query. First, we can use all forms of renaming in one query. In fact, all of the select list items can be used in the same query. For example, this query is legal:

Tip

```
select *, zip, *
   from authors
```

Second, the WHERE clause uses the real column names, not the headings. If we had written the WHERE clause as:

```
'Last Name' > 'M'
```

the query would return no rows. This is because SQL Server interprets 'Last Name' as a literal string, and 'L' is not greater than 'M'. Finally, notice that in the ORDER BY statement you *can* use the column headings.

Using expressions

Cross-Reference

One of the great flexibilities of Transact-SQL is that you can use almost any kind of expression as a "column" in your queries. An expression includes constants, column names, functions, and subqueries. We reserve subqueries, which are queries within queries, for Chapter 9. Here we would like to discuss constants and functions.

Putting constants in a query

You can put constants, such as numeric or character data, in your SELECT statements. Therefore, you can write a query such as this:

```
SELECT 'The author is named', au_lname, ',', au_fname
   FROM authors
   WHERE state = 'UT'
   ORDER BY 2, 4
```

And your output will be (spaces deleted for brevity):

```
                    au_lname   au_fname state
-------------------------
The author is named Ringer    , Albert   UT
The author is named Ringer    , Anne     UT
```

Secret

At first this feature might seem to be of limited utility, until you realize that you can use literal strings in combination with the system tables to build database administration queries. We will use this idea extensively in the rest of the book. We are getting a little bit a head of ourselves by mentioning it now, but here's a quick example. Suppose you want to see the distinct values for every column of the authors. This is nine queries you have to write. It might be faster just to write this query:

```
SELECT 'SELECT DISTINCT', name, 'FROM authors ORDER BY 1'
   FROM syscolumns
   WHERE id = OBJECT_ID( 'authors' )
   ORDER BY name
```

Cross-Reference

We discuss the OBJECT_ID function in the "System Functions" section of this chapter; the syscolumns table is Chapter 11. For now just know that this query finds the names of the columns in the authors table so that the output is

```
               name
-----------------------------
SELECT DISTINCT address      FROM authors ORDER BY 1
SELECT DISTINCT au_fname     FROM authors ORDER BY 1
SELECT DISTINCT au_id        FROM authors ORDER BY 1
SELECT DISTINCT au_lname     FROM authors ORDER BY 1
SELECT DISTINCT city         FROM authors ORDER BY 1
SELECT DISTINCT contract     FROM authors ORDER BY 1
SELECT DISTINCT phone        FROM authors ORDER BY 1
SELECT DISTINCT state        FROM authors ORDER BY 1
SELECT DISTINCT zip          FROM authors ORDER BY 1
```

This happens to be exactly the set of queries you were going to write! Just cut and paste them from the results tab back into the query tab and run them. Notice that there is no column heading for the literal strings. You must use the renaming techniques provided earlier whenever you use constants or functions to ensure your output has the headers you want.

Using String Functions

If you have a database with a fair amount of character data, as we do, the string functions of Transact-SQL are invaluable. The string functions are +, ASCII, CHAR, CHARINDEX, DIFFERENCE, LOWER, LTRIM, PATINDEX, REPLICATE, REVERSE, RIGHT, RTRIM, SOUNDEX, SPACE, STR, STUFF, SUBSTRING, and UPPER. Below we examine the string functions we find most useful. In this section, we will use partial SELECT statements of the form SELECT select_list. We leave off the "FROM authors" for brevity.

Concatenation (+)

You can combine any number of columns and strings with the + operator: SELECT au_lname+', '+au_fname. This produces output like the following:

```
White, Johnson
Green, Marjorie
Carson, Cheryl
```

If you wrote SELECT au_lname, ',', au_fname instead, you would have less readable output:

```
White                                   , Johnson
Green                                   , Marjorie
Carson                                  , Cheryl
```

ASCII(char_expr)

This returns the ASCII value of the first character in char_expr. This is the only way you can differentiate by case in a case-insensitive environment. If your server has a case-insensitive sort order, the phrase WHERE column_name = 'A' will return all cases where column_name is 'A' or 'a'. To restrict column_name to just capital 'A' you must write WHERE ASCII(column_name) = 65.

CHAR(integer_expr)

This returns the ASCII character for integer_expr when integer_expr is between 0 and 255; otherwise, it returns null. We use this a lot to format queries. For example, instead of writing

```
SELECT 'SELECT DISTINCT', name, 'FROM authors ORDER BY 1'
   FROM syscolumns
   WHERE id = OBJECT_ID( 'authors' )
```

As we did above, we would usually write

```
SELECT 'SELECT DISTINCT', name,char(13)+char(9)+'FROM authors',
      char(13)+char(9)+'ORDER BY 1'
   FROM syscolumns
   WHERE id = OBJECT_ID( 'authors' )
```

This puts a return and a tab in front of the keywords FROM and ORDER BY. We could get the same effect by writing

```
SELECT 'SELECT DISTINCT', name,'

        FROM authors', '

        ORDER BY 1'

   FROM syscolumns
   WHERE id = OBJECT_ID( 'authors' )
```

However, we find this more difficult to read, both in this book and in the Query Analyzer.

STR (float_expr [, length [, decimal]])

This function converts a number to a string. You can use integers as well as have floating point numbers. This function will become important if you are transferring data out of SQL Server and into another RDBMS. The utility for doing this, BCP, which we discuss in Chapter 16, left-justifies all numbers. This creates problems for other systems, such as IBM's SQL/DS or DB2. You can force numbers to be right-justified by making a view with STR.◀

SUBSTRING (expression, start, length)

The last, and probably most important, string function that we will mention is substring. This lets you chop strings into smaller pieces. It is very convenient, but over use of SUBSTRING leads to bad database design (see Chapter 12) and poor query performance (see Chapter 29).◀

Using system functions

SQL Server tracks almost all objects in your database with integer tags. This is where you get object ids, user ids, column ids, and so on. The trouble with these ids is that whereas SQL Server can figure out in an instant that object id 16003088 is "authors" in your database, you have to write a complex query to figure out the same thing. To smooth this over SQL Server gives you system functions for converting an id to a name and vice versa. The system functions are COALESCE, COL_LENGTH, COL_NAME, DATALENGTH, DB_ID, DB_NAME, GETANSINULL, HOST_ID, HOST_NAME, IDENT_INCR, IDENT_SEED, INDEX_COL, ISNULL, NULLIF, OBJECT_ID, OBJECT_NAME, STATS_DATE, SUSER_ID, SUSER_NAME, USER_ID, and USER_NAME.

GROUP BY AND HAVING

So far, we have taken a table and created another table that was a subset of the first table in some way, shape, or form. What we haven't done is to summarize the data in the table in any way or add any new information. Now, we will. You can choose any subset of a table's columns and declare it to be a group. When you designate groups three things happen in the SELECT statement:

- You will see each distinct combination of the designated columns only once.
- You can add summary information about your groups to the SELECT list.
- You can limit your result set based on the summary information.

This summary information is supplied by Transact-SQL's *vector aggregate* functions, which are

- SUM(numericExpression)
- AVG(numericExpression)
- MIN(expression)
- MAX(expression)
- COUNT(expression), and
- COUNT(*)

The first two are for numeric data only and give you the sum or average of the expression, which may simply be a numeric column. The next two work on any expression and give you the minimum or maximum. COUNT(expression) counts the number of non-null values in the expression. COUNT(*) is a special way of saying "count the number of rows in the group." The general syntax of a SELECT statement, including the GROUP BY and HAVING, is

```
SELECT [ALL | DISTINCT] select_list
   [FROM table_name [, table_name2 [..., table_name16]]
   [WHERE clause]
   [GROUP BY clause]
   [HAVING clause]
   [ORDER BY clause]
```

The select list in this case must contain the same columns as the GROUP BY clause, plus any number of aggregate functions. The GROUP BY can contain expressions, including functions such as SUBSTRING. Notice that GROUP BY and HAVING precede the ORDER BY clause.

To illustrate the subtleties of GROUP BY and HAVING, let's make up some financial data for a table called financialData, shown in Table 8-1.

Table 8-1
Financial Data Illustrating GROUP BY and HAVING

Year	*Month*	*Profit*
1995	Sep	75
1995	Oct	-95
1995	Nov	50
1995	Dec	-35
1996	Jan	40
1996	Feb	110
1996	Mar	-10

Here is a sample query:

```
SELECT Year, SUM(Profit) SumP, AVG(Profit) AvgP, MIN(Profit) MinP, Max(Profit)
MaxP,
      COUNT(*) NumMonths
   FROM financialData
   GROUP BY Year
```

And the results:

```
Year      SumP      AvgP      MinP      MaxP      NumMonths
-----------------------------------
1995       -5        -1        -95        75          4
1996      140        46        -10       110          3
```

So in this query, we're grouping by year and doing a bunch of calculations on the rows in each year's group.

The difference between WHERE and HAVING

HAVING is similar to WHERE because they both restrict which rows go in the result table. The difference is that WHERE acts on rows and HAVING acts on groups, for example:

```
SELECT Year, SUM(Profit) SumP, AVG(Profit) AvgP, COUNT(*) NumMonths
   FROM financialData
   WHERE Profit > 0
   GROUP BY Year
```

says "Show us the total and average profits, by year, for the months that had a positive profit." The result is

```
Year        SumP        AvgP        NumMonths
----        ----        ----        ---------
1995        125         62          2
1996        150         75          2
```

This says that 1995 and 1996 both had two profitable months. From looking at the original data, you can see that these are September and November for 1995, and January and February for 1996.

On the other hand, this query:

```
SELECT Year, SUM(Profit) SumP, AVG(Profit) AvgP, COUNT(*) NumMonths
   FROM financialData
   GROUP BY Year
   HAVING SUM(Profit) > 0
```

says "Show us the total and average profits for the years that had a net profit." It returns

```
Year        SumP    AvgP    NumMonths
----        ----    ----    ---------
1996        140     46      3
```

because the sum of the monthly profits in 1995 was less than 0; it was -5.

CUBE and ROLLUP

If you have a sizeable amount of data, you will probably be interested in the higher level values of your aggregate functions, as well as the values for the entire table. Let's create a table named XYZ with the bland column names of X, Y, Z, and Quantity. (The choice of column names will become clear in a minute.) Suppose table XYZ has a lot of rows and you want to see the sum of the Quantity column grouped by X, Y, and Z. The query you will write is

```
SELECT X, Y, Z, 'Sum' = sum( Quantity )
   FROM XYZ
   GROUP BY X, Y, Z
   ORDER BY X, Y, Z
```

Your result will look like this:

```
X  Y  Z  Sum
-------------
X1 Y1 Z1 13
X1 Y1 Z2 17
X1 Y1 Z3 15
X1 Y2 Z1 33
X1 Y2 Z2 47
X1 Y2 Z3 15
X1 Y3 Z1 8
.
.
.
```

Understanding ROLLUP

In this case, the first set of higher level totals would be the total sum for X1, Y1, regardless of what Z is, then the total sum for X1, Y2, and so on. Finally, you could ask for the total sum for X1, regardless of what Y or Z is, the total for X2, and so on. The ROLLUP operator makes this possible. You simple append the phrase "WITH ROLLUP" to the end of the GROUP BY clause:

```
SELECT X, Y, Z, 'Sum' = sum( Quantity )
   FROM XYZ
   GROUP BY X, Y, Z WITH ROLLUP
   ORDER BY X, Y, Z
```

Now the results look like this:

```
X       Y       Z       Sum
------------------------
X1      Y1      Z1      13
X1      Y1      Z2      17
X1      Y1      Z3      15
X1      Y1      (null) 45
X1      Y2      Z1      33
.
.
.
X3      Y3      Z3      13
X3      Y3      (null) 92
X3      (null) (null) 232
(null) (null) (null) 696
```

SQL Server has calculated all the intermediate totals for you and listed them with nulls. Whereas the normal GROUP BY gave you the X,Y,Z totals, you now have X,Y totals; X totals, and the grand total.

Understanding CUBE

Having the ROLLUP totals is nice, you say, but what if you want to see the total for all of Z1, regardless of what X or Y are? You are treating this group of data as a cube, and you want to see totals along all axes. This is what CUBE is for. Simply replace "WITH ROLLUP" with "WITH CUBE" and you get all the output you got before, plus this:

```
(null) Y1       Z1      39
(null) Y1       Z2      51
(null) Y1       Z3      45
(null) Y1       (null) 135
(null) Y2       Z1      99
(null) Y2       Z2      141
(null) Y2       Z3      45
(null) Y2       (null) 285
(null) Y3       Z1      24
(null) Y3       Z2      213
(null) Y3       Z3      39
(null) Y3       (null) 276
X1      (null) Z1      54
X2      (null) Z1      54
X3      (null) Z1      54
(null) (null) Z1      162
```

(continued)

(continued)

```
X1      (null) Z2     135
X2      (null) Z2     135
X3      (null) Z2     135
(null) (null) Z2      405
X1      (null) Z3     43
X2      (null) Z3     43
X3      (null) Z3     43
(null) (null) Z3      129
```

You now have the higher level totals from every perspective: Y,Z totals; X,Z totals; Y totals, and Z totals. The importance of having SQL Server do these calculations is the performance gain. Prior to SQL Server 6.5, if you wanted these kinds of calculations, either you did them in your client application (a poor choice) or you wrote additional queries or stored procedures to get SQL Server to do the work. The problem with the addition queries, however, is that SQL Server is creating the same kinds of worktables over and over. CUBE lets SQL Server calculate all the desired results all in one shot.

Summary

Transact-SQL is the language you use to retrieve data. It is also the foundation of the SQL Enterprise Manager. You can run your SQL in a variety of applications; we like the Query Analyzer window of the SQL Enterprise Manager the best. The command for retrieving data is the SELECT statement. You can write a basic SELECT statement that simply returns all the data in a table with no effort at all. As you become more sophisticated, you will want to specify which columns the SELECT statement should return, as well as the ordering of the rows and columns. You can restrict which rows the SELECT statement retrieves with the WHERE clause. SELECT statements allow functions and other expressions instead of column names; if you use an expression, you should assign a name to the output column. The GROUP BY keyword collects data into groups, which allows you to use aggregate functions and the HAVING clause. The latest additions to the GROUP BY syntax are the CUBE and ROLLUP operators, which show higher level aggregations of data within one query.

REVIEW QUESTIONS

Q: What features does Transact-SQL have that qualify it as a programming language?

A: It has control of flow, variables, input and output, and stored procedures.

Q: What form does both the input and output of the SELECT statement take?

A: Tables.

Q: What kind of partitioning can you do with a SELECT statement?

A: Both vertical and horizontal partitioning.

Q: Can you rename a column in a SELECT statement to something that isn't a valid SQL Server identifier, such as "This has spaces in it"?

A: Yes, simply enclose the column header in quotes.

Q: Can you use column headers in WHERE clauses, GROUP BY clauses, or ORDER BY clauses?

A: You can only use them in ORDER BY clauses

Q: How do you concatenate strings in SQL Server?

A: Use the + operator.

Q: What is the difference between WHERE and HAVING?

A: WHERE acts on rows; HAVING acts on groups.

Q: Which command returns more data, CUBE or ROLLUP?

A: CUBE. The CUBE results are a superset of the ROLLUP results.

Chapter

MORE SQL!

9

In the last chapter, you learned the basics of using the SELECT statement to retrieve data. In this chapter, you'll learn about some of the more advanced aspects of Transact-SQL (TSQL), and we'll give you some ideas on where to use them. This chapter is not an all-encompassing reference for Transact-SQL. Microsoft ships one of those with SQL Server 6.5. Instead, you should think of this chapter as an extension of Microsoft's Transact-SQL Reference. By the time you are done with this chapter, you will be well on your way to becoming a Transact-SQL guru.

WHAT'S IN THIS CHAPTER

In this chapter you will learn

- Some of the niftier things you can do with the SELECT statement
- What a subquery is and how to use it
- How to correctly use outer joins
- The Transact SQL control flow statements
- The basics of transactions

SELECTED AGAIN!

You already know the basics of using the SELECT statement, but there are many more features of this command. Here, we introduce you to COMPUTE BY, SELECT INTO, outer joins, subqueries and search conditions, and unions.

Printing summary rows with COMPUTE BY

The COMPUTE BY clause allows you to group and aggregate data as well as print separate total lines. For example, let's say you wanted to see a report based on the employees table shown in Table 9-1 that identified all the employees grouped by years of service and you also wanted to see the average salary for each year.

Table 9-1
Employees Table

Id_no	*Full_Name*	*Salary*	*Years*
1	John Osborn	100,000	10
2	Clare Mansfield	50,000	7
3	Amy Pederson	100,000	10
4	Darah Whelihan	35,000	1
5	Andrew Fedorchek	30,000	1
6	Dave Rensin	30,000	1

A simple *SELECT* from employees* would then yield the following:

```
id_no       full_name         salary          years
-----       ---------------   ----------      -----
1           John Osborn       100,000.00       10
2           Clare Mansfield   50,000.00        7
3           Amy Pederson      100,000.00       10
4           Darah Whelihan    35,000.00        1
5           Andrew Fedorchek  30,000.00        1
6           Dave Rensin       30,000.00        1
```

Unfortunately, this output isn't of much use. Luckily for you, SQL Server gives you some other choices in formatting your output. One of the most intriguing involves the use of the COMPUTE BY clause. The SQL for outputting the average salary for employees by number of years of service would look like this:

```
SELECT * FROM employees
ORDER BY years ASC, full_name ASC
COMPUTE avg(salary) BY years
```

The first line retrieves all the data from the table, the second line orders it, and the last line computes the average salary for each year of service. The resulting output looks like this:

```
id_no      full_name            salary              years
-----      ----------------     ---------           -----
5          Andrew Fedorchek     30,000.00           1
4          Darah Whelihan       35,000.00           1
6          Dave Rensin          30,000.00           1

                                avg
                                ==========================
                                31,666.67

id_no      full_name            salary              years
-----      ----------------     ---------           -----
2          Clare Mansfield      50,000.00           7

                                avg
                                ==========================
                                50,000.00

id_no      full_name            salary              years
-----      ----------------     ----------          -----
3          Amy Pederson         100,000.00          10
1          John Osborn          100,000.00          10

                                avg
                                ==========================
                                100,000.00
```

The COMPUTE BY clause allows a user to print aggregated summary information for subgroups of the table data. Each resultant calculation appears on a separate line. The syntax for this clause is

```
COMPUTE aggregate(columnA)[,aggregate(columnN)] [BY column1[,columnN]]
```

where *aggregate* is one of five functions (SUM, AVG, MIN, MAX, and COUNT).

The *BY* part of the clause is optional. If you omit it, the aggregates will not be grouped and will print after the data. If you do choose to use the BY part of the clause, though, there are a few restrictions:

- The use of BY in a COMPUTE clause requires the use of an ORDER BY clause in the SELECT statement.
- The columns in the COMPUTE BY section must be in the same order as the columns in the ORDER BY clause.
- You may not skip any columns, unless they are at the end. For example, if the SELECT statement contains ORDER BY a, b, c then you can specify columns a, b, and c; a and b; or just *a* in the COMPUTE BY clause.

The following output shows the effect of running the previous query without using the BY part of the COMPUTE BY clause:

```
id_no        full_name             salary               years
-----        -------------------   -----------          ------
5            Andrew Fedorchek      30,000.00            1
4            Darah Whelihan        35,000.00            1
6            Dave Rensin           30,000.00            1
2            Clare Mansfield       50,000.00            7
3            Amy Pederson          100,000.00           10
1            John Osborn           100,000.00           10

                                   avg
                                   ==========================
                                   57,500.00
```

Creating tables with SELECT INTO

One of the niftiest SQL extensions in Transact-SQL is the SELECT INTO clause. Using this statement will allow you to create and populate a new table without having to create it first using the CREATE TABLE command. For example, if you wanted to make an identical copy of the *employees* table to a new table named *new_table*, you would use the following command:

```
SELECT * INTO new_table FROM employees
```

This will create a new table named *new_table* that will have the same structure as *employees*, as well as the same data.

Cross-Reference

One of the things SELECT INTO will not do is re-establish any primary keys (Chapter 13), indexes (Chapter 13), or triggers (Chapter 14). You will be able to get a complete copy of the data, but not of any of the constraints. SELECT INTO will, however, re-create identity columns.

When using the SELECT INTO statement, you should be aware of a few things. First, you can create three types of tables: permanent, local temporary, and global temporary. You create a local temporary table by beginning its name with a hash (#). Global temporary tables are created by beginning their names with two hashes (##).

Cross-Reference

Second, you cannot create a permanent table with SELECT INTO unless the select into/bulk copy option (Chapter 6) is enabled for the database.◀

Cross-Reference

Finally, the SELECT INTO statement will re-create identity columns (Chapter 13) as long as the following conditions are met:

- The SELECT statement does not contain a join, GROUP BY clause, or aggregate function (MIN, MAX, AVG, SUM, COUNT, and so on).
- You don't use a UNION expression. (More on UNIONs later.)
- The identity column is not listed more than once in the column list.
- The identity column is not part of an expression.◀

Let's look at a practical example using SELECT INTO. The following code creates a stored procedure named copy_table that creates a new table identical to a preexisting one. The syntax for the routine is copy_table source, dest.

Cross-Reference

If you don't know how to create a stored procedure, you should see Chapter 14.◀

Warning

Please be careful when typing in this procedure. When we first wrote it, we did not include parentheses in the execute line. Without them, execute tries to run the contents of @sql_statement as if it were a variable holding the name of a stored procedure. This caused our server to work until it ran out of memory and had to be restarted. We duplicated it three more times just to be sure:

```
create procedure copy_table
@src_table char(255), @dest_table char(255)
as

   declare @sql_statement char(255)

   select @sql_statement = 'SELECT * INTO ' + rtrim(@dest_table) +        ' FROM '
   + rtrim(@src_table)
   execute (@sql_statement)

GO
```

◀

CD-ROM

Before we continue any further, we need to clarify a few things. First, you should *always* put comments and error checking in your stored procedures and triggers. That having been said, you are probably wondering why we don't have such things in the last example. The answer is simple: When we put those things in, they double the size of the code. That's fine if you are writing routines so that other people can maintain them but lousy if you are trying to give an example. All the code that ships on the companion CD-ROM is correctly commented and contains the appropriate error checking.◀

Outer joins are your friends

In this section, we are going to explain a useful little concept called an *outer join*. For the purposes of explanation, we are going to add another table to the employees table. It is called phone_messages and will hold the telephone messages for each employee. The structure and data of phone_messages is shown in Table 9-2.

Table 9-2
The Phone Messages Table

id_no	message_no	message_text
1	1	Bill Called
1	2	Joe Called
1	3	Paul Called
2	4	Mark Called
2	5	Jane Called
3	6	Annette Called
3	7	Barbara Called
4	8	Joanne Called
4	9	Lia Called
4	10	Cheryl Called

Let's assume that you want to see a list of all of the employees and their phone messages. You would probably use a SQL statement like the following:

```
SELECT full_name, message_text
FROM employees e, phone_messages p
WHERE e.id_no = p.id_no
```

This generates the following output:

```
full_name           message_text
---------------     --------------
John Osborn         Bill Called
John Osborn         Joe Called
John Osborn         Paul Called
Clare Mansfield     Mark Called
Clare Mansfield     Jane Called
Amy Pederson        Annette Called
Amy Pederson        Barbara Called
Darah Whelihan      Joanne Called
Darah Whelihan      Lia Called
Darah Whelihan      Cheryl Called
```

There's a problem here, though. Not all of the employees are listed. This is because employees with no messages have no rows in the phone_messages table and, therefore, will not show up with this kind of query, called a *natural join*. A natural join shows all rows that have matches in both tables. For this example, we want a way to show all employees, whether or not they have any phone messages. You do this with an outer join.

An outer join returns all rows from one table, even if they do not have corresponding rows in the related table. Missing values are displayed as nulls. There are two types of outer joins: a *left outer join* and a *right outer join*. A left outer join means that the table on the left-hand side of the equals sign (=) returns all rows, including ones that do not occur in the table on the right-hand side of the expression. A right outer join is just the opposite.

In Transact-SQL, outer joins are typically expressed with either the *= symbol (for left outer joins) or the =* symbol (for right outer joins). With this in mind, the previous SQL should be written as:

```
SELECT full_name, message_text
FROM employees e, phone_messages p
WHERE e.id_no *= p.id_no
```

This generates the following output:

```
full_name           message_text
---------------     --------------
John Osborn         Bill Called
John Osborn         Joe Called
John Osborn         Paul Called
Clare Mansfield     Mark Called
```

(continued)

(continued)

```
Clare Mansfield     Jane Called
Amy Pederson        Annette Called
Amy Pederson        Barbara Called
Darah Whelihan      Joanne Called
Darah Whelihan      Lia Called
Darah Whelihan      Cheryl Called
Andrew Fedorchek    (null)
Dave Rensin         (null)
```

As you might suspect, outer joins operate under a few constraints:

Cross-Reference

- You cannot perform an outer join on text or image columns (Chapter 13).◄
- Bit columns cannot contain null values, so they will show up as zero.
- Null values in joining columns will never match each other.

SQL-92 outer joins

Cross-Reference

As many of you probably know, there is an industry standard for SQL called *SQL-92,* published by the American National Standards Institute (ANSI). This standard is an attempt to unify the many SQL dialects implemented by various database vendors. We will cover the SQL-92 standard in greater detail in Chapter 10. For now, all you need to know is that Microsoft has enhanced the capabilities of Transact-SQL language to meet this standard. Part of this enhancement was to add SQL-92 ways of implementing joins, which we'll look at here. ◄

Inner joins

An *inner join* retrieves records from two tables where a certain set of criteria are met. The old way of doing an inner join in T-SQL looks something like this:

```
SELECT emp.firstname, emp.lastname, div.name
FROM div, emp
WHERE div.div_id = emp.div_id
```

The SQL-92 standard, however, specifies that the join conditions are part of the FROM clause. You specify the two tables you're joining, and you use an ON clause to specify which columns must match to join the tables. If there's a matching column name in both tables and that column is the column you're joining by, you can just specify that column name in the ON clause. Therefore, the last query in SQL-92 (and SQL Server 6.5 syntax) would be

```
SELECT emp.firstname, emp.lastname, div.name
FROM div JOIN emp ON div_id
```

Left and right outer joins

A little earlier in this chapter, you learned how to perform left and right outer joins using the *= and =* operators. In this section, you learn how to perform the same operations with SQL Server 6.5's new join syntax.

The following code is the original example used in this chapter to demonstrate the left outer join:

```
SELECT full_name, message_text
FROM employees e, phone_messages p
WHERE e.id_no *= p.id_no
```

This same code written in the new join syntax is as follows:

```
SELECT full_name, message_text
FROM employees left outer join phone_messages
  ON id_
```

Once again, please note that the join condition has moved from the WHERE clause to the FROM clause.

Full outer joins

Assume, for the moment, that you have two tables: a and b. Also, assume that there are rows in both tables that correlate to each other. If you wanted a list of all records from a that included correlating records from b, you would use an outer join, for example:

```
SELECT * FROM a,b WHERE a.id *= b.id
```

Alternately, if you wanted a list of all records from b that included any correlating values from a, you would code the following:

```
SELECT * FROM a,b WHERE a.id =* b.id
```

However, what if you wanted all records from both a and b, including any correlating values? In previous versions of TSQL, you would have to use a UNION (we discuss UNION later in this chapter). For example:

```
SELECT * FROM a,b WHERE a.id *= b.id
UNION
SELECT * FROM a,b WHERE a.id =* b.id
```

If you use the SQL-92–style joins, you can use a new type of join operator called a *full outer join*. The syntax for this is as follows:

```
SELECT * FROM a FULL OUTER JOIN  b On id
```

As you can see, this is quite a savings in code and improves readability.

Design problems?

Should you find yourself in the position where a full outer join is your only solution for a query, you may have a poorly designed table scheme. The effects of a full outer join can often be duplicated with a better set of table designs and a simpler query. For example, assume the following:

You have two tables: english and math. english holds the names, GPAs, and IDs of all the students in a particular English class, while math holds the same information for a particular math class. You can retrieve all the students from both classes with a full outer join:

```
SELECT * FROM english JOIN math ON id
```

In truth, however, this is not a good table design. A better way to do this is to have two different tables. The first would be called students and would hold the names and IDs of students in the school. The second table would be called classes and would hold the student ID, class name, and GPA (or grades) for each of the students in their respective class. If you want a list of all the students in both the Math and English classes, you simply use the following.

```
SELECT s.name
FROM students s JOIN classes c ON id
WHERE c.name in ('math', 'english')

SELECT s.name FROM students s, classes c
    WHERE s.id = c.id and
        c.name IN ('math', 'english')
```

This query, although longer than the first, runs faster for large tables than its predecessor. This set of table structures, although not nearly optimal, is better than the older version because it's more flexible. Don't believe us? Okay, how would you get a complete list of all students in the school from the first set of tables? The answer is that you still need a full outer join. This may seem fine now, but what happens when you have 100 classes? You would need to write a 100-way full outer join. That's a lot of SQL!

With the second set of tables, you can always get a complete list of students with a simple SELECT statement. It doesn't matter how many classes you add.

Tip

The SQL-92 join syntax represents a big change if you're used to the old T-SQL–style of doing things. In some cases, like a simple inner join, the older style will be easier to use and read. In others, like the full outer join, the new style is greatly preferred. Which style you use is completely up to you. We recommend that you begin to get used to the new style of joins as it is likely to become more common. In the meantime, however, there is one thing you absolutely *must* remember: you *cannot* mix old- and new-style joins in the same SQL statement.◀

Subqueries and search conditions

Joins are nifty, no doubt about it. The true power of the SELECT statement, (and SQL in general), comes, however, from the capability to use subqueries and search conditions. In the next few sections, we will discuss these things and how to make effective use of them.

Subqueries

Joins are not the only way to relate data in SQL Server. You can also use something called a *subquery*. A subquery is a SELECT statement that is nested within an expression that returns TRUE or FALSE. Subqueries are most commonly found in WHERE and HAVING clauses.

A short example should help.

Consider the employees and phone_messages tables. Let's say you wanted a list of the employees who had phone messages, but you did not want duplicate rows. You would have two choices. You first option is to construct a SQL statement that looks like the following:

```
SELECT DISTINCT full_name
FROM employees e, phone_messages p
WHERE e.id_no = p.id_no.
```

Your second option, however, is to construct your SQL with a subquery:

```
SELECT full_name
FROM employees e
WHERE e.id_no IN
    (SELECT p.id_no
     FROM phone_messages)
```

In this example, we used a second SELECT statement in the middle of our WHERE clause. This is an example of a simple subquery. In this instance, you are probably better off with the first set of SQL because it will use indexes and, therefore, be faster. There are, however, cases when a subquery is the only way to get the data you need. For example, assume that you have another table named other_employees that holds information about employees in another division. Also, assume that you want a list of employees from the employees table who make more than all of the employees in the other_employees table. You cannot get this with a regular set of joins. You must use a subquery. The following SQL shows you how:

```
SELECT full_name
FROM employees e
WHERE e.salary > (SELECT max(o.salary) FROM other_employees o)
```

Another nice feature of subqueries is that they can be nested as deep as you need. For example, you can have something like:

```
SELECT field1
FROM a
WHERE a.field2 IN
    (SELECT b.field2
     FROM b
     WHERE b.field3 IN
        (SELECT c.field3
         from c))
```

Search conditions

SQL Server provides a number of useful conditional operators that help you construct flexible queries. In this section, we will go over these items and give you examples of how to use each.

AND

This operator combines two conditional expressions into a single expression. The combined expression is TRUE when both expressions are TRUE, otherwise, it's FALSE.

For example:

```
SELECT *
FROM a
WHERE a.col1 = 1 AND
    a.col2 = 'Dave'
```

This code selects all rows from a where column 1 has a value of 1 and column 2 has a value of dave.

ALL

This conditional returns TRUE when *all* the values to its left meet some condition with respect to all the values to its right. For example:

```
SELECT *
FROM a
WHERE a.col1 > ALL
    (SELECT b.col1
     FROM b)
```

This code returns all rows from a where the value in column 1 is greater than *all* the values of column 1 in table b.

ANY

This item is similar to the ALL operator except that it says to compare to ANY value in the subquery. For example:

```
SELECT *
FROM a
WHERE a.col1 > ANY
    (SELECT b.col1
     FROM b)
```

This code returns all rows from a where the value in column 1 is greater than any the values of column 1 in table b.

BETWEEN

This operator tests to see if the value to the left falls between the values to its right. For example:

```
SELECT *
FROM a
WHERE col1 BETWEEN col2 AND col3
```

This code retrieves rows from table a where the value of column 1 is in between the values of columns 2 and 3.

The use of the BETWEEN clause is logically synonymous to the use of the >= and <= operators. In other words, the phrase *a between b and c* is equivalent to *a* >= *b and a* <= *c*. So “5 BETWEEN 3 AND 10” is TRUE, as is “5 BETWEEN 5 AND 5”.◄

EXISTS

This operator is TRUE if the query to its right returns any rows. Here's a simple example:

```
if EXISTS (SELECT * FROM employees) print "There are records."
```

When used in a SELECT statement, however, it is often used like this:

```
SELECT *
FROM a
WHERE EXISTS
    (SELECT b.col1
     FROM b
     WHERE b.col1 = a.col1)
```

When used in this way, the EXISTS operator acts much the same as the IN operator.

IN

This operator evaluates to TRUE when the value on the left is contained in the list on the right. A simple example would be something like this:

```
SELECT a_name FROM authors WHERE home_state IN ('MD','VA','CA')
```

This code returns the names of those authors who live in either Maryland, Virginia, or California. A more common usage of the IN predicate, however, is demonstrated by the following:

```
SELECT *
FROM employees e
WHERE e.id_no IN
    (SELECT p.id_no
     FROM phone_messages)
```

In this context, the IN predicate is acting identically to the EXISTS predicate, except that the outer queries table is not referenced in the subquery, as in the EXISTS example. In just a minute, we will discuss the merits of using EXISTS versus IN.

IS [NOT] NULL

As you might expect, this condition checks to see if the expression to its left is null.

You can also use the construct "= NULL" to check for null values. Here's a quick example:

```
SELECT * FROM employees WHERE salary is not null
```

LIKE

This operator performs a match of an expression on the left with a pattern on the right. The patterns are formed from the SQL-Server – supported wildcards. You can use this item with char, varchar, and datetime data. Table 9-3 shows the SQL Server wildcards and their functions. Note that the LIKE operator, like the rest of the string operators, will have different behavior depending on the case-sensitivity of your server.

Table 9-3
SQL Server Wildcards

Wildcard	*Function*
%	Matches any string of characters. For example, when used with LIKE, 'abc%' will match any string that starts with *abc*; '%abc' will match any string that ends with the letters *abc*. '%abc%' will match any string that contains the substring 'abc' .
_ (Underscore)	Matches any single character. The pattern '_at' will match *cat*, *hat*, *rat*, and so on.
[ ]	Matches any single character within a range or set. For example, '[a-q]' will match any character that is between *a* and *q* while '[art]' will only match the characters *a*, *r*, and *t*.
[^]	Matches any single character *not* within a range or set. For example, '[^a-q]' will match any character that is not in the range *a-q*.

Examples

Here are some examples of how to apply these items in your searches.

This query will return the names 'Thomson', 'Thames', 'Thimmly', and so on:

```
SELECT au_lname FROM authors WHERE au_lname like 'th_m%'
```

This next example will only retrieve messages that begin with the letters "a" through "z":

```
SELECT message_text
FROM phone_messages
WHERE message_text like '[a-z]%'
```

This example will return names that do not begin with "c":

```
SELECT au_lname FROM authors WHERE au_lname LIKE '[^c%]'
```

Alternately, you can write it this way:

```
SELECT au_lname FROM authors WHERE au_lname NOT LIKE 'c%'
```

EXISTS versus IN

As we mentioned earlier, the EXISTS and IN operators can often be used interchangeably. Given this, you might wonder which you ought to use. Our answer to this is emphatic: Use EXISTS! We say this because constructing your syntax with the EXISTS predicate will cause SQL Server to return data several times faster than with the IN clause. As the number of rows returned by the subquery grows, this difference will become more acute. A quick look at both syntaxes should explain why.

Here is a simple example of the IN clause:

```
SELECT * from employees e
WHERE e.id_no IN
    (SELECT p.id_no
     FROM phone_messages)
```

First, SQL Server will process the subquery. In this case, it will have to retrieve all the rows in the phone_messages table. If this table is very large, this process could take a while. Next, SQL Server must compare each id_no value in the employees table to the set of values returned from the subquery. It is doing all of this with brute force. In other words, SQL Server has no opportunity to take advantage of any indexes you may have on your tables.

Now, look at the same code written with the EXISTS predicate:

```
SELECT * from employees e
WHERE exists
    (SELECT p.id_no
     FROM phone_messages p
     WHERE p.id_no = e.id_no)
```

Once again, SQL Server will process the subquery first. This time, however, it can use any indexes you may have on the respective id_no columns. This means that the subquery results will come back a lot quicker. It is because of this added efficiency that we highly recommend that you use the EXISTS syntax wherever possible.

Unions

There will be times when you want to combine sets of data that do not necessarily relate or that have no common key. When this happens, you need to use a UNION. The UNION operator combines the results of two SELECT statements into one final result set. The general form for a UNION is as follows:

```
SELECT select_list [INTO clause]
    [FROM clause]
    [WHERE clause]
    [GROUP BY clause]
    [HAVING clause]
[UNION [ALL]
SELECT select_list
    [FROM clause]
    [WHERE clause]
    [GROUP BY clause]
    [HAVING clause]...]
[ORDER BY clause]
[COMPUTE clause]
```

You have seen all of these parameters before, except for the UNION [ALL] clause. The following scenario is an example of when a UNION is appropriate. Previously, we defined a table named employees to hold data about employees in one division and another table named other_employees to hold data about employees in another division. If, for example, you wanted a complete list of all employees in both divisions, you would use the following SQL:

```
SELECT * FROM employees
UNION
SELECT * FROM other_employees
```

UNION ALL

Normally, when SQL Server constructs the result set from a UNION, it discards duplicate rows. If you do not want SQL Server to do this, you need to use the UNION ALL clause. The advantage to doing this is that SQL Server will not have to spend processing time on discarding duplicate rows. For this reason, you *always* want to use the UNION ALL clause when you are dealing with sets of data that will never intersect. An example is the employees and other_employees tables. Because it is not possible for one person to be working in two divisions at the same time, you can say that the two tables hold sets of data that never intersect. For this reason, you would want to use the UNION ALL statement as follows:

```
SELECT * FROM employees
UNION ALL
SELECT * FROM other_employess
```

UNION rules and behavior

There are a few additional things to keep in mind when using the UNION operator:

- If you want to place your result set into a new table, you need only include the INTO clause with the first SELECT statement.
- If you try to UNION two columns that have incompatible data types, SQL Server will return an error.
- If you attempt to UNION two char or binary columns that are defined with different lengths, SQL Server will define the result column to be the size of the larger of the two.
- If you UNION two varbinary or varchar columns, SQL Server will create the result column with a length equal to the longest entry in both sets.
- Both SELECT statements must return the same number of columns. This is because the result of the UNION is still a table with a fixed number of columns.
- Note that the column names don't have to match, and this can be very advantagious when dealing with two tables with similar, but not identical, structures.

Bitwise Operators

SQL Server supports four bitwise operators. A *bitwise operator* is a mathematical symbol used to perform calculations on numbers at the binary level. The four supported functions are

- &: AND
- |: OR
- ^: Exclusive OR
- ~: NOT

For the next few examples, assume that A = 17 and B = 11.

&: AND

The bitwise AND operator returns TRUE if both bits are set to 1. Otherwise, it returns FALSE. If we apply the bitwise AND operator to A and B, we get the following:

```
(A & B)
10001 - 17
01011 - 11
----------
00001 - 1
```

In other words, this query will return the value 1:

```
select 11 & 17
```

|: OR

The bitwise *OR* operator returns TRUE if one or both bits are set to 1. Otherwise, it returnsFALSE. If we apply the OR operator to A and B, we get the following:

```
(A | B)
10001 - 17
01011 - 11
----------
11011 - 27
```

^: Exclusive OR

The bitwise Exclusive OR (XOR) operator returns TRUE if only one bit is set to 1. If both or none of the bits are set to 1, it returns FALSE. If we apply the XOR operator to A and B, we get the following:

```
(A ^ B)
10001 - 17
01011 - 11
----------
11010 - 26
```

~: NOT

The NOT operator switches the bits in a single value. ~1 = 0. NOT only takes one operand, for example:

```
~A
10001 - 17
----------
01110 - 14
```

Controlling the Flow of Execution

SQL Server provides several programming mechanisms to control the flow of execution in your programs. In this section, we will review them and explain how they are used.

BEGIN...END

A single SQL command is called a *statement*. A group of related statements is a *block*. Each statement block must begin with the BEGIN statement and end with the END statement. For example, this following is a valid statement block:

```
BEGIN
    select * from a
    select * from b
    select * from c
END
```

If you have programmed in C, then you can consider the BEGIN and END statements to be equivalent to curly braces "{ }."◀

IF...ELSE

Perhaps the most well-known set of flow-control statements in all of programming is the IF...ELSE group. In SQL Server, the general form of this set is as follows:

```
IF expression
    sql_statement | statement block
```

```
ELSE
    sql_statement | statement block
```

The following is an example of this sequence.

```
IF @myVar > 0
    BEGIN
        UPDATE myTable SET someValue = @myVar
        PRINT 'myVar was greater than zero.'
    END
ELSE
    PRINT 'myVar was less than or equal to zero.'
```

WAITFOR

The *WAITFOR* statement causes SQL Server to wait for a certain delay or until a certain time is reached. The syntax for this statement is

```
WAITFOR {DELAY 'time' | TIME 'time'}
```

The *TIME* identifier tells SQL Server to wait until a specific time has come, while the *DELAY* identifier tells SQL Server to wait for a certain delay. For example, the following line will wait until 11:59:00 pm before continuing the script:

```
WAITFOR TIME '23:59:99'
```

You can use any valid time format for the argument to the WAITFOR clause (see your SQL Server companion documentation for a list of valid time formats).◀

WHILE

The WHILE construct is another very famous flow-control statement. In SQL Server, the WHILE loop takes on the following form:

```
WHILE expression
    sql_statement | statement_block
    [BREAK]
    sql_statement | statement_block
    [CONTINUE]
```

The BREAK statement causes the loop to exit, and the CONTINUE statement causes control to jump back to the start for the next set. The following code demonstrates a basic WHILE loop:

```
DECLARE @ctr int

SELECT @ctr = 1000

WHILE @ctr > 0
    SELECT @ctr = @ctr - 1

PRINT 'finished loop'
```

This next example demonstrates a more complicated loop with the use of both the BREAK and CONTINUE statements:

```
DECLARE @ctr int

SELECT @ctr = 1000

WHILE @ctr > 0
    BEGIN
        SELECT @ctr = @ctr - 1

        IF @ctr = 50
            CONTINUE

        IF @ctr = 1
            BREAK
    END

PRINT 'finished loop'
```

CASE

Another nice addition to SQL Server 6.5 is an ANSI SQL-92–compliant CASE expression. The CASE statement is used to evaluate a set of related alternatives and return a value. If you are programmer, this behavior is a little different than what you might expect. In many languages, the CASE statement, or its counterpart, evaluates an expression and then performs an action.

In Transact-SQL, however, CASE is an expression, not a statement. Therefore, it can only return a value.

The CASE statement comes in two flavors: *simple* and *searched*.

The simple CASE expression

The simple CASE expression evaluates a possible set of values for the same expression. Its format is as follows:

```
CASE expression
    WHEN expression1 THEN return1
    [[WHEN expression2 THEN return2] [...]]
    [ELSE expressionN]
END
```

In this syntax, *expression* is evaluated, and its result value is compared against *expression1, expression2, ... expression*N. If, for example, the result value matches *expression1*, *return1* is returned. The following is a quick example of this form:

```
DECLARE @nVal int, @textName char(15)

SELECT @nVal = 1

SELECT @textName =
    CASE @nVal
        when 0 then 'Zero'
        when 1 then 'One'
        when 2 then 'Two'
        else 'Greater Than Two'
    END
```

In this example, *if @nVal* is zero, then *@textVal* is set to 'Zero'. This comparison repeats for 1 and 2, and finally returns 'Greater Than Two' if it cannot match *@nVal* to any of the comparison values. Of course, you can see that the result will clearly be "One."

The searched CASE expression

The searched CASE expression tries to match several Boolean (true/false) expressions and return the appropriate value. The general form of this is the following:

```
CASE
    WHEN Boolean_expression1 THEN expression1
    [[WHEN Boolean_expression2 THEN expression2] [...]]
    [ELSE expressionN]
END
```

This form of the CASE expression is very similar to using multiple IF statements. The following is an example of using this form:

```
declare @nVal int, @textName char(20)

select @nVal = col1
from some_table
where some_column = another_column

select @textName =
    case
        when @nval < 0 then 'Less Than Zero'
        when @nval between 0 and 3 then '0-3'
        when @nval between 4 and 7 then '4-7'
        else 'Greater Than Seven'
    end
```

Simple verus searched CASE expressions

Our rule of thumb for the use of the CASE expression is that you should use the simple form when possible and the searched form only when needed. We're not saying that there is anything wrong with the searched form. We just think that the simple form is easier to read.

A good example of when you absolutely cannot use the simple form of the CASE expression is the previous code snippet. You could not have written that code as the following:

```
select @textName =
    case @nval
        when < 0 then 'Less Than Zero'
        when between 0 and 3 then '0-3'
        when between 4 and 7 then '4-7'
        else 'Greater Than Seven'
    end
```

Therefore, you have to use the searched form when you need to evaluate a set of Boolean expressions.

A CASE for every case

The CASE expression can be used *anywhere* an expression is called for. This means that you can apply it in UPDATE statements, as well. The following example gives a raise to employees based on the number of years they have been with the company:

```
update employees
    set salary =
        case
            when years between 0 and 2 then salary * 1.3
            when years between 3 and 5 then salary * 1.5
            when years between 5 and 7 then salary * 1.75
            else salary * 2
        end
```

Transactions

All SQL Server actions are performed within the context of an item called a *transaction*. A transaction is the smallest unit of work known to SQL Server and can be either implicit or explicit.

For example, the following SQL is actually executed via three transactions, one for each statement:

```
select * from a
select * from b
select * from c
```

These transactions are *implicit* because they are generated by the system and hidden from the user.

You can, however, define your own transactions to encapsulate several otherwise-independent SQL statements into a single unit of work. These are known as *explicit* transactions. Explicit transactions are created with the use of the BEGIN TRANSACTION and COMMIT TRANSACTION statements. For example, the set of SQL statements can be contained in a single transaction, like so:

```
begin transaction
select * from a
select * from b
select * from c
end transaction
```

The value of being able to declare a user-defined transaction is that you can commit or cancel your changes in stages. As you may have guessed, the COMMIT TRANSACTION statement commits your changes to the database. Also, if any of the statements in the block fail, the *entire* transaction is rolled back.

Rollback transaction

If, however, you have not committed a change to your database and want to cancel it, you can do so by using the ROLLBACK TRANSACTION statement. Consider the following scenario. You want to perform a set of actions against one table and then want to check to see if those changes have had the desired effect. If they have, you want to commit the changes permanently; otherwise, you want to cancel them. The following pseudocode shows this basic process:

```
begin transaction
...
some SQL statements
...
if (some validation condition) then
    commit transaction
else
    rollback transaction
```

This process of change and validation is the single biggest reason why you might use an explicit transaction.

Another reason that you might want to encapsulate some code in an explicit transaction is to guarantee the consistency of certain data for a given period of time. Consider the following situation.

You are writing some SQL that changes the values in a certain column to 1. Somewhere later in the SQL, you perform some other operation against the table that assumes that those values in that column are still 1. If you are operating in a multiuser environment, this is not necessarily a valid assumption. After all, some other process may have changed the values in that column.

There are two possible solutions to this problem. First, you could explicitly check the value of the column each time you are about to perform the critical operation. This will guarantee that you are not making any false assumptions. The problem with this, of course, is that it will mean extra code and time for the process.

The other solution is to put the code that changes the column values and the code that assumes the changes in the same explicit transaction. By doing this, you can guarantee that you will have a lock on those values for the duration of the process. The biggest problem with this method is that very large transactions can choke SQL Server and cause it to run out of memory. As a matter of fact, we have done this before. We once wrote a stored procedure that executed all of its code within a single transaction. We did this to guarantee that certain changes we made earlier in the procedure would still be valid later. When we tested the procedure it worked fine. Later, however, as more users began to use the system, we found that we were running out of memory. The problem turned out to be that many people were trying to run the procedure at the same time and were choking the system. We finally decided to bite the bullet and put in all the extra code to do the data checking throughout our procedure and break the code up into several smaller transactions.

Additional transaction rules

There are few statements that you cannot use with an explicit transaction. They are

- ALTER DATABASE
- DISK INIT
- LOAD TRANSACTION
- CREATE DATABASE
- DROP *<objname>*
- RECONFIGURE
- CREATE INDEX
- DUMP TRANSACTION
- SELECT INTO
- CREATE PROCEDURE
- GRANT or REVOKE
- TRUNCATE TABLE
- CREATE TABLE
- LOAD DATABASE
- UPDATE STATISTICS
- CREATE VIEW

The other important thing to remember about transactions is that any remote procedure calls made within a transaction cannot be rolled back with the ROLLBACK TRANSACTION statement.

Summary

In this chapter, you learned some more advanced concepts of Transact-SQL, such as subqueries, searched case expressions, bitwise operators, and outer joins. This, however, has certainly *not* been an exhaustive look at all the capabilities of Transact-SQL. For that, we refer you to your SQL Server manuals. The point here was to explore some of its more important concepts and expose you to some of the often overlooked capabilities of the language.

Review Questions

Q: Will the SELECT INTO statement re-create primary keys or indexes?

A: No.

Q: Under what circumstances will the SELECT INTO statement not properly create identity values?

A: When any of the following occurs:

- The SELECT statement contains a join, GROUP BY clause, or aggregate function.
- Multiple SELECT statements are joined with UNION.
- The identity column is listed more than once in the column list.
- The identity column is part of an expression.

Q: What's the biggest difference between T-SQL joins and SQL-92 joins?

A: SQL-92 joins are specified in the FROM clause, while T-SQL joins are set in the WHERE clause.

Q: When are full outer joins necessary?

A: In our opinion, never. In our view, the absolute need for a full outer join usually denotes a problem with the table design.

Q: What is the atomic unit of work in SQL Server?

A: The transaction.

Q: How do you undo the actions of a particular transaction?

A: Issue a rollback.

Q: What does the following expression return? (10 & 2) | 3

A: 3

Chapter 10

ANSI SQL VERSUS TRANSACT-SQL

In the last chapter, we introduced ANSI SQL-92, the set of standards for SQL published by the American National Standards Institute (ANSI), an attempt to unify the various dialects of SQL implemented by various vendors. The SQL Server 6.5 manuals claim that Transact-SQL "has been enhanced to meet American National Standards Institute (ANSI) SQL-92 standards," but this does *not* mean that Transact-SQL has been certified as ANSI SQL-92 – compliant; it just means that Transact-SQL has been further enhanced to meet the specifications of the standard. In this chapter, we cover the differences between ANSI SQL and Transact-SQL, and what keeps Transact-SQL from being truly ANSI SQL-92 – compliant.

WHAT'S IN THIS CHAPTER

In this chapter, you learn about the differences between ANSI SQL-92 and Microsoft Transact-SQL, including

- Data types and conversion mechanisms
- Concepts of ordering a relational system
- Terminology
- Table column alterations
- Data retrieval

We also tell you where we think ANSI SQL-92 is superior to Transact-SQL and vice versa and give a look at what's ahead beyond SQL-92.

Note

Before we begin, we have a confession to make. When we first outlined this book, we wanted a chapter comparing Transact-SQL with the ANSI SQL-92 standard, but we hadn't done a feature-by-feature comparison. We reasoned that this kind of comparison would help you understand where Transact-SQL fits in the database world and would make learning other SQL dialects easier. We expected to find that Transact-SQL was a far more extended implementation of the ANSI standard, providing greater functionality. Boy, were we in for a surprise! What we found is that, by and large, ANSI SQL-92 is a broader specification of the SQL language and that vendors are trying to catch up.◀

Because of the greater general sophistication of the ANSI SQL-92 standard, this chapter focuses on features of that standard as an illustration of where we think database vendors, including Microsoft, will be going. In other words, this chapter looks toward the future of Microsoft SQL Server and all other SQL-based DBMSs. It is our hope that, after you have finished this chapter, you will have a better understanding of where the database world and its major players are headed in the next few years.

A Quick History

Cross-Reference

As we note in Chapter 8, SQL started in the 1970s at IBM. Actually, the language was first named SEQUEL, which stood for *Structured English Query Language*. (This is no doubt why the acronym SQL is commonly pronounced "sequel.") By the time IBM introduced its first product that used SQL (SQL/DS, in 1981), other database vendors were in the process of building their own implementations. As a matter of fact, the first product to market that used SQL was by a little company named Relational Software, Inc. That little company is now Oracle!◀

In 1983 IBM introduced the first version of its incredibly successful DB2 product. The popularity of this product solidified SQL as the standard on which all database vendors would eventually settle.

In the 1986 the American National Standards Institute (ANSI) published its first standard for the SQL language, SQL-86. Three years later, it published a moderately updated version, SQL-89. By this time, however, database vendors were already going full steam ahead with their own implementations of SQL.

You may be wondering why the ANSI SQL-86 and SQL-89 standards are at all important. The reason is simple. One of the biggest complaints in the computer industry is that every vendor has its own implementation. Over the years, though, vendors have sought to avoid this problem by building their products to be compliant with the relevant ANSI standards. Actually, the usual strategy is to build an ANSI-compliant product and then add a bunch of enhancements and extensions.

Remember, compliance with a standard means that it will be easier to implement a given language on different platforms. That's a *huge* selling point for a language. (Go to any software store and look at the boxes for the C compilers. We guarantee that you will find a reference to ANSI compliance on every product!)

A bad standard is worse than no standard

Standards are a good and worthwhile thing, as long as they are complete. Unfortunately, the SQL-86 and SQL-89 standards were far from complete. For example, SQL-89 provided no way for a user or database owner to alter the structure of a database once it was defined. That's right, there was no way to create a new table once a database had been established. Obviously, the leading DBMS vendors found the standard to be less than useful for commercial applications.

As a result, software makers went their own way. This is one of the principal reasons that SQL implementations vary so greatly among database products. The other reason, of course, is that a new and exciting language extension is just one more feature that makes product A better than product B. Therefore, the incentive is for the software makers to extend their languages as far as possible, which pretty much describes the state of the world until 1992.

Going 100 miles an hour — in the wrong direction!

In 1992, the rules of the game changed. In the old days, vendors could count on the fact that an ANSI standard would be a least-common-denominator approach to defining a language. ANSI SQL-92 broke that tradition in a big way. Not only did it include functions necessary for a commercial implementation, but it also extended the language in directions that the database vendors never thought would happen.

ANSI SQL compliance went, in one fell swoop, from being a bare minimum for a DBMS, to being a long-term goal. The new standard added such things as new data types, support for dynamic SQL execution, Remote Data Access (RDA), and new set and join operators. To this day, most vendors are still trying to implement all of these features. Microsoft is no exception.

In the following sections we cover some of the features of ANSI SQL-92 that are not yet implemented, or implemented fully, in Transact-SQL.

Data Types

The SQL-92 standard defines some data types and conversion mechanisms that are not included or fully implemented in Microsoft SQL Server.

Bit varying (varbit) and bit(n)

SQL Server and SQL-92 both define a data type called *bit*. A variable of this type can only hold either a zero or a 1. SQL-92, however, goes a step further and lets you define the *bit* field to be of a given length so that you can store several bit values, for example:

```
DECLARE myVar as bit(4)
SELECT myVar = CAST ('0110' as bit(4))
```

This code creates a new variable named *myVar* that holds a string of four bits. Considering the number of fields in the SQL Server system tables that store strings of bits as integers, this data type would be a logical, although not necessarily beneficial, future addition to Transact-SQL.

SQL is the standard language for the relational database model. To this end, it has continually expanded its referential capabilities. However, the inclusion of a *bit* data type that can have a width greater than one seems, to us, to encourage non-relational behavior. In other words, the inclusion of this data type would seem to imply a tacit approval for the technique of storing multiple values in a single field by turning certain bits off and on. This is a curious little contradiction, as performing such operations would greatly subvert the intentions of the first normal form and would, therefore, serve to undermine one of the cornerstone principles of SQL.◀

SQL-92 also defines a new data type called *bit varying* or *varbit*. This type allows you to store a series of bits of an arbitrary length. This is analogous to the *char varying* or *varchar* types in Transact-SQL.

Dates, times, and intervals

In SQL Server, dates and times are treated as discrete units. In other words, SQL Server is equipped to store and manipulate values that represent single moments in time. In this respect, Transact-SQL and SQL-92 are very similar. In fact, other than a couple of syntax differences, the two implementations are almost identical. There are, however, two important differences that deserve to be highlighted. SQL-92 allows date values to have a range from January 1, 0001 to December 31, 9999. Transact-SQL, however, only allows for a range of January 1, 1753 to December 31, 9999. Why does Transact-SQL have this restriction? We don't know. It just does.

The second difference is that SQL-92 defines a data type called *Time With Timezone*. This data type allows you to store explicitly what time zone the value is from. It does this by storing, along with the time value, a time-zone value expressed as an offset from Universal Coordinated Time (UCT).

UCT (previously known as Greenwich Mean Time or GMT) is used internationally as a common measure for the earth's time. All places on earth are designated as having a specific offset from UCT time. The East Coast of the United States, for example, has an offset of UCT – 5. Therefore, twelve o'clock noon in New York is actually 12:00:00 p.m., UCT – 5. Why have a UCT time at all? The reason is simple: if there were no standard mechanism for determining time, the process would be left to each individual community and would therefore be subject to political constraints. For example, the time in Nepal is always 15 minutes different than the time in India. Nepal does this as a sign of political independence and freedom. This is yet another example of when a standard is a good thing.◀

With the exception of these discrepancies, SQL-92 and Transact-SQL operate in very similar fashions on data that represents a discrete moment in time. SQL-92, however, extends its treatment of dates and time to include a new data type: the *interval*. The interval data type is used to represent a period or length of time. For example, in SQL-92, the subtraction of one date from another yields a result that is an interval. In this scheme, interval values come in two forms: *year-month* and *day-time*. In other words, you can express an interval in terms of years and months or days and time. You cannot, however, express an interval in terms of years, months, days, and time. You also cannot mix year-month and day-time intervals in the same expression.

National characters

Another area where SQL-92 is further along than Transact-SQL is in the treatment of international character sets and data. In SQL-92 (but not Transact SQL), you can define the columns of your table to hold characters from different character sets. For example, you can use the following statement to create a table that holds three types of characters:

```
CREATE TABLE myTable (
    col1 char (30) CHARACTER SET ENGLISH,
    col2 char (30) CHARACTER SET HEBREW,
    col3 char (30) CHARACTER SET FRENCH
)
```

The table *myTable* can now hold data for Hebrew, French, and English characters. This specification of character type can be used anywhere a character is defined. For example, the following code defines a user-defined-type called *french_name*.

```
CREATE DOMAIN french_name character (30) character set FRENCH;
```

As you might expect, SQL-92 also provides a mechanism whereby you can translate between different character sets. This is accomplished with the TRANSLATE function. Assume that you have a column named *english_col* that holds text in the English character set. If you wanted to display that column and its equivalent Hebrew value, you could use the following code:

```
SELECT english_col, TRANSLATE (english_col USING HEBREW)
FROM myTable
```

The differences between SQL-92 and Transact-SQL, however, are not just confined to subtle differences in data. There is a general disagreement between the two on how to order a relational system more generally. The next section discusses this.

A Different View of the World

SQL-92 defines a certain hierarchy for the relational world. According to this model, *databases* contain *catalogs*. *Catalogs* contain *schemas,* and *schemas* contain *tables.*

The SQL Server model, however, is similar but less flexible. It says that *servers* contain *databases*. Though SQL Server doesn't usually refer to it this way, you can view *databases* as containing *users* that contain *tables*. (All your SQL Server manuals will say simply that *databases* contain *tables* that are owned by *users*.) Table 10-1 compares the terminology of Transact-SQL with that of ANSI SQL-92, from the top of the hierarchy to the bottom.

Table 10-1
Data Hierarchies in SQL Server and ANSI SQL-92

SQL Server	*ANSI SQL-92*
servers	databases
databases	catalogs
users	schemas
tables	tables

The relationship between these two models is a lot easier to understand if you approach it from the bottom up.

Tables

There's not much to say here. The SQL 92 view of tables and the Transact SQL view of tables are very similar. We just promised you that we would start from the bottom up!

Schemas

SQL Server 6.5 follows the old SQL-86 and SQL-89 standards, which say that a *schema* is an identifier that lets users create their own tables without fear of using the same name as someone else. The identifier is the username, so the schema is basically synonymous with the user. The trouble with this is that users are stuck with only one identifier, their name. In SQL-92, however, a schema is associated with an *authorization identifier* (user), but a given user can have multiple schemas. In other words, a SQL 92 schema is an abstract umbrella that keeps table names unique. The important thing to remember here is that a user can own multiple schemas. This is not the case in Transact SQL.

Note that although SQL Server 6.5 includes a CREATE SCHEMA command for "ANSI compliance," it has not actually complied with the standard at all. SQL Server's command is

```
CREATE SCHEMA AUTHORIZATION OWNER [schema_element]
```

The ANSI standard is

```
CREATE SCHEMA schema_name AUTHORIZATION OWNER [schema_element]
```

In SQL Server, you can't give a name to a schema, which was the whole point of introducing schemas in SQL-92.

Another interesting difference between the two implementations is what happens when a schema is dropped. In SQL Server, you can't drop a user who owns tables, which is a double limitation:

- You can't drop a whole schema in SQL Server. You have to drop the objects of a schema one by one. Remember that a schema here is the same as a user.
- In SQL Server, if you want to drop users, you must drop their schemas. You can't transfer ownership of schemas.

In SQL-92, however, you have a lot of choices. First of all, you can drop a schema. If you use the CASCADE clause when issuing a DROP SCHEMA statement, you will not only drop the named schema and its data but also delete any other objects in any other schemas that reference any objects in the schema being dropped. SQL-92 also gives you the option of dropping your schemas in a safer manner by using the RESTRICT clause. When this option is used, a particular schema will only be dropped if all of its tables and data have first been deleted.

Catalogs

In SQL-92, collections of schemas are held in larger entities known as *catalogs*. Each catalog has a specific schema called the INFORMATION_SCHEMA. This schema holds the definitions for all other the schemas in the catalog. Here's where it gets confusing. A SQL Server *database* is equivalent to a SQL-92 *catalog*. The SQL Server database catalog is equivalent to the SQL-92 INFORMATION_SCHEMA.

Databases

In SQL-92, related groups of catalogs are held in a larger collection called a *database*. This is analogous to the SQL Server *server*.

Confusing, isn't it?

The differences between the two models would probably be a lot easier to articulate if it were not for the contradictory meaning of the term *database*. In spite of this, it is probably reasonable to assume that Microsoft will implement the true schema functionality in future versions of SQL Server.

Table Column Alterations

In Transact-SQL, you are limited in the ways that you can alter a table once you have created it. You can add columns to a table with the ALTER TABLE statement, but you have no means with which to alter or drop individual columns from the table. SQL-92, however, contains provisions in the ALTER TABLE statement to allow the user to alter the definition of a column or drop it altogether. Assume the following table exists in a DBMS that is ANSI SQL-92–compliant.

Server_Machines

machine_name char(30)	building char(10)	room_number char(4)	dba_name char(50)

The following SQL will, in SQL-92,

1. Alter machine_name to be 50 characters in length.
2. Drop the column building:

```
ALTER TABLE server_machines
    ALTER COLUMN machine_name character(50)
ALTER TABLE server_machines
    DROP COLUMN building
```

Data Retrieval Differences

Without a doubt, the largest degree of difference between Transact-SQL and SQL-92 exists in the area of data retrieval. In general, SQL-92 provides a greater array of methods for constructing queries. In Transact-SQL these queries require more complex logic or multiple statements. This section will highlight some of the more important distinctions.

Row value constructors

In Transact-SQL, operations and comparisons are performed on individual values and columns. The SQL-92 standard, however, allows most of these operations to be performed on a parenthesized set of values known as a *row value constructor*.

For example, in Transact-SQL, a query that compares multiple columns needs to be written as follows:

```
SELECT a.first_name, b.book_title
FROM authors a, books b
WHERE a.au_id = b.au_id AND
   a.publisher = b.publisher
```

This query can get pretty complicated as the number of columns to compare increases. The addition of row value constructors, however, allows the previous example to be written much more simply in SQL-92:

```
SELECT a.first_name, b.book_title
FROM authors a, books b
WHERE (a.au_id, a.publisher) = (b.au_id, b.publisher)
```

In our opinion, this feature is just plain cool! It is an even greater convenience when you need to compare columns and sort them in dictionary order. Here's the Transact-SQL:

```
SELECT a.first_name, b.book_title
FROM authors a, books b
WHERE (a.au_id < b.au_id) OR
   ((a.au_id = b.au_id) AND (a.publisher < b.publisher))
```

In SQL-92 this is simply:

```
SELECT a.first_name, b.book_title
FROM authors a, books b
WHERE (a.au_id, a.publisher) < (b.au_id, b.publisher)
```

Set operators and predicates

As mentioned earlier, the relational data model is the product of the practical application of mathematical set theory to conventional database systems. In this section, we will briefly explore some of the set operators and predicates that are defined in SQL-92, but do not yet exist in Transact-SQL.

INTERSECT

One of the most basic operations in set theory is to find the elements that any two sets share. This subset is called the *intersection* and is illustrated in Figure 10-1.

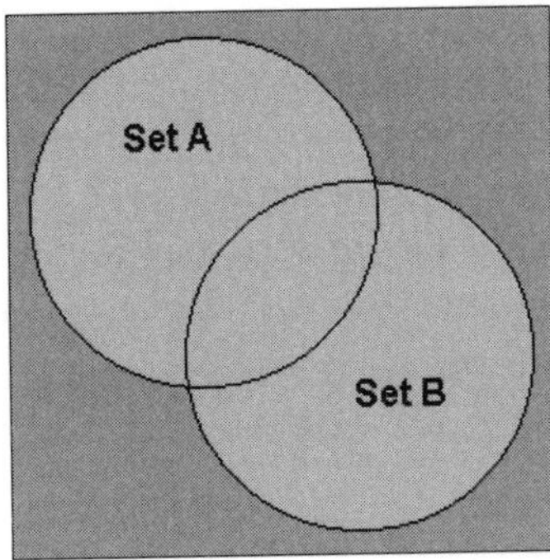

Figure 10-1:
This is a simple intersection.

To that end, SQL-92 defines an operator named INTERSECTION that computes the relevant shared values of any two sets of data. For example, the following will produce all rows that exist both in table *a* and table *b*:

```
SELECT * from a
INTERSECT
SELECT * from b
```

By default, this will use all columns in *a* and *b* with the same name for the comparison. You can also specify which columns are relevant to the intersection by using the CORRESPONDING BY clause:

```
SELECT * from a
INTERSECT CORRESPONDING BY (col1, col2, col3)
SELECT * from b
```

In Transact-SQL, you can only get this with a join:

```
SELECT a.*, b.*
   FROM A, B
   WHERE A.col1 = B.col1
      AND A.col2 = B.col2
      AND A.col3 = B.col3
```

EXCEPT

SQL-92 also defines another extremely useful operator called EXCEPT. The purpose of this keyword is to allow the user to determine all rows from a table that do not exist in another table. For example, the following code returns rows from A that do not exist in B:

```
SELECT * from a
EXCEPT
SELECT * from b
```

As with the INTERSECTION operator, EXCEPT uses same-name columns by default. It also can be used with a CORRESPONDING BY clause to specifically enumerate the fields to be compared

```
SELECT * from a
EXCEPT CORRESPONDING BY (col1, col2, col3)
SELECT * from b
```

This is really hard to do in Transact-SQL; in fact, we find that very few people know the correct way to phrase the query. The correct syntax is

```
SELECT *
   FROM A
   WHERE NOT EXISTS (SELECT *
         FROM B
         WHERE A.col1 = B.col1
            AND A.col2 = B.col2
            AND A.col3 = B.col3)
```

OVERLAPS

As we mentioned earlier, SQL-92 contains several more features with which to store and manipulate date and time data than does Transact-SQL. Among the most useful is the OVERLAPS predicate. This keyword checks to see if two time intervals intersect one another. Its general syntax is as follows:

```
(start-time, end-time | interval) OVERLAPS (start-time, end-time | interval)
```

The following example should help explain:

```
(TIME '11:00:00', INTERVAL '2' HOUR)
OVERLAPS
(TIME '12:30:00', TIME '13:00:00')
```

This query checks to see if an interval of time starting at 11 a.m. and spanning for two hours will intersect an interval of time starting at 12:30 pm and ending at 1:00 p.m. The Transact-SQL is less elegant. To be honest, there is no elegant way to do this in Transact SQL.

UNIQUE

You have already learned about the use of the predicate EXISTS to check for the existence of a particular value in a set. SQL-92 extends this logic a little further by also defining a predicate named UNIQUE to check that none of the values in a particular set repeats. For example, the following expression will return TRUE if none of the rows in table *a* are duplicates:

```
UNIQUE (SELECT * FROM a)
```

In Transact-SQL you would need

```
NOT EXISTS (SELECT count(*) FROM a GROUP BY col1, col2, …, coln HAVING COUNT(*) > 1)
```

Where *col1, col2, ..., col*n is a listing of all the columns in the table. Since you can't group by more than 16 columns, on tables with 17 columns or more you would have to use

```
EXISTS (SELECT *
   FROM A A1 JOIN A A2
   ON A1.col1 = A2.col1
      AND A1.col2 = A2.col2
      .
      .
      .
      AND A1.coln = A2.coln)
```

WHERE TRANSACT-SQL BEATS SQL-92

The news isn't all bad for Transact SQL. There are a few areas where it still blows away the SQL-92 standard:

- SQL-92 has no support for triggers.
- SQL-92 has no support for stored procedures.
- SQL-92 has no definition for data replication.

Let's take these one at a time. First, the lack of support for triggers. This addition was apparently a hotly contested issue in the standardization process but never made it in to the SQL-92 specification because of a general lack of agreement. Having spent the better part of the last several years knee-deep in the trenches of database management, we can tell you that triggers are an indispensable tool for any database owner. (We cover triggers and stored procedures in Chapter 14.)◀

Second, SQL-92 has no support for stored procedures. For this reason alone, any DBMS that chooses to develop its SQL only to the point of SQL-92 compliance will surely be useless in the client/server arena.

And last, SQL-92 has no definition for data replication. As databases become more distributed across far-flung enterprises, the need for automated data mirroring and synchronization will become paramount. This issue is completely ignored in the SQL-92 standard and will certainly have to be addressed in the next standard.

Beyond SQL-92: SQL3

Almost immediately after the release of SQL-92, work began on a new ANSI standard called SQL3. (It's called SQL3 because SQL-89 and SQL-92 are generally regarded as SQL1 and SQL2.) The SQL3 standard will address the basic issues of stored procedures and triggers, as well as some newer and more complicated issues, such as:

- Object-oriented SQL
- Multimedia SQL
- Temporal SQL

In the following sections we consider each of these developments.

Object-oriented SQL?

We know more than a few database owners and developers who have been trying to avoid learning an object-oriented (OO) language because the concepts are so radically different from a standard procedural language.

Sorry to burst your bubble, but SQL3 will have wide-reaching specifications for the storage of persistent objects in a database. It seems that the worlds of the object database model and the relational database model will finally meet. If you, as a database owner/manager, don't want to be out of a job soon, you had better get yourself to a bookstore and start reading up on object-oriented principles and design. If you are a programmer and don't know anything about object-oriented principles, it's a wonder you still *have* a job! We are not kidding.

It used to be that database programming was the last refuge of the procedural coder. This will be no more. Most companies do not yet expect their database owners to be OO gurus, but that skill is quickly becoming a prerequisite for a programmer. Once these features make it into mainstream DBMSs, there will be no escape.

Multimedia SQL: SQL/MM

The emergence and proliferation of multimedia applications since the publication of the SQL-92 standard have led many people to believe that the next SQL standard should have some mechanisms for the storage, manipulation, and retrieval of multimedia data. The work of the SQL/MM group, specifically, is focused on the development of a set of SQL Abstract Data Types (ADTs) to handle this kind of data. In fact, SQL3 refers to *abstract data types* for object definitions, instead of the more commonly accepted term *classes*. (At the time of this writing, SQL/MM is not an official part of the SQL3 standard. Whether it makes it in before the standard goes to press is entirely unclear.)

Technically, this work is not part of the official SQL3 specification, but you can bet you are going to see it implemented anyway. There's just too much need for it. Witness the hoopla about video on demand, the new technology that most cable companies and some phone companies are promising that will allow media watchers to choose a movie or event from a menu and see it immediately.

All of this data has to be stored *somewhere*, and it will be kept in the next generation of multimedia databases. Oracle and Bell Atlantic are already experimenting with such a technology in the Washington, D.C. metropolitan area. And what about all the cool new multimedia stuff out on the Internet? You guessed it. It's also going to have to be managed with multimedia-aware DBMSs.

Describing time: SQL/Temporal

Another facet of the SQL3 development that is the subject of much discussion is how the new SQL standard will deal with certain attributes of time. The problem breaks down like this: Databases are currently set up to store instantaneous values — snapshots in time. There are no real provisions to deal with how the progression of time affects the data.

One of the most cited examples of where theses abilities would be helpful is in the tracking of stock market data. There are many people who feel that a user should be able to store a stock's performance over time as a single value in a table. Then, the user could use computational operators (min, max, avg, and so on) to extract needed information from the series. The idea is that there is value added by storing this information as a single value rather than as multiple rows in a table.

Examples aside, the basic complaint is that the current types for date, time, and intervals do not do an adequate job of capturing data changes over time. At this point, it is unclear how much of the SQL/Temporal work will make it into the SQL3 standard, but it continues to be a hotly contested issue among those involved in the standardization process.

Summary

In this chapter, we have tried to give you some perspective on where SQL Server and Transact-SQL fit in the world of relational database management and how they are likely to change over time. It is our hope that this insight will help you better prepare for the future so that the databases you construct now will still be relevant in five years. Transact-SQL may not be perfect, but it is generally a good implementation of the SQL-92 standard. In some areas it lacks the robustness defined in the ANSI SQL-92 standard, but excels in other areas. In our opinion, its benefits far outweigh its shortcomings.

Review Questions

Q: Why did SQL become the standard data manipulation language for RDBMSs and not some other language?

A: There are two reasons. First, SQL was a simple answer to a much larger problem of allowing users to formulate and execute their own queries. Second, SQL was backed by IBM. It might as well have been blessed by the Pope, himself!

Q: If the original SQL standards were so simple and elegant, why did so many DBMS vendors extend it in so many different directions?

A: Neither the SQL-86 or SQL-89 standards were complete enough to use for a commercial DBMS. For example, SQL-89 does not have any DATE datatypes. Most companies did start with these ideas in mind, but soon found that they needed to extend the specifications in order to meet real-world needs. Some of these extensions wound up being supported by SQL-92, while others became obsolete.

Q: Why would the ANSI committee in charge of SQL-92 include a *bit(n)* and *bit varying* type if their use would tend to violate the first normal form?

A: We really don't know the answer to that. If we had to guess, though, we would have to say the committee included them for completeness. If database owners and developers abuse the standards, that's not the committee's fault!

Q: Why are there so many more levels of abstraction in the SQL-92 model than in the Transact-SQL model?

A: In one form or another, the committees involved in the SQL standardization process have always been concerned with the interoperability of SQL with other environments. This includes the interoperability of one SQL-based system with another. They were also acutely aware of the problem that conflicting entity names can play in a database. To resolve this problem, they put in place several extra layers of abstraction so as to reduce the possibility of name redundancy and to further help identify elements in an enterprise-wide system.

Chapter

SQL Server System Tables and Procedures

11

*I*f you were going to build an RDBMS to manage tables of data, where would you put all the administrative information about those tables? In more tables, of course! SQL Server system tables contain all the information that describes your SQL Server system and its databases.

What's in This Chapter

In this chapter you'll find out:

- How SQL Server stores information in system tables and how to retrieve it
- The critical knowledge each DBA must have about the database system tables
- Advanced system table usage
- What system tables in the master database you should use regularly

Knowing your way around the system tables is very important to you as a system administrator or database owner. The system tables tell you about potential problems in your database that you cannot see easily with the SQL Enterprise Manager. You can also leverage the system tables to make a large number of changes in a matter of seconds, changes that would take a lot of time-consuming, redundant work from the user interface of the SQL Enterprise Manager. Furthermore, Microsoft provides lots of stored procedures to query and modify the system tables. This chapter not only explains the system tables but also covers the procedures that SQL Server provides for using them.

What we are *not* going to do in this chapter is list each system table column, each index, and the procedures that reference the tables. The SQL Server manuals do that. We may highlight specific columns or procedures, but we are primarily going to talk about how to use the system tables to get information. After you read this chapter, you can make your own listing of the system tables, including columns, indexes, and procedures, if you wish. Throughout this chapter, we use *a lot* of SQL. If you want to follow along by running the SQL yourself, you can do so with the SQL Query Tool, which is available within the SQL Enterprise Manager or as a standalone application. We covered how to use this tool back in Chapter 3. Note that there is a 16-bit version of the SQL Query Tool, so even if you are using a Windows for Workgroups machine, you can run the queries in this chapter.◀

Preliminary Observations

Before we dive right into the first system table, there are some global issues to get out of the way. Specifically, you will want to know:

- What kinds of system tables SQL Server has.
- The conventions Microsoft uses in system tables data storage, especially integer IDs and integer bit flags.
- How to create SQL commands from system tables.

Categories of system tables

Not all system tables are in all databases. Where you will find a given table depends on what category it is in. Microsoft groups the tables into categories based on related functions:

- **System catalogs.** These are tables that contain server-wide information, such things as who is authorized to log in to the server and what databases are on the server. They are found only in the master database.

- **Database catalogs.** These tables contain information specific to a database, such as who is authorized to use a database and what tables are in the database. All databases, including master and tempdb, have a database catalog. The database catalog contains data about your data, commonly called *meta-data*.

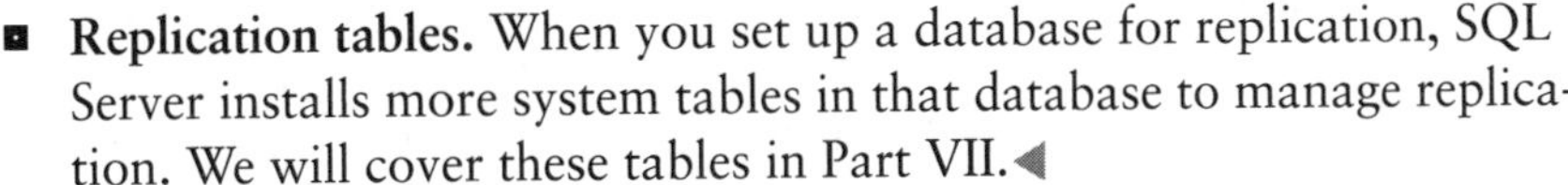

- **Replication tables.** When you set up a database for replication, SQL Server installs more system tables in that database to manage replication. We will cover these tables in Part VII.◀

- **SQL executive tables.** These are the tables in the msdb database that SQL Server uses to manage the SQL Executive tasks. We will cover these tables in Part VI.◀

Integer ids

Throughout the system catalog you will find no less than 30 different "id" variables, including all these obscure names: altsuid, artid, colid, constid, csid, dbid, depdbid, depid, depsiteid, fkeydbid, fkeyid, gid, id, indid, kpid, langid, objid, pubid, remoteserverid, rkeydbid, rkeyid, rkeyindid, soid, spid, srvid, suid, sync_objid, taskid, uid, xactid. Every one of these, except for xactid (a timestamp), is some kind of integer, either a tinyint (1 byte), a smallint (2 bytes), or an integer (4 bytes). SQL Server uses integers to track and identify objects and all "things" in the system tables, rather than using character string names. There are a number of good reasons for using integer ids:

- They boost the performance of SQL Server. A computer can manipulate integer variables must faster than the standard 30 character strings SQL Server uses for names.
- They save space. The largest integer id, is an int datatype, which is only four bytes. A name can take up to 30 bytes of storage.
- They make SQL Server more flexible. Suppose you want to rename a column, a table, *a database*? No problem! All SQL Server has to do to update the system tables is change the character string in one table. If SQL Server tracked objects by name, changing a name would mean changing every single occurrence of that name everywhere the system tables held information about the object. Here's another example: if Microsoft ever decides to increase the length of the standard SQL Server identifier, it will be less painful for the company because of the integer ids.

Cross-Reference

Of course, there are a few down sides to all these integer ids. The leading issue you will face is that the ids are hard for a human being to make sense out of. If we tell you that "table 178099675, owned by user 6, is referentially linked to table 338100245, owned by user 8," we haven't given you much information. It is much better to be able to say that "the table Hugh.authors is linked to the table Deb.titleauthor." However, this requires being able to decipher the darned ids. Your friends here are the system functions (refer to Chapter 8) for translating ids to names and vice versa.◀

Using bits in integers as flags

In almost all system tables, you will find that yes/no information is stored not in bit fields, but in various bits of integers. This allowed Microsoft to keep the structure of the system tables more stable during development because an integer, having 32 bits, automatically reserves 32 yes/no flags. Thus, if today they need 7 flags but tomorrow they need 10 flags, they don't have to alter the system tables. This is great for Microsoft, but the down side for you is that you have to do some extra work in querying the system tables.

Cross-Reference

Now, you might be thinking that these 'status integers' aren't in 3NF. Good for you. In fact they are not even 1NF: they violate the atomicity rule. (See Chapter 12 for a complete discussion of the normal forms and the atomicity rule.) We can't recommend this kind of denormalization. It wouldn't have been too much trouble to do it the right way; we will show you how it should have been done in the next section.◀

Querying for bit flags

The way to determine if bit number *x* is on, where *x* ranges from zero to 31, is to use the following predicate:

```
WHERE column_name & power(2,x) > 0
```

Don't make the mistake of testing for

```
WHERE column_name & power(2,x) = 1
```

The expression *column_name & power(2,x)* returns either zero or power(2,x), not zero or 1.

You will see some system stored procedures with WHERE clause, for example:

```
WHERE column_name & 509
```

or

```
WHERE column_name & 0x01fd,
```

leaving you to figure out for yourself what they mean. A useful trick is to set up a table of integers, *n*, as follows:

```
CREATE TABLE n (n int PRIMARY KEY)
INSERT n VALUES (1)
WHILE (SELECT MAX(n) FROM n) < 32 INSERT n SELECT n+(SELECT MAX(n) FROM n) FROM n
INSERT n VALUES (0)
```

At first *n* has just one row, with n = 1. Then, 2 gets inserted, then 3 and 4, then 5, 6, 7, and 8, and so on. Thus, *n* gets populated with 0, 1, 2,...32. Now you can resolve something like *0x01fd* with this stored procedure:

```
CREATE PROCEDURE bitmask @test int AS
   /* If you call bitmask with a binary value for the @test parameter,
      it SQL Server will automatically convert the binary to an int. */
   SET NOCOUNT ON /* We don't want to see all the row counts */
   SELECT 'Hexadecimal', convert( binary(8), @test),
      '= Integer', CONVERT( int, @test)
   PRINT 'Bitmask'
   SELECT SIGN(@test & power(2,n)) 'on', n bit, POWER( 2, n) integer,
         CONVERT(binary(4), power(2,n)) hex
      FROM n
      WHERE n <= ceiling( log( convert( int, @test))/ log(2))
         /* The ceiling( log( etc. makes it so that the proc stops
            with the last power of 2 it needs */
      ORDER BY n
```

Bitmask 0x01fd returns the following:

```
Hexadecimal 0x0000000000000203 = Integer 515
Bitmask
on          bit         integer     hex
----------- ----------- ----------- ----------
1           0           1           0x00000001
1           1           2           0x00000002
0           2           4           0x00000004
0           3           8           0x00000008
0           4           16          0x00000010
0           5           32          0x00000020
0           6           64          0x00000040
0           7           128         0x00000080
0           8           256         0x00000100
1           9           512         0x00000200
```

The results tell us that 0x01fd is actually 515 base 10, 100000011 base 2, and that the first, second, and ninth bits are on. This is all the conversion information we could possibly need.

Pseudodynamic SQL

Throughout this chapter, there will be lots of examples of creating SQL statements with other SQL statements. Suppose you want to grant select authority on all your tables to *public.* (See Chapter 7 for more information about GRANT.) If you guessed that you could simply write

```
GRANT SELECT ON ALL TO public /* Wrong! */
```

Guess again. 'SELECT ON ALL' isn't legal Transact-SQL. You have to execute the GRANT command separately for every single table. We will cover the sysobjects table later, but for right now we will tell you that it includes the names of all your tables. Therefore, you could create the SQL to grant select authority on all tables in a database with this SELECT statement:

```
SELECT 'GRANT SELECT ON '+name+' TO public'
   FROM sysobjects
   WHERE type = 'u'
   ORDER BY 1
```

If you run this query in the pubs database, you get the following:

```
GRANT SELECT ON authors to public
GRANT SELECT ON discounts to public
GRANT SELECT ON employee to public
GRANT SELECT ON jobs  to public
GRANT SELECT ON pub_info to public
GRANT SELECT ON publishers to public
GRANT SELECT ON roysched to public
GRANT SELECT ON sales to public
GRANT SELECT ON stores to public
GRANT SELECT ON titleauthor to public
GRANT SELECT ON titles to public
```

You can cut and paste this SQL from the Results tab of the Query window back into your Query tab, and run it to do the grants. If you can type the SELECT 'GRANT...' query quickly or if you already have the query saved on your hard drive, this little cut and paste operation is faster than the

GUI tools. If you have a database of hundreds of tables, this query is the *only* way to accomplish the task. The only thing we could improve on is the 'cut and paste' part.

First of all the default configuration of the SQL Query Tool puts headers and row counts on your query results:

```
----------------------------------------------------
GRANT SELECT ON authors TO public
.
.
.
GRANT SELECT ON titles TO public
 (11 row(s) affected)
```

You don't want to cut and paste the dashed line or the row count. If you want to remove them from the output, click the Query Options button to bring up Figure 11-1, the Query Options dialog box. By default you are looking at the Query Flag tab. Check the "No Count Display" box. Now switch to the Format Options tab, Figure 11-2, verify that the "Result Output Format" is "Column Aligned", and clear the "Print Headers" box.

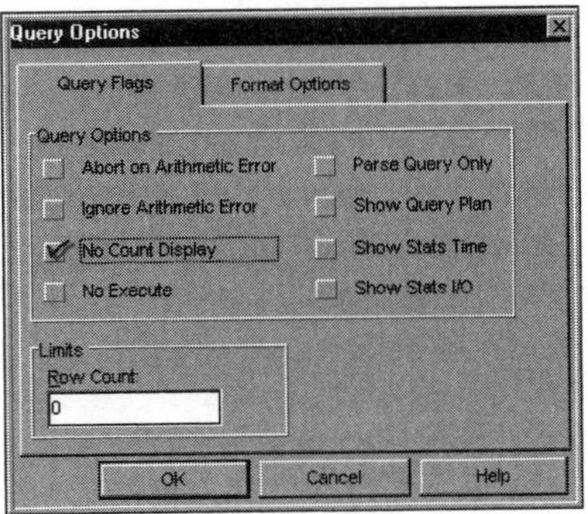

Figure 11-1:
Use the Query Flags to turn off the row count in your query results.

This is minor improvement, but the real question is "Why can't we just have the grants run dynamically?" In fact we can, with some minor modifications. Remember that the way to run SQL dynamically is by using the EXECUTE command. So:

```
EXECUTE('GRANT SELECT ON authors to public')
```

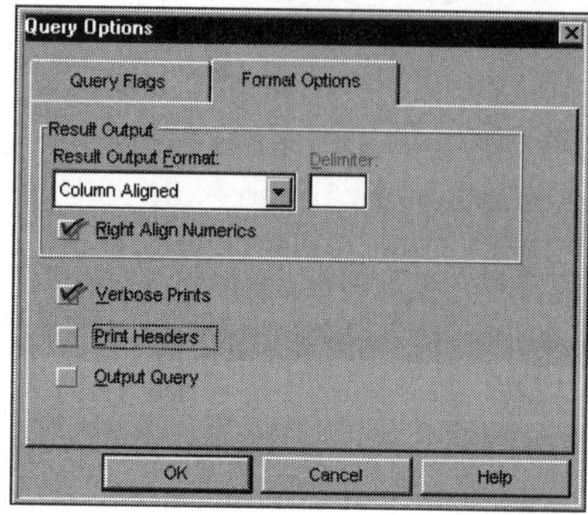

Figure 11-2:
Use the Format Options to suppress the column headings in your query results.

sends the string 'GRANT SELECT ON authors to public' to SQL Server for execution. Therefore, all we need to do is take the 11 GRANT statements above and use them one by one as strings to the EXECUTE command. As you will recall from Chapter 9, when you need to access rows from a table one at a time, you use a CURSOR:

```
DECLARE c_grant_select CURSOR FOR
SELECT 'GRANT SELECT ON '+name+' to public'
   FROM sysobjects
   WHERE type = 'u'
   ORDER BY 1
FOR READ ONLY
OPEN c_grant_select
DECLARE @s_grant_select varchar(255)
FETCH c_grant_select INTO @s_grant_select
WHILE @@FETCH_STATUS = 0 BEGIN
   EXECUTE(@s_grant_select)
   FETCH c_grant_select INTO @s_grant_select
END
CLOSE c_grant_select
DEALLOCATE c_grant_select
```

The SELECT statement we used to build the SQL is exactly the same. We have simply packaged it in a cursor, and we are running it with an EXECUTE statement. When you are writing and testing a query that generates SQL, it is typically easier to use the cut and paste method. We call this *pseudodynamic SQL*. When you are satisfied with your query, you should wrap it up in a cursor and compile it in a stored procedure. For the sake of both brevity and clarity, we will not include the CURSOR or EXECUTE statements the examples in this chapter. However, you should remember to use them in your code.

Essential System Table Knowledge

There are certain tables that are an absolute must for studying. These are the system tables you will use over and over again. These are the tables that not only the DBA should know but also any user writing SQL should know. Our list of must-know tables is

- sysobjects
- sysindexes
- syscolumns

Sysobjects

You will never stop using the sysobjects table. It lists all the objects in your database, together with who owns them and all kinds of other nifty information. When we say "objects", we include all of the following: CHECK constraints, DEFAULT constraints, defaults (non-DRI), FOREIGN KEY constraints, PRIMARY KEY and UNIQUE constraints, stored procedures, rules, stored procedures for replication, system tables, triggers, user tables, views, and extended stored procedures. There is a one row in sysobjects for each object in any of these categories.

Help on sysobjects

To see all the pertinent information about sysobjects, type **sysobjects** anywhere in your Query tab. Highlight the word *sysobjects* (you can highlight a word by double clicking it), and press ALT-F1. The Results tab shows this information:

```
sysobjects      dbo             system table       Feb 24 1996  7:56AM
system

name            sysname         30                 no    yes   no
id              int             4     10     0     no    (n/a) (n/a)
uid             smallint        2     5      0     no    (n/a) (n/a)
type            char            2                  no    yes   no
userstat        smallint        2     5      0     no    (n/a) (n/a)
sysstat         smallint        2     5      0     no    (n/a) (n/a)
indexdel        smallint        2     5      0     no    (n/a) (n/a)
schema_ver      smallint        2     5      0     no    (n/a) (n/a)
refdate         datetime        8                  no    (n/a) (n/a)
```

(continued)

(continued)

```
crdate          datetime      8                  no     (n/a) (n/a)
version         int           4     10     0     no     (n/a) (n/a)
deltrig         int           4     10     0     no     (n/a) (n/a)
instrig         int           4     10     0     no     (n/a) (n/a)
updtrig         int           4     10     0     no     (n/a) (n/a)
seltrig         int           4     10     0     no     (n/a) (n/a)
category        int           4     10     0     no     (n/a) (n/a)
cache           smallint      2     5      0     no     (n/a) (n/a)

No identity column defined.    (null)      (null)

sysobjects      clustered, unique located on system       id
ncsysobjects    nonclustered, unique located on system    name, uid

No constraints have been defined for this object.

No foreign keys reference this table.
```

When you pressed ALT-F1, the SQL Query Tool executed the stored procedure sp_help 'sysobjects'. You can do this with any object in the database: highlight it and press ALT-F1 to run sp_help. You can also run sp_help directly. Its syntax is simply:

```
sp_help [objname]
```

If you run sp_help without an object name, sp_help summarizes the objects in your database. When you are finished reading this "Essential System Table Knowledge Section", you will be able to write your own sp_help procedure.

Using sysobjects in queries

Returning to sysobjects, we list the columns you will need most in Table 11-1. Let's start by selecting the first five of these columns from sysobjects in pubs:

```
SELECT name, id, uid, type, crdate
   FROM sysobjects
   ORDER by id
```

Table 11-1
The Most Commonly Used Columns in Sysobjects

Column	Description/Values	Value Description
name	name of the object	
id	integer id for the object	
uid	id of the owner of the object	
type	the type of the object:	
-	C	CHECK constraint
-	D	Default or DEFAULT constraint
-	F	FOREIGN KEY constraint
-	K	PRIMARY KEY or UNIQUE constraint
-	P	Stored procedure
-	R	Rule
-	RF	Stored procedure for replication
-	S	System table
-	TR	Trigger
-	U	User table
-	V	View
-	X	Extended stored procedure
crdate	the date the object was created	
deltrig	the object id of the delete trigger	
instrig	the object id of the insert trigger	
updtrig	the object id of the update trigger	

Notice that this will give us the top line of the information we got from sp_help. The result of the query begins this way:

```
name                id         uid    type crdate
------------------- ---------- ------ ---- -------------------------

sysobjects          1          1      S    Feb 24 1996  7:56AM
sysindexes          2          1      S    Feb 24 1996  7:56AM
syscolumns          3          1      S    Feb 24 1996  7:56AM
systypes            4          1      S    Feb 24 1996  7:56AM
sysprocedures       5          1      S    Feb 24 1996  7:56AM
syscomments         6          1      S    Feb 24 1996  7:56AM
syssegments         7          1      S    Feb 24 1996  7:56AM
syslogs             8          1      S    Feb 24 1996  7:56AM
sysprotects         9          1      S    Feb 24 1996  7:56AM
sysusers            10         1      S    Feb 24 1996  7:56AM
sysalternates       11         1      S    Feb 24 1996  7:56AM
sysdepends          12         1      S    Feb 24 1996  7:56AM
syskeys             13         1      S    Feb 24 1996  7:56AM
sysreferences       14         1      S    Feb 24 1996  7:56AM
sysconstraints      15         1      S    Feb 24 1996  7:56AM
```

(continued)

(continued)

```
sysarticles         16         1    S    Feb 24 1996  7:56AM
syspublications     17         1    S    Feb 24 1996  7:56AM
syssubscriptions    18         1    S    Feb 24 1996  7:56AM
authors             16003088   1    U    Feb 24 1996  8:02AM
UPKCL_auidind       32003145   1    K    Feb 24 1996  8:02AM
```

The output goes on for another 50 rows or so; you can run the query if you want to see it all. We are happy to stop right here because we now have a list of the very objects this chapter is about: the system tables! Notice that the tables we consider critical just happen to be numbers 1, 2, and 3. Obviously, someone at Microsoft agrees with us. It is no accident that the system tables have sequential ids. Microsoft assigns ids of 50 or lower to the system tables. All other objects have large integers generated from a hashing algorithm. Notice that there are 18 system tables in the database catalog.

When we defined the system catalog, which resides only in master, we didn't tell you which tables were in that catalog. You can find that out for yourself simply by knowing the structure of sysobjects:

```
SELECT name, id
   FROM master.dbo.sysobjects m
   WHERE NOT EXISTS (SELECT *
         FROM pubs.dbo.sysobjects
         WHERE id = m.id)
      AND type = 'S'
   ORDER BY id
```

The result is this:

```
name                 id
-------------------- -----------
sysdatabases         30
sysusages            31
sysprocesses         32
syslogins            33
syslocks             34
sysdevices           35
sysmessages          36
sysconfigures        37
syscurconfigs        38
sysservers           40
sysremotelogins      41
syslanguages         44
syscharsets          45
```

Psuedo-Dynamic SQL from sysobjects

A perfect example of the kind of SQL you can write by querying sysobjects query is the set of GRANT statements we presented as we discussed pseudo-dynamic SQL. There is no end to this kind of mulit-object manipulation. Another example is to unload all the data from a entire database into operating system files.

```
SELECT 'exec master.dbo.xp_cmdshell ''bcp',
      +DB_NAME()+'.'+USER_NAME(uid)+'.'+name, 'out',
      +USER_NAME(uid)+'.'+name, ' /n /T'''
   FROM sysobjects
   WHERE type = 'u'
   ORDER BY USER_NAME(uid), name
```

Cross-Reference

Running the SQL from this query will copy all the data out to SQL Server's default directory on the server machine (more about the bcp utility in Chapter 17). In pubs this query yields

```
exec xp_cmdshell 'bcp pubs.dbo.authors     out dbo.authors     /n /T'
exec xp_cmdshell 'bcp pubs.dbo.discounts   out dbo.discounts   /n /T'
exec xp_cmdshell 'bcp pubs.dbo.employee    out dbo.employee    /n /T'
exec xp_cmdshell 'bcp pubs.dbo.jobs        out dbo.jobs        /n /T'
exec xp_cmdshell 'bcp pubs.dbo.pub_info    out dbo.pub_info    /n /T'
exec xp_cmdshell 'bcp pubs.dbo.publishers  out dbo.publishers  /n /T'
exec xp_cmdshell 'bcp pubs.dbo.roysched    out dbo.roysched    /n /T'
exec xp_cmdshell 'bcp pubs.dbo.sales       out dbo.sales       /n /T'
exec xp_cmdshell 'bcp pubs.dbo.stores      out dbo.stores      /n /T'
exec xp_cmdshell 'bcp pubs.dbo.titleauthor out dbo.titleauthor /n /T'
exec xp_cmdshell 'bcp pubs.dbo.titles      out dbo.titles      /n /T'
```

Each of these commands opens an operating system command shell and runs the bcp utility to copy data out of a SQL Server table to an operating system file. Because we generated one command for each user table, we have the entire database.

Other uses of sysobjects

Depending on how complex your SQL Server implementation is, you may have a huge number of objects. We have over 2,000 objects, with an average of 300 objects per type. Scrolling through drop down list boxes in the SQL Enterprise ceases to be effective when you reach this level. Hot keying on the first letter of an object name is helpful, but typically many of our object names begin with the same handful of letters. However, we never have any trouble finding the names of objects that we have forgotten. We just query sysobjects for name LIKE '%<whatever>%', where we fill in the string we want.

In many of the queries in this book, you will see joins on sysobjects for one of two reasons: to get an object's owner or to get an object's type. While SQL Server gives you an OBJECT_NAME function, there is no OBJECT_OWNER nor OBJECT_TYPE function. We think these would make outstanding additions to the system function set.

Sysindexes

Without question, the next most important system table to a database administrator is sysindexes. There is one row in sysindexes for each index on a table. Additionally, there is one row in sysindexes for each table that has no clustered index. A clustered index is the one index on a table for which you have instructed SQL Server to store the data in the same order as the index. Finally, there is one row in sysindexes for each table that contains text or image data. The presence of these non-index rows in sysindexes can be confusing until you get used to it. In Chapter 12 we will point out how the non-index rows violate the relation model and normalization; in Chapter 28 we will see how the data retrieval algorithms of SQL Server make it somewhat reasonable to put non-index rows in sysindexes. Table 11-2 lists the most commonly used columns of sysindexes. Remember that you can use sp_help to see a summary of sysindexes.◀

Table 11-2
The Most Commonly Used Columns in Sysindexes

Column	Description/Values	Value Description
name	name of index, unless indid = 0	
id	the ID of object that owns the index	
indid	the ID of the index	
-	0	table with no clustered indexes
-	1	clustered index
	2-250	non-clustered index
	255	entry for a table with text or image data
dpages	number of leaf level pages in the index	
reserved	number of pages allocated to the index	
used	number of pages actually being used by the index	

(continued)

Column	Description/Values	Value Description
rows	a row count for the table	
status	integer of bit flags	
-	1	Cancel command if attempt to insert duplicate key
-	2	Unique index
-	4	Cancel command if attempt to insert duplicate row
-	16	Clustered index
-	64	Index allows duplicate rows
-	2048	Index used to enforce PRIMARY KEY constraint
-	4096	Index used to enforce UNIQUE constraint
keycnt	number of keys in index	
keys1	Description of key columns (if entry is an index)	
keys2	Description of key columns (if entry is an index)	
UpdateStamp	A timestamp of when sysindexes data last changed	

You will notice that there is some redundant information in sysindexes. For example, you can determine which entries are clustered indexes either from the indid column or the status column. If they are consistent, this query should return no rows:

```
SELECT *
   FROM sysindexes
   WHERE (indid != 1 AND status & 16 = 16)
      OR (indid = 1 AND status & 16 = 0)
```

On our server, these columns are indeed consistent: the query above returns no rows.

Reading index information

Recall that the sp_help stored procedure returned information like this about the sysobjects table:

```
sysobjects     clustered, unique located on system      id
ncsysobjects   nonclustered, unique located on system   name, uid
```

How might we go about getting this information? The index name and type are stored in the table, alright, but what about the key names? They are imbedded in varbinary(255) columns. We have to use the INDEX_COL function to pull them out. Suppose we only want to get index information about the system tables? First, we cheat a little bit by seeing how many keys we are dealing with:

```
SELECT MAX(keycnt)
   FROM sysindexes
   WHERE id < 50
```

The result of this query is 6, which tells us that no system table has more that 6 columns in a key. Then we can combine what we know in this query:

```
SELECT OBJECT_NAME(id) objname,
      name indexname,
      CASE indid WHEN 1 THEN 'clustered' ELSE 'nonclustered' END
      +CASE WHEN status & 2 = 2 THEN ', unique' END indextype,
      INDEX_COL( OBJECT_NAME(id), indid, 1) indexcol1,
      INDEX_COL( OBJECT_NAME(id), indid, 2) indexcol2,
      INDEX_COL( OBJECT_NAME(id), indid, 3) indexcol3,
      INDEX_COL( OBJECT_NAME(id), indid, 4) indexcol4,
      INDEX_COL( OBJECT_NAME(id), indid, 5) indexcol5,
      INDEX_COL( OBJECT_NAME(id), indid, 6) indexcol6
   FROM sysindexes
   WHERE id < 50
      AND indid BETWEEN 1 AND 250
   ORDER BY id, indid
```

Though the formatting isn't quite as nice as sp_help, this query returns the critical information about system table indexes. For the first three system tables, the output looks like this:

```
objname      indexname      indextype           icol1  icol2  icol3
------------ -------------- ------------------- ------ ------ ------
sysobjects   sysobjects     clustered, unique   id     (null) (null)
sysobjects   ncsysobjects   nonclustered, unique name  uid    (null)
sysindexes   sysindexes     clustered, unique   id     indid  (null)
syscolumns   syscolumns     clustered, unique   id     number colid
```

We omitted the last three columns for readability because they contained only nulls.

Primary keys for the system tables

Now that you know how to query sysindexes you can find out which system tables have primary keys:

```
SELECT OBJECT_NAME(id)
   FROM sysindexes
   WHERE id < 50
      AND status & 2048 > 0
```

This query returns no rows! There are no primary keys on the system tables, which means they have no foreign keys either. How can Microsoft get away with this? Easy. First of all, they do have unique indexes on most of their tables, so they aren't worried about duplicate rows creeping in. Second, the only way that you are supposed to modify the system tables is via Microsoft's stored procedures, and presumably they have checked these to make sure they won't break the relationship among the system tables.

Syscolumns

The last table of our must-know trio is syscolumns. This table contains one row for every column in a table or view and one row for every parameter of each stored procedure in the database. Table 11-3 lists the important columns of syscolumns. With this information we can almost go ahead and write the query that displays the columns of all the system tables. The only thing we are missing is an English description of the types. That we get from systypes, the system table that defines the types of the database.

Table 11-3
The Most Commonly Used Columns in Syscolumns

Column	Description/Values	Value Description
id	ID of the table or view for which this is column, or the ID of the procedure for which this is a parameter.	
Colid	ID of the column itself. This in the order in which you see the columns of tables	
status	Integer of bit flags	
-	0x08	The column allow nulls
-	0x80	The column is an identity
type	The actual storage type of the column	
length	How many bytes of storage the column requires	
usertype	The datatype specified when the table was created	
name	The name of the column or parameter	

```
SELECT OBJECT_NAME(id) objname, colid, c.name,
      t.name type, c.length,
      CASE WHEN status & 0x08 = 0x08 THEN 'NULL' ELSE '' END 'null'
   FROM syscolumns c
   JOIN systypes t ON c.usertype = t.usertype
   ORDER BY id, colid
```

For the syscolumns system table itself, the result is the following:

```
objname        colid name           type           length null
-------------- ----- -------------- -------------- ------ ----
syscolumns     1     id             int            4
syscolumns     2     number         smallint       2
syscolumns     3     colid          tinyint        1
syscolumns     4     status         tinyint        1
syscolumns     5     type           tinyint        1
syscolumns     6     length         tinyint        1
syscolumns     7     offset         smallint       2
syscolumns     8     usertype       smallint       2
syscolumns     9     cdefault       int            4
syscolumns     10    domain         int            4
syscolumns     11    name           sysname        30
syscolumns     12    printfmt       varchar        255    NULL
syscolumns     13    prec           tinyint        1      NULL
syscolumns     14    scale          tinyint        1      NULL
```

As you can imagine, applications like the SQL Enterprise Manager are querying the syscolumns table all the time to retrieve information about tables.

The Rest of the Database Catalog

Though we have called special attention to sysobjects, sysindexes, and syscolumns, don't ignore the rest of the database catalog. (Recall that we listed the other 15 database catalog tables in the sysobjects section). We have already touched on systypes; there isn't much more we want to say about them. We postpone discussion of sysarticles, syspublications, and syssubscriptions to Chapter 22, because they are replication tables. That leaves us with the following tables that we would like to introduce:

- sysprocedures
- syscomments
- syssegments

- syslogs
- sysprotects
- sysusers
- sysalternates
- sysdepends
- syskeys
- sysreferences
- sysconstraints◀

For some of these tables (especially sysprocedures, syssegments, and syslogs) we will have little to say because they don't do a lot for you if you try to query them. The remaining system table can be real assets in your bag of tricks.

Sysprocedures

This table contains a binary plan or sequence tree for each object that requires one, including views, defaults, rules, triggers, CHECK constraints, DEFAULT constraints, and stored procedures. This table is really for SQL Server internal use. Our only interaction with it has been when it becomes corrupted, which has happened to us twice in the last three years. In both cases it was unfixable: we either had to restore from backups or rebuild the database.

Syscomments

Whenever you create an object that requires some custom SQL text, such as a view or a stored procedure, SQL Server stores the text is the syscomments table. Sp_help for syscomments shows this (abbreviated) output:

```
id               int            4
number           smallint       2
colid            tinyint        1
texttype         smallint       2
language         smallint       2
text             varchar        255

syscomments      clustered, unique located on system
                 id, number, colid, texttype
```

This just about tells the whole story. The unique index is identified by id (the object id), number (the stored procedure number, if it is a compound stored procedure), colid (a counter), and texttype (User-suplied, System-supplied, or Encrypted comments.) After that there is language, which is not used, and text, a varchar(255) to hold your text. The colid is used when you have objects with more than 255 characters of text. The text will be stored in 255 character chunks with colid 1, 2,... . To get an idea of what syscomments data look like, try this query:

```
SELECT colid, text
   FROM syscomments
   WHERE id = OBJECT_ID( 'sp_help' )
   ORDER BY colid
```

The first row of output (there are 38 rows), looks like this:

```
colid text
----- -------------------------------------------------------------
    1 create procedure sp_help  -- 1995/09/13 18:23
    @objname varchar(92) = NULL      /* object name we're after */
as

declare @objid int         /* id of the object */
declare @sysstat smallint     /* the type of the object */
declare @dbname varchar
```

The raw output is pratically impossible to read because of the carriage returns embedded in the text field. However, there are two things we want you to keep in mind about syscomments:

Cross-Reference

- Syscomments doesn't change automatically when you rename objects. If we rename 'sp_help' to 'sp_help_object', the text in syscomments won't reflect the change. We will have a lot to say about the problems this creates in Chapter 18.◄
- Syscomments lets you search object definitions for particular strings. Suppose you want to know if any system-stored procedures contain the word *magic* in their definitions (it would probably be in a comment, not actual SQL.) You can search for the string with this query:

```
SELECT DISTINCT OBJECT_NAME(id)
   FROM syscomments
   WHERE text LIKE '%magic%'
   ORDER BY 1
```

The result is two stored procedures, sp_stored_procedures and sp_tables. You can see where searches like this are powerful tools for the DBA.

Syssegments

Cross-Reference

We won't talk much about segments in this book. In Chapter 1 we advised you not to use them, but to set up RAID instead. We have heard rumors that Microsoft will eliminate segments in the next release of SQL Server. If you are still interested, syssegments contains the segment defined for your database.◄

Syslogs

This table is your transaction log. You can't really query it with SQL; for example, a typical SELECT * FROM syslogs looks like this:

```
xactid         op
-------------- ---
0x031500001b00   7
0x021500000100   0
0x000000000000  17
0x021500000100   9
0x021500000100   9
0x021500000100   9
```

Cross-Reference

DBCC (Chapter 26) is the best way to find out what is going on in syslogs.◄

Sysusers

Just as the syslogins table lists SQL Server users in the system catalog, sysusers lists valid users for the database. It tells you the following:

- The SQL Server login for the user. This is tracked by the *suid* (the smallint), not the name (the varchar(30)).
- The unique identifier for the user within the database, a smallint called *uid*. All other tables in the database catalog refer to a user's *uid*. The database owner is always *uid* = *1*.
- The name for the *uid*, which must be unique within a database, but which does *not* have to match the name for the *suid* (though often they are the same).
- The group ID of the group to which the user belongs.

By combining this table with others, you can identify some interesting and useful things, such as the following.

Users with no logins

Database backups present an interesting problem for syslogins and sysusers. Suppose you have a database backup of a database called YourDatabase, made on a server named SERVER1, that you want to restore on a different server, SERVER2. Further assume that on SERVER1 there is a user named "Andrea", who has a *suid* of 361, and is a user in YourDatabase. It is quite possible that there is no such *suid* in SERVER2. What should SQL Server do about this? Causing the backup to fail would be unreasonable. Letting SQL Server automatically add *suid* 361 to SERVER2 is dangerous because SQL doesn't know what to use as a password, default database, language, and so on.

A warning would be nice, but instead SQL Server simply allows a backup to put undefined *suid* in sysusers without even telling you about it. Here's what to do:

Identify the problem

A simple NOT EXISTS query suffices to identify this situation:

```
SELECT *
   FROM YourDatabase..sysusers u
   WHERE suid > 0
      AND NOT EXISTS (SELECT *
      FROM master..syslogins
         WHERE suid = u.suid)
```

We specify *suid > 0* because public and guest have *suids* of –2 and –1, respectively. Furthermore, groups will be entered in sysusers with negative *suids*.

The query above will find disconnects in YourDatabase, but if you are the system administrator, you want to check all databases. In that case you need to run this SQL:

```
DECLARE c_use_db CURSOR FOR
SELECT 'use '+name
   FROM master..sysdatabases
   ORDER BY 1
FOR READ ONLY
OPEN c_use_db
declare @s_use_db varchar(255)
FETCH c_use_db INTO @s_use_db
WHILE @@FETCH_STATUS = 0 BEGIN
   EXECUTE(@s_use_db)
   SELECT @s_use_db - Optional. Tells you which database you are currently in.
   SELECT *
      FROM sysusers u
```

```
      WHERE suid > 0
         AND NOT EXISTS (SELECT *
            FROM master..syslogins
            WHERE suid = u.suid)
   FETCH c_use_db INTO @s_use_db
END
CLOSE c_use_db
DEALLOCATE c_use_db
```

Notice the query in the BEGIN...END loop is the same query: we have simply packaged it in a cursor that runs it for each database. We will have occasion to use this again, and in the future we will simply write

```
use <each database in turn>
SELECT *
   FROM sysusers u
   WHERE suid > 0
      AND NOT EXISTS (SELECT *
      FROM master..syslogins
         WHERE suid = u.suid)
```

We will agree that 'use <each database in turn>' means to wrap the query in the cursor loop above.

Fix the problem

In SQL Server 6.5 Microsoft gives you a stored procedure to fix the situation above. It is called sp_change_users_login, and you can run it in three modes: Report, Update_One, and Auto_Fix. Running it in Report mode does about the same thing as the query above. With Update_One you tell SQL Server to fix one login. Auto_Fix is the dangerous one; there, you give SQL Server the freedom to guess what to do.

Users with the wrong login

Your problems with sysusers don't end here, however. Suppose in YourDatabase in SERVER1 you have a user named FEDORCHEK, with a *suid* of 361. You restore a backup of YourDatabase into SERVER2, but it just so happens that in SERVER2 syslogins has a user named RENSIN with a *suid* of 361. You have a problem. FEDORCHEK wants access to YourDatabase. You add a login for him, which happens to get a *suid* of 400. You attempt to add FEDORCHEK as a user of YourDatabase, but (surprise!) you can't because the user name FEDORCHEK is taken by *suid* 361. Furthermore, RENSIN has access to YourDatabase, and he isn't supposed to. What a mess. You can identify *possible* occurrences of this problem with the following:

```
use <each database in turn>
SELECT *
   FROM sysusers u, master..syslogins l
   WHERE u.suid > 0
      AND u.uid > 1 /* Exclude the database owner */
      AND l.suid = u.suid
      AND l.name <> u.name
```

This only works if you accept the SQL Server defaults and let each sysusers name be the same as the syslogins name, which we recommend. Once you identify problems, you can fix them with the Update_One option of *sp_change_users_login*.

Users not allowed in their default database

You can have logins who are not allowed into their default database, either because the database owner dropped the users or because the logins were never set up right to begin with. The sysusers table is your key to fixing this, as shown here:

```
use <each database in turn>
SELECT suid, name, dbname
      FROM syslogins l
      WHERE dbname = 'YourDatabase'
         AND NOT EXISTS (SELECT *
            FROM YourDatabase..sysusers
            WHERE suid = l.suid)
```

We leave it as an exercise for you to modify this SQL to correct the problem automatically.

Sysdepends

The sysdepends system table contains one row for each table, view, or stored procedure that is referenced by a view, stored procedure, or trigger. As such it can be a wealth of information. The two columns you want to focus are simply depid, which is the object being referenced, and id, the object doing the referencing. For example, to find all the stored procedures that reference sysdepends, you would write

```
SELECT OBJECT_NAME(id) objname
   FROM sysdepends
   WHERE depid = OBJECT_ID('sysdepends')
   ORDER BY 1
```

This returns the following:

```
objname
------------------------------
sp_depends
sp_MSdependencies
sp_MSobject_dependencies
sp_rename
```

Queries of this kind are very helpful because they tell you more than you get in the SQL Server Books Online about what references what. For example, only the first and last procedures above are listed it the Online books.

Syskeys

Syskeys is a holdover from all the way back to SQL Server 4.2. It used to hold primary key foreign definition.

THE SYSTEM CATALOG

The system catalog tables contain server-wide information, and they are extremely valuable to the system administrator. The system tables are only in the master database. Therefore, either you should preface all the SQL you see below with

```
use master
go
```

or you should put 'master.dbo.' in front of each system table name. As you will recall, we queried sysobjects earlier to produce a list of the tables in the system catalog. The result was

```
name                id
------------------- -----------
sysdatabases        30
sysusages           31
sysprocesses        32
syslogins           33
syslocks            34
sysdevices          35
sysmessages         36
```

(continued)

(continued)

```
sysconfigures       37
syscurconfigs       38
sysservers          40
sysremotelogins     41
syslanguages        44
syscharsets         45
```

Of these, we would like to focus on sysdatabases, sysprocesses, syslogins, and sysdevices.

Sysdatabases

In the sysdatabases table, we have one entry per database. This table stores such information as what options are set in the database, who the owner is, when the database was created, and so on. The important columns here are

- **name.**The name of database.
- **dbid.** The integer SQL Server uses to track your database. If you've ever watched SQL Server recover, you might have noticed it recovers databases in *dbid* order.
- **suid.** The OWNER of the database (not necessarily the creator). This column can be changed with *sp_changedbowner*.
- **status.** A holder of all the status bits. You can use this to query database options.
- **crdate.** When the database was created.
- **dumptrdate.** The date of the last dump transaction. Query this field to see a summary of what was backed up when.

The SQL Enterprise Manager GUI doesn't let you summarize database information. If you have only a handful of databases, this probably doesn't bother you, but once you have more than a few, you will appreciate this table. The sp_helpdb procedure summarizes sysdatabases. An especially useful idea is to collect all the sysdatabases information for an entire enterprise. For example, you could define a table in the structure of the output of sp_helpdb and populate it for all your remote servers. Once you have data in this table, you can look for such things as how many databases are owned by the system administrator with a query like this:

```
SELECT srvname, name
  FROM enterprise_sysdatabases
  WHERE suid = 1 /* The system administrator is the owner */
    AND name NOT IN ( 'master', 'model', 'msdb', 'pubs', 'tempdb' )
  ORDER by 1, 2
```

You will be concerned if there are a lot of databases returned by this query; that tells you that your database owners all have system administrator access. Give them ownership of their databases and reserve the system administrator access for those who truly need it.

Sysprocesses

The sysprocesses table gives you information about the current SQL Server processes. This is not technically a table because it doesn't exist until you query it. SQL Server builds it dynamically. There is a wealth of information here, and Microsoft has added more information with SQL Server 6.5. Table 11-4 lists all the fields available to you in sysprocesses.

Table 11-4
Columns in Sysprocesses

Column	Datatype	Description
spid	smallint	Process ID
kpid	smallint	Windows NT thread ID
status	char(10)	Process ID status (for example, runnable, sleeping, and so on)
suid	smallint	Server user ID of user who executed command
hostname	char(10)	Name of workstation
program_name	char(16)	Name of application program
hostprocess	char(8)	Workstation process ID number
cmd	char(16)	Command currently being executed
cpu	int	Cumulative CPU time for process
physical_io	int	Cumulative disk reads and writes for process
memusage	int	Number of 2K pages of the procedure cache that are currently allocated to the process
blocked	smallint	Process ID of blocking process, if any
waittype	binary	Reserved
dbid	smallint	Database ID
uid	smallint	ID of user who executed command
gid	smallint	Group ID of user who executed command

There are several system procedures available to you to query this table, including sp_who, sp_who2, and sp_processinfo. Experiment with them. They won't always provide the data you need. That's why we explicitly listed the columns above: so you will know what you are missing out on.

Keep these points in mind for sysprocesses:

- At any instant in time, the vast majority of the processes will be sleeping. When you have hundreds of people logged in, you may want to limit your query with:

  ```
  WHERE NOT (status = 'sleeping' and cmd = 'awaiting command')
  ```

  This will screen out the connections that aren't doing anything interesting.
- There is always going to be at least one process running: your query of sysprocesses. It will show up with a cmd of SELECT. If you are running several SELECT statements at once, it can be difficult to determine which is which.
- One field to watch like a hawk is blocked. If blocked is anything other than zero, the process isn't getting anywhere. If the blocked query is running in the Query Analyzer, the user can watch the globe spin for minute after minute and get no answer back from SQL Server. The number in the blocked field is the spid of process that is locking out the blocked process. The system administrator can kill that process if necessary.

Syslogins

The syslogins tables lists the logins of your SQL Server. Each login is identified within SQL Server by *suid*, a smallint that is stored in this table. This integer is how SQL Server tracks logins. The name of the login is also stored in this table and must be unique. Also in this table are the default database and an encrypted password string. After reading about the last few tables, you probably expect that there is a sp_helplogin procedure, right? Close, but no cigar. Microsoft went plural on this one; it is *sp_helplogins*.

You can use syslogins for a variety of purposes. Here are a few of our favorites.

Finding a login

When you need to check on whether a login was created, you can just query syslogins. For example, you know there has to be login for someone whose name is David Andrew Smith, but you aren't sure if it is dsmith, smithd, dasmith, smithda, or what. If you have hundreds of logins, you won't want to search in the Server Manager window. It is simply easier to query:

```
SELECT *
   FROM syslogins
   WHERE name like '%smith%'
   ORDER BY name
```

Taking an action for all logins

Suppose you want to send a quick mail message to all your SQL Server users. Execute the SQL that this generates

```
SELECT 'master..xp_sendmail '''+name+''', ', '''The SQL Server will be down this
Saturday while we upgrade the operating system to Windows NT 4.0'''
   FROM syslogins
```

Warning

What happens when your SQL Server login is FEDORCHE, but your mail account is FEDORCHEK? xp_sendmail will fail. This is yet another reason to keep the logins standardized on your network.◀

You can easily extend this kind of query to such things as adding all logins as users to a new database, changing the default database from one database to another, and so on.

Changing the name of a login

When people in your organization change last names and want new logins, it can be a royal pain, especially in SQL Server. Suppose you have a user named Andrea Teague, with a login of TEAGUEA, and she wants to change to FEDORCHA because she changed her last name. How would you normally do this? You would have to drop the login TEAGUEA and add it back as FEDORCHA. However, there are lots of catches:

1. You first have to drop TEAGUEA out of all databases of which she is a user.
2. If TEAGUEA owns any objects in a database, you are going to have to drop those objects before you can drop TEAGUEA as a user. Assuming she wants the objects back, you have to bulk copy all her data and make scripts for all her objects.
3. When you do finally drop TEAGUEA, you will lose all her user information, like her default database, her encrypted password string, and so on.

This is a mess. Because SQL Server is really tracking TEAGUEA by her *suid*, you should be able just to change her name there. Why Microsoft doesn't offer this feature isn't clear; the steps are simple enough:

1. Configure the server to allow updates to the system catalog:

```
sp_configure 'allow', 1
reconfigure with override
```

2. Create a procedure that renames userids. You will want to add error checking to this, such as making sure the new name is a valid SQL Server identifier as so on:

```
CREATE PROC sp_renamelogin @old_name sysname, @new_name sysname AS
IF NOT EXISTS (SELECT * FROM syslogins WHERE name = @new_name) BEGIN
UPDATE syslogins
   SET name = @new_name
   WHERE name = @old_name
END
```

3. Reconfigure the system catalog to disallow updates:

```
sp_configure 'allow', 0
reconfigure with override
```

Warning

Bear in mind that this isn't part of Microsoft's supported feature set, so if something goes wrong, you are on your own.◀

Searching for null or obvious passwords

If you are using standard or mixed security mode, you want all your logins to have passwords, hopefully good ones. Unfortunately, users are notorious for setting their passwords to the easiest thing for them to remember. All too common are logins with no password, the login name itself as the password, or 'password' as the password. With syslogins you can find these situations easily:

```
SELECT name
   FROM syslogins
   WHERE password is null
      or pwdcompare(name, password) = 1
      or pwdcompare('password', password) = 1
   ORDER BY name
```

After you read Chapters 19 and 20 on tasks and mail, you might consider setting this up to run each night and e-mail any violations to you. If you have a table with employee information, you can check more stuff, such as spouse's names, birthdates, and so on. If you really want to be aggressive, you could load a list of English words into a table and compare the passwords against that.◀

Finding logins whose default database doesn't exist

In SQL Server you can drop or rename a database that is the default database for one or more logins. The default database doesn't get fixed automatically, nor do you get any warnings that you have orphaned some logins. Those logins can still access SQL Server, but they will get a non-fatal error and be connected to master because their default database doesn't exist. The trouble is, this error message makes some applications, such as MS Query, disallow the connection altogether, leaving users unable to log in.

You can find this problem with the system catalog:

```
SELECT name, dbname
   FROM syslogins log
   WHERE NOT EXISTS (SELECT *
         FROM sysdatabases
         WHERE log.dbname = name)
   ORDER BY name
```

Sysdevices

We'll close our system table tour with the sysdevices table. Early on in the book we had you create devices. This table lists the devices you have created in your SQL Server. Here you find helpful information, such as the operating system name of your devices. You may have noticed that there is no way to get a list of these operating system names from the SQL Enterprise Manager GUI. You can only see the names one by one with Manage⇨Devices⇨Edit Device. However, you can get this list from sysdevices with:

```
SELECT phyname
      FROM sysdevices
      WHERE cntrltype = 0 /* We only want non CD-ROM database devices */
      ORDER BY 1
```

Reconcile this list with the contents of your MSSQL\DATA directory once in a while. If you have files in this directory that are not in the list above, they are left over from devices you have already dropped. You should delete these files to recover disk space. The stored procedure sp_helpdevice presents the sysdevices table in a more readable format.

Tip

When you delete old device files, make sure SQL Server is running when you do the deletes: it will then prevent you from deleting an active device by mistake. If you are trying to delete a file for a device you just recently dropped, you might have to stop and start SQL Server, but you still want to do the deletes with SQL Server running.◀

Summary

There is no end to what you can do if you know the system tables and how to manipulate them with Transact-SQL. There are four main catalogs: the system, database, replication, and executive catalogs. We covered the first two in this chapter. SQL Server tracks all objects with integer IDs and gives you functions to convert the most frequently used IDs to names. Querying the system tables effectively requires interpreting status columns and the ability to build SQL statements in a query. Sysobjects is the key to all the system tables, followed closely by sysindexes and syscolums. With these tables, you can list your database objects and get important information about them. The rest of the database catalog is often quite helpful, too, but also contains tables that only mean something to SQL Server. The system catalog in the master database contains information pertinent to the server as a whole, such as lists of logins, databases, devices, and active processes.

Review Questions

Q: Why does SQL Server use integer ids to track objects instead of names?

A: The IDs allow faster execution, save space, and provide flexibility.

Q: What are the four categories of system tables, and where are they found?

A: The system catalog, in master only; the database catalog, in each database; replication tables, which are in various databases; and SQL Executive tables, which are in the msdb database.

Q: What is the clearest (easiest to read) way to query for a particular bit of an int?

A: Using the "POWER(2,*n*) & status", where *n* is the bit location and status is the column you are querying.

Q: Where can you go to get a list of all your objects?

A: Sysobjects

Q: Name four pieces of information you can get from sysobjects based on an object id.

A: The object name, owner, type, and creation date.

Q: What does sysindexes tell you?

A: What indexes you have on a table and whatever their attributes are (unique, clustered, and so on.)

Q: Why is sysdepends import?

A: It tells you which objects depend on other objects.

Q: How do you use sysdatabases with a cursor to save yourself a lot of work?

A: You can execute a query in all databases automatically if you set up the correct cursor.

Q: What makes sysprocesses different from all the other tables discussed in this chapter?

A: It isn't really stored on disk. SQL Server creates it on the fly when you issue a query to it.

Part

IV

DATABASE ADMINISTRATION

This part covers the creative work that you do as a database developer. A robust SQL Server database contains a rich variety of objects, all designed by you.

In Chapter 12, we begin with the foundation of your design, the relational model. In particular, we focus on SQL Server's support for the fundamental elements of the relational model. We discuss which features to use, how to use them, and perhaps most importantly, how not to use them. Next we proceed to a quick tour of normalization, which guides your decision on what data goes in what tables. We finish Chapter 12 with a thorough explanation of how to implement SQL Server's Declarative Referential Integrity, the single most important tool for a database administrator in establishing and maintaining data integrity.

With a sound design in mind, you are ready to begin creating your tables, and Chapter 13 is your guide. First, you want to know what building blocks are available to you in SQL Server, namely what types of data you can put in each column. Our discussion includes not just SQL Server datatypes, but other considerations such as SQL Server identifiers, keywords, quoted identifiers, and identity columns. With this background, we then cover using the SQL Enterprise Manager to create full-featured tables of every description.

As a good DBA, you will instinctively want to create several other objects the instant you create each table, and Chapter 13 follows through by covering these items as well. You will want to index your tables and know how to keep your index statistics current. You may need to set up views on your table. Views are an extremely powerful tool because they present a logical table to a user based on your physical tables. As such, they allow you divide, combine, reorder, rename, and filter to your heart's content with consuming any physical storage. Finally, Chapter 13 reviews granting permissions on your tables and views, so that everyone can use your creations.

One of the best features by far in SQL Server is the combining of several SQL statements into one compiled group called a *stored procedure*. As we explain in Chapter 14, fully utilizing stored procedures is a vital part of designing good client-server applications. Therefore, we give a complete discussion of stored procedure syntax, including using parameters with stored procedures and the various options you have in creating stored procedures. Next, we cover how SQL Server deals with stored procedures, especially the compilation of procedures and the storage of a procedure plan in the procedure cache of your server's memory. The second half of Chapter 14 is all about a specific kind of procedure called a *trigger*. Called automatically when you INSERT, UPDATE, or DELETE data in a table, triggers let you encode complex business logic directly into SQL Server.

We close out Part IV with SQL Server rules and defaults, Chapter 15. They are another option for you as a DBA to preserving the integrity of your data, in addition to the DRI we cover in Chapter 12 and the triggers we discuss in Chapter 14.

Chapter

Database Design 12

If you want information on developing a database, you'll typically find two kinds of books out there:

- Academic books on design that talk about no product in particular and don't even talk about the data definition language (DDL) commands of SQL, leaving you wondering how to implement the theory.
- Product-specific books that discuss DDL commands and interfaces in great detail, but give little information on what constitutes good design, other than to say it is "beyond the scope" of the book.

We prefer a different approach. Because this is a book on SQL Server, we do, of course, go into great detail on the commands and interfaces that implement your database design. However, in this chapter we cover the larger design concepts into which these commands fit.

What's in This Chapter

In this chapter, we cover two key areas of database design: the relational model and normalization. You will hear these two words used interchangeably, but they are different. The *relational model* is a standard for designing relational database management systems (RDBMSs); *normalization* is standard for designing the tables of a database. After you read this chapter you will

- Know exactly what a relation is and how to make sure your tables are really relations
- Know the difference between the normal forms
- Understand the importance of Declarative Referential Integrity (DRI)

Using the Relational Model

Scientists tell us that in the Jurassic period of computers (roughly a couple of decades ago, based on carbon-14 dating of transistors and vacuum tubes), businesses used hierarchical and network databases (see the sidebar, "Are Hierarchical Databases Really Dead?"). In these systems, the relationships between various data elements were explicitly stored with pointers and other links. The links were exposed to the users and programmers, so in order to query or update the data, you had to understand how it was stored. This limited the accessibility of the data to the select few who understood, in detail, the workings of the specific hierarchical or network database.

Then, in 1968, a man working at IBM named Edgar F. Codd proposed the *relational model*, a new paradigm for managing databases. The main goals of the relational model, which are still valid today, are the following:

1. *Simplifying the interaction with the data by users*

    who have large databases

    who need not be familiar with programming

    who normally conceive their interactions independently from all other users

2. *Substantially increasing the productivity of those users who are professional programmers*
3. *Supporting a much more powerful tool for the database administrator to use in controlling who has access to what information and for what purpose, as well as in controlling the integrity of the database*

---

*from E.F. Codd's *Relational Model for Database Management, Version 2*: pg. 11, Addison-Wesley, 1990

Are Hierarchical Databases Really Dead?

RDBMS folks don't like to admit it, but hierarchical databases do still have their place. Here's one: The Registry of Windows NT or Window 95.

A hierarchy works here because Microsoft is absolutely sure that the database will be accessed *only* through the interface Microsoft has written.

Over two decades of experience with Codd's relational model have shown that it is the simplest, most powerful, most flexible, and most reliable way to manage data. However, users reap these benefits only if the relational model is implemented correctly. In implementing the model correctly in SQL Server, two key players emerge

- **Microsoft.** The vendor's job is to deliver to you a DBMS that gives you all the tools you need to manage data in the context of the relational model. In our opinion, Microsoft is ahead of the pack in this regard, especially when you consider all of SQL Server's graphical tools for database administration.
- **You, the database developer.** That's right, you. Your role is actually more important. You actually have to create the database in SQL Server that simplifies user interaction and increases programmer productivity. You have to use the tools Microsoft gave you.

This second point may seem a bit silly. After all, if you are reading this book, you are clearly using SQL Server, so doesn't it follow that you are using the tools of the relational model and delivering a relational database to your users? No, it doesn't follow. Codd has articulated the relational model to the DMBS vendors as a list of features, hundreds of features in fact, that must be supported to comply with the relational model. Either by necessity or out of the vendors' desire to deliver maximum flexibility, the majority of these features are *optional* in any RDBMS, including SQL Server. Therefore, in the following section we will discuss which of the optional SQL Server features support the relational model and how using these features achieves the goals outlined for the relational model.

What is a relation?

The first, and most fundamental, point of the relational model is that all data is stored in relations. A relation is a set of rows and columns with the following properties:

- The values contained in the rows and columns are atomic (we'll define this in a moment).
- The ordering of the rows and columns doesn't matter.
- There are no duplicate rows.

These three items pack quite a wallop, and we'll consider them one by one.

The values in a relation are atomic

When values are *atomic*, it simply means that an RDBMS cannot decompose the value of a specific column in a specific row into smaller pieces. (If you're thinking, "But what about the SUBSTRING function?" we'll talk about that in a minute.) For folks who have only used a RDBMS, it is impossible to imagine how *not* to comply with this rule. So, let's take an example. Suppose we tell you to create a table in SQL Server that is to store test scores of students in a class. This table is to have two, and only two, columns. Furthermore, there must be no more than one row per student. The first column is a 30-character field called student, the second is to be an integer called score. Enter these values in Table 12-1.

Table 12-1
An Example of Non-Atomic Data

student	***score***
Fedorchek	89
	90
	95
Rensin	99
	97
	83
	90

This obviously wouldn't work if we're only allowed to have two columns and two rows. How would you do it? You can't store data this way in SQL Server, which is the whole point. Atomicity is one of the few features of the relational model that isn't optional. It is designed in at the lowest level. Non-atomic storage was possible in hierarchical databases; however, and the languages supporting them provide syntax for accessing data stored in this way.

The way to fix this problem is to relax the requirements restricting the number of rows and columns. The proper way to store the data would be like in Table 12-2.

Table 12-2
A Corrected Example

student	*score_number*	*score*
Fedorchek	1	89
Fedorchek	2	90
Fedorchek	3	95
Rensin	1	99
Rensin	2	97
Rensin	3	83
Rensin	4	90

How to get yourself in trouble with atomicity

Although SQL Server doesn't let you directly break the atomicity rule of relations, you as a database developer can still violate the spirit of the rule in many ways. As the database owner, your job is to weed out non-atomic data from your design. The following examples are the common mistakes we have seen, but there are others. Don't let your customers tell you these poor designs are required for convenience or that "it has worked so far." The point is that these non-atomic structures prevent you from using the relational model tools Microsoft worked so hard to put in SQL Server.

Using SUBSTRING to violate atomcity

SUBSTRING is an invaluable function — you simply couldn't manage character data without it — but it opens a Pandora's box in relational databases. To an RDBMS the only compound (non-atomic) data supported is supposed to be the relation. You can't make a new structure (like with the struct operator in C) and put it in a cell of a table. This limitation is an intentional attempt to keep the relational model, and the languages supporting it, simple. But as any C programmer will tell you, a character string is an inherently compound data type; it is an array of characters.

Let's try to make another table, this time of employee addresses. Again we will have two columns, a 30-character employee column and a 255-character address column. We will call the table addresses, and we want to enter the data shown in Table 12-3.

Table 12-3
An Example of Poor Database Design

employee	*address*
Fedorchek, Andrew M.	1020 N Quincy St 711 Arlington VA 22201
Rensin, David K.	1231 S Ciderbarrel Rd Fair Oaks VA 22405

This is a table you really can create and enter into SQL Server, but it isn't a relation. Both columns are non-atomic. Suppose this table had thousands of entries, and further suppose that "Ciderbarrel Rd" in Fair Oaks, VA, gets renamed to "Applecider Cir." How would you update your data? Good luck. You could try this:

```
UPDATE addresses
   SET address = STUFF(address,PATINDEX('Ciderbarrel Rd',address),14,'Applecider
Cir')
   WHERE address like '%Ciderbarrel Rd%Fair Oaks VA%'
```

Not only is this extremely awkward, there is no guarantee it will work. Suppose someone entered an address as "Ciderbarrel Road", or listed the town and state as "Fair Oaks, VA"? Furthermore, if this is a really large table, your performance searching in the address field will be abysmal because no indexes can be used. What you needed was a better original design, as in Table 12-4.

Table 12-4
An Example of a Better Design

emp_lname	***add_no***	***st_name***	***st_type***	***apt_no***	***town***	***state***	***zip***
Fedorchek	1020	N Quincy	St	711	Arlington	VA	22201
Rensin	1231	Ciderbarrel	Rd	null	Fair Oaks	VA	22405

Now you can make your change with this:

```
UPDATE addresses
   SET st_name = 'Applecider', st_type = 'Cir'
   WHERE st_name = 'Ciderbarrel'
      AND st_type = 'Rd'
      AND town = 'Fair Oaks'
      AND state = 'VA'
```

This UPDATE statement is easier to write, and because you can now index *town* and *state*, it will probably run faster. (We cover indexes in Chapter 13.) Furthermore, you don't have to worry about the difference between "Fair Oaks VA" and "Fair Oaks, VA" because these quantities are explicitly separated into separate fields. Finally, you can use the tools of the RDBMS to restrict the acceptable values for st_type to your own list, such as 'Rd', 'St', 'Dr', 'Cir', 'Ave', and so on, so no one can enter "Road" instead of "Rd".◀

Using an integer to store bit flags

Our favorite non-atomic trouble spot is using an integer to store bit flags because Microsoft does it all over the place in its system tables. Suppose you needed to store a bunch of true/false values in a table. What would you do? You could set up a bit column for each question. This would at least meet the atomicity standard of a relation. There is an even better way we will discuss below in normalization. The wrong way is to put on your C programmer hat and say, "Hey, 23 in binary is 10111, so I can just use one integer field to store my true/false values. 23 would mean true for the first, third, fourth, and fifth questions." Now you don't have a relation any more.

Have you ever tried to query sysindexes to find which indexes on a given table, if any, have a particular column anywhere in the key? Good luck. The correct query is this:

```
SELECT i.name
FROM sysindexes i
   JOIN syscolumns c ON i.id = c.id
   WHERE i.id = OBJECT_ID(<the_table_you_want>)
      AND indid NOT IN (0,255)
      AND c.name = <the_column_you_want>
      AND (SUBSTRING(keys1,3 + 0*16,1) = colid
         OR SUBSTRING(keys1,3 + 1*16,1) = colid
         OR SUBSTRING(keys1,3 + 2*16,1) = colid
         OR SUBSTRING(keys1,3 + 3*16,1) = colid
         OR SUBSTRING(keys1,3 + 4*16,1) = colid
         OR SUBSTRING(keys1,3 + 5*16,1) = colid
         OR SUBSTRING(keys1,3 + 6*16,1) = colid
         OR SUBSTRING(keys1,3 + 7*16,1) = colid
         OR SUBSTRING(keys1,3 + 8*16,1) = colid
         OR SUBSTRING(keys1,3 + 9*16,1) = colid
         OR SUBSTRING(keys1,3 + 10*16,1) = colid
         OR SUBSTRING(keys1,3 + 11*16,1) = colid
         OR SUBSTRING(keys1,3 + 12*16,1) = colid
         OR SUBSTRING(keys1,3 + 13*16,1) = colid
         OR SUBSTRING(keys1,3 + 14*16,1) = colid
         OR SUBSTRING(keys1,3 + 15*16,1) = colid
         OR SUBSTRING(keys1,3 + 16*16,1) = colid)
   ORDER BY 1
```

We chose not to use the INDEX_COL function in this query to emphasize the fact that you are really using a SUBSTRING. This is the kind of burden you place on users if you store non-atomic values.

Appending a letter designator to a description

Another common atomicity problem is caused by appending a letter designator to a description. Almost all databases have made-up codes that mean something to the users. Whether it is a part number or a project billing number, it is just easier to refer to a code such as "FEDBP012" in a database, rather than to have to write out explicitly "Business process redesign study for Department of Redundancy Department." You will of course have a separate table defining the descriptions of codes like "FEDBP012." But what if someone decides to record the completion of a project by altering its description to say "Business process redesign study for Department of Redundancy Department (C)"? Or maybe they will append the completion date on the description. Either way is wrong. Create a separate column to record this new information. The ALTER TABLE command makes this so easy that you have no excuse not to give your users a new column.

Using compound codes

Yet another atomicity problem involves using compound codes. Continuing with the previous example, you may find that what "FEDBP012" means is that is the twelfth (the 012 part) business process redesign study (the BP part) that your company has done in support of the federal government (the FED part). Furthermore, all codes have to be of the form AAABB###, where AAA is chosen from a list of customers you support, BB is chosen from a list of project categories, and ### is just a sequential number. You have three fields here; you ought to have three fields in your table. Otherwise, you have to do a lot of application-specific logic to keep people from dreaming up codes in the wrong format.

Giving a field column more than one meaning

This usually happens out of laziness. You have a table that contains some information. You get a new requirement to track a new piece of information. How inconvenient. Now you not only have to alter the table (this isn't too much work, but this alone makes a lot of database owners say "no"), but you also have to change your applications: the input screens, the internal logic, the reports, and so on. Then you get a "bright" idea. You notice that the data for this new requirement could be accommodated in an existing column, so you stuff the data there, making it a multi-use column. Let's look at an example.

Suppose you have a table that lists all company employees, both workers and managers. You have a column in this table called supervisor, which is the employee's immediate boss. You leave supervisor blank for all vice presidents because as far as you can see they are accountable to no one. The new requirement is to add data for employees who will now be getting company cars, and it just so happens that only vice presidents are eligible for this perk. Therefore, to save work, you store the license plate of each vice president's car in the supervisor column. This is a good solution, right?

Wrong! You have made a mess of the database that will haunt you and everyone else later. Among your problems are

- Even if everyone swore up and down that no one but vice presidents would get cars, they will change their minds. You won't be able to cope, and you will have to change your structures. Change it now and get it right.
- You can neither link this multi-use column to the list of valid supervisors nor to the list of valid company license plate numbers, so you have to write special logic that will take more time to write, debug, and maintain.
- Someone not privy to your unique ideas about how to store data will query the table and get incorrect results. For example, someone will count the number of distinct values in the supervisor column to see how many people in the company are supervisors. All those license plate numbers will fictitiously add to the count. The relational model stresses that you can't anticipate all the way people will access the data.

Speaking of columns that change meaning, we can go right back to the sysindexes table to find an example. What does the name column mean? Sysindexes does have a row for each index in your database, but it also has a row for each table that has no indexes. If we are really talking about an index row, then name is the index name. Otherwise, it is the table name.◀

The ordering of the rows and columns doesn't matter

The second defining aspect of a relation is that the order of rows and columns doesn't matter. This simply means that the database shouldn't show you counters, pointers, or any internal ordering scheme and require you to use them. When you create a table it has the columns you specify, period. In this model, unlike dBASE, there is no record number you can reach. The value of not having explicit counters is that you never have to worry about a query or an application going haywire because somehow the record numbers ended up in an unexpected state. Like the principle of atomicity, this is fundamental to SQL Server's design, so you have to go out of your way to violate this precept of the relational model. However, it can still happen; here's how:

Using the clustered index instead of ORDER BY

Different RDBMSs have different methods of implementing clustered indexes. In DB2, when you first load a table it will be in clustering index order. Though DB2 tries to stay faithful to the clustering index with inserts and deletes, the data will drift out of clustering index order. Therefore, you can never predict the order a simple SELECT * FROM table_name will have. In SQL Server it is different. If defined, data is always stored in clustered unique index order, although the data is not necessarily returned in that order.

Tip

Don't ever write a query, a cursor, or an application that expects the data to be returned in clustered unique index order. Always use an ORDER BY clause when the result set of the query will be more than one row. It doesn't take any extra effort on your part, and it often takes minimal extra effort on SQL Server's part. If you fail to include the ORDER BY clause, you are in effect treating the table as if it has some intrinsic order. You will get a rude surprise if someone changes the clustered index order or if the SQL Server optimizer just happens to provide your result set in a different order.◀

Explicitly creating record numbers

There are lots of ways to create record numbers, even if SQL Server doesn't give them to you. You can use the timestamp data type, you can apply the identity property to a column, or you can implement your own custom method for generating record numbers. These are all okay if you are using these fields as surrogate keys, a denormalization technique in which you replace a long, composite primary key with a small single column key in hopes of getting better performance. The timestamps and identities aren't okay if you are creating them to function as record numbers. If you have no other way to query and manipulate the data other than your surrogate keys and if there is no other unique way to identify a row, you have record numbers. The biggest problem with true record numbers is that from the user's perspective, SQL Server isn't set up to handle them and the performance of any record-by-record operation is almost universally slow. CURSORs themselves are slow and, unfortunately, are the only real mechanism SQL Server provides for one-row-at-a-time access.

You find record numbers all the time in SQL Server databases when you need to store character data that is more than 255 characters, but not too much more. What happens is that you have some text that you need to store that may be as little as a line or two but could be as much as a couple hundred characters, even a few thousand characters. What do you do? A char data type is limited to 255 characters. You can use a text data type, but they suck up a 2K page for each entry, even if all you store is "Hello." Besides that, the text data type requires special commands like WRITETEXT, so it is more work for you and your programmers. The typical solution is to use two columns: a sequence_number column that is an int and a text column that is char(255). Then, you would break your text into 255-character chunks and store them with sequence numbers of 0, 1, 2, and so on. This is how the syscomments table in SQL Server works.

Dealing with large amounts of character data is admittedly the Achilles Heel of a RDBMS. Having said that, we encourage you to use the text data type if at all possible. The sequence_number column solution doesn't fit into the relational model, and it leads to problems, such as these:

- One person decides to start numbering at zero, and another person figures the first entry should be labeled as 1.
- The keyword LIKE may fail to find a string because it is split across rows. For example, if the string "Fedorchek" breaks so that "Fedor" is the last five characters of sequence_number 1 and "chek" is the first four characters of sequence_number 2, you won't find the string with text LIKE '%Fedorchek%'.
- You have to concatenate the strings back together yourself for display purposes, which is a pain.

If you have the space to spare, give the text data type a shot.

There are no duplicate rows in a relation

Here is the third part of the definition of a relation. There must be a column or combination of columns in a relation, even if it is all the columns, that uniquely determine each row. Therefore, the example in Table 12-5 is not a relation.

The names "Andrew" and "Dave" appear twice. Tables like this where rows cannot be uniquely identified are called corrupted relations. They have been a source of great debate for the life of the relational model. We fall on Codd's side of the fence. Our combined experience in working with many different databases has yet to show us an example were duplicate rows were needed or provided any meaningful information. There are whole papers and chapters of books about why corrupted relations are bad; we will summarize the problems with just three points:

Table 12-5
An Example of a Corrupted Relation

friends
Andrew
Andrea
Dave
Lia
Scott
Fred
Jackie
Chris
Dave
Andrew

- There is no support in SQL for corrupted relations. If you try to create the table above in SQL Server with just the single column called friends and then use SQL to update one, and only one, of the "Andrew" rows to "Mark", you can't do it. You have to delete both "Andrew" rows, and then insert an "Andrew" and a "Mark" row. Use your imagination to picture a real-life example with hundreds of megabytes of data to see what you are in for with corrupted relations.
- There is no consistent way to interpret duplicate rows. This is Codd's principal objection to using duplicate rows.
- You lose lots of functionality with corrupted relations. You can't use the table to define the domain of values for another table. You can't replicate such a table. You can't edit such a table with Microsoft Query or Microsoft Access.

We would like to see the RDBMS vendors eliminate support for corrupted relations, and we would like to see the ANSI SQL3 standard specify that all SQL queries must return true relations. Until this happens, the burden of enforcing the relational model is on you, the database developer. We will tell you how to adhere to the uniqueness rule, but first we need to define a primary key. A primary key is a subset of the columns of the table such that:

- Specifying the values for this subset uniquely determines a row in the table.
- There is no smaller subset of the primary key set which would still have this property, that is, there is no smaller subset whose values are enough to determine a row uniquely.

We will talk about how SQL Server implements primary keys in the Chapter 13. In order to make sure your database adheres to, and gets the benefits of, the relational model you *must:*

- Always, always, *always* put a primary key on a table. The SQL Enterprise Manager doesn't even warn you if you use it to create a table without a primary key; in fact, you have to click a special button just to get the primary key interface to appear (it is normally hidden). This is poor database design. Always use primary keys.
- Use SELECT DISTINCT on all queries where there is the slightest chance you will get duplicate rows returned. Even if you aren't putting the SELECT results into a table, it is still important for closure. A SELECT retrieves information from relations, and it should always have a relation as its output.◀

There are still a couple of trouble spots to watch for with regard to primary keys, such as:

- Tables created with SELECT INTO. This command does not allow you to specify a primary key. Always follow it with an ALTER TABLE command to put the primary key back on.
- Temporary tables, especially temporary tables created inside stored procedures. For some reason, programmers tend to forget about primary keys on temporary tables, apparently thinking, "What could it matter for something that isn't permanent?" It matters. You get all the same problems.

NORMALIZATION

So far, the only thing we have said about database *design* is to encourage you to make sure all your tables are relations. This will go a long way toward ensuring that you reap the benefits of an RDBMS. However, there is a whole discipline of design called *normalization* that we would like to discuss. Normalization specifies a succession of increasingly more demanding standards for table design that are unimaginatively named first normal form (1NF), second normal form (2NF), third normal form (3NF), Boyce-Codd normal form (BCNF), fourth normal form (4NF), and fifth normal form (5NF). Each of these standards helps prevent certain anomalies that would otherwise occur if you didn't follow these standards. Realizing the performance and flexibility potential of any relational database depends on your ability to understand and enforce the rules of the normal forms. If you screw that up you pay the price everywhere else. Worse yet, you may not even realize where you are losing out. You may have just learned to live with a certain amount of debugging time, a certain amount of poor application performance, a certain amount of inflexibility. The collective experience of database owners over the years shows that using the first three normal forms is sufficient to avoid the vast majority of pitfalls in data management, so we will focus on them.

First normal form (1NF)

A first normal form table must have atomic values and a primary key, and the order of its rows and columns must not matter. Sound familiar? All relations are in the 1NF. We have already covered the problems of not using relations in the first half of this chapter in great depth.

Second normal form (2NF)

The second normal form requires that all non-key columns depend on the whole primary key. Therefore, if the primary key of a table is one column, it is automatically in the second normal form. Suppose you make a table of the files on your hard drive that has fields such as directory char(255), file_name char(255), extension char(255), and assoc_app char(255). Assume the first three are the primary key. This is not in 2NF because assoc_app doesn't depend on the whole primary key. Only the extension is required to determine the association. Therefore, you should split this table into two tables: one with directory, file_name, and extension and the other with just extension and assoc_app.

The 2NF corrects certain problems. Suppose you have a new application called "AndrewsEditor.EXE," and you want to record the fact that files with the extension .AMF are used with this file. You can't capture this information until you actually have an .AMF file. Likewise, suppose you clean up your hard drive and get rid of all your .DBF files (because you now use only Microsoft Access). With only the 1NF table you wouldn't be able to associate .DBF files with the dBASE application.

Third normal form

The third normal form requires that there be no transitive dependencies among non-key columns. This means that you cannot have one non-key column dependent on another non-key column for its definition. Consider the following: You have a table that stores information about automobiles (Table 12-6). It stores the name of the car, the make of tire it ships with, and the expected life (in miles) of the tire.

Table 12-6
Improper Third Normal Form

Auto_make	*tire_make*	*tire_life*
1995 Mazda Protégé	Michelin XJ11	50,000
1995 Acura Integra	Michelin XJ11	50,000
1995 Porsche 911	Parelli ABQ-32	112,000

The problem with this data is that the value in tire_life has nothing to do with the value in auto_make. It is really dependent on the value in tire_make (another non-key column).

The correct way to handle this situation is to have two tables: autos (Table 12-7) and *tires* (Table 12-8).

Table 12-7
Autos Table

Auto_make	*tire_make*
1995 Mazda Protégé	Michelin XJ11
1995 Acura Integra	Michelin XJ11
1995 Porsche 911	Parelli ABQ-32

Table 12-8
Tires Table

tire_make	*tire_life*
Michelin XJ11	50,000
Parelli ABQ-32	112,000

The reformatting of the data in this form has done several things. First, it has more formally established the dependency of tire_life on tire_make. Second, as you add more values to the autos table, you will greatly reduce the amount of data needed in the tires table and, therefore, the amount of data in your database. Last, if you change a value for which tire a car ships with, it will not mean a change in the value of the tire life.

INTEGRITY CONSTRAINTS

At this point, you know what a relation is and how to make sure your tables are relations. We can now safely pull apart the words "Relational Database Management System" to say that your main job as a database owner is to manage your relations. A huge part of this managing relations is maintaining *integrity*, the quality and consistency of your data. You have to make sure you don't have incorrectly typed values, missing values, incorrectly formatted values, and so on. You do this with integrity constraints. There are five kinds of integrity constraints in the relational model:

- Domain integrity
- Column integrity
- Entity integrity
- Referential integrity
- User-defined integrity

These five areas don't perfectly correspond to what you find in the SQL Server manuals or the ANSI-92 SQL standard, unfortunately. In this section, we'll guide you through how SQL Server lets you enforce these integrity constraints and where it falls short. We will be covering what Microsoft calls Declarative Referential Integrity (DRI), which includes CHECK, DEFAULT, PRIMARY KEY, UNIQUE, and FOREIGN KEY (referential integrity) constraints, all of which we define below. We will also comment on related issues such as user-defined datatypes and triggers, but those topics are covered in detail in subsequent chapters.

Domain integrity

By definition, a *domain* is the set of values over which a specific column in a relation is defined. This is the single biggest area where all RDBMSs, including SQL Server, don't do what the relational model demands. The relational model requires the ability to:

- Define new domains beyond those given to you by the RDBMS
- Limit the range of values for a domain
- Specify whether comparison operators apply on the domain

Let's examine SQL Server support for these three requiremnents.

Defining new domains beyond those given with the RDBMS

You can do this in SQL Server, but not in the way specified by the ANSI SQL-92 standard. We will have more to say about this in Chapter 15, but here's a quick overview. In SQL-92 the command for creating a new domain is CREATE DOMAIN. This falls right in line with all the other CREATE commands, such as CREATE TABLE, CREATE VIEW, CREATE INDEX, and so forth. Domains in the SQL-92 standard have owners, just like tables, views, and other objects. The SQL-92 syntax is

```
CREATE DOMAIN  [database.[owner].]domain_name datatype [constraint [constraint
[...constraint]]]
```

The constraints can be CHECK and DEFAULT constraints. These constraints use the keyword VALUE to refer to the domain column, for example:

```
CREATE DOMAIN FedorcheksFavorite char(4) DEFAULT ('NONE') CHECK (VALUE BETWEEN 'A'
AND 'F')
```

This isn't what SQL Server does. In SQL Server you create new domain by creating a new user defined datatype. The "command" is the stored procedure sp_addtype. The syntax is

```
sp_addtype typename, phystype [, nulltype]
```

Notice that all you specify is a name, a base datatype, and whether the column is null, for example:

```
sp_addtype 'FedorcheksFavorite', 'char(4)', null
```

Adding in the other information is kludgy. As we explain in Chapter 15, the inclusion of a default requires creating a default with CREATE DEFAULT and then binding the default to the datatype with sp_bindefault. Adding a check of some kind is, likewise, obscure; you must create a rule with

CREATE RULE and then bind it with sp_bindrule. You can't put a foreign key on a datatype in SQL Server.◀

Specifying a range of values for a domain

You can specify a range of values for a domain in SQL Server, but again it is not the ANSI SQL-92 standard way. Notice that in our SQL-92 example above we simply said "CHECK(VALUE BETWEEN 'A' and 'F')". As we said above, to do this in SQL Server requires the CREATE RULE command and the sp_bindrule stored procedure. In our opinion, you are better off enforcing this kind of stuff with either column or referential integrity. (We'll talk about these soon.)

Specifying whether the comparison operators (<, >) apply to the domain.

You simply can't do this in SQL Server, nor is there a work-around. The feature just isn't supported. The idea of the relational model is that you might have a column in one table that records the number of employees working on a project, and in some other column somewhere else specify the amount of money spent on various pieces of the project. You would likely make the former an int data type and the latter a money data type in SQL Server. Even though these are different data types, SQL Server allows you to do nonsensical things like compare them, add them together, and so on. According to the relational model, if you create a "people" domain and a "dollars" domain, even if they have the *same* base data type (such as int), you still couldn't compare them unless you explicitly told the RDBMS to convert one to another. The relational model specifies other kinds of type-checking, too, such as making sure that a UNION marries up values in the same domain.

Though it isn't required by the relational model, one kind of integrity you do get with domains is defaults. You can specify the default value for any column in your user-defined domain, which will be used in the absence of a supplied value.

Column integrity

Column integrity in the relational model involves any specific rules that don't apply to a domain as a whole, but do apply to a specific column. These rules limit the range of acceptable values for the column. SQL Server supports such rules nicely with the CHECK constraint. A CHECK constraint limits the values you put in columns of a table. SQL Server CHECK constraints are either column level constraints or table level constraints. Each column of a table can have at most one column level constraint but can be referenced by any number of table level constraints. Only the column level constraints enforce column integrity; table level CHECK constraints are for user-defined integrity, which we get to a little bit later. The syntax for a CHECK constraint itself is

```
[CONSTRAINT constraint_name] CHECK [NOT FOR REPLICATION] (expression)
```

Cross-Reference

The optional constraint name must conform to the SQL Server rules for identifiers. If you do not want data being replicated from another server subject to your constraint, you may specify "NOT FOR REPLICATION". The mandatory expression must be Boolean and must not contain any subqueries. You can use this syntax either in the SQL Enterprise Manager interface (Chapter 13) or inside a CREATE TABLE or ALTER TABLE command, for example:

```
CREATE TABLE ColumnIntegrityTest (
 name varchar(30) CHECK(name LIKE '[_@#a-z]%'
      AND name NOT LIKE '%[^a-z0-9_@$#]%'))
```

In this example, we have confined the column name to beginning with a letter or the symbols _, @, and #, and we have restricted all characters to letters, numbers, or the symbols _, @, #, and $. In other words, a valid SQL Server identifier! Notice that we gave no name to the constraint; SQL Server assigns a name for us. You can find the name from the sp_help stored procedure (highlight "ColumnIntegrityTest" in the Query Analyzer and press ALT-F1), or from this query:

```
SELECT 'Constraint Name' = OBJECT_NAME( constid )
    FROM sysconstraints con
    JOIN syscolumns col ON con.id = col.id
        AND con.colid = col.colid
    WHERE con.id = OBJECT_ID( 'ColumnIntegrityTest' )
        AND col.name = 'name'
```

In our case, the constraint name ends up being "CK__ColumnInte__name__0856260D". If you wish to specify the constraint name explictly, you may do so:

```
CREATE TABLE ColumnIntegrityTest (
   name varchar(30) Constraint Valid_SQL_Server_Identifier
      CHECK(name LIKE '[_@#a-z]%'
      AND name NOT LIKE '%[^a-z0-9_@$#]%'))
```

For a given database user, constraint names must be unique in the database.

Column Level verses Table Level

There is a very subtle difference between the examples above and this CREATE TABLE statement:

```
CREATE TABLE ColumnIntegrityTest (
  name varchar(30), CHECK(name LIKE '[_@#a-z]%'
      AND name NOT LIKE '%[^a-z0-9_@$#]%'))
```

Do you see the difference? This CREATE TABLE statement has a comma immediately after the datatype of the column. It is still syntactically correct, but that one little comma tells SQL Server that this is a table level constraint. The same holds true if you are naming the constraint yourself:

```
CREATE TABLE ColumnIntegrityTest (
   name varchar(30), Constraint Valid_SQL_Server_Identifier
      CHECK(name LIKE '[_@#a-z]%'
      AND name NOT LIKE '%[^a-z0-9_@$#]%'))
```

This is a table level constraint, too.

Adding CHECK Constraints with ALTER TABLE

If you have already created a table, you can still add whatever constraints you need. Unless you specify NOCHECK, SQL Server checks all the data in the table to see if it meets the constraint you want to create. If any of the rows violate the constraint, SQL Server gives you an error and does not create the constraint. The syntax is the following:

```
ALTER TABLE [database.[owner.]]table_name
[WITH {CHECK | NOCHECK}]
   [ADD
      {col_name column_properties [column_constraints]
      | [[, ] table_constraint]}
         [, {next_col_name | next_table_constraint}]...]
```

Let's say we created our table simply as:

```
CREATE TABLE ColumnIntegrityTest (name varchar(30))
```

Now we can add the constraint we created before with the command:

```
ALTER TABLE ColumnIntegrityTest ADD CHECK(name LIKE '[_@#a-z]%' AND name NOT LIKE
'%[^a-z0-9_@$#]%')
```

Or we can name the constraint explicitly:

```
ALTER TABLE ColumnIntegrityTest ADD CONSTRAINT Valid_SQL_Server_Identifier
CHECK(name LIKE '[_@#a-z]%' AND name NOT LIKE '%[^a-z0-9_@$#]%')
```

There are two important points to note when you add CHECK constraints with the ALTER TABLE command to a column that is already in the table:

- SQL Server always designates the constraint as a table level constraint. There is no way to tell SQL Server that the constraint is for one specific column.
- You have the option of overriding the CHECK at creation.

The second bullet refers to "WITH NOCHECK". If you create the constraint with the command:

```
ALTER TABLE ColumnIntegrityTest WITH NOCHECK ADD CHECK(name LIKE '[_@#a-z]%' AND
name NOT LIKE '%[^a-z0-9_@$#]%')
```

Warning

SQL Server will not check your data at constraint creation time for adherence to the constraint. However, any time you try to UPDATE a row in the future, SQL Server will check this constraint, even if you are updating a column not affected by the constraint. This produces madding bugs. We advise you not to use NOCHECK unless it is to reapply a constraint that you just dropped a minute earlier, and even then only if you feel you can't afford the performance hit of a full check.◀

Adding Columns and CHECK Constraints with ALTER TABLE

When you add a column to a table, you can put column level constraints on at the same time. To continue our example, you might write

```
ALTER TABLE ColumnIntegrityTest ADD owner varchar(30) null
   CHECK(owner = USER_NAME()
      OR owner = SUSER_NAME()
      OR owner IN ('Andrew','Dave'))
```

The virtue of adding your CHECK constraint as you add your column is that SQL Server will record your constraint as a column lever constraint attached to that specific column. This example also shows that you can use functions in your CHECK constraints. As before, you can explicitly name your constraint if you so desire.

Suspending or dropping CHECK Constraints

Once created, a SQL Server enforces your CHECK constraints on all INSERTs and UPDATEs. The bulkcopy program (BCP.EXE) is always exempt from CHECK constraints, and you may exempt the replication process with NOT FOR REPLICATION. If you need to allow some normal INSERT or UPDATE statements to violate the constraint, the ALTER TABLE command allows you to do so. The syntax is

```
ALTER TABLE [database.[owner.]]table_name
    {{CHECK | NOCHECK} CONSTRAINT {constraint_name | ALL}
```

To lift our favorite example check we would write

```
ALTER TABLE ColumnIntegrityTest NOCHECK CONSTRAINT Valid_SQL_Server_Identifier
```

This leaves the constraint off until we turn it back on with the CHECK option in the ALTER TABLE command. We offer the same warning as we did before about NOCHECK: don't use it.

If you want to modify a check, you must drop it and re-create it. The syntax is

```
ALTER TABLE [database.[owner.]]table_name
    [DROP CONSTRAINT]
    constraint_name [, constraint_name2]...]}
```

Renaming columns with CHECK Constraints

The text that defines your CHECK constraint is stored in syscomments. If you want to see it you can use the SQL Enterprise Manager, sp_help, or query syscomments directly. If your constraint is named 'CK__ColumnInte__name__23FE4082' the query would be

```
SELECT colid, text
    FROM syscomments
    WHERE id = OBJECT_ID( 'CK__ColumnInte__name__23FE4082' )
    ORDER BY colid
```

Secret

It is important to order the query by colid because if you have more than 255 characters of text in your CHECK constraint, it spills over into a second line in syscomments. Furthermore, SQL Server will often pad your CHECK constraint with parentheses, and SQL Server converts all "IN" expressions to "OR" expressions. This increases the length of your CHECK constraint. Note that sp_help doesn't give you more than the first line of your check constraint when you have a long constraint.◀

Now here's a question for you: What happens when you rename a column in your table with sp_rename? Does the constraint still work? Yes, because it is compiled. However, you should clean up this inconsistency by dropping and recreating the constraint with the correct column name. Otherwise, you leave behind a problem that will surface when you try to script the table.

DEFAULT Constraints

Strictly speaking, the capability to specify a default value for a column isn't part of the column's data integrity, but it is often talked about as such. Let's talk about this handy feature. As you know from our discussion of SQL, you can choose to insert data only into a subset of a table's columns when you insert a row. You do this by using the optional column list after the INSERT command:

```
INSERT [INTO]
    {table_name | view_name} [(column_list)]
{DEFAULT VALUES | values_list | select_statement}
```

Normally, SQL Server puts a null in the columns for which you did not supply a value. If one of the columns doesn't allow nulls, your INSERT fails. DEFAULT Constraints allow you to specify a value that SQL Server should use instead of a null when you don't supply a value. The syntax for a DEFAULT Constraint is

```
[CONSTRAINT constraint_name]
    DEFAULT {constant_expression | niladic-function | NULL}
        [FOR col_name]
```

Constant expression means things, "Andrew", and 29. A niladic-function is one that requires no arguments, such as USER_NAME(), DB_NAME(), and so on. You can even combine constants and expressions, for example:

```
DEFAULT (USER_NAME()+' was using '+DB_NAME())
```

What use you might possibly have for this eludes us, but you can do it if you need to. You incorporate DEFAULT constraints into your tables in the same way you handle CHECK constraints. Here are a few quick examples.

```
/*Unnamed default*/
CREATE TABLE DefaultTest (
   Column_A varchar(30) DEFAULT ('Fedorchek'))

/*Named default*/
CREATE TABLE DefaultTest (
   Column_A varchar(30) CONSTRAINT Default_A DEFAULT ('Rensin'))

/*ALTER TABLE default*/
ALTER TABLE DefaultTest ADD DEFAULT ('Pines') FOR Column_A
```

Entity integrity

The relational model demands that every relation have a primary key and that no column of the primary key be null. SQL Server supports this with the PRIMARY KEY constraint. When you specify a primary key, SQL Server automatically creates a unique index to enforce the key. SQL Server always enforces the primary key, period. Nothing, not bulkcopy, not replication, nothing, can violate the primary key. SQL Server also lets you define UNIQUE constraints, which do allow nulls. However, when a UNIQUE constraint spans more than one column, only one row can have null values for all the UNIQUE constraint columns. Each table can have at most one primary key, but up to 249 unique keys.

The syntax for UNIQUE and PRIMARY KEY constraints is identical, so we will cover only the primary key case. The syntax for a primary key constraint is

```
[CONSTRAINT constraint_name]
    PRIMARY KEY [CLUSTERED | NONCLUSTERED]
        (col_name [, col_name2 [..., col_name16]])
        [ON segment_name]
```

Cross-Reference

Primary key names must be unique by *uid* in the database, and they must be valid identifiers. The use of this syntax is similar to what we just discussed with CHECK constraints. You can apply the primary key in the SQL Enterprise Manager (Chapter 13), or you can forge ahead in the Query Analyzer. To create a primary key when you create a table, you have a number of options, depending on whether you have multiple columns in the primary key and whether you want to name the constraint.◀

Single Column PRIMARY KEYs

If your primary key consists of only one column, you can use this abbreviated syntax on CREATE TABLE statements:

```
[CONSTRAINT constraint_name]
    PRIMARY KEY [CLUSTERED | NONCLUSTERED]
```

You would put the code above immediately after your column name, for example:

```
CREATE TABLE PrimaryKeyTest (
    Column1 int null,
    TheKeyColumn int PRIMARY KEY,
    Column3 int null)
```

You can name the primary key if you wish:

```
CREATE TABLE PrimaryKeyTest (
    TheColumn int CONSTRAINT PK__PrimaryKeyTest PRIMARY KEY )
```

To find the primary key name, you can use sp_help, but this stored procedure truncates the name of the primary key. The most direct approach is simply to query syscontraints:

```
SELECT OBJECT_NAME( constid )
    FROM sysconstraints
    WHERE id = OBJECT_ID( 'PrimaryKeyTest' )
```

You can specify the primary key when you use ALTER TABLE, but then you must explictly list the column names. We cover that case next. Note that you can't add a column and make it your primary key. Any column you add must allow nulls, but by definition the primary key can't allow nulls. You can, however, specify that a new column be unique:

```
ALTER TABLE UniqueKeyTest ADD UniqueColumn int null UNIQUE
```

Single or Multiple Column PRIMARY KEYs

The usual syntax for specify primary keys is to list the key values, for example:

```
CREATE TABLE PrimaryKeyTest (
    Column_A int,
    Column_B int PRIMARY KEY ( Column_A, Column_B ),
    Column_C varchar(255) null)
```

The primary key declaration must come after you have defined the columns of the primary key, so this is illegal:

```
CREATE TABLE PrimaryKeyTest (
    Column_A int PRIMARY KEY ( Column_A, Column_B ),
    Column_B int,
    Column_C varchar(255) null)
```

However, this is okay:

```
CREATE TABLE PrimaryKeyTest (
    Column_A int,
    Column_B int,
    Column_C varchar(255) null, PRIMARY KEY ( Column_A, Column_B ))
```

If you look carefully, you will see we slipped a comma in right before the primary key declaration this time. In the first example this comma was optional; here it is mandatory. Leave the comma out, and SQL Server will warn you about creating a primary key on the nullable column Column_C. This is a bug as far as we are concerned. As with the CHECK constraints and the single column primary key examples, you can explicitly name the primary keys, just precede the keywords PRIMARY KEY with CONSTRAINT constraint_name.

ALTER TABLE and PRIMARY KEY

You can add a primary key to a table that already exists with the ALTER TABLE command. SQL Server will check the data to make sure the primary key is valid. If data exists in the table that violates the primary key, the ALTER TABLE command fails. There is no "NOCHECK" for creating primary keys. The syntax is

```
ALTER TABLE [database.[owner.]]table_name
    ADD primary_key_constraint
    |
    [DROP CONSTRAINT]
    primary_key_constraint
```

If you created a table without a primary key, such as:

```
CREATE TABLE PrimaryKeyTest (
    Column_A int,
    Column_B int,
    Column_C varchar(255) null)
```

you can add the primary key with:

```
ALTER TABLE PrimaryKeyTest ADD PRIMARY KEY ( Column_A, Column_B )
```

Dropping the constraint is just as easy:

```
ALTER TABLE PrimaryKeyTest DROP CONSTRAINT PK__PrimaryKeyTest__4376EBDB
```

Referential integrity

Referential integrity in the relational model means that each value for a set of columns in one relation must have a corresponding value in *some* relation with a primary key over the *same domain*. This is not how referential integrity is supported in most RDBMSs, including SQL Server. SQL Server supports referential integrity with foreign keys, and the concept foreign keys support is this: each value of a set of columns in a table must have a corresponding value in the primary or unique key of another table. The key differences are as follows:

- The relational model expands coverage of the values to multiple tables. If table A has the set of columns on which we are trying to set up referential integrity, the relational model says some of the values might be defined in table B, but some might be defined in table C, table D, and so on. All that is required is that B, C, D, and so on, all have the same primary key. In contrast, SQL Server allows table A to refer to only one specific table.
- The relational model restricts referential integrity to sets of columns in the same domain. SQL Server only demands that the common columns of the two tables have the same base datatype and the same length.

SQL Server is less robust than the relational model in its enforcement of referential integrity, but so are most RDBMSs. In SQL, there is no support for a foreign key referencing multiple tables with the same primary key, and the concept of the domain isn't even considered. Don't get the idea that referential integrity is weak in SQL Server, however. The inclusion of true foreign keys in SQL Server was a major advance in SQL Server 6.0. Proper use of relational integrity will save you no end of headaches down the road. As you saw with normalization, most database designs split databases into lots of little tables. Keeping those tables synchronized would be a full-time job if you didn't have SQL Server's foreign keys. Declarative Referential Integrity (DRI) is the only way to manage these relationships. (The language can get confusing. DRI is Microsoft's term for all constraints that are defined when you create a table, namely CHECK, DEFAULT, PRIMARY KEY, UNIQUE, and FOREIGN KEY constraints. Referential integrity, on the other hand, refers only to foreign keys.)

The database alternative to DRI, triggers, is an administrative nightmare when it comes to referential integrity (see the section "Why DRI is far superior to trigger RI"), and you don't want to try to manage these relationships in your application programs because it is easier and more reliable with SQL Server. Users may access the data without using your application. They can't access the data without SQL Server.

What foreign keys do

SQL Server FOREIGN KEY constraints affect updates and deletes on the referenced tables and inserts and deletes on the foreign key tables. (In this section, we will call the table with the primary key or unique constraint the referenced table, and the table with the foreign key the foreign key table.) Before a primary or unique key value is updated or deleted in a referenced table, SQL Server must ensure that this will not orphan a foreign key value. The UPDATE or DELETE will be allowed only if there is no foreign key referencing the key values to be changed. Before a non-null foreign key value is inserted or updated in the foreign key table, SQL Server checks to make sure that value exists in the referenced table. Incidentally, there is no reason why the referenced table and foreign key table can't be the same tables.

As long as we are on the subject of nulls, one of Codd's ideas that no one else in the field agreed with was the idea of two nulls. Codd's relational model specifies that missing values are either missing and unavailable (such as when you don't know someone's middle name) or missing and inapplicable (such as when someone has no middle name). Technically, only missing and inapplicable nulls should be exempted from foreign key enforcement.◀

Defining FOREIGN KEY constraints

If you have read the previous sections on CHECK, DEFAULT, PRIMARY KEY, and UNIQUE constraints, you can already guess what the rules are going to be for creating foreign keys. Namely, you can

- Specify FOREIGN KEY constraints either with the SQL Enterprise Manager or with the CREATE TABLE or ALTER TABLE statements
- Pick your own names for FOREIGN KEY constraints or let SQL Server pick them
- Use a short-cut syntax when defining a single column foreign key
- Tell SQL Server not to check the foreign key when you add it with ALTER TABLE

- Suspend a FOREIGN KEY constraint temporarily
- Exempt replication from FOREIGN KEY checks
- Drop a FOREIGN KEY altogether with ALTER TABLE

There are a few extra curve balls in FOREIGN KEY constraints; we will highlight those, too. As before, we cover only the command line syntax here; we discuss the GUI interface of the SQL Enterprise Manager in Chapter 13. The syntax for a FOREIGN KEY constraint is

```
[CONSTRAINT constraint_name]
    [FOREIGN KEY (col_name [, col_name2 [..., col_name16]])]
        REFERENCES [owner.]ref_table [(ref_col [, ref_col2
            [..., ref_col16]])]
```

You can create up to 31 FOREIGN KEY constraints per table, each of which can have up to 16 columns. A FOREIGN KEY constraint references the PRIMARY KEY or UNIQUE constraint of some table *in the same database*. This last little bit is the kicker, and a major factor in your decision of how to divide your data into multiple databases. Don't get so excited about parceling your applications out into separate databases that you deny yourself the opportunity to use foreign keys. We have several major applications that need to be referentially linked, and we have all their tables in one database. Unless the resulting database is so large that you can't back it up over night, this is what we recommend.

In order to create a FOREIGN KEY constraint, you must have REFERENCES permission on the referenced table; SELECT permission alone is not sufficient. SELECT permission means you can actually query the referenced table; REFERENCES permission specifically means you can set up FOREIGN KEYs, even though you may not have SELECT permission.

Creating a foreign key, unlike creating a primary key or unique constraint, does not create an index. You may very well want an index, in which case you have to make it yourself. We will have a lot more to say about how and when SQL Server uses indexes in Chapter 28, but for now we make one simple observation. When you are constantly inserting and updating the foreign key table, the indexes you need are the indexes on the referenced table, which SQL Server has already created for you. In this case, the index on your foreign key column is actually slowing you down: SQL Server has to maintain this index on the fly as you insert and update. On the other hand, if your are doing a lot of updates and deletes to the referenced table, a good index on the foreign key table helps tremendously.

For the purposes of our FOREIGN KEY examples, let us create two tables we can reference

```
CREATE TABLE SingleColumnKey (
    PK int PRIMARY KEY,
    UQ int UNIQUE)
CREATE TABLE LotsOfKeys (
    PK1 int,
    PK2 int PRIMARY KEY (PK1, PK2),
    UQ1 int null,
    UQ2 int null UNIQUE(UQ1, UQ2))
```

Now we can create foreign keys to our hearts' content. Here are examples of the main uses of foreign key syntax:

CREATE TABLE and the Single Column Foreign Key

The simplest possible foreign key example is

```
CREATE TABLE ForeignKeyTest (
    Column_A int REFERENCES SingleColumnKey)
```

When you don't tell SQL Server which columns of the referenced table you want, SQL Server assumes you want the primary key. To reference a UNIQUE constraint, you must explicitly name the columns of the referenced table:

```
CREATE TABLE ForeignKeyTest (
    Column_A int REFERENCES SingleColumnKey (UQ))
```

You can supply your own name, if you don't want to get stuck with something like FK__ForeignKe__Colum__76026BA8:

```
CREATE TABLE ForeignKeyTest (
    Column_A int CONSTRAINT The_Foreign_Key
    REFERENCES SingleColumnKey)
```

ALTER TABLE and the Single Column Foreign Key

The syntax for ALTER TABLE follows in the same pattern, but now you have to specify to which column you are applying the key:

```
ALTER TABLE ForeignKeyTest ADD FOREIGN KEY (Column_A)
   REFERENCES SingleColumnKey
ALTER TABLE ForeignKeyTest FOREIGN KEY ADD (Column_A)
   REFERENCES SingleColumnKey (UQ)
ALTER TABLE ForeignKeyTest ADD CONSTRAINT The_Foreign_Key FOREIGN KEY (Column_A)
   REFERENCES SingleColumnKey
```

Multiple Column Foreign Keys

When you have more than one column in the foreign key, you must use the FOREIGN KEY (*col_name* [, *col_name2* [..., *col_name16*]]) syntax to tell SQL Server which columns are to be in the key:

```
CREATE TABLE ForeignKeyTest (
    Column_A int,
    Column_B int FOREIGN KEY (Column_A, Column_B)
        REFERENCES LotsOfKeys)
```

You can name the constraint by inserting CONSTRAINT constraint_name before the keywords FOREIGN KEY; you can specify the UNIQUE constraint of the referenced table by listing the columns you want to reference, UQ1 and UQ2. The ALTER TABLE command is just like the ALTER TABLE commands above but with more than one column in the named lists.

FOREIGN KEYS referencing a table not yet created

You will occasionally have use for a foreign key that references the table itself. The syntax for this is no different than any other foreign key:

```
CREATE TABLE ForeignKeyTest (
    Column_A int REFERENCES ForeignKeyTest,
    Column_B int PRIMARY KEY)
```

The really exciting question is what to do when you have two tables, First and Second, and each has to reference the other. The straight forward approach isn't going to work:

```
CREATE TABLE First (
    Column_A int PRIMARY KEY,
    Column_B int REFERENCES Second)
CREATE TABLE Second (
    Column_B int PRIMARY KEY,
    Column_A int REFERENCES First)
```

Obviously, you will get an error when you try to create the table named First. You can make it work by splitting the defintion of First into two steps:

```
CREATE TABLE First (
    Column_A int PRIMARY KEY,
    Column_B int)
CREATE TABLE Second (
    Column_B int PRIMARY KEY,
    Column_A int REFERENCES First)
ALTER TABLE First ADD FOREIGN KEY (Column_B) REFERENCES Second
```

However, there is a more elegant way. The CREATE SCHEMA command was invented for just this kind of situation. It tells SQL Server to group the CREATE TABLE commands together and evaluate their validity at the end. All you need to do is preface the first CREATE TABLE command with CREATE SCHEMA, and the statements will run without error.

Bypassing and dropping foreign keys

Tip

SQL Server gives you the flexibility to bypass Referential Integrity when you first apply it, using the NOCHECK option of ALTER TABLE. SQL Server then enforces the foreign key from that point forward. Don't do this. We have regretted it each time we granted ourselves this exception. Be aware that the bulk copy program (BCP.EXE) also bypasses foreign keys. We would prefer to see SQL Server take a page out of DB2's book and put a table in a hold status after a bulk copy until the table owner lets the DBMS check the DRI. Almost as bad as the NOCHECK option in creating a foreign key is the NOCHECK option for suspending a foreign key. If you need to use this command, ask yourself why you bother having the foreign keys to begin with. ◀

Why DRI is far superior to trigger RI

We should mention that you do have another option for enforcing referential integrity in SQL Server: triggers. If any of you hearken back to the SQL Server 4.*x* days, the only way you could enforce referential integrity at that time was to treat it as custom business logic and use triggers. This is a very error-prone way to enforce referential integrity because you immediately have four times as much work: You have to worry about the update and delete triggers of the referenced table and the insert and update triggers of the foreign key table. Furthermore, you have to write the SQL to enforce the constraint, which is easy to screw up. Finally, you have no way to query the system tables and know for sure where your foreign keys are. SQL Server 4.*x* had some software and stored procedures to buffer this, but DRI is still far superior. The only reasons you might still resort to triggers to enforce your referential integrity are as follows:

- You have cross-database referential integrity. If it is a case of one or two tables, this might be okay, but any more than that and we recommend you take a long, hard look at why these tables are in separate databases.
- You want custom error messages. Give us break. The SQL Server error messages aren't that unreadable, and if you really hate them, write logic into your application to provide custom error messages. Don't do that in SQL Server.

User-defined integrity

User-defined integrity includes any business rules that don't fit into the other categories of integrity. Whenever you have such rules, you should always use SQL Server to enforce them, even if you intend to check this stuff with an application. The reason for this double-checking is that you never know who else will be changing the data or how they will be changing the data. At a minimum, the application programmers themselves almost always need to modify tables directly. They are the ones most likely to violate some obscure business rule because they don't know the data as well as the end users. Furthermore, there may be applications that come along years later that need to modify the data. The only sure-fire way to protect your data is with user-defined integrity.

SQL Server gives you two options here: CHECK constraints and triggers. CHECK constraints are better because you define a rule once and SQL Server enforces it on all three modification commands: INSERT, UPDATE, and DELETE. With triggers, you frequently have to write a rule three times because you attach triggers to each of the INSERT, UPDATE, and DELETE actions. If the rules that you want to apply to any two or all three of these are identical, you can combine the triggers, but that is rarely the case.

CHECK constraints and user-defined integrity

When we say that CHECK constraints enforce user-defined integrity, we are talking now about table level constraints, or constraints that involve more than one column of your table. These constraints are defined much the same way as the column level constraints, except that they are always separated from column definitions and column level constraints by commas, for example:

```
CREATE TABLE UserDefinedIntegrityTest (
    Column_A int,
    Column_B int, CHECK( Column_A + Column_B < 10000 ))
```

If you try to run this without the comma before the keyword CHECK, you will get an error telling you that you can't create a column level constraint on Column_B that references Column_A.

CHECK constraints and IF THEN logic

One of hardest things to sort out in your head is to translate IF THEN logic into CHECK constraints. For example, you will wish you could write a constraint along these lines:

```
IF Column_A BETWEEN 16 AND 30 THEN CHECK(Column_B > 100000)
```

This isn't legal syntax of course, and you might be tempted just to resort to a trigger:

```
CREATE TRIGGER Unnecessary ON UserDefinedIntegrityTest FOR INSERT, UPDATE AS
BEGIN
    IF EXISTS (SELECT *
        FROM inserted
        WHERE Column_A BETWEEN 16 AND 30)
            AND NOT (Column_B > 100000))
            BEGIN
                RAISERROR( 'Game Over', 16, -1)
                ROLLBACK TRAN
            END
        END
END
```

Don't do it! Your criteria here is if something is true about Column_A, then you want to check a condition on Column_B. Another way of saying that is that every row of the table must either *fall outside the criteria* for Column_A or be subject to the check on Column_B. Convince yourself that this CHECK constraint does the same job as the trigger:

```
ALTER TABLE UserDefinedIntegrityTest ADD CHECK(Column_A NOT BETWEEN 16 AND 30 OR
Column_B > 100000)
```

When to use triggers

Triggers, which we discuss in Chapter 14, are best used for the following cases:

- Checks that involve analyzing combinations of rows. Without subqueries, you can't do such things as apply aggregate functions (SUM, AVG, COUNT, and the like). You must use triggers.
- Custom security measures. If the basic GRANT functionality doesn't do what you need, triggers are your answer.
- Checks that involve other tables, but do not have referential integrity. This again means using subqueries, which CHECK constraints don't allow.

Summary

The relational model has set the standard for DBMS work, yielding databases that are vastly more productive. The relational model dictates a set of features that SQL Server *should* provide to you, but in many cases the features are options that you must choose. You want all your tables to be true relations, which means atomic data, no intrinsic ordering, and no duplicate rows. Databases that follow the relational model are automatically in first normal form, but there are higher forms that are used in database design to eliminate the potential of incompletely or incorrectly recording information in relations. The principal way to guard your data in the relational model is through integrity constraints. SQL Server supports these constraints in various ways, including CHECK, DEFAULT, PRIMARY KEY, UNIQUE, and FOREIGN KEY constraints. Triggers provide custom business rule enforcement, but triggers should never be used when a true constraint applies.

Review Questions

Q: What is the problem with hierarchical and network databases?

A: The user or programmer has to understand how all the data is explicitly linked to retrieve or update information.

Q: What is the difference between a SQL Server table and a relation?

A: A relation has no duplicate rows; a SQL Server table allows duplicates.

Q: What does normalization do for you?

A: It protects you from incorrect information and potential loss of information.

Q: How can you enforce column integrity in SQL Server?

A: Use a CHECK constraint.

Q: Does the SQL Enterprise Manager prompt you for a primary key, much like Microsoft Access?

A: No, you have to remember to put one on.

Q: Can a primary key allow nulls? Can a unique constraint?

A: Columns that are nullable can't be part of the primary key, but they can be in a unique constraint.

Q: Can foreign key reference unique constraints?

A: Yes. This is one way to establish a foreign key to a group of columns that must include some nulls.

Q: Can foreign keys reference more than one primary key?

A: No, but this is part of what the relational model requires.

Q: When might you use triggers instead of CHECK constraints.

A: Any time that you need a subquery or you are doing some special kind of security enforcement.

Chapter

TABLES, VIEWS, AND INDEXES

13

Think about it. You probably could manage without indexes (though your performance would be terrible), stored procedures, triggers, and all the other niceties that make up a top-notch RDBMS. The things you could *not* live without, however, are the tables. Without tables, you have no place to store your data. Without data, databases become nothing more than an expensive way to waste disk space. To this end, it is absolutely critical that you understand the basics of this thing called a *table* and its cousin, the *view*. By the time you finish this chapter, you will have such a comprehension.

Because indexes, in our opinion, run a close second behind tables as the most important part of a database, we will also introduce them to you here.

Be advised, however, that we dedicate an entire chapter (Chapter 28) to optimizing your queries with indexes. Therefore, the discussion of indexes in this chapter will be very basic.◀

What's in This Chapter

This chapter includes coverage of the following topics:

- The single most important items in any RDBMS: Tables
- The second most important items in any RDBMS: Indexes

Tables: A Formal Definition

Microsoft, in part, defines a table as "a collection of rows (or records) that have associated columns (or fields)." In other words, a *table* is a collection of related data that is held in a common structure. This definition may seem a little broad because a table can be an ambiguous concept. It is, therefore, probably not a good idea to try to pinpoint a good definition for a table; consequently, we will spend the effort defining what makes a *good* table. After all, if your tables are the most important objects in your databases, then it stands to reason that one of the most important things you can do is to design good tables.

If you are coming from a FoxPro or dBASE environment, a table is the same as a .dbf file. A collection of .dbf files would be considered a database. In Paradox, tables are stored in .db files. In Access, an .mdb file is a database.◀

The Basics

As we mentioned earlier, a table is an object in a database. This means that you can edit or view a table the same way you edit or view any other object in a database: through the SQL Enterprise Manager. To view a specific table in the SQL Enterprise Manager, expand the Objects⇨Tables tree of the desired database (see Figure 13-1). This picture shows a table called 'dave.'

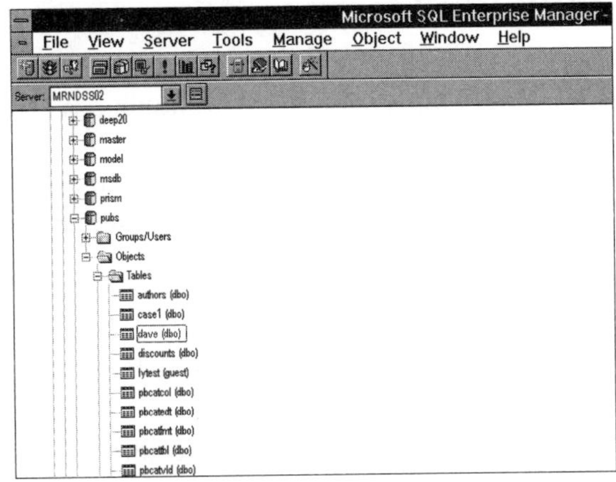

Figure 13-1:
The 'dave' table.

The easiest way to understand the elements of a table is to create a new one. To do this, right-click the Tables node of the open tree and select New Table. The window shown in Figure 13-2 opens.

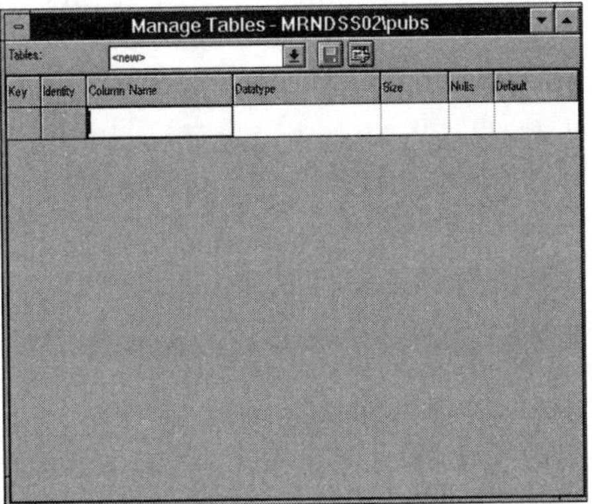

Figure 13-2:
This screen lets you create a new table.

In the next several sections, we will discuss the specific parts of this screen.

Column name

A *column name* is the identifier you use to address a specific field in a table. Column names must adhere to the following rules:

- Column names can contain from 1 to 30 characters, including letters, symbols, and numbers, and must be unique within a table.
- The first character of a column name must be a letter or the symbols _ or #.
- Characters following the first character can include letters, digits, or the symbols #, $, or _.
- By default, no other characters are allowed in column names. However, you can flip a switch in SQL Server to use *any* characters in column names. More on that later.

As long as you follow the preceding rules, you can name a column anything you want. We think, however, there are a couple of additional rules of thumb that you should follow so that your column names are *good* column names:

- Do not name a column the same as an SQL keyword. (for example, SELECT, IN, DECLARE, DESC, and so forth). If you do, you run the risk of confusing the SQL parser. Just imagine trying to retrieve the values of a column named "select." The SQL would be something like SELECT select FROM my_table. Yikes! You will *really* confuse your users. You can, however, get away with this if you use *quoted identifiers,* although we recommend that you don't. We'll get to that in a moment.
- Make your column names relevant to the data that the column will hold. For example, if your column will hold a social security number, choose a name like "soc_number" or "social_security_number." This will help you remember what data a column holds and will make your SQL far more readable.

Quoted identifiers

Earlier, we told you that it is a bad idea to name your columns using SQL keywords. In most cases, you will only confuse people who are trying to use your tables. SQL Server, as a rule, won't even let you name a column something stupid like "select." There is an exception, though. You can use something called a *quoted identifier.*

One of the new features in SQL Server 6.0 was the capability to tell the SQL parser that anything in double quotes ("") refers to a database object or column name. This means that you can use SQL keywords and other previously disallowed strings as column and table names. The following bit of code demonstrates this:

```
set QUOTED_IDENTIFIER ON
go

CREATE TABLE dave ("this is a test" int, "select" int)
```

This SQL first enables the use of quoted identifiers by using the SET QUOTED_IDENTIFIER ON command and then creates a table called dave that has columns named this is a test, and select. Normally, the first column name would be invalid because it contains spaces, and the second column name would be invalid because it is an SQL keyword. You can, however, use them without incident as long as you first execute the SET QUOTED_IDENTIFIER ON command and then wrap them in double quotes. For example, the following will yield an error:

```
SELECT "this is a test", "select" FROM dave
```

On the other hand, this will work fine:

```
SET QUOTED_IDENTIFIER ON
go

SELECT "this is a test", "select" FROM dave
```

Our advice to you is to not mess with quoted identifiers or columns that are named the same as SQL keywords. It is more trouble than it is worth!

Transact SQL keywords

Table 13-1 consists of a list of keywords in SQL Server 6.*x*. We include it here so that you can easily refer to it when naming your columns.

Can't Fool the 'Ole SQL Enterprise Manager!

The SQL Enterprise Manager *will not* allow you to use spaces in a column name, even if you have previously used the SET QUOTED_IDENTIFIER ON command. This is why the previous examples were done in SQL and not through the SQL Enterprise Manager. In fact, the SQL Enterprise Manager behaves unpredictably when you try to use it with a table that uses a quoted identifier.

Table 13-1
Transact SQL Reserved Keywords

ADD	ALL	ALTER
AND	ANY	AS
ASC	AVG	BEGIN
BETWEEN	BREAK	BROWSE
BULK	BY	CASE
CHECK	CHECKPOINT	CLOSE
CLUSTERED	COALESCE	COMMIT
COMMITTED	COMPUTE	CONFIRM
CONSTRAINT	CONTINUE	CONTROLROW
CONVERT	COUNT	CREATE
CURRENT	CURRENT_DATE	CURRENT_TIME
CURRENT_TIMESTAMP	CURRENT_USER	CURSOR
DATABASE	DBCC	DEALLOCATE
DECLARE	DEFAULT	DELETE
DESC	DISK	DISTINCT
DOUBLE	DROP	DUMMY
DUMP	ELSE	END
ERRLVL	ERROREXIT	EXCEPT
EXEC	EXECUTE	EXISTS
EXIT	FETCH	FILLFACTOR
FLOPPY	FOR	FOREIGN
FROM	GOTO	GRANT
GROUP	HAVING	HOLDLOCK
IDENTITY	IDENTITY_INSERT	IDENTITYCOL
IF	IN	INDEX
INSENSITIVE	INSERT	INTERSECT
INTO	IS	ISOLATION
KEY	KILL	LEVEL
LIKE	LINENO	LOAD
MAX	MIN	MIRROREXIT
NOCHECK	NONCLUSTERED	NOT
NULL	NULLIF	OF
OFF	OFFSETS	ON
ONCE	ONLY	OPEN
OPTION	OR	ORDER
OVER	PERM	PERMANENT
PIPE	PLAN	PRECISION
PREPARE	PRIMARY	PRINT
PROC	PROCEDURE	PROCESSEXIT
PUBLIC	RAISERROR	READ

(continued)

RECONFIGURE	REFERENCES	REPEATABLE
REPLICATION	RETURN	REVOKE
ROLLBACK	ROWCOUNT	RULE
SAVE	SCROLL	SELECT
SERIALIZABLE	SESSION_USER	SET
SETUSER	SHUTDOWN	SOME
STATISTICS	SUM	SYSTEM_USER
TABLE	TAPE	TEMP
TEMPORARY	TEXTSIZE	THEN
TO	TRAN	TRANSACTION
TRIGGER	TRUNCATE	TSEQUAL
UNCOMMITTED	UNION	UNIQUE
UPDATE	UPDATETEXT	USE
USER	VALUES	VARYING
VIEW	WAITFOR	WHEN
WHERE	WHILE	WITH
WRITETEXT		

Datatype

The next thing you need to do when creating a new column in a table is to define what kind of data the field will hold. The basic Transact SQL datatypes break down into the following categories:

- **Binary** (binary, varbinary): As you might expect, these datatypes hold binary data. You might use these type to hold bitmaps or sounds.
- **Character** (char, varchar): These datatypes hold character data.
- **Date and time** (datetime, smalldatetime): These datatypes hold dates and times.
- **Exact numeric** (decimal, numeric): These datatypes hold precise numeric values.
- **Approximate numeric** (float, real): These datatypes hold approximate numeric data. For example, 2/3 might be stored as 6.6666666666666666667 in the system. That's not the *exact* value of 2/3. It's an approximation.
- **Integer** (int, smallint, tinyint): These datatypes hold integer data.
- **Monetary** (money, smallmoney): These datatypes hold numeric data for decimal currency.

- **Special** (timestamp, user-defined datatypes): A timestamp is an exact value of time. It is most often used as a unique row identifier. We will cover user-defined datatypes a little later.
- **Text and image** (text, image): Text and image datatypes are used to hold very large character and binary data. They have their own set of functions and operators.

In addition to the items just addressed, you have a few other things to consider when setting up your columns:

- Think about the possible values that can be placed in the column. For example, if you are defining a column that will hold numeric data that might be greater than 2,147,483,647 (32 bits in length) or will need a decimal point, you will not want to define your column as an integer field. In this case, perhaps an exact numeric would be appropriate.
- Be aware that varchars will in general provide slower updates but faster selects. By definition, the amount of storage they use is variable. Suppose that you have a varchar(255) field in a row that just happens to contain the string "TNT". If you update that to "trinitrotoluene," there might not be enough room on the 2K data page. This forces SQL Server to split a page, which slows down the update. Conversely, if you are SELECTing from a table with a great deal of less-than-full varchars, the table will be smaller, the indexes will be smaller, and your selects will run more quickly. You have to decide what is best for your application. In general, small varchars (less than 50 characters or so) aren't worth it. Use char for them.
- Know the precision (how many decimal places are supported) for each datatype. Floats have double the precision of reals, and so on. Your online help will tell you these things.
- You can't change a datatype without dropping (destroying) and recreating a table, so try to get it right the first time.

Size

This *size* part of a column definition refers to how many characters the column will accept. Some datatypes, such as char, allow you to enter a size, and others, such as int, do not. The idea here is to keep your column sizes as small as is feasible. Obviously, the smaller your columns are, the less space your table will occupy.

There is one caveat, though. Just like the datatype, you can't change the size of a column without dropping the whole table, so again, you want to be sure about what you enter.

Nulls

This option determines whether or not a particular column will allow Null values. As we said earlier, the columns that will uniquely identify any given row of data should not allow Nulls. One more important tidbit about Nulls: A Char column that allows Nulls is stored as a Varchar internally by SQL Server.

Another important feature of nulls is that they are exempt from a foreign key check. In other words, if you have a column that will not always be filled in, but when it is filled in it must be among the primary key values of another table, you should let that column allow nulls.

In addition to these, there are a couple of other important things to remember about nulls:

- A column that is defined as allowing NULL cannot be used as part of the primary key.
- Nullability (the capability to store a missing entry) can't be changed after a column is created.

Default

If you try to insert a new row of data into a table but fail to specify data for all the columns, SQL Server attempts to insert a NULL into the unspecified fields. If any of those fields do not allow Nulls, the insertion fails. This is where a *default* becomes handy. If there is a value in the *default* portion of a column definition, SQL Server inserts that value into the specified column, rather than trying to insert a NULL.

If this were all that defaults could do, they would still be pretty handy. Lucky for you, though, they can do a lot more! One of the coolest things about defaults is that you can include system functions in them. Let's say that you create a column that is a date. You can set the default value to be the getdate() function. This way, when a user inserts a row without specifying a date, the server simply inserts the system date.

The Not-So-Basics

You probably noticed that there are two column-definition items on your screen that we did not discuss: Key and Identity. They are a little more complicated than the others, so we thought we would leave them for here.

Key

At some point in your career, you may have used a database system that allowed you to refer to a specific row of data in a table by a row number. (Those of you who have used either FoxPro or dBASE know what we are talking about.) The nice part about being able to refer to a specific row of data via a row number was that you always had a unique way of identifying a row. This is not the case in SQL Server. If you want to guarantee that you will always be able to identify any row of data in a table, you must either declare a *primary key* for it or create a unique index on it. Don't worry, we'll cover indexes a little later.

To refresh your memory, a *primary key* is a column, or the minimal set of columns, that will always uniquely identify a row of data. For example, if your table will hold personnel information, a social security number would be a good choice for a primary key.

To declare a primary key for a table, click the Advanced Options button (it's the one that has the plus (+) sign on it) in the table creation window. The screen shown in Figure 13-3 appears.

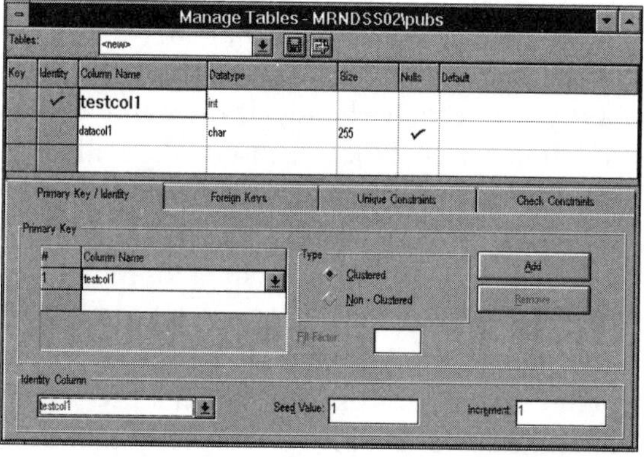

Figure 13-3:
The advanced options for creating a table.

The Primary Key/Identity tab should be active. First, you need to select the columns that will make up the primary key. You do this by choosing them from the Column Name list box. You may notice that some of the fields in the table are not available as a choice for a primary key. This is because a column cannot be a candidate for a primary key if it allows Nulls or if its datatype is bit.

A primary key enforces its uniqueness via a unique index. This is what the Clustered and Non-Clustered options pertain to. For the time being, leave this option the way it is. We'll go over clustered versus nonclustered indexes a little later.◀

When you have finished choosing your new key, click the Add button.

Identities

In SQL Server 6.0, Microsoft introduced a new column property called *identity*. Essentially, a column with this characteristic will hold a numeric value that is system generated.

This eliminates the need for timestamps as surrogate keys, which is what you had to do in SQL Server 4.21. You actually had to have *two* columns, one timestamp and one binary(8), and then an INSERT trigger to copy the timestamp to the binary because the timestamp will change on UPDATE.◀

The truth of the matter is that you can insert your own values into an identity field by using the SET IDENTITY_INSERT command. We'll talk about this a little later, but we thought we would bring it up now so that you wouldn't think we were liars!

The nice thing about having a field that is an identity type is that it is a perfect candidate for a primary key.◀

I Didn't Pick That Name!

The SQL Enterprise Manager doesn't let you enter a name for your Primary Key, which is a design flaw, in our opinion. It is going to pick a name for you that will be something like "PK___1__10" for a table you are creating from scratch. If you add the primary key later, you will get a name like "PK_Table_Name_2__10". True, you can rename these primary keys with sp_rename, but that's a bother, and it's not available in the user interface.

Identity columns must follow a few simple rules:

- Because identity columns hold numeric values, they must be either tinyint, smallint, int, decimal, or numeric.
- There can be only one identity column in a table.
- Identity columns cannot allow Nulls or have a default value defined for them.

To designate a column with the identity property, open the Advanced Options screen, select the desired field from the Identity Column list, and enter a Seed Value (the value at which the column will start) and an Increment (the amount of change with each new row).

Warning

The SQL Enterprise Manager has an annoying little bug in the way it allows a user to define an identity column. It will only allow positive numbers in the Seed Value and Increment fields. If, however, you declare an identity column using the CREATE TABLE command, you can use negative numbers. Uuuggghhh!◄

Warning! Geeky stuff ahead!

When we first sat down to write this book, we decided that we were going to guide you through a personal tour of the innards of SQL Server. Although we have always tried to keep the material accessible, there are going to be times when the geek factor of this book shoots through the roof. This is one of those times. It's not that we have tried any less hard to make the following easy to understand, it's just that it gets pretty complicated. But hey, that's why you're reading a *SECRETS* book!

Overriding an identity value

Assume, for the moment, that you have created a table called *idtest* that contains two columns: *uid* and *name*. *Uid* is defined as an identity column with a seed value of 1 and an increment of 1, and *name* is defined as char(20). If you were to execute the following SQL:

```
INSERT INTO idtest (name) VALUES ("Andrew Fedorchek")
INSERT INTO idtest (name) VALUES ("Dave Rensin")
INSERT INTO idtest (name) VALUES ("John Osborn")
```

you would expect the data in idtest to look like this:

```
uid          name
---          ----------------
1            Andrew Fedorchek
2            Dave Rensin
3            John Osborn
```

If, however, you had tried the following code:

```
INSERT INTO idtest (uid, name) VALUES (4, "John Osborn")
```

you would have received the following error:

```
Msg 544, Level 16, State 1
Attempting to insert explicit value for identity column in table 'idtest' when
IDENTITY_INSERT is set to OFF
```

SQL Server is not a happy camper when you explicitly try to assign a value to a column that it thinks it ought to have final say over.

Should you ever need to insert a specific value into an identity column (for what reason we know not), you can override SQL Server's objections by using the SET IDENTITY_INSERT <table_name> ON command. This statement enables you to insert values into an identity column for the table <table_name>. The following code remedies the preceding error:

```
SET IDENTITY_INSERT idtest ON
go
INSERT INTO idtest (uid, name) VALUES (4, "John Osborn")
```

Identity does not mean unique

Just because a column has the identity property, it does not mean that it will always be unique. You can insert a duplicate value using the previously mentioned technique, and SQL Server will go along merrily. However, this will only happen if *you* insert the non-unique values. If you only have SQL Server generate the values, you will not get duplicates. If you want to guarantee that your identity column will always be unique, you can do one of three things:

- Make it your primary key or add a UNIQUE constraint.
- Declare a unique index on it (more on this later).
- *Never* use the SET IDENTIY INSERT <table_name> ON command.

Just in Case You're Wondering

John Osborn is our acquisitions editor at IDG. You will find that we like to use the names of people we know in our examples. If you look at the inside cover of the book and read the dedication and acknowledgments, you will be able to figure out who all these people are.

The one and only

As we mentioned earlier, there can only be one column in a given table that has the identity property. Because of this fact, SQL Server allows you to refer to the identity column of a table as IDENTITYCOL. In other words, you don't have to know the name of the column to get data from it. For example, the two following statements are identical with respect to the *idtest* table:

```
SELECT * FROM idtest WHERE uid > 1
SELECT * FROM idtest WHERE IDENTITYCOL > 1
```

@@IDENTITY

SQL Server provides a global variable named @@IDENTITY to hold the last used identity value in the database. This does *not* mean that it will necessarily hold the largest or smallest identity value, just the last one used. Under most circumstances, this variable is of little practical value. There is one example, however, where it can have an interesting use.

Assume, for the moment, that you have specified the identity column in your table as the primary key column. The following SQL will show you the last row of data entered in your table:

```
SELECT * FROM yourTable WHERE IDENTITYCOL = @@IDENTITY
```

This procedure will work even if users have been entering their own values for the identity column by using the SET IDENTITY INSERT statement.

One quick note, though, about the @@IDENTITY variable. If you delete all the rows in a table, @@IDENTITY doesn't reset. If, however, you *truncate* the table, it does.◀

What Works for One Is Lousy for Many

One of the problems with the @@IDENTITY variable is that it holds the last used identity values for *all* tables in the database.

Although the previous example works great in a database where there is only one table with an identity column, it breaks down when you have many tables that use an identity column as a primary key.

Select Into and Identity Columns

When selecting an existing identity column into a new table, the new column inherits the identity property. The following example illustrates this point:

```
CREATE TABLE #temp (col1 int identity)

/* insert 3 new values */
INSERT INTO #temp DEFAULT VALUES
INSERT INTO #temp DEFAULT VALUES
INSERT INTO #temp DEFAULT VALUES

/* create #tmp2 with a select into */
SELECT * INTO #tmp2 FROM #temp

/* insert another value into #tmp2 */
INSERT INTO #tmp2 DEFAULT VALUES

/* view the values in #tmp2 */
SELECT * FROM #tmp2
```

You should get the following:

```
(1 row(s) affected)


(1 row(s) affected)


(1 row(s) affected)


(3 row(s) affected)


(1 row(s) affected)

col1
```

(continued)

(continued)

```
----------
1
2
3
4

(4 row(s) affected)
```

If, however, one of the following conditions is true, the new column does not inherit the identity property:

- The SELECT statement contains a UNION, JOIN, GROUP BY, or aggregate function.
- The identity column is selected more than once.
- The identity column is part of an expression.

If any of these conditions is true, the column is created NOT NULL instead of inheriting the identity property.

Foreign keys

The next tab in the Advanced Options window of the table editor deals with foreign keys. As you learned in the chapter on DRI (Chapter 12), a foreign key is a column (or set of columns) in a table that matches a column (or set of columns) that is the primary key of another table. For example, suppose you have a table Customers that has a primary key column of CustID. Also suppose that you have a table Orders, which has a primary key column of OrderID and a non-primary key, or dependent, column CustID. Also assume that you do not want to be able to enter a value for Orders.CustID unless that value already exists in Customers.CustID. You enforce this relationship through the use of a foreign key.◀

To establish a column of your table as foreign key into another table, choose the primary key table from the referenced table list. The columns that make up its primary key will be listed in the key columns column. Next, choose the columns from your table that will correspond to the primary key columns from the referenced table.

What's in a Name?

It is generally considered good form to keep the names of your data elements consistent within your database. For example, if two tables store the same user id, it would be considered bad form to name one column user_id and the other userid. It's also really handy when writing joins because you can simplify your query if the matching columns have the same name.

This convention will really help a lot when it comes time to establish foreign key relationships.

Unique constraints

Another tab in the Advanced Options window of the table editor deals with something called a *unique constraint.* A unique constraint simply means that you are restricting a column, or set of columns, to hold unique values always.

Tip

If you are thinking that this feature has little or no value because of the existence of unique indexes, you are right. Microsoft implements unique constraints with unique indexes. They only include unique constraints for ANSI compliance!◀

Check constraints

The last tab in the advanced options window is where you specify *check constraints.* A check constraint is an additional logical constraint you can place on your columns. This is a good place to implement certain business and data rules. For example, suppose that you have a column named department_number and you want to make sure that no value is ever entered into that column that is greater than 9. All you need to do is create a new constraint that says "department_number <= 9." If anyone tries to insert data that holds a value for department_number that is greater than 9, the INSERT statement will fail.

Permissions

We have spent a lot of time talking about various security issues related to SQL Server. Up to this point, though, these issues have concentrated mostly on how to protect yourself from unwanted users logging in to your database server. The remaining component of a good security scheme is to decide who can perform what operation on your data. To this end, we will spend some time here talking about how to assign various security privileges that relate to your tables. These privileges are also known as *permissions*. A table has five distinct permissions associated with it. They are the following:

- **SELECT.** Having this permission allows a user or group to retrieve data from the table.
- **INSERT.** This permission allows users or groups to insert new data into the table.
- **UPDATE.** This permission allows users or groups to update existing data in the table.
- **DELETE.** A user or group with this permission can delete data from a table.
- **REFERENCE.** This permission gives the user the right to reference the table without having the ability to SELECT from it. This is useful for tables that have foreign key relationships, because it allows SQL Server to validate a value in a dependent table without giving the user the right to retrieve data from the master table.

You can edit a table's permissions in the SQL Enterprise Manager by right-clicking the desired table and selecting Permissions. The window shown in Figure 13-4 appears.

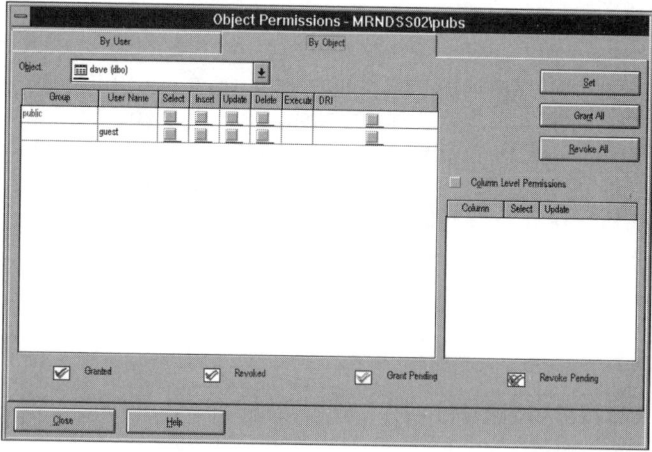

Figure 13-4:
The table permissions window.

The list on the left is a list of all groups and users in your database, and their the row of checkboxes shows permissions for the current table.

The DRI check box is actually the REFERENCE permission.◀

The SELECT and UPDATE permissions have the added advantage that they can be assigned at the column level. This means that you can grant a user the right to see certain columns in a table but not others. You can edit the column-specific permissions of a table by clicking the Column Level Permissions and selecting the items you want.

Views

One of the great strengths of an RDBMS is the capability to define virtual data sets derived from real tables. In the following sections, we explain how to define such things in SQL Server 6.*x* and show you some practical uses for them.

A definition

A *view* is a virtual table that contains one or more subsets of data from one or more tables or views. A view is constructed from SQL, not data. A view looks like a table and acts like a table, but is not a table. It is, in fact, just a set of SQL statements that return data. You can, in most cases, perform the same operations on a view as you can on a normal table.

Didn't I See Keys on Views in SQL Server 4.21

Yes, you did. SQL Server 4.21 didn't have true primary or foreign keys. All that happened when you declared a key was this: SQL Server recorded your declaration in syskeys, and the next time you used the trigger builder, the SQL Object Manager generated the triggers you needed to enforce the relationship. This kind of loose enforcement works with views as well as tables, so you could declare keys on views. You can still do that now, if you have a copy of the SQL Object Manager.

A purpose

Views have a great many uses in an RDBMS. Here are some of them:

- **Security.** You can GRANT and REVOKE permissions on certain views so as to limit what data certain people can see.
- **Application stability.** Though the name of the table, the names and numbers, and even types of columns may change, you can keep things constant for an application with a view.
- **Code Reuse.** This saves commonly used SELECT statements, especially complex joins, for everyone to use.

Views have certain drawbacks, too. Among them are the following:

- Certain views are either partially or entirely non-updatable.
- You cannot put indexes on views.
- You cannot put constraints on views.

Consider the following example. You have a table that contains all the financial information for your corporation. You decide, though, that you do not want everyone with access to the table to be able to read all the data. Certain groups of users should only be able to read certain portions of the data, and others should be able to read all the data. We will also assume that you have gone ahead and created three distinct groups of users in your system: serfs, lords, and kings.

In order to partition your data, you could create three separate tables for each group. The problem, of course, is that you have no real way to keep the data synchronized across tables. Your other choice is to create a virtual table (view) for each group and give access for each group to their corresponding view.

The advantage to creating views is that you do not have to repeat any data. If you insert new data into your master table, it will show up in the appropriate view.

No GUIs Allowed

There is no real GUI way of creating views in SQL Server. The closest thing to it that you can do is, while in the SQL Enterprise Manager, to highlight the database in which you want to create your view and select the Manage⇨Views menu option.

A window opens that enables you to type the definition for your view.

Don't worry, we will show you specifically how to create the appropriate views for serfs, lords, and kings after we first explain the general process for creating a view.

A way

Views, in SQL Server, are created with the CREATE VIEW command.

The syntax for the CREATE VIEW statement is as follows:

```
CREATE VIEW [owner.]view_name
[(column_name [, column_name]...)]
[WITH ENCRYPTION]
AS select_statement [WITH CHECK OPTION]
```

In this syntax, the following are what's what:

- **view_name.** The name you want to assign to the view. View names must follow the same rules as table names.
- **column_name.** You can explicitly define the names of the result columns in a view by including column names. If you do not explicitly name the result columns, SQL Server takes the names from the SELECT statement. As a result, the only times you will ever consider using this option will be when the default names will not suffice. For example, if you reference a computed column in your SELECT statement, you may want to name it to something more useful than SQL Server's default name for a computed field. You might also use this to give a friendlier name to an existing obscure name, like Soc_sec_number if the name in the base table is something like EMP_FED_SSN.
- **ENCRYPTION.** View definitions are stored in the syscomments system table. If you specify WITH ENCRYPTION, SQL Server encrypts the definition stored there so that no one can read it.
- **AS select_statement.** The SELECT statement you use to define your view can be as complex as you like and need only follow a few rules:
  - You cannot include ORDER BY, COMPUTE, or COMPUTE BY clauses.
  - You cannot include the INTO keyword.
  - You cannot reference a temporary table.
- **WITH CHECK OPTION.** This option forces all data modification statements executed against the view to comply with any restrictions set forth in the SELECT statement. This means that if your select statement has a WHERE clause that restricts the query to WHERE state = 'NY'

<<use straight quotes>>, you won't be able to INSERT rows into the view where the state = 'ME'.

There are also a few more restrictions to which a view must adhere:

- A view can reference no more than 250 columns.
- If a view is defined with a SELECT * statement, the result columns are fixed. If you later add more columns to the appropriate tables, they will not show up in the view. You will need to delete and recreate the view for them to appear. The reason for this is that SQL Server expands the asterisk (*) at the time the view is created to the complete column list.
- If you create a view on a table that is then dropped, users will get an error message if they attempt to execute the view. If you later re-add the missing table, the errors will stop.

Some examples

While in the SQL Enterprise Manager, highlight the database in which you want to create your view and choose Manage⇨Views. You should see the window shown in Figure 13-5.

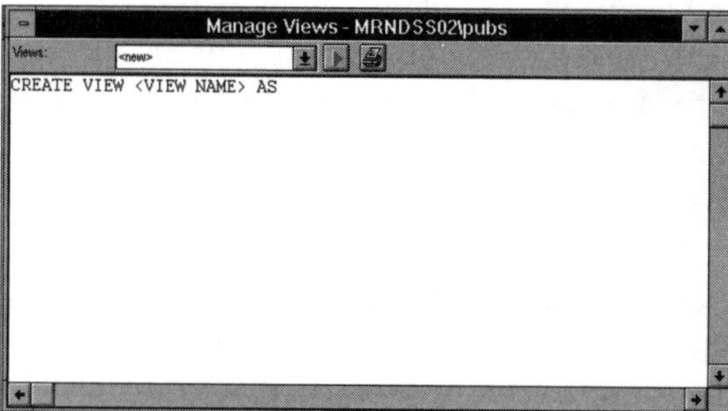

Figure 13-5:
From this screen you can manage your views.

Replace <VIEW NAME> with the name you want to assign your view. Do not keep the brackets (<>)! The statement to create the *serfs* view might look like this:

```
CREATE VIEW vSerfs AS

SELECT year, net_revenue, gross_revenue
FROM corporate_data
```

The *v* in front of vSerfs means (to us) that this object is a view. SQL Server doesn't know anything about the name. If you then remove the capability of the serfs group to read the corporate_data table, they will only be able to see the data you want:

```
REVOKE select ON corporate_data FROM serfs
```

The second user group we discussed was lords. We defined the lords group as having the ability to see all the serf data plus a few other columns. The definition of the lords view would look similar to this:

```
CREATE VIEW vLords AS
SELECT a.*, b.some_field, b.some_other_field
FROM vSerfs a, corporate_data b
REVOKE select ON corporate_data FROM lords
```

The last group we talked about was kings. We said that the kings group could read any data from the table. We really don't have to create a view for the kings group. We just have to make sure that they have access to the corporate_data table.

Updatability rules for views

As you might expect, a few restrictions govern the way you can use data modification statements with views. They are the following:

- Data modification statements (INSERT or UPDATE) are allowed on multitable views (views defined with a JOIN) if the data modification statement affects only one table. In other words, you cannot use data modification statements on more than one table in a single statement.
- INSERT statements are not allowed if a computed column exists within the view.
- INSERT statements are not accepted unless all the NOT NULL columns without defaults in the underlying table or view are included in the view through which you are inserting new rows. Without this restriction, SQL Server would be put in the position of trying to insert a value into a column that is non-null, but does not have a default value.
- All columns being modified must adhere to all restrictions for the data modification statement as if it were executed directly against the base table. This applies to column nullability, constraints, identity columns, and columns with rules or defaults (or both) and base table triggers.

- UPDATE statements cannot change any column in a view that is a computation, nor can they change a view that includes aggregate functions, built-in functions, a GROUP BY clause, or DISTINCT.
- You cannot use READTEXT or WRITETEXT on *text* or *image* columns in views.
- By default, data modification statements on views are not checked to determine whether the rows affected will be within the scope of the view. You can issue an INSERT statement on a view to add a row to the underlying base table which would not be visible through the view. Similarly, you can issue an UPDATE statement that changes a row so that the row no longer meets the criteria for the view. If all modifications should be checked, use the WITH CHECK option when you create the VIEW.

Indexes

Over time, it will become clear to you that your users use certain columns from your tables to perform searches. You can greatly increase the retrieval performance of these queries by creating indexes on those columns. An *index* is a structure that holds a specific key value and a pointer to the physical place in the table where the row corresponding to that key exists. It acts just like an index for a book. In this case, however, you decide what columns are stored.

Index types

There are three types of indexes in SQL Server: *unique*, *non-unique*, *and clustered.* A unique index allows you to store only one instance of any key value. Primary keys, for example, are enforced in SQL Server through the use of a unique index. A non-unique index, however, allows you to store multiple references to any particular key value. This means that underlying table can have multiple rows with the same key value. A clustered index arranges the data on disk in indexed order.

The type of index you choose to create will very much depend on the nature of the data in your table. Here's a quick example to illustrate our point. Assume that you have an employee table with five fields: employee_id, first_name, last_name, home_phone, and street_address.

Tip

The first thing you need to know is that a unique index will always give you the best retrieval times. Therefore, it should be your goal to make as many of your indexes unique as possible. With this in mind, you would want to declare employee_id as your primary key because it is always unique. When you do this, SQL Server creates a unique index on the column.◀

Sometimes, however, you need to have a good retrieval time for fields that are not unique. Good examples of this are the first_name and last_name fields. It is very likely that people are going to want to search these fields. There is, however, no way to guarantee that either is going to be unique. Your best bet is to create non-unique indexes on both fields.

Clustered versus nonclustered

SQL Server provides the capability for you to specify how the data in your index is physically stored. You can specify one index in a table to store similar key values physically together in the index. This is called *clustering*. Clustering has the advantage that it will boost performance for queries that use that index. If you have a particular index that you expect will be used a lot more than the others, it is a good candidate for clustering. Be careful, though, clustering does have its disadvantages. Physically ordering an index on a set of key values may make indexes based on other keys less efficient. At this point, you are probably thinking that clustering is not a good idea if your indexes are going to be used equally. We don't agree. We think that you always want a clustered index. They work so much better. If you need to, flip a coin to pick one index for clustering.

Creating an index

To create a new index on a table, right-click the desired table and choose Indexes. The screen shown in Figure 13-6 appears.

The first thing you need to do is choose, from the list on the left, the column(s) that you want to define your index. You do this by clicking a column and then choosing the Add button. The next thing you have to decide is what attribute you want your new index to have. You can choose from the following:

- **Unique Keys.** If you check this option, the index will be created as a unique index. Otherwise, it will be created as a non-unique index.

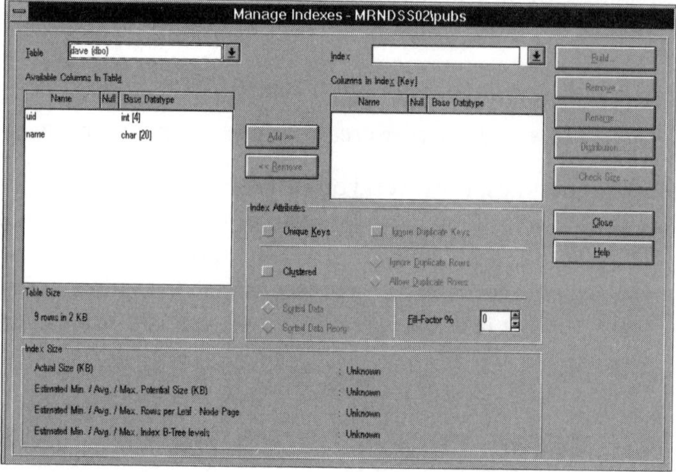

Figure 13-6:
Create an index here.

- **Ignore Duplicate Keys.** Normally, if you try to insert a row of data into a table that contains a duplicate key value, SQL Server returns an error. If, however, you enable this option, SQL Server returns only a warning. It will, however, still reject the duplicate data.
- **Clustered.** This option specifies whether you want the index to be clustered. The default is nonclustered.
- **Ignore Duplicate Rows.** If this option is enabled, SQL Server will not allow duplicate rows of data in a table. Note that this pertains to an entire row of data, not just a key value.
- **Allow Duplicate Rows.** This option allows duplicate rows of data in the table. It is enabled by default.
- **Sorted Data.** If this item is enabled, SQL Server assumes that the data in your table is sorted before it tries to create the index. If it finds that the data is not sorted, the index creation fails. The advantage to this option is that if your data is already sorted, the index-creation process goes a little faster. For clustered indexes, though, the creation process will go *a lot* faster.
- **Un-Sorted Data.** This item tells SQL Server that the data is not already sorted and that it should sort the data before creating the index.

- **Fill Factor %.** This option tells SQL Server how full to make each index page at creation time. This is important because, if SQL Server needs to span pages to create the index, the entire process will take longer. The truth of the matter is, though, that this fill factor is not maintained throughout the life of the index and is seldom relevant. Our advice is to accept the value that SQL Server gives. If you would like more information on the special cases where a fill factor is important, please refer to Chapter 4.◀

Index performance reporting

Although this chapter intentionally does not cover many performance-tuning aspects of SQL Server, there is one that we would like to show you now. Go ahead and pick a table that has more than 200 rows in it and select Manage⇨Indexes. When the index window appears, select one of the indexes and then click the Distribution button. The Index Distribution Statistics window appears. If there is no information in the window, click the Update button (See Figure 13-7).

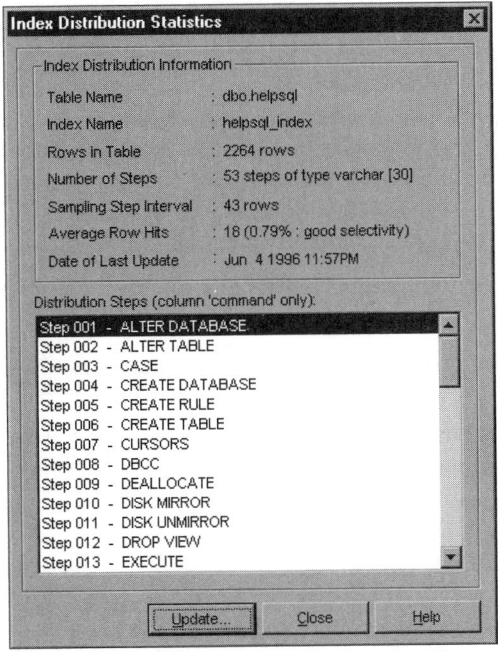

Figure 13-7:
This screen show you your index distribution for a table.

The index distribution window shows you how well your index is constructed and is likely to perform. In a nutshell, it shows you how worthwhile it is to have the index in question.

The first three items in the display (table name, index name, and rows in table) are self explanatory. The next three, however, are where the value is. The Number of Steps value indicates how many steps it took SQL Server to traverse the index when it was compiling its sample. The Sampling Step Interval shows the number of index rows between sample points. The Average Row Hits value, however, is the most important statistic. This value shows the average number of rows that would be returned by this index if you sent SQL Server a fully qualified query.

For example, assume that you have an index on last names. The Average Row Hits statistic would show you the average number of rows you would be likely to get back if you sent a SELECT statement with a WHERE clause like where lastname = 'Jones'. The closer that number is to 1, the better. For tables that have more than 200 rows, SQL Server also gives you a brief phrase that gives its opinion of your index performance. The possible outcomes are the following:

- **Optimal.** Your index returns an average of exactly 1 row per qualified query.
- **Very Good.** The index returns more than 1 row but less than 0.5 percent of all rows.
- **Good.** The index returns more than 0.5 percent of all rows, but less than 1 percent of all rows.
- **Fair.** On average, the index returns between 1 percent and 2.5 percent of all rows per qualified query.
- **Poor.** The index returns more than 2.5 percent but less than 5 percent of all rows.
- **Very Poor.** The index returns more than 5 percent of all rows.

In general, indexes that are performing at fair or worse performance are good candidates for removal. We will cover index and query optimization later in this book, but we thought this would be a good thing to introduce to you now.

SUMMARY

In this chapter, you have learned some of the most important things you can ever know about using your SQL Server system effectively. A good table, index, and view structure will help you in a multitude of areas of system management. These areas include speed, security, data integrity, and ease of use. Although you certainly have not learned *everything* there is to know about these topics, you are well on your way to mastering them.

Cross-Reference

For further reading, we suggest you consult the chapter on system tables and stored procedures (Chapter 11). The items in this chapter will give you even greater insights into your tables, indexes, and views.◀

REVIEW QUESTIONS

Q: What are the rules for column names?

A: A column name should comply with the following rules:

- The first character of a column name must be a letter or the symbols _ or #.
- Characters following the first character can include letters, digits, or the symbols #, $, or _.
- By default, no embedded spaces are allowed in column names.

Q: What are some good rules of thumb for column names?

A: The following are strongly recommended rules of thumb for the naming of columns:

- Do not name a column the same as an SQL keyword. (for example, SELECT, IN, DECLARE, and so on). If you do, you run the risk of confusing the SQL parser.
- Make your column names relevant to the data that the column will hold.

Q: Is it a good idea to use quoted identifiers?

A: No. You don't gain much by using them and will substantially increase your risk of error.

Q: Which is better as a column type, a char that allows nulls or a varchar that allows nulls?

A: They are the same. SQL Server stores all chars that allow nulls as varchars.

Q: Is there a way to have SQL Server automatically generate my primary key values?

A: Yes, use identity columns.

Q: Is this method foolproof?

A: Not a chance! If you use the SET IDENTITY INSERT statement, you can really hose your keys!

Q: Why would anyone use a view? After all, they seem to be more trouble than they are worth.

A: Wrong! Views are really handy in two major areas. First, you can use a view to control access rights for certain tables. Second, there will be times when it will be programmatically easier to deal with an aggregate or un-normalized table. Rather than destroying your nice table scheme by introducing poorly formatted data, you can create a view.

Q: When is it a bad idea to use a clustered index?

A: Never! We feel very strongly that it is *always* a good idea to use them, but only one per table.

Chapter

14

STORED PROCEDURES AND TRIGGERS

Up to this point, we have spent our time discussing SQL Server's capabilities to store data. The true power of SQL Server, however, is in the way you can program it to process your data. If you are approaching this book from the point of view of a programmer, you will especially appreciate stored procedures. If, however, your main concern is as a DBA, you will, no doubt, find triggers of interest. In this chapter, we discuss both concepts and give you ideas on what roles they can play in your system.

WHAT'S IN THIS CHAPTER

This chapter includes coverage of the following topics:

- What is a stored procedure?
- What is a trigger?
- How do the two differ?
- Where are each appropriate?
- How can I use each to simplify my life?

THE CLIENT-SERVER MODEL

If you have even glanced at a computer magazine in the last two years, you have undoubtedly seen a lot written about the client-server model of computing and how it is changing the way applications are being written. In this section, we give a brief overview of the concepts and how they apply here.

Once upon a time

Back in the Jurassic period of computing (see Chapter 12), all processing was done on a central machine. Each user would then connect to that machine via a *dumb terminal*. A dumb terminal was a computer that had just enough brains to connect to a mainframe. All the commands and processing being done by the user were being executed in the memory of the central mainframe. The introduction of the PC, however, changed all that. Over time, programs were written to run directly on a user's computer. The need for central mainframes and networks began to diminish. This was good because it allowed a much broader group of people to take advantage of software. It was also a problem, though, because most personal computers did not have anywhere near the processing power of their mainframe predecessors.◀

From this dilemma, the client-server model was born. In essence, the program that the user interfaces with (the client) requests data from a centralized machine (the server). All or almost all of the raw database retrievals and calculations are performed by the server and returned to the client. In fact, one of the most difficult jobs for a programmer writing for a client-server environment is figuring out which processes to delegate to the server and which to keep for the client. As you soon will see, stored procedures and triggers are critical tools for implementing a good client-server model with SQL Server.

STORED PROCEDURES

A *stored procedure* is a compiled piece of SQL code that is executed by SQL Server. It may contain variables, control flow statements, calls to other stored procedures, and a host of other programming niceties. If you are a programmer, you can consider a stored procedure a precompiled function or library. If you are a DBA, you can think of stored procedures as just plain cool.

Getting started

The easiest way to create a stored procedure is in the SQL Enterprise Manager. Click the database in which you want to create the procedure and choose Manage⇨Stored Procedures. The screen shown in Figure 14-1 appears.

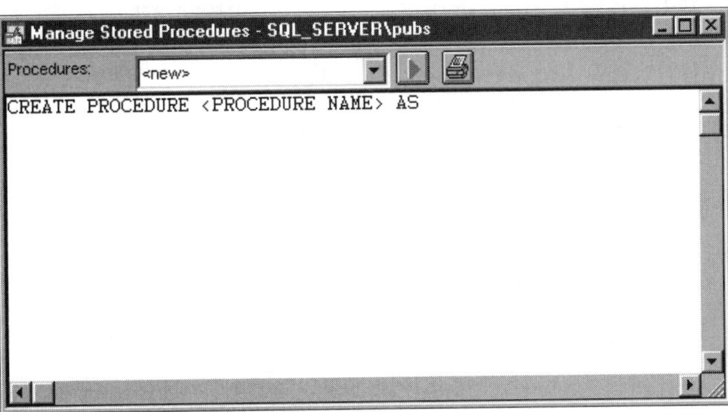

Figure 14-1:
The Manage Stored Procedure screen.

The first thing you've probably noticed is that you are confronted with SQL. Well, you guessed it, there's no real GUI way of creating a stored procedure. You have to define it with the CREATE PROCEDURE statement. For the time being, though, give your new procedure a name by replacing <PROCEDURE NAME> with something like p_myTestProc and enter the following code on the next line:

```
SELECT * FROM authors
```

When you are finished, click the green arrow. If all went well, your procedure should disappear and you should see a blank window identical to the first.

You may have noticed that we asked you to create your procedure with the prefix *p_*. The reason for this is simple. When you are looking at a list of objects in your database, the *p_* prefix will indicate to you that you are looking at a stored procedure that you created. (The system stored procedures all start with *sp_*.)◀

What happened?

At this point, it is probably worthwhile to talk about what SQL Server did with your new procedure. First, SQL Server creates a more efficient representation, called a *normalized form,* or *query tree*, of the stored procedure. It does this by replacing object references, such as table and column names, with their respective object ids. This information is then stored in the sysprocedures table while the original format of the procedure is stored in the syscomments table.

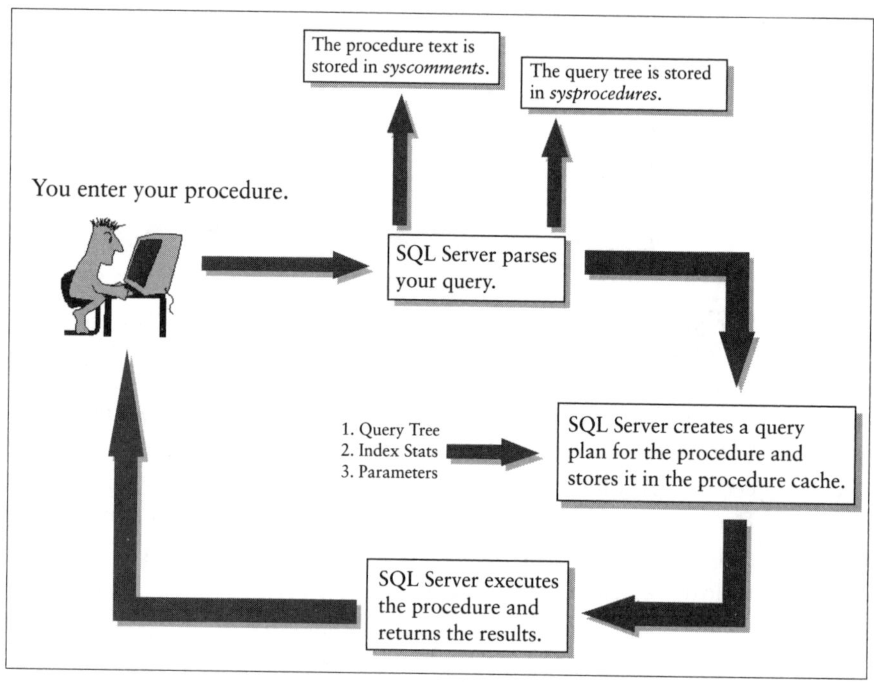

Figure 14-2:
This is what happens when you create and run a stored procedure.

The first time you run your procedure, SQL Server creates something called a *query plan* for the procedure. A query plan is the optimal path for executing a stored procedure. SQL Server uses three criteria for building a query plan:

- The SQL statements stored in the query tree. Please note that this information is taken from the query tree and *not* the original procedure text. This is because the query tree is a more efficient, and thus better, representation of the procedure logic.

- The statistics for any table or index referenced in the procedure. You learned earlier that SQL Server keeps performance statistics about its tables and indexes. This information is critical for SQL Server to choose the fastest execution path for the procedure.
- The values of any parameters you may have passed into the procedure the *first* time is what was executed. Obviously, the parameters you pass can have a great effect on the indexes SQL Server chooses for the procedure execution.

Query plans are stored in SQL Server's procedure cache. This means that SQL Server will need to recompile each procedure (create a new query plan) the first time it is run after the server has been restarted.◀

As you might expect, there are a few more things to talk about with respect to how SQL Server treats stored procedures internally. We are leaving that for a little later in the chapter, however.

A syntactical description

As you have already seen, stored procedures are created by using the CREATE PROCEDURE statement. The exact syntax for CREATE PROCEDURE is as follows:

```
CREATE PROCEDURE [owner.]procedure_name[;number]
    [(parm1 [, parm2]...[parm255])]
[{FOR REPLICATION}|{WITH RECOMPILE}
    [{[WITH]|[,]} ENCRYPTION]]
AS sql_statements
```

The following paragraphs explain each component of this syntax.

Procedure_name[;number]

You must give each stored procedure you create a name that is unique for the database in which it resides. Names must adhere to the same rules that govern table names and can also be used as quoted identifiers. The only other restriction you need to know about procedure names is that they can be no more than 20 characters long.

The purpose of the [;number] parameter is to enable you to group procedures together. This is helpful if you want to drop a group of procedures. For example, if you create two procedures, sp_grouped;1 and sp_grouped;2, and then issued a DROP PROCEDURE sp_grouped, *both* procedures would be dropped. We don't recommend that you use this numbering feature because it's too easy to drop procedures you never meant to delete.

You can also create private and global temporary stored procedures by starting their names with # and ##, respectively. For example, #myTmpProc would be a private temporary procedure, whereas ##myOtherProc would be a global temporary procedure. We will give an example of a temporary procedure a little later.

Parameters

You can also pass parameters into a stored procedure. They are specified in the following way:

```
parameter = @parameter_name datatype [= default] [OUTPUT]
```

@parameter_name is the name that you want to give your parameter. There a few rules to be aware of when dealing with parameters to a stored procedure:

- All parameter names must start with an @ and must conform to the rules governing identifiers.
- Parameters are always local to the procedure. This means that other procedures and routines can use parameters with the same name and there will be no conflict.
- A parameter can only be used for *r-values* (items on the right side of an operator). This means that you cannot use parameters for things like table and column names.
- A stored procedure can have up to 255 parameters.

The datatype portion specifies which datatype the parameter will be. You may use any datatype you want except image.

The default option enables you to specify what the default value of the parameter should be. This allows the user to execute the procedure without specifying any parameters. Normally, if users don't supply parameters to a stored procedure that expects them, they get an error message. The default value for any parameter can be any valid value of the specified datatype. This also includes NULL.

The OUPUT flag indicates that the parameter will be used to return data to the calling procedure.

All parameters are considered input parameters. The OUTPUT flag simply means that the given parameter will also return data.◀

The only restriction here is that you cannot use text parameters for output.

When we say *text*, we literally mean the SQL Server text datatype.◀

For Replication

This one gets a little hairy. The short answer is that this option is used when you want to create a filter procedure for use during replication. Don't worry because we'll go over this and all the other related items in the section that deals with replication (Part VII).◀

With Recompile

If you specify this option, SQL Server will not store a query plan for the stored procedure. This means that it will be recompiled each time it executes. The biggest disadvantage to this approach is that your procedure will take longer to execute because it has to be recompiled. If, however, you expect that the parameters you pass will not likely yield the same query plan each time you call the procedure, using this option may be your best bet. A procedure's execution time can be longer if it is using a query plan that is not optimal for the parameters that have been passed. A good example of this is when you intend to include wildcard characters in your parameters or plan to identify which columns to use. Here's a brief example of a stored procedure with which you probably want to use the WITH RECOMPILE option:

```
CREATE PROCEDURE p_recompile_test @tableNo int = 1 WITH RECOMPILE AS

IF @tableNo = 1
    SELECT * FROM pubs..authors

IF @tableNo = 2
    SELECT * FROM pubs..discounts

IF @tableNo = 3
    SELECT * FROM pubs..publishers
```

If, for example, this procedure first executes with a parameter of 1, and then the query plan will be optimized for the authors table. Clearly, a plan that is optimal for authors will not be so for discounts or publishers. Because of this fact, this procedure is a good candidate for the WITH RECOMPILE flag.

With Encryption

Specifying this flag encrypts the syscomments table entry that contains the text of your procedure. The problem with this is that when a database is upgraded, syscomments entries are required in order to recreate procedures. Obviously, the encrypted entries won't be any good. Use this option only if you absolutely need to make sure that no one can read the text of your stored procedure. Our advice to you, though, is *not* to use this option. You will have to recreate all of your procedures if you ever upgrade your software. Quite frankly, there are too many other good security precautions you can take to prevent unauthorized access to your system. We think you can pretty much ignore this one.

Other Rules

There are a few other rules of which you need to be aware when creating a stored procedure:

- If you are using SQL Server 6.0, the procedure can include any SQL statements, with the exception of the following: CREATE VIEW, CREATE TRIGGER, CREATE DEFAULT, CREATE PROCEDURE, and CREATE RULE. SQL Server 6.5, however, eliminates this restriction.
- You can reference an object created in the same procedure as long as it is created *before* it is referenced.
- You cannot do the following in a stored procedure: create an object, drop it, and then create a new object with the same name.
- You can use SET statements within a stored procedure. They will, however, only be in effect during the execution of the procedure.
- If you create a private temporary table inside a procedure, the temporary table is dropped when the procedure exits.
- You can declare as many variables as you like in a stored procedure, as long as there is enough memory for them.

Examples

The following are some examples that better illustrate some of the items we have discussed thus far.

Input/output parameters

This code creates, runs, and drops a procedure that retrieves the syntax of a given stored procedure. It is important to note here that we are using one variable as both an input and output parameter.

```
/* Section 1 */
CREATE PROCEDURE #p_getSyntax @proc_name char(255) OUTPUT AS

SELECT @proc_name = text
    FROM syscomments
    WHERE id = object_id(@proc_name)
GO

DECLARE @rval char(255)
SELECT @rval = 'p_recompile_test'

/* Section 2 */

EXECUTE #p_getSyntax @rval OUTPUT

/* Section 3 */

PRINT 'The syntax is:'
PRINT ' '
SELECT @rval

/* Section 4 */

DROP PROCEDURE #p_getSyntax
GO
```

Section 1 declares a procedure named #p_getSyntax that accepts one parameter, @proc_name. There are a couple of important things to note here. First, #p_getSyntax is a private temporary procedure. It will not exist from one transaction to the other. Second, the parameter @proc_name is both an input and output parameter. All parameters to a stored procedure are, by default, input parameters; therefore, all you need to do to get data back from them is also to include the keyword OUTPUT.

Section 2 declares a variable named @rval and sets it to the value #p_getSyntax. This section also executes the stored procedure. It is important also to include the OUTPUT keyword in the execution statement, or the procedure will not return data to the parameter.

Section 3 simply prints the new value of @rval, and Section 4 drops the procedure.

Grouping procedures

The following code demonstrates the concept of grouping procedures together so that they can be dropped easily:

```
/* Create stored procedures */

CREATE PROCEDURE p_group_test;1 AS
PRINT 'proc 1'
GO

CREATE PROCEDURE p_group_test;2 AS
PRINT 'proc 2'
GO

CREATE PROCEDURE p_group_test;3 AS
PRINT 'proc 3'
GO

/* Execute procedures */

EXECUTE p_group_test;1
EXECUTE p_group_test;2
EXECUTE p_group_test;3

/* Drop procedures */

PRINT ''
PRINT 'Dropping group..'

DROP procedure p_group_test

PRINT 'done.'
PRINT ''

/* Prove that ALL the procedures were dropped */

PRINT 'Trying to execute after drop...'
PRINT ''

EXECUTE p_group_test;1
EXECUTE p_group_test;2
EXECUTE p_group_test;3

go
```

The output of this process is the following:

```
proc 1
proc 2
proc 3

Dropping group..
done.

Trying to execute after drop...

Msg 2812, Level 16, State 4
Stored procedure 'p_group_test' not found.
```

As you can see, all the procedures in the group were dropped. There are a few other things you ought to know about grouping stored procedures, such as the following:

- All procedure groups MUST have a ";1" procedure. In other words, you cannot create procedure_group;2 until procedure_group;1 exists.
- If you leave off a ";" number, ";1" is implied. This means that creating p_myProc and p_myProc;1 is identical. It also means that if you execute p_myProc, it will run p_myProc;1.
- You can skip numbers in groups as long as you have a ";1" procedure. Yes, that means you can create p_myproc;1, p_myproc;7, and p_myProc;9.
- You can create procedures out of order, as long as you first create the ";1" procedure.

The blood and guts of stored procedures

This last section on stored procedures addresses some of the inner workings of how SQL Server executes a particular procedure. Although the material is pretty technical, it is still *very* important. A clear understanding of the concepts in this section will help you work through certain common errors and performance issues.

One for you, and one for me

Stored procedures are reusable, but not reentrant. *Reusable code* means that multiple users can use a given piece of code at the same time. They are, however, using their own copy of that code. *Reentrant code*, on the other hand, means that multiple users can use the *same* instance of code in memory at the same time.

Consider this scenario. You create a procedure called myProc without the WITH RECOMPILE option. This first time you execute myProc after starting SQL Server, SQL Server will retrieve its query tree from sysprocedures, create a query plan, place it in the procedure cache, and execute the code. Each subsequent time you execute myProc, however, SQL Server will use the query plan it stored in the procedure cache. This means that subsequent calls to the procedure will be faster, because SQL Server will not have to recompile it.

What if, however, you try to execute myProc while someone else is already using it? The answer is that SQL Server will generate a new query plan for you and leave it in the procedure cache. This means that you can now have two people using the procedure at the same time without SQL Server having to recompile it.

Stored procedure schizophrenia

The capability to have multiple query plans in the procedure cache, however, raises some potential problems. Consider the following scenario: User A and user B both execute the same stored procedure at the same time with very different parameters. When the procedures are finished, SQL Server stores both query plans in the procedure cache. A short time later, user A and user B both execute the procedure again. This time, though, A uses exactly the same parameters as B. What happens? The answer is that one of the users gets better performance from SQL Server than the other. The reason is that one of them is guaranteed to get a nonoptimal query plan for his or her query. Actually, they could *both* get nonoptimal plans if they use parameters that would cause the two plans in the cache to perform badly. The point is that having multiple query plans in memory can begin to cause performance headaches for certain stored procedures.

Fortunately, there are a few things you can do to alleviate this problem. First, you can execute the stored procedure with the WITH RECOMPILE option. This forces SQL Server to create a new query plan for you. The problem, though, is that it takes longer to run this procedure because SQL Server has to do more work.

The second thing you can do is periodically drop and recreate your procedures. When you do this, SQL Server automatically flushes all query plans for that procedure from memory. This is actually very easy to do in the SQL Enterprise manager. Choose the relevant database and then select Manage⇨Stored Procedures. When the empty procedure window opens, select the procedure you want to flush from the list at the top. *So far, you are performing the same steps you would perform if you were going to edit the procedure*. Notice an important thing about the way SQL Server is displaying your procedure code. It has put a few lines at the top that check for the existence of the procedure and then drop it. The rest of the code recreates the procedure. Therefore, all you need to do is click the run button to execute the T-SQL code in the window. By dropping and recreating the procedure, SQL Server automatically flushes your query plans from memory. Flushing another procedure is as easy as selecting it from the list and pushing the green button. Do this periodically for your most heavily used procedures.

Auto execution stored procedures

One of the cool new features of SQL Server 6.0 was the capability to specify certain stored procedures to execute immediately when the server starts up. There are, however, a few things that we need to point out:

- All such procedures must be created by the system administrator.
- Startup procedures cannot require any parameters.
- Each startup procedure runs with its own connection. This means that if you start 20 procedures in parallel, you will use 20 connections. You can run procedures in serial if you have one procedure call another.
- Each procedure will run as a background process with the system administrator id.
- The startup procedures are launched *after* the last database has been recovered.

To create a startup stored procedure, you must be logged in as system administrator and create the stored procedure in the *master* database.

To make an existing stored procedure a startup procedure, type the following:

```
sp_makestartup procedure_name
```

To stop a procedure from executing at startup, type this:

```
sp_unmakestartup procedure_name
```

To view a list of all startup procedures, type the following:

```
sp_helpstartup
```

Beyond Client-Server: Three-Tier Partitioning

The purpose of the client-server model is to provide a way to distribute the processing load of your application across two or more machines. One of the problems with it, though, is that if any of your business rules change, you may need to change program code in two different places: the client program and the server stored procedures. This complicates matters considerably for the people who have to maintain your code. Over time, however, programmers and system architects have devised a scheme to alleviate this problem. It is called *three-tier partitioning*. In this system, client-server applications are divided into three logical segments: the user interface, the database logic, and the business rules and logic.

The user interface

The *user interface* portion of the three-tier model consists of that program code with which the user directly interacts. In a Windows environment, for example, that would be any menus, windows, or other controls with which the user sees and works. The idea is to divide the interface code logically from the rest of the system so that interface design changes can be made with little or no impact on the program code for the business rules and database logic.

Database logic

The *database logic* is that portion of the program code that is responsible for the maintenance of data in the system. This code will usually retrieve and update data, but will seldom perform much analysis on it. Most database

Beyond Three-Tier: N-Tier

Developers have already begun working on the next step beyond the three-tier architecture: the N-tier architecture. In essence, this model says that an application can be partitioned into as many logical segments as needed in order to maintain maximum flexibility and component interoperability. The fastest growth of this concept is in the area of distributed program objects. In a nutshell, this area is focused on keeping compiled bits of program code (not necessarily in the same language) on different servers so that a wide variety applications can use them.

These ideas are very much beyond the scope of this book, but we thought that you ought to be aware of the direction that things are headed. If you are a programmer, you will certainly encounter these concepts again.

logic is run on the database server and is, therefore, most commonly implemented with stored procedures and other similar mechanisms. In a SQL Server environment, that portion of your database logic that resides on your server will be performed by stored procedures and SQL Server's new Declarative Referential Integrity (DRI) functions.

Business rules and logic

Business rules and logic are those constraints and procedures that are driven by the nature of the process in which you are engaged. In other words, they are typically additional relationships and constraints that you create for your data that have little or nothing to do with good database design and form. You can violate a business rule without taking your tables out of the third normal form.

A quick example should help clarify the distinction between the two. Assume that you have decided that no employee in your company who has the job title gopher may earn more than $30,000 a year. Also assume that you have a table that holds the following:

- Employee ID (emp_id)
- Employee Name (emp_name)
- Employee Job Title (job_title)
- Employee Salary (emp_salary)

It would be very helpful to be able to tell SQL Server to check the value of the Employee Salary field every time someone tries to insert a new record or update an existing value in the Employee Job Title field. This way, you could make sure that no user can ever enter an invalid salary value for a given job title. This is a good example of a business rule. It is a constraint on the data that is beyond the scope of a normal database restriction. In SQL Server, business rules are most commonly implemented by *triggers*, although very simple rules can be implemented with other things, such as defaults.

A business process, on the other hand, is a series of steps that is requested by the user. A good example of this would be aggregating financial data from a series of tables in order to prepare a yearly tax report. This kind of process would best be encapsulated in a stored procedure. That way, if the business process needs to change (if the tax law is altered, for example), all you need to do is fix the stored procedure to compute the new values correctly.

Triggers

A *trigger* is a specialized kind of stored procedure that executes when a certain event happens to a table. Triggers can be defined for three distinct table actions: updates, deletions, and insertions.

Creating triggers

To create a new trigger, select the desired target database in the SQL Enterprise Manager and choose Manage⇨Triggers. The window shown in Figure 14-3 appears.

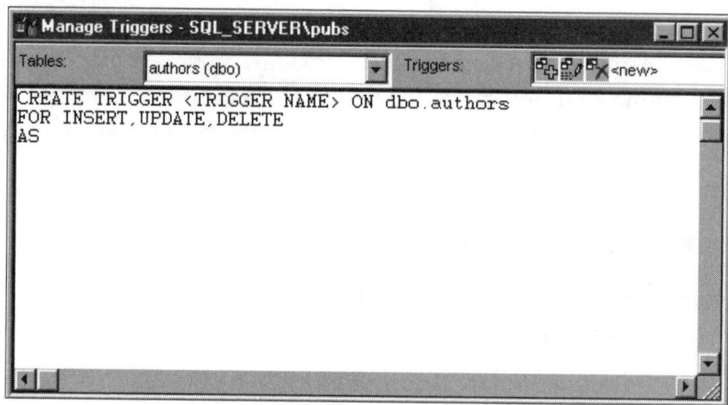

Figure 14-3:
You can manage your triggers from this window.

This window is very similar to the window in which you created your stored procedures. The first thing you need to do is choose the table on which you want to create your trigger. You do this by choosing it from the list in the top left of the window. After you have done this, you must modify the CREATE TRIGGER statement.

The CREATE TRIGGER statement

Like regular stored procedures, triggers can only be created and edited through the use of SQL. There is no GUI tool to help you through the process. As a result, we will take some time in this section to explain the basics of the CREATE TRIGGER statement.

The syntax for the CREATE TRIGGER statement is as follows:

```
CREATE TRIGGER [owner.]trigger_name
ON [owner.]table_name
FOR {INSERT, UPDATE, DELETE}
[WITH ENCRYPTION]
AS sql_statements
```

The only thing that should seem unusual to you about this syntax is the introduction of the FOR {INSERT, UPDATE, DELETE} clause. As we mentioned earlier, triggers are fired for one of three events: a table update, a table delete, and a table insert. You can also specify more than one condition in this clause. In other words, you can have the same trigger fire for an insert and an update.

Warning

A table can have one and only one trigger defined for its insert, delete, and update events. That means a maximum of three triggers per table. No exceptions!◀

The inserted and deleted tables

Triggers recognize two special tables named *inserted* and *deleted*. When you perform an insert operation, the data you insert are stored in the inserted table. Likewise, when you perform a delete operation, the data you delete are stored in the deleted table. When you perform an update operation, the original data are stored in the deleted table, and the new data are stored in the inserted table.

Note

The inserted and deleted tables are imaginary tables that SQL Server creates just to help with the syntax. They don't really exist and cannot be referenced outside the trigger.◀

Knowing about these tables can help you determine whether a specific business rule has been followed. The following is a brief example to illustrate this point:

```
CREATE TRIGGER t_good_salary
ON employee
FOR INSERT, UPDATE
AS
DECLARE @salary real, jobTitle char(255)

SELECT @salary = emp_salary, @jobTitle = job_title
FROM inserted
```

(*continued*)

(*continued*)

```
IF @job_title = 'gopher' and @salary > 30000
    BEGIN
        raiserror('you lose!',1,1)
        ROLLBACK TRANSACION
    END
```

This trigger is fired every time there is an insert or an update operation against the employee table. All it does is check to see whether the row being inserted or updated meets the business rule. If it doesn't, the code causes an error message and rolls back the transaction.

Checking multiple rows

Assume for the moment that you execute the following SQL with the preceding trigger still in place:

```
update employee set emp_salary = 100000
```

No matter how many rows are affected by the SQL, the t_good_salary trigger will only be fired once. This means that you must somehow iterate through the inserted table to check the values of the inserted rows. You can do this by declaring a cursor and stepping through each row.

SQL Server also provides a way for you to find out how many rows were affected by the actions that caused the trigger. This value is stored in the global variable @@ROWCOUNT.

Conditional triggers and the IF UPDATE clause

There will certainly be cases when you will want to enforce different business rules for different columns in the same table. In order to do this, though, you must first determine which column is being updated. You can accomplish this in a trigger by using the IF UPDATE clause. The following

Now You See It, Now You Don't

Be careful when using the @@ROCOUNT variable. Certain actions within a trigger can reset its value to zero. Our advice to you is to declare an integer variable at the beginning of your trigger and set it to @@ROWCOUNT.

This way, you will not have to worry about whether or not @@ROWCOUNT will keep its value.

example should help. Assume that you are using the same employee table as before with the same restriction on salary. Also assume that you do not allow employee id numbers lower than 100 to be inserted into the table. You can enforce these rules with the following trigger:

```
CREATE TRIGGER t_good_data
ON employee
FOR INSERT, UPDATE
AS

/* Check the salary info */

IF update(emp_salary)
BEGIN

    DECLARE @salary real, jobTitle char(255)

    SELECT @salary = emp_salary, @jobTitle = job_title
    FROM inserted

    IF @job_title = 'gopher' and @salary > 30000
    BEGIN
        raiserror('you lose!',1,1)
        ROLLBACK TRANSACTION
END

END

/* Check the employee id info */

IF update(employee_id)
BEGIN

    DECLARE @eid int
    SELECT @eid = employee_id FROM inserted

    IF @eid < 100
    BEGIN
        RAISEERROR('you lose again',2,2)
        ROLLBACK TRANSACTION
END

END
```

This code is really divided into two separate sections. The first section validates that the data does not violate the rule on salary for people with the job title "gopher." The second section checks to see that the employee id being inserted or updated is not less than 100.

The key thing in this example is the use of the IF UPDATE clause. It is used here to check which column is being updated so that the trigger can apply the correct rule. The other thing to notice here is the use of the RAISERROR statement. This command returns an error of a user-specified type to SQL Server. It is not important that you understand the syntax of the command right now. We only point it out here because the trigger returns a different error for each business rule. By doing this, your program code can easily discern which rule failed.

Additional rules for triggers

If you are using SQL Server 6.0, there are some things you can do in a regular stored procedure that you cannot do in a trigger. For example, the following SQL cannot be used in a trigger:

- All CREATE statements
- All DROP statements
- ALTER TABLE and ALTER DATABASE
- TRUNCATE TABLE
- GRANT and REVOKE
- UPDATE STATISTICS
- RECONFIGURE
- LOAD DATABASE and LOAD TRANSACTION
- All DISK statements
- SELECT INTO

The only way to circumvent these rules is to upgrade to SQL Server 6.5. For example, you cannot create a stored procedure that uses a SELECT INTO and then have your trigger execute the stored procedure.

As long as we are on the topic of stored procedures, there are some other things of which you ought to be aware. In our preceding example, we used the IF UPDATE clause to check whether certain columns were being updated. We then executed code that was specific to those columns. The problem is that the entire code listing of the trigger can get pretty messy if you have more than a couple of IF UPDATE statements in there. Our first thought was to put the logic for each column in a stored procedure and simply execute the correct procedure. There was one problem. Even if a stored procedure is executed from a trigger, it cannot see the special inserted and deleted virtual tables. This greatly limits the use of that approach.

Examples

Now that we have covered the basics of triggers, it's time for some examples. The next few sections should help clarify the concepts just introduced.

Analyzing all the rows: Using aggregates

Previously, we mentioned that a trigger is fired for each SQL statement, not for each affected row. In other words, if you execute an update statement that affects 20 rows in a particular table, the update trigger for that table will fire only once. As a result, you need to write your trigger to loop through all the rows of the inserted table in order to see whether the proposed data meets your needs.

Earlier in the chapter, we gave an example of a simple trigger to check that a person with the job title "gopher" was not getting more than $30,000 a year in salary. Here is that code:

```
CREATE TRIGGER t_good_salary
ON employee
FOR INSERT, UPDATE
AS

DECLARE @salary real, jobTitle char(255)

SELECT @salary = emp_salary, @jobTitle = job_title
FROM inserted

IF @job_title = 'gopher' and @salary > 30000
    BEGIN
        raiserror('you lose!',1,1)
        ROLLBACK TRANSACTION
END
```

The problem is that this trigger checks only the *first* row of the inserted table. An offending item of data could occur later and would be allowed in the table. In this specific case, we have two choices regarding how to rewrite the trigger. The easiest way to do it is to use SQL Server's MAX function. The following code illustrates the point:

```
CREATE TRIGGER t_good_salary
ON employee
FOR INSERT, UPDATE
AS
DECLARE @salary real
```

(*continued*)

(*continued*)

```
SELECT @salary = max(emp_salary)
FROM inserted
WHERE job_title = 'gopher'

IF @salary > 30000
    BEGIN
        raiserror('you lose!',1,1)
        ROLLBACK TRANSACTION
END
```

Because we have to cancel the entire update statement if there is even one offending record, we can simply find the maximum salary being entered into the table for all employees with the job title "gopher." The problem with this approach, however, is that it doesn't let the person executing the SQL know *which* record caused the problem. We can, however, fix this problem by adding some additional logic, as follows:

```
CREATE TRIGGER t_good_salary
ON employee
FOR INSERT, UPDATE
AS

DECLARE @salary real, @employee_name char(255)

SELECT @salary = max(emp_salary)
FROM inserted
WHERE job_title = 'gopher'

IF @salary > 30000
    BEGIN
        SELECT @employee_name = employee_name
            FROM employee
            WHERE job_title = 'gopher' and
                SALARY = @salary

raiserror('Employee %s has a salary of %d. (employees with  the job title gopher
cannot have salaries above 30,000',1,1,@employee_name, @salary)

        ROLLBACK TRANSACTION
    END
```

This trigger tells the user *which* record caused the problem so that he or she can fix the data.

Analyzing all the rows: Using cursors

The other way to analyze the entire contents of the inserted and deleted tables is to declare a cursor and go through them row by row. The following is a simple example of such an approach:

```
CREATE TRIGGER t_good_salary
ON employee
FOR INSERT, UPDATE
AS

DECLARE @salary real, @employee_name char(255), @job_title char(255)

DECLARE e_cursor CURSOR
   FOR SELECT emloyee_name, salary, job_title FROM employee

OPEN e_cursor

WHILE @@FETCH_STATUS <> -1
   BEGIN
      FETCH NEXT FROM e_cursor INTO @employee_name, @salary, @job_title

      IF @job_title = 'gopher' and @salary > 30000
      BEGIN
         raiserror('You Lose',1,1)
         ROLLBACK TRANSACTION
      END
   END

CLOSE authors_cursor

DEALLOCATE authors_cursor
```

With the aid of a cursor, this trigger can process each row of the inserted table separately.

The truth of the matter is, though, that you will be able to use SQL Server's aggregate functions to do this processing in the vast majority of cases where you need a trigger. It is useful to know how to use a cursor in a trigger, but it is seldom needed.

Summary

In this chapter, you learned how to unload some of your processing chores to SQL Server by using stored procedures and triggers. If you are a DBA, you can certainly appreciate how trigger and stored procedure can help you keep your data clean. If you are a programmer, however, the appeal of these topics is likely the fact that you can now more evenly distribute the processing duties of your program between your client machine and your SQL Server machine. All in all, stored procedures and triggers are possibly the most useful tools you have as SQL Server users and administrators.

Review Questions

Q: What is a stored procedure?

A: A stored procedure is a compiled piece of SQL code that is executed by SQL Server. It may contain variables, control flow statements, calls to other stored procedures, and a host of other programming niceties.

Q: What is a trigger?

A: A trigger is a specialized kind of stored procedure that executes when a certain event happens to a table. Triggers can be defined for three distinct table actions: updates, deletions, and insertions.

Q: How do triggers and stored procedures differ?

A: A trigger can only be executed by SQL Server when a defined action occurs in a table. Triggers cannot take parameters or be grouped.

Q: How are triggers and stored procedures the same?

A: They are both compiled code, and they are both used to enforce business rules and to balance processing load between the client and server machines.

Q: What are the two ways to process all the rows affected by an INSERT, UPDATE, or DELETE statement?

A: You can either use aggregate functions to check for certain criteria, or you can use a cursor to go through the inserted and deleted tables.

Q: If two users run the same stored procedure with the same parameters, are they guaranteed to have the same response time from SQL Server?

A: No. If there is already more than one query plan in memory for that procedure, the two users can get very different performance times.

Q: Is it a good idea to encrypt my stored procedures and triggers?

A: Not really. If you ever want to upgrade your version of SQL Server, you will be out of luck.

Q: If you use a SET statement in a trigger or a stored procedure, how long is it in effect?

A: It remains in effect either until you issue another SET statement that contradicts it or until the trigger/procedure finishes.

Chapter

Other Database Objects 15

Our focus in database administration so far has been Declarative Referential Integrity (DRI). This is usually both the simplest and the most powerful way to define relationships in data. However, there are some things that aren't easily done with DRI. This chapter discusses how to identify these requirements and what SQL Server gives you to solve them.

What's in This Chapter

After reading this chapter you will be able to:

- Recognize when you need to create your own datatypes
- Set up user-defined datatypes in SQL Server
- Create your own rules and defaults

User-Defined Datatypes

User-defined datatypes in SQL Server give you another option for enforcing data integrity. You can pick a basic SQL Server datatype (binary, char, float, money, and so on) and assign it a length if appropriate, a default, a rule, and a nullability. This then becomes a new datatype. User-defined datatypes are a weak attempt at supporting the relational model concept of the *domain,* the set from which a column draws its values. *In The Relational Model for Database Management, Version 2,* E. F. Codd writes, "Omission of support for domains in the most serious deficiency in today's relational DBMS products." You will agree after you read this section.

Pros and cons of user datatypes

If you find that you are using a particular datatype over and over again, you can formally declare it as a user datatype. This gets you the following advantages:

- You do less typing.
- You can assign a default and a rule to your user datatype, which may make your life easier when you need to change the default or rule of a column common to many tables.
- You put more information into your meta-data for your own reference.

That's it. If you have ever used a robust programming language, such as C++, that lets you define datatypes that are full and equal partners with the system-supplied datatypes, SQL Server isn't giving you much. The limitations of user datatypes include the following:

- You don't get the real domains of the relational model. In the relational model, each column should have a domain, and comparisons across domains aren't valid. For example, you should be able to declare a user type of "staffsize" as an int to count the number of people in your company services, and another type called "books_sold" as an int to track the number of books you sell. In the relational model, you can't do a nonsensical thing, such as add a number of type "books_sold" to a number of type "staffsize" without an explicit type casting. SQL Server offers no such protection.
- You cannot create a new user-defined datatype based on other user-defined datatypes.

- Users can override some of what you define when creating a table, such as the nullability.
- You get no extra type checking from SQL Server. If you make a user type called YourType that is char(7) not null, it behaves like all other character data types. There are no features preventing you from putting a char(50) null value into YourType. Instead, the char(50) string just gets truncated without warning. We have learned to live with this behavior for basic char types, but user datatypes should be more robust.
- Your user type can be nothing more than a system datatype, a width if appropriate, nullability, a default, and a rule. You can't set up anything more elaborate, such as vectors, lists, arrays, and so forth. Of course, these kinds of datatypes would violate the atomicity rule of the relational model, so we can't really fault SQL Server on this one.

Permissions and user-defined datatypes

For reasons that are not particularly clear to us, user-defined datatypes are outside of the SQL Server permission structure. Anyone can set up a user-defined datatype. Anyone can see and use anyone else's user-defined datatype. If you find it necessary to restrict the permission to create user-defined datatypes in a specific database, log in as the dbo of the database, *choose that database,* and execute the following command in the Query Analyzer:

```
CREATE PROC sp_addtype @typename varchar(30), @phystype varchar(30),
  @nulltype varchar(8) = null as
exec sp_addtype @typename, @phystype, @nulltype
```

This looks as if it has nothing to do with permissions, but it does. Because there is no such thing as "create datatype" permission, you have to use the backdoor of revoking execute authority on the underlying system procedure, sp_addtype. You could just go into master and revoke execute on sp_addtype from public, but then no one could create user-defined datatypes in any database. Instead, you want to revoke execute authority in a specific database. SQL Server doesn't directly support this either, but you can create a stored procedure in your database with the same name as a procedure in master and have that procedure do nothing more than call the one in master. Now, anytime a call is made to sp_addtype in your database, including any made by the SQL Enterprise Manager, *your* procedure gets called. Finally, because you granted no permission on the preceding procedure, no one but the dbo can execute it.

If you have some really sharp users, they will realize that they can still create a user defined datatype by explicitly calling master..sp_addtype, but that only works from the Query Analyzer. An application like the SQL Enterprise Manager will be locked out.

Setting up user datatypes

To set up a user-defined datatype, select the database you want in the Server Manager window. Now you can do one of the following:

- Choose Manage⇨User-Defined Datatypes.
- Expand the database icon, right-click Objects, and choose New User-Defined Datatype.
- Expand Objects, right-click User-Defined Datatypes, and choose New UDDT.

All of these procedures bring up the dialog box shown in Figure 15-1.

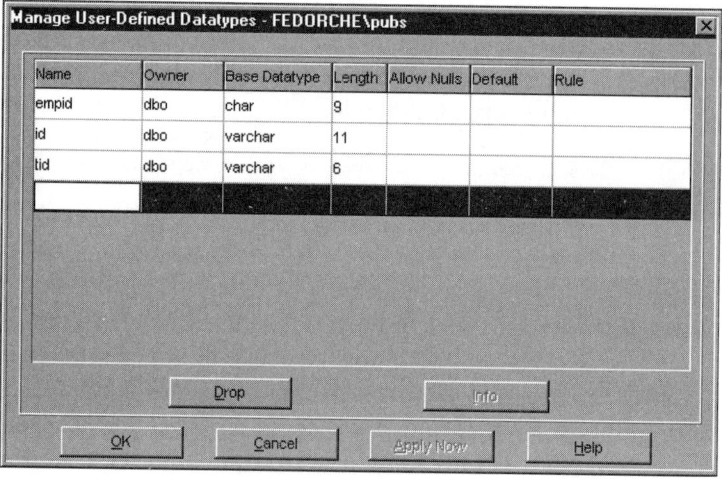

Figure 15-1:
Enter your new datatypes in the Manage User-Defined Datatypes window.

From here, follow these steps:

1. Pick a name. Although the SQL Enterprise Manager groups User-Defined Datatypes under objects, like tables, views, and so on, SQL Server doesn't handle them that way. First of all, the rules for naming user-defined datatypes are a little different from those for other objects. The names of user-defined datatypes must be unique, regardless of the owner. Second, the names of user-defined datatypes do not have to be distinct from the name of true objects in the database. There can be both a table called authors and a user-defined datatype called authors, but there cannot be both a fedorchek.authors type and a rensin.authors type.
2. Tab past the Owner box. The cursor is there after you enter a name, but you cannot change the Owner.
3. Pick a base datatype. It is no accident that timestamp isn't one of your choices. SQL Server doesn't allow that because it is really a binary.
4. Enter a length, if appropriate. Fields like int don't allow a length, whereas char does. Numeric accepts two parameters, precision and scale. If you don't enter a length, you get the default. There are defaults for all datatypes, even though some, like binary, don't display their defaults.
5. Put a check in Allow Nulls if you want the field to have nulls *by default.* (This can be overridden when creating an object.)
6. Choose a default, if you want one. This isn't like creating a table, where you can just type in a default value. You have to create the default first as a separate database object. We discuss that in this chapter. You can change the default for a user-defined datatype later.
7. Choose a rule, if you want one. These, too, can be changed later.
8. Enter more datatypes if you want.
9. When you want to save your datatypes in the database but continue working in the dialog box, click Apply Now. When you want to save and exit, click OK.

Editing and dropping user-defined datatypes

You edit or drop user-defined datatypes by right-clicking the datatype and choosing Edit or by any of the methods you used to create a new user-defined datatype. (They all bring up the same dialog box, shown as Figure 15-1.) All you can do, as far as editing, is change the name. Anything more substantial, such as changing the length, requires you to drop and recreate the datatype. You can't drop user-defined datatypes that are in use by any table or stored procedure. If you try, the SQL Enterprise Manager will tell you so.◀

Stored procedures for managing user-defined datatypes

The graphical interface of the SQL Enterprise Manager works fine, for user-defined datatypes, but the Transact-SQL is very simple, too.

Adding a user-defined datatype

The stored procedures for managing user-defined datatypes are very straightforward. Add a type with the following code:

```
sp_addtype typename, phystype [, nulltype]
```

For this stored procedure, *typename* is the name you pick, for example, "MyDatatype"; *phystype* is the SQL Server datatype, for example, "binary(8)"; and *nulltype* is either "null" or "not null". This parameter is optional. You can check on what you added in at least two ways:

- Highlight the typename and press Alt+F1 (equivalent to "sp_help 'MyDatatype'").
- Execute the following query:

```
SELECT *
   FROM systypes
   WHERE usertype > 100

   /* The reason for "usertype > 100" is that usertype values of 100 or under are
   reserved for SQL Server's datatypes. */
```

You will notice that default and rule are not options of sp_addtype. You have to bind them separately, which we discuss later in this chapter.

Dropping a user-defined datatype

It doesn't get any easier than this:

```
sp_droptype typename
```

If the type is in use, SQL Server will tell you so and list the tables using the type. SQL Server is smart enough to prevent you from dropping a type that you do not own, so you don't have to worry about everyone having execute authority on sp_droptype.

Renaming a user-defined datatype

The stored procedure sp_rename is the generic way to rename any object. However, because you can have both an entry in sysobjects and an entry in systypes with the same name, you should specify 'userdatatype' when using sp_rename:

```
sp_rename oldname, newname [,USERDATATYPE]
```

How SQL Server user-defined datatypes differ from the SQL92 standard

There are two important differences between SQL Server user-defined datatypes and the SQL92 standard:

- In SQL92, the command is "CREATE DOMAIN MyDatatype... ." This speaks volumes. We see that user-defined datatypes should be objects in the database, recorded in the sysobjects table. We should see the ability to "GRANT CREATE DOMAIN... ." We should find that user-defined datatype names must be unique within a *uid*, but not within the database as a whole. In short, user-defined datatypes should behave like tables, views, and all other objects.
- SQL92 specifies that you can bind a CHECK constraint to a domain. You can't bind a CHECK constraint to a user-defined datatype.

If you haven't already figured out that we aren't impressed with SQL Server's implementation of user-defined datatypes, here's one last nail for the coffin: We don't use them anywhere in any of our systems.

Non-DRI Defaults and Rules

In Chapter 12, we presented the default and check constraints for tables. There is another way for you to enforce this kind of integrity: standalone database defaults and rules. The procedures for handling them are very similar, so we are going to discuss them both at the same time.

You create the definitions for rules and defaults without references to any particular table, and then you bind (link) them to specific columns or to user-defined datatypes. The reasons for doing this might include the following:

- You have a default or rule that you will use with multiple tables.
- You want to link a default or rule to a user-defined datatype.

Obviously, you can't have both a DEFAULT constraint and a non-DRI default on the same column in a table, but you can have both CHECK constraints and a rule on a column. SQL Server enforces the rule first, and then all of your CHECK constraints.

Tip

Though you can use user-defined datatypes in the parameters and variables of stored procedures, neither the defaults nor the rules will apply there.◀

How rules are described

A rule is expressed as the kind of conditional expression that goes in a WHERE clause. You can use relational operators: IN, LIKE, BETWEEN, and so on. You can use functions, including system functions such as OBJECT_ID(), OBJECT_NAME(), and so forth. You can't reference other tables or columns, which means that you can't do any subqueries. You must use a variable that represents the column to be tested. The name of this variable doesn't have to be the name of the real column of the table you intend to bind the rule to; indeed, you will most likely be binding the rule to columns of different names in different tables. Think of this as a parameter of a stored procedure.

You do not specify anywhere what the type of the variable is; SQL Server is trusting you to be consistent in your use of the variable and the column types to which you bind it. For example, you could write a rule that says the following:

```
@variable like 'sys%' or  @variable < 50
```

You can even bind this rule to both character and integer datatypes, but you will get an error the first time you try to insert a row because you can't compare a number to the string 'sys%', nor can you compare characters to the number 50.

A typical rule would be to check that a column adheres to an acceptable range of years, as follows:

```
@year between 1980 and 2019
```

Or, if @year is to be char(4):

```
@year like '19[89][0-9]' or @year like '20[01][0-9]'
```

How defaults are described

A default is a "constant expression," but you have to understand what SQL Server considers constant. In addition to using true constants, such as 28, "N/A", and 0x0ab0, you can use any constant, built-in function, mathematical expression, or global variable, in other words, any legal r-value expression. You can also put comments in your defaults. For example, all of the following are legal defaults:

```
'Unknown'

rand() /* Random number */

CONVERT(CHAR(3),GETDATE()) -- three letter abbreviation of the month

OBJECT_NAME(@@PROCID) -- name of the procedure doing the update
```

What you can't use in a default is any reference to tables or columns of tables.

Creating a new rule or default

The processes for creating and manipulating rules and defaults are identical. Here we give the steps for rules only. To manage defaults, simply apply the same steps.

To create a rule, follow these steps:

1. Select a database in the Server Manager window.
2. Choose Manage⇨Rules or right-click Objects⇨New Rule or right-click Rules⇨New Rule. You get the Manage Rules dialog box with the Rules tab (see Figure 15-2).
3. Type a name for the rule. Because rules are database objects, they must be unique within an owner. You can't give a rule the same name as a table, view, and so on that you own. You *can* use a name that someone else has already used for a rule.
4. Enter the rule constraint in the Description box.
5. Click Add.

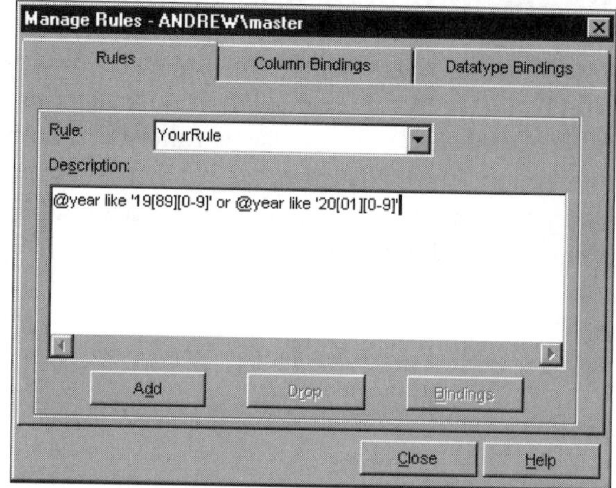

Figure 15-2:
Create your rules in the Manage Rules Window.

Binding and dropping

Linking a rule or default to a column or datatype is called *binding*. After you bind a rule of default to something, you cannot drop that rule or default — you have to unbind it first. This makes life difficult when you want to change a rule or default because, although you may see "Edit" in their pop-up menus, you can't really edit them. That is, you can't change the value of a default or the definition of a rule. The only way to change either is to drop and recreate it, but to drop a rule or default, you have to break all its bindings. This would seem to reduce their value substantially because, if you have a rule bound to a dozen columns, you have to do a dozen unbindings, drop the rule, recreate it, rebind it to the dozen columns, and hope you don't miss any.

Fortunately, there is a better, though less obvious, way. If you have a rule or default that is going to be bound to a whole bunch of columns *with a common type and length*, you are better off creating a user-defined datatype for that common type and length and then using that datatype in your tables. You then do *one* binding of the rule or default to that datatype. You can unbind the rule or default from the datatype even though tables may be using the datatype. Then you can drop, recreate, and rebind the rule or default.

Connecting a rule to a column

The next thing you will no doubt want to do is to bind your rule to a column. If you want to unbind a rule we cover that here, too. The process is the same. To bind rule to a column, follow these steps:

1. Open the Manage Rules dialog box, if you don't already have it open.
2. Choose the Column Bindings tab.
3. Select a table with which to work. Only user tables will be listed.
4. Select a column.
5. Click in the Binding area, and a drop-down list box of rules appears. If there is already a rule bound to the column, it is displayed, too.
6. Choose a rule to bind to the column. If another rule is already bound, choosing a new rule automatically unbinds the old one. Choose none to unbind the old rule and not bind any new one.◀

Tip

7. Click Bind to save your changes.

There is a big difference between what happens when you add a CHECK constraint to a table and when you bind a rule to a column. When you add a CHECK constraint, SQL Server will check the data already in the table against the constraint. If any data violate the constraint, you receive an error and you must either correct the data or add the constraint with the NOCHECK option. However, when you add a rule the existing data in the table is not checked. The rule will only apply to future inserts or updates to the table.

Binding a rule to a datatype

This one is really easy:

1. Open the Manage Rules dialog box, if you don't already have it open.
2. Choose the Datatype Bindings tab.
3. Click the Binding cell of the datatype you want. A drop-down list box of rules appears. If there is already a rule bound to the datatype, it is displayed, too.
4. Choose a rule to bind to the datatype. If another rule is already bound, choosing a new rule automatically unbinds the old one. Choose none to unbind the old rule and not bind any new one.

5. If you want your change to affect only the future use of this datatype, check Future Only. Otherwise, you are changing the rule for tables that are currently using it.
6. Click Bind to save your changes.

Transact-SQL for rules and defaults

As always, our preference is for using the SQL instead of the user interface. We do have to concede, however, that the SQL Enterprise Manager does a great job of rolling several different commands into one window. Here's what you need to do in SQL.

Creating and dropping Rules

Not surprisingly, the command for creating rules is CREATE RULE. The syntax is

```
CREATE RULE [owner.]rule_name AS condition_expression
```

The rule name and condition_expression are the same things you typed into the SQL Enterprise Manager, for example:

```
CREATE RULE YourRule AS @year like '19[89][0-9]' or @year like '20[01][0-9]'
```

The command for dropping a rule is

```
DROP RULE [owner.]rule_name [, [owner.]rule_name...]
```

Binding and unbinding rules with SQL

The way to bind a rule is with sp_bindrule:

```
sp_bindrule rulename, objname [, futureonly]
```

The objname is either a column of a table or a user-defined datatype. If it is a column, you must use the format 'table_name.column_name'. The quotes are required because of the (.) in the middle of the string. The futureonly option is the same futureonly we discussed earlier: it means you only want the rule to apply to future bindings of the datatype. When you want to unbind the rule, you use the companion command, sp_unbindrule. Its syntax is

```
sp_unbindrule objname [, futureonly]
```

You will notice right away that rulename is not a parameter. If you want to unbind all the bindings on a rule, you have to be more sophisticated. This query will return the SQL that you must cut and paste back into the query window and execute (replace 'YourRule' with the actual name of your rule):

```
select 'exec sp_unbindrule '''+object_name( id )+'.'+name+''''
     from syscolumns
     where domain = object_id( 'YourRule' )
```

SQL for defaults

Once again, we won't bore you will covering the same ground twice. Replace "RULE" with "DEFAULT" above, and you get the commands you need: CREATE DEFAULT, DROP DEFAULT, sp_bindefault, & sp_unbindefault. (Notice that the stored procedures are *not* sp_binddefault and sp_unbinddefault.) To drop all binding for a default, you must replace 'domain' with 'cdefault' in the query above.

Summary

An alternative to DRI is to use user-defined datatypes, rules, and defaults. User-defined datatypes fall far short of the relation model's domain, which limits their utility. User-defined datatypes specify a base datatype, a length, and nullability. You can override the nullability when you create tables. Rules and defaults provide an alternative to CHECK and DEFAULT constraints. They can be bound to any number of columns, and they can be bound to user-defined datatypes. This lets you create a rule or default once and use it many times, which is handy. The syntax for rules and defaults is virtually identical.

Review Questions

Q: What relational model concept are UDDTs supposed to support?

A: Domains.

Q: Can you put a CHECK constraint on a UDDT?

A: No, but you can bind a rule to it.

Q: Can a rule include subqueries?

A: No. It can't reference any table or any columns other than the one column or datatype for which the rule is used.

Q: Can you drop a rule or default that is bound to column?

A: No, you must unbind it first.

Part

V

TRANSFERRING DATA

At times in your life as a DBA, it will be necessary for you to transfer data in and out of your database en masse. Luckily for you, SQL Server comes with a few tools to help make this process easier. In this part of the book, we cover those tools.

We begin our discussion with SQL Server's Bulk Copy Program (BCP) utility in Chapter 16. This is one of the most powerful and underutilized tools in the SQL Server arsenal. By the time you finish the chapter, you will be ready to take full advantage of its capabilities.

Next, we cover what is perhaps the most important task a DBA can perform: backing up and restoring (Chapter 17). In this chapter, we show you how to backup and restore your data through the SQL Enterprise Manager and discuss various backup methodologies. By the time you finish this chapter, you will have enough information to decide which backup plan is right for you.

Finally, we turn our attention to the business of transferring and scripting the definitions of your database objects (such as tables, stored procedures, and so on). In Chapter 18, we cover how to save the definitions of your objects in plain text successfully for easy regeneration of your database schema. We also show you some pitfalls of Microsoft's built-in capability for this and how to avoid them.

Chapter

The Bulk Copy Program

16

The Bulk Copy Program (BCP) is a fast, flexible, command-line utility for moving data between tables (or views) and disk files. Command-line? That's right. BCP is one of the few SQL Server functions that has to be done from the command line. Microsoft has said that BCP doesn't have a GUI, strictly for performance reasons. In fact, a previous version of SQL Server (4.21) had a GUI front end for BCP, but Microsoft chose to do away with it in subsequent releases. Unfortunately, BCP is still one of the most misunderstood and misapplied tools in the SQL Server arsenal. In our opinion, the lack of a GUI won't help that fact.

What's In This Chapter

This chapter includes coverage of the following topics:

- How to get up and running with BCP
- What a format file is and how it can help you
- How to use BCP to generate basic reports
- Various caveats and pitfalls to avoid with BCP

How to Get into a Lot of Trouble

If you are really adventurous, you can use the old 4.21 NT Object Manager utility for bulk copy operations. There are, however, a few drawbacks:

Warning

- The performance is a lot worse than the command-line version.
- The SQL Server 4.21 Object Manager has no clue what an identity column is and is not going to warn you if you try. Do not try to copy identity columns into your tables!
- This tool will also try to drop your indexes in order to rebuild them later. *Don't let it!* Lots of other stuff will bomb.◀

In our opinion, using the SQL Server 4.21 Object Manager for SQL Server 6.x bulk copy operations is a bad idea. It's far too easy to destroy your data.

BCP can do a lot of nifty things. As a result, it has a lot of possible parameters. These can become very confusing for the uninitiated. Don't worry. By the time you are finished with this chapter, you will be a bona fide BCP deity. Before we get into that, though, it is important for you to understand exactly what this utility can and cannot do. BCP has very few limitations when it is extracting data from a table or view, but has quite a few limitations when it tries to insert or apply data to a table. These limitations become very important as your databases become more complicated.

BCP *can* do the following:

- Enforce primary keys
- Enforce UNIQUE constraints
- Use defaults
- Log transactions if a table has indexes
- Enforce nullability rules

BCP *cannot* do the following:

- Enforce foreign keys
- Enforce CHECK constraints
- Check rules
- Execute triggers
- Log transactions when a table doesn't have indexes

Who Can Run BCP?

Anyone can run BCP. What they can do with it, however, depends on the kind of access they have in your databases. For example, if users can issue a SELECT against a table or view, they can BCP data out of that table or view. If they can issue INSERT statements against that data, they can probably BCP data into those tables.

You cannot BCP data into a view, only a table. A lot of people get confused on this point because you can copy *out* of a view.◀

Where to Run BCP

This may seem like a silly thing to discuss. After all, BCP is a command-line client utility. That means it is run at an MS-DOS prompt on a client machine. Right? Not necessarily. It is certainly true that most of the time you will be running BCP from an MS-DOS prompt on a client machine. There is, however, another option. SQL Server has a built-in stored procedure called xp_cmdshell. This code allows authorized users to run any valid Windows NT program or command as if they were sitting at the server console. There are a few times when this is a good thing. For example, what if you want to BCP out some data to a disk that is local to the server, but that disk is not a shared resource? The way you would do this would be to use xp_cmdshell to execute the BCP operation as if you were sitting at the NT machine. The other virtue of xp_cmdshell is that if you are on a Windows for Workgroups client, you can get to the 32-bit BCP.

To Log or Not to Log, That Is the Question

The idea behind BCP is to be able to transfer as much data as possible in or out of a table in the shortest possible time. To this end, you can perform a *fast bulk copy*. This means that the data being inserted into the table will not be reported in the transaction log. This can speed up the process a great deal. The problem is that the table must have *no* indexes defined in order to BCP in data and not have it logged. That's right, you have to drop all your indexes, perform the BCP, and then recreate the indexes. Doing this can cause data-integrity problems if you are relying on indexes to keep your data unique.

The Select Into/Bulk-Copy option must be enabled for the table or you cannot perform a fast BCP. If the option is not set, you can still use BCP, but all inserts will be logged.◀

There is no way around this dilemma. You cannot use a primary key or a UNIQUE constraint to circumvent this issue because both of these things use indexes to enforce their uniqueness.

Nuts and Bolts

Now that you have had an overview of the BCP utility, it's time to talk about how to use it. The simple syntax to BCP data out of a table is as follows:

```
BCP <table_name> out <filename> /c /U<user_name> /S<server_name>
```

A lot of people get confused with the BCP syntax. They wonder if they have to use forward slashes or dashes. The answer is that you can use both.◀

For example, the following command will copy the table pubs..authors on server my_server to the file authors.txt:

```
C:\SQL> BCP pubs..authors out authors.txt /c /Usa /S my_server
Password:

Starting copy...

23 rows copied.
Network packet size (bytes): 4096
Clock Time (ms.): total =    170 Avg =      7 (135.29 rows per sec.)
```

Copying data back into a table is just as easy. The syntax for that is the same as the above except that the word *out* is replaced with the word *in*, for example:

```
C:\TEMP> BCP pubs..authors in authors.txt /c /Usa /S my_server
Password:

Starting copy...
23 rows copied.
Network packet size (bytes): 4096
Clock Time (ms.): total =    170 Avg =      7 (135.29 rows per sec.)
```

That's it! That's all you need to do very basic BCP operations.

BCP a la carte

One of the nice things about the SQL Server client utilities is that they have more options than a new luxury sedan. BCP is no exception. This section explains the various options for BCP and their usage.

/a packet_size

This option specifies the size, in bytes, of each network packet sent to and received from the server. This option is usually set in the Configuration section of the SQL Enterprise Manager. Valid values for this option range from 512 to 65,535.

The Windows NT-ased BCP utility has 4,096 as its default packet size, whereas the MS-DOS-based program uses a default size of 512.

Increasing the network packet size may speed up BCP operations. Microsoft recommends a packet size between 4,096 and 8,192 bytes. If the server is unable to grant the request for a larger packet, a default value of 512 is used. Actual packet sizes and performance statistics are shown on the screen after each BCP operation.

/b batchsize

This option is the number of rows per batch of data copied (the default copies all the rows in one batch).

/c

This option tells BCP to perform the copy operation with a character data type as the default. This option does not prompt for each field; it uses char as the default storage type, no prefixes, \t (tab) as the default field separator, and \n (new line) as the default row terminator. It is the simplest way to BCP data but may not be the best way.

/E

This option tells BCP how to treat identity columns. Normally, when you BCP data into a table, SQL Server assigns each identity column a value of zero and then reassigns a unique value later. If the /E option is used, however, SQL Server takes the identity value from the identity columns in the data file. This flag is only useful if you have BCPd out data that contains an identity column and you want to keep those identity values when you BCP the data back in. If you prefer that SQL Server generate new identity values after you BCP in the data, it's probably easier just to omit your identity columns from your format file.

This option is in effect only during BCP in. It has no effect during BCP out.

/e errfile

This option specifies the name of the error file to create. BCP copies any rows that it cannot insert into the table from your data file into the error file. Error messages will still be displayed on your screen. If you do not include this option, no error file is used.

/F firstrow

This option is the number of the first row to copy (the default is the first row).

/f formatfile

BCP supports a special file called a *format file*. This file specifies how to format each column of the source table. This option is useful when you have already created a format file and want to use it to help format your inserted data. If you do not use either this option or the /c option, you are asked to provide format information. We cover format files in greater depth at the end of this section.

/i inputfile

This option sets the name of a file that redirects input to BCP. You can usually ignore this option and use a format file.

/L lastrow

This option is the number of the last row to copy (the default is the last row).

/m maxerrors

This option specifies the maximum number of errors BCP will allow before the copy is aborted. The default is 10.

/n

This option is like the /c option, except that it instructs BCP to perform the copy operation using the data's native (database) datatypes as the default.

/o outputfile

This item sets the name of a file that receives output redirected from BCP. This is similar to redirecting the BCP screen output using the MSDOS > command (that is, BCP > output.txt).

/P password

This option sets the password to use with the username specified in the /U option. If this item is not used, BCP prompts you for one.

/r row_term

This option is the default row terminator. It is usually \n (new line).

/S servername

This option specifies which SQL Server to connect to. The servername is the name of the server computer on the network. This option is required when you are executing BCP from a remote computer on the network.

/t field_term

This option is the default field terminator. It is usually \t (tab).

/U login_id

This option sets the login ID for this operation.

/v

This option causes BCP to report the current DB-Library version number.

Format Files: A Description

A BCP format file is a text file that tells SQL Server and BCP how to treat data being bulk copied in and out of tables. The basic structure of a format file is as follows:

```
<SQL Ver>
<# of columns>
<Col #>  <Type>  <PrefixLen>  <Len>  <Terminator>  <Table Col>  <Name>
<Col #>  <Type>  <PrefixLen>  <Len>  <Terminator>  <Table Col>  <Name>
<Col #>  <Type>  <PrefixLen>  <Len>  <Terminator>  <Table Col>  <Name>
.
.
.
<Col #>  <Type>  <Prefix>  <Len>  <Terminator>  <Table Col#>  <Name>
```

The following paragraphs describe the various options in this syntax.

SQL Ver

This is the SQL Server version number. In this case, it is 6.5.

Warning

You cannot have blank lines in a format file. If you do, BCP chokes. We know because we had a blank line in a big format file and it took us at least an hour to figure out the problem.◀

of columns

This is the number of column definitions to be read by BCP from the format file. You can, for example, have 5 columns defined in the format file. If, though, this value is set to 3, BCP will only read the definitions of the first 3 columns.

Type

This is the SQL Server data type. Valid entries are shown in Table 16-1.

Table 16-1
SQL Server Data Types Versus Format File Storage Types

SQL Server Data Type	Format File Storage Type
binary, varbinary	SQLBINARY
bit	SQLBIT
char, varchar	SQLCHAR
datetime	SQLDATETIME
decimal	SQLDECIMAL
float	SQLFLT8
image	SQLIMAGE
int	SQLINT4
money	SQLMONEY
numeric	SQLNUMERIC
smallint	SQLINT2
text	SQLTEXT
tinyint	SQLINT1

PrefixLen

BCP precedes each field (other than those defined as character) with an ASCII string of one or more characters that indicates the length of the field. By doing this, BCP doesn't need to delimit each field with a special character, because it knows how long each item is. If, for example, the length of the column is 11 characters, the prefix character will be *one* character that is an ASCII 11.

To store data with no prefix before the column, use a prefix length of 0. Each stored field is padded with spaces to the full length specified at the next prompt for length of field.

Len

This entry specifies the maximum column length for the data.

Beware of Truncation

This is an area where a lot of people get into trouble. If you specify a length that is too small for actual data, BCP truncates the data and prints an overflow message.

If you are converting datetime data to character data and you specify a length of less than 26 bytes, the data is silently truncated.

The amount of space your data will actually take depends on the values of the len, prefix len, and terminator entries (that is, len + prefix len + terminator).

If you specify a prefix length of 1, 2, or 4, the storage space used is the actual length of the data, plus the length of the prefix, plus any terminators. In this case, the actual storage space for each row does not depend on the value of len.

If you specify a prefix length of 0 and no terminator, BCP allocates the maximum amount of space specified in len. In other words, the field is treated as if it were of fixed length so that it is possible to determine where one field ends and the next begins.

For example, if the field is defined as varchar(10), it will occupy 10 characters in the output file, even if some of the values are only 1 character long.

This fixed length format is sometimes called SDF, for system data format.

Terminator

The terminator entry specifies what characters, if any, should terminate that column. Field terminators can be up to 10 characters long and consist of the following:

\t	a tab character
\r	a carriage return
\n	a newline
\\	a backslash
\0	a NULL (ASCII 0 character)

Any printable character (that is, A,b,c,$,#,!, and so on)

It is very important to choose a field terminator that will never exist in the column. It would be a bad idea, for example, to choose a backslash as the field terminator of a character column because a backslash can occur in the data. BCP would choose the first occurrence of the backslash as the field terminator and the copy would probably fail.

NULL is Not None

A field terminator of "" means that there is no terminator for that column. An entry of "\0", on the other hand, means that an ASCII 0 character will be stored in the output file after the field. In both cases, you will see no apparent termination of the field if you look at it in notepad, but BCP and SQL Server know the difference.

Table Col#

This entry tells BCP in what column the field is located in the database table. In other words, field 6 in the data file could actually be field 2 in the database table. BCP arranges your data in this order when it tries to copy back into the table.

Name

This is the name of the column in the SQL Server table. In reality, it is not important if this value matches the name of the column because BCP uses the value in the Table Col# entry to arrange the data. The only criteria for the Name entry is that it not be left blank.

FORMAT FILES: SOME EXAMPLES

Now that you have a basic idea of what a format file is, we will show you how to use it. For the purposes of the next few examples, we assume that the following simple table (Table 16-2), called Deep_Spacers, exists in your database.

Table 16-2
Deep_Spacers - Data Definition

Field Name	Field Type	Field Length
First_Name	Char	15
Last_Name	Char	20
Sex	Char	1
Social_Security_No	Char	11

Table 16-3 shows the data in the table.

Table 16-3
Deep_Spacers - Data Elements

First Name	Last Name	Sex	Social Security No.
Benjamin	Cisco	M	111-11-1111
Kira	Narise	F	222-22-2222
Jadzia	Dax	F	333-33-3333
Miles	O'Brian	M	444-44-4444
Julian	Bashir	M	555-55-6666

The basic file

Given the preceding data definitions, our format file should look like this:

```
6.5
4
1   SQLCHAR   0   15   ","     1   first_name
2   SQLCHAR   0   20   ","     2   last_name
3   SQLCHAR   0   1    ","     3   sex
4   SQLCHAR   0   11   "\r\n"  4   social_security_no
```

This file will produce an output file in which each field is terminated with a comma and each row is ended with a carriage return and line feed pair. If the format file is named DS9.fmt, our BCP command will look like this:

```
BCP tv_shows..Deep_Spacers out DS9.txt /Usa /P"sapassword" /S my_server /f DS9.fmt
```

The resulting file, DS9.txt, will look like the following:

```
Benjamin,Cisco,M,111-11-1111
Kira,Narise,F,222-22-2222
Jadzia,Dax,F,333-33-3333
Miles,O'Brian,M,444-44-4444
Julian,Bashir,M,555-55-5555
```

Column aligned

One of the most common problems faced by people using BCP is how to create an output file where all the columns are lined up. The answer is to create your format file so that there are no prefixes and no field terminators. In the case of Deep_Spacers, that file would look like the following:

```
6.5
4
1   SQLCHAR   0   15   ""      1   first_name
2   SQLCHAR   0   20   ""      2   last_name
3   SQLCHAR   0   1    ""      3   sex
4   SQLCHAR   0   11   "\r\n"  4   social_security_no
```

If BCP is run with a format file in this configuration, the resulting data will look like this:

```
Benjamin       Cisco               M111-11-1111
Kira           Narise              F222-22-2222
Jadzia         Dax                 F333-33-3333
```

```
Miles          O'Brian             M444-44-4444
Julian         Bashir              M555-55-5555
```

This output has only one small problem. The sex field and the social_security_no field are running together. This is a common problem when dealing with fields where all the available positions are likely to be filled. The way to fix this problem is to increase the field length in the format file. If we change the value of len for the sex field from 1 character to 4, the output will look like this:

```
Benjamin       Cisco               M   111-11-1111
Kira           Narise              F   222-22-2222
Jadzia         Dax                 F   333-33-3333
Miles          O'Brian             M   444-44-4444
Julian         Bashir              M   555-55-5555
```

The problem with this solution, of course, is that BCP will whine about data overflow if you try to BCP back in with the same file.

Changing column orders

There will be times when you will want to BCP out data in a different column order than what is in the table. This is no problem. All you need to do is put the column definitions in the order you want. Let's say, for example, that you want the preceding output with the first and last names reversed. This is accomplished with the following format file:

```
6.5
4
1   SQLCHAR   0   20   ""       2   last_name
2   SQLCHAR   0   15   ""       1   first_name
3   SQLCHAR   0   4    ""       3   sex
4   SQLCHAR   0   11   "\r\n"   4   social_security_no
```

See the difference? In this file, we have specified that we want table column 2 to be the first column in our output file, and table column 1 to be the second column in our output file. When this format file is used, the output looks like this:

```
Cisco               Benjamin      M   111-11-1111
Narise              Kira          F   222-22-2222
Dax                 Jadzia        F   333-33-3333
O'Brian             Miles         M   444-44-4444
Bashir              Julian        M   555-55-5555
```

Readability formatting

Up to this point, all the format files we have shown you have had the same field terminator. This is not necessary. You can mix and match field terminators any way you want. Suppose that you want your output file to be in the following format:

```
last_name, first_name Gender: sex SSN: social_security_no
(i.e. Cisco, Benjamin Gender: M SSN: 111-11-1111)
```

You would accomplish this with the following format file:

```
6.5
4
1   SQLCHAR   0   20   ", "          2   last_name
2   SQLCHAR   0   15   " Gender: "   1   first_name
3   SQLCHAR   0   4    " SSN: "      3   sex
4   SQLCHAR   0   11   "\r\n"        4   social_security_no
```

Notice that the 'Gender' terminator is on the line with the definition for 'first_name' because we want it following 'firstname' and preceding 'sex' column.

Consider the possibilities. You can now use BCP to create basic reports. By embedding more carriage return/line feed pairs, you can extend this technique to create some very nice looking output. Consider the following format file:

```
6.5
4
1   SQLCHAR   0   20   ", "          2   last_name
2   SQLCHAR   0   15   "\r\n\t"      1   first_name
3   SQLCHAR   0   4    "\r\n\t"      3   sex
4   SQLCHAR   0   11   "\r\n\r\n"    4   social_security_no
```

This gives you the following output:

```
Cisco, Benjamin
        M
        111-11-1111

Narise, Kira
        F
        222-22-2222
```

```
Dax, Jadzia
        F
        333-33-3333

O'Brian, Miles
        M
        444-44-4444

Bashir, Julian
        M
        555-55-5555
```

There is an interesting and very useful side effect to being able to create such a diverse set of format definitions. You can use these complicated format files to BCP in data that is formatted in a nonstandard way. Think about it. If you had been given the preceding output file before you learned about BCP, you would have had to write a custom program to parse the data and apply it against your table.

Inputting formatted files

You just learned that a good format file can save you a lot of time and effort when importing data from an oddly formatted file. There are, however, a couple of pointers we would like to share with you that will make this process easier.

Get a good binary editor

This is *very* important when trying to import formatted data. You need to view the source data in an editor that shows any embedded, nonprintable characters. NULLS are the biggest problem. Many files you will get will have a NULL ("\0") or an end-of-file (EOF) character written as the last character of the file. You need to delete it or BCP will not be able to copy the data.

A good binary editor also has another key advantage: it helps you determine whether the indenting you see is due to tabs (\t) or spaces. In other words, if you were to view the output file from the previous exercise on your screen, you would have no way of determining whether the sex and social_security_no fields were indented as a result of a tab or three spaces. This is an important piece of information to have when creating your format file.

Use a dummy table

No matter how much practice and experience you get with format files, you will seldom create the correct format file the first time. After all, how many times have you written a flawless program or document the first time through? Create a dummy table in your database so you can BCP in the source data without fear of destroying any production data.

Skipping columns

Sometimes, it will be important for you to skip columns as you are BCPing data in or out. In the next couple of sections we will cover how to do this.

Coming out

There will be times when you don't want to copy out all the columns from your table. Perhaps you need only the first and last names. It can be a painfully long process to edit out of an output file the data you don't want. Thankfully, you don't have to. You can easily skip columns when BCPing out data by simply not including them in your format file. If, for example, you only want the last name and gender from the *Deep_spacers* table, your format file would be as follows:

```
6.5
2
1    SQLCHAR    0    20    ""        2    last_name
2    SQLCHAR    0    4     "\r\n"    3    sex
```

Going in

Okay, okay. That last example was easy. Try this one. Let's say you have an output file with all four columns from the *Deep_spacers* table, but only want to BCP in two of them. Maybe you've created a new table called DS9_Lite that has only a last_name field and a gender field. How would you BCP just those columns from your output file into DS9_Lite? You can't simply omit the definitions for the columns you want to skip because BCP will get hopelessly confused when it finds more columns than you have defined. Give up?

There is one thing you have to do to the format file definitions of the omitted columns: Set the table column number to 0. It is still important to specify a column length, prefix length, and field terminator so that BCP knows how many bytes to skip for the column. In our DS9 example, the format file looks like this:

```
6.5
4
1   SQLCHAR   0   20   ""       1   last_name
2   SQLCHAR   0   15   ""       0   first_name
3   SQLCHAR   0   4    ""       3   sex
4   SQLCHAR   0   11   "\r\n"   0   social_security_no
```

By setting the table column entries to 0, you are telling BCP not to insert the data found in the corresponding output file column to any particular column in the destination table.

The columns you are skipping need either to allow null or to have defaults.◀

Using temporary tables

You have already learned that you can BCP out of both tables and views and into tables. What about temporary tables? The answer is yes. You can BCP data in and out of temporary tables just as you can with regular tables. The only difference is that you must give the complete 30-character table name. This also includes the beginning pound signs (##). Here's an example:

```
xp_cmdshell "BCP tempdb..##some_temp_db out test.dat /c /Usa /P"
```

Empty trailing fields

We once encountered a really annoying problem that serves as a good example here. We had a lot of data on a mainframe that we needed in an SQL Server table, so we had the mainframe spit out a text file. The problem was that the last column of the data was sometimes empty and the program we used to transfer the file between our mainframe and our PC trimmed the rows that had spaces at the end. The effect was to get a file where some rows were 149 characters long and others that were 145 characters long. When we tried to BCP in that data, SQL Server treated the "\r\n" pair at the end of those bad rows as data and kept reading into the next line. The effect was to skip every other line of data. The problem we found was not in our format file, but in our table design. When we added a default value to the offending table column, SQL Server inserted the default when it encountered the "\r\n" instead of treating the terminator as data.

This actually makes sense. BCP got to a valid field terminator and became confused. On the one hand, if it treated the "\r\n" as a field terminator, it would have to try to insert no data into a column that did not allow NULLS or have a default. This certainly wouldn't do, so it decided to treat the "\r\n" as data and press on. Beware of this situation. It took us at least a couple of hours to figure it out!

Datetime truncation

If you attempt to BCP out a column of data that is defined as a datetime, you will find that SQL Server chops off the seconds and milliseconds. This is not a bug; it's a deliberate design choice. If you want to get around this problem, you need to create a view that defines your datetime field as *convert(char(23),your_field,13)*. This converts the offending field to a character field that preserves the seconds and milliseconds. Don't worry about BCPing the data back in. SQL Server takes the expanded format just fine.

Summary

In this chapter, you learned how to harness the power of BCP to do tasks such as produce simple reports and read in oddly formatted data. If you take anything from this chapter, it should be that the true power of BCP lies in the format files. Each of the examples we gave are real-world problems that we have faced — and still face — on a daily basis.

Review Questions

Q: Why is there no GUI for BCP?

A: Microsoft did away with it for performance reasons.

Q: How do we know this?

A: At every technical conference/demo for SQL Server 4.21 we went to, the technical presenters told us that they always used BCP from the command-line because the performance from the GUI tool was too bad. Lo and behold, there is no BCP GUI in SQL Server 6.0/6.5. Hey, it doesn't take a Pentium to know that 2 + 2 = 3.9999999!

Q: Can I still use the SQL Server 4.21 BCP GUI tool?

A: Only if you want to be sued for malpractice! There are too many enhancements to SQL Server 6.*x*, including new data types, that will easily confuse the older tool and cause a lot of data damage.

Q: Who can run BCP?

A: Anyone who has a valid login.

Q: What benefits do you gain by running BCP by using xp_cmdshell.

A: There are three. First, you can run the process with the speed and power of your server, and second, you can take advantage of a 32-bit BCP from a Windows for Workgroups machine. Finally, you'll have greatly reduced network traffic.

Q: What is the advantage to *fast BCP*?

A: It is substantially faster than standard BCP operations.

Q: What is the disadvantage of *fast BCP*?

A: You have to drop all your indexes, primary keys, and UNIQUE constraints.

Q: What's the difference in using a dash (-) instead of a slash (/) for BCP command-line options?

A: None whatsoever.

Q: What is a prefix length?

A: The prefix length specifies how many characters are to be set aside at the beginning of the field so that SQL Server can store the length of the field. A prefix length of 1 means that one character is set aside. Because a character may have an ASCII value of up to 255, a prefix length of 1 can indicate a column as large as 255 characters.

Q: What are valid field terminators?

A: Field terminators can be up to 10 characters long and consist of the following:

\t	a tab character
\r	a carriage return
\n	a newline
\\	a backslash
\0	a NULL

Any printable character (that is, A,b,c,$,#,!, and so on)

Q: What is a good field terminator?

A: Any character or set of characters that will never occur in the field that they terminate.

Chapter

Backing Up and Restoring

17

Backing up a database is one of the more boring tasks a DBA has to perform. We know it, and you know it. Despite this fact, though, good DBAs do this chore on a regular basis to insure that their production systems aren't down for any serious length of time.

What's in This Chapter

In this chapter, you will learn the following:

- Backing up a database is a lot like writing a SQL procedure; there are more ways to do it than you think.
- Choosing what backup plan is best for you and how to implement it.

Gee, Mom, Do I Have to Do This Now?

We are going to assume that you don't need to be convinced that you should back up your databases periodically. It's common sense. If you haven't been backing up your data and your system goes down, you will be fired! The real debate is not should you back up your data, but how frequently should you back up your data. No matter what size your system is, we have the same recommendation: do it nightly.

Schedule your system to back itself up at some obscure time in the wee hours of the morning. If you faithfully follow this plan, you will never lose more than one day of transactions, which is an acceptable recovery rate in most cases.

There is a second good reason for performing nightly backups: the process will take a lot less time. This is obvious but, nonetheless, important. The more frequently you back up your data, the fewer changes there will be to capture.

At this point, you are probably wondering whether it's worth your while to back up more frequently than once a day. The answer, in the majority of cases, is no. Users in a live environment don't want to have their systems slow down once or twice a day so that the DBA can perform backups. That cuts into their productivity.

OK, OK. So How Do I Do This?

There are only two general classes of database backups a DBA can perform: a *full backup* and an *incremental backup*. A full backup is when the DBA backs up the entire database. In some cases, though, this is a little excessive. An incremental backup, however, is when the DBA backs up only those things that have changed since the last backup. As you might expect, each type has distinct advantages and disadvantages. The remainder of this chapter is devoted to discussing the various methods used to perform each (including how to restore from each), and how to choose which one is best for you.

One Fell Swoop

Backing up an entire database, especially if it is large, can be a long and tedious task that requires the DBA to be present for the entire process. It has some serious advantages, as well, though. We will discuss both sides of the issue.

Disadvantages

As the amount of data that needs to be backed up increases, so does the likelihood that the backups for a given night will not fit neatly onto a single tape. This means that you, as a DBA, cannot just schedule the process to run at 3 a.m. and go home. You need to be there to switch the tapes. Of course, you can always buy a tape drive with a huge capacity. This is, however, an added cost.

The other main disadvantage with this approach is the amount of time it takes. Several gigabytes of data can take several hours to back up. You may not have enough time in any one evening to back it all up. That means you have to stagger your backups across more than one evening. So much for nightly backups!

Advantages

Restoring a lost database from a full backup can be a lot easier than restoring from an incremental backup. This is the biggest advantage to this process. All you need to do is switch tapes. In an incremental restore, however, you have to restore the transaction logs from each day and reapply them against your tables. What a pain!

The choices

There are three basic ways that you can back up an entire database: dumping, mirroring, and replicating. We will discuss each.

Dumping

Cross-Reference

Dumping is the most common way to back up data, and it involves copying the data in a specialized format to a dump device. (See Chapter 6 for a description of how to create and manage a dump device.) You can send data to a dump device either by using the SQL Enterprise Manager or by using the DUMP statement. We describe this process using the SQL Enterprise Manager.◀

Before we talk about how to perform a dump, however, we need to discuss a few interesting points about dump devices. First, a dump device can be either a file on disk or a file on tape. In other words, you don't have to be limited to backing up your data only to tape. This is the most common scenario, but is not necessarily the most appropriate. In fact, you can eliminate most of the disadvantages of dumping an entire database by using dump devices located on a disk. We'll get to that in a moment. The second thing that is important about dump devices is that they can reside on a machine other than your SQL Server machine. This presents several interesting possibilities, as the following example will demonstrate.

Let's say that you want to back up ten databases, each of which is 2GB in size. It is probably not reasonable to expect that you will be able to back up all 20GB of data in any one evening. Even if you could, you would have to be there to switch tapes, right? Wrong! Don't use tape.

Get an old 486, install Windows for Workgroups on it, and use it as a dump machine. In other words, you can create a dump device that is defined as the file \\another_machine\some_drive\some_file.dat. If this machine has enough drive space, you can dump your databases to it nightly. This method holds two key advantages:

- You don't have to be present because there is no need to switch media.
- It's a lot faster to dump to disk than it is to dump to tape.

It is unlikely that you will ever have so much data that you will not be able to dump your entire data set every night. This is a great solution for very large production environments, but it is probably overkill if your data can fit nicely onto one or two tapes.

It is not a good idea to back up your databases to a fixed-disk dump device that resides on the same machine as your server. If your machine is ever damaged, you will lose both your data and your backups. This is a dangerous practice.◀

Now that you have a good conceptual understanding of this process, we will take you through it step by step:

1. In the SQL Enterprise Manager, right-click the Dump Devices folder and select New Dump Device. The screen shown in Figure 17-1 appears.
2. Enter a unique name in the Device Name field and a unique filename in the Device File field. If you are creating a dump device on another machine, this entry will look something like the following:

   ```
   \\MyOtherMachine\Drive_C\dumps\MyDumpDevice.Dat
   ```

   When you are satisfied, click the Add button.

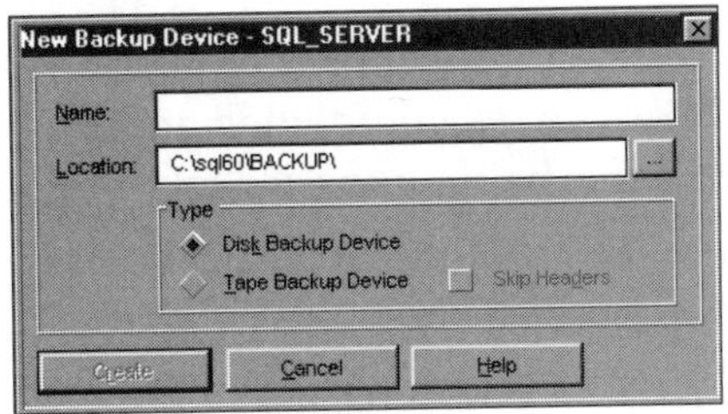

Figure 17-1:
Create a new dump device here.

Now that you have created a valid dump device, here's how to back up your data:

1. Right-click the database you want to back up and then select Backup/Restore. The screen shown in Figure 17-2 appears.

   This screen is divided into three parts: the device listing, the backup options, and the backup destination listing.

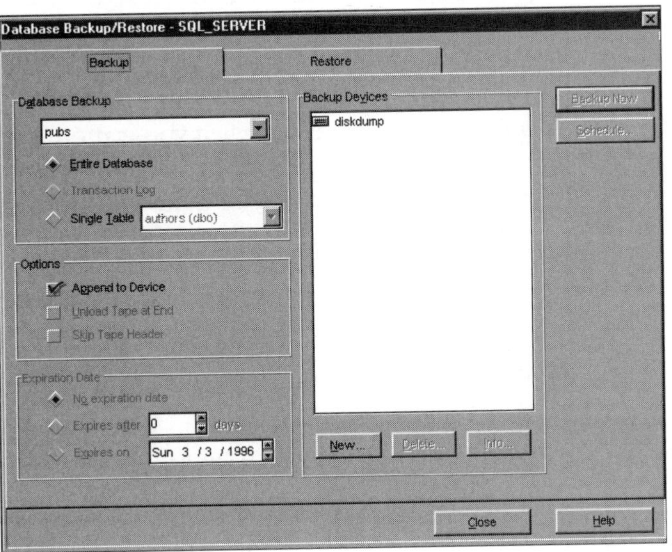

Figure 17-2:
Backup your databases here.

- **Backup Devices.** This listing shows all the installed dump devices on the server. You can create a new device by clicking the New button, and you can see information about what is currently backed up on that device by choosing the Info button.
- **Entire Database.** Selecting this option causes SQL Server to dump the entire database.
- **Transaction Log.** Selecting this option causes SQL Server to dump only the transaction log. In order to use this option, though, your database must meet a few conditions. First, your transaction log must reside on a device separate from your data. Second, the Truncate Log On Checkpoint option must be enabled for the database.
- **Single Table.** One of the new features of SQL Server 6.5 is that you can now back up a single table at a time.
- **Append To Device.** One of the new features of SQL Server 6.*x* is that you can back up many databases to the same dump device. You accomplish this by selecting the Append to Device option. If you disable this item, SQL Server attempts to overwrite any data on the dump device.
- **Skip Tape Header.** When SQL Server writes a database dump to a tape, it creates a small header that contains important pieces of information about the dump. Selecting this option tells SQL Server to ignore the tape header on the device when it tries to perform the dump. There are two cases when you want to select this option. The first case is when you want to overwrite data that has not expired yet. Because the expiration date for a dump is stored in the tape header, you can prevent SQL Server from warning you about nonexpired data by skipping the tape header. The second case in which this option is useful is when you are dumping to a tape for the first time. Selecting this option in this instance reduces the time SQL Server takes to start the dump because it won't search for a tape header that does not exist.
- **Unload Tape At End.** This option causes SQL Server to rewind and unload the tape after the current dump.
- **Data Expiration.** In order to safeguard against overwriting previous backups, you can give your data dumps expiration dates. By doing this, you cause SQL Server to warn you anytime you try to overwrite a data set that has not expired yet. The Expires On option lets you set a specific date on which the dump expires, and the Expires After option lets you tell SQL Server to expire the data after a certain number of days. Finally, setting the No Expiration Date option forgoes this warning mechanism altogether.

2. After you have set any backup options you want, you must tell SQL Server what dump devices to use. You do this by clicking a device from the Dump Devices section.
3. When you are satisfied with your options, click the Backup Now button to start the operation, or click the Schedule button to schedule the job for later. We cover scheduling a little later in the chapter.

Mirroring

Some DBAs forego the process of nightly backups completely and instead choose to mirror their data devices. The biggest advantage to this practice is that after mirroring has been installed, it is seamless, requires no user intervention, and can bring a server back up in a matter of seconds. If you do decide to mirror your data instead of performing nightly backups, there are a few things you need to consider.

There is a common misconception that you cannot mirror a data device to a disk that resides on a machine other than SQL Server. This is not true. It is true that you cannot refer to a mirror device in the form of \\machine\device\file when you create the device, but you can attach a network drive via File Manager and refer to the new logical drive when you create your mirror. In other words, if you have a network machine named NetMachine and you want to mirror a data device to that machine, you cannot create a mirror device as \\NetMachine\drive\file.mir. You must attach (or map) a logical drive letter to that resource in File Manager (say, E:) and refer to it that way when you create your device. In our example, that would be E:\file.mir. Using this technique, you can mirror to a separate machine, just as you can dump to a separate machine.

Warning

There are, however, some huge concerns with this option. If you do decide to mirror to a separate machine, you need to be absolutely sure that the physical connection to the mirror machine will never be broken. If it is and SQL Server can't complete a mirror operation, your server will hang and your users will be very upset.◀

You can, of course, always mirror to a device on the same machine as SQL Server. This, however, has the same problem as dumping to a device on the same machine. If the machine is destroyed or stolen, so are your data and your backup.

No matter what type of mirroring scheme you choose, though, it is our strongest recommendation that you periodically dump all your databases to tape. Perhaps you do this once a week or even twice a month. The important thing is to minimize the damage in case your mirroring scheme becomes corrupted.

Replicating

One of the most highly touted features of SQL Server 6.*x* is a capability called *replication*. This is a process wherein any number of remote machines periodically can get copies of parts of your database or complete databases from you server. The primary purpose of this new feature is to partition your data across servers more easily and, therefore, maximize throughput enterprise wide. In principle, you can also use replication as a means of backing up your data. We don't recommend using it to this end, but it is an option. Because replication is a very complicated topic with far-reaching effects on your enterprise, we have dedicated an entire section of the book to it. In other words, we aren't going to cover it here. We just wanted you to be aware of the fact that you can use it to back up your data.

Inch by Inch

We have spent the last several pages discussing the various methods for backing up entire databases in one sitting. As you have learned already, you do not necessarily have to take this approach in order to preserve your data. You can choose to perform an incremental backup. As mentioned earlier, an incremental backup means that you back up your entire database once and then only the transaction logs thereafter. If you ever need to restore, you simply restore your old database and reapply all the backed-up logs.

Disadvantages

The biggest disadvantage to this practice comes when you need to restore you data. Depending on how long it's been since your last full backup, you may have to reapply hundreds of transaction logs in order to get to your current state. This can be a very long and involved process.

Advantages

As you might expect, however, backing up your data incrementally holds a few nice advantages. First, 99.99 percent of the time it is faster and takes less space to back up a transaction log than it does to back up an entire database. This means that you can use a lower capacity tape and leave your backups running unattended.

The 'choice'

Unlike backing up an entire database, there is really only one way to perform incremental backups: dumping.

The process of dumping a transaction log is identical to the process for dumping an entire database with one exception. Instead of choosing Entire Database from the backup options tab, you select Transaction Log. Everything else is the same. This means that you can also dump a transaction log to a network drive.

Actually, the concept of dumping a log to a shared drive presents some interesting possibilities. Consider this scenario. You schedule a full database dump to a particular network device every Friday evening and a log dump every Monday through Thursday evening. The log operations are set to append to the dump device, whereas the entire dump operation is set to overwrite the device. Figure 17-3 shows this graphically.

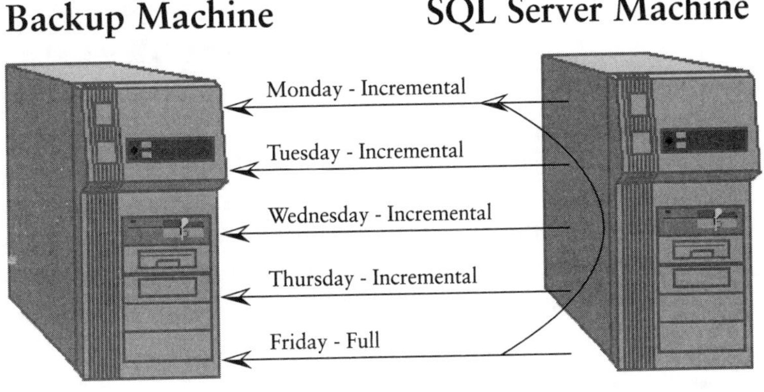

Figure 17-3:
A typical dump schedule.

This means that if, for example, your system dies on Friday morning, you can restore last Friday's database and reapply the logs from the past four days. In an environment where you have to dump several large databases, this kind of scheduling could be perfect. After all, it certainly won't take more than a weekend to dump all your data, just as it will never take more than an evening to dump one day's worth of logs.

Scheduling Your Backups

We have alluded several times in this chapter to the process of scheduling your backups to run at certain times or intervals. We have purposely not explained this in any further deatil until this point. To schedule a backup, right-click the desired database, select Backup/Restore, complete the appropriate information, and click Schedule. A screen similar to Figure 17-4 appears.

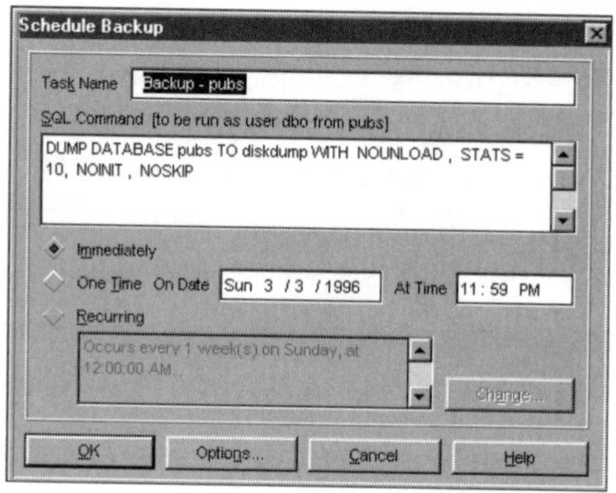

Figure 17-4:
You can schedule your backups here.

This is an interface to SQL Server's built-in process scheduler. This dialog box enables you to set some basic options about the scheduled process. The following short sections discuss the parts of this dialog box.

Task Name

This is the task name under which the process will run.

SQL Command

This is the SQL command that will be run at the appropriate time. This statement will be run as the database owner (dbo) from the selected database.

Immediately

This option causes SQL Server to begin the process as soon as the OK button is clicked. This is the same as clicking the Backup Now button shown in Figure 17-2.

On Time

This option lets you specify a certain day and time to run this process.

Recurring

This setting enables you to schedule this process to run at a certain interval. We'll get to this in a minute.

Notifications

Another nice feature of SQL Server is the capability to notify a user via e-mail and pager about the success or failure of a backup process. This is accomplished by clicking the Options button on the scheduler screen. When you do so, you see the window in Figure 17-5.

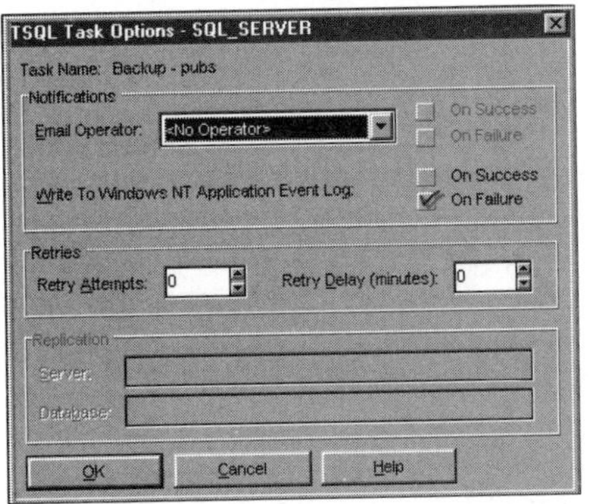

Figure 17-5:
Configure your scheduling options here.

You can ignore the Replication fields that are grayed out at the bottom. They are for notifications specific to replication. The Email Operator list box lets you select a person to e-mail or page in the event of a success or failure of the backup process. The Write to NT Application Event Log option enables you to specify whether NT indicates the process success status in the event log.

If this is the first time you are attempting to use e-mail or pager notification, the only two options available to you in the Email Operator list are <No Operator> and <New Operator>. To add a person to be notified, select the <New Operator> option. Figure 17-6 shows the screen that appears.

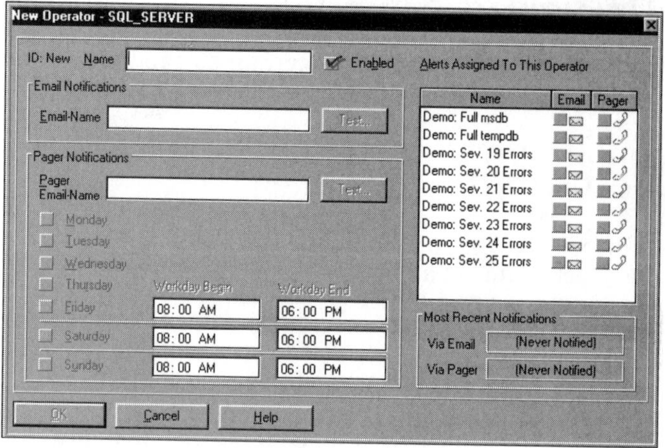

Figure 17-6:
Add a new e-mail operator here.

The following sections discuss the parts of the New Operator screen.

Name

This is the name you want to give the new operator. This name does not have to correspond to a valid SQL Server user. For example, you could give a name of "Alerts about my db."

Enabled

This setting indicates whether this operator is enabled. When you create a new operator, it is automatically added to the operator list. You can use this setting to temporarily enable or disable an operator without deleting it.

Email Name

This is a valid MAPI e-mail address. It can be a user name or a group name. Enter this value to enable mail notifications. When you are finished, click the Test button to send a test message to the address.

Pager Email-Name

If you have pager services installed for Microsoft Mail, you can send a page to people to report the process status. This field is the name of the pager e-mail address to which you want to send the message. When you enter a name in this field, you can also specify what days, or what weekend hours, you want the operator paged. When you have finished configuring the pager e-mail settings, you can test them by clicking the Test button.

Alerts Assigned To This Operator

This list contains all the defined alerts for the database. You can specify what alert is sent and whether it is sent via e-mail, pager, or both by clicking in the appropriate fields.

RESTORING

Cross-Reference

Now that you have a good understanding of how to back up your data, it's time we discuss the process of restoring it. Recovering your data from an archive depends on what process you used to back it up in the first place. Because you have already learned how to recover from a mirror device (see Chapter 6) and we have not covered using replication in any depth, the only thing to cover here is how to restore from either a dumped database or a dumped log.◀

To restore from a data or log dump, right-click the target database, select Backup/Restore, and click the Restore tab. You see the window shown in Figure 17-7.

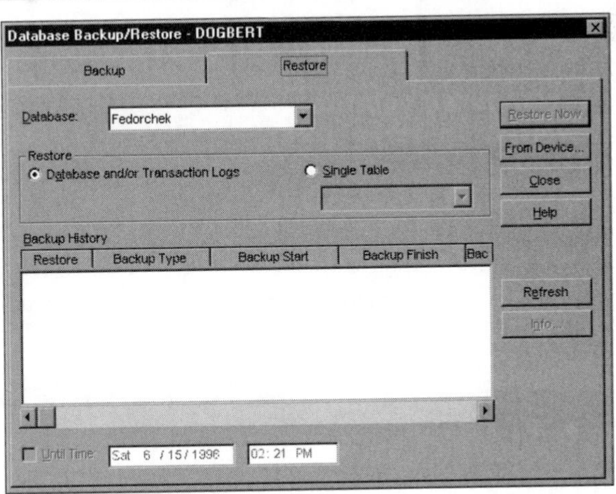

Figure 17-7:
Restore your data from here.

The items on this tab enable you to specify certain things about the restoration process. These things are covered in the following sections.

Database

From this list, select the database to which you want to restore your data.

Database and/or Transaction Logs

Select this option to restore the entire database or transaction log.

Single Table

Select this option to restore a specific table from the backup set.

Backup History

This section shows the basic backup history of this backup device.

Info

This button will bring up a screen that shows a more detailed backup history for this device.

Until Time

These options allow you to set through when to restore data. In other words, only data up through the moment in time will be restored.

Don't Believe Everything You Read

The online help for the SQL Enterprise Manager quite clearly states that "[y]ou cannot restore from floppy disk dump devices when using SQL Enterprise Manager." This is not true.

We backed up and restored many small databases this way while writing this chapter.

Restore Now

Click this to begin the restoration process.

From Device

Click this to choose a new dump device.

Refresh

Click this button to refresh the information on this screen.

Summary

There are a lot more options when it comes to backing up and restoring a database than you probably thought. When choosing the correct procedure for your system, you must consider your data size, how often you want to back up, and how much money you have to spend on extra hardware. No matter what kind of configuration you choose, stick to it! It's easy to get lazy and forget to back up a database or two. The problem is that DBAs usually pick the time right before a crash to forget to do a backup.

The backup procedures you choose depend on your resources. This includes drive space, time, money, and how much effort you are willing to exert to restore lost data. The following is a concise list of your choices. Our recommendations are in bold.

- Method: **Dump**, Mirror, Replicate
- Media: Tape, Local Disk, **Remote Disk**
- Scope: Incremental, **Complete**
- Frequency: Hourly, **Daily**, Weekly, Monthly

Review Questions

Q: What's the difference between a full backup and an incremental backup?

A: A full backup means that the complete database is backed up, whereas an incremental backup just archives the transaction log for a database.

Q: What is the main advantage of a full backup?

A: Restoring the data is simple.

Q: What is the main disadvantage of a full backup?

A: It can take a lot of time.

Q: Is it ever a good idea to mirror a database device to a drive that is not on the server machine?

A: Almost never. If the remote connection goes down for any reason, so will your server.

Q: Scenario: You are trying to overwrite a tape backup, and SQL Server keeps preventing you from doing so because the backup has not expired. What do you do?

A: You have two choices:

- Append to the tape instead of overwriting it.
- Select the Skip Tape Header option on the backup screen.

Chapter

Scripts and Transfers

18

We have spent a good bit of time talking about backing things up. Backing up is helpful for circumstances when the data on your production database becomes corrupted. Backups are less helpful when you want to move a full or partial copy of your database elsewhere — to another SQL Server, for example. In fact, if the destination server has a different sort order or character set, you can't even use the backups. Now what?

You have to build the database from the ground up. All the commands you executed to create tables, views, stored procedures, triggers, logins, and so on, must be re-executed in the destination database. You *did* save all your notes and files when you were building your database, right? What? Your dog ate them? Not to worry, Microsoft has given you a tool to recreate all these commands, which are collectively called the *script* for a database. You can create the script alone, you can create the script and transfer the data, or you can just transfer the data. This chapter covers the tools for these operations.

What's in This Chapter

This chapter includes coverage of the following topics:

- Using the Script Generator to get any or all of the data that describes your database, your metadata
- Compensating for the various shortcomings of the script-generation process
- Becoming an expert on the new SQL Server 6.5 Transfer utility in the SQL Enterprise Manager

You have two menu choices in the SQL Enterprise Manager for scripting and transferring: Object⇨Generate SQL Scripts and Tools⇨Database/Object Transfer. The second one of these actually has to make scripts as a first step, so we first talk about scripting issues common to both menu choices.

Scripts

The scripts for a database are all the SQL commands required to construct a database. Everything you do within a database in the SQL Enterprise Manager actually sends SQL commands to SQL Server. If you ever needed to re-create that work, you certainly couldn't sit at the SQL Enterprise Manager and redo all the pointing and clicking. Nor do you want to rely on a bunch of text files you may have saved when you originally created the objects — how do you know they are up-to-date? Even if you used SQL Trace to capture the SQL the Enterprise Manager generated when you created the tables, what would you do about all the alterations you made to your objects over time? Our production database has over 300 tables with about 800 DRI constraints, 200 views, and another 350 or so stored procedures. Trying to recreate it without help would be absolutely impossible.

Recreating all the objects of your database is what scripts are for. They provide a complete record of your Data Definition Language (DDL), so between scripts and dumping your data to files with the bcp utility (See Chapter 16), you have every single scrap of information in your database. The reasons you need scripts are many:

- Scripts, combined with the bcp utility or used in Tools⇨Database/Object Transfer, provide a way to transfer an entire database to another SQL Server. Scripts are not the only way: you can restore a backup of one server into another. However, this only works if the destination server has the same character set and sort order as the source. You can use replication to transfer data and table definitions, but scripts and the bcp utility are the best way for a one-time transfer of a large number of tables. Replication won't transfer your views, stored procedures, and so forth.

- Scripts can serve as selective partial backups. Suppose that you have inadvertently dropped a view or stored procedure you need (see Chapters 13 and 14). Even though you could find it in a backup, you don't want to replace your whole database, just this one view or procedure. Restoring the backup would cause you to lose all the other changes made in your data. You could get the object from the backup by restoring the backup into another database. For large systems, this consumes a lot of space and time. To make matters worse, suppose that you don't know *which* backup tape has the missing item because you might have dropped it several backups ago. Now you have to restore a whole bunch of backups until you find it. Scripts solve this problem.◀
- Combined with the bcp utility, scripts serve as a safety net to whole backups. A couple of years ago when we were just starting with SQL Server 4.21, we had a database that was corrupted and *all the backups were corrupted, too.* It is true that this was partially our fault, but hindsight is 20/20. The only way we were able to bail ourselves out was with scripts and the bulk copy program.
- Scripts may be the only way to copy your database tables to another RDBMS. SQL Server does support replication to Oracle and other ODBC data-sources, but you will run into systems to which you can't replicate. It might be that you can't establish an electronic link, that the link is too slow for you to use it for the initial load of the data, or that SQL Server just doesn't replicate at all to the RDBMS you need to support.
- Running a script for your entire database is a valuable tool for finding problems in your metadata. As you see in this chapter, there are lots of little bugs in how your metadata is stored. Running a database script in some empty test database turns on the light and sends the bugs scurrying out like cockroaches.

How Script Generation Works

All the information needed to make a script is stored in the system tables of SQL Server. In some cases, such as views and procedures, the text itself is explicitly stored. In other cases, such as tables and DRI, the system tables store the information needed to create the text. The Script Generator is a GUI tool that lets you pick and choose what scripts you want. It reads the system tables and carries out the difficult process of converting them into SQL text.

A critical part of script generation in SQL Server 6.5 is determining the order in which to create objects. Consider the titleauthor table in the pubs database. Because titleauthor has a foreign key pointing back to authors, we have to create the authors table first. It also has a foreign key pointing back to titles, so we have to create that before titleauthor, too. But wait! Titles has a foreign key referencing publishers, so we have to create *it* before we create titles. This is a mess the script generator has to sort out. With pubs it's not too difficult, but when you have hundreds of referentially linked tables, it is a nightmare! Furthermore, you have to consider the ordering of your views, which procedures depend on which tables and views, and so on.

SQL Server 6.5 creates objects is this order to resolve the dependency issues:

1. **Logins.**
2. **Groups.**
3. **Users.** Notice that we have to create the logins before we can create the users, and it is easier to create the groups first so that we can specify the groups for users as we add them to the database.
4. **Tables.** Within tables SQL Server gives you the option of ordering the tables by dependency order, which lets you ensure that they will create successfully.
5. **Views.** Views can depend on tables and other views, so with the tables already created, we can safely make the views. Again, we have to be careful about the dependencies within views as we order the CREATE VIEW statements.
6. **Stored Procedures.** Stored Procedures can reference tables and views, so SQL Server is now ready to create them.
7. **Triggers.** Triggers can reference all of the above: tables, views, and stored procedures. However, nothing can reference a trigger, not even another trigger, so we can safely create the triggers last.

You may wonder if you can get into a circular loop on table dependencies, where A depends on B, which depends on C, which in turn depends on A. Not only can this happen, SQL Server explicitly supports this with the CREATE SCHEMA command:

```
create schema authorization Andrew
create table A (
    c1 int primary key,
    c2 int references C )
```

```
create table B (
    c1 int primary key,
    c2 int references A )
create table C (
    c1 int primary key,
    c2 int references B )
```

Regrettably, the script generator can't handle this; you as the DBA have to fix it.

Creating the Scripts for Your Database

You are now ready to create the script for your database. Switch to your database and choose Object⇨Generate SQL Scripts. You see the screen shown in Figure 18-1.

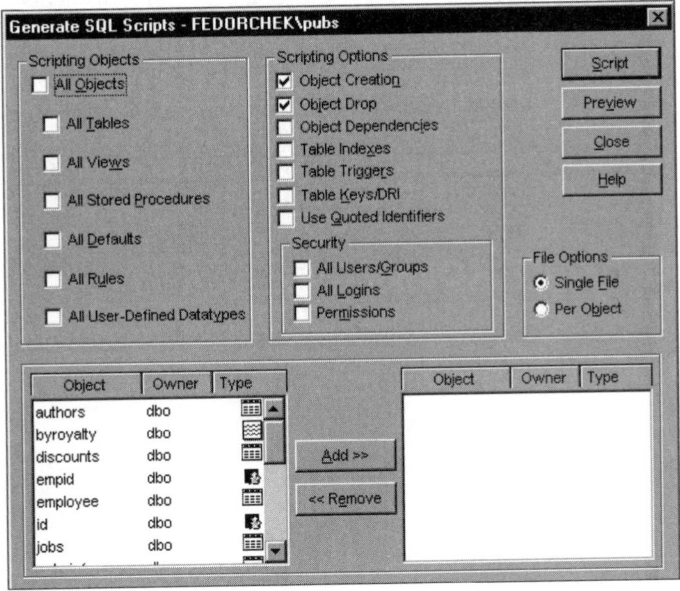

Figure 18-1:
Use the Generate SQL Scripts window to choose your scripting options.

Here you have a busy group of choices. The following sections discuss these options.

Scripting Objects

This one is simple: you can choose either all objects or all the objects of one or more types. When you check a box, wait a second. You will see all the object names of that type move from the left side box below to the right side box, indicating that you have selected them. You can also use the Add and Remove buttons to include or exclude object names that you highlight. One of the most obnoxious bugs in the SQL Enterprise manager is that your objects are sorted *case-sensitive* in the Generate SQL Scripts dialog box, no matter what the sort order of your server is. It is also frustrating that you can sort neither by owner nor by object type, even though these columns are listed in the boxes of object names.◀

If you have hundreds of objects, picking and choosing the objects you want can be a real pain, especially if you want to use some criteria that don't fall into the given categories, such as all the objects for a particular user. Here's how you can cheat the SQL Enterprise Manager. Create a userid for scripting, such as "Script". Then, create a view on sysobjects named "script.sysobjects" which tailors sysobjects to what you want. If you run the script generator with that userid, you will get only the objects you want! Even better, you don't have to reregister the server to switch to the script userid. You just have to use the SETUSER command on the spid the SQL Enterprise Manager is using, which you can access from the Manage...Window. The steps to follow are the following:

1. Open the Manage Stored Procedures Window.
2. In place of the "CREATE PROCEDURE <PROCEDURE NAME> AS" text, type this:

   ```
   SETUSER script
   GO
   CREATE VIEW sysobjects AS
   SELECT *
      FROM sysobjects
      WHERE uid = 4
   ```

   and execute it.
3. Open the Generate SQL Scripts window as you normally would. You will see only the objects owned by userid 4. Make whatever scripts you want.
4. Open the Manage Stored Procedures Window and execute simply "SETUSER" to return to being the dbo.◀

Scripting Options

Here you can choose any combination of the following:

- **Object Creation.** Makes your CREATE statements. Whether this makes CREATE TABLE, CREATE VIEW, CREATE PROCEDURE, and so on depends on the scripting options you checked.
- **Object Drop.** Includes the appropriate DROP TABLE, DROP VIEW, DROP PROCEDURE, and other statements.
- **Object Dependencies.** This is a tricky one. You have to select this to make sure your script has the correct dependency order we discussed above. However, checking it can include other objects you did not originally check.
- **Table Indexes.** Creates the non-DRI indexes for your tables.
- **Table Triggers.** Creates the triggers for your tables.
- **Table Keys/DRI.** This option scripts all DRI: DEFAULT, CHECK, PRIMARY KEY, UNIQUE, and FOREIGN KEY constraints. With DRI it is all or nothing: you can't script only a specific type of DRI constraint. Note that this will also create your PRIMARY KEY and UNIQUE indexes.
- **Use Quoted Identifiers.** Encloses objects names in double quotes (" ") and puts the SET QUOTED_IDENTIFIER ON command in the script.

You will get some interesting interaction between these options and the scripting objects if you don't know what to expect. For example, to create all triggers, and only the triggers, you have to check "All Tables" and "Table Triggers". If you just check "Table Triggers" alone, you will get an empty file because you haven't told SQL Server which tables to make trigger scripts for. To add DROP commands to your trigger script you have to check "Object Drop," but that includes the table drops! There is nothing you can do to get only the trigger drops without the table drops. Note that you do not select "Object Creation": that would script your tables, too.

As we mentioned above, you must select "Object Dependencies" to ensure that referentially linked tables are created in the correct order. You may include in your script tables that you did not explicitly include. If you choose only "All Views" and check "Object Dependencies", the script generator will order your views correctly, but it will put all tables the views reference in the script. Likewise, "All Stored Procedures" with "Object Dependencies" will include both tables and views that the procedures need, regardless of whether you selected them. Fortunately, the CREATE TABLE and CREATE VIEW commands are grouped together, so you can delete them if you need to.

Security

If you want to create the 'sp_addlogin' or 'sp_adduser' commands to add your server logins or database users to another server or database, check the appropriate boxes.◀

Contrary to what the help for the SQL Enterprise Manager tells you, "All Logins" really means every single login on the server, not just logins associated with the database. *SQL Server will not transfer the passwords of the logins.* The logins are scripted with null passwords. Refer to Chapter 7 for a discussion of how to transfer passwords from one server to another. Selecting Permissions means both object permission and database permissions will be included in the script.◀

File Options

Up until now, you have probably imagined that you were making one big file for your database scripts. One of the cool things about this tool is that it will make a file for each object. Choose Per Object if you want this. You don't have to specify any file or directory names now. That comes when you click the script button.

Go for it

You are ready. Your choices are Script or Preview. If you select Preview, the script generator will let you see and edit the file before you save it. If you selected Per Object for your file option, the Preview button overrides that choice and gives you one single file to look at. If you select Script, you will be prompted for a filename if you selected the Single File option. Otherwise, you select only a directory, Figure 18-2. SQL Server will use default file names of the form user_name.object_name.object_type, where object type is a three character abbreviation of the object type.

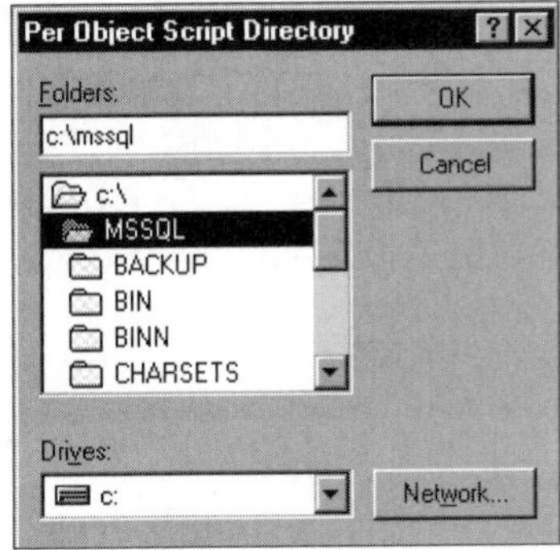

Figure 18-2:
If you select Per Object you can only specify a directory name.

Running Your Script

When your script finishes, we strongly recommend that you test it right away. Create a new database and run the script in a query window. The size of this test database will have to be large enough to allow each index or non-clustered table definition to occupy an extent and accommodate your database catalog. You can estimate the size you need for the data with this query:

```
select (select sum( reserved ) * 2
   from sysindexes
   where id < 50
      and indid < 2)
+(select 16 * count(*)
   from sysindexes
   where id > 50)
```

When you run your script, you will probably see some errors in your output. If you are unlucky, you will see a huge number of errors. It is important that you resolve each and every one of them. If Microsoft had made a perfect script generator and you were a perfect database administrator, there would be no errors. We don't how good you are as a database administrator, but we can tell you that there are some problems with the script files.

Database options aren't scripted

If your database has the SELECT INTO/BULK COPY option turned on, you can create procedures that use SELECT INTO. If you forget to turn this option on in the target database, the script will bomb. The script generator probable should insert the sp_dboption command, but it doesn't.

Bogus lengths on user defined datatypes

If you have a table in your database with columns of type sysname, SQL Server will script those columns as being of type sysname (30). This produces warning messages when you run the script, but the tables do create successfully. You can save yourself the warnings by globally replacing "sysname (30)" with "sysname" in your script.

Failed grants on non-dbo objects

When you have tables that are not owned by the dbo, SQL Server will correctly script them and their indexes within the 'user_name.table_name' format. Unfortunately, the dbo can't issue a GRANT statement in the 'user_name.table_name' format. Instead, the dbo must use the SETUSER command. That's what the script generator should do, but it doesn't. Therefore, the grants are all scripted as if the dbo owned the objects. At best, the grants fail with an error that they reference objects that don't exist. At worst, the grants of a non-dbo–owned object corrupt the grants of the dbo owned object with the same name.

If Your Script Has Errors

Though you may not realize it, your database may contain a whole bunch of inconsistencies in the system tables, especially if you have many objects and you make many changes. These inconsistencies don't affect your day-to-day operations, but they throw a major monkey wrench into script generation. All these problems show up as errors in the results when you run your script. For small databases it is feasible just to let these errors happen and deal with them when they occur.

The Problem with Objects Owned by Other Users in SQL Server 6.0

The Script Generator in SQL Server 6.0 has a problem with objects owned by other users: it fails to put the user's name in the CREATE statement for the object. Thus, you see something like the following for a table named test, owned by user rensin. (We have deleted some blank lines and spaces for brevity):

```
if exists (select * from sysobjects where id = object_id('rensin.test')
and sysstat & 0xf = 3)
   drop table rensin.test
GO
CREATE TABLE test
(  i int NOT NULL ,
   j int NOT NULL ,
   CONSTRAINT PK__test__i__4C4B5DA7 PRIMARY KEY  CLUSTERED (i))
GO
CREATE  INDEX j ON rensin.test(j)
GO
GRANT  SELECT  ON test  TO public
GO
```

When you run this script logged in as the dbo, here is what happens:

1. The table rensin.test, if it exists, gets dropped.
2. If there is an object (not necessarily a table) called dbo.test in the database, you get an error. If there is no object called dbo.test, the preceding table is created as dbo.test. Either way, there will be no table called rensin.test.
3. You get this error on the create index statement:

```
Cannot create and index on table 'test', because this table does not exist
in database '<dbname>'.
```

4. The grants may or may not work. If SQL Server created dbo.test, the grants work. If there was already some other table ***or view*** called dbo.test, the grants get applied to that other object. If there was already a dbo.test that was not a table or view, you get errors like the following: GRANTED/REVOKED privilege...not compatible with object.

Worse yet, suppose your database has a dbo.test and a rensin.test and you create a script for all objects. When you run the script in an empty database, only one of the two objects will be in the database, and you don't know which one it will be until you look.

For rich databases, that isn't feasible. (A rich database has a large number of objects.) We would have *thousands* of lines of errors if we naively let the script generator do its thing with no help from us. Rather than going through a dozen iterations of generating and executing scripts, we like to get it right the first time. Follow the steps discussed in subsequent sections to avoid the headaches we found in those thousands of lines of errors.

Unrecorded dependencies

Cross-Reference

As we discussed in Chapter 11, when one object depends on another, SQL Server records that fact in sysdepends.◀

Suppose that you create a view on authors, like this:

```
CREATE VIEW names AS
SELECT au_lname, au_fname
   FROM authors
```

Now, create a view on top of that view, as follows:

```
CREATE VIEW full_names AS
SELECT au_fname+' '+au_lname
   FROM names
```

You can see that full_names depends on names by running this system procedure:

```
sp_depends full_names
```

That procedure returns the following:

```
In the current database the specified object references:
name                 type            updated selected
-------------------- --------------- ------- --------
dbo.names            view            no      no
```

Now we are going to change names:

```
DROP VIEW names
GO
CREATE VIEW names AS
SELECT au_lname, au_fname, city
   FROM authors
```

In SQL Server, you can drop the view names even though full_names depends on it. After you recreate names, the view full_names is still valid, and you can still select rows from it. But if you run sp_depends full_names again, you get nothing. Why? When you created names, SQL Server assigned it some integer, like 1040006736, to track it. When you created full_names, SQL Server recorded the fact that full_names depends on object number 1040006736. When you drop and recreate names, SQL Server gives it a new number, say 1072006850. Although the view full_names is still valid, SQL Server never records the fact that it now depends on object number 1072006850, unless you drop and recreate full_names.

The result of this is that the script generator loses information. It won't know that full_names depends on names, and because it goes in alphabetical order for objects that don't depend on one another, the script generator puts the CREATE VIEW statement for full_names first. When you run the script, you get the following error:

```
Msg 208, Level 16, State 1
Invalid object name 'names'.
```

And full_names isn't created at all!

Updating dependency information

You can find disconnects like the preceding one in your database by looking for depids in sysdepends that are not defined is sysobjects (which means using a NOT EXISTS clause). Finally, you have to join your results with sysobjects to get the owner and type of the object. The correct query is

```
SELECT DISTINCT o.name, user_name(o.uid) owner, o.type
   FROM sysobjects o JOIN sysdepends d
      ON o.id = d.id /* This join is just to get the object owner and type */
      WHERE NOT EXISTS (SELECT *
            FROM sysobjects
            WHERE d.depid = id) /* Find depid in sysdepends that aren't real id's
*/
   ORDER BY o.name, user_name(o.uid), o.type
```

You have to open each object listed by this query in its respective Manage windows and re-create it. When you do, you have one of three cases described in the next sections.

ANSI SQL92 Joins Verses Old Style Joins

If you are using SQL Server 6.0, you would have to write the query this way:

```
SELECT DISTINCT o.name, user_name(o.uid) owner, o.type
   FROM sysobjects o, sysdepends d
   WHERE o.id = d.id
      AND NOT EXISTS (SELECT *
            FROM sysobjects
            WHERE d.depid = id)
   ORDER BY o.name, user_name(o.uid), o.type
```

The conversion from the ANSI SQL92 joins down to the SQL89 joins is straightforward, so we list only the SQL92 style joins in the rest of this chapter.

A successful recompile

You re-create the object, and the next time you run the query the object isn't on the list. All is well. By re-creating the object, you updated the dependency information SQL Server needs.

Invalid Object Name

You may see the screen shown in Figure 18-3 in the SQL Enterprise Manager when you try to recompile the procedure or trigger or view. You can't re-create the object because it depends on something that isn't there. In this case, you have to figure out what is wrong. The object is broken: the next time someone tries to use it, he or she gets the same error. You can drop the object, fix the missing reference, or comment out the offending section (if it is a stored procedure.) Here is a trivial example of how to create this problem:

```
CREATE PROC theMissingObject AS
PRINT "Hello World"
GO
CREATE PROC theBrokenObject AS
EXEC theMissingObject
GO
DROP PROC theMissingObject
```

Notice that when you drop theMissingObject, you get no warning that something else depends on it. (This is the same type of thing we did above with the views full_names and names, but this time we don't recreate theMissingObject.)

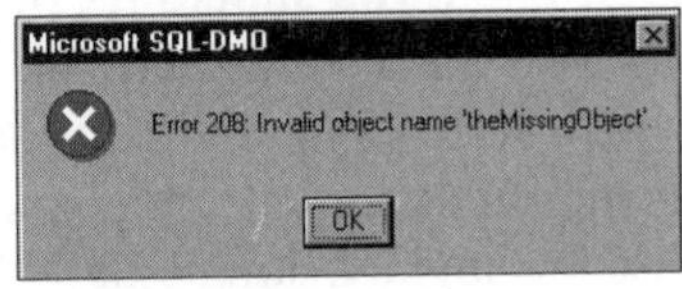

Figure 18-3:
What happens when you recompile an object that depends on a missing object.

A successful recompile, but the object is still on the query's list

This is a ghost problem. Consider what this kind of procedure will do

```
CREATE PROC createAndDropTable AS
CREATE TABLE thePhantomTable (
   column1 int PRIMARY KEY)
SELECT *
   FROM thePhantomTable
DROP TABLE thePhantomTable
```

Imagine this as part of a real stored procedure with lots of other logic. What we have here is a permanent table, thePhantomTable, which either should have been declared as a temporary table or should be kept as permanent and not dropped at the end of the stored procedure. The design of the procedure is sloppy, but it won't be a problem when the script runs.

Finding users whose default database doesn't exist

One option in the script generator lets you generate login script information. These scripts will fail if the default database doesn't exist. You can have this situation for at least two reasons:

- You are going to run this script on a server that doesn't have one of the databases you do. In this case, you should just search and replace the database name with the name of whatever database you want the logins to have as a default.
- You are going to run this script on your own server, but you have logins pointing to databases you either dropped or renamed.

The second problem you should fix right away because not only does it mess up your scripts, but also it screws up logging in for those users. When you try to log in to SQL Server and your default database doesn't exist, SQL Server logs you in, leaves you in master, and returns an error to the application that you used to login. Though all SQL Server applications (SQL Enterprise Manager, ISQL/w, and so forth) know what to do with this error, some applications, such as Microsoft Access, misinterpret the error and deny the user a connection altogether.

To find users with nonexistent default databases, you must search for entries in the master.dbo.syslogins table which refer to databases that are not listed in the master.dbo.sysdatabases table. Therefore, the query you want is

```
SELECT *
   FROM master.dbo.syslogins l
   WHERE NOT EXISTS (SELECT *
         FROM master.dbo.sysdatabases
         WHERE name = l.dbname)
```

Use the Manage⇨Logins window to change their default databases.

Excluding objects that reference other databases

You can write procedures, triggers, and views that reference objects in other databases. If you try to run the scripts for these procedures, triggers, and views on another server, you may get errors. The possible causes for the errors are that the other databases don't exist, the other databases have different names, or the objects you want in the other databases don't exist. SQL Server will not create these procedures, triggers, or views because they reference nonexistent objects.

The way to find objects in your database that reference other databases is to look for other database names in the text of your objects. You have to be a little bit careful, however, because:

- SQL Server stores text in 255-character chunks. You don't want to miss a reference that spans the end of one block and the beginning of the other.
- You have to exclude references that are commented out. This is difficult, because a comment in SQL Server can be delimited either by the pair (/*, */) or the pair (--, char(13)).

Though you can do this in Transact-SQL, the language doesn't lend itself to the task. Our choice would be to write a C program; we leave that as an exercise for the C programmers among you. If you want to attempt the search in SQL, you can start by simply searching for the database names without worrying about the comments. The text of your objects is recorded in syscomments; the database names are in sysdatabases. Therefore, you have to join these two tables. However, you also have to join syscomments with itself to catch database names that cross the boundaries of the varchar(255) text column is syscomments. The "straightforward" query for this search is the first problem:

```
SELECT DISTINCT OBJECT_NAME(id) object_name, name database_name
   FROM syscomments c JOIN master..sysdatabases d
   ON text LIKE '%[ ,]'+name+'.%.%'
   WHERE name NOT IN ('master','tempdb','model')
UNION
SELECT DISTINCT OBJECT_NAME(a.id) object_name, name database_name
   FROM syscomments a JOIN syscomments b
   ON a.id = b.id
      AND a.colid+1 = b.colid
      AND a.number = b.number
      AND a.texttype = b.texttype
   JOIN master.dbo.sysdatabases
   ON substring(a.text,128,128)+b.text LIKE '%[ ,]'+name+'.%.%'
   WHERE name NOT IN ('master','tempdb','model')
ORDER BY 1
```

Warning

Cross-Reference

As we discuss in Chapter 29, this query is horribly inefficient. This is why we recommend a C program. Note that this query will return a superset of the objects that reference other databases. Look over the output list of the query: you probably will want to exclude some of these objects from a script you plan to run on a server where the referenced databases don't exist. Some of the objects on the list may not concern you because the reference to another database is buried in a comment.◀

A cascading problem

Depending on how you have structured your databases, you could be in for a real mess if you are transferring one database that has a lot of references to another. The preceding query grabs all the objects that will potentially fail to be created on the destination server. However, if they fail to be created, views or triggers that reference *them* will fail to be created, which could cause other object-creation failures, which would...you get the idea. If this happens, you are probably looking at a system that should have been *one* database, not two.

Renamed objects

When you rename an object, SQL Server changes the name attached to the integer that tracks the object. SQL Server doesn't change the text associated with the object. For example, go into the pubs database, expand Objects⇨Views⇨titleview, and right-click. From the pop-up menu choose Rename titleview. Enter some other name and click OK. Now, right click on that new name, and choose Edit from the pop-up menu. Notice that it still contains the line "CREATE VIEW titleview." However, the drop and grants all have the correct name. This is because the CREATE VIEW text is stored directly in SQL Server, and it didn't change just because you renamed the object. The drop and grants, on the other hand, are generated from the system tables, and they are correct.

If you try to run this script in the Manage Views window without editing it, you get an error telling you that your new object name doesn't exist. Exit this window, and in the Server Manager window, right-click on the Views icon, and choose Refresh in the pop-up menu. Now titleview is back. Edit it, and you find the grants are gone. What happened was that SQL Server first successfully dropped the object with the new name. Then, it created titleview. Next, it tried to do grants on the new object name, which failed. Finally, when you exited the Manage Views window, the information about the grants was lost forever.

In summary:

- Your object was created with the old (wrong) name.
- You lost all permissions on the object.

This is what will happen when you run the script for your database. Worse yet, if you have other objects that reference the new name of the object, they won't create properly, either.

An ounce of prevention is worth a pound of cure

The way to prevent this problem is to be careful about renaming. Always rename a procedure, trigger, or view by doing the following:

1. Execute sp_depends @objname to find out what objects depend on the @objname you are about to rename.
2. Open the object in a Manage Stored Procedures, Manage Triggers, or Manage Views window and replace the name there, both in the CREATE line and in the GRANT lines.

3. Immediately do Steps 1 and 2 for the objects that depend on your renamed object. These objects are invalid until you do this.

Clearly, renaming one object can lead to a lot of work, but unfortunately, that's life. You don't save yourself any work with sp_rename, you just postpone it. Objects can get recompiled by SQL Server without warning, and the recompiles will fail. Fix your problems early. You can identify renaming problems you already have by searching for objects where there is no entry in syscomments containing the appropriate CREATE statement. In SQL that translates to:

```
SELECT type, USER_NAME(uid)+'.'+name object
   FROM sysobjects o
   WHERE type IN ( 'P', 'TR', 'V' )
      AND NOT EXISTS (SELECT *
         FROM syscomments c
         WHERE c.id = o.id
            AND colid = 1
            AND text LIKE '%create%'
               +CASE o.type
                  WHEN 'P' THEN 'proc'
                  WHEN 'TR' THEN 'trigger'
                  WHEN 'V' THEN 'view'
               END+'%'+o.name+'%')
   ORDER BY 1, 2
```

Once again we are victimized by the non-3NF structure of syscomments: the appropriate CREATE statement may span two adjacent colids, most likely colid = 1 and colid = 2. This can happen if you have a long comment before your CREATE statement. We err on the side of caution by including in the query anything that *might* be a problem.

Tip

Renamed objects with incorrect entries in syscomments are the kind of problem that you should be continually on the watch for and that you should correct right away. Therefore, the preceding query is an excellent candidate for running as a nightly task that e-mails a list to you if it finds something. More on that in Part VII.◀

Objects with text referencing renamed objects

Your problems with renamed objects can go even deeper if you have a rich database (one with lots and lots of objects, especially lots of procedures, triggers, and views.) Consider this code:

```
CREATE PROC aboutToBeRenamed AS
PRINT "Hello World"
GO
CREATE PROC soonToBeInvalid AS
PRINT "Andrew says:"
EXEC aboutToBeRenamed
GO
sp_rename 'aboutToBeRenamed', 'hasBeenRenamed'
EXEC soonToBeInvalid
```

Your output should be the following:

```
Warning - Procedures, views or triggers reference this object and will become
invalid.
Object name has been changed.
Andrew says:
Hello World
```

For right now, the stored procedure soonToBeInvalid does work, but not for long. Sometime soon when you run it, you will get:

```
Andrew says:
Msg 2812, Level 16, State 4
Stored procedure 'aboutToBeRenamed' not found.
```

Problems like this are time bombs in your database waiting to explode. Find them and fix them. You can identify them with the same kind of logic we used to find bad CREATE statements. This time we are looking for an object that depends on objects not contained it in the definition text of the first object. Our NOT EXISTS clause still references syscomments, but the outer query must join sysdepends and sysobjects:

```
SELECT o.type, o.name, OBJECT_NAME(depid) dependsOn
   FROM sysobjects o JOIN sysdepends d
   ON o.id = d.id
   WHERE o.type IN ( 'P', 'TR', 'V' )
      AND OBJECT_NAME(depid) IS NOT NULL
      AND NOT EXISTS (SELECT *
         FROM syscomments c
         WHERE c.id = d.id
            AND text LIKE
               '%['+CHAR(9)+CHAR(10)+CHAR(13)
               +' .,]'+OBJECT_NAME(d.depid)+'%')
   ORDER BY 1, 2
```

The LIKE string takes advantage of the fact that table name must be preceded by a tab, a carriage return, a space, a period, or a comma. Once again, because of the fact that syscomments isn't a true relation (because of the colid intrinsic ordering), it is difficult to search for a string with total accuracy. This query will thus return a superset of the potential problems, which is better than having it miss something. For example, a procedure might depend on syscomments, but the text column might hold "... sysco" for colid 1 and "mments ..." for colid 2. This will never be found with "text LIKE '%syscomments%'". However, we can do better. The more complete approach would be to UNION the previous query with a query that joins syscomments with itself in the NOT EXIST clause. That query is particularly difficult for the SQL Server optimizer to decipher, so we break it up with a temporary table. We make our own version of syscomments that contains the concatenated comments as well as normal comments:

```
CREATE TABLE #comments (
   id int,
   number smallint,
   colid int PRIMARY KEY (id, number, colid),
   text varchar(255))
INSERT #comments
SELECT id, number, colid, text
   FROM syscomments
   WHERE texttype = 2
INSERT #comments
SELECT a.id, a.number, a.colid*256+b.colid,
      SUBSTRING(a.text, 128, 128)+b.text
   FROM syscomments a
   JOIN syscomments b
      ON a.id = b.id
      AND a.number = b.number
      AND a.colid + 1 = b.colid
   WHERE a.texttype = 2
      AND b.texttype = 2
```

Now, we can replace "syscomments" in the original query with "#comments" and get only the problem children. These are objects you must fix.

Renamed columns

So far, we have confined our concerns to objects that have been renamed, but you can rename columns as well. As you can now see, these renamed columns will be a problem for you when you try to create scripts for your database. In addition to fouling up your views, procedures, and triggers, renamed columns will wreck your CHECK constraints, for example:

```
CREATE TABLE ColumnRenameTest (
   c1 varchar(30) PRIMARY KEY CHECK (c1 LIKE '[A-Z]%'))
EXEC sp_rename 'ColumnRenameTest.c1', 'NewName', 'column'
INSERT ColumnRenameTest VALUES ('Andrew Fedorchek')
EXEC sp_help 'ColumnRenameTest'
```

Notice three things when you run this SQL:

- When you rename the column c1, SQL Server doesn't warn you that a CHECK constraint references that column
- You can still insert data after you rename the column, which shows the constraint still works.
- sp_help shows the old name of the column in the CHECK constraint, as will the script generator.

By now the SQL for ferreting out this disconnects should be familiar:

```
SELECT OBJECT_NAME(con.id) 'Table Name',
      COL_NAME(con.id, colid) 'Column Name',
      o.name 'Constraint Name'
   FROM sysconstraints con
   JOIN sysobjects o
   ON constid = o.id
   WHERE colid != 0
      AND o.type = 'C'
      AND NOT EXISTS (SELECT *
         FROM syscomments
         WHERE con.constid = id
            AND text like '%'+col_name(con.id, con.colid)+'%')
```

Unfortunately, there is no clean way to identify procedures, triggers, or views that reference renamed columns because no system table records this dependency.

Objects with no stored text whatsoever

This shouldn't be possible, but it is. If you create a view with the EXECUTE command, the text isn't recorded, yet the view works, for example:

```
EXECUTE("create view CanYouSeeMe as select * from sysobjects" )
```

When you run the Script Generator, this object will be skipped entirely, without warning. The good news is that there is a bulletproof way to identify this problem: run the following query. The bad news is that you are on your own in trying to fix it. You can run procedures like sp_help and sp_depends to get some information about the object, but if you don't have the text stored in a file somewhere, you're hosed. Fortunately, this problem is rare. Here's the query you want

```
SELECT type, USER_NAME(uid)+'.'+name
   FROM sysobjects o
   WHERE type IN ( 'D', 'P', 'R', 'TR', 'V' )
         AND NOT EXISTS (SELECT *
            FROM syscomments c
            WHERE c.id = o.id)
   ORDER BY 1, 2
```

Objects with encrypted text

These will bomb for sure. You can't do anything about it, either. Aren't you glad you used encryption? If you want to know where these monsters are, search on syscomments WHERE power(2,2) & texttype != 0.

The Trigger Order Flaw of SQL Server 6.0

As discussed earlier, the Script Generator tries to create objects in the proper order to avoid errors. If you use triggers to enforce custom business rules or referential integrity, this order is very important. Assume that you have two tables, A and B, and each table has triggers that reference the other table, named T_A_DELETE, . . ., T_B_UPDATE. Further assume that B has a foreign key referencing A. In what order should these two tables and six triggers be created?

1. Table A comes first, because B needs it for DRI.
2. Table B comes second.
3. The triggers come last, in any order among themselves.

Here it is:

```
CREATE TABLE A (
    A int PRIMARY KEY)
CREATE TABLE B (
    B int PRIMARY KEY REFERENCES A)
GO
CREATE TRIGGER T_A_ALL ON A FOR INSERT, UPDATE, DELETE AS
SELECT A,B
```

(continued)

The Trigger Order Flaw of SQL Server 6.0 (continued)

```
   FROM A CROSS JOIN B
GO
CREATE TRIGGER T_B_ALL ON B FOR INSERT, UPDATE, DELETE AS
SELECT A,B
   FROM A CROSS JOIN B
```

The critical part here is that you have to create *both* tables before you create either table's triggers. In fact, you are always safe in putting triggers last because nothing can depend on a trigger. This basic fact eluded the SQL Server 6.0 implementation of the Script Generator. It always, but *always*, puts the triggers right after their tables in the script file, like this (we have shortened the Script Generator output for brevity):

```
CREATE TABLE A (
     A int PRIMARY KEY)
GO
CREATE TRIGGER T_A_ALL ON A FOR INSERT, UPDATE, DELETE AS
SELECT A,B
   FROM A CROSS JOIN B
GO
CREATE TABLE B (
     B int PRIMARY KEY REFERENCES A)
GO
CREATE TRIGGER T_B_ALL ON B FOR INSERT, UPDATE, DELETE AS
SELECT A,B
   FROM A CROSS JOIN B
```

Thus, if you run the script in an empty database, it would create table A and then attempt — and fail — to create A's triggers.

If you haven't upgraded to SQL Server 6.5, the easy solution for this is to use the Script Generator to make two files: one that is everything but the triggers, and a second that is the triggers only. Run them in that order. Another alternative is to run one complete script twice in the new database because on the second pass, tables such as B will already exist at the time creation of triggers such as T_A_ALL runs. Be prepared to see an avalanche of other errors, mostly of the following variety:

```
Msg 3726, Level 16, State 1
Could not drop object 'A'.  It is being referenced by a foreign key con-
straint.
Msg 2714, Level 16, State 1
There is already an object named 'A' in the database.
```

You can ignore these kinds of messages on the second pass.

TRANSFERRING OBJECTS

With what you have now learned about SQL scripts, you can transfer all or part of your database to any server you want: simply make the scripts and do the bulk copies. However, if you are going from one SQL Server to another, it seems reasonable that SQL Server should be able to do even *more* of the work for you. Specifically, SQL Server should run the script for you, if you plan to run it anyway, and SQL Server should do the bulk copying for you. That is the purpose of the Object transfer management interface.

Interestingly enough, however, the transfer management interface doesn't do its scripts exactly the same way that the script generator does. The major differences are

- Whereas the script generator either makes one great big file or individual files for each object, the transfer management makes a different file for each object type. You have no choice about this with the transfer management interface. All you can specify is a directory into which the files will go. In this regard, the script generator is much more flexible.
- The transfer manager takes an entirely different approach to DRI. The script generator goes to the trouble of ordering tables correctly but creates all DRI constraints with the table. The transfer manager simply creates all tables without any DRI whatsoever. Then, it creates all the primary keys and all the foreign keys. The transfer manager approach is more robust because it cannot fail on circular dependencies.
- The transfer manager lets you choose to convert User Defined Datatypes (UDDT) to base datatypes.
- The transfer manager gives you the flexibility to choose between scripting clustered indexes and non-clustered indexes.
- With the transfer manager you can choose whether you want Object Permissions, Statement Permissions, or both.

Pick any server and select Tools⇨Database/Object Transfer. You will see the dialog box is Figure 18-4. Let's look at the options you have here.

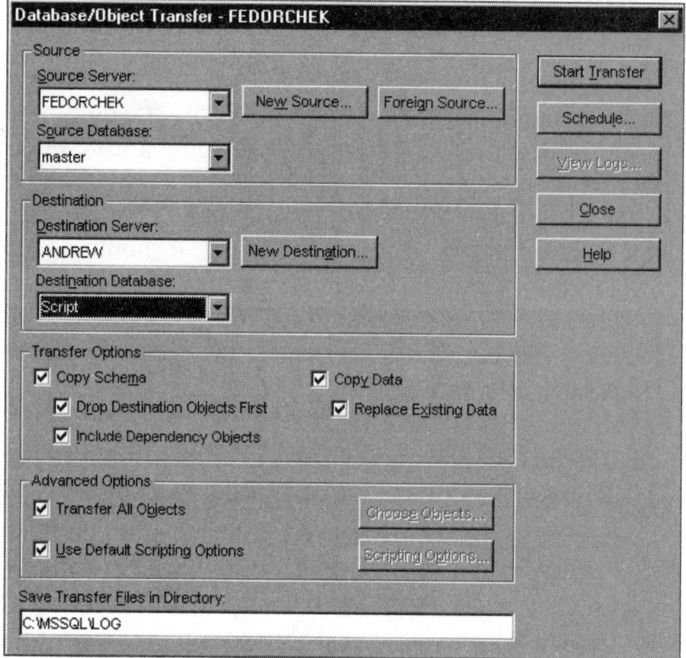

Figure 18-4:
The Database/Object Transfer dialog box pushes scripts and data to another server.

Source

The top of the dialog box allows you to choose any SQL Server running version 6.*x* or 4.*x*, or a server running SYBASE System 10. The Source Server drop-down list box shows you the servers you have registered in the SQL Enterprise Manager (which will of course be only SQL Servers). To register another SQL Server, press the New Source to bring up the standard Register Server dialog box (see Chapter 5). The Foreign Source button brings up the foreign source dialog box, Figure 18-5. Here, you simply supply a server, login id, and password. You can use this dialog box to transfer from a SQL Server that you do not wish to register or to transfer from a SYBASE System 10 server. The Source Database drop-down list box lists the databases of the server displayed in Source Server. ◀

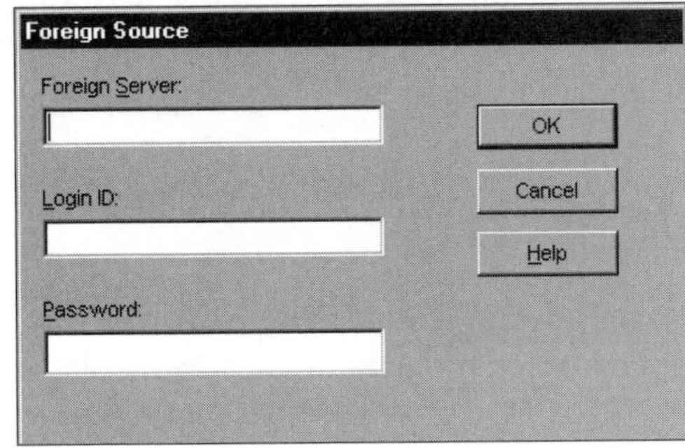

Figure 18-5:
Enter an unregistered SQL Server or a SYBASE System 10 server in the Foreign Source dialog box.

Destination

The Destination Server drop-down list box shows you the SQL Server 6.5 servers you have registered in the SQL Enterprise Manager. No, you can't use this interface to transfer into SQL Server 6.0 utilities. This really leaves you hanging high and dry if you still have SQL Server 6.0 running anywhere, especially because the Transfer Manager application of SQL Server 6.0 doesn't transfer DRI. The only solutions we can recommend are that you do the scripts and bulk copies yourself or upgrade everything to SQL Server 6.5.

Like the New Source button, the New Destination button lets you register another server so that you can use it. The Destination Database drop down list box will show you the databases on the server you have selected.

Transfer Options

In the transfer options group you have five choices:

- **Copy Schema.** In other words, do you want the script? You can choose to transfer only data. If you deselect this, the next two items gray themselves out.
- **Drop Destination Objects First.** Same as Scripting Options/Object Drop in Figure 18-1.

- **Include Dependency Objects.** Same Scripting Options/Object Dependency as in Figure 18-1. Be ready for the fact that the transfer manager seems to screw up the dependencies of views.
- **Copy Data.** Do you want to transfer the data? If you deselect this, you are making scripts only (though SQL Server will run the scripts on the destination database.)
- **Replace Existing Data.** If you clear this box, the data you transfer will be appended to the data already in the destination tables, if any.

Advanced Options

The Advanced Options bring up pieces of the Generate SQL Scripts dialog box you saw in Figure 18-1. By default, both check boxes are selected, which means both buttons are grayed out. If you clear a check box, the button next to it becomes active.

Choose Objects

The Choose Objects button opens Figure 18-6, the Choose Objects to be Transferred dialog box. Here we see an interface very similar to the Generate SQL Scripts dialog box. The Add/Remove Objects section lets you highlight individual objects to include or exclude; the Object Types sections allows you to include or exclude entire types of objects.

Scripting Options

The Scripting Options button brings up Figure 18-7, the Transfer Scripting Options dialog box. This, too, is quite similar to the Generate SQL Scripts dialog box. The differences are

- A Table Binding option to bind rules and defaults to tables.
- A Use Base Type Only option to convert UDDTs to the basic SQL Server datatypes.
- Object Permission/Statement Permission check boxes so you can differentiate between the two kinds of permissions
- Three Index Scripting options. You can choose whether to include non-DRI non-clustered indexes and non-DRI clustered indexes. (The DRI indexes are included based on the "Table DRI" Object Scripting option.) Finally, you can choose to use the sorted data option in creating keys

and indexes. If you know that the sort orders of the two servers are the same, checking this option speeds things up substantially.

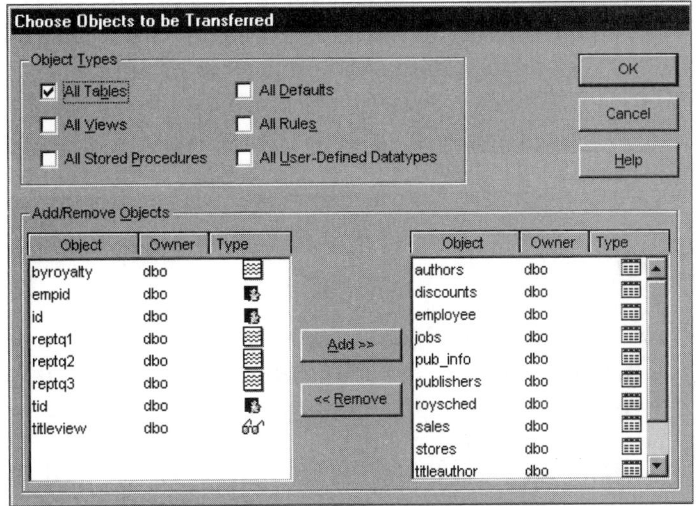

Figure 18-6:
Choose Objects to be Transferred window groups objects by type.

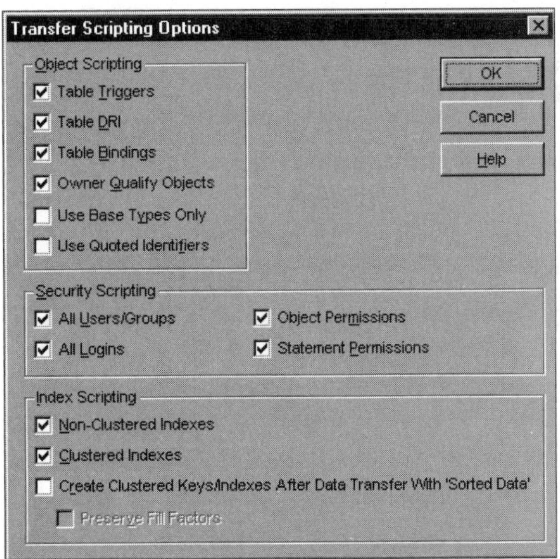

Figure 18-7:
Use the Transfer Scripting Options to fine tune your scripting.

Wrapping it up

The directory you pick in Save Transfer Files in Directory is where all the script files will go. When you are ready, you can click either Start Transfer to launch the transfer immediately or Schedule to schedule a time for a one-time or recurring transfer. After the transfer runs, it will display for you the error log. These errors are going to be the same kind of errors you dealt with in script generation.

Summary

The SQL Enterprise Manager gives you some robust tools for generating the SQL to recreate your database. You can choose to make the SQL alone or to transfer the scripts and data to another server. The major issues in recreating a database elsewhere are the order in which to issue CREATE commands and how to cope with objects that have been renamed. The tools themselves that are discussed in this chapter are not difficult to use. The inconsistencies SQL Server allows in its database catalog are what can make this experience a living hell. We have done our best to help you use right away what we learned by trial and error.

Review Questions

Q: Where does the information to make a script originate?

A: The database catalog.

Q: Why is scripting order even an issue?

A: When one object depends on another, the first object can't be created until after the other one is.

Q: If an object is renamed, why is its old name a problem? Where is the old name found?

A: The old name is in syscomments, and this causes an object either to get scripted with the wrong name or to fail to create when the script runs.

Q: Which SQL Server versions can the Object Transfer menu item transfer into? Out of?

A: Object Transfer can transfer *into* SQL Server 6.5 only, but it can transfer *out of* any version.

Q: What happens if you don't make all the corrections outlined in this chapter?

A: If your database is relatively simple, maybe nothing. More than likely, though, you will be missing objects on the destination side.

Part

VI

ADVANCED FEATURES

This part deals with more advanced features that SQL Server has to offer. At this point, if you have carefully read the previous chapters, you should be ready to get into the darkest and dustiest corners of SQL Server.

We begin our journey with a discussion of SQLMail (Chapter 19). This chapter covers SQL Server's capability to interact with any MAPI-compliant e-mail system and how to get the most from it. In this chapter we also cover some shortcomings of Microsoft's implementation and how to successfully reduce their impact.

Wouldn't it be nice if you could be warned *before* a serious system error occurs? Better still, wouldn't it be nicer if you could teach SQL Server to fix the problem without having to involve you? You can, and in Chapter 20 we show you how.

Finally, we wrap up our discussion of these advanced features with a presentation on one of the most compelling features to emerge from SQL Server 6.5: distributed transactions. In Chapter 21, we teach you how SQL Server implements the idea of distributed transactions and how you can use them to balance the processing load across your network and increase the fault tolerance of your systems. Although the concepts are relatively simple, distributed transactions provide a nearly infinite capability for creativity and expansion.

Chapter

SQLMAIL

19

Not so many pages ago, you were told that you could have SQL Server send e-mail to a user (or set of users) when a certain backup or restore event occurs. The truth of the matter is, though, that SQL Server is capable of interacting with an e-mail system in a much more robust manner than simple process alerts. In fact, you can set up your SQL Server machine to handle a whole host of e-mail requests — and even answer user queries remotely. In this chapter, you learn the ins and outs of these processes and how to use them to aid those users who do not have a direct LAN connection to your server.

WHAT'S IN THIS CHAPTER

In this chapter, you will learn the following:

- The basics of the SQLMail stored procedures
- How to get around some of the limitations of SQLMail
- How to write some truly nifty applications using the SQLMail stored procedures

When we first decided to include SQLMail in this book, we debated a great variety of presentation styles. More specifically, we debated between having several small examples or one large project. In the end — in our usual decisive manner — we decided on both. To that end, this chapter is structured a little differently than most of the other chapters in this book.

This first half of the chapter is an explanation of the basic procedures and commands for the SQLMail capability. It is specifically written so that you can refer to it as a quick reference.

The second half of the chapter, though, concentrates on building a sample project called a *listserver*. A listserver — for the purposes of this book — is a program that accepts and processes e-mail from users and returns results. In this chapter, we show you how to build such a program completely with Transact SQL and SQLMail. Our program includes security, support for canned queries, user-defined (or ad-hoc) queries, and a basic macro language.

SQLMail: An Overview

SQL Server spends most of its time acting in the capacity of a *server*. In other words, it spends this time providing services and information to other applications and users: its *clients*. In rare instances, however, SQL Server acts as a client. SQLMail is such a case. SQL Server has a set of system stored procedures that enable it to log into any valid MAPI messaging system as a user and then read, send, and delete mail.

To enable the SQLMail facilities of SQL Server, you must perform the following steps:

1. Install and configure a MAPI-compliant e-mail system on a server on your network, such as Microsoft Exchange.
2. Create a user account through which SQL Server can log in.
3. Configure the SQLMail parameters of your SQL Server with the userid and password of a valid account for the mail post-office.

Configuring the SQLMail Parameters

Configuring SQLMail is easy enough. Basically, you have two choices: Have SQLMail start every time the SQL Executive starts, or start SQLMail by hand.

> **What If It Doesn't Work ?**
>
> We have seen cases in which both MS Mail and SQL Server seem to be configured correctly, but SQLMail refuses to start. In these cases, there is often an easy solution. Go to the NT machine that is running SQL Server, start the MS Mail client program, and log in as the account you want SQL Server to use. When you have successfully logged in, open the SQL Enterprise Manager, right-click the SQL Mail option, and select Start. If SQL Server sees that a mail session is already running on the machine, it will use that session to perform its operations. If this strategy doesn't work, you have probably misconfigured something along the way.

To have SQLMail start every time the SQL Executive starts, you need to run the SQL Setup utility from the NT machine on which you are running SQL Server. Select the Set Server Options button, and click the Auto Start Mail Client check box. When you are prompted for a name and password, enter the userid and password of the mail account you want SQL Server to use.

Your other option, when configuring SQLMail, is to start and stop it manually. You can do this either with the xp_startmail stored procedure (which we talk about a little later) or through the SQL Enterprise Manager. For the moment, we'll talk about the GUI way of doing it.

To start SQLMail through the SQL Enterprise Manager, right-click the SQL Mail icon. Click the Configure option to set the name and password, and click the Start option to start SQLMail.

Starting and Stopping SQLMail

If you don't configure SQL Server to start its SQLMail services automatically when it initializes, you have to start and stop those services yourself. Simply right-click the SQL Mail icon under a server's tree and select Start. You can also start mail within a stored procedure; you do this with the xp_startmail and xp_stopmail extended stored procedures. A description of each follows.

xp_startmail

The syntax for the xp_startmail procedure is

```
xp_startmail ['user'] [, 'password']
```

The parameters *user* and *password* are optional strings that specify the userid and password of the mail account to use. If you do not provide these parameters, SQL Server attempts to use the information provided in the SQLMail configuration. If the information SQL Server uses (whether it comes from parameters or a configuration) is incorrect, xp_startmail returns an error. You may also use variables as these parameters.

By default, only the system administrator has permission to use the SQLMail stored procedures. If other users or groups need this functionality, it must be explicitly GRANTed to them.◀

xp_stopmail

The syntax for xp_stopmail is simply:

```
xp_stopmail
```

This command takes no parameters. If it is executed when no mail session is present an error is returned.

Processing Messages by Hand

In the next several sections, we introduce you to the four procedures that allow you to process mail with SQL Server: xp_findnextmsg, xp_readmail, xp_sendmail, and xp_deletemail.

xp_findnextmsg

Assuming, for the moment, that you have successfully started an SQLMail session, the first thing you will probably want to do is check your mail spool for any incoming messages. You accomplish this task with the xp_findnextmsg procedure. The syntax for this command is

```
xp_findnextmsg [@msg_id = msg_id [OUTPUT]]
    [, @type = type]
    [, @unread_only = {'true' | 'false'}])
```

The following sections discuss various parts of this syntax.

@msg_id

The *@msg_id* parameter is an input *and* output parameter that specifies the unique string identifier (USI) of the message on input and the USI of the next message on output. The only time you would ever place a value for input in *@msg_id* is if you wanted to search for the presence of a message with a specific USI.

@type

The *@type* parameter specifies the type of message for which you are searching. The message type is defined by the MAPI mail definition:

```
IP[M | C].Vendorname.subclass
```

If you leave this parameter NULL, messages whose type begins with IPM will be returned by the procedure. Because the IPM message type is the most common, you will seldom have to specify this parameter. If, however, you want to return messages whose type begins with IPC, you have to specify this value. The default value for *@type* is NULL.

@unread_only

The *@unread_only* parameter specifies whether xp_ findnextmsg should return all messages in the inbox or just those that have not been read. Valid values for this option are 'true' or 'false'. The default for this parameter is 'true'.

Return value

This procedure returns a 0 if it succeeded and a 1 if it did not. All failures other than invalid parameters are logged to the Windows NT event log.

MAPI Message Types

All MAPI messages are of a specific type. What type that is depends largely on your environment. Specifically, the vendorname and subclass portions of the message type depend greatly on the program that generated the message. The only thing you really need to know about this standard is that the messages you will be concerned about will all begin with the IPM specification. To this end, we recommend that you leave the *@type* parameter out of any calls to the xp_findnextmsg procedure. If you are interested in learning more about the MAPI specification, you can get white papers from Microsoft that detail the API.

xp_readmail

After you have determined that there are messages in your inbox, you probably will want to read them. You do this by using the xp_readmail stored procedure. The syntax for this procedure is as follows:

```
xp_readmail ([@msg_id = msg_id] [, @type = type [OUTPUT]]
     [, @peek = {'true' | 'false'}]
     [, @suppress_attach = {'true' | 'false'}]
     [, @originator = @sender OUTPUT]
     [, @subject = @subject_line OUTPUT]
     [, @message = @body_of_message OUTPUT]
     [, @recipients = @recipient_list OUTPUT]
     [, @cc_list = @cc_list OUTPUT]
     [, @bcc_list = @bcc_list OUTPUT]
     [, @date_received = @date OUTPUT]
     [, @unread = {'true' | 'false'}]
     [, @attachments = @temp_file_paths OUTPUT])
     [, @skip_bytes = @bytes_to skip OUTPUT]
     [, @msg_length = @length_in_bytes OUTPUT])
```

The following section cover the parts of this syntax.

@msg_id

This parameter specifies the ID of the message to read.

@type

Use this parameter to return the message type of the item being read.

@peek

This parameter enables SQL Server to view the message without changing its status to read. You are, in essence, being allowed to *peek* at the message without affecting its status. This item accepts the values 'true' and 'false'. The default value of 'false' signifies that the message status *will* be changed.

@suppress_attach

Attachments can pose an interesting problem for any program that is trying to deal with e-mail. The *@suppress_attach* parameter allows you to read the message without also reading the attachments. Normally, when an attachment is read, it is stored in a temporary file on disk. This process wastes drive space and increases the overall time it takes to process the spool. By specifying a value of 'true' for this option, though, you can tell SQL Server to ignore the attachments. The default value for this option is 'true'.

@originator

This item is an output parameter that returns the mail address of the message sender. In order to reserve enough space for the entire e-mail address, we recommend that you pass a variable that has been defined as varchar(255).

@subject

This output parameter returns the subject line of the message. Again, we advise that you pass a variable that has been defined as varchar(255).

@message

This output parameter returns up to 255 bytes of the message text. When used in conjunction with the @msg_length and @skip_bytes parameters, the entire message text can be read, regardless of its length. We go into how to do this a little later.

@recipients

This parameter returns the list of the recipients of the mail message. Recipients' names are separated by a semicolon (;). Again, define this variable as varchar(255).

@cc_list

This parameter returns the list of the copied recipients (cc:'ed) of the mail message. Recipients' names are separated by a semicolon (;). As always, define this variable as varchar(255).

@bcc_list

This parameter returns the list of people who were blind cc:'ed on the message. It behaves just like the @cc_list parameter.

@date_received

This parameter returns the date on which the message was received. This variable also needs to be defined as a varchar(255). If you need to do any date arithmetic or comparisons, you need to use the CONVERT function.

@unread

This parameter specifies whether or not only unread messages are considered. Like the other true/false options, the acceptable input values for this item are 'true' and 'false'. The default value for this parameter is 'true'.

@attachments

As we mentioned earlier, when a message that contains attachments is processed — and you've instructed SQL Server not to ignore them — the attached files are stored on disk in temporary files. This parameter returns a semicolon-separated (;) list of those temporary files. The list will be in the order of the attachments.

@skip_bytes

If a value other than 0 is passed for input, this parameter specifies the number of bytes to skip before reading the next 255 bytes (max) of the message into the @body_of_message output parameter. When @skip_bytes is used, @body_of_message will include the next portion of the message, and @bytes_to_skip will return with the next starting point within the message (the previous @bytes_to_skip plus the length of @body_of_message).

@msg_length

This parameter returns the total number of bytes in the message. When this message is used in conjunction with the @skip_bytes parameter, you can process messages of an arbitrary length.

We will give examples of xp_readmail in our listserver application. For now, we forge ahead with the definition of xp_sendmail.

xp_sendmail

OK, you've now found the messages addressed to you and read them. Surely, some of them require replies! You can reply by using the xp_sendmail procedure. The syntax for it is as follows:

```
xp_sendmail @recipient = recipient [; recipientn; ]
     [, @message = message]
     [, @query = query]
     [, @attachments = attachments]
     [, @copy_recipients = recipient [; recipientn]
     [, @blind_copy_recipients = recipient [; recipientn;]
     [, @subject = subject]
     [, @type = type]
     [, @attach_results = {'true' | 'false'}]
     [, @no_output = {'true' | 'false'}]
     [, @no_header = {'true' | 'false'}]
     [, @width = width]
     [, @separator = separator]
     [, @echo_error = {'true' | 'false'}]
     [, @set_user = user]
     [, @dbuse = dbname]
```

The following sections cover the parameters of this syntax.

@recipient

This required parameter specifies the list of addresses to whom you want to send your message. If you need to send the item to more than one recipient, simply separate them by semicolons (;).

@message

This parameter specifies the text of the message being sent.

@query

If you specify this parameter, SQL Server attempts to execute its contents as a query and send the results.

@attachments

This parameter specifies any files that need to be sent as attachments to the message. Once again, if you need to send more than one file, simply list them here separated by semicolons.

@copy_recipients

This parameter contains the addresses of the users to whom you want to cc: the message.

@blind_copy_recipients

This parameter contains the addresses of the users to whom you want to bcc: the message.

@subject

This is an optional parameter that specifies the subject of the e-mail. If you do not specify a subject, "SQL Server Message" will be used.

@type

This parameter holds the message type for the e-mail. See our explanation in the section dealing with the xp_findnextmsg procedure for a more in-depth discussion of this setting.

@attach_results

This parameter indicates whether SQL Server should send the results of @query as an attached text file or appended to the main message text. The default parameter 'false' means that the results are not sent as a separate file, but are appended to the message text.

If this value is set to 'true', however, one of two things will occur:

- If the parameter @attachments is not NULL, SQL Server uses the first filename specified for the name of the attached results file.
- If @attachments is NULL, SQL Server generates a new filename with a .TXT extension for the results.

@no_output

This setting determines whether anything is returned to the client session that sent the e-mail. The default value of 'false' means that the session *does* receive output from the mail operation.

@no_header

This parameter specifies whether column header information is sent with the query results. The default value of 'false' means that column headings *will* be sent.

@width

This parameter sets the line width of the output text for a message that uses the @query parameter. For queries that produce long output rows, use @width together with @attach_results to send the output without line breaks in the middle of result lines. The default width is 80 characters. If your output lines are longer than this value, they will wrap.

@separator

This setting specifies the column separator (field terminator) for each column of the results set. This is particularly handy if you expect that the sent results will need to be imported into another application, such as a spreadsheet or word processor. This is identical to the /t parameter of BCP or isql.

@echo_error

This parameter allows SQL Server to capture any error messages that may occur when running the instructions in the *@query* parameter and append them to the end of the mail message. This will prevent those errors from being reflected in the error log. The only other important thing to realize with this parameter is that if you set it to 'false', the xp_sendmail procedure will always return 0.

@set_user

This setting specifies the security context in which the query should be run. The default is 'guest' (the *guest* user).

@dbuse

This parameter specifies the database context in which the query should be run. The default is NULL (which means the user is placed in his or her default database).

xp_deletemail

After you have read and responded to a particular e-mail message, you probably will want to delete it. You do this by using the xp_deletemail stored procedure. Its syntax is as follows:

```
xp_deletemail [@msg_id = ] msg_id
```

SQLMail and Security

When the @query parameter is used, xp_sendmail establishes another connection to your SQL Server machine as the user specified in the @set_user parameter. This happens so that a user cannot inadvertently run a query that he or she would not normally have been able to run. (Remember, the xp_sendmail procedure normally has the same rights as the SA!) The other implication of this security feature is that the xp_sendmail procedure can have its query operations blocked by another query. In other words, you still have the same contention issues with this procedure as you do with a normal user.

@msg_id

This parameter specifies the ID (as assigned by xp_findnextmsg) of the mail message in the inbox that should be deleted.

Inelegant, Ugly, and Just Plain Bad!

At this point, we feel we really need to mention something that we regard as a *major* shortcoming of SQL Server: the inability to handle character strings greater than 255 characters gracefully. Wait a minute! We know what you are thinking. Yes, SQL Server does have a column type called *text* that can handle a huge amount of character data. The problem, though, is this: You cannot declare a variable of type *text*, only a column. Here are a few examples of what we are discussing.

Big messages, big problems

Let's say that you want to send a message, using xp_sendmail, that has a list of recipients greater than 255 characters. How do you do it? The answer is that you can't — at least not all in the same message. The reason is that the *varchar* datatype only supports up to 255 characters. In our opinion, it should support up to 32K of character data. (We choose this number because it is what a number of other DBMSs do, and we have found it to be quite adequate.)

OK, so you don't think that's a big deal. Try this one on for size. How do you send a note with a message that's greater than 255 characters? Give up? The answer is that you have to create a table with a varchar(255) column, insert your message as rows in the table, and use the @query parameter of xp_sendmail. The following code illustrates this:

```
create table foo (mtext varchar(255))

insert into foo values ('this is ')
insert into foo values ('a really stupid ')
insert into foo values ('way to ')
insert into foo values ('have to ')
insert into foo values ('do things.')

execute xp_sendmail
     @recipients='root',
     @query='select rtrim(mtext) from foo',
     @no_header='true'

drop table foo
```

Now, admit it! That's a little less than elegant. This point will become even more important when we discuss sp_processmail.

Processing Messages Automatically with sp_processmail

The last several sections of this chapter have been spent talking about the various stored procedures you can use to process e-mail with SQL Server. This section shows you how to put it all together.

Microsoft includes a stored procedure with SQL Server called sp_processmail. This procedure processes all the e-mail in a particular inbox by treating all the messages as SQL queries. The results are then returned to the sender and anyone who may have been cc:'d on the original message.

The syntax for sp_processmail is as follows:

```
sp_processmail [@subject = subject] [[,] @filetype = filetype]
     [[,] @separator = separator] [[,] @set_user = user] [[,]
  @dbuse = bname]
```

@subject

This parameter specifies the subject line of mail messages to interpret as queries for SQL Server. When specified, sp_processmail processes only messages that have this subject. By default, SQL Server processes all mail messages as though they were queries.

@filetype

This parameter specifies the file extension to be used when sending the results set file back to the message sender. The default is .TXT.

@separator

This parameter specifies the column separator (field terminator) for each column of the results set (this information is passed to the xp_sendmail extended stored procedure to return the results set back to the message sender). The default is 'TAB', which is a special case for the tab character to be used between columns.

@set_user

This parameter specifies the security context in which the query should be run. The default is 'guest' (the *guest* user).

@dbuse

@dbuse specifies the database context in which the query should be run. The default is the *master* database.

SP_PROCESSMAIL AS A LEARNING EXAMPLE

The sp_processmail procedure is a good starting point to really understand how to use all the SQLMail components. The following is the commented source code to sp_processmail. (The comments were added by us!) Take a minute and read through it. Afterwards, we will cover a few important points about the code and the process.

```
/***********************
  Variable Declarations
************************/
```

```
declare @status int
declare @msg_id varchar(64)
declare @originator varchar(255)
declare @cc_list varchar(255)
declare @msgsubject varchar(255)
declare @query varchar(255)
declare @messages int
declare @mapifailure int
declare @resultmsg varchar(80)
declare @filename varchar(12)

select @messages=0
select @mapifailure=0

if @separator='tab' select @separator=CHAR(9)


/****************************************
  Begin main loop. The (1=1) test in the
  while statement would normally cause
  this loop to run forever. The presence
  of the break statements, however, fixes
  that problem.
****************************************/

while (1=1)
  begin

    /****************************************
       Get next message. If there are none,
       exit the main loop.
     ****************************************/

    exec @status = xp_findnextmsg
              @msg_id=@msg_id output,
              @unread_only='true'

    if @status <> 0
              begin
                        select @mapifailure=1
                        break
              end

    if @msg_id is null break

    /****************************************
      Read the found message. Exit on error.
     ****************************************/
```

(continued)

(continued)

```
  exec @status = xp_readmail
            @msg_id=@msg_id,
            @originator=@originator output,
            @cc_list=@cc_list output,
            @subject=@msgsubject output,
            @message=@query output,
            @peek='true',
            @suppress_attach='true'

   if @status <> 0
            begin
                    select @mapifailure=1
                    break
            end

    /**************************************
      If this message should be processed,
      generate a random filename, return a
      message with the query results attached
      as an attachment with that filename,
      and delete the message.
     **************************************/

if ((@subject IS NULL) OR (@subject=@msgsubject))
begin

     select @filename='SQL' +
     convert(varchar,ROUND(RAND()*100000,0)) + '.' + @filetype

     exec @status = xp_sendmail
                    @recipients=@originator,
                    @copy_recipients=@cc_list,
                    @message=@query,
                    @query=@query,
                    @subject='Query Results',
                    @separator=@separator,
                    @width=256,
                    @attachments=@filename,
                    @attach_results='true',
                    @no_output='true',
                    @echo_error='true',
                    @set_user=@set_user,
                    @dbuse=@dbuse

            if @status <> 0
                    begin
                            select @mapifailure=1
```

```
                    break
              end

        select @messages=@messages+1

        exec xp_deletemail @msg_id

    end
end

/***************************************
  When the main loop is exited, raise an
  error that reports the number of
  successfully processed messages. Error
  15079 is defined in the sysmessages
  table as "Queries Processed: %d."
 ***************************************/

 if @mapifailure=0
       begin
          raiserror(15079,-1,-1,@messages)
          return(1)
       end
 else
    return(0)
```

The biggest shortcoming of this code is that it absolutely cannot handle a query greater than 255 characters. Quite frankly, that's just plain unreasonable because it's very easy to construct a meaningful query that exceeds that amount. As a result, this code is going to need some serious reworking.

WARNING — kludge ahead!◀

The following code is a kludge. It works, but it's ugly and inelegant. The only reason we are showing it to you is that we can't figure out any other way to do it!

Solution #1: The kludge

The basic strategy to handle a large query is this:

1. Create a table with two columns. The first is an integer field and will be used to keep the message chunks in order. The second column is a varchar(255). We will use this column to store each chunk of the message returned by xp_readmail.

2. Read each chunk (in order) from the table into a set of variables. Yes, this is the most efficient way. If you try to assign the variables directly with each call to xp_readmail, you will find that you will have to hard code as many calls to xp_readmail as you have predefined variables — in this case, 40.
3. Dynamically create a view with the variables you have populated. Yes, the view is necessary. We'll go into a little more detail a little later.
4. Send the message out with the @query parameter set to 'select * from <created_view>', where created_view is the name of the view you made with the populated variables.

The following code reads the next message in the inbox and processes it according to the preceding steps. This code should probably be put in a stored procedure with the @mId variable passed in as a parameter. Please try to keep the preceding steps in mind as you read it. Afterwards, we will cover some of the important issues surrounding this implementation.

```
use tempdb

create table foo (c1 int, c2 varchar(255))

/**********************************
     Insert Query Into Table
**********************************/

declare @mId varchar(255)
declare @mText varchar(255)
declare @sBytes int
declare @mLength int
declare @iCtr int
declare @sRecipients varchar(255)

select @iCtr = 1

exec master..xp_findnextmsg @msg_id = @mId OUTPUT

exec master.. xp_readmail
     @msg_id = @mid,
     @peek = 'true',
     @message = @mText OUTPUT,
     @skip_bytes = @sBytes OUTPUT,
     @originator = @sRecipients OUTPUT,
     @msg_length = @mLength OUTPUT

insert into foo values (@iCtr, @mText)
select @iCtr = @iCtr + 1
```

```
while (@sBytes < @mLength)
begin
      exec master..xp_readmail
              @msg_id = @mid,
              @peek = 'true',
              @message = @mText OUTPUT,
              @skip_bytes = @sBytes OUTPUT

      insert into foo values (@iCtr, @mText)
      select @iCtr = @iCtr + 1

end

exec master..xp_deletemail @mid

/*****************************
      Process Query
*****************************/

declare @1 varchar(255), @2 varchar(255), @3 varchar(255),
      @4 varchar(255), @5 varchar(255), @6 varchar(255),
      @7 varchar(255), @8 varchar(255), @9 varchar(255),
      @10 varchar(255), @11 varchar(255), @12 varchar(255),
      @13 varchar(255), @14 varchar(255), @15 varchar(255),
      @16 varchar(255), @17 varchar(255), @18 varchar(255),
      @19 varchar(255), @20 varchar(255), @21 varchar(255),
      @22 varchar(255), @23 varchar(255), @24 varchar(255),
      @25 varchar(255), @26 varchar(255), @27 varchar(255),
      @28 varchar(255), @29 varchar(255), @30 varchar(255),
      @31 varchar(255), @32 varchar(255), @33 varchar(255),
      @34 varchar(255), @35 varchar(255), @36 varchar(255),
      @37 varchar(255), @38 varchar(255), @39 varchar(255),
      @40 varchar(255)

select @1 = c2 from foo where c1 = 1
select @2 = c2 from foo where c1 = 2
select @3 = c2 from foo where c1 = 3
select @4 = c2 from foo where c1 = 4
select @5 = c2 from foo where c1 = 5
select @6 = c2 from foo where c1 = 6
select @7 = c2 from foo where c1 = 7
select @8 = c2 from foo where c1 = 8
select @9 = c2 from foo where c1 = 9
select @10 = c2 from foo where c1 = 10
select @11 = c2 from foo where c1 = 11
select @12 = c2 from foo where c1 = 12
select @13 = c2 from foo where c1 = 13
select @14 = c2 from foo where c1 = 14
```

(continued)

(continued)

```
select @15 = c2 from foo where c1 = 15
select @16 = c2 from foo where c1 = 16
select @17 = c2 from foo where c1 = 17
select @18 = c2 from foo where c1 = 18
select @19 = c2 from foo where c1 = 19
select @20 = c2 from foo where c1 = 20
select @21 = c2 from foo where c1 = 21
select @23 = c2 from foo where c1 = 22
select @23 = c2 from foo where c1 = 23
select @24 = c2 from foo where c1 = 24
select @25 = c2 from foo where c1 = 25
select @26 = c2 from foo where c1 = 26
select @27 = c2 from foo where c1 = 27
select @28 = c2 from foo where c1 = 28
select @29 = c2 from foo where c1 = 29
select @30 = c2 from foo where c1 = 30
select @31 = c2 from foo where c1 = 31
select @32 = c2 from foo where c1 = 32
select @33 = c2 from foo where c1 = 33
select @34 = c2 from foo where c1 = 34
select @35 = c2 from foo where c1 = 35
select @36 = c2 from foo where c1 = 36
select @37 = c2 from foo where c1 = 37
select @38 = c2 from foo where c1 = 38
select @39 = c2 from foo where c1 = 39
select @40 = c2 from foo where c1 = 40

execute('create view vTmp as ' +
      @1+@2+@3+@4+@5+@6+@7+@8+@9+@10+
      @11+@12+@13+@14+@15+@16+@17+@18+@19+@20+
      @21+@22+@23+@24+@25+@26+@27+@28+@29+@30+
      @31+@32+@33+@34+@35+@36+@37+@38+@39+@40)

execute master..xp_sendmail
      @recipients=@sRecipients,
      @query = 'select * from tempdb..vTmp',
      @width = 255

drop table foo
drop view vTmp
use master
```

There are a few things we would like to point out about this code. First, it has a couple of limitations:

- The query it processes must be valid for the CREATE VIEW command. If it is not, this routine will generate an error.
- This code will only handle queries up to 10K in size. (40 variables × 255 characters per variable = 10,200 characters.) If you need it to do more, then you have to hard code more variables.

There are also probably a few things in the preceding implementation that don't seem immediately obvious. In the next couple of pages, we will explain our reasons for this odd strategy.

Why read the message into a table?

The first thing that you are probably curious about is why we read the message chunks into a table, instead of directly into variables. We do this to save a lot of space, time, and trouble. If the chunks were not read into the table, the following line of code would have to be executed for each of the 40 variables:

```
if (@sBytes >0)
begin
   exec master.. xp_readmail
         @msg_id = @mid,
         @peek = 'true',
         @message = @1 OUTPUT,
         @skip_bytes = @sBytes OUTPUT
end
```

So, then, why don't we just use dynamic SQL in some kind of loop? Perhaps something like this:

```
declare @sSQL varchar(255)

select @sSQL = "exec master.. xp_readmail
   @msg_id = @mid,
   @peek = 'true',
   @message = @1 OUTPUT,
   @skip_bytes = @sBytes OUTPUT"

execute (@sSQL)
```

Clearly, if we put this code in some kind of while loop, we can overcome the need for tables, right? Wrong! The problem is that execute will not recognize the local variables. For example, the following will *not* work.

```
declare @myVar varchar(255)
select @myVar = 'This is a test'
execute("select 'myVar is:' + @myVar")
```

The reason is that execute runs in its own transaction. Therefore, it cannot see any variables that are local to other transactions.

Why bother creating the view?

The odd thing about our implementation is that we needed to create a view. Why not just set the @query parameter to xp_sendmail to @1+@2+@3...+@40? This one is easy. What do you do if the length of the string produced by @1+@2+@3...+@40 is greater than 255 characters? After all, the @query parameter in xp_sendmail is defined as a varchar(255).

A couple of parting shots

The entire reason this kludge even works is that execute takes parameters that are in excess of 255 characters. It simply converts the resulting string to a *text* type. That's right, we said a *text* type! Apparently, SQL Server *can* handle strings larger than 255 characters, but, for some reason, Microsoft elected not share this capability with us mere mortals.

Solution #2: Canned, planned, and happy

Even with the preceding extensions, supporting ad hoc queries via e-mail is a real nightmare. We recommend a much simpler approach: a listserver. A *listserver*, at least for the purposes of this book, is a program that accepts e-mail and processes prebuilt queries. Think about it: users can send mail with a subject like

```
"run monthly exception report using 'John Smith', 1, 02/18/96"
```

and get back meaningful results. In our experience, this approach has been much easier to write and maintain.

How to

The crux of this system is a lookup table that you keep that has the common name of a query and the name of the stored procedure that actually implements it, for example:

common_name	stored_proc_name
monthly exception report	sp_mo_ex_rpt
mailing list	sp_mail_list
inventory list	sp_inventory_list

The only thing you would have to write is a routine to interpret the subject line. For example, assume that @subject holds the subject line and @sender is the address of the sender of the e-mail. The following code runs the correct query and e-mails the results back:

```
declare @uIndex int
declare @commonName varchar(255)
declare @parms varchar(255)
declare @spName varchar(255)
declare @sCommand varchar(255)

if (SUBSTRING(@subject,1,3) = 'RUN')
begin
     select @uIndex = CHARINDEX('USING', @subject)
     select @commonName = SUBSTRING(@subject,4,@uIndex - 4)
     select @parms = SUBSTRING(@subject,@uIndex + 5,255)
end

select @spName = stored_proc_name
from lookup_table
where common_name = @common_name

select @sCommand = 'execute ' + @spName + ' ' + @parms

execute master..xp_sendmail
   @recipients=@sender,
   @query = @sCommand,
   @width = 255
```

Of course, this approach has a downside. Your users cannot run any ad-hoc queries. They all must be pre-built and maintained by the SA or DBO. In the end, of course, the choice is yours.

Summary

Integrating SQL Server with e-mail can be both practical and fun. You can certainly do more with it than simply report errors or log alerts. In this chapter, you learned the ins and outs of how to use SQLMail more effectively as a regular part of your DBMS strategy. Specifically, you learned that you can use SQLMail to extend the accessibility beyond the confines of your corporate network — to the entire world!

Review Questions

Q: What are the three basic steps for setting up SQLMail?

A: The steps are the following:

1. Install and configure a MAPI-compliant e-mail system on a server on your network.
2. Create a user account through which SQL Server can log in.
3. Configure the SQLMail parameters of your SQL Server with the userid and password of a valid account for the mail post-office.

Q: How do I send a message that is larger than 255 characters?

A: Create a table that has a varchar(255) column and insert your message there. Then, use the @query option of xp_sendmail and set it to "select * from my_table". For example:

```
create table foo (mtext varchar(255))

insert into foo values ('this is ')
insert into foo values ('a really stupid ')
insert into foo values ('way to ')
insert into foo values ('have to ')
insert into foo values ('do things.')

execute xp_sendmail
  @recipients='root',
  @query='select rtrim(mtext) from foo',
  @no_header='true'

drop table foo
```

Q: How do I have SQL Server check and answer mail every *n* minutes ?

A: Create a stored procedure that performs the mail functions and create a task that runs it every *n* minutes. Don't worry; tasks are covered in the next chapter!

Chapter

Alerts and Tasks

20

If you are like most people who administer a database, your office isn't in the same place as your server. This means you probably find out about server problems when angry users start calling you! There is a better way. You can set up a series of notifications called *alerts*, which can let you know when a situation is occurring that might cause a problem. As you begin to find out which of these problems are likely to occur again, you can also set up routines to run automatically to fix them. These routines are called *tasks*.

What's in This Chapter

In this chapter, we examine two of the best weapons you have against catastrophic server problems: *alerts* and *tasks*. We also show some practical things you can do with these tools to make your life as an administrator a lot easier. These things include

- Using alerts to supplement your office time
- Detecting and dealing with unwanted system users
- Using performance based alerts

Danger, Will Robinson!

Wouldn't it be nice if your database server could warn you before a bad thing was about to happen? Think about it: your users would never get upset at you. Well, we are happy to tell you that you can make this pipe dream a reality. All you need is a little time and some ingenuity.

One of the really nice features of SQL Server is that it has the capability to notify you via e-mail or pager when certain user-defined events occur. These notifications are called *alerts*. To configure the alerts for your server, simply click a server in the SQL Enterprise Manager and select Server⇨ Alerts. The window shown in Figure 20-1 appears.

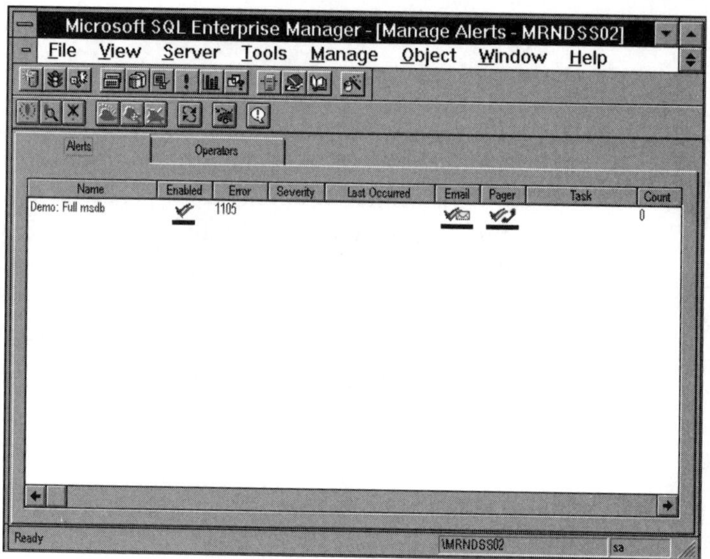

Figure 20-1:
This window shows you all the alerts that are currently defined for your server.

Operators

The purpose of defining an alert is so that the server can automatically notify someone of a certain event. These people are known as *operators*. If you click the Operators tab, the current window changes to the one shown in Figure 20-2.

At this point, you probably don't have any operators defined for your system. In order to explain and demonstrate alerts better, it's a good idea for you to go ahead and define one operator. To do this, click the new operator toolbar button. The screen shown in Figure 20-3 will appear.

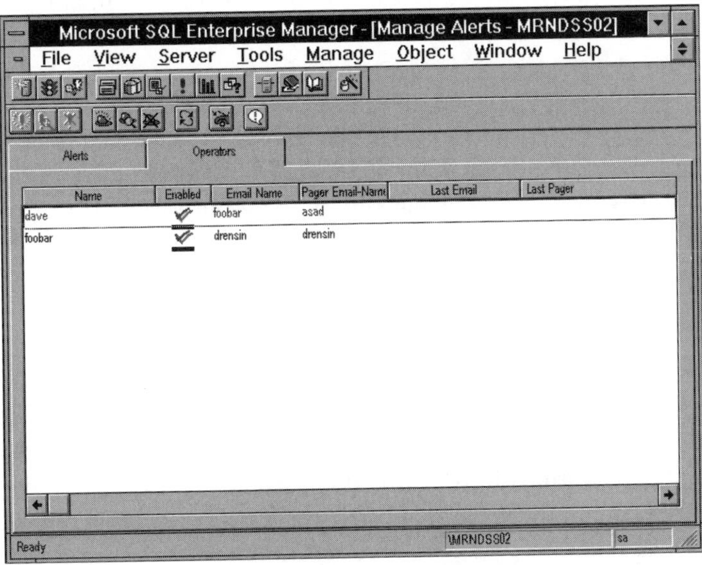

Figure 20-2:
This view shows all the operators that have been defined for this server. Remember, an operator is just someone who needs to be notified for a certain event.

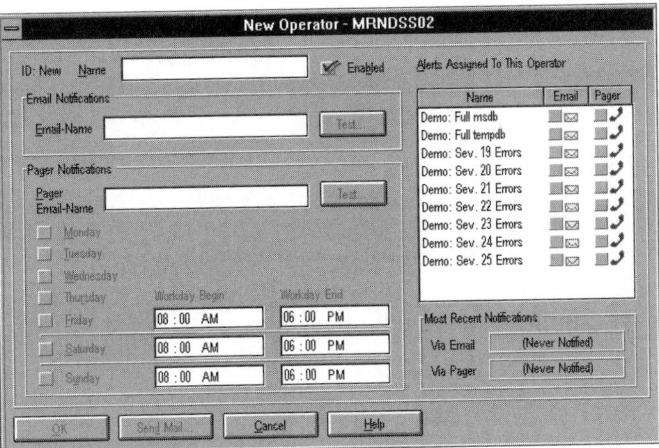

Figure 20-3:
This window lets you create a new operator for your system.

The following sections discuss the various options available in this window.

Name

Type the name you want to use for this operator. For example, if you plan to e-mail notifications of fatal events to a certain operator, you may want to choose a name like "Critical events operator."

Email-Name

This box holds the e-mail address of the operator. You can have SQL Server verify the address by clicking the Test button. SQL Server tells you whether the address you typed is valid.

Pager Notifications

Some e-mail systems are set up so that mail to a certain address triggers a machine to dial a phone number and send a message to a pager. If you have such a system, you can tell SQL Server to page this operator by filling in the Pager Notifications information. You can even specify which days to allow pages and during which hours by selecting the appropriate check boxes.

When you have finished setting up your operator, click the OK button.

Creating an alert

Now that you have created an operator to receive your notifications, it's time to create an alert. To do this, go back to the Alerts tab and click the New Alert toolbar item. The window shown in Figure 20-4 appears.

The following sections describe the parts of this New Alert window.

Name

This is the field where you put the name of your alert. It is best to keep this name as meaningful as possible. For example, if you are creating an alert for when the tempdb database fills up, you may want to give a name like "tempdb is full."

Alert Definition

This section of the window enables you to define what types of things will trigger your new alert. If you know the exact error number of the item that you want to trigger the alert, you can enter it in the Error Number box. If, on the other hand, you want to trap an entire class of errors, you can elect to have your alert fire for every error that has a certain severity level. You choose this option by selecting from the Severity list.

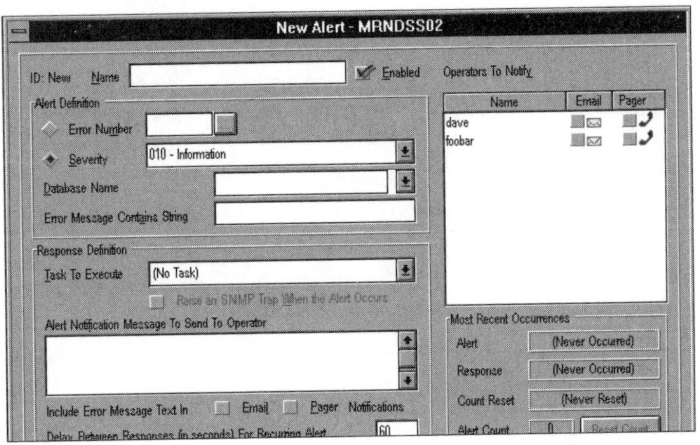

Figure 20-4:
This is the New Alert window. From here, you can define your new alert.

In many cases, you will only want to trigger an alert for an error that occurs in a specific database. To set this option, choose the appropriate database from the Database Name list.

Sometimes, you will want to lump together errors that do not share the same severity or error number. If, however, they share similar text, you can choose to signal the alert for them by entering their common text in the Error Message Contains String box. For example, SQL Server comes with four separate error messages defined with the word "fatal" in them. They all have different error numbers and severity levels. If you wanted to trigger the same alert for all of them, though, you would simply enter the word **fatal** in this box.

Response Definition

After you have defined which error(s) you want to trigger your alert, you must decide how you want your server to respond. The first thing you have to decide is whether you want your server to run a specific task when this alert is triggered. We haven't covered tasks yet, so we'll skip this for now. We'll come back to it, though.

Raising an SNMP Trap

SNMP stands for Simple Network Management Protocol. This is a standard set of messaging commands that can be used in conjunction with special monitoring software to keep better track of certain network processes. One of the new features of SQL Server 6.5 is support for the SNMP protocol. The process basically works like this: When a certain alert is triggered, SQL Server raises an SNMP trap. A *trap* is just a mechanism to notify some process (an agent) that a certain condition has occurred. Upon receipt of the trap, the agent forwards a message to a predefined set of workstations that a certain event has occurred. These workstations are running special monitoring programs that allow the users to read and interpret these messages. This system is very useful for anyone who has to manage several resources that are not in the same physical place. If you want your alert to raise an SNMP trap, check the Raise An SNMP Trap When The Alert Occurs check box.

The next thing you need to decide is what message you want to send to the operator. You type this in the Alert Notification Message To Send To Operator box. In our example, an appropriate message might be "The tempdb database is full. You'd better hurry up and do something, or you're gonna' get fired!"

Because all error messages have some text of their own, you probably will want to include it in the e-mail or page that you send to your operator. To do this, check the appropriate boxes on the Include Error Message Text In line.

The last thing you need to decide in this section is what to do about recurring errors. For example, if you elect to trigger an alert when the tempdb database fills up, you could be receiving a lot of messages in a very short period of time. You can mitigate this by choosing a delay between message responses. For example, if you choose a delay of 60 seconds, and 150 errors that meet your alert condition are triggered within a 59 second time frame, you will only receive notification of the first one. This is option is a great way to keep your e-mail box from filling up with unnecessary messages.

Operators To Notify

The last section of this window enables you to choose which operators to notify and whether to notify them by e-mail, pager, or both. Simply check the appropriate boxes to set this up.

Using alerts to supplement your office time

Let's say that you are working on your server enough during the day that you don't really need to set up alerts. After all, if a serious error occurs, you'll know about it. What do you do if a problem develops overnight or on the weekend? Unless you're the first person in the office, someone is bound to notice. A simple and unobtrusive solution to this problem to decide what kind of errors require your attention on a weekend or evening and set up alerts for them. Then create an operator whose pager e-mail is an address that you routinely check from home. By setting the pager e-mail to your address, you can control when the messages are sent. For example, you might define the alerts to send mail during the hours of 6 p.m. to 1 a.m. during the weekdays 10 a.m. to 1 a.m. on the weekends. That way, you can check your e-mail at your convenience for any problems that require your attention and you don't have to bother with an annoying pager.

Alert engine options

Another nice set of features in SQL Server is the capability to contend with failed alerts or to manage alerts for a set of servers from a centralized place. To access these options, click the Alert Engine Options button. The window shown in Figure 20-5 appears.

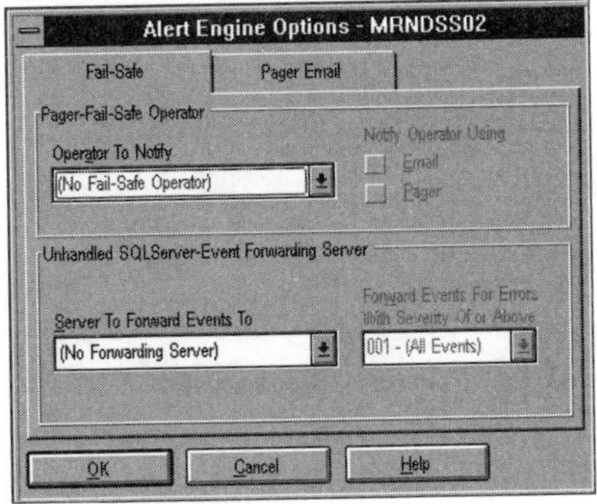

Figure 20-5:
This window allows you to set the alert engine options.

The Fail-Safe tab specifies how you want SQL Server to handle alerts that fail. An alert can fail because of an incorrect pager address, a problem with the e-mail system, or a gap in the pager schedules. When this occurs, you can have a certain operator paged or e-mailed. You specify this in the Operator To Notify box.

SQL Server also enables you to manage all events for a given group of servers from a central machine. Suppose that you have four machines acting as database servers. It would sure be nice not to have to add an alert to all four machines every time you want to trap another kind of event. You can avoid this problem by specifying a *forwarded event server*. A forwarded event server is a machine to which you want to send all events that do not have associated local alerts. When the remote server receives these events, it triggers any of its alerts that apply. These received events appear to the remote server as if they were generated locally. To specify a forwarded event server (that is, the server *receiving* the forwarded alerts), choose one of your predefined servers from the Server To Forward Events To list.

The other nice part of this window is the Pager Email tab (see Figure 20-6).

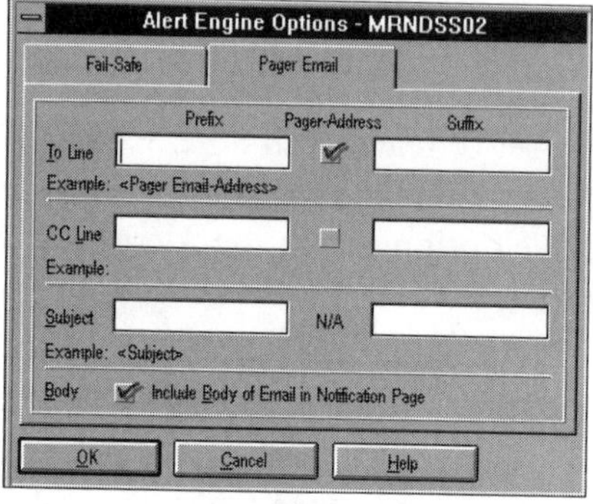

Figure 20-6:
You can set the Pager Email options from this window.

Forwarder Beware!

Electing to forward your events to a central server is great for event management but lousy for network bandwidth. SQL Server generates an awful lot of errors and events. If you have too many of them forwarding to another server, you can bring your network to a crawl.

The other problem is that you cannot have your alerts run tasks to fix the problems if the machine that the alert being triggered on is not the same machine from which the error came. In general, it is our recommendation that you forgo event forwarding and simply take care to keep your servers synchronized.

Using this tab, you set options that are specific to your e-mail paging system. Some systems require a special prefix or suffix for a pager e-mail address. For example, if Joe Smith has a pager e-mail account set up at a specific post office, his full address might be @PGRPO:jsmith. You can specify these special prefixes or suffixes in this tab for the To: and CC: lines of your e-mail message. You can also specify that the subject of your mail has a certain prefix. For example, perhaps you want all pager notifications to begin with "***PAGE*** ."

TASKS

Alerts are only half useful if all you can do is trap the errors that come predefined by SQL Server. The real power of alerts comes when you can run your own processes to deal with problems. These processes are called *tasks*. A task is really nothing more than a certain command, or set of commands, that is scheduled to run at a certain time or during a certain interval with a given frequency. To manage the tasks for your server, choose Server⇨Tasks in the SQL Enterprise Manager. The window shown in Figure 20-7 appears.

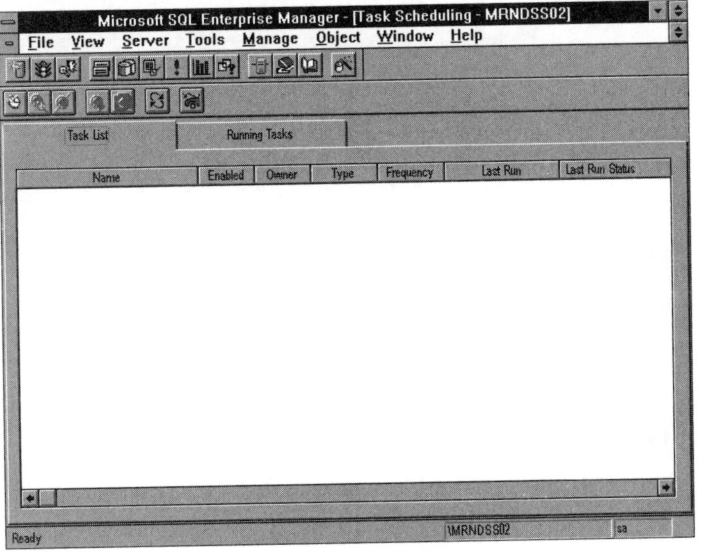

Figure 20-7:
The Server⇨Tasks menu gives you this window.

This is the list of all the tasks currently defined for your system. At this point, it's probably blank. No problem, that's easily remedied.

Creating a new task

To create a new task, click the New Task toolbar button. The window shown in Figure 20-8 opens.

The following sections discuss the parts of this window.

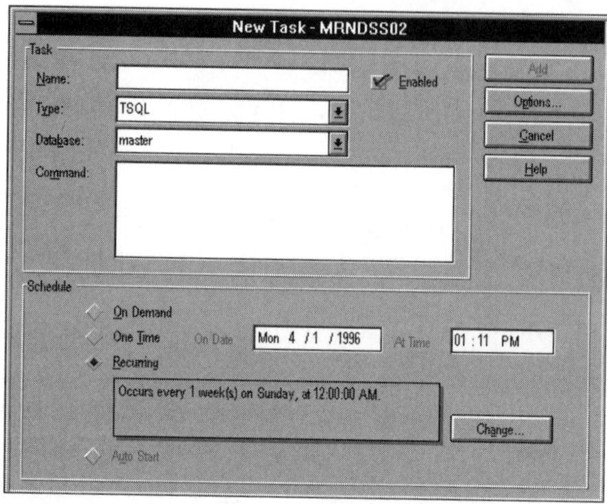

Figure 20-8:
You can create a new task in this window.

Name

This box holds the name you want to call your task. Again, you should name your tasks with something meaningful.

Type

A task can be one of five different types. They are the following:

- **CmdExec.** Specifies an operating-system command, or a .CMD or .EXE file to run. The command cannot contain UI components, such as Notepad or Paintbrush.

- **Distribution.** Specifies a replication distribution process command.
- **LogReader.** Specifies a replication log reader process command.
- **Sync.** Specifies a replication synchronization process command.
- **TSQL.** Specifies a Transact-SQL statement to be run against the selected database. The statement is limited to 255 characters and cannot contain embedded GO commands.

Database

Select from this list the database in which you want your task to run.

Command

This box is where you enter the actual command that constitutes your task. There are only a couple of restrictions here:

- You may not enter more than 255 characters.
- The commands you enter must match the type you specified in the Type option. For example, if you specified that the task is of type TSQL and you enter a command of **del c:\mydir*.***, the task generates an error because the command is not a valid Transact-SQL command.

Scheduling your new task

After you define what commands make up your new task, you have to decide when you want it to run. This is determined in the Schedule section of the New Task window.

On Demand

This option means that the task runs only when you specifically call it. There are two ways you can call a specific task. First, you can click the Run Task toolbar button from the main task list window. Second, you can make a call to the undocumented stored procedure sp_schedulersignal.

One Time

Use these options if you only want your task to run once.

sp_schedulersignal

sp_schedulersignal is a stored procedure that SQL Server uses to trigger scheduler events. It takes two parameters: @OpType (operation type) and @ID (the task id). Operation types can be any of the following: R, O, I, T, A, G, D, or E. Because this procedure is not documented anywhere, we don't know what these codes mean. What we *do* know is that an operation type of O (the letter O) runs the task specified by the @ID parameter. For example, the command *exec sp_schedulersignal 'O', 1* runs task 1.

Recurring

This option enables you to set your new task to run at certain times or during certain intervals. The default value is

```
Occurs every 1 week(s) on Sunday, at 12:00:00 AM.
```

To change this value, click the Change button. The window shown in Figure 20-9 opens.

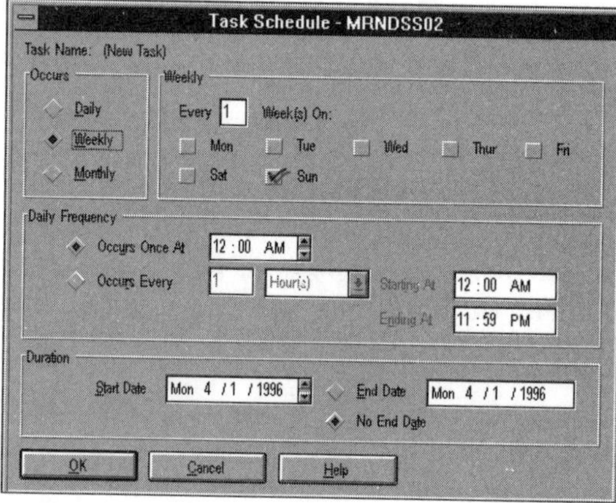

Figure 20-9:
This screen lets you change when the task runs.

This screen enables you to set your recurrence options. It's pretty self-explanatory, so we won't go into it here. When you have finished editing these options, click the OK button.

Task Options

Like alerts, tasks have certain other advanced options associated with them. To access these settings, click the Options button. The screen shown in Figure 20-10 appears.

Figure 20-10:
Edit the advanced task options here.

From this screen, you can specify whether or not someone is sent e-mail or a page to indicate successful or failed task executions, whether to log the event in the Windows NT event log options, and whether to retry the task. Of these, the Retries and Replication sections merit some further discussion.

The Retries options enable you to set the number of retry attempts for a failed task. It is important to note here that you cannot set retry attempts for Transact-SQL tasks. To modify the default retry behavior of a task (which is not to retry), change the Retry Attempts setting to any value between 0 and 256 and the Retry Delay setting to the number of minutes you want SQL Server to wait between attempts.

The Replication sections options specify a remote target server and database for LogReader and Distribution tasks only. It is unavailable for all other task types. When you have finished these options, click the OK button.

PUTTING IT ALL TOGETHER

In the last several sections, you have learned the basics of creating and maintaining your own tasks and alerts. In this section, we give you several practical examples of how to use tasks to make your life easier.

Intruder alert!

Oftentimes, it will become necessary for you to allow access to your SQL Server machine by users outside your corporate domain. In those cases, you probably will want to know when these people are actually logged on. In this section, we show you how to set up a monitoring process.

The basic process is as follows:

1. A given process runs periodically to determine how many users outside the domain are currently connected.
2. If that number is greater than 0, the process raises a user-defined error.
3. A specific alert fires for that event and sends e-mail to an operator to warn him or her of the intrusion.

The first thing you have to do is create a procedure that checks to see whether anyone outside your domain is using your server. Because the master..sysprocesses table keeps track of this for you already, this query should be pretty simple. The following is the code for it:

```
CREATE PROCEDURE usp_checkForIntruders @domainName varchar(255) AS

DECLARE @intruders int
DECLARE @msg varchar(255)

SELECT distinct rtrim(nt_domain) + '\' + nt_username full_name
      INTO #foo
      FROM sysprocesses
      WHERE nt_domain <> @domainName AND
              datalength(rtrim(nt_domain)) <> 0

SELECT @intruders = count(*) FROM #foo

SELECT @msg = 'There are %d users logged in to your system who are not members of
the domain ' + @domainName

IF (@intruders > 0)
raiserror (@msg,10,1,@intruders)

DROP TABLE #foo
GO
```

Next, we add a task that runs the new procedure once every half hour. Use your own domain name instead of home_net. Figure 20-11 shows this.

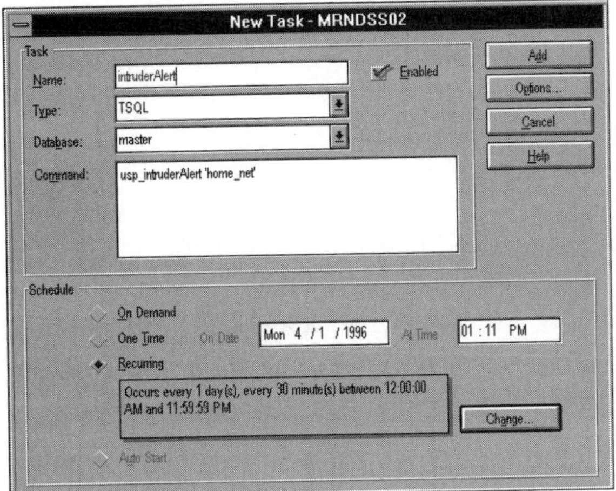

Figure 20-11:
Our completed task.

Finally, we create an alert to trap our new error. Figure 20-12 shows the completed alert.

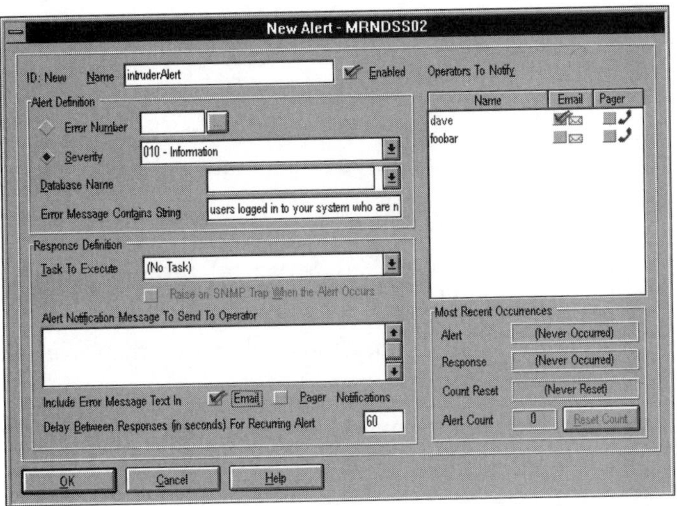

Figure 20-12:
Our completed alert.

Performance-based alerts

One of the biggest headaches an SA can face is when his or her production machine gets overloaded. When this happens, users can't connect, queries don't run, and everyone is generally annoyed. Wouldn't it be great if you could have your machine alert you when its CPU load was over a certain percentage? Think about it: you could kill runaway processes before they ate all of your CPU. Microsoft thought you might want to do this, so it gave the Performance Monitor utility the capability to generate alerts. In this section, we briefly discuss how to set an alert threshold for CPU load in the SQL Performance Monitor.

To generate an alert for a CPU threshold, you first need to define an error that represents the specific event you want to trap. For example, say that you want to get an alert each time your server exceeds 75 percent CPU usage. You can create a user-defined error by using the sp_addmessage procedure, as follows:

```
sp_addmessage 50003, 10, 'CPU Usage Is Over 75%', 'us_english', 'true'
```

This code adds a new message (number 50003), which has a severity level of 10, a text of 'CPU Usage Is Over 75%', uses a default language of *us_english*, and is logged to the Windows NT Event Log.

In order to get *any* event to trigger an alert, the event *must* be set to log to the Windows NT Event Log.◀

Now that the appropriate message has been created, the performance monitor must be configured to generate the alert. To do this, follow these steps:

1. From the Microsoft SQL Server 6.5 program group, choose the SQL Performance Monitor icon.
2. From the View menu, choose Alert, and then from the Edit menu, choose Add to Alert.
3. From the Object box, select a SQL Server object (in this case, % Processor Time), and then from the Counter box, select a counter.
4. In the Alert If box, select either the Over or Under option, and then type a threshold (a number) in the Alert If box. In this example, you want to choose the Over option and enter a value of **75.00**.
5. Enter a SQLALRTR.EXE command in the Run Program on Alert box. Type: **sqlalrtr /E50003**. When the event occurs (processor time over

75%), the program SQLALRTR.EXE will run, and it will post an error 50003, the message we created earlier.

6. In the Run Program on Alert box, choose the Every Time option.
7. Choose Add.
8. Choose Done.

Summary

In this chapter, you learned how to preemptively strike against those errors that can keep system administrators pulling their hair out. With a little creativity, you can configure your systems to take care of many common and annoying administration headaches. At the very least, you can be warned before certain critical situations become fatal.

For example, you can actually expand the intruder alert example to kill the offending connections. With a little effort, you might also create a procedure to kill processes until the CPU load falls under a certain threshold. This way, you could prevent your servers from ever being overloaded!

These are just two examples of how you can build on the things you have learned in this chapter to help make your job easier and more manageable.

Review Questions

Q: What are the advantages to alert forwarding?

A: The big advantage to alert forwarding is the ability to maintain and trap alerts from a central server.

Q: What are the disadvantages to alert forwarding?

A: There are two big problems with it.

- If you have many servers forwarding many alerts, you can chew up a lot of network bandwidth.
- If you manage all alerts in an enterprise from a central server, you have no way to know which servers generated the alert. Worse still, you cannot automatically run tasks to deal with the problem because the tasks will run on the central machine, not the machine that generated the error.

Q: Why should you create a stored procedure for each task you want to run?

A: You don't have to. It's a good idea, though, because you are limited to 255 characters for the command you can enter when defining a task. Because stored procedure names are less than 255 characters, this is a good way to beat this restriction.

Q: If the sp_schedulersignal stored procedure is undocumented, how did we discover it ?

A: Patience! We will show you how to discover all sorts of neat little undocumented things in the next part of the book!

Chapter

The Microsoft Distributed Transaction Coordinator

21

The early 1990s ushered in a new era of applications computing with the widespread adoption of the client/server paradigm. Six years later, the computing world is beginning to shift again. This time, though, the new pattern of distribution is not with the data, but with the actual application execution components. The new model looks something like the one in Figure 21-1.

The idea is that there are three types of servers in the environment: file servers, database servers, and process servers.

- **File Servers.** These machines share common file space among machines in the enterprise.
- **Database Servers.** These machines share data among machines in the enterprise.
- **Process Servers.** These machines share computing processes among many machines in the enterprise.

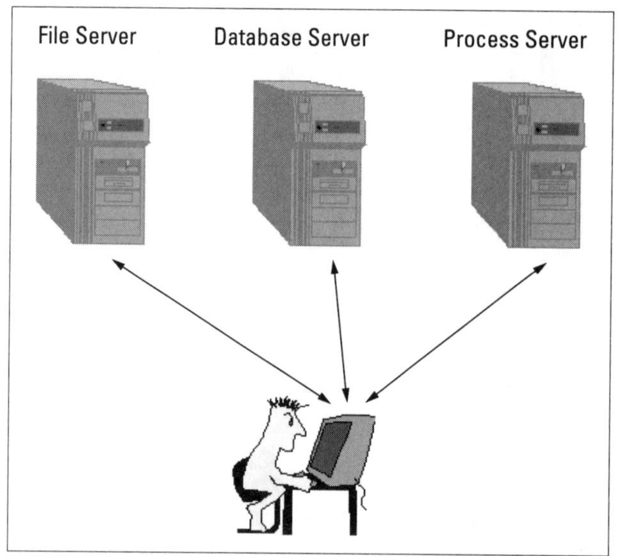

Figure 21-1:
This is a basic distributed processing architecture.

This movement toward the distribution of application processes is known as *distributed computing*. With SQL Server 6.5, Microsoft provides developers with the beginning steps toward enterprise-wide distributed computing. This is implemented with the Microsoft Distributed Transaction Coordinator (MS DTC).

What's in This Chapter

In this chapter, you will learn the basics of the Microsoft Distributed Transaction Coordinator. Some of the topics we will cover are the following:

- What is a distributed transaction?
- What are the tools used to monitor and control distributed transactions, and how are they used?
- How can the principles of distributed transactions be used to create a more fault-tolerant system, to balance processing load, and to improve application power?

The Distributed Transaction Model

In a nutshell, a *distributed* transaction is special type of transaction whose disposition depends on processes running on two different machines. A brief example can help demonstrate this arrangement:

```
begin distributed transaction

insert into myTable values ('a',1)
execute wally.pubs..addToMytable 'a', 1
/* note that the full name of this stored procedure includes the servername,
'wally', as well as the database, 'pubs' */

commit transaction
go
```

This code is a simple illustration of a powerful concept. If either the INSERT statement or the remote stored procedure fails, *both* statements are rolled back. This is the power of a distributed transaction.

Here's what's happening behind the scenes when a distributed transaction is being processed:

1. The server on which you are running the original query (the local machine) starts processing a SQL query and detects a distributed transaction. It logs into the specified remote server and sends the requested action to its MS DTC.
2. The local machine finishes processing the SQL and sends the resultant disposition (whether the SQL succeeded) to the remote MS DTC.
3. If the local query encounters an error, the remote DTC rolls back the actions of the remote procedure.
4. If the remote procedure encounters an error, the local machine rolls back the effect of the local procedure.

Setting Up Distributed Transaction Processing

Setting up your servers to handle distributed transaction processing requires only two basic steps:

1. Configure the MS DTC.
2. Set up remote logins.

Configuring the MS DTC

The easiest way to configure the MS DTC for a server is through the SQL Enterprise Manager. Simply expand the tree for the target server, right-click the item named Distributed Transaction Coordinator, and choose the Configure option. Figure 21-2 shows the window that appears.

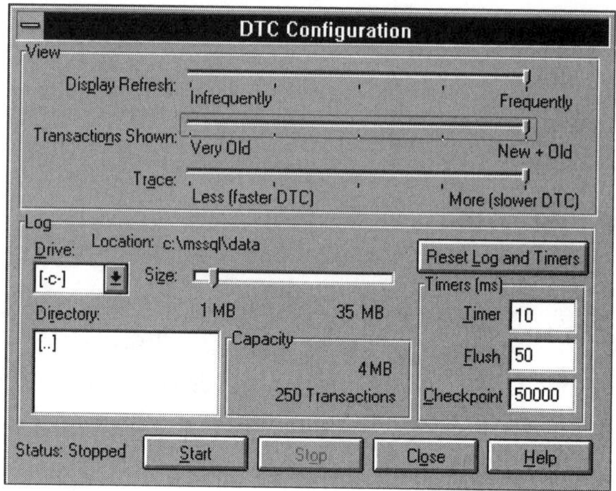

Figure 21-2:
Configure your MS DTC settings here.

You can control the MS DTC from the SQL Enterprise Manager only if you are running Windows NT. In other words, you cannot start, stop, or configure the MS DTC of a remote server using the SQL Enterprise Manager from a Windows 95 machine! ◀

The following sections describe the parts of the screen shown in Figure 21-2.

Display Refresh

This setting controls how often trace, statistical information, and the transaction list are sent from the MS DTC to the various view windows. More frequent updates increase the amount of resources needed and slow down overall DTC processing. The upside, though, is that more frequent display refreshes also provide more accurate information on the running MS DTC. The following values are used in the slider to indicate the update timing (left to right):

- Update the display every 20 seconds (default).
- Update the display every 10 seconds.
- Update the display every 5 seconds.
- Update the display every 3 seconds.
- Update the display every 1 second.

Transactions Shown

This setting controls how long a transaction must be active before being displayed in the Transactions view window. The following values are used in the slider to indicate the lengths of time (left to right):

- Show 5 minute-old transactions.
- Show 1 minute-old transactions.
- Show 30 second-old transactions (default).
- Show 10 second-old transactions.
- Show 1 second-old transactions.

Trace

This item controls the level of traces sent to the Trace view window. The following values are used in the slider to indicate the level of tracing (left to right):

- Send no tracing.
- Send only error traces (default).
- Send error and warning traces.
- Send error, warning, and informational traces.
- Send all traces.

Log

The MS DTC log file is always called MSDTC.LOG. These settings control various attributes of the file.

- **Location:** The location of the MS DTC log file, based on the Drive and Directory settings.
- **Drive:** The drive on which the MS DTC log file is located.

- **Directory.** The directory on which the log file is located.
- **Size.** The slider can be used to change the size of the MS DTC log file.
- **Capacity.** The current size of the MS DTC log file and the number of allowable concurrent transactions.

Warning

In order to change the size or location of the MS DTC log safely, you must do the following: Stop the MS DTC, change the desired settings, click the Reset Log and Timers button, and restart the MS DTC.◀

Setting up remote servers and logins

After you have configured the MS DTCs of the server you want to use, you need to define remote logins for them. To do so, click a server in the SQL Enterprise Manager, and choose Server⇨Remote Servers (see Figure 21-3).

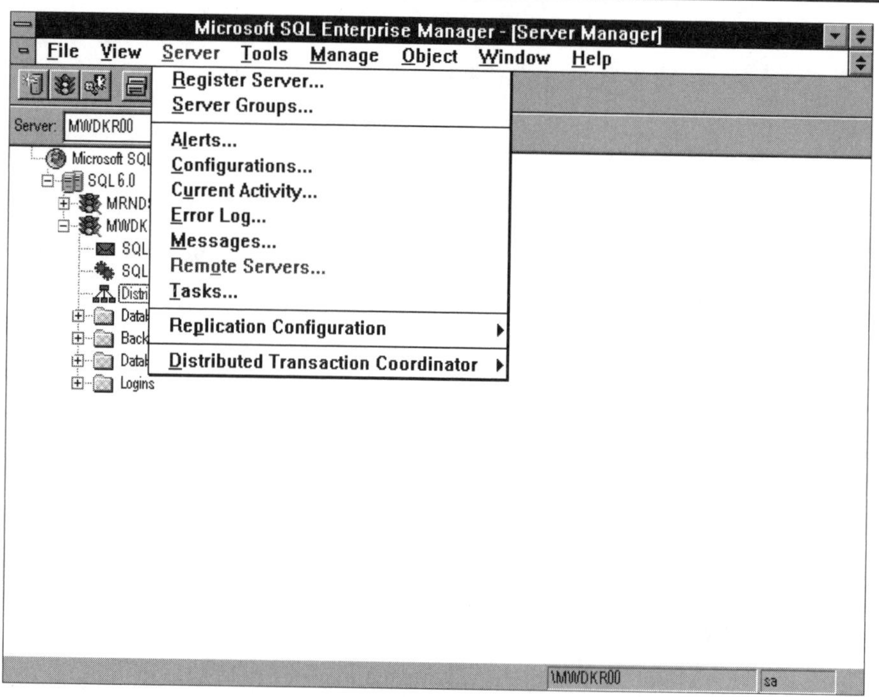

Figure 21-3:
Configure remote logins here.

The window shown in Figure 21-4 appears.

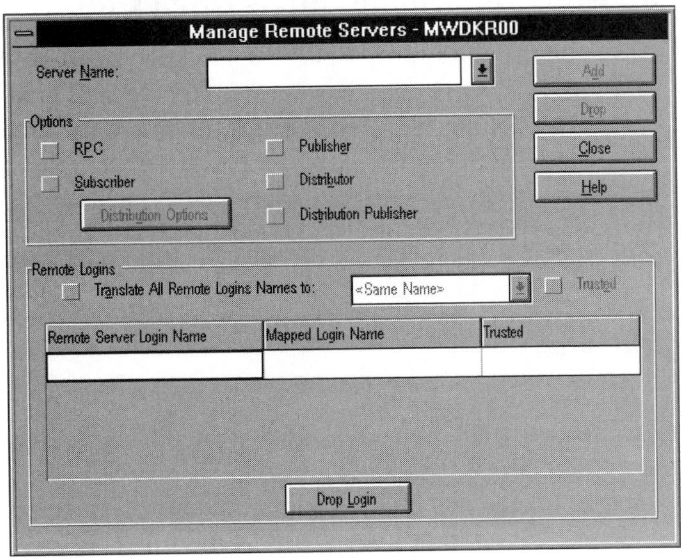

Figure 21-4:
You can set your MS DTC remote login options here.

The following sections cover the options on this window.

Server Name

This item holds the name of the remote server you want to configure. If you have already configured a machine and want to edit it, simply select it from the list box.

Options

Cross-Reference

This section is where you configure what type of services for which you want to use the remote server. For the purposes of this chapter, we will only cover the RPC (Remote Procedure Calls) option. You will become familiar with the other options in the Replication section (Part VII) of this book.◀

In order for one server to call a stored procedure on another server, the target machine must be configured to support Remote Procedure Calls (RPC). RPC is a standard that enables two servers to coordinate certain actions by logging in to one another. In this case, the two servers are coordinating the disposition of a transaction. If you are unsure whether your server is configured for RPC support, don't worry. We'll show you how to check it in a few pages.

Translate All Remote Logins Names to

This option enables you to specify a valid user id on the remote server to which all local names will be mapped. For example, if you choose probe, all RPC calls from the local machine will attempt to log in to the remote server with the user id of probe. The problem with this option is that you circumvent any security you have put on the remote machine. We recommend that you leave this option set to <Same Name> and simply make sure that users who need to do RPCs have access to the remote machine.

Trusted

If this box is checked, Windows NT handles all security for your RPCs. Because we already recommended that you use trusted security for your SQL Server machine, we also think that using this option is a good idea. Otherwise, you have to maintain a synchronized list of logins on multiple machines.

Individual Login Mapping

The last section of this window lets you individually map remote logins to different local names. For example, a value of Joe in the Remote Server Login Name field and a value of sa in the Mapped Login Name field mean that anytime the remote userid Joe tries to make an RPC, it will first have to be validated as the local login sa.

Configuring Windows NT For RPC Services

In order for the MS DTC to work correctly, you must have the Windows NT machine that SQL Server is running on configured for RPC Services. In this section, we show you how to do this. Follow these steps:

1. Open the Control Panel, and double-click the Network icon. A window appears similar to that shown in Figure 21-5.
2. Click the Add Software button, and choose RPC Configuration from the Add Network Software list. The screen in Figure 21-6 appears.
3. Follow the directions on the screen, and reboot your computer.

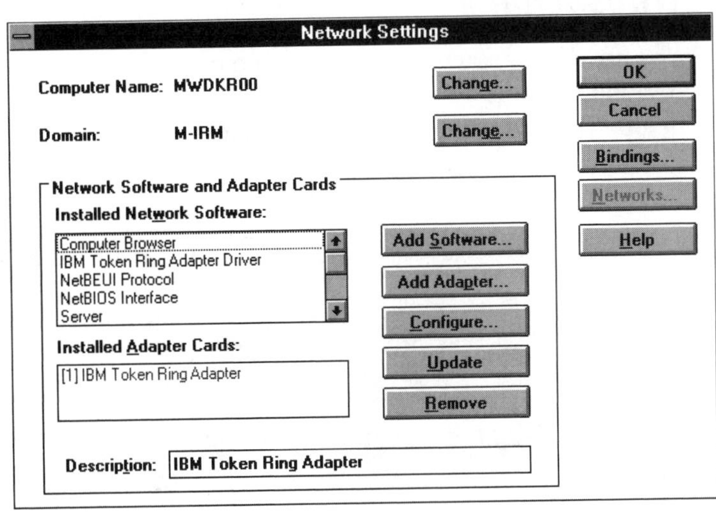

Figure 21-5:
The Windows NT Network Control Applet.

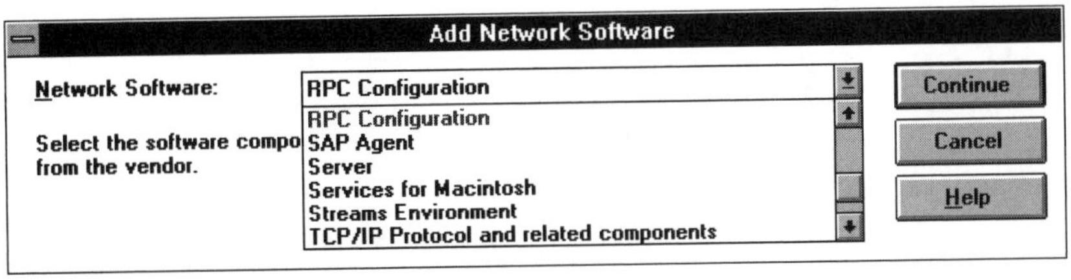

Figure 21-6:
Add RPC Support Here.

MONITORING DTC ACTIVITY

Occasionally, you will want to see the progress of the remote transactions on a given machine. To do this, you use one of the three view windows provided by the MS DTC. They are the transactions view, the trace view, and the statistics view.

Transactions

You use the Transactions Window to monitor the status of a transaction or to resolve a transaction manually. To open this window, right-click the DTC of a particular server and select the Transactions option. The DTC Transactions window appears (see Figure 21-7).

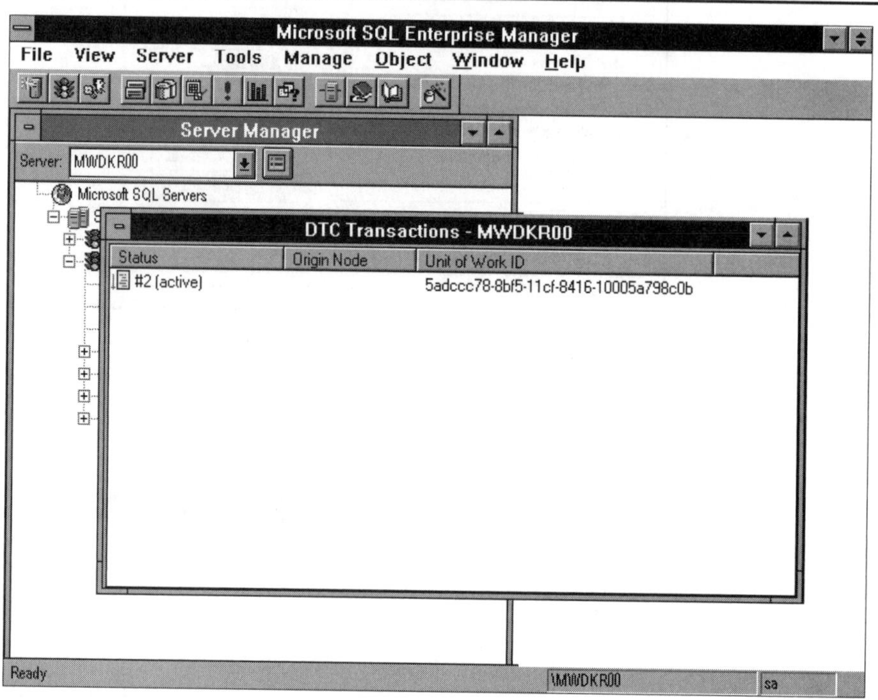

Figure 21-7:
Control the status of your open transactions here.

Monitoring a transaction

Transactions are displayed in the window by icons that represent the current state of each transaction. The possible transaction states are as follows:

- **Active.** The transaction has been started and some work has been performed with respect to this transaction.

- **Aborting.** The transaction is aborting. The DTC is notifying all SQL Servers and subordinate DTCs that the transaction must abort. It is not possible to change the state of the transaction at this point.
- **Aborted.** All servers and subordinate transaction coordinators have been notified or are currently unavailable. After a transaction has aborted, it is immediately removed from the transaction list in the Transactions window. It is not possible to change the state of the transaction at this point.
- **Preparing.** A commit request has been issued by the client application. The DTC is polling all relevant SQL Servers and subordinate DTCs to see whether it's okay to commit the transaction.
- **Prepared.** All relevant SQL Servers and DTCs have signaled that it is okay to commit the transaction.
- **In-doubt.** The transaction is prepared and was initiated on a different server (and is, therefore, coordinated by a different DTC), and the coordinating MS DTC is unavailable. The administrator can force the transaction to commit or abort by using the right-click context menu and selecting Resolve/Commit or Resolve/Abort. After a forced outcome is executed, the transaction goes through commit or abort sequences. If a forced outcome is selected, the transaction is designated as Forced Commit or Forced Abort.
- **Forced Commit.** In-doubt transaction was forced to commit by the administrator.
- **Forced Abort.** In-doubt transaction was forced to abort by the administrator.
- **Notifying Committed.** The transaction has prepared successfully (all participants have agreed to allow the transaction to commit). The DTC is notifying the relevant SQL Servers and subordinate DTCs that the transaction has been committed. MS DTC does not forget the transaction until all participants have acknowledged receiving (and logging) the commit request. It is not possible to change the state of the transaction at this point.
- **Only Failed Remain to Notify.** The DTC has notified all connected subordinates (DTCs) and SQL Servers of the transaction commit. The only ones left are not available. It is possible to force the DTC to forget the transaction at this point by using Resolve/Forget.
- **Committed.** The transaction has committed, and all subordinates have been notified. After a transaction commits, it is immediately removed from the transactions list in the Transactions window. It is not possible to change the state of the transaction at this point.

Changing the view options

You can right-click any transaction's icon to display a menu that enables you to change the way that icons are displayed in the window:

- **Large Icon:** Displays transactions in large icons that are arranged sequentially in rows across the screen.
- **Small Icon:** Displays transactions in small icons arranged sequentially in rows across the screen.
- **Details:** Lists transactions in a single column and provides an additional two columns of information: the network node on which the transaction originated and the unit of work ID associated with each transaction. This is the transaction's global unique identifier, which is generated by the MS DTC when the transaction begins. This is the view shown in Figure 21-7.
- **List:** Displays transactions sequentially in columns down the screen.
- **Clear:** Removes all currently displayed icons from the screen.

Manually resolving a transaction

You can right-click a transaction's icon to display a menu that enables you to resolve the transaction manually:

- **Commit:** Commits the transaction on the local MS DTC.
- **Abort:** Aborts the transaction on the local MS DTC.
- **Forget:** Deletes the transaction record from the log file of the local MS DTC.

Trace

The Trace Window lists current trace messages issued by the DTC. Tracing allows the system administrator to view the current status of various DTC activities, such as startup and shutdown, and to track potential problems by viewing additional debugging information. You can filter the displayed information by severity level by adjusting the Trace slider in the Configuration dialog box. To open the Trace window, right-click the DTC of a server and select Trace. You see the window shown in Figure 21-8.

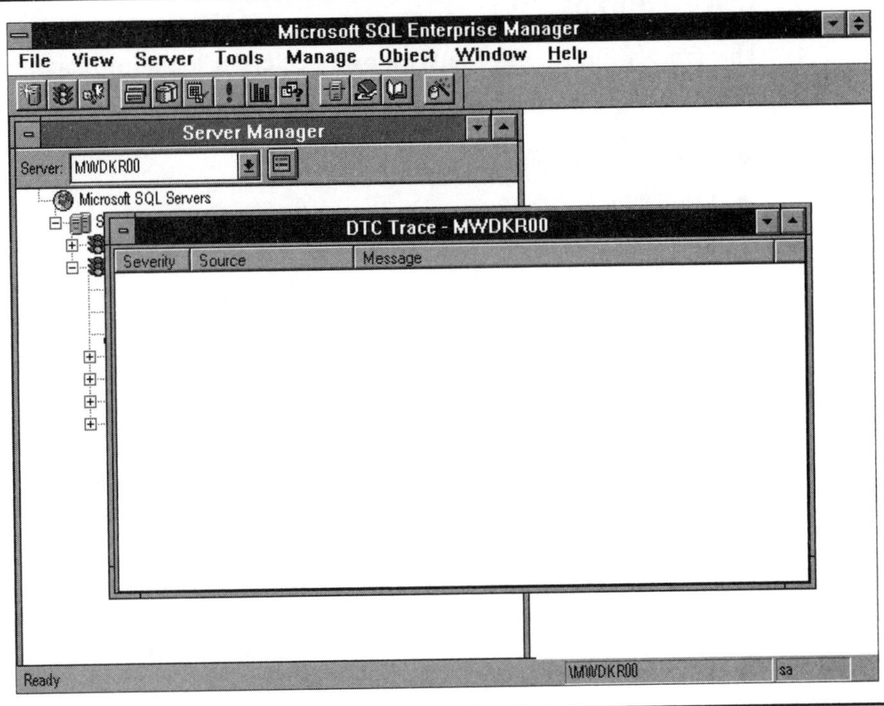

Figure 21-8:
You can trace your transactions here.

Trace severity levels

MS DTC tracing supports the following levels of severity:

- **Errors.** Cause the DTC to malfunction or need a restart. An example is a detected corrupt log file.
- **Warnings.** Information about something that might go wrong soon.
- **Information.** Useful information about infrequent events, such as startup and shutdown.
- **Debugging.** Information, such as new connections being established with clients or servers.

  All error, warning, and informational traces are routed to the Windows NT event log regardless of whether SQL Enterprise Manager is running and regardless of the trace view slider setting.

Trace sources

The Trace window and the Windows NT event log allow each message to be tagged with its source. The tags are as follows:

- **Source.** Description
- **SVC.** The MS DTC Service
- **LOG.** The MS DTC log
- **CM.** The MS DTC network connection manager

Statistics

The Statistics Window allows you to view statistical information about the transactions in which a server participated. Some of the statistics are cumulative, others reflect current performance. It is important to remember that should you ever stop the DTC, the values of all cumulative statistics will reset to zero when you restart the DTC. To open this window, right-click the DTC of a particular server and select the Statistics option. The DTC Statistics window appears (see Figure 21-9).

Current statistics

The Current group shows the following:

- **Active.** The current number of transactions that have not yet completed the two-phase commit protocol.
- **Max. Active.** The highest number of active transactions at any time during the period in which the DTC was operational.
- **Indoubt.** The current number of in-doubt transactions. In-doubt transactions might require administrator intervention. You can view and manage in-doubt transactions in the Transactions window.

The size of the DTC log file determines the maximum allowable number of concurrent transactions. After a transaction has committed or aborted, it is deleted from the log file. Should the log file at any point become full, however, the DTC on the local server will refuse to accept any new transaction until sufficient space has been cleared in the log file to record the new transaction or until the log is expanded.

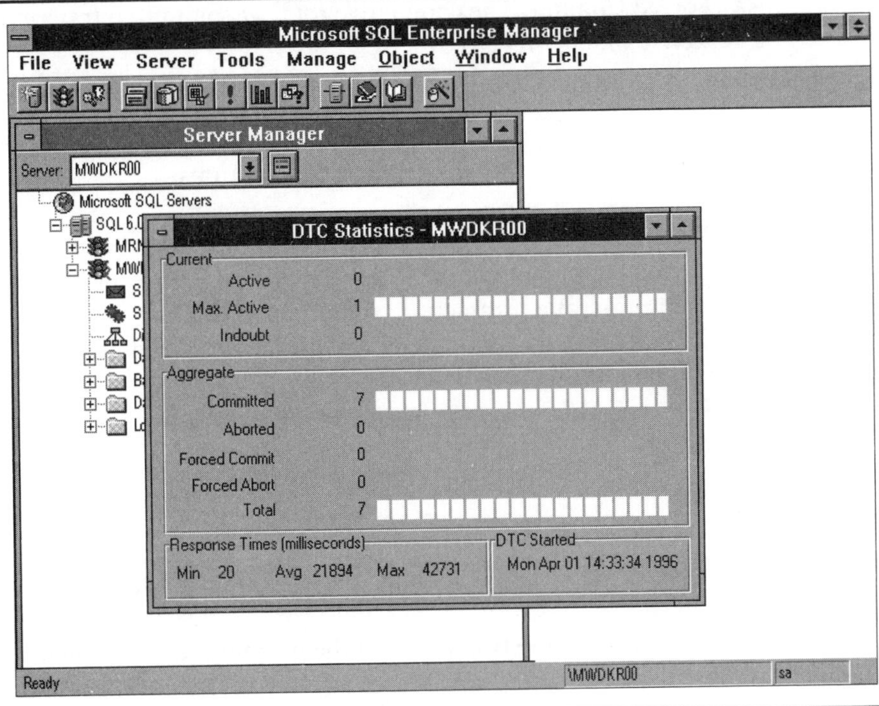

Figure 21-9:
You can view your MS DTC statistics here.

Active statistics enable you to measure the transaction load on a particular DTC. If, for example, the number of current transactions approaches the historical maximum, the system administrator may decide to increase the size of the log file to allow for more transactions. If, on the other hand, the number of current transactions is well below the maximum, the administrator may decrease the size of the log file to conserve resources such as memory.

Cumulative statistics

The Aggregate group shows the following:

- **Committed.** The cumulative total of committed transactions. This number does not include forced (manually resolved) commits.
- **Aborted.** The cumulative total of aborted transactions. This number does not include forced (manually resolved) aborts.

- **Forced Commit.** The cumulative total of committed transactions that were manually resolved.
- **Forced Abort.** The cumulative total of aborted transactions that were manually resolved.
- **Total.** The cumulative total of all transactions.

The Response Times group shows the minimum, average, and maximum transaction response times in milliseconds. Response time refers specifically to the duration of a transaction from the point that it began to the point that its outcome is known: the point at which it is definitively committed by the commit coordinator.

The DTC Started group shows the date and time that the current DTC started.

Implementing Distributed Transactions

After you have properly configured the machines that will manage your transactions, you are actually ready to *do* something. In truth, the vast majority of the work you will ever have to do with distributed transactions is done when you have finished configuring your systems.

Distributed transactions are implemented with the addition of a single word to the normal BEGIN TRANSACTION statement: DISTRIBUTED, for example:

```
BEGIN DISTRIBUTED TRANSACTION
INSERT INTO myTable VALUES (1,'a','Joe')
EXECUTE wally.pubs..addToMyTable 1, 'a', 'Joe'
COMMIT TRANSACTION
GO
```

If either the INSERT or the EXEC statements cause errors, both statements will be rolled back. Consider, however, what happens with the following statement:

```
begin transaction
insert into myTable values (1,'a','Joe')
exec otherserver.pubs.dbo.sp_insertIntoMyTable 1, 'a', 'Joe'
commit
```

Even though the INSERT and EXEC statements are in the same transaction, their outcomes are independent of one another. One can fail while the other succeeds. Why, you ask? The answer is that these statements are really being executed in two separate transactions. This stems from the fact that remote stored procedures are executed in their own transaction space on the *otherserver* machine. Its results have already been committed or rolled back before the overall transaction finished. Figure 21-10 shows this graphically.

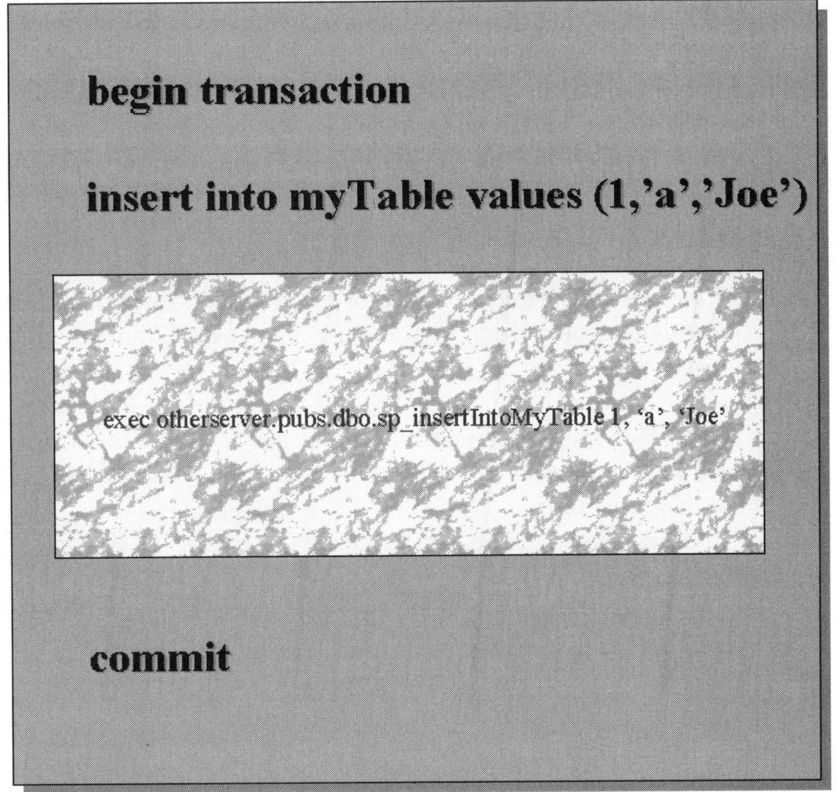
begin transaction
insert into myTable values (1,'a','Joe')
exec otherserver.pubs.dbo.sp_insertIntoMyTable 1, 'a', 'Joe'
commit

Figure 21-10:
The anatomy of combination code.

The removal of the single word *DISTRIBUTED* completely changed the nature of the code. That's it! There are no other SQL statements to learn! That having been said, it's time for some examples.

A Practical Example

Perhaps the most compelling scenario in which distributed transactions would be the most helpful is the classic "cross boundary process" problem. In a nutshell, the issue boils down to this: how do you accommodate processes that need data from servers that reside across organizational boundaries? It's a classic client/server problem that happens to be easily solved by the distributed transaction model.

Consider the following situation. Your company has three major departments: sales, production, and personnel. Each group maintains its own SQL Server machine and databases. After several years of operation, you decide that you want to develop a set of applications that will better coordinate efforts between the three departments. During your analysis, however, you discover that certain — hitherto unknown — dependencies exist between tables in different databases on different servers.

For example, suppose you decide that when a contract has been signed by the sales department, you want the resulting order to be placed in the incoming queue for the production department. You really only have three choices here.

First, you could move all the sales and production data to the same server. This is not a very attractive option, of course, because it will probably break most of your other applications and confuse the heck out of all of the displaced users.

Your second option is to replicate the sales table periodically to the production machine. That way, you could poll the data at certain intervals and make the appropriate changes to the production queue. The problem here, though, is that your data will only be as current as you replicate it. The other major problem with this approach is that there is no easy way to replicate your changes back to the sales server.

Replication would work if you had horizontal partitions. If you could horizontally partition the data such that you had mutually exclusive subsets of rows, each updated only in one place, you could use replication. This example, however, doesn't afford such a partition.◀

Your final option is to use distributed transaction processing. This way, you can cross-modify tables on the two different servers without concern that some data are going to be committed and others are not. The downside to this process, though, is that you will have to create different remote procedures to change the data. In our opinion, though, this is a small price to pay for the benefits of the distributed transaction model.

SUMMARY

When the computing age began, all processes ran on one server. As time went on, though, processes began to move off the server and onto the client. This led to the current state of client/server computing. As information systems move into the next century, however, a new model is emerging in which a client runs processes on multiple servers. We are witnessing the birth of the age of distributed computing. Soon, the line between process server and process client will be blurred. In some sense, the state of applications networking is moving to a point where many peers will act as one large computing entity. This represents the ultimate in scalability and flexibility.

In this chapter, you learned how to apply the principles of distributed computing to your database configuration and administration. More importantly, though, you took your first steps into the next great paradigm in information computing.

REVIEW QUESTIONS

Q: What types of servers make up a distributed processing environment?

A: There are three basic servers in this arena. They are

- **File Servers.** These machines share common file space among machines in the enterprise.
- **Database Servers.** These machines share data among machines in the enterprise.
- **Process Servers.** These machines share computing processes among many machines in the enterprise.

Q: What service is required on the Windows NT machines involved in distributed transactions processing?

A: In order for the SQL Server DTC to operate correctly, the RPC Configuration software must be added to the network control panel.

Q: Should I start the MS DTC service if I'm not using distributed transactions?

A: Only if you want your server to run at less than optimal performance! The MS DTC adds a great deal of overhead on a server that you shouldn't otherwise incur unless you really need it. Don't laugh. We've seen plenty of DBA's that enabled all the nifty bells and whistles of SQL Server without properly considering their resource requirements.

Part

VII

REPLICATION

The number and size of client-server database applications is growing dramatically as more and more businesses trust mission-critical processes to powerful RDBMS tools such as SQL Server. To support these high-powered applications, companies will have anywhere from a half dozen to several hundred database servers. Keeping common data synchronized among many servers is one of the biggest challenges faced by system administrators. SQL Server's tool for meeting this challenge is *replication*, a facility for keeping data consistent between servers.

In Chapter 22, we set the stage for covering replication from A to Z. We define the terms you see throughout the rest of this part. We examine step by step how replication works, paying particular attention to the translation of INSERT, UPDATE, and DELETE statements into commands for the replication to use. We look at the system tables that SQL Server uses to control replication, which gives insight into how to design a replication scheme. We conclude with a strategy for assigning replication jobs to various servers.

Once you have designed your replication plan, you are ready to use the SQL Enterprise Manager to put it into action. Chapter 23 guides you through the basic setup tasks for replication. You learn what you need to do to a server so that it can be a source for replicated data, a transfer agent, or a receiver of replicated data. You see how to specify exactly which data you want to replicate, and we guide you through a daunting group of options. Finally, we discuss linking the whole thing up, and who has the permissions to do what to make replication happen.

Every company wants to buy products that can exchange information with other products doing the same function. Your purchase of SQL Server is no different: you have every right to want to see your SQL Server data exchanged with other RDBMS applications. In Chapter 24, we look at Microsoft's answer to this concern, replication to ODBC data sources. After reading Chapter 24, you will hopefully find this kind of replication as easy as replication from one SQL Server to another. You will know what to do to set up replication to ODBC data sources, and what your limitations are.

The challenge for any product whose audience has a diverse skill level is to make each feature easy for a novice to use, while still giving advanced users unlimited flexibility and customization. Welcome to Chapter 25. Here, we delve into the special kinds of replication scenarios you may need, such as using stored procedures or manual synchronization. We also present our experience in troubleshooting the replication process when it doesn't behave the way you know it should.

Chapter

Replication Overview

22

When we migrated our production systems on the mainframe to the client-server environment, we had few complaints. Everything worked out as well as or better than we expected. We didn't miss the mainframe in the least — with one exception, which we expect is a common problem:

Suppose that before you moved to SQL Server, all your data was in DB2 in an IBM ES9000. Everyone in your company, thousands of users across wide geographic locations, may have used the data in this one ES9000. This was super convenient for the system administrators and database owners because all the data was in one place. Unfortunately, the mainframe business paradigm costs many millions annually to maintain (not to mention the fact that MVS is quite unfriendly to use), so you migrated your business to a client-server database. For a variety of reasons that we will discuss in this chapter, your data is now going to be dispersed across many different SQL Servers. How in the world are you going to do all the work you did before *and* keep the data synchronized on all these servers?

Before SQL Server 6.0, this was a real pain, and we migrated from the mainframe long before SQL Server 6.0 was released. You have already read the chapters on generating SQL Scripts, BCP, and transferring objects. That's one way — the old way — of keeping your data synchronized. The new way is *replication*. SQL Server gives you the built-in utilities to do just about anything, as far as keeping multiple copies of data up-to-date goes.

What's in This Chapter

SQL Server is doing an enormous amount of work here, so correctly setting up replication takes some thought. Just as you should take the time to design your database before you dive in and start creating tables, so should you sit down and set up a replication strategy *before* you try to do it. That's the crux of this chapter. This chapter is also important because understanding the theory behind replication is critical in troubleshooting replication problems. You will learn

- Why you need so many database servers on your network
- What SQL Server replication is
- The SQL Server replication paradigm
- The intricate details of each replication step
- The database design considerations for replication
- How to design your replication topology

This chapter presents all the concepts behind replication; the subsequent chapters discuss how actually to set up and administer replication using these concepts.

Why Bother with Multiple Database Servers?

Those of you in large companies might laugh at this question. If you have a small or medium size organization, however, you may not have multiple database servers (yet), and you might be wondering if and why this is necessary. Good question. No doubt all the hardware vendors are telling you that if you buy just *one* of their flagship machines, you will never need anything else. We don't agree. Here are some of the reasons why:

- You need at least two machines so that you will not have a single point of failure. Not only do you have to worry about hardware failure, but software, too. No matter *what* Microsoft tells you, SQL Server and even Windows NT do occasionally hang. Replication isn't intended as a hot backup, but for some organizations, it actually works better than having to restore from backup tapes.

A very specific set of circumstances needs to be true to use replication as any kind of backup. Among the most important constraints is that the database schema must be static, and it must be acceptable to lose at least a few minutes of work.◀

- You should have different machines for Online Transaction Processing (OLTP) and Decision Support Systems (DSS). These machine will be configured differently in their fault tolerance, their transaction logs, tempdb, and so on. You will then replicate from the OLTP server to the DSS server.
- SQL Server and Windows NT are not as advanced in allocating processor resources as we would like. Try setting up one SQL Server machine so that all users from one department receive top priority, with everyone else secondary. You can't. You need another server for your high priority department, with replication to and from the other servers.
- You may need to run different network protocols on different machines. Though most companies have standardized on TCP/IP, not eveyone uses this protocol. One of the authors works in an office that still uses NetBEUI.
- You may have to support Internet connections to retrieve database information, but you want some layer of protection for your mission-critical data. A good solution is a production server running integrated security and hidden behind a strong firewall, replicating to a DSS server open to Internet connections.
- You may grow into connecting with other companies and organizations. When you first set up your databases, you probably didn't need to exchange information with other organizations. Most likely you now do, or will soon. It isn't feasible for any organization to give up its server totally and use someone else's. You should just replicate between them.
- You might need to pass on SQL Server data to other OBDC data sources. Suppose that your company mostly uses Oracle, and you are leading the crusade to switch gradually to SQL Server. As you change over, the SQL Server data needs to be visible in Oracle. Replication makes this happen.
- If your company really grows, multiple servers become a fact of life. Hardware vendors are working to expand the limit of how many users one machine can support, but there will always be a limit. After you cross it, you are stuck with keeping lots of servers synchronized.

Now that you understand why you will likely have multiple servers, we will talk a little bit about how to share data between them. In this case, we are referring specifically to replication. In the next few sections, we attempt to define exactly what we mean by the term *replication*.

What is Replication?

Replication is a SQL Server process for keeping specific user tables (or partitions of those tables) loosely consistent between a source database and any number of destination databases. Let's break this down to the lowest level.

Who is replicating?

SQL Server 6.*x* does the work. Specifically, a SQL Server task runs all the time, looking for data in a database to replicate. When the task finds some, it passes it off to other tasks. These tasks transfer the data to the destinations.

What is being replicated?

SQL Server replicates whatever user tables you designate. Period. There is no explicit replication of any other database objects, such as views, stored procedures, system tables, and so on. Nor can you specify that an entire database is to be replicated. All you can do is designate that all the user tables in the database are to be replicated. If you add tables to your database, you also have to add them to your replication scheme. You can replicate a subset of a table: that is, you can limit which columns or rows of a table are replicated.

If you need to replicate other database objects, don't worry; there is a way, but it involves transmitting the data through the only thing you can replicate: user tables. We cover this in Chapter 25.◀

When is the replication happening?

The replication happens at specified intervals, which may be as small as one minute or as large as several months. It is not instantaneous, however, so the copies are not guaranteed to be constantly the same as the original. This is where *loose consistency* comes in. Loose consistency means that there is a time lag between when data is changed in the source and when it is changed in the destination. It also means that the commits are resolved only on the originating server. If a change fails on a subscriber, that has no effect on the originating server.

Where is the data replicated?

SQL Server 6.5 servers can replicate to ODBC Level 1 data sources. Because SQL Server is ODBC-compliant, you can replicate from SQL Server 6.*x* to other SQL Servers 6.*x*. You can also replicate to such systems as Oracle, Microsoft Access, and so forth. If your source server is still running SQL Server 6.0, it can only replicate to other SQL Server 6.*x* servers. Replication to ODBC databases is new with SQL Server 6.5. If you are wondering whether you can replicate to SQL Server 4.2*x*, see the sidebar that follows.

The Basic Replication Paradigm

In this section, we discuss in detail how replication works. This is not an explanation of how to set up replication; that follows in subsequent chapters.

Replication definitions

We use several terms that you will also find in the SQL Enterprise Manager and the Microsoft documentation. We list them in the following sections in their logical order, not alphabetical order.

Can I Replicate to SQL Server 4.2?

Yes, but not cleanly. If you haven't upgraded your SQL Server 4.2 server by now, you are well behind the power curve. Upgrade without delay. You might think that you could define your SQL Server 4.2 server as an ODBC data source and get basic replication to work, but you will have significant problems. For starters, replication to ODBC data sources uses quoted identifiers, which SQL Server 4.2 doesn't support. We will show you how to get around all this, but it would be better if you just upgrade.

SQL Server roles

A machine can play various roles in the replication process. Any SQL Server in your network might act in any one, two, or all of these roles.

Publication server or publisher

Any server that is the source of data you want to replicate is a *publication server*. The tables you want to replicate are actually updated here. This server must be running SQL Server 6.*x*.

Subscription server or subscriber

Any server that is the destination of data you want to replicate is a *subscription server*. The tables for replication are read-only here. This does *not* mean that the database has the read-only option set; it just means that unless you are doing some advanced replication, you will screw up the replication process by making changes it doesn't know about.

Distribution server or distributor

The server that transfers data between the publisher and the subscribers is the *distribution server*, and it is running SQL Server 6.*x*. Keep in mind that the distribution server can, and often will, be the same machine as the publication server or the subscription server. Each publication server uses one, and only one, distribution server. However, multiple publishers, as well as multiple subscribers may use one distribution server. Furthermore, one subscription server may receive data from multiple distributors. A the end of this chapter, we discuss how to impose some order on this free-for-all.

Replication components

SQL Server manages replication with articles, publications, and databases.

Article

An *article* is the smallest object of replication. It is tied to a specific user table and specifies everything you might want to know about the replication of that table. You can do a lot of customization with articles.

Publication

A *publication* is nothing more than a collection of articles *in a single database* that you want to administer as a group. A server can subscribe to an entire publication at once, saving a lot of detail work. SQL Server synchronizes all articles in a publication together, which guarantees that foreign key relationships between members of a publication will be preserved.

Publication database

A database that is allowed to contain articles and publications is, logically, a *publication database*. You designate your existing databases to allow publication. Think of this as another attribute of your database, just like whether a database allows "select into/bulkcopy." The publication databases are in the publication server.

Distribution database

This is a completely separate database that SQL Server sets up for you to manage the distribution. It is not an attribute of one of your existing databases, and you should not be using the distribution database for anything other than distribution. All the data you will be replicating funnels through the distribution database; it holds on to the data until it can send it off to the subscription databases. As you probably guessed, the distribution database is in the distribution server.

Subscription database or destination database

Any database that you have allowed to receive replicated data is dubbed a "subscription" database. Other than this, the term implies nothing special about a database. We use the terms *destination database* and *subscription database* interchangeably.

Destination tables

The tables within the destination databases that receive data from your articles are called *destination tables*. The idea of publications and articles has no meaning in the destination database because it doesn't really see these constructs. All the destination database sees is an automated process sending changes just like any user might.

Replication concepts

We refer to a few fundamental replication concepts over and over again. They are described in the following sections.

Synchronization

To *synchronize* a publication or an article means to bulk copy all the data out of the publisher and bulk copy it into the subscriber. This is a complete replace operation, and it is done once at the start of the replication process.

Filtering

This is used in advanced replication. It is a means to restrict what data is replicated either vertically (only certain columns replicate) or horizontally (only certain rows replicate).

Subscription

A *subscription* is the connection between one destination database and one publication or article. We refer to the result of subscribing as a subscription.

Push subscription

A *push subscription* is a subscription set up from the publication server. Such subscriptions are publication-centric: you can set up a bunch of push subscriptions for one publication all at once. Doing so eases the load of synchronization because the bulk copy can be done just once.

Pull subscription

A *pull subscription* is a subscription set up from a subscription server. Such subscriptions are destination-centric: you can set up one destination server with everything it needs.

Don't read too much into the push versus pull terminology. It only has meaning for the administration of the initial setup. The two types have nothing to do with how replication works; the distribution database always has the active role in replication. There is no kind of subscription where the subscriber logs into the distributor looking for data.◀

What really happens: An overview

Okay, let's get to the guts of it. Just how does this replication thing work? We will lay out the basic steps and then cover them in detail after you have the big picture. Here's an outline of the steps:

1. You set up a SQL Server machine to allow publishing, which means specifying where the distribution database is going to reside. It can either be on the publishing SQL Server machine, in which case your publication and distribution servers are the same, or your distribution database can be on another machine. If the distribution database is to be on the publisher, the SQL Enterprise Manager creates it for you at this time, and it creates tables within the distribution database to support replication.

2. You specify one or more databases to be publication databases. SQL Server adds a task for each database, called the *log reader task*, which will convert transaction log records into SQL statements for replication. These tasks later start scanning the transaction logs, looking for data to replicate.
3. You create publications, which are administrative groups into which you will put articles. SQL Server sets up a task for each publication. This task looks for subscriptions.
4. You define articles for publication with all kinds of options that we get into later. SQL Server makes scripts for creating the tables on the destination servers. SQL Server updates the replication system tables in the publication database to reflect what you defined.
5. You define for the distribution server how to connect to the subscription servers. For SQL Server subscription servers, this means making them remote servers to the distribution server. For ODBC data sources, it means setting up an ODBC data source in the Windows NT Control Panel and then pointing to that source in the distribution server. Basically, what we are doing here is making sure that the distributor can talk to the subscribers. SQL Server creates replication clean-up tasks for the subscribers.
6. A subscription is set up, either by your setting it up from the Publication Server or by the subscriber's setting it up from the subscription server. Among other things, you specify whether you want to send a complete replacement of the data at periodic intervals or whether you want to send changes. SQL Server now adds a job to the distribution database list of jobs for the initial synchronization. SQL Server bulk copies all the data out of the table to file.
7. The initial synchronization occurs. Depending on the options you choose, the Distribution Server bulk copies the data into the Subscription Server, or you do it, or there is no initial synchronization.
8. Log-based replication starts. SQL Server reads the transaction log of the publication database and converts it into INSERT, UPDATE, and DELETE statements. SQL Server logs into the subscription server and executes these SQL commands to publish the information. If you choose to replicate snapshots, SQL Server simply resynchronizes the tables at period intervals.

Replication in More Detail

That was the nickel tour of replication. Now we delve into the details.

Replication system tables

In Chapter 23, we cover all of the graphical work you do in the SQL Enterprise Manager to set up publication. This setup work turns into Transact-SQL sent to SQL Server, which in turn changes the system tables and adds a bunch of user objects. Therefore, we examine the system tables to understand what it really means to publish.◀

Effects on the system catalog

Just what exactly happens when a server becomes a publisher? We start with the system catalog. After you have set up publishing, you should look at the *sysservers* table:

```
SELECT *
   FROM master..sysservers
```

You see a list of servers that includes, at a minimum, your local server and the distributor (if it is different from the local server). The local server will always be srvid 0; the rest are listed in the order they were added. The exciting field here is srvstatus — run sp_helpserver to translate the numbers into the five statuses: dist (Distribution Server), dpub (Combined publisher/subscriber), pub (publication server), rpc (remote server), and sub (subscription server). The status of your server will have changed to show that it now publishes. This is what SQL Server reads to see whether you have publishing installed on your server.

The other system table used by publication is *sysdatabases*. The category field tells you whether a database is publishing (category = 1), subscribing (category = 2), or both (category = 3). When SQL Server wants to show you which databases are publishing, this is the table it queries.

Effects on the database catalog

Four tables control replication:

- syspublications
- sysobjects

- sysarticles
- syspublications

We present these tables in detail because if you have any trouble with replication, you will have to query them extensively.

Syspublications

This is the list of the publications in your database. It is empty right now, but by looking at its columns, you can learn a lot about the purpose of publications. (See Table 22-1.)

Table 22-1

Syspublications Shows You What Information is Controlled at the Publication Level

Column	Datatype	Description
description	varchar(255)	Your description of the publication
Name	varchar(30)	The unique name of the publication, must be a valid identifier
Pubid	int	The integer used to track the publication, an identity column
repl_freq	tinyint	0 if transaction based; 1 if scheduled table refresh
Restricted	bit	Security of the publication: 1 if restricted; 0 if unrestricted
Status	tinyint	0 if log-based; 1 if not log-based
sync_method	tinyint	0 if native bcp; 1 if char bcp
Taskid	int	The task id for this publication

This is the relational model at its finest; by looking at this table, you can see exactly what is controlled at the publication level, versus the article level. Specifically, the following are constant for all articles in a publication:

- **The replication method.** All articles in a publication are either handled by log-based replication or scheduled refreshes. This is the fundamental reason for having a publication: to keep a group of tables in synch on subscription servers.
- **The security method.** If you have some articles for which you want to restrict subscriptions, you have to put them in a separate publication. You cannot restrict individual articles within a publication. This rule permits the great convenience that a subscription server can subscribe to an entire publication at once.
- **The synchronization method.** Does this have to be standard for a publication? No. This is the default method for a publication. A subscriber can override it, as we shall see.

- **The replication task id.** Your distribution server does not get cluttered with tasks for each article, nor for each subscriber. There is just *the* task for a publication.

Sysobjects

The category column of sysobjects tracks which tables are publishing. This is a bit redundant because you could obtain this information from sysarticles, which we discuss next. The real value of sysobjects is that it defines the valid tables of the database.

Sysarticles

Table 22-2 shows what you have in sysarticles.

Table 22-2
Look at Sysarticles to See What Options You Have in Defining Articles

Column	*Datatype*	*Description*
artid	int	The unique number used to track the article; an identity column
Columns	varbinary(32)	A cryptic, non-3NF way of storing which columns are published
Creation script	varchar(127)	Path to the creation script for the article
del_cmd	varchar(255)	If desired, a special command for running on a delete
Description	varchar(255)	Your description of the article
Dest_table	varchar(30)	The name of the destination table
Filter	int	The ID of the stored procedure you will use for a horizontal filter
filter_clause	text	The WHERE clause you will use for a horizontal filter
ins_cmd	varchar(255)	If desired, a special command for running on an insert
Name	varchar(30)	The name of the article, unique within a publication
Objid	int	The object ID of the table being published
Pubid	int	ID of the publication of which the article is a member
pre_creation cmd	tinyint	Specifies drop, delete, or truncate target table
Status	tinyint	Bitmap used to describe various properties
sync_objid	int	The ID of the table or view that will be used to synchronize
Type	tinyint	Information about whether there are filters or views
upd_cmd	varchar(255)	If desired, a special command for running on an update

This table neatly summarizes the flexibility you get with articles. All the fancy options have defaults so that you don't have to be burdened with features you don't need. However, if you do need special replication features, you can do the following:

- Customize the SQL that the distributor will use to create a destination table. When you create an article, SQL Server writes the CREATE TABLE statement it needs to file. This distribution task logs into distribution servers and runs this script. You can modify it to include *any* SQL that you want.
- Specify special actions for insert, updates, and deletes. Normally, the idea of replication is to keep tables on two servers in synch, so you would let SQL Server replicate all transactions as they occur. However, you can specify that SQL Server either take no action or run a special stored procedure in replication.
- Give a different name to the table on the destination server. This is particularly useful when communicating with another organization that perceives the data differently and has different names for the tables. For example, one office might call the authors table "writers". Notice that you *can't* rename the columns.
- Filter your data either horizontally or vertically. You might use this to prevent sensitive information from getting out.
- Tell SQL Server what to do if the destination table already exists: nothing, DROP (which means SQL Server will then CREATE the table), TRUNCATE (a non-logged DELETE of an entire table), or DELETE.
- Give a special view for use in synchronization. This works in coordination with the filters: if you are going to restrict which rows or columns you will replicate, you probably don't want them to be included in the initial synchronization.

The main thing about the preceding options is that there was no mention of using specific options on specific servers. For example, you can't set up one article that will have one name on one subscriber but a different name on another. For that, you need to set up two articles on the same table. You must do likewise for any of the other options.

Syssubscriptions

The last table (Table 22-3) added to a database by installing publishing is *syssubscriptions*.

Not much is managed at the subscription level: the article is what has all the features. However, the subscriber does control *the method* by which it is synchronized.

Table 22-3
Syssubscriptions Keeps Track of Who Has Subscribed to What

Column	Datatype	Description
artid	int	The article ID from *sysarticles*
srvid	smallint	The Server ID from *sysservers*
dest_db	varchar(30)	The name of the destination database from *sysdatabases* of the subscriber
status	tinyint	Tells you whether the subscription is active
sync_type	tinyint	How an article is to be synchronized: by SQL Server, by you, or not at all
timestamp	timestamp	Initial "time" of subscription (recall that timestamps aren't date-times)

What's in the distributor?

When you let SQL Server set up distribution, you get a database made for you that has six user tables and a bunch of stored procedures for administering them. Understanding these six tables is fundamental to understanding what the distribution database is doing for you. For the rest of this chapter, we assume that you named your distribution database the default name *distribution*. You can find the new tables with the following:

```
SELECT name, crdate
   FROM distribution.dbo.sysobjects
   WHERE uid = 1
```

The list you expect to see is MSjob_commands, MSjob_subscriptions, MSjobs, MSsubscriber_info, MSsubscriber_jobs, and MSsubscriber_status. Let's look at them.

MSjobs

This lists the "jobs" of replication. A *job* is a transaction in the publication database that affects a table being replicated. For example, if you are replicating the authors table in the pubs database, this UPDATE statement would spawn one job:

```
UPDATE authors
   SET au_lname = 'Fedorchek'
   WHERE au_id = '998-72-3567'
```

And this SQL statement would be one replication job:

```
INSERT authors
SELECT *
    FROM ##new_authors
    /* Assume you have just loaded some new authors into
    the global temporary table ##'new_authors */
```

And so would this one:

```
DELETE authors
```

The first example affects one row in authors, the second affects a bunch of rows, and the last affects all the rows. Yet each statement, if run by itself, comprises only one job in replication. If you run them together, they are each considered automatic transactions, and thus you have three separate jobs. Finally, if you encapsulate all three within a BEGIN TRAN / COMMIT pair, their outcomes become mutually dependent, and they appear as one job for replication. The point is that the number of rows you change with your SQL statement does not affect how many jobs you get. It is the number of transactions that is relevent.

Table 22-4 shows the structure of MSjobs is.

Table 22-4
MSjobs Lists All the Jobs for Distribution

Column	*Datatype*	*Description*
publisher_id	smallint	The local server ID of the publishing server, from *sysservers*
publisher_db	varchar(30)	The name of the published database
job_id	int	The job ID
type	tinyint	The transaction type
xactid_page	int	If the event is log-based, the page of the transaction
xactid_row	smallint	If the event is log-based, the row of the transaction
xactid_ts	binary(8)	The timestamp of the transaction
entry_time	datetime	The time the row was added to the table

The unique index of MSjobs is publisher_id, publisher_db, job_id. The transaction type specifies whether we are dealing with a SQL Script, a bcp, an SQL command, and so on. This table makes it quite clear that the jobs are tied to the transaction log of the publishing database.

MSjob_commands

All jobs have at least one command. They may have many commands, however, so the unique index of MSjob_commands is publisher_id, publisher_db, job_id, and command_id. It has the structure shown in Table 22-5.

Table 22-5
MSjob_commands Lists the Actual Commands the Distributor Will Execute

Column	Datatype	Description
publisher_id	smallint	The local server ID of the publishing server, from sysservers
publisher_db	varchar(30)	The name of the published database
job_id	int	The job ID (these first three reference MS_jobs)
command_id	int	The command ID: a sequential number
art_id	int	The article ID, from sysarticles of the published database
incomplete	bit	Indicates whether this is the full command; SQL can become broken into multiple lines
command	varchar(255)	The actual command or command fragment

The command column in this table holds text you can recognize. The log reader puts actual INSERT, UPDATE, and DELETE commands in here. This table, and this column in particular, is your major space consumer in the distribution database.

MSsubscriber_info

So far, we have found tables to list the jobs that the distributor is doing for publishers and the commands for those jobs. Now, we need to define subscribers to receive these commands. Remember that machines which can subscribe will be listed in sysservers of master. In the distribution database, however, we have specific details about the relationship of a subscriber to a publisher in Mssubscriber_info. (See Table 22-6.)

Table 22-6
MSsubscriber_info Defines the Relationship of a Subscriber to a Publisher

Column	Datatype	Description
publisher	varchar(30)	The name of the publisher, from sysservers
subscriber	varchar(30)	The name of the subscriber, from sysservers
type	tinyint	Whether the subscriber is a SQL Server
login	varchar(30)	The login to be used
password	varchar(30)	The password to be used
commit_batch_size	int	The number of transactions executed on the subscriber before a commit is issued
status_batch_size	int	The number of transactions before the status state is updated
flush_frequency	int	Rentention time for distributed transactions
frequency_type	int	Whether this is Daily, Monthly, and so on

(continued)

Column	Datatype	Description
frequency_interval	int	The interval of frequency_type
frequency_relative interval	int	The relative interval for day of the month when the freqtype is monthly (32)
Frequency recurrence_factor	int	The recurrence factor based on the frequency_type
frequency_subday	int	The reschedule occurrence based on frequency_interval; once, every second, every minute, every hour
frequency_subday interval	int	The amount of time per frequency_subday when it is a unit of time
active_start time_of_day	int	The time of day when this task is active
active_end time_of_day	int	The time of day this task is no longer active
Active_start_date	int	The date and time after which this task may be scheduled
Active_end_date	int	The date and time after which this task may no longer be scheduled
Retryattempts	int	The number of retry attempts when a task execution fails
Retrydelay	int	The delay, in minutes, between retry attempts

Warning

Why does this table use the names of the publishers and subscribers, rather than the ids? No good reason that we know of. It is, in our opinion, confusing and inconsistent.◀

Clearly, there is a boat load of parameters for when subscribers and publishers talk. The user interface makes these parameters clear, so we will not dwell on them. There is one important point here: the *flush_frequency*. After the distribution database has sent the *commands* of MSjob_commands successfully to all subscribers, it doesn't need them, right? Not exactly. They are worth keeping around for a while in case one of the subscriber databases crashes. They can be resent after a crash.

Synchronization considerations

You have a bunch of options on synchronization, both in how you create the script and in how you obtain the data from the publisher to the subscriber. We will cover the script options in detail when we start talking about the user interface for them. Right now, we want to focus on the how and why of the options in transferring data.

Let the replication process do it

The simplest way of synchronizing is when SQL Server does it via replication. The following steps tell how it works in general terms:

1. A subscription server subscribes to an article. This makes an entry in MSjob_subscriptions.
2. The task for the publication finds this entry in MSjob_subscriptions. The task puts a halt to *all* publications to that database so that it can do a synchronization. This means that no other articles obtain their data until the synchronization of this article is complete.
3. The SQL Executive logs into the subscriber and bulk copies the data in.
4. The replication resumes.

Under this scenario, you do no work; SQL Server has done it all.

You transfer the data, but you tell SQL Server to wait

This is otherwise known as *manual synchronization*, which is misleading. In all likelihood, you *will* synchronize. The difference here is that when you defined the subscription, the synchronization is already done, so SQL Server has the green light to start replicating.

Log-based replication

After the initial synchronization, SQL Server uses log-based replication (unless you choose to replicate only snapshots). We discussed the transaction log in detail in Chapter 17, but we will highlight the key points again now. Every time you change the data in a table — either directly with an insert, an update, or a delete, or by running a stored procedure — SQL Server *logs* the change. There is one table in each database, called *syslogs*, which SQL Server uses to guarantee transaction integrity. Before making a change to a given row, SQL Server records the before and after images of the affected rows and the associated indexes. Up until now, the only uses we have discussed for this are backup/restore and recovery. However, this log does nicely for replication, too. When you specify an article for replication and activate a subscription, the entries in syslogs for that table are tagged. For each publication database, there is a log reader task that reads its transaction log, searching for entries tagged for replication. When the log reader tasks find changes for an article in the log, it converts them into SQL and records them in a table in the distribution database. The distribution database has a separate task running that will log into the subscription servers and run this SQL. Let's look at an example.◀

You have decided to replicate the authors table. You make this change:

```
UPDATE authors
   SET au_lname = 'PINES'
   WHERE au_lname = 'Ringer'
```

This UPDATE statement affects two rows in the authors table. The before and after images of the rows, and their index entries, are recorded in syslogs. The before images of the two "Ringer" rows, as displayed by DBCC (refer to Chapter 26), are

```
00ce8e44:  01180500 0d030000 12000000 80000000  ................
00ce8e54:  1030f400 68010000 23070000 01000000  .0..h...#.......
00ce8e64:  d7100000 01000000 db100000 07033830  ..............80
00ce8e74:  31203832 362d3037 35320154 00393938  1 826-0752.T.998
00ce8e84:  2d37322d 33353637 52696e67 6572416c  -72-3567RingerAl
00ce8e94:  62657274 36372053 6576656e 74682041  bert67 Seventh A
00ce8ea4:  762e5361 6c74204c 616b6520 43697479  v.Salt Lake City
00ce8eb4:  55543834 31353208 4b464436 28221c11  UT84152.KFD6("..

00ce8f08:  011a0502 0d030000 12000000 80000000  ................
00ce8f18:  1030f400 68010000 d1060000 01000000  .0..h...........
00ce8f28:  db100000 01000000 dd100000 07043830  ..............80
00ce8f38:  31203832 362d3037 35320152 00383939  1 826-0752.R.899
00ce8f48:  2d34362d 32303335 52696e67 6572416e  -46-2035RingerAn
00ce8f58:  6e653637 20536576 656e7468 2041762e  ne67 Seventh Av.
00ce8f68:  53616c74 204c616b 65204369 74795554  Salt Lake CityUT
00ce8f78:  38343135 32084944 42342622 1c110000  84152.IDB4&"....
```

and these are the after images:

```
00ce8d1c:  01140b01 0d030000 12000000 64000000  ............d...
00ce8d2c:  07033830 31203832 362d3037 35320153  ..801 826-0752.S
00ce8d3c:  00393938 2d37322d 33353637 50494e45  .998-72-3567PINE
00ce8d4c:  53416c62 65727436 37205365 76656e74  SAlbert67 Sevent
00ce8d5c:  68204176 2e53616c 74204c61 6b652043  h Av.Salt Lake C
00ce8d6c:  69747955 54383431 3532084a 45433527  ityUT84152.JEC5'
00ce8d7c:  211c1100                             !...

00ce8d98:  01160b03 0d030000 12000000 64000000  ............d...
00ce8da8:  07043830 31203832 362d3037 35320151  ..801 826-0752.Q
00ce8db8:  00383939 2d34362d 32303335 50494e45  .899-46-2035PINE
```

(continued)

(continued)

```
00ce8dc8:  53416e6e 65363720 53657665 6e746820  SAnne67 Seventh
00ce8dd8:  41762e53 616c7420 4c616b65 20436974  Av.Salt Lake Cit
00ce8de8:  79555438 34313532 08484341 3325211c  yUT84152.HCA3%!.
00ce8df8:  11000000                             ....
```

Clearly syslogs doesn't store data in a format that is easy for you to read, but the change is there. You can see the string "PINES" where "Ringer" used to be. Next, the log reader task for the pubs database comes along and converts what's in the log to this (we added the carriage returns for readability):

```
delete from "authors"
   where "au_id" = '998-72-3567'
delete from "authors"
   where "au_id" = '899-46-2035'
insert into "authors"
   values ('998-72-3567', 'PINES', 'Albert', '801 826-0752',
   '67 Seventh Av.', 'Salt Lake City', 'UT', '84152', 1)
insert into "authors"
   values ('899-46-2035', 'PINES', 'Anne', '801 826-0752',
   '67 Seventh Av.', 'Salt Lake City', 'UT', '84152', 1)
```

These SQL strings are recorded in a table in the distribution database; SQL Server will execute the SQL on the subscribers. Now, let's answer some common questions about this process.

What happened to my SQL?

You will notice several things about this SQL:

What was a single command from your perspective is now many commands, as far as replication is concerned

This is how log-based replication works. It always deals with changes on a row-by-row basis. If you change 1,000 rows, you can expect at least 1,000 separate commands to appear in the distribution database.

Your UPDATE was converted to a DELETE and an INSERT

Understanding that replication works row by row, you might have expected to see the following:

```
UPDATE "authors"
   SET "au_lname" = 'PINES'
```

```
   WHERE "au_id" = '899-46-2035'
UPDATE "authors"
   SET "au_lname" = 'PINES'
   WHERE "au_id" = '998-72-3567'
```

Instead, you got a DELETE and an INSERT. This won't always happen either; sometimes you will get an UPDATE command back. Everything depends on how SQL Server does the update. When an UPDATE is converted to a DELETE and an INSERT, it can mess up your foreign keys in the destination database. More on that later.

Your WHERE clause changed

On UPDATEs and DELETEs, the WHERE clause is always an explicit listing of the primary key values. For this reason, you can only use log-based replication with tables that have a primary key. SQL Server restricts you to snapshot replication for tables without primary keys.

Everything is in quoted identifiers

Again, that is how replication works.

How does the log reader work if you set "truncate log on checkpoint"?

As you will recall, "truncate log on checkpoint" flushes your log at regular intervals, often every few seconds. By default, the log reader task runs every five minutes. What happens if the transactions it needs have already been truncated? SQL Server doesn't allow this. Transactions for replication cannot be truncated on checkpoints until the log reader reaches them. Therefore, it is possible for your transaction log to grow and grow, even if you have set "truncate log on checkpoint". You should set alerts on both the transaction log size and on failed replications to tell you when you are in danger of your transaction log filling up.

Just when are the replication transactions removed from the log?

After the log reader has read a transaction, the transactions can be dumped on the next DUMP TRANSACTION or DUMP DATABASE. Notice that if the log reader task is failing, you will not be able to get these transactions out of the log, even with a DUMP DATABASE.

Are the transactions retained anywhere after they are read and applied to the subscriber?

Yes. The SQL for the transactions is retained in the distribution database. You set a retention parameter to specify how long the transactions are retained.

Won't you always need the transactions in the distribution database, just in case future subscribers show up?

No. You know that when you set up the subscription for an article, SQL Server bulk copied out all the data. SQL Server then used this data to synchronize the subscriber(s) initially. What happens if a new subscriber comes along a month later? Is SQL Server going to bulk copy this month-old data in and then need to refer back to a month's worth of transactions in the distribution database? No. SQL Server performs a fresh bulk copy for new subscribers.

What happens if you truncate a table, which is a nonlogged operation?

Easy. You can't truncate a table that is being replicated.

In what order are transactions sent to a subscriber?

The transactions are sent in the exact time order in which they were executed in the database.

Database Design Considerations

The replication process has some heavy impact on the design of your databases, both on the publication and the subscription side. Let's look at the main points to consider.

Primary keys

Any table that you want to publish with transaction-based replication must have a primary key. In our opinion, *all* your tables should have primary keys, so hopefully your tables already meet this requirement. If not, you have to establish primary keys now. If you want to replicate a table for which you cannot find a group of fields that uniquely determine rows, you will have to introduce a surrogate key with an identity column. This will be a pain because, if you try to put the new identity column with an ALTER TABLE, your column will have to allow nulls, which means it cannot be the primary key. Therefore, you have to drop and recreate the table.

Though it is a requirement that the replicated table have a primary key, by default SQL Server does *not* transfer that primary key to the subscriber. Why this is so eludes us. This creates a host of problems, not the least of which is that you lose the ability to use your subscriber as a publisher for other databases for the table. We recommend that your replication plan always include transferring the primary key.◀

Other DRI, other indexes, and triggers

If you create the script for a table with a script generator, you get the following options:

- Object Creation
- Object Drop
- Table Indexes
- Table Triggers
- Table DRI

When you create a script through replication, however, your options are the following:

- Specifying some action for handling a table that already exists (dropping it, truncating it, doing nothing, and so on)
- Transferring the clustered index
- Transferring the nonclustered indexes
- Transferring the primary key

In other words, SQL Server's replication GUI tools don't give you the option of scripting triggers or DRI. You can still work that into your replication plan, but you have to do it yourself. We recommend that you *do* include all DRI in your scripts. If replication is working correctly, there should never be a DRI violation. If you do get a DRI violation, it will alert you to the fact that something is amiss. To include DRI in your scripts requires some work and requires understanding the NOT FOR REPLICATION option on constraints.

Not for replication

Regrettably, there was a major problem with replication and foreign keys in SQL Server 6.0. Here's the problem: Suppose that you are replicating two tables, such as the authors and titleauthor table of pubs. There is a foreign key on au_id in titleauthor referencing authors. Suppose further that it is important to you that the foreign key exist both in the publication database and in the destination database. This might be the case under an advanced replication scenario in which the tables are horizontally partitioned, with all East Coast authors updated on one server, but all West Coast authors on another, each replicating changes to the other. What happens when you execute the command we gave as an example earlier?◀

```
UPDATE authors
   SET au_lname = 'PINES'
   WHERE au_lname = 'Ringer'
```

The very first command that comes out of this is as follows:

```
delete from "authors"
   where "au_id" = '998-72-3567'
```

The SQL Executive logs into the destination server and tries to issue this command, but because this au_id has entries in titleauthors, SQL Executive receives a foreign key violation, the transaction is rolled back *on the destination server only*, and replication stops. Game over.

In SQL Server 6.0, you really didn't have much choice but to drop the foreign key. In SQL Server 6.5, your "solution" is to create the foreign key constraint on the destination titleauthor table with the keywords NOT FOR REPLICATION. This exempts the replication process from having to adhere to the foreign key. This gets you going, but it still isn't perfect. The problem here is that *real* foreign key violations can get through. Suppose that someone on the publication server executed the following command:

```
DELETE authors
   WHERE au_id = '998-72-3567'
```

This is a case where you may *want* to have a foreign key violation occur. The publication server may not have any references to au_id '998-72-3567', but you do. The real solution, which Microsoft hasn't given us, is what is called an *update in place*. An UPDATE on the publication server should generate an UPDATE command. Period.

There is also a NOT FOR REPLICATION option on CHECK constraints. This feature is supported in both SQL Server 6.5 and 6.0.

If you are still using SQL Server 6.0 or if you are really worried about letting true foreign key violations through, we offer a work-around in Chapter 25.◀

Create scripts with DRI

If you are going to keep foreign keys in the destination database, you have little choice but to create your own script and run it yourself. Then, you should set up your articles so that they do not drop existing tables. We'll show you how to do this in Chapter 23. The reasons for doing this are twofold. First of all, the SQL Server replication process won't even make CREATE TABLE scripts with foreign keys, so you would have to go out of your way to set up replication with such scripts. Second, even if you did this, there would be no guarantee that they would run in the correct order. Any script that ran and tried to reference a table not yet created would bomb, upsetting the entire apple cart.◀

How to divvy up articles into publications

SQL Server publications are meant to simplify the process. You reap the benefits of this simplification by using exactly the number of publications you need and no more. A group of tables that need to be always in synch, of course, will be in one publication. Any group of tables with common replication characteristics, however, should be in the same publication.

Other considerations

Stablize your table definitions

Realize that after you create an article for a table, you can't drop that table. If you find that you must drop and recreate the table, you will have to unsubscribe all the subscribers. Not only will this force you to redo the work of establishing the subscriptions, but you will be burdening the network with a resynchronization.

You *can* ALTER, but don't! It seems reasonable to us that certain ALTER TABLE commands should be prohibited on a table that is being replicated. At the bare minimum, SQL Server should stop you from dropping the primary key. No such luck. You can do whatever ALTER TABLE changes you want. You can drop the primary key. You can add columns. You can change any other constraints you want. Replication will continue to function by assuming that the original definition still applies. New columns will not be replicated; the old primary key will be treated as the key. Don't set yourself up for this kind of chaos. If you must ALTER a table that has an article on it, drop and readd all the subscribers.◀

Have a plan for timestamps, identities, and user-defined datatypes (UDDT)

Replication converts UDDTs to their base data types. This hasn't been a problem for us, but you will have to decide what this means for your databases. Identity columns will be replicated without their identity property, and timestamps will be converted to varbinary(8). This makes perfect sense because you want the destination table to have exactly the same values as the publication table. Therefore, you can't have the subscription server making up its own identity and timestamp values.

Cross-Reference

You will recall from Chapter 15 that we were very critical of SQL Server's UDDTs. The fact that they don't participate in replication just reinforces the point that UDDTs fall far short of what is needed to truly support the relational concept of domains.◀

Replication Topology Design

Whether you have two servers or 200, you have some design work to do on setting up publication, distribution, and subscription servers. SQL Server gives you enormous flexibility, and you want to take advantage of it.

Who has the data, and who needs it?

Ideally, the answer to this question should be dictating your replication setup, not the other way around. For example, if you have one table that needs to be updated on two different servers, it would be a shame to force all the updates to happen on just one server for the sake of your replication design. We attack this problem as follows:

1. Come up with a list of which servers need to have copies of which tables.
2. Make another list of which servers need to update which tables.

3. Find any cases where two servers need to update the same table. These you must resolve with horizontal or vertical partitions. (If you can't, you have to resort to a two-phase commit.) At the end, you should have a list of publishers and subscribers with information by tables. Now, you just have to connect the dots with distribution servers. There are really two critical questions:

   - Do you need any publishing subscribers? A publishing subscriber subscribes to articles published by some server and then republishes them. Think of this as a photocopy of a photocopy. The reason for doing this is to lighten network and server loads. If you have one machine that has to publish to 250 servers, it is going to do little else except publish. It would probably be better to break this into two or three layers. Have the main server publish to 15 subscribers, which in turn publish to 15 or 16 more subscribers. If this is too much of a load, you could have the main server publish to just six other servers, each of which publishes to six more, which in turn publishes to five or six more.
   - How many distribution servers do you need, and will they be combined with either publishers or subscribers? The key point to bear in mind is that a publisher and its distributor must be connected by a reliable, high-speed communications link.

Summary

SQL Server replication is a flexible, powerful way to keep copies of data on multiple servers. SQL Server uses loose consistency, which means that there is a time lag between when changes are made on the publisher and when they are made on the subscriber. Three logic servers are involved in replication: the publisher, the distributor, and the subscriber. You replicate user tables by defining articles on them. These user tables must have primary keys. Articles are grouped into publications. Subscribers can subscribe to articles or whole publications. SQL Server reads changes to published tables out of the transaction log and stores the corresponding SQL in the distribution database. The SQL Executive logs into remote servers and runs this SQL to keep the destination tables up to date. A table that is being published can't be dropped. If you have more than a couple of servers, you will have to plan the use and location of distribution servers to minimize your cost and to maximize your throughput.

Review Questions

Q: If you have on OLTP server and a DSS server, which one is the publisher? the subscriber? the distributor?

A: Because the data is actually being updated on the OLTP server, it is the publisher. The DSS server is the subscriber. Usually, you do not want an OLTP publisher to bear the load of distribution, so if you don't have a third machine, you will probably put the distribution database on the subscriber.

Q: What database objects can you replicate? All tables? Tables and Views? All objects?

A: You can replicate only user tables. No other database, not even system tables, can be replicated.

Q: What versions of SQL Server can publish? distribute? subscribe?

A: Only SQL Server 6.0 and SQL Server 6.5 can publish or distribute. Only SQL Server 6.5 can publish to ODBC data sources. All SQL Servers can subscribe, but the process for subscribing an SQL Server 4.2*x* server is messy.

Q: What are the two major ODBC subscribers that Microsoft is targeting with SQL Server 6.5?

A: Microsoft Access and Oracle.

Q: Can you replicate snapshots at specified intervals, instead of doing log-based replication?

A: Yes.

Q: Can you combine the two? In other words, can you replicate transactions as they occur but still do a complete refresh once a week?

A: No, that is not directly supported. You could rig it yourself, however, by creating a weekly task that unsubscribes and then resubscribes all articles in a publication. That will force resynchronization.

Q: How do push and pull subscriptions vary in how the distributor and subscriber exchange transactions?

A: They don't. Push and pull subscriptions refer only to how you administer things, not to how replication works.

Q: If replication hiccups, how will you know?

A: Replication is handled by tasks, so you can look at the task manager. You can also set up e-mail notification.

Q: How do database/transaction dumps interact with the log reader?

A: You cannot dump unreplicated transactions.

Q: Why is replication a problem when destination tables have foreign keys?

A: Some updates are changed into DELETEs followed by INSERTs.

Q: Can you replicate a table without a primary key?

A: No. There must be a primary key defined on a table when you set up replication. You can drop that key later, but you shouldn't.

Q: Can you have one single table that is updated on two servers, with each replicating changes back to the other?

A: Yes, but you must have mutually exclusive horizontal partitions defined for this to work.

Chapter

Setting Up Replication

23

*I*n the preceding chapter, we covered what replication is and how it works. Here we get right down to the nuts and bolts. This chapter will be your guide as you set up replication and your reference when you modify replication.

What's in This Chapter

In this chapter, we discuss

- Installing a distribution database
- Enabling servers and databases to publish
- Enabling servers and databases to subscribe
- Defining publications and articles
- Subscribing to publications and articles
- Setting up database owners with replications permissions and logins

Installing a Distribution Database

The first thing you need for replication is a distribution database. It can be on the same server as your publishing databases, on the same server as your subscribing databases, or on a separate server altogether. Wherever it will be, you now set it up. In this chapter, we will create a distribution database on a server named DISTRIBUTOR.

Note

Some replication tasks can only be done by the system administrator; others can be done by a database owner. We will discuss these subtleties after we get the basic process out of the way. Therefore, we assume that you are logged in as the system administrator (sa) in the sections that follow.◀

Memory check

If your distribution server will be the same as your publication server, that server has to be configured to use at least 16MB of RAM. Check to see how much RAM you have allotted to SQL Server by doing one of the following:

- Choose the server you want in the SQL Enterprise Manager, select Server⇨Configurations, and then choose the Configuration tab. Check that the "memory" configuration is at least 8192. If not, change it and restart the server.
- From the query window type the following:

  ```
  sp_configure
  ```

  See that the memory option is at least 8192. If not, type the following:

  ```
  sp_configure 'memory', 8192
  RECONFIGURE
  ```

  Again, you must restart SQL Server.

Tip

If you don't have the RAM to support replication, you can cheat and run replication anyway, but at a big performance hit. sp_configure doesn't check to make sure that you have enough physical memory to cover what you allocate.◀

Device size check

You will need to create devices for your distribution database, unless you already have free space on other devices. How much space do you need? As always, estimating database size is difficult. Microsoft recommends that you start with 30MB for data and 15MB for the log. If you have a fair idea of what your transaction load will be, you can certainly refine these estimates. The largest space consumer in the distribution database will probably be MSjob_commands. As we discussed in the preceding chapter, this table holds the SQL commands to be sent to the subscription servers. You will be storing a lot of commands like the following:

```
DELETE FROM "table_name" WHERE "pk_col1" = value1, "pk_col2" = value2, …
INSERT INTO "table_name" VALUES ('col1', 'col2', …)
```

If you go to the trouble of counting all this mess, you are looking roughly at this equation for each row UPDATED:

> 25 + 6 × *number of primary key columns* + *total length of table name and primary key column names* + 25 + 4 × *number of columns* + *average row size*

These are just heuristics, so we will say you are looking at roughly 100 plus double your average row size. Let's say that you have set the retention parameter to two days, and you expect about 1,000 updates a day on a table where the total length of the rows is 300. You might guess that you need room for 2 × 1,000 × (100 + 2 × 300) = roughly 1.5MB of data for the SQL commands! When considering the other tables in the distribution database, 30MB seems a reasonable start, but if you plan to replicate 10,000 updates per day, you probably should start much larger.

As always, remember to put your log on a separate device so that you can dump the log. Whatever size you choose for the data device, we recommend that you make the log device at least half that size. This is a database where there will be a very high volume of changes.

The topology diagram

When it comes to replication, Microsoft has provided you with the ultimate GUI. Select a server in the Server Manager Window and choose Server⇨Replication Configuration⇨Topology. A window of mostly white space with your chosen server in the center appears (see Figure 23-1).

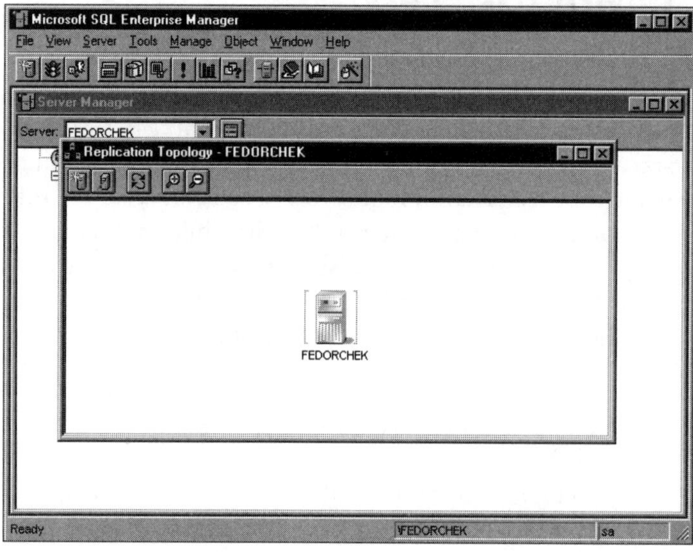

Figure 23-1:
Use the Install Replication Publishing dialog box to create a distribution database.

Big deal, you say. Maybe it doesn't look too exciting right now, but we are just getting started. Right-click the server, and choose Install Publishing.

Creating the distribution database

We are now going to create the distribution database. If you didn't follow the preceding steps, you can get to the right place by selecting a server from the Server Manager window and choosing Server➪Replication Configuration➪Install Publishing. Even if you don't want to configure a server *publishing* per se, just distribution, you still have to use this menu item. The Install Replication Publishing dialog box appears (see Figure 23-2).

If the Install Publishing option is grayed out, someone has already installed publishing. If you are absolutely sure that you need to reinstall it, skip ahead to "Uninstalling Publishing," in Chapter 25.◀

You have to choose one of two radio buttons: local or remote. You want local because you are creating a distribution database. Now, all you have to do is specify the name and sizes of your data and log devices. Both text boxes have <new> as an option, enabling you to create devices here if need be. Click OK, and you are off and running.

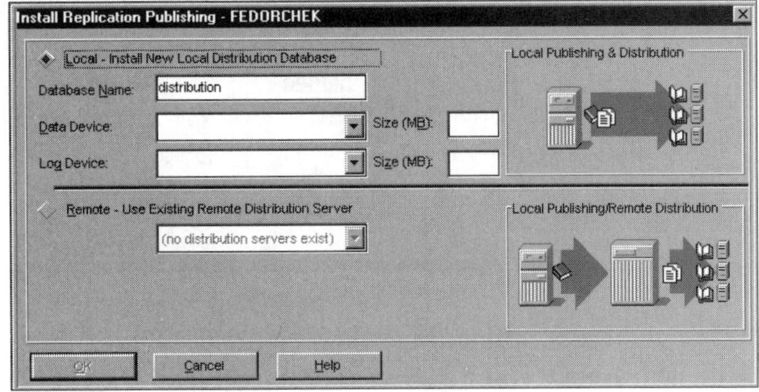

Figure 23-2:
Use the Install Replication Publishing dialog box to create a distribution database.

There is only one dialog box you want to see when you are done, Figure 23-3. How long it will take to get there depends on how long it takes your server to create databases.

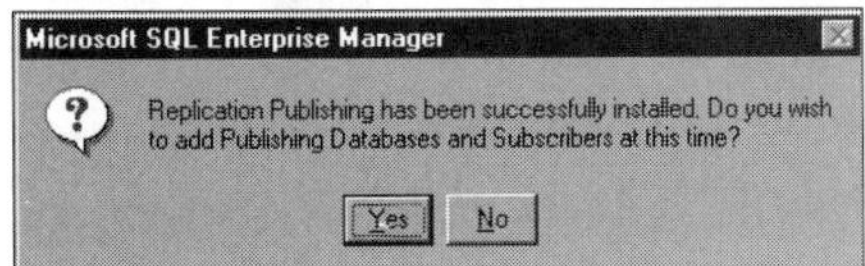

Figure 23-3:
The successful installation dialog box tells you everything worked.

Gotcha! The SQL Enterprise Manager Still Demands 16MB

As you know, if you are just setting up a distribution server, you don't need 16MB of RAM for SQL Server (though it would be nice). As soon as you choose this menu item, however, you get an error message if you don't have 16MB RAM allocated to SQL Server. How do you tell SQL Server that this is just a distribution server? You can't. This is a bug. You have two choices. You can either lie to SQL Server by configuring it for 16MB temporarily (even though you don't really have 16MB to give it), or you can install the distribution database with SQL alone, which is a pain. In that case, you will have to update the Windows NT Registry, too. It would be better to set your SQL Server memory fictitiously to 16MB (8,192 2K pages), install the distribution database, and then switch SQL Server back to 8MB (4,096 2K pages).

How Not to Name Your Servers

In one case, we got the dumb idea of naming our distribution server REPLICATION. Bad move. This is a SQL Server keyword, and the SQL Enterprise Manager choked on setting up replication. Fortunately, you can rename a server from within Windows NT. Then, you have to use sp_dropserver and sp_addserver to tell SQL Server about the name change.

If you get anything other than Figure 23-3, worry. Your distribution database is most likely not correct. Try to correct the error and reinstall publishing. You might have to uninstall publishing first. One error you might see is

```
Unable to connect to site '0' because "" is unavailable.
```

In this case, you or someone else has messed up the sysservers table, and there is no entry for srvid = 0, the local server. This most often happens when you have tried to uninstall publishing; we cover how to correct this problem there.

If you are ready to specify publishing databases and subscribers at this time, you can select Yes in the Successful Installation dialog box. If you are already late for your carpool, don't worry, you can always get back here from the SQL Enterprise Manager menus.

Checking your progress

If you want some further reassurance that all is well, go look at the tables in the new distribution database. There should be six of them. If you SELECT * FROM master.dbo.sysservers, you will find that the status of your server has changed.

Setting Up Subscribers and Publishing Databases

Let's go back to that Replication Topology window. You have just defined a publication/distribution server, and you want some of the servers you have registered in the SQL Enterprise Manager to be subscribers to that publisher. Simply drag the server's icon from the Server Manager window into anywhere in the Replication Topology window. The server is now prepared to accept subscriptions. You can right-click a subscriber to specify which of its databases will actually be receiving publications.

Setting up subscribers and publishing databases from the menu

If you select Yes in the successful installation dialog box or choose Server⇨Replication Configuration⇨Install Publishing⇨Publishing, the Replication-Publishing dialog box appears (see Figure 23-4).

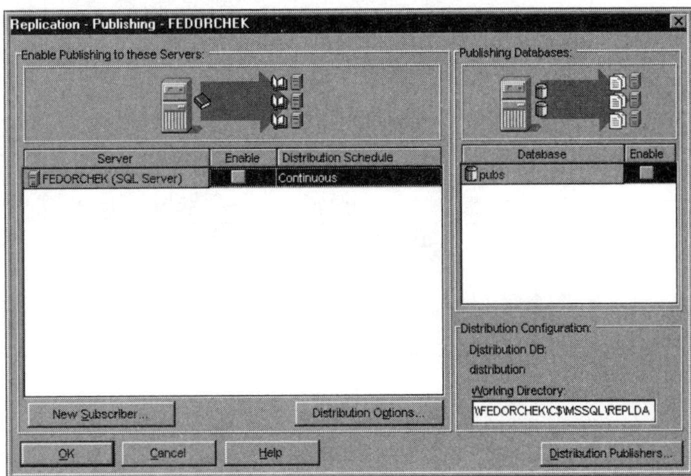

Figure 23-4:
Use the Replication-Publishing dialog box to enable servers to subscribe and databases to publish.

What you see listed on the left side are all the servers registered in the SQL Enterprise Manager you are using, plus all servers defined as remote servers to your new distribution server. Click New Server if you need to register another server. Regrettably, differences in case can cause a server to appear twice in this window. For example, if you have "DISTRIBUTOR" registered in your SQL Enterprise Manager and "distributor" listed in sysservers, you see two entries. If this bothers you, you will have to drop the remote servers and re-add them in all caps (use sp_dropserver and sp_addserver).

Check the servers that you want to be able to subscribe to this publisher. This is one direction of a two-way street. You designate which servers you will allow to subscribe; they will also have to allow you to publish to them. As you enable servers to receive publications, you can change the Distribution Schedule for each one by clicking the Distribution Options button, which displays the Distribution Options dialog box (see Figure 23-5). Incidentally, when you used the Replication Topology window, it was able to set up both directions for you because you had to have both servers registered to use that window.

Your options here are described in the following sections.

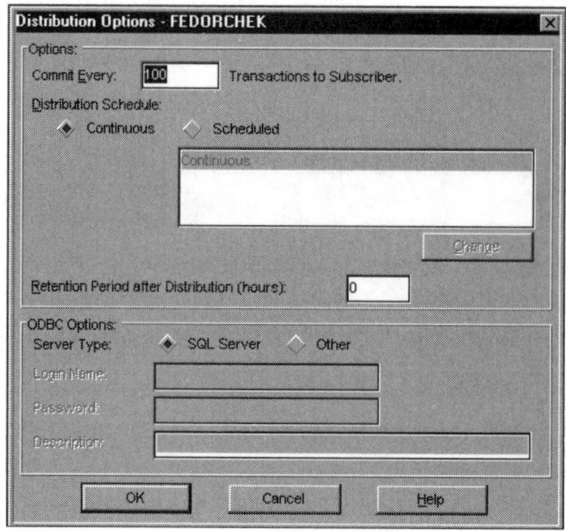

Figure 23-5:
Use the Distribution Options dialog box to set the distribution schedule and retention period.

Commit Every <X> Transactions to Subscriber

Microsoft's use of the word *Transactions* here causes no end of confusion. Remember from Chapter 22 that each transaction in your database corresponds to a replication job. The log-reader takes each transaction and breaks it apart into separate SQL statements for each row. Thus, the insert of 541 rows from a single INSERT statement is one transaction and one job, but it generates 541 separate INSERT commands to be sent to the subscriber. Ideally, you would like all 541 INSERT statements to be encapsulated in one BEGIN TRAN / COMMIT TRAN pair on the subscriber. However, in balancing the load on your network and your servers, you may decide that there is an upper limit on how many SQL statements you want to send to the subscriber at one time.◀

SQL Server lets you specify a maximum number of SQL statements to send to the subscriber: this option. Thus, you are not specifying the number of transactions from your publication database to commit on the subscriber, but the number of job commands. For example, with the default value of

100, suppose a user issues the transaction that inserts 541 rows. These would be sent to the subscriber in five blocks of 100 and a final block of 41. You can play with this value to adjust the load on your network. We have never had any trouble with the default values. Notice that this number is a *ceiling*, not a floor. If someone changes just one row, that one change will be sent when it is read: SQL Server doesn't wait for 99 other changes to accumulate.

Distribution Schedule and Change Button

If you know you don't need the changes published more often than once an hour, or once a day, and so on, this is the place to set them for all publications going from the publisher to the subscriber. You can tinker with the frequency of individual tasks later, so go ahead and choose whatever will be best for most of the subscriptions. The default, Continuous, is a bit misleading. This really means changes start moving through the replication process as soon as the log reader finds them, and by default, the log reader polls every 10 seconds. Therefore, we have a scheduled transactions of a very tiny interval!

Retention Period after Distribution (hours)

The reason you retain transactions after they have been applied to a subscription server is for recovery of the subscription server. Suppose that you have a subscription server named SUBSCRIBER and you back it up every morning at 03:00. Let's say that it has a disk failure at 17:45 (that's 5:45 p.m. for you U.S.-born or nonmilitary people) that same day. If you restore the backup from 03:00, you have lost almost 15 hours worth of replicated transactions. However, if you had set your retention period in DISTRIBUTOR to 24 hours, SQL Server is smart enough to reapply the transactions you lost. The downside to setting a high retention period is that is consumes disk space. We keep it right at the default of 0 (zero) because in our case, it would be acceptable just to resynchronize all the publications.

When you have set all the Distribution Options to your satisfaction, click OK to return to the Replication-Publishing dialog box.

The publishing databases

In order to add publications to your databases, you have to check them off here. SQL Server adds some extra system tables to the databases and sets up a log reader task for each publishing database.

The default directory

Don't be in such a rush to click OK that you forget to verify the Working Directory. If the directory doesn't exist, SQL Server isn't going to create it for you; instead, you will get error messages on your replication tasks.

The Distribution Publishers button

If you are setting up a distribution database, you can specify publication servers that you want to allow to use this distribution database. By definition, these would be servers that you have *not* yet set up for publishing.

If you had set up publishing on them, you would have already chosen their distribution server. Earlier, we talked about the two-way street, and it applies here as well. You still have to install publishing on these servers, but you select Remote instead of Local.◀

Checking your progress

At this point, you expect to see a bunch of tasks added to the distribution server. There should be a clean-up task for each subscription server. On the publication server, you expect to see this:

- After you refresh your database listing in the Server Manager window, the publishing databases have a "share" hand underneath them.
- There is a log reader task for each publishing database.

Setting Up the Subscription Database

The publishing set up was the difficult part. Enabling a server to subscribe involves a lot less. Choose Server➪Replication Configuration➪Subscribing. The Replication Subscribing dialog box appears (see Figure 23-6).

On the left, you check the servers from which you want to receive publications; on the right side, you have a list of databases for whichever server is currently highlighted on the left. You pick the databases for each server which you will subscribe to publications. This puts one table into a subscribing database for replication to use. The only thing difficult about this step is actually remembering to do it. It is easy just to skip into defining publications and articles, but if you do, the Subscribers button will be grayed out.

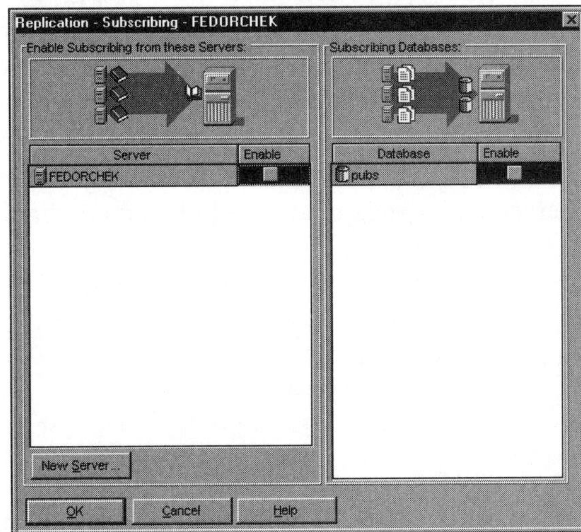

Figure 23-6:
Use the Replication-Subscribing dialog box to authorize servers to publish and databases to subscribe.

What to look for now

At this point, any database that is allowed to subscribe has a table called MS_job_commands_info. SELECT * FROM this table, and you will see that it lists your publisher.

Not so fast

If it seemed to you that defining both subscribers and publishers was a bit too easy, you have good instincts. In fact, a lot of replication problems are being swept under the rug right here. Though you may have specified any number of publisher-subscriber relationships, you have no guarantee that these servers can actually talk to each other. Here's an example of what can happen.

You have a publisher called PUBLISHER running NetBEUI. It functions as its own distribution server. You have a subscriber called SUBSCRIBER running IPX/SPX. There is no common network protocol that both machines are using. You are working at a machine called WORKSTATION, which is running *both* NetBEUI and IPX/SPX, so you can register both PUBLISHER and SUBSCRIBER in your SQL Enterprise Manager. Therefore, you can set up replication as just described, and you will get no error messages. Not one single transaction is going to be replicated between those two machines, however, until you get them talking on a common protocol.

We could go on with other examples, but you get the point. This isn't completely the SQL Enterprise Manager's fault, mind you. You need the flexibility to set up replication for a server that is temporary unavailable, so SQL Server can't categorically exclude servers that it can't find on the network. A warning would be nice, though.

If you are dealing with servers that you think are up and running and you think the communications link is active, do yourself a favor and verify the connection with an ODBC ping:

```
exec master..xp_cmdshell "c:\sql60\binn\odbcping /Sservername /Ulogin_id
/Ppassword"
```

This runs the ODBCPING.EXE utility in your SQL Server directory. The syntax is

```
ODBCPING [-S Server | -D DSN] [-U Login Id] [-P Password]
```

For example, from within the Query window you could verify a connection to a server named SUBSCRIBER via xp_cmdshell:

```
exec master..xp_cmdshell 'ODBCPING /S SUBSCRIBER /U sa'
```

The expected result is 'CONNECTED TO SQL SERVER'. You have a problem if you see 'COULD NOT CONNECT TO SQL SERVER'.

Defining Publications and Articles

Now that you have installed publishing, you can set up publications within your databases. Remember that within a database, you have any number of publications, and within publications, you have articles, which are the lowest level replication objects. Every article must be in one and only one publication, though one base table could be the foundation of more than one article.

Creating a publication in the SQL Enterprise Manager

Expand the database for which you will define a publication. Whereas before you saw just an Objects and a Logins folder, you now have a Publications folder. Right-click it and choose New Publication. The Edit Publications dialog box appears (see Figure 23-7).

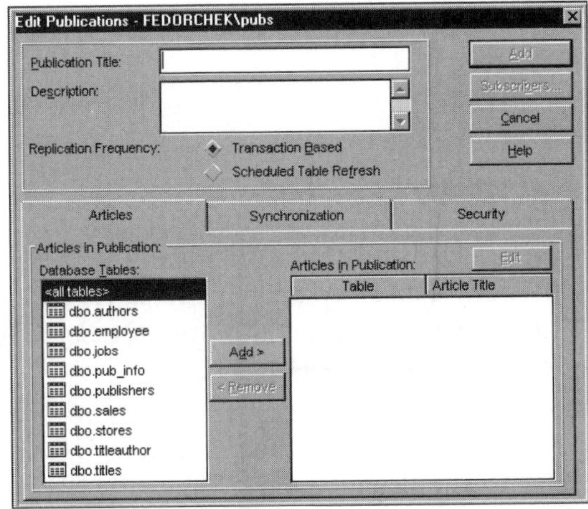

Figure 23-7:
Use the Edit Publications dialog box to create and change publications.

You need to supply the three pieces of information, as described in the following section.

Publication title

This must be a valid identifier, of course.

- **Description.** Optional. This will be passed on to those who will be trying to decide whether they should be subscribing to your publication, so you might include whatever information they need here.
- **Replication Frequency.** There is a huge difference between these two radio buttons. Transaction-based activities read the transaction log and send SQL statements as replacements. Schedule Table Refresh means that at specific intervals, you will dump all your data and apply a new copy. The former spreads the load of replication out over time; the latter keeps network activity minimal and then causes the demand for resources to spike tremendously with the interval you choose.

Defining an article

Warning

A publication can exist without an article in it, but the SQL Enterprise Manager won't let you set that up directly. Therefore, the Add button is grayed out until you add at least one article. For adding articles, you have the standard Add/Remove pair of boxes, which also has the unfortunately standard flaw: you can't highlight a group of tables for addition. Your list on the left for adds is filled with the user tables of your database because you have to base each article on a user table. Any customization you want to do comes later. (For horizontal or vertical filtering, see "The Filters tab" later in this chapter.)◀

Synchronization tab

The other two tabs are straightforward. Under Synchronization, you get to choose between native bcp and character. As the dialog box points out, native is faster and the best choice for SQL Server 6.*x* to SQL Server 6.*x* replication. You choose character if:

- You expect ODBC subscribers, such as ORACLE or Access. They won't be able to handle native bcp. You really have to plan ahead for this kind of heterogeneous replication. If you choose native and later want to add an ODBC subscriber, SQL Server won't let you do it.
- You are doing something advanced that would choke on native bcp. If you plan to have destination tables with columns whose nullability isn't the same as your source table (this is asking for trouble), you need character.

Tip

Don't forget that character bcp drops the millisecond information off of datetimes. This will mess you up if a datetime field is part of the primary key of the table.◀

The frequency is listed later on with the default of every five minutes. The change button brings up the standard task interface for you to specify whatever frequency you want.

Security tab

This is pretty simple. If you want to restrict this publication, you check off the subscribers who can have access. All other servers won't even be able to see that this publication exists, let alone subscribe to it.

Edit article

Switch back to the Articles tab. If you don't want to mess with any of the defaults, you can just add a bunch of tables and be done with it. If you are replicating from SQL Server 6.*x* to another SQL Server 6.*x*, we do *not* recommend accepting the defaults. At a minimum, you want to include the primary key option. Do yourself a favor and click the Edit button of your first article. The Manage Article dialog box appears (see Figure 23-8).

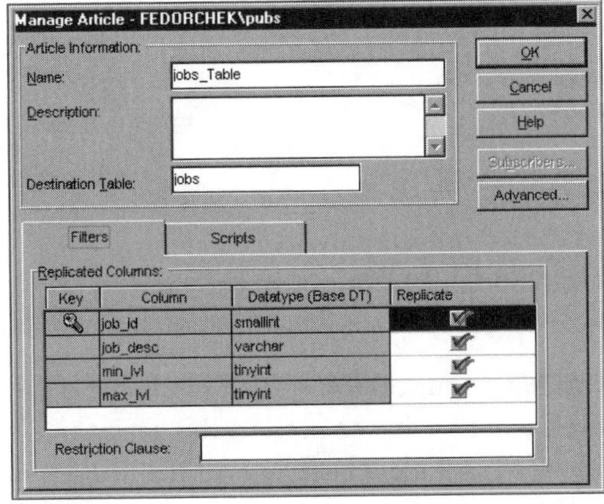

Figure 23-8:
Use the Manage Article dialog box to edit articles.

Just as with the publication, you specify a name and an optional description. The SQL Enterprise Manager appends the word *table* to your table's name, which is redundant for most folks. You might need this if you are setting up more than one article on a table based on various restriction clauses. You also get the very convenient feature of pairing this table with a destination table of a different name.

The Filters tab

The Filters tab is currently showing. If you want to restrict the columns of the article, this is a nice interface for it. There are straightforward stored procedures for defining publications and articles, if you want to go that route, but defining columns with stored procedures is a good bit of work. Make your selections here instead.

The Restriction box is for a WHERE clause, if appropriate. Don't type the word *WHERE* itself, just the clause. SQL Server will use this WHERE clause for both the initial synchronization and the log-based replication.

The Scripts tab

This tab is for both the creation script and the customization of SQL that will go to your destination table. By default, changes to the source table will produce the same end result on the destination table. However, you can make these changes do virtually anything you want. Simply click Custom for whatever command you want to change. You must then enter one of two things in the adjoining text box:

```
none
```

or

```
call procedure_name
```

In the latter case, procedure_name is a stored procedure *in the subscription server*. A stored procedure with this name must exist in each separate subscription server, though it need not be the same exact procedure in each subscriber. We will cover the syntax for creating these procedures in Chapter 25.◀

If you have your own script all ready for creating the table in the subscription server, you type in the path to this script in the Creation Script text box. This script can include whatever you want. For example, you could include the scripts for your custom insert, update, and delete stored procedure. Leaving this box blank causes SQL Server to create the script for you. Click Generate to view and edit the options for creating this script. This is where we recommend you check Include DRI - PK. Notice that primary keys are the only DRI option. If you want anything else, you have to provide the script.

When you have finished with the article

When you are satisfied with your article definition, click OK, and you return to the Edit Publications dialog box. If you have more than one article, you have to Edit each of them separately. This becomes tedious very quickly. Consider using the sp_addarticle command discussed in Chapter 25 to save yourself a lot of repetitive work.◀

Defining Subscribers

If you have finished setting up the publication and the article, you may be ready to set up subscribers, but the Subscribers button is still grayed out. You didn't miss anything. You have to choose Add and define the publication without subscribers as your first step. Then, you can immediately right-click and choose Edit to edit the publication to put the subscribers on. Now you are off and running with replication!

Publication Permissions for DBOs

Until now, we have swept permissions under the rug by setting up replication as the system administrator. The tasks of setting up the distribution database and configuring a server for publication are reserved to the system administrator and cannot be delegated. This is the customary approach for such server-level tasks. Unfortunately, it is also reserved for the sa to configure a database for publishing, to set up publications, and to set up subscriptions. Why this is so is less clear.

The remaining tasks, managing existing publications and subscriptions, are available to the database owners. However, the database owners must be members of MSDB and distribution databases on the distribution server. When the publishing server holds the distribution database, this is a simple matter of adding the logins for the database owners to these two databases. When you have a remote distributor, you have some extra steps to deal with. You must do the following:

1. Make logins in the distribution server for the publishing database owners.
2. Map the remote logins between the two servers as trusted logins with sp_addremotelogin.
3. Add the logins to the MSDB and distribution databases on the distribution server.

A database owner of a subscription database must be mapped to repl_subscriber of the publisher(s).

Summary

Setting up replication for the SQL Enterprise Manager is straightforward. The first thing you do is let SQL Server create your distribution database and install publishing. You pick databases to enable for publishing and servers to enable for subscription. The Edit Publication dialog box guides you through defining publications and articles from creation to subscriptions. Database owners have restricted roles in the process; the process is geared mostly to system administrators.

REVIEW QUESTIONS

Q: Can you install a distribution database with less than 16MB of memory allocated to SQL Server?

A: No, but that just means you have to configure SQL Server to grab 16MB of RAM. How much you really have is another story.

Q: Can you replicate a non-dbo owned table?

A: Yes, but such a table will be a dbo-owned table on the subscription servers.

Q: Can you define a publication with no articles?

A: With stored procedures, yes; with the SQL Enterprise Manager, no.

Q: Why would you want to synchronize with native bcp? With character?

A: Native bcp is faster and better for datetime and image data. Character is required for ODBC subscribers.

Q: How do you subscribe a bunch of servers to one publication in such a way that all subscribers are synchronized at the same time?

A: You schedule the initial synchronization for a time when all servers will be available and you will have finished setting up the subscriptions.

Chapter

Replication to ODBC Data Sources

24

A new feature of SQL Server 6.5 is the capability to replicate to ODBC data sources. This is an important step for SQL Server and for Microsoft because it means that you can now run SQL Server and other major RDBMS on the same network and have non-SQL Server applications stay current with data in SQL Server.

Of course, the major player we are after here is Oracle, and that is what Microsoft targeted in its development. The other big ODBC data source Microsoft invested some time in was Microsoft Access, a welcome addition if your office uses all Microsoft products. This emphatically does *not* mean that you are limited to these two; it just means that Microsoft put extra effort into getting them right.

What's in This Chapter

- The rules for translating from SQL Server to ODBC data sources
- How to set up replication to ODBC data sources
- Replication between SQL Server 6.5 and SQL Server 4.21 using ODBC

THE RULES OF ENGAGEMENT

Replication to ODBC data sources is quite a task because other systems will have different data types, different methods for loading data, and so on. Bridging these gaps required a lot of design decisions. Among the key rules are these:

- You can publish from SQL Server to an ODBC data sources. Data doesn't flow the other way.
- All SQL is created with quoted identifiers. Thus, an insert statement for the *employee* table will begin with the following:

  ```
  INSERT INTO "employee"
  ```

  This seems to be a reasonable safety precaution, but it does become annoying.
- You cannot group transactions in batches. Removing this functionality widens the playing field of ODBC sources to which SQL Server can talk.
- The ODBC Datasource Name (DSN) must conform to the rules for identifiers — a reasonable request. Because this is just the ODBC DSN, you can still do things like replicate to an MS Access database named "This is not a valid SQL Server identifier.MDB". You just have to give such data sources a valid identifier as its ODBC DSN name, like ACCESS DATA.
- You cannot truncate the destination table if it exists. You have to use DELETE instead. This frees us from making any assumption about if and how an ODBC data source implements a nonlogged table delete.
- Microsoft has established fixed mappings of SQL Server datatypes to the datatypes of each ODBC data source. You don't get to pick what maps to what. Refer to your Microsoft SQL Server documentation for the latest information about what ODBC data sources are supported and what the datatype mappings are. These mappings will sometimes limit the ranges of acceptable values for datatypes.
- The ODBC driver must be 32-bit. Certainly this is appropriate: there is no reason to drag 16-bit applications into this just for backwards "contemptibility."
- The ODBC driver must be for the same processor architecture as the distribution server. This means that if your distribution server is a DEC Alpha, you need to use the DEC Alpha version of the ODBC driver. Now we are hitting a few speed bumps, but this doesn't have to stop you from doing any replicating. No matter what processor architecture your publisher has, it can talk to a distributor with a different architecture. At worst, you will be forced to devote a few more machines on your network to replication.

How to Replicate to ODBC Data Sources

Out of necessity, this involves steps that you can't do in the SQL Enterprise Manager. In particular, you need physical access to the distribution server. So much for remote administration.

Setting up an ODBC Data Source

Before you start, you must install whatever ODBC drivers you will need *on the distribution server*. Note that it really doesn't matter at all whether your workstation or even your publisher can connect to the ODBC data source to which you want to replicate. It is the distribution server that must be able to connect. Microsoft ships a set of ODBC drivers with the SQL Server 6.5 CD-ROM, and you can run the ODBC driver setup from there.

After you install the drivers, you have to run the ODBC configuration utility in the Control Panel *of the distribution server* to define your specific data sources. Go ahead and do that now, if you can. These are the steps to follow:

1. Open the Control Panel and select the 32-bit ODBC icon. You will see Figure 24-1.

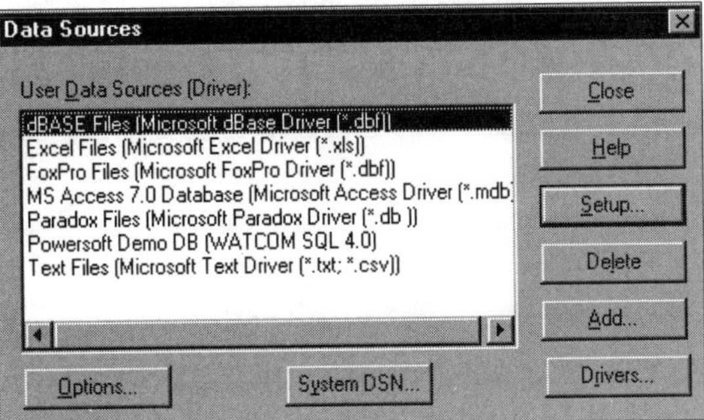

Figure 24-1:
Launch the ODBC Data Sources dialog box from the Control Panel.

2. Do not click Add. You want the Data Sources to be visible to all users and services, not just the current user, so click System DSN. This brings up Figure 24-2, System Data Sources.

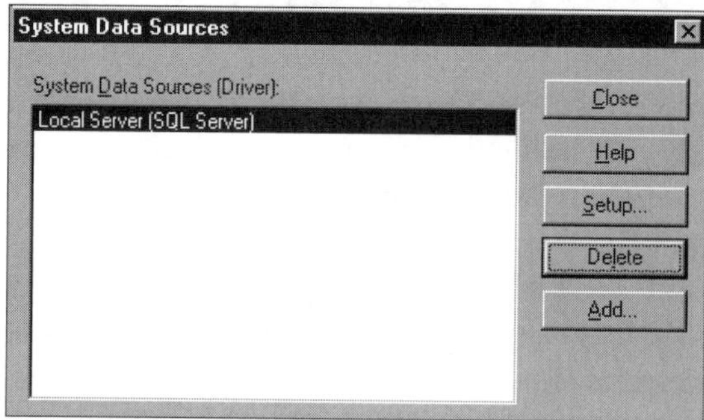

Figure 24-2:
Click System DSN to open the System Data Sources dialog box.

3. Now you should click Add, which opens Figure 24-3, Add Data Source.

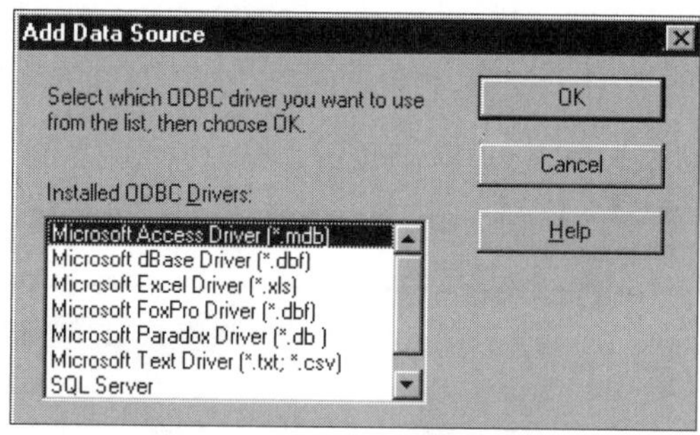

Figure 24-3:
Choose the appropriate driver in the Add Data Source dialog box.

4. Choose the appropriate Driver, for example, Microsoft Access Driver. Then, click OK. Now you will see Driver specific dialog boxes. We shall continue with the Access-specific dialog boxes, which means you will see Figure 24-4, ODBC Microsoft Access 7.0 Setup.
5. Enter a SQL Server identifier for the Data Source Name, for example, SECRETS. You can type whatever you want in the Description, including leaving it blank. Then either choose Select to connect to an existing database or Create to make a new one.
6. Click OK, click Close, and click Close again. You have now defined a new OBDC datasource.

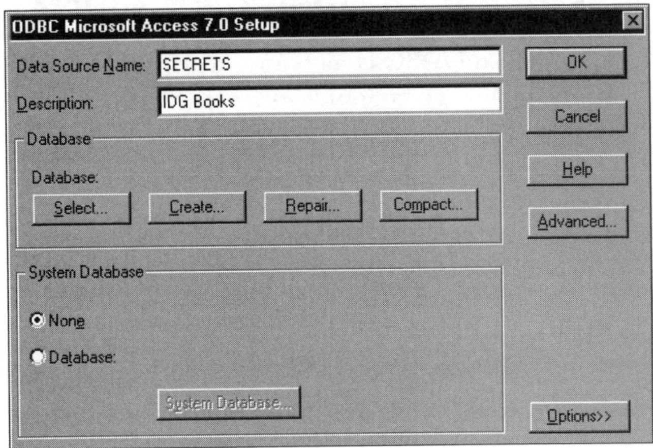

Figure 24-4:
The ODBC Microsoft Access 7.0 Setup dialog box is specific to MS Access.

If you absolutely have to install the ODBC driver remotely, you have no choice but to add the registry key directly using remote registry editing. (See Chapter 7 for an example of this). Copy an existing key for the same ODBC driver, and change the appropriate information. You will not be able to copy the key while replication is using the Data Source. Note also that you have to edit the ODBC.INI file in the WINNT directory of the distribution server. Hopefully, future releases of either Windows NT or SQL Server will support remote installing of ODBC Data Sources.◀

Verifying your connectivity

Next, we recommend trying to connect to the ODBC data source from the distribution server with MS Query. SQL Server 6.5 Setup installs a copy of this application automatically when you install the server, so you definitely have it on the distribution server. If you can't get to the ODBC data source with Microsoft Query, you know replication isn't going to work. It is much easier to troubleshoot replication this way rather than set up all the replication and then have to decipher why it isn't working. Once you see that you have correctly set up the ODBC Data Source, try to ping it from the publication and subscription servers with ODBCPING.EXE (Chapter 23).

Subscribing an ODBC Data Source

To subscribe an ODBC Data Source to your publications, you must first define the ODBC Data Source as a new subscriber, which you can do from the Replication Publishing Window, Figure 24-5. There are a number of ways to open this Window. Our favorite is

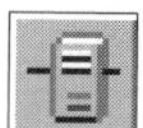

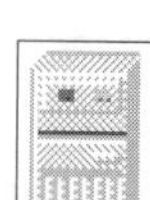

1. Select a server in the Server Manager window.
2. Click the Replication Topology tool bar button.
3. Right click on the server icon for your server.
4. Choose Replication Configuration⇨Publishing from the pop-up menu. Now you are in the Replication Publishing dialog box, Figure 24-5.

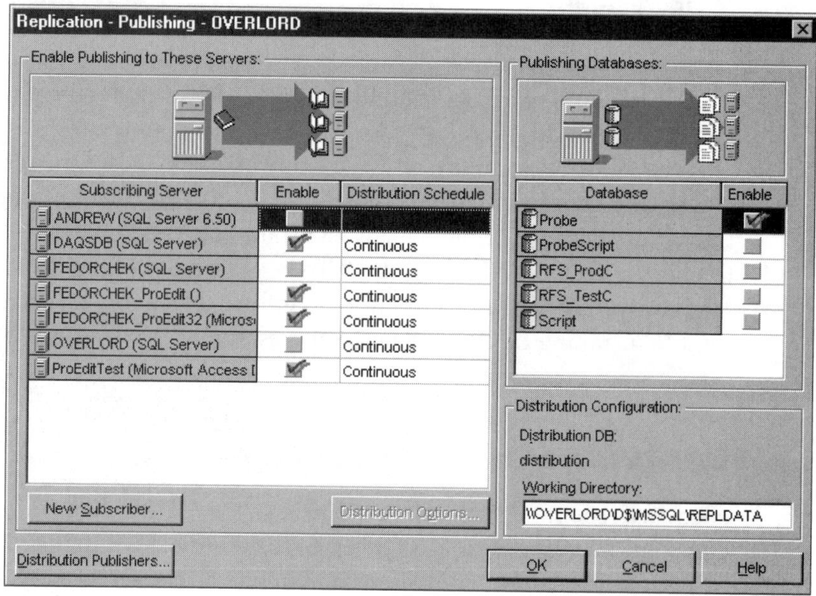

Figure 24-5:
The Replication Publishing window is the first step to defining an ODBC Data Source as a subscriber.

There is a button for New Subscriber. Click it and you get the New Subscriber dialog box. This in turn has a button labeled ODBC Subscriber. Click that and you see the New ODBC Subscriber dialog box, Figure 24-6. The distributor's DSN drop-down list box shows the ODBC data sources known to the distribution server that you have not already specified as subscribers. Again, remember that this list is not what is set up on your machine nor the publication server: it is the ODBC Data Sources of the distribution server.

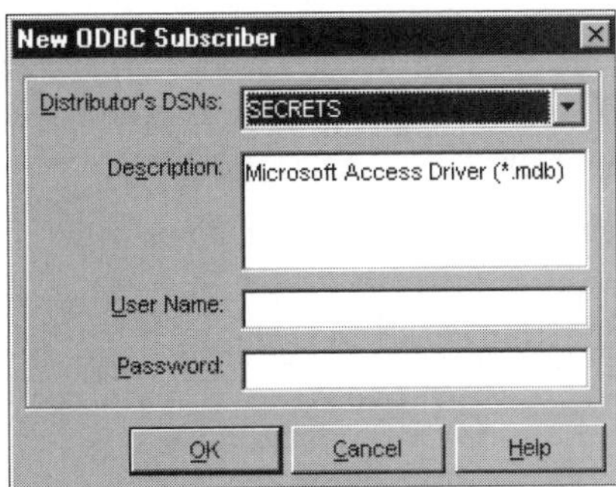

Figure 24-6:
Use the New ODBC Subscriber dialog box to make an ODBC Data Source a new subscriber.

If you supply a login and password, the new login will override the login defined in the ODBC data source, if you defined one there. Make sure that you use a login that has the authority to create tables. Click OK, and SQL Server tries to connect to the ODBC data source and create the MSjob_last_info table in the destination database. If this works, SQL Server returns you to the New Subscriber dialog box, and you are well on your way.

If it doesn't work, you might get any number of ODBC error messages, for example, Figure 24-7. In this case the error message says "Not enough information to connect to this DSN." We intentionally skipped part of the ODBC Data Source definition to produce this error: we didn't pick an MDB file for the Data Source. If we go back and fix it, everything is fine. Note that this error would have been caught both by attempting to connect with MS Query, as we recommended, and by using ODBCPING, as we recommended.

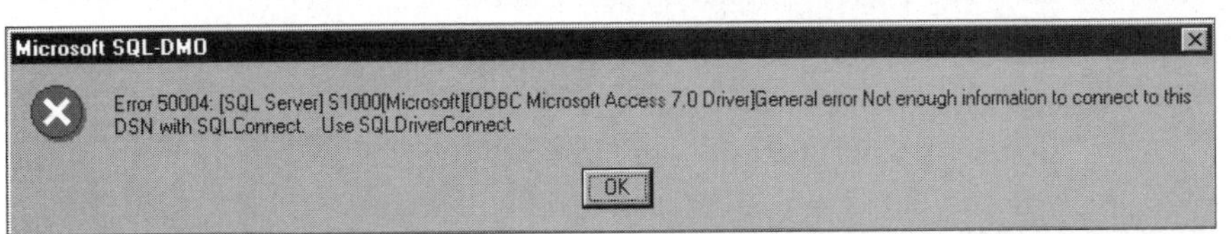

Figure 24-7:
There are any number of errors you might get if SQL Server can't connect to the ODBC Data Source.

Subscribing ODBC Data Sources to publications

The rest of replication set up for creating publications and articles is the same for ODBC as it is for SQL Server subscribers, but remember these points:

- Don't put a primary key into the table-creation script unless you know the ODBC data source supports both primary keys and ANSI SQL for their creation.
- Make sure that you use character bulk copy program (bcp) for synchronization, not native bcp.
- You have to select automatic or manual synchronization.

Troubleshooting ODBC replication

Trying to troubleshoot ODBC replication isn't much fun because you will be getting all kinds of ODBC-specific error messages with which you may or may not be familiar. The best route to deciphering it all is to connect to the ODBC data source outside of SQL Server and try to run each of the commands in MSjob_commands yourself.

An ODBC Example: SQL Server 4.21

We knew we needed to pick some example of ODBC replication to show you, and we wanted to pick something that would be a little challenging. If you read Microsoft's documentation, you will find that it is fairly vague on the subject of replicating to SQL Server 4.21. Clearly, this is an ODBC data source, but Microsoft doesn't come out and say that you can replicate to it. They don't say you can't, either. Our guess is that they really want you to invest in an upgrade (which you should, but that's not the issue here), so they don't bother to tell you what you need to know.

We have already tipped our hand as to what the problem is going to be earlier in this chapter: quoted identifiers. In this case study, however, we will first set up replication — as if we didn't already know this — just to show you the debugging process, too. Here we go.

Step 1: Making sure you can talk to SQL Server 4.21

If you happen to have SQL Server 4.21 running on the same machine as SQL Server 6.*x*, they can't both use the same Named Pipe. The default for both is \\.\pipe\sql\query. Earlier, we discussed changing the pipe for SQL Server 6.5. Let's change the pipe for SQL Server 4.21 here. (Remember you only need to do this if you have SQL Server 4.21 and SQL Server 6.5 running on the same machine.)

1. Stop SQL Server 4.21, if it is running.
2. Run REGEDT32.EXE, and edit the connection string under the HKEY_LOCAL_MACHINE

    SOFTWARE

        Microsoft

            SQLServer

                Server

                    ListenOn

    to be \\.\pipe\sql42\query.
3. Start SQL Server 4.21.
4. Run the client-configuration utility on the distribution server to specify a server name and connection string for this machine. We will use the server name SQLSERVER42.
5. Register SQLSERVER42 in the distribution server SQL Enterprise Manager to make sure that you got it right.

We are not suggesting here that your subscription server be the same as your publication or distribution server. The instance of SQL Server running on this subscription server might not even be involved in the replication.

Step 2: Setting up an ODBC data source for SQLSERVER42

If we didn't have the correct ODBC drivers installed, we would have to do that now, but because the SQL Server ODBC driver has to be on the distribution machine (because SQL Server 6.5 is), we are all set. We just need to follow these steps:

1. Double-click the ODBC32 icon in the Control Panel.
2. Click System DSN.
3. Click Add.
4. Choose SQL Server and click OK.
5. To keep things simple, let the Data Source Name be the same name as your server, SQLSERVER42, though you could enter whatever you want.
6. In the server box, type in whatever name you gave to the client configuration utility, SQLSERVER42 in our case. Notice that we don't enter any pipe names in the ODBC definition; that's what the Client Configuration Utility is for.
7. Click Options and specify the database you want to be the subscription database.
8. Click OK.
9. Click Close.
10. Click Close again.

Step 3: Use MS Query to make sure that you got it right

As we have stressed throughout our discussion of replication, one of the most important things you can do to ensure success is to verify your connection to the subscription server before you set up replication. This is particularly important in cases like this, where you are connecting to a server which you seldom use or which has some special circumstances.

1. Run MS Query from the Microsoft SQL Server 6.5 folder.
2. Choose File➪New.
3. Choose Other.
4. Select SQLSERVER42 and double-click.
5. Log in as the system administrator. (Yes, you could use another id, but that just adds more things that could go wrong. We will have enough trouble as it is; we promise.)

   If you get in, great. If you get any of the typical ODBC errors, like

```
Connection failed:
SQLState: '28000'
SQL Server Error: 4002
[Microsoft][ODBC SQL Server Driver][SQL Server]Login failed
```

you have obviously done something wrong.

Step 4: Define SQLSERVER42 as a subscriber, and subscribe it to a publication

We covered these steps earlier in this chapter. We will use a publication called simply test, with a lone article (again called test), based on the following table:

```
CREATE TABLE test (
    column1 varchar(30) primary key,
    column2 int)
```

What data are in this table doesn't matter; let's just populate it with

```
INSERT INTO test SELECT name, id
    FROM master.dbo.sysobjects
    WHERE uid = 1
```

Create the publication and the article with all the default parameters, except that you have to choose character bcp. If you did everything correctly, you will find in the default replication directory that a script for the table is generated, as well as a .TMP file for synchronization. Log into SQLSERVER42, and you will find MSlast_job_info in the destination database. Test isn't there, however, and it isn't coming no matter how long you wait.

Step 5: Troubleshooting the tasks

Cross-Reference

If you look at the history of the tasks in the distribution server by selecting Server⇨Scheduled Tasks, there should be a bright red failed distribution task for SQLSERVER42. Double click the task to open the edit task window and click the history button. (Refer to Chapter 20 for more information on task management.) The message you will see is

```
Incorrect syntax near 'test'
```

What could this mean? Let's go to the distribution database and find the commands for this article. Get the art_id from *sysarticles* of the publishing database, and query MSjob_commands. You should see just three commands (assuming that you didn't change any data in *test* yet). The first command is

```
drop table "test"
```

Try running that in SQLSERVER42. You get exactly the same error. Now we're getting somewhere. Clearly, this command needed to be just

```
drop table test
```

We can fix this directly in MSjob_commands. Update the command column for this row to the SQL above. Restart the failed task from the task window, wait a few minutes, and go look for test again in SQLSERVER42. Lo and behold, there it is, complete with data!

Step 6: Testing log-based replication

Now you know that replication can do the synch task. Make any changes you like to test in the publication database. We will simply do this:

```
INSERT INTO test VALUES ( 'Testing', 0)
```

Wait as long as you want; this change won't appear in SQLSERVER42. Let's query MSjob_commands again to look for this SQL. Sure enough, we find

```
insert into "test" values ( "Testing", 0)
```

Obviously, we have the same quoted identifier problem. If we look at the task errors, we find the same kind of syntax error message. Well, now what? We could change the SQL in MSjob_commands again, but we can't be doing this every single time. We need a way to get the data over to SQLSERVER42 without referencing test explicitly. Every time test appears in the SQL, we are going to get quotes. The solution is to use custom replication procedures.

Step 7: Setting up custom replication procedures

If you set up custom replication procedures, the command column in MSjob_commands has simply the text

```
call procedure value1, value2, …
```

Another Approach

A different way to attack this problem is to write a trigger on the MSjob_commands table that strips out the quotes. This is an excellent idea for handling the drop commands. It becomes really, really messy on UPDATE statements, however, because not only is the table name in quotes, but so are all the column names. We think you will agree that the custom stored procedures are a lot simpler.

No quoted identifiers! We cover custom procedures more in the next chapter, but for now, we will create these procedures in SQLSERVER42 for a test:

```
CREATE PROC insert_test @column1 varchar(30), @column2 int AS
INSERT INTO test VALUES (@column1, @column2)
GO
CREATE PROC update_test @column1 varchar(30), @column2 int, @old_column1 var-
char(30) AS
UPDATE test SET column1 = @column1, column2 = @column2 WHERE column1 = @old_column1
GO
CREATE PROC delete_test @column1 varchar(30 AS
DELETE test WHERE column1 = @column1
GO
```

Drop the subscription to article test, modify the article to call these procedures, and resubscribe. Try it as before, and now replication finally works to this ODBC data source.

Summary

A significant enhancement to replication in SQL Server 6.5 is that you can now replicate to ODBC data sources. There are several restrictions to keep in mind, the most significant of which is that you can only replicate data out of SQL Server 6.5 to an ODBC data source, not the other way around. Setting up replication for ODBC requires only minor adjustments to the process you have already learned. The biggest hurdle is getting the right drivers and creating the data sources. You can replicate to SQL Server 4.2 via ODBC, but you will need custom stored procedures to do it.

Review Questions

Q: Can SQL Server 6.0 replicate to any ODBC data sources at all, such as just Microsoft Access?

A: No. This is strictly a SQL Server 6.5 feature.

Q: What is the maximum batch size (the -c parameter) for ODBC replication?

A: It doesn't matter at all what you set for -c, the batch size is always 1.

Q: Can you replicate SQL Server datatypes that have no equivalent type in the ODBC data source?

A: Yes. SQL Server will convert its datatypes into the ODBC data source's types.

Chapter

Advanced Replication

25

The basic replication we outlined in Chapters 24 and 25 gets you started, but everyone will need to do advanced work in replication. Here we cover what you need to know to handle any replication scenario.

What's in This Chapter

In this chapter, we cover the follow topics. Each section stands on its own, so you can skip to reading the ones that are of the most interest to you.

- Using some SQL to save work
- Building scripts from your publishing databases
- Using your own replication stored procedures
- Working around the foreign key problem
- Troubleshooting replication
- Uninstalling publishing

Using Some SQL to Save Work

Though we are big fans of Transact-SQL and stored procedures, we do use the GUI a lot. Setting up replication manually from start to finish entirely with SQL is a lot of work for no reason. Having said that, there are definitely times when you should use stored procedures instead of the SQL Enterprise Manager.

Setting up articles with sp_addarticle

The graphical interface of the SQL Enterprise Manager is certainly nice, but if you have more than a handful of articles to publish, it becomes tedious in a hurry. Suppose that you have 75 tables you want to publish, with no foreign keys to worry about, and the way you know which tables to publish is that they all have names ending in "_gov." Furthermore, you want their primary keys included in the scripts, and you want the destination tables to have the "_gov" suffix stripped off. You will be working all day to set this up through the SQL Enterprise Manager. The better way to do this is with sp_addarticle. Its syntax is

```
sp_addarticle publication, article, source_table [, destination_table]
    [, vertical_partition] [, type] [, filter] [, sync_object] [, ins_cmd]
    [, del_cmd] [, upd_cmd] [, creation_script] [, description]
    [, pre_creation_cmd] [, filter_clause]
```

The parameters are as listed in Table 25-1.

Table 25-1
Use sp_addarticle with These Parameters

Parameter	Default	Explanation
publication		Name of the publication that will contain the article.
article		Name of the article; must be unique in the publication.
source_table		Name of the table on which you are basing your article.
destination table	source table	Name you want used in the destination server(s).
vertical partition	false	Whether there is to be a vertical partition. If true, only the primary key columns are initially flagged for replication. You have to add more columns with sp_articlecolumn.
type	1	Specifies the type of article. Can be 1 Log-based article (the default)

Parameter	Default	Explanation
		3 Log-based article with manual filter 5 Log based article with manual view 7 Log-based article with manual filter and manual view
filter	null	The name of a stored procedure you want to use for filtering.
sync_object	null	The name of the view you want to use for fitering.
ins_cmd	SQL	If not SQL, your command to be executed on INSERT.
del_cmd	SQL	If not SQL, your command to be executed on DELETE.
upd_cmd	SQL	If not SQL, your command to be executed on UPDATE.
creation script	null	Path to your custom script for the article creation script.
description	null	Your 255-character-or-less description of the article.
pre_creation cmd	'none'	Can be: 'None', 'Drop', 'Delete', 'Truncate'.
filter clause	null	Your WHERE clause for limiting what gets replicated.

Certainly, you will not need a lot of these parameters in any given situation. To return to our example, you would do the following:

1. Use Object⇨Generate SQL Scripts to make scripts for all your tables, with the DRI option checked and Save Scripted Objects To Separate Files checked. Let's say the path you chose was C:\MyPath.
2. Run a query against the sysobjects system table to create the sp_addarticle commands.

```
SELECT 'exec sp_addarticle, MyPublication,' , name , ',' , name , ',' ,
      substring(name,1,abs(datalength(name)-4)) , ',' ,
      '@creation_script = ''c:\myPath\'+name+'.SQL'''
FROM sysobjects
       WHERE type = 'u'
          AND name LIKE '%[_]gov'
```

   This produces output like the following:

```
    exec sp_addarticle, MyPublication, myFirstTable_gov, myFirstTable_gov,
myFirstTable,
       @creation_script = 'c:\myPath\myFirstTable_gov.SQL'
exec sp_addarticle, MyPublication, mySecondTable_gov, mySecondTable_gov,
mySecondTable,
   @creation_script = 'c:\myPath\mySecondTable_gov.SQL'
```

3. All you have to do now is run the script.

Why Does Drop All Run Slowly?

If you do have a stack of 75 articles, 'sp_droparticle publication, all' runs for several spins of the little Query Analyzer globe. If you build the 75 individual sp_droparticle commands and run them in one batch, they run much faster. The reason is that the first method uses a cursor. This is a good example of how cursors slow you down.

Dropping articles

As you might imagine, there is an sp_droparticle stored procedure, too. Though you could use a procedure similar to the preceding one to drop all the articles in your publication, there is an easier way. The syntax of sp_droparticle is as follows:

```
sp_droparticle publication, article
```

Publication and *article* are the names of your publication and article, respectively. When you want to drop all articles, simply pass the string 'all' as the article.

Building Scripts from Your Publishing Databases

One of the major drawbacks of the SQL Enterprise Manager script generator is that it does not build scripts for your replication system tables. In fact, replication is the only part of a database definition that Microsoft ignored in the script generator. Hopefully, it will be included in a future release. Until then, you have to do it yourself, but we provide the SQL for doing so. This can be dressed with a Visual Basic or Visual C++ program if you have the time and inclination. Before we start, let's discuss why you might want this. Just as in regular SQL Scripts, you will need this if:

- You are in a situation where restoring from a backup is impossible. It may be that you want to set up your entire database, replication and all, on a machine with a different sort order or a different character set.
- Restoring from a backup is unacceptable. Perhaps you have accidentally dropped all the articles of a publication with the nifty command we just discussed, but nothing else is wrong with the database. If the last backup

is from two days ago and will take hours to restore, none of your users are going to agree to all the down time and lost work because of your mistake. You won't be able to restore that backup; you need a script.

- You need to drop and recreate all your publications quickly. Suppose that you have to alter some of your tables, which means the articles associated with them must be dropped.

What we are *not* going to do here is provide scripts for setting up the distribution database. You can quickly set that up from the SQL Enterprise Manager, even if you have to start over from square one.

Publications

You recreate your publications with sp_addpublication. We have not yet presented its syntax. It is as follows:

```
sp_addpublication publication, taskid,
   [, @restricted = {'true'|'false'}
   [, @sync_method = {'native'|'character'}
   [, @repl_freq = {'continuous'|'snapshot'}
   [, @description = 'string description'
   [, @status= {'inactive'|'active'}]]]]]
```

This stores a bunch of information is syspublications; reversing it is straightforward:

```
SELECT 'exec sp_addpublication', name, ',', taskid, ',',
      case restricted when 0 then 'false' when 1 then 'true' end, ',',
      case sync_method when 0 then 'native' when 1 then 'character' end, ',',
      case repl_freq when 0 then 'continuous' when 1 then 'snapshot' end, ',',
      description, ',',
      case status when 0 then 'inactive' when 1 then 'active' end
   FROM syspublications
   ORDER BY name
```

The output from this query will depend on what you have set up for your publications, but if you have three publications named pub1, pub2, and pub3, you might see something like this:

```
exec sp_addpublication pub1,  6, false, character, continuous, , active
exec sp_addpublication pub2, 13, false, character, continuous, , active
exec sp_addpublication pub3, 10, false, character, continuous, , active
```

Articles

Next come your articles. The syntax for sp_addarticle is

```
sp_addarticle publication,  article,  source_table [, destination_table]
   [, vertical_partition] [, type] [, filter] [, sync_object] [, ins_cmd]
   [, del_cmd] [, upd_cmd] [, creation_script] [, description]
   [, pre_creation_cmd] [, filter_clause]
```

as follows:

```
SELECT 'exec sp_addarticle',
      p.name, ',',
      a.name, ',',
      ''''+USER_NAME(uid)+'.'+o.name+''',',
      dest_table, ',',
      'true, ',
      a.type, ',' ,
      OBJECT_NAME(sync_objid), ',',
      ''''+ins_cmd+''',',
      ''''+del_cmd+''',',
      ''''+upd_cmd+''',',
      ''''+creation_script+''',',
      ''''+a.description+''',',
      CASE pre_creation_cmd
         WHEN 0 THEN 'none'
         WHEN 1 THEN 'drop'
         WHEN 2 THEN 'delete'
         WHEN 3 THEN 'truncate'
      end, ',',
      ''''+CONVERT( varchar(255), filter_clause)+''''
   FROM sysarticles a
   JOIN syspublications p ON a.pubid = p.pubid
   JOIN sysobjects o ON a.objid = o.id
   ORDER BY a.name
```

Once again, the output depends on what articles you have defined, but you can expect something like this:

```
exec sp_addarticle art1 , art1_Table , 'dbo.art1', art1 , true, 1 , art1 , '', '', '',
'\\SERVERNAME\D$\MSSQL\REPLDATA\SERVERNAME_dbname_art1_art1_Table.SCH', '', drop , ''
```

USING YOUR OWN REPLICATION STORED PROCEDURES

Up until now, we have always talked about replication commands that simply mimic the INSERTs, UPDATEs, and DELETEs executed in the publication database. Normally, this is exactly what you want because your whole intent is to keep the destination tables exactly the same as your publication tables. However, there may be circumstances when you want to do something entirely different. Following is an example.

We mentioned earlier that you can't replicate objects other than tables. Views, for example, don't get replicated. How can you replicate them anyway? Well, the information about views is stored in system tables. Of course, you can't replicate them because:

- The replication process won't let you.
- It would create chaos in the destination database if you could.

The solution involves FOR REPLICATION user-stored procedures. SQL Server lets you define custom stored procedures to run instead of the logreader process on any or all INSERTs, UPDATEs, and DELETEs.

In our example, we start by dumping the appropriate system table information into a user table. For simplicity, we will stick to database owner-owned views, as follows:

```
CREATE TABLE repl_views (
   name sysname,
   colid int PRIMARY KEY (name, colid),
   id int,
   num_lines int, /* Why is necessary will be clear when we write the procedure. */
   text varchar(255))
```

This should be two tables, one with colums id (PK), name, num_lines; the second with id, colid PK(id, colid), text. We have stuffed all the data in one table to keep the example short.

Next, we will fill it with the current view information:

```
INSERT repl_views
SELECT o.name, colid, c.id, (SELECT max(colid) FROM syscomments a WHERE a.id =
c.id), text
   FROM sysobjects o, syscomments c
   WHERE o.id = c.id
      AND uid = 1
      AND o.type = 'v'
```

Our plan is to create a task that will update this table periodically. Then, we will use replication to create the views in the destination server. (This, of course, assumes that the destination databases will have the old tables and views on which the new views depend.) When a view is changed, it must be dropped, so we will never be updating repl_views. We will only be deleting and inserting. Thus, the stored procedure for keeping repl_views current is as follows:

```
CREATE PROC refresh_repl_views AS
DELETE repl_views
   FROM repl_views r
   WHERE NOT EXISTS (SELECT *
         FROM sysobjects s
         WHERE s.id = r.id)
INSERT repl_views
SELECT o.name, colid, c.id,
      (SELECT max(colid) FROM syscomments a WHERE a.id = c.id), text
   FROM sysobjects o, syscomments c
   WHERE o.id = c.id
      AND uid = 1
      AND o.type = 'v'
      AND NOT EXISTS (SELECT *
         FROM repl_views
         WHERE id = c.id)
```

Now we are finally in a position to define custom procedures for replication. The syntax for a delete procedure for replication is

```
CREATE PROCedure procedure_name pkc1, pkc2, …, pkcn FOR REPLICATION AS sql_statements
```

Where pkc1, pkc2, …, pkc*n* are the primary key columns. The "FOR REPLICATION" makes it so that *only* the replication process can use the procedure in the destination database.

In our case, we want to drop views that have been dropped in the publication database, so we have

```
CREATE PROC repl_view_delete @name sysname, @colid int FOR REPLICATION AS
EXEC('IF EXISTS (SELECT *
   FROM sysobjects
   WHERE name = '''+@name+''')
   DROP VIEW '+@name)
DELETE repl_views
   WHERE name = @name
      AND colid = @colid
```

Finally, the exciting one: the insert. The syntax for an insert procedure for replication is the following:

```
CREATE PROCedure procedure_name c1, c2, …, cn FOR REPLICATION AS sql_statements
```

Our custom procedure will be the following:

```
CREATE PROC repl_view_insert
   @name sysname, @colid int, @id int, @num_lines int, @text varchar(255)
   FOR REPLICATION AS
INSERT repl_views VALUES(name, @colid, @id, @num_lines, @text)
IF (SELECT COUNT(*) FROM repl_views WHERE name = @name) = @num_lines BEGIN
   DECLARE @1 varchar(255), @2 varchar(255), @3 varchar(255), @4 varchar(255),
      @5 varchar(255), @6 varchar(255), @7 varchar(255), @8 varchar(255),
      @9 varchar(255), @a varchar(255), @b varchar(255), @c varchar(255),
      @d varchar(255), @e varchar(255), @f varchar(255)
   SELECT @1 = text FROM repl_views WHERE name = @name AND colid = 1
   SELECT @2 = text FROM repl_views WHERE name = @name AND colid = 2
   SELECT @3 = text FROM repl_views WHERE name = @name AND colid = 3
   SELECT @4 = text FROM repl_views WHERE name = @name AND colid = 4
   SELECT @5 = text FROM repl_views WHERE name = @name AND colid = 5
   SELECT @6 = text FROM repl_views WHERE name = @name AND colid = 6
   SELECT @7 = text FROM repl_views WHERE name = @name AND colid = 7
   SELECT @8 = text FROM repl_views WHERE name = @name AND colid = 8
   SELECT @9 = text FROM repl_views WHERE name = @name AND colid = 9
   SELECT @a = text FROM repl_views WHERE name = @name AND colid = 10
   SELECT @b = text FROM repl_views WHERE name = @name AND colid = 11
   SELECT @c = text FROM repl_views WHERE name = @name AND colid = 12
   SELECT @d = text FROM repl_views WHERE name = @name AND colid = 13
   SELECT @e = text FROM repl_views WHERE name = @name AND colid = 14
   SELECT @f = text FROM repl_views WHERE name = @name AND colid = 15
   EXEC(@1+@2+@3+@4+@5+@6+@7+@8+@9+@a+@b+@c+@d+@e+@f)
END
```

The reason for including num_lines is so that each call to num_lines will include the information about how many total lines to wait for. Otherwise, we could have a CREATE VIEW attempting to fire without all the text that it needs.

To link these into an article, you check the CUSTOM buttons on the Scripts tab of Manage Article and type in CALL proc_name. For the insert, you would type CALL repl_views_insert.

Working around the Foreign Key Problem

You will recall from Chapter 22 that there is a problem in how replication handles foreign keys. The NOT FOR REPLICATION mitigates this somewhat, but it isn't a perfect solution. Furthermore, there may be many of you still using SQL Server 6.0 who don't have this the luxury of even this partial solution. Therefore, we will take this opportunity to present an alternative solution.◀

To review, our difficulty is this: SQL Server replication will sometimes convert an UPDATE into a DELETE/INSERT pair. This conversion can happen even when only nonkey fields are being UPDATEd. If you defined foreign keys on the destination side, you will be in trouble when the DELETE comes along. It may try to DELETE a record that is being referenced by a foreign key.

At first, you might think that a custom UPDATE procedure FOR REPLICATION will be your way out. No, this doesn't work because if the log reader converts an UPDATE into a DELETE/INSERT, it won't call your custom UPDATE. It will call your custom DELETE and custom INSERT, if you have them.

Instead, we will log all the changes to the publication table as follows (assume that the table to be published is called yourTable):

1. Make a table called log_yourTable with this structure:

```
CREATE TABLE log_yourTable (
   timestamp PRIMARY KEY,
   command char(6) CHECK (command in ('insert','update','delete')),
   <all the columns of yourTable>)
```

2. Make triggers on yourTable to log changes in log_yourTable, as in the following:

```
CREATE TRIGGER TR__yourTable__ins FOR INSERT AS
   INSERT log_yourTable (command, <all the columns of yourTable>)
   SELECT 'INSERT', i.* FROM inserted i
```

   The update and delete triggers are similar. In the update trigger, be sure to insert into log_yourTable the new values, that is, the inserted table values.

3. Set up replication on log_yourTable. Notice that log_yourTable is only inserted into; it should never be updated or deleted.
4. Define custom procedures on the destination server to process the insert, update, and delete commands. Here you have beaten the replication process because the UPDATE trigger on yourTable guarantees that you will know when an actual UPDATE happened.

Troubleshooting Replication

Regrettably, the need to troubleshoot the replication task comes up more often that we would like. We will break the process down into pieces in the order in which they should occur.

Completing the replication setup

This falls in the same category as "Is it plugged in?", but it still needs to be checked. Make sure that you hit all these points as you installed replication:

- You created a distribution database.
- You installed publishing on a server and received a dialog box saying the installation was successful.
- You now have a distribution database with six user tables starting with the letters *MS*.

If any of the preceding are not true, you should reinstall publishing. Skip to the "uninstall" section in this chapter. Charging ahead, did you:

- Enable a database on the publisher to publish?
- Check to make sure this database has sysarticles, syspublications, and syssubscriptions?
- Check to see that the log reader task for this database exists?
- Enable a server to receive subscriptions?
- Check for the clean-up task for that subscriber on the distribution server?
- Enable a database on that server to subscribe?
- Check for MSlast_job_info in that database?

If you answered No to any of these, you should try simply repeating the appropriate steps for whatever you are lacking. Finally, we have to ask

- Did you define a publication?
- Did you check for the distribution task for that publication?
- Did you define at least one article in that publication?
- Is there at least one subscription to that article?
- Is there a script file for that article in whatever directory you specified?

If any of these are not true, you should attempt to redefine the publication, article, or subscription as appropriate.

The only other thing to check in the "Is it plugged in?" category is whether the SQL Executive is running, and whether it is using something other that the local system account. In the Server Manager window, make sure that the SQL Executive icon is colored green inside the little gears. If not, right-click it and choose Start. If it fails to start, you have found your problem. To check which account it is using, right-click the SQL Executive and choose Configure. The "local system" account box should be cleared, and there should be an account and password filled in below. When you install publishing, the SQL Enterprise Manager checked to make sure that this is so, but someone could have changed it.

The log reader

After you have checked all the preceding stuff, the log reader should be running, scanning your transaction log for transactions to replicate.

Seeing what is in the log

There are two extended stored procedures to use here, sp_repltrans and sp_replcmds. The first shows you transactions that the log reader has not passed to the distribution database; the second shows you the commands for these transactions. sp_repltrans takes no parameters, so just make sure that you are in the publication database when you run it. If you get no results, everything is okay as far as the log reader is concerned. If you do see rows, you have unreplicated transactions. Run sp_replcmds to see what these transactions really are. The syntax is as follows:

```
sp_replcmds [maxtrans]
```

Maxtrans is the maximum number of transactions for which you want to see information.

Changing the log reader frequency

If you have transactions that aren't getting out of the log, you want to know why. Let's switch to the Task Manager and follow these steps:

1. Select the log reader task for the database in question and edit it.

2. Right now it is set as an autostart task. Change the frequency so that it runs every minute, and modify the task. (Refer to Chapter 20 for details on task management.)◀
3. Stop and start the SQL Executive. This is necessary to get the log reader to start running with the new frequency you specified.
4. After a few minutes, look at the history of the task. There should be some error there for you to see that will shed light on what is wrong.

How to truncate your log

If you have a lot of changes going on in your database, your transaction log is filling up rapidly while you are trying to figure this mess out. You can't truncate unreplicated transactions out of this log. What can you do to keep the log from filling up? You have three choices:

- **Drop your articles and publications.** Not a very desirable solution. This will stop further transactions from getting marked for replication all right, but it does nothing about what is in the log. Even if you dropped the tables to which these transactions correspond, the transactions would still be pinned in the log.
- **Extend the log size.** You will need a larger log for replication anyway, so this might be a good idea, especially if you feel confident that after the extension you will not be in danger of filling up the log before you fix replication.
- **Unmark the replication transactions.** You can't truncate a bunch of transactions out of your log because they are tagged as needing to be replicated. You can, as the system administrator, lie to SQL Server and make it look as though these transactions have been read. The good part about this is that you don't have to drop any articles or publications. The bad part is that after you pull this stunt, you really need to unsubscribe and resubscribe everything to make sure that things are synchronized. If you want to do this, all you need is the following:

```
sp_repldone 0, 0, NULL, 0, 0, 1
```

Passing the ball to distribution

After the log reader reads tasks, it should put them in MSjob_commands in the distribution database. SELECT from this table to see if you find the transaction you seek. If you do, you know for sure that the log reader is not your problem. Now, it's on to the distribution task.

The distribution task

At this point, we have verified that the commands needed for replication are waiting in the MSjob_commands table for the distribution task to grab. Now, we will micromanage that task to make sure that it is doing its job by doing the following:

1. Follow the steps for "Changing the log reader frequency" to change the frequency of the distribution task to the same interval: every minute.
2. Edit the command of the task so that the -c parameter reads -c1. Normally, the distribution task commits in batches: this switches it to commit on the subscription servers command by command.
3. After you have stopped and started the SQL Executive, you should start to get errors in the task history after a few minutes.

Common errors and solutions

This is where you will have the bulk of your trouble with replication. Let's discuss some common errors.

Login errors

Any flavor of error along the lines of "server does not exist", "not a valid user of trusted connection", "database in single user mode," and so on is basically telling you that the distribution task could not get to the server or the database it needed. You can solve that with what you already know about the SQL Enterprise Manager. Use that tool to verify the server status, verify that the repl_publisher login exists, and so forth.

No jobs found

If you have botched up your replication set, and especially if you have incorrectly reinstalled publishing, you will get an error about "no jobs found with an id > X." What is happening here is that repl_publisher logged in successfully, connected to the destination database, and queried MSlast_job_info to find out what transactions to send. That table led the repl_publisher to conclude that no commands needed to be sent. You will have to update this table to get it in line with what the distribution database says.

Standard INSERT, UPDATE, or DELETE errors

The last likely scenario is that the distribution task did log into the subscriber and it did try to execute the appropriate command (an INSERT, UPDATE, DELETE, or one of your custom procedures), and the command bombed. Hopefully, it will be clear to you what went wrong. Perhaps you created a CHECK constraint on the target table and you failed to specify NOT FOR REPLICATION when you needed to. Maybe you have a primary key violation, which would indicate either that the tables are not synchronized or that someone is updating the destination side table. Whatever the problem, you have four ways to implement your solution:

- You can fix the situation on the subscription side. When the distribution task retries its command, everything should work.
- You edit the SQL in the MSjob_commands table. When the distribution task attempts a retry, it will use your new SQL, and everything should work.
- You can kill the job. The command is

  ```
  sp_MSkill_job job_id, publisher, publisher_db
  ```

  You find the values for the three parameters by looking at the MSjob_-commands table. Killing the job allows the distribution task to pick up with the next task.
- You yourself can run the SQL that is failing, and after you get it to work, kill the job.

Uninstalling Publishing

There are reasons that you may need to uninstall publishing, not the least of which is that you need a fresh start. Here's what to do:

1. Script your articles and publications, if desired, with the method outlined earlier in this chapter.
2. Remove all your publishing databases from the publishing list. Choose Server⇨Replication Configuration⇨Publishing, and clear the check boxes for all Publishing Databases.
3. Clear the check boxes for all servers to which you have currently enabled subscribing.
4. Clear your publication server's flag. The correct command is as follows:

   ```
   sp_serveroption DISTRIBUTOR,'dist', false
   ```

   DISTRIBUTOR is the name of your distribution server.

5. Disconnect from and reconnect to the server. This forces the SQL Enterprise to requery sysservers.
6. If the distribution database was being used for this publisher alone, you may now drop it.

Tip

The preceding procedure *should* uninstall replication. However, we have occasionally had to go as far as running REGEDT32.EXE and deleting the REPLICATION registry key. If you are serious about removing replication, you can do that if all else fails.

Summary

In this chapter, we covered a variety of special things you can do with replication, depending on what kinds of advanced requirements you have.

Review Questions

Q: Is there any part of setting up publishing that can't be done with SQL and stored procedures?

A: Yes, you have to make entries into the Windows NT Registry. You could do this with extended stored procedures, of course.

Q: What part of article definitions did we leave out of our scripts?

A: Vertical partitions: that is, restricting the columns of a base table.

Q: Can you mix custom stored procedures with standard processing so that perhaps you call a stored procedure on update but let the log reader make INSERT and DELETE SQL commands?

A: Absolutely.

Part

VIII

TROUBLESHOOTING AND OPTIMIZATION

Without a doubt, this one of the most exciting sections of the book. The techniques presented here are ones you will probably use when something is running too slowly, or worse yet, not running at all. This can be quite frustrating until you learn the reasons SQL Server does what it does; then it is truly exciting. You will sweep in, fix a problem, and in no time have things working better than they were before.

If there is one command that is the nerdy command of SQL Server, it is the Database Consistency Checker (DBCC) command. DBCC is really the umbrella command for invoking any number of other SQL Server specific commands that generally get into the weeds of what SQL Server is doing. Chapter 26 reveals everything you could want to know about DBCC. We start with trace flags, which let you customize SQL Server to behave the way you want it to behave. This includes getting SQL Server to revert to the behavior of previous versions, turning off various ANSI-standard features, and turning on all kinds of extra output to dissect your SQL. Armed with this knowledge, you are ready to use preventive maintenance DBCC commands to find problems in your database *before* they find you. Recognizing that you can't find everything, however, we next discuss the DBCC commands you need to bail yourself out of a disaster. Finally, we discuss how to use DBCC to manage memory, a critical performance issue.

Though we have packed Part VIII with as many troubleshooting hints as we can fit, you will inevitably run into a situation not documented here. Therefore, we offer Chapter 27 to show you how to craft your own solutions to SQL Server problems. In our experience, at least half of all SQL Server problems can be solved by shoving the client application out of the way and looking at the actual Transact-SQL going to the server. Either the client application is not running the Transact-SQL you think it is, or it is hiding a vital error message from SQL Server. For this reason, the SQL Trace utility discussed in Chapter 27 is one of the single greatest features of SQL Server 6.5. We discuss it in depth in Chapter 27, as well as other techniques we have used to crack open the hood of SQL Server.

The optimization section of Part VIII begins with Chapter 28. Getting SELECT, INSERT, UPDATE, and DELETE statements to work quickly is the most important part of designing a database application, bar none. Entire data models get revised and rearranged in the name of query performance. Developers let query performance dictate what functionality their application can and can't have, rather than the other way around. Chapters 28 and 29 tell you everything you need to know to get the very last drop of performance out of SQL Server. Read these chapters *before* you butcher your data model or your application design.

In Chapter 28 we begin with a detailed discussion of how SQL Server stores data in the actual operating system files. We get very detailed here so that there is absolutely no doubt in your mind what SQL Server goes through to retrieve data. With that in mind, we discuss how indexes help in getting data off the disk quickly, and why some indexes are much, much better than others. The second half of Chapter 28 presents a step-by-step approach to indexing an entire database, whether it has ten tables or 10,000. The techniques we offer get you up to speed quickly, solving most of your optimization problems with one master stroke.

You notice we said most of your optimization problems. That is where Chapter 29 comes into play. You can have a greatest index structure in the world and still write a query that literally runs 100 times longer that it should. Chapter 29 discusses query optimization from soup to nuts. First of all, we show you that not all SQL is equal — cases where two commands are equivalent in SQL, but one runs enormously faster than another. Next, we get SQL Server to tell us *how* is it executing a query. Often when we see the path SQL Server has chosen, we see that we need another index or that our query is poorly written. Once we are satisfied that a quick path to the data does exist, but SQL Server isn't choosing this path, we use trace flags to examine *why* SQL Server is executing a query the way it is. At this point, the mystery is all over. If we don't like what SQL Server is doing, we force it to run the query our way.

Chapter

26

Database Consistency Checker

Relational Database Management Systems (RDBMSs) are rather unusual compared to other software systems because you almost expect that there will be disconnects and inconsistencies. The problems we are referring to here are not what you usually think of as bugs. They are errors in the devices, databases, and objects that SQL Server is managing for you. These errors may be the result of bugs in the SQL Server application, but they may be flaws that the SQL Server application intentionally allows for some reason, usually to get better performance. The flaw can be outside of SQL Server, too; this might indicate a hardware error or maybe something *you* did. Because these disconnects are in your databases — not some EXE file that shipped with SQL Server — they can be fixed when you find them, if you have the tools. The Database Consistency Checker (DBCC) is that tool. You use it to do the following:

- Identify and diagnose flaws in your databases
- Fix those flaws
- Get special information not accessible via SQL Server
- Run other special tasks

As it turns out, you have to use DBCC to interpret the output of DBCC, which forces a specific order on this chapter. First, we talk about the way DBCC lets you display information; then, we get into other broad areas of checking. This chapter explains how to use DBCC to your best advantage.

What's in This Chapter

This chapter includes coverage of the following topics:

- Preventive maintenance on inconsistencies
- Dealing with problems that are already in progress
- Managing your memory
- Snooping around where you shouldn't be

DBCC in General

Learning the syntax of DBCC is simple. It is always of the form:

```
DBCC command ( parameter1, parameter2, ... )
```

The complete syntax for the supported DBCC command set is the following:

```
DBCC {
    CHECKALLOC [(database_name [, NOINDEX])]|
    CHECKCATALOG [(database_name)]|
    CHECKTABLE (table_name [, NOINDEX|index_id])|
    CHECKDB [(database_name [, NOINDEX])]|
    CHECKIDENT [(table_name)]|
    DBREPAIR (database_name, DROPDB [, NOINIT])|
    dllname (FREE)|
    INPUTBUFFER (spid)|
    MEMUSAGE|
    NEWALLOC [(database_name [, NOINDEX])]|
    OPENTRAN ({database_name}|{database_id})
        [WITH TABLERESULTS]|
    OUTPUTBUFFER (spid)|
    PERFMON|
    PINTABLE (database_id, table_id)|
    SHOW_STATISTICS (table_name, index_name)|
```

```
    SHOWCONTIG (table_id, [index_id])|
    SHRINKDB (database_name [, new_size [, 'MASTEROVERRIDE']])|
    SQLPERF ({IOSTATS|LRUSTATS|NETSTATS|RASTATS [, CLEAR]} |
        {THREADS}|{LOGSPACE})|
    TEXTALL [({database_name|database_id}[, FULL|FAST])]|
    TEXTALLOC [({table_name|table_id}[, FULL|FAST])]|
    TRACEOFF (trace#)|
    TRACEON (trace#) |
    TRACESTATUS (trace# [, trace#...])|
    UNPINTABLE (database_id, table_id)|
    UPDATEUSAGE ({0|database_name} [, table_name [, index_id]]) |
    USEROPTIONS}
[WITH NO_INFOMSGS]
```

You will find that there is a name/id schizophrenia to DBCC. Sometimes DBCC wants an object name, sometimes the object itself. Sometimes DBCC takes both, sometimes it doesn't.◀

What we are going to do in the rest of this chapter is explore these individual commands in detail. We will group the commands by functionality, rather than go through them alphabetically.

DBCC Permissions

Who can execute DBCC depends on the particular DBCC command. The general rule is this:

- A DBCC command that affects just one object (usually an individual table) can be run by the object owner. Any DBCC command that can be run by an object owner can also be run by the database owner or the system administrator.
- A DBCC command that affects just one database but sweeps across all objects in the database can be run by the database owner or the system administrator.
- All remaining DBCC commands, which are usually server-wide in their scope, can be run only by the system administrator.

You cannot transfer DBCC permissions. Period. There is no command like GRANT DBCC ON... or GRANT EXECUTE ON DBCC... . You can't even fake out SQL Server with stored procedures. For example, the following doesn't work:

```
CREATE PROC my_DBCC_CHECKCATALOG
DBCC CHECKCATALOG
GO
GRANT EXECUTE ON my_DBCC_CHECKCATALOG TO PUBLIC
```

You can certainly run these SQL statements and create the procedure, but if someone other than the DBO tries to execute my_DBCC_CHECK-CATALOG, this error results:

```
Only the DBO of database database_name may run the DBCC CHECKCATALOG command.
```

Trace Flags

Many other DBCC commands hinge upon being able to do further DBCC research using trace flags, so we start here. Trace flags are used for two main reasons:

- To get SQL Server to turn on or off some special functionality. Usually, you are turning on some non-ANSI standard behavior or some function an earlier version of SQL Server allowed.
- To have SQL Server provide special output or information.

The fact that trace flags let SQL Server 6.5 mimic the functionality of earlier versions is vital information to keep in mind as you upgrade. Rather than hold off upgrading for two months while you clean up application programs to comply with the particular quirks of version 6.5, you may be able to turn on a few flags and upgrade tomorrow!

The syntax for turning on trace flags is the following:

```
DBCC TRACEON ( tracenum [, tracenum ... ] )
```

Microsoft's Disclaimer

Microsoft makes a point of telling you in its documentation that it doesn't support trace flags, which means that it won't commit to providing a particular flag in a future release, nor will Microsoft provide you any help or answer questions about trace flags.

Don't let that discourage you because you will miss out on some cool stuff.

For example:

```
DBCC TRACEON ( 3604, 302 )
```

The only curve ball is that if you mistype the *tracenum* parameter, (that is, you meant to type **3604**, but instead you type **3064**), you will get no error or warning, even though the number you put in was not a valid flag.

Turning off trace flags is just as easy. The syntax is as follows:

```
DBCC TRACEOFF ( tracenum [, tracenum ... ] )
```

If you want to check which flags you have on, the command is the following:

```
DBCC TRACESTATUS ( tracenum [, tracenum ... ] )
```

Finally, you can see which flags are in effect by typing

```
DBCC TRACESTATUS ( -1 )
```

If you need to have particular flags in effect at the moment SQL Server starts, you can send those flags as parameters to the SQLSERVR.EXE executable with the -T option, as follows:

```
SQLSERVR /T3609
```

The SQL Enterprise Manager provides an interface for this in the Options tab of the Server Configuration window. Click the parameter button, and you can type in your options.

Your SQL Server documentation has a complete list of currently supported trace flags. Here we list the ones that, in our opinion, are particularly useful.

-1 Using this trace number with another makes the other trace flag apply to all connections, for example:

```
    DBCC TRACEON ( 3604 ) /* Applies just to this spid */
    DBCC TRACEON ( 3604, -1 ) /* Trace flag 3604 is now in effect for all
present and future SQL Server connections, until SQL Server restarts. */
```

110 Trace flag 110 disables the ANSI SELECT features. In ANSI SQL certain redundant table listing are illegal. For example, suppose you need to do an UPDATE like this:

```
CREATE TABLE ##110 (
     c1 int PRIMARY KEY,
     c2 int)
UPDATE ##110
     SET a.c2 = b.c2
     FROM ##110 a, ##110 b
     WHERE a.c1 = b.c1
             AND a.c2 < b.c2
```

This will get you the following error message:

```
Msg 8154, Level 16, State 1
The table '##110' is ambiguous.
```

Trace flag 110 will allow your update to work.

204 This flag allows you to put columns in a SELECT statement that are not in aggregate functions and not in your GROUP BY clause. SQL Server 4.2 allowed this all the time, but it was removed with SQL Server 6.0 because it is not ANSI-standard behavior. It is, however, quite useful. For example, you want to see the names, types, owners, and creation dates of all objects where two different users own objects with the same name. Without this flag you have to write

```
SELECT name, USER_NAME(uid), type, crdate
   FROM sysobjects
   WHERE name IN ( SELECT name
      FROM sysobjects
      GROUP BY name
      HAVING COUNT( * ) > 1 )
```

With flag 204 set, the query is simply the following:

```
SELECT name, USER_NAME(uid), type, crdate
   FROM sysobjects
   GROUP BY name
   HAVING COUNT( * ) > 1
```

Notice that this query would ordinarily be illegal in SQL Server 6.*x* because USER_NAME(uid), type, crdate are not in the GROUP BY clause.

This flag also enables you to put columns in your ORDER BY clause that are not in a SELECT DISTINCT clause. We used this flag a lot when we were running SQL Server 6.0, but we had to give it up with SQL Server 6.5 because flag 204 now turns off ANSI-style joins, which we want.

237 With SQL Server 6.5 you must have REFERENCES permission on a table to create a FOREIGN KEY. SELECT permission is not enough. For example, this will return an error:

```
CREATE TABLE TraceFlag237TestA (
      c1 int PRIMARY KEY)
GRANT SELECT ON TraceFlag237TestA TO public
SETUSER 'guest'
CREATE TABLE TraceFlag237TestB (
      c1 int REFERENCES TraceFlag237TestA)
```

If you set Trace flag 237, SELECT permission alone is sufficient to create FOREIGN KEYs, and the SQL above will work.

246 A regrettable flaw in SQL Server 6.0 and earlier versions was that you could have one column name be null in a view or a table created by SELECT INTO, for example:

```
SELECT type, min(name)
   INTO sloppy
   FROM sysobjects
```

The second column has no name. If you still need this behavior, you can turn it on with flag 246.

1200 This flag let's you see what kind of locks you are requesting. After you run

```
DBCC TRACEON ( 1200 )
```

When you execute any query, such as the following:

```
SELECT *
   FROM sysobjects
```

You get to see what kind of locks you requested, for example:

```
Process 11 requesting table lock of type SH_INT on 6 3
chaining lock onto PSS chain
Process 11 requesting page lock of type SH_PAGE on 6 48
chaining lock onto PSS chain
Process 11 releasing page lock of type SH_PAGE on 6 48
Process 11 releasing table lock of type SH_INT on 6 3
Process 11 requesting table lock of type SH_INT on 6 3
chaining lock onto PSS chain
Process 11 requesting page lock of type SH_PAGE on 6 48
```

(continued)

(*continued*)

```
chaining lock onto PSS chain
Process 11 releasing page lock of type SH_PAGE on 6 48
Process 11 releasing table lock of type SH_INT on 6 3
Process 11 requesting page lock of type SH_PAGE on 6 24
chaining lock onto PSS chain
Process 11 releasing page lock of type SH_PAGE on 6 24
```

1204 This flag and the next one give you information about deadlocks when they occur. You must have the flag on before the deadlock starts, however. Therefore, there are two ways to approach this flag. Either you keep it on all the time, or you turn it on when you have a deadlock you can reproduce.

1205 More detailed information supporting flag 1204.

3604 This flag sends trace and DBCC output to your screen. This is a very important flag. If you forget to use it, many other DBCC commands will give you messages like the following:

```
    DBCC execution completed. If DBCC printed error messages, see your System
Administrator.
```

If you were expecting some real output and got the preceding message instead, make sure that flag 3604 is set.

Tip

Only certain trace flags and DBCC commands require flag 3604 to be set. Others will give you full output no matter what. Furthermore, some DBCC commands, such as TRACEON, have no output. In that case, you always get the "DBCC execution completed" response.◀

3609 Use this flag when you start SQL Server; this skips creating tempdb. This capability is useful when you know something is wrong with tempdb.

4022 Used when you start SQL Server, it skips the execution of the start-up stored procedures. Quite handy.

DBCC Help

You are now ready to get help on DBCC when it is available. First, you have to send DBCC and TRACE output to the client with

```
DBCC TRACEON ( 3604 )
```

And you can now request help on a DBCC command with DBCC HELP. The syntax is as follows:

```
DBCC HELP ( dbcc_command )
```

For example, to get HELP on TRACEON use

```
DBCC HELP ( TRACEON )
```

For reasons known only to Microsoft, this is not part of the supported DBCC feature set, which means that you have no guarantee it will be available in future releases, nor is there any guarantee that help is available for all commands. When no help is available DBCC Help tells you so, and when the dbcc_command is not a valid DBCC command, Help tells you that, too.

Finding Flaws

Before you go searching for disconnects in SQL Server, you might wonder just what in the world you are trying to find. Mostly, you are looking for inconsistencies in database meta-data and database data storage. A perfect example is this: SQL Server stores data in doubly linked 2K pages. Therefore, if page X points to page Y as its next page, page Y had better point to page X as its previous page. When this is not the case, something is seriously wrong.

The next group of DBCC commands we want to discuss are commands you should run periodically just to see if you have any problems in your database. How often you will run the commands depends on how long it takes the commands to run for your databases. In our case, we can get by with running the command each night, and so we do. You also want to run these command immediately *after* a backup, if you can. The reason for not checking the consistency of your database before you back it up is that in theory something could happen to corrupt your database in the few seconds after the DBCC finishes and before the backup starts. In that case, the DBCC would erroneously lead you to believe your backup is clean.

CHECKDB

If you pick only one command in this chapter to add to your bag of tricks, let it be this one. CHECKDB checks the following on a table-by-table basis:

- All data pages are properly linked. As we said earlier, in a doubly linked list, you have pointers going in both directions. If X points to a successor Y, Y had better point to a predecessor X.
- All index pages are properly linked.
- All indexes are in the correct sort order.
- The data on each data page is reasonable.
- The row offsets on each page are reasonable. A *row offset* specifies the location of a row on a data page.

When a table fails any of these criteria and DBCC can't fix the problem, the DBCC tells you that the table is corrupted. This will require your attention to fix. CHECKDB checks system tables, too because they can also become corrupted. In fact, this has happened to us at least twice. When DBCC finds a corrupted table, it does nothing more than tell you in the output. DBCC doesn't flag the table or take it offline or anything of that nature. (DBCC does tell you *which* table, fortunately.)

Running CHECKDB

The syntax of CHECKDB is as follows:

```
DBCC CHECKDB [(database_name [, NOINDEX])] [WITH NO_INFOMSGS]
```

The database name is optional; if you leave it out, DBCC checks your current database. If you wish to check tables only and not their indexes, you can specify the NOINDEX option. We always go ahead and check both the tables and indexes. You will like the WITH NO_INFOMSGS in this command because, otherwise, you get several lines of output per table, which really adds up if you have a couple hundred tables, for example, to check *master*:

```
DBCC CHECKDB( master )
```

Your first few lines of output will look like this:

```
Checking master
Checking 1
The total number of data pages in this table is 24.
Table has 355 data rows.
Checking 2
The total number of data pages in this table is 6.
```

```
Table has 65 data rows.
Checking 3
The total number of data pages in this table is 41.
The number of rows in Sysindexes for this table was 1133.  It has been corrected to
1132.
Table has 1132 data rows.
```

This is all normal output, including the fact that DBCC changed the rows column of sysindexes. The "Checking n" refers to object number *n* in sysobjects. What isn't normal is something like this:

```
Table Corrupt: Page linkage is not consistent; check the following pages: (current
page#=%ld; page# pointing to this page=%ld; previous page# indicated in this
page=%ld)
```

In fact, any message starting with the words "Table Corrupt" is very bad. You also should be concerned about any message with severity level higher that 16, such as this:

```
Msg 605, Level 21, State 1
Attempt to fetch logical page 114128 in database 'YourDatabase' belongs to object
'ObjectA', not to object 'ObjectB'.
```

The behavior you will get when using a corrupt table is undefined. A SELECT * from the table could lead to a loop, where SQL Server attempts to return an infinite number of rows to the query. Even so, you might be able to use this table while it is corrupt for weeks, as long as SQL Server never has to read the bad page. This is why the DBCC is so important: It may be the only way you find out about the dangers waiting for you.

How to fix a corrupted table

OK, so DBCC told you the table is corrupt. Now what? Well the strategy is basically this:

1. Figure out which object specifically is corrupt. (It could be a corrupt index instead of a corrupt table.)
2. Drop and recreate the corrupted object.

Clearly, we are using a machete when a surgeon's scalpel would be more appropriate, but this is the only safe way for a user to fix the problem.

Identifying the index id (indid) for a corrupted table

If DBCC tells you that a specific page number of a specific object number is corrupt, you want to know which object specifically, and whether the corrupt page is an index or an object. Finding out which object you are dealing with is easy. If the object id is 732529643, for example, run this query:

```
SELECT USER_NAME( uid ), name
    FROM sysobjects
    WHERE id = 732529643
```

Finding the index id requires DBCC again. The relevant command is DBCC PAGE, which has this syntax:

```
DBCC PAGE ( dbid, pagenum [, printopt={0|1|2} ][, cache={0|1} ][,logical={1|0} ] )
```

Like Help, Microsoft considers this command outside the supported feature set. As with most nonsupported commands, you must set trace flag 3604 (output to client). You can find the database id (dbid) of your current database with:

```
SELECT DB_ID()
```

For example, if your dbid is 6 and your pageno is 133032, you would run

```
DBCC TRACEON( 3604 )
DBCC PAGE( 6, 133032 )
```

Your output will look something like this:

```
DATABASE:6   OBJECT:732529643   PAGE:133032 (0x207a8)
Page header for page 0x23ff000
pageno=133032 nextpg=133033 prevpg=0 objid=732529643 timestamp=0001
019e14ea
nextrno=27 level=0 indid=0  freeoff=1974 minlen=18
page status bits: 0x1
```

In the output, you will see the word *indid*, followed by the actual number of the index id. You may remember that 0 means a table with no clustered index, 1 means a clustered index, anything from 3 – 250 is a nonclustered index. However, in the DBCC output, indid = 1 only for the non-leaf pages of a clustered index. The leaf pages have indid = 0. If you have a nonclustered index that is corrupt, you got off easy. Query sysindexes to find the index name, drop the index, and recreate it. Notice that the object id is repeated by this command, so you can always find the object id based on the page alone.

If indid = 1, you have a corrupted non-leaf page of the clustered index. Try to drop and recreate the index and cross your fingers.

If you have a corrupt table or corrupted leaf page of a clustered index, you have to drop the table. Ideally, you can restore this table alone from a backup. If you aren't thrilled about how much work this will make you lose, you might be able to preserve some or all of the current data, but remember, BCP could fail just as SELECT * could fail. You will have to play with breaking up the data, depending on how SELECT * behaves. You may want to see the actual data of the corrupt page, which you can do with the following:

```
DBCC PAGE ( 6, 732529643, 1 )
```

Now you see the actual rows of your table, and you can possibly see where your table is breaking up.

What to do when a system table is corrupt

We wouldn't wish this on anyone, but twice we have had a system table become corrupted, once in SQL Server 4.2 and once in SQL Server 6.0. This is a mess because you can't very well drop a system table. This is what we recommend:

1. Call Microsoft. See if the company has any ideas.
2. Make a backup of your database and keep it separate from your usual backups. We have found that you can usually back up a corrupted database, and when you restore, it will still be corrupted. This is important because you will probably fix this problem long before your support channel bails you out. You want a copy of the situation so that hopefully they can figure out what happened.
3. Restore from a backup.
4. Immediately do a DBCC on the database after you have restored it. Don't be shocked to find out that your most recent backup is corrupted, too. Ours was.
5. If your last several backups are corrupt, consider bulk copying your data out for your user tables. Then, you will have to drop the whole database and recreate it from a script.

One final word: Though CHECKDB is quite helpful, it doesn't find everything. Don't assume that a valid CHECKDB output means you can relax. Try some of the other DBCC checks.

CHECKTABLE (table_name [, NOINDEX|index_id])

This is simply a version of CHECKDB that lets you focus on a specific table. This can be handy if CHECKDB takes too long; you can use CHECKTABLE to inspect your most important and most frequently updated tables. For very large databases this command is essential — DBCC takes too long.

CHECKCATALOG [(database name)]

As you know, the system tables don't have foreign keys, so maintaining the consistency of those tables is up to the stored procedures Microsoft wrote. The CHECKCATALOG commands searches for some obvious disconnects. In our many years with SQL Server, we have gotten only one error message out of CHECKCATALOG — it found some entries in syscolumns using ids not in sysobjects. What to do about the errors is always a judgment call. In our case, we just deleted the offending records out of syscomments.

NEWALLOC [(database_name [, NOINDEX])]

The least important of our fishing expeditions, NEWALLOC verifies the allocation of extents in the database. We will cover extents in greater detail in our "Query Optimization" chapter, but for now, we will just mention that your database is divided into allocation units of 512K each, and each allocation unit is divided into 32 *extents* of 16K each. SQL Server only puts one object in each extent, but an object can own multiple extents. Each index is in its own extent as well. Yes, even an empty table consumes 16K of disk space. As objects are created and destroyed, SQL Server is busy allocating and deallocating extents. DBCC NEWALLOC comes along with a broom to clean up any mess left behind by this process. This is definitely a command to run with the NO_INFOMSGS parameter, as follows:

```
DBCC NEWALLOC WITH NO_INFOMSGS
```

This will hopefully produce the simple

```
DBCC execution completed. If DBCC printed error messages, see your System
Administrator.
```

If you are inclined to see all the output, you will first get a message like this:

```
Checking Fedorchek
Database 'Fedorchek' is not in single user mode - may find spurious allocation
problems due to transactions in progress.
```

Because NEWALLOC can take a while to run, it is entirely possible that someone will be doing something to change the extent allocation while you are running NEWALLOC. We don't worry about this message. Rare is the time when we have the luxury of putting the database in single-user mode. No matter what time we pick, someone complains.

Next, you will find that for each object you will get this kind of summary:

```
***************************************************************
TABLE: yourtable        OBJID = 678293476
INDID=1      FIRST=12560      ROOT=12664      DPAGES=57     SORT=0
    Data level: 1.  57 Data  Pages in 8 extents.
    Indid      : 1.  2 Index Pages in 1 extents.
INDID=2      FIRST=12792      ROOT=12809      DPAGES=21     SORT=0
    Indid      : 2.  23 Index Pages in 4 extents.
TOTAL # of extents = 13
***************************************************************
```

The most interesting part of DBCC NEWALLOC is what you get at the very end:

```
Processed 53 entries in the Sysindexes for dbid 4.
Alloc page 0 (# of extent=31 used pages=51 ref pages=51)
Alloc page 256 (# of extent=31 used pages=46 ref pages=46)
Alloc page 512 (# of extent=14 used pages=31 ref pages=31)
Alloc page 768 (# of extent=2 used pages=15 ref pages=8)
Alloc page 1024 (# of extent=1 used pages=1 ref pages=1)
Alloc page 1280 (# of extent=1 used pages=1 ref pages=1)
Total (# of extent=80 used pages=145 ref pages=138) in this database
```

This is the output for pubs; for a larger database, you see much more. What we have here is a summary of the allocation pages for your database, both for the data devices and the log devices. Pubs is 2M of data + 1M of log = 3M, which is 80 extents. The allocation units with "used pages = 1" are currently empty.

Rebuilding indexes

As we mentioned earlier, the pages of a SQL Server table are a doubly linked list. When you initially load a table (from BCP, for example), SQL Server tries to keep the page links in order so that page 14983 links to 14984, which links to 14985, and so on. In so doing, SQL Server can make best use of a read-ahead cache. However, in the process of all the inserts, updates, and deletes over time, the links lose this monotonic sequence. Eventually, reading the table begins to look like a ping-pong match. DBCC provides a utility for identifying when a table is fragmented like this and, with SQL Server 6.5, provides a utility for fixing it.

SHOWCONTIG (*table_id*, [*index_id*])

This command scans a table for fragmentation. Like most DBCC commands, you are forced to look up the object id yourself. (Why DBCC doesn't do this eludes us.) To run SHOWCONTIG for 'yourtable':

```
select object_id( 'yourtable' )
```

Now you can run DBCC itself. By default, it scans indid 0 or 1, whichever applies, if you don't give it an indid:

```
DBCC SHOWCONTIG scanning 'yourtable' table...
[SHOW_CONTIG - SCAN ANALYSIS]
Table: 'yourtable' (646293362)  Indid: 1  dbid:6
TABLE level scan performed.
- Pages Scanned................................: 93
- Extent Switches..............................: 92
- Avg. Pages per Extent........................: 7.8
- Scan Density [Best Count:Actual Count].......: 12.90% [12:93]
- Avg. Bytes free per page.....................: 795.7
- Avg. Page density (full).....................: 60.49%
- Overflow Pages...............................: 0
- Disconnected Overflow Pages..................: 0
```

Not the Same as DB2 REORG

If you come from the DB2 crowd, know that SQL Server fragmentation is not the same as the fragmentation there. SQL Server uses B-tree indexes; DB2 doesn't. In DB2, a table with a clustering index may become less clustered over time, but in this case, the rows themselves on the DB2 data pages are no longer in clustering order.

That *never* happens in SQL Server. SQL Server rearranges rows on a page on the fly to keep them in order. When no room is left on a page, SQL Server splits the page into two. This is the power of a linked list, but it leads to this kind of fragmentation.

The number you want to zoom in on is the Scan Density. 100 percent is optimal. In our example, we have 12.90 percent, which stinks. Our table has 93 pages, which means we will need at least 93/8 = 12 (rounding up) extents. Therefore, we expect there will have to be at least 12 Extent Switches, meaning SQL Server leaves one extent and enters another while traversing the page linkage. However, SQL was forced to switch 92 times on this table.

Another pair of key statistics are the Avg. Bytes free per page and Avg. Page density. The table above shows 795.7 free bytes per page on average. If you run this query

```
select minlen, maxlen
   from sysindexes
   where id = 646293362
```

you can find the minimum and maximum lengths of a row on data page. In our case, they are 60 and 95. Therefore, we have room for at least 8 more rows per page. The average page density tells us we are almost 40 percent empty, which means that SQL Server is loading a lot of white space into the cache for this table.

The solution is to rebuild the index. In SQL Server 6.0, the only way to do this was to drop and recreate the index. However, you can't drop a primary key index without dropping the primary key, and you can't drop a primary key without dropping all the foreign keys that reference it. This hassle is enough to dissuade most folks from rebuilding indexes. SQL Server 6.5 has a better way.

DBCC DBREINDEX

The purpose of DBCC REINDEX is to fix the fragmentation we just found. The syntax is the following:

```
DBCC DBREINDEX (['database.owner.table_name' [, index_name
[, fillfactor [, {SORTED_DATA|SORTED_DATA_REORG}]]]])
[WITH NOINFOMSGS]
```

For example, to fix 'yourtable', you can simply do as follows:

```
dbcc dbreindex ( 'yourtable' )
```

For comparison, here is the output of SHOWCONTIG after the reindexing. Take particular note of the Scan Density and the Average Page Density. You will also see that the total number of pages for this index dropped from 93 down to 57:

```
DBCC SHOWCONTIG scanning 'yourtable' table...
[SHOW_CONTIG - SCAN ANALYSIS]
Table: 'yourtable' (646293362)  Indid: 1  dbid:6
TABLE level scan performed.
- Pages Scanned................................: 57
- Extent Switches..............................: 7
- Avg. Pages per Extent........................: 7.1
- Scan Density [Best Count:Actual Count].......: 100.00% [7:8]
- Avg. Bytes free per page.....................: 42.1
- Avg. Page density (full).....................: 97.91%
- Overflow Pages...............................: 0
- Disconnected Overflow Pages..................: 0
```

Updating sysindexes

Secret

The sysindexes table has a wealth of information about your indexes, including some statistics that become out of date over time. In particular, SQL Server does not automatically update the used, reserved, dpages, or rows columns of sysindexes for performance reasons. These first three columns are all measures of how many data pages an index is using; rows is literally the number of rows in the index. If you use the SQL Enterprise Manager to check the size of your database, you probably aren't getting an accurate measurement. Likewise, stored procedures such as sp_spaceused are using out-of-date information from sysindexes. The way to update this data is with DBCC UPDATEUSAGE. The syntax is

```
DBCC UPDATEUSAGE ({0 | database_name} [, table_name [, index_id]])
[WITH COUNT_ROWS]
```

If you pass in a parameter of 0 for your database name, SQL Server checks your current database. You can check your whole database, one specific table, or one specific index. The last option, WITH COUNT_ROWS, tells SQL Server to update the rows column in addition to used, reserved, and dpages. There is a *major* difference in execution time between using this parameter and not. You might run UPDATEUSAGE in a batch like this:

```
EXEC sp_spaceused /* See how big your database appears to be */
SELECT GETDATE() /* Record when you started */
GO
DBCC UPDATEUSAGE( 0 ) WITH COUNT_ROWS
GO
SELECT GETDATE() /* Record when you finished */
EXEC sp_spaceused /* See how big your database really is */
```

The output will look like this:

```
DBCC UPDATEUSAGE: Sysindexes row for Table 'YourTable' (IndexId=8) updated:
     USED Pages: Changed from (886) to (2142) pages
     RSVD Pages: Changed from (896) to (2363) pages
DBCC UPDATEUSAGE: Sysindexes row for Table 'YourTable' (IndexId=7) updated:
     USED Pages: Changed from (973) to (2342) pages
     RSVD Pages: Changed from (984) to (2557) pages
DBCC UPDATEUSAGE: Sysindexes row for Table 'YourTable' (IndexId=5) updated:
     USED Pages: Changed from (973) to (2495) pages
     RSVD Pages: Changed from (984) to (2761) pages
DBCC UPDATEUSAGE: Sysindexes row for Table 'YourTable' (IndexId=2) updated:
     USED Pages: Changed from (1149) to (2890) pages
     RSVD Pages: Changed from (1160) to (3178) pages
DBCC UPDATEUSAGE: Sysindexes row for Table 'YourTable' (IndexId=1) updated:
     USED Pages: Changed from (22982) to (23044) pages
     RSVD Pages: Changed from (24186) to (24375) pages
```

Checks for Trouble after it Happens

Up until now, we have been trying to get ahead of the game by seeking out errors and performance problems. DBCC can also help when trouble occurs.

INPUTBUFFER

This is a wonderful command. When you find that a process has hung or is dragging the processors down, you really need to know what SQL is causing the problem. SQL Server 6.5 includes SQLTrace for just this purpose, but it only traps SQL *after* you turn it on. What if you want to find the SQL a user has already sent to server?

```
DBCC INPUTBUFFER( spid )
```

You can get the spid from sp_who or by querying sysprocesses. The only drawback is that you get only the first 256 characters, which isn't enough for some long SQL statements people might write. You can use a companion command, DBCC OUTPUTBUFFER, if you want to see what SQL Server sent back to the user.

OPENTRAN

Just yesterday, we had a minor catastrophe in our database. The log was filling up excessively, despite the fact that we have 'truncate log on checkpoint' set. Why would this happen? Because we had an uncommitted transaction in our log. We found it with DBCC OPENTRAN. The syntax is

```
OPENTRAN ({database_name}|{database_id}) [WITH TABLERESULTS]
```

For example, the output when a transaction is actively running looks like this:

```
Transaction Information for database: Fedorchek

Oldest active transaction:
        SPID         : 16
        UID          : 1
        SUID         : 1
        Name         : YourProc
        RID          : (32777 , 16)
        Time Stamp   : 0001 00022C89
        Start Time   : May  6 1996 11:15:35:026AM
```

In this case, the open transaction was the creation of a procedure named 'YourProc'. If the Start Time is unreasonably old, you may have an uncommitted transaction. Of course *unreasonable* is a subjective judgment based on your knowledge of your operations. For us, anything over an hour is unreasonable. Use KILL to terminate the spid, 16 in this case. If that doesn't work, shut the server down immediately. We failed to shut ours down because of user complaints that they couldn't accept the down time. Many hours later, we had to shut it down anyway because we were running out of log space and the recovery took two hours and fifteen minutes. The moral of the story is that the users got stuck with a lot more down time by postponing solving the problem.

Memory Checks

DBCC provides a command for checking the SQL Server's usage of memory. Let's review what we know about memory and SQL Server thus far:

- SQL Server is initially configured to use 8M of memory. You changed that, or at least you should have, when you first installed SQL Server. If not, refer to Chapter 4 immediately. Reading this section on memory checks is a waste of time otherwise.◀

- You may or may not be putting tempdb in RAM.
- SQL Server caches datapages for your tables, thus saving disk I/O.
- SQL Server caches the optimized execution plan for stored procedures.

You might have a lot of legitimate questions, such as whether you have allocated enough memory to SQL Server, whether you have enough memory left over to put tempdb in RAM, and whether the stored procedure cache is large enough. DBCC can help. There are two commands we want to discuss, DBCC PERFMON and DBCC MEMUASGE.

DBCC PERFMON

DBCC PERFMON gives you a plethora of performance statistics. The syntax is simply:

```
DBCC PERFMON
```

Let your server run for a few days, then fire off this command. The output has four sections: I/O Statistics, Cache Statistics, Network Use, and Read Ahead Statistics. It looks like this:

```
Statistic                          Value
------------------------------ -----------------------
Log Flush Requests                        2650.0
Log Logical Page IO                       2983.0
Log Physical IO                           2122.0
Log Flush Average                         1.24882
Log Logical IO Average                    1.40575
Batch Writes                              2091.0
Batch Average Size                        10.0048
Batch Max Size                            8.0
Page Reads                                177784.0
Single Page Writes                        1397.0
Reads Outstanding                         0.0
Writes Outstanding                        0.0
Transactions                              45910.0
Transactions/Log Write                    21.6353
------------------------------ -----------------------
Cache Hit Ratio                           52.0153
Cache Flushes                             6.0
Free Page Scan (Avg)                      1.0134
Free Page Scan (Max)                      787.0
Min Free Buffers                          2457.0
```

(continued)

(continued)

```
Cache Size                                      30923.0
Free Buffers                                     2529.0
------------------------------ -----------------------
Network Reads                                       0.0
Network Writes                                  48700.0
Command Queue Length                                0.0
Max Command Queue Length                            0.0
Worker Threads                                      8.0
Max Worker Threads                                  8.0
Network Threads                                     0.0
Max Network Threads                                 0.0
------------------------------ -----------------------
RA Pages Found in Cache                         25165.0
RA Pages Placed in Cache                        42184.0
RA Physical IO                                   5916.0
Used Slots                                          0.0
```

Out of all of these numbers, you want to zoom in on Cache Flushes and Free Page Scan (Avg). They are 6.0 and 1.0134, respectively, in our example. After your server has been up for a few days, you want these two figures to be less than 100, and less than 10 respectively. We are in great shape on our server. If your figures routinely come out over 100 and 10, you need more memory for your data cache.

DBCC MEMUSAGE

DBCC MEMUSAGE gives you detailed output on SQL Server's memory usage. Its syntax is simply:

```
DBCC MEMUSAGE
```

There are three sections to the output you get from MEMUSAGE. The first is a summary of how memory is divided up:

```
Memory Usage:


                         Meg.    2K Blks        Bytes


 Configured Memory: 96.0000      49152    100663296
         Code size:  1.7166        879      1800000
 Static Structures:  0.3544        182       371600
             Locks:  0.2861        147       300000
      Open Objects:  0.2289        118       240000
    Open Databases:  0.0031          2         3220
```

```
User Context Areas:  2.9504      1511       3093732
        Page Cache: 63.2278     32373      66299104
      Proc Headers:  1.5233       780       1597346
   Proc Cache Bufs: 25.5742     13094      26816512
```

The word *Usage* is a bit misleading here. This is reporting allocated memory to each item, not what is really being used. For example, this tells you that the page cache can hold up to 1,702 pages. It doesn't mean 1,702 data pages are in the cache right now.

The Data Cache

The next section of MEMUSAGE is more important:

```
Buffer Cache, Top 20:

     DB Id  Object Id        Index Id 2K Buffers

         6  484964854               0     12350
         6 1909581841               0      8506
         6  213575799               0      1913
         6  672005425               0      1756
         6  384004399               0      1081
         6  593489243               0       843
         6         99               0       532
         6  296440180               0       240
         6  569053063               0       185
         6  352004285               0       159
         6  365960380               0       156
         6  252527933               0        53
         6  320004171               0        53
         6  316528161               0        48
         6  537052949               0        39
         6  512004855               0        36
         6  412528503               0        31
         6  452964740               0        25
         6  416004513               0        22
```

Here, you are looking at the top 20 (by size) tables in your data cache. As SQL Server processes queries, it first looks in the data cache for the page it wants. If it finds it, great. You just saved yourself a disk read. If not, SQL Server fetches the data page from the disk. SQL Server saves each page it fetches in RAM, in the data cache. When the cache is full, SQL Server kicks out the oldest data pages to make room for new ones. *Oldest* doesn't mean the time the page was initially read from the disk, it means the last time a page was read period. Therefore, the pages that SQL Server needs most often stay in the cache.

This section of DBCC MEMUSAGE has the most meaning after you have been doing heavy processing. (When you first turn SQL Server on, there won't be much in the cache.) Optimizing the data cache size can really be a black art, but we will try to give you a few rules of thumb. First of all, you need to resolve the object ids into real table names to see what is going on. Then you should have a list, by name, of what is in your cache. Does the list of tables seem reasonable to you? Are there any tables you think should be there and aren't? You are particularly looking for tables that you know are being queried all the time. If the data cache is filled with all your active tables, but still missing some tables, you may need a larger data cache.

If the sum of the 2K Buffers column is close to the page cache size of the previous section, you might consider giving more memory to SQL Server. If MEMUSAGE listed the Top X, where X is less than 20, definitely consider giving SQL Server more memory. The reasoning here is that if it only takes you twenty tables or less to max out your data cache, your cache hit ratio can't be very good. In other words, if you do not have many tables in your cache, most of your queries are probably generating disk I/O. This is something to check with the performance monitor. You want your queries to find the data they need in RAM.

Procedure Cache

The last and most important section of the MEMUSAGE is the procedure cache, which tells you the size of procedures in the cache. What we want to do with this is figure out the average size of the procedures you are using. Start with this query in your production database:

```
select id, count(*) row_count
    into #large_procs
    from sysprocedures
    group by id
set rowcount 20
select object_name(id) name, row_count
    from #large_procs
    order by 2 desc
```

Cross-Reference

The reason for the temporary table is an optimization issue, which we will explain in Chapter 29. For comparison, the output of this SQL in master is

```
name                          row_count
----------------------------- -----------
sp_helprotect                 543
sp_rename                     543
sp_MSdependencies             523
```

```
sp_create_removable          430
sp_helpconstraint            407
sp_changesubstatus           402
sp_changearticle             386
sp_fallback_activate_svr_db  372
sp_checknames                371
sp_ddopen                    333
sp_foreignkey                315
sp_fallback_MS_verify_ri     314
sp_helpsort                  312
sp_MStablekeys               311
sp_db_upgrade1               304
sp_MSdbuserprofile           303
sp_addarticle                300
sp_db_upgrade2               298
sp_helparticle               296
sp_helpdb                    295
```

These are your largest stored procedures. Recompile and execute the very largest one, and run MEMUSAGE. You see it first in the third section of the output:

```
Procedure Name: large_procedure
Database Id: 6
Object Id: 130815528
Version: 1
Uid: 1
Type: stored procedure
Number of trees: 0
Size of trees: 0.000000 Mb, 0.000000 bytes, 0 pages
Number of plans: 1
Size of plans: 0.166811 Mb, 174914.000000 bytes, 86 pages
```

This shows you the size of your maximum procedure plan for this database. If you have other databases using a lot of stored procedures, do this test for them as well. Microsoft's heuristic for initial procedure cache estimate size is Procedure Cache = (Maximum Concurrent Users) * (Size of Largest Plan) * 1.25. For example, if we expect a maximum of 50 concurrent users, we would need a 50 * 0.166811 * 1.25 = 10.4MB procedure cache. Our OLTP server has 128MB of RAM with 112MB for SQL Server, so we are in good shape.

If you don't have a large enough procedure cache, you can either alter the ratio of the data cache to the procedure cache or you can buy more memory. Before you rush to the store for RAM chips, try the first option.

If you have fairly detailed knowledge of your system at the stored procedure level, you can afford to be more sophisticated in your estimate. There may be certain procedures you know you run all the time. The cache should be large enough to hold *all* of these plans at once. By running each of the procedures and looking at MEMUSAGE, you can find the size of each of their plans. Your total cache size must be larger than that.

DBCC PROCCACHE

If you want to see at a glance where the procedure cache is without waiting for a full MEMUSAGE, you can simply run this command:

```
DBCC PROCCACHE
```

Your output will be something like this:

```
num buffs    buffs used    buffs active    cache size    cache used    cache active
---------    ----------    ------------    ----------    ----------    ------------
688          15            0               679           272           0
```

This command is normally used by the Performance Monitor.

Pinning tables

Our discussion of memory isn't complete without a mention of *pinning tables*. If you have a table you want to stay fixed in the cache, you can "pin" it with DBCC PINTABLE. The syntax is

```
PINTABLE (database_id, table_id)
```

After you run this command, pages from this table will stay in the cache forever after SQL Server reads them. Notice SQL Server doesn't read the table into memory immediately. The pages will enter memory from the normal reads associated with queries.

We think PINTABLE falls in the same category at FORCEPLAN — they are both bad ideas. You spent all this money for a high-speed RDBMS like SQL Server so it could manage page caching for you. SQL Server is almost always going to do a better job than you will. We don't use PINTABLE. If you have pinned a table and need to unpin it, use this command:

```
UNPINTABLE (database_id, table_id)
```

Undocumented and Unsupported DBCC Commands

There is a wealth of other DBCC commands that are useful in various circumstances that Microsoft doesn't document or support. You can find out about them in third-party books, TechNet, and word of mouth. Table 26-1 presents the most comprehensive list of DBCC commands we know, along with comments about some of them.

Warning

You couldn't possibly be on thinner ice than this. Microsoft doesn't guarantee these commands will exist is the future, won't answer questions about them, and won't help you if you break your database with them. Play with these commands in a development environment. If you find one you think will be useful in your production environment, confirm with your primary support provider that it is a good idea.◀

Table 26-1
Complete List of DBCC Commands

Command	Help (if available)
addextendedproc	
adduserobject	
allocdump	allocdump(dbid, page)
allocmap	
allow11load	
bhash	bhash({ print_bufs|no_print }, bucket_limit)
bufcount	
buffer	buffer([dbid][, objid][, nbufs], printopt = { 0|1|2 }, buftype)
bytes	bytes(startaddress, length)
capture_tds	
catalogcheck	
checkalloc	checkalloc([dbname])
checkcatalog	
checkdb	checkdb([dbname])
checkident	
checktable	checktable(tablename)
convert_34to42	
dbcontrol	dbcontrol(dbname,ONLINE|OFFLINE)
dbinfo	dbinfo([dbname])
dbrecover	
dbreindex	
dbrepair	dbrepair(dbid, option = { dropdb|fixindex|fixsysindex }, table, indexid)

(continued)

Table 26-1 *(continued)*
Complete List of DBCC Commands

Command	*Help (if available)*
dbtable	dbtable(dbid)
delbuff	
delete_row	delete_row(dbid, pageid, delete_by_row = { 1|0 }, rownum)
des	des([dbid][, objid])
descount	
devcontrol	
dropextendedproc	
dropuserobject	
extentchain	extentchain(dbid, objid, indexid, sort={1|0}, display={1|0} [,order={1|0}])
extentcheck	extentcheck(dbid, objid, indexid, sort = {1|0})
extentdump	extentdump(dbid, page)
extentzap	extentzap(dbid, objid, indexid, sort)
findnotfullextents	findnotfullextents(dbid, objid, indexid, sort = { 1|0 })
fix_al	
gaminit	
gammon	
getvalue	
help	help(dbcc_command)
ind	ind(dbid, objid, printopt = { 0|1|2 })
inputbuffer	
locateindexpgs	locateindexpgs(dbid, objid, page, indexid, level)
lock	lock
log	log([dbid][,objid][,page][,row][,nrecords][,type={-1..36}], printopt={0|1})
memstats	
memusage	memusage
mrulru	
newalloc	newalloc(dbname, option = { 1|2|3 })
no_print	
opentran	
outputbuffer	
page	page(dbid, pagenum [, printopt={0|1|2}][, cache={0|1}] [,logical={1|0}])
perflog	
perfmon	
pglinkage	pglinkage(dbid, start, number, printopt={0|1|2}, target, order={1|0})
pintable	

(continued)

Command	Help (if available)
print_bufs	
procbuf	procbuf(dbid, objid, nbufs, printopt = { 0|1 })
proccache	
prtipage	prtipage(dbid, objid, indexid, indexpage)
pss	pss(suid, spid, printopt = { 1|0 })
rebuild_log	
rebuildextents	rebuildextents(dbid, objid, indexid)
report_al	
resource	resource
save_rebuild_log	
show_bucket	show_bucket(dbid, pageid, lookup_type)
show_statistics	
showcontig	
showtext	
shrinkdb	
sqlper60	
sqlperf	
tab	tab(dbid, objid, printopt = { 0|1|2 })
textall	
textalloc	
traceoff	traceoff(tracenum [, tracenum ...])
traceon	traceon(tracenum [, tracenum ...])
tracestatus	
undo	undo(dbid, pageno, rowno)
unpintable	
updateusage	
upgradedb	
usedextents	
userlicestats	
useroptions	
wakeup	

Remember that you have to use DBCC TRACEON(3604) in order to see the output of many DBCC commands.

ALLOCMAP(dbid)

This gives you a summary of which allocation units are active (have data) at a glance.

DBCONTROL(dbname,ONLINE|OFFLINE)

In the hierarchy of restricting database access, you first have 'dbo use only', which limits access to user aliases to the database owner and those using the system administrator account. Then you have 'single user' mode, which means just one connection. Last, you can take a database offline, which is a zero user mode. Nobody, not even the system administrator, can use the database until it is put back online.

DBINFO(dbname)

This lists a slew of nerdy parameters for your database, such as which page the last checkpoint touched and what the next objectid should be. Here's an example:

```
DBINFO STRUCTURE:

dbi_lastrid: page 136, offset 0
dbi_dpbegxact: page 32282, offset 2
dbi_oldseqnum: Jan  1 1900 12:00:00:000AM
dbi_curseqnum: May  6 1996  8:46:58:426AM
dbi_nextseqnum: Jan  1 1900 12:00:00:000AM
dbi_deallocpgs: -14417919
dbi_drprowcnt: 34
dbi_pgcnt: 0
dbi_rowcnt: 0
dbi_llpage: 0
dbi_dbid: 6
dbi_suid: 1
dbi_version: 408
dbi_status: 0xc
dbi_checkpt: page = 32282, offset = 11
dbi_nextid: 162815642
dbi_complete: 1207959552
dbi_crdate: May  5 1996  1:51:11:176PM
dbi_dbname: Fedorchek
dbi_ldstate: 4
dbi_allocmap: 0x8a3560
```

SUMMARY

Managing a database still requires a lot of human intervention, despite the best efforts of Microsoft and other vendors to make systems that require minimal supervision. Over the course of time, a database will at best show a performance drag, and at worst it will become corrupted. The catch-all tool for finding and fixing problems is the Database Consistency Checker (DBCC). You should run DBCC to check the consistency of your database, to make sure that your tables are not fragmented, and to check the consistency of your catalog. You can use DBCC to see what is going on when you have a runaway query. DBCC is the tool that enables you to analyze your memory management. DBCC happens to be the door to using trace flags, which enables you to turn on or off special behavior in SQL Server. If you are feeling adventurous, you can run all kinds of unsupported DBCC commands to see whether they are of use to you.

REVIEW QUESTIONS

Q: Why are consistency checks even necessary? Why isn't SQL Server robust enough to stay perfectly consistent and optimized?

A: SQL Server is faced with competing goals. The requirements of fast transaction processing are at odds with wanting to do DBCC-type housecleaning.

Q: What is a trace flag?

A: A trace flag turns on or off some SQL Server behavior. Some of the behaviors are nothing more than providing more information to the client; others affect how SQL Server processes SQL.

Q: Why are trace flags important when you want to upgrade SQL Server?

A: You will almost always have applications that depend on some behavior of SQL Server that are modified or eliminated in the next release. Trace flags let your applications continue to run until you have time to fix them.

Q: Name two ways to turn trace flags on.

A: DBCC TRACEON and starting the SQL Server executable file with the /Tflagno parameter.

Q: How is CHECKDB different from NEWALLOC?

A: CHECKDB does things such as verify page linkages and the reasonableness of data pages. NEWALLOC reviews the allocation units and their extents.

Q: What does it mean for an SQL Server table to be fragmented? Aren't the rows always in clustered index order?

A: A SQL Server table is fragmented when the pages aren't next to each other in the extents. It has nothing to do with rows.

Q: How do you find fragmentation, and how do you fix it?

A: Use DBCC SHOWCONTIG and DBCC DBREINDEX, respectively.

Q: What are the two main consumers of memory for SQL Server that you have some control over?

A: The data cache and the procedure cache.

Q: How do you decide if your procedure cache is big enough?

A: You can estimate either based on the size of your largest procedure plan and your number of concurrent users, or based on the size of all the procedures you expect to stay resident in the cache.

Chapter

Finding Hidden SQL Server Features

27

Throughout this book, we have showed you things in SQL Server that are not documented anywhere else. All this time, you have probably been wondering how we came to know these things. In this chapter, we teach you some very powerful techniques for divining your own, hitherto unknown, secrets of SQL Server.

What's in This Chapter

In this chapter, we will cover the three basic techniques you can use to unravel some of SQL Server's most closely guarded mysteries. These techniques include the following:

- Editing executables
- Searching for undocumented stored procedures
- Spying on SQL calls with SQL Trace

Inside Information

Probably the easiest way to learn an undocumented feature of SQL Server is to know someone at Microsoft. We, however, do not know any such people and, therefore, cannot speak with any authority on the subject. We just thought we'd toss it in for completeness.

Executable Editing

Back in the very early days of PCs, many software companies branded their tools with unique serial numbers. You couldn't install the product unless you knew the special code. This information was generally kept in the user manual. The theory was that if you had the user manual, you must have bought the product.

The problem with this theory was that the serial numbers were often stored as plain text within the executable. In other words, all you needed to do to "crack" the software was open the executable in a binary editor and begin searching for strings. Eventually, you would find the string that was the needed serial number.

That's not very bright!

The reason this method of searching was so effective was not because of any stupidity on the part of the software houses but because of an inherent truth with most compilers.

Most language compilers store string literals as plain text in the resulting executable. This is less true today, but it is still pretty common. Let's say that you have the following line of code in a C program:

```
myVar = 'This is a test'
```

When you compile your executable, there's a good chance that you can open the .exe in an editor and see the string *'This is a test.'*

In the early days of PC software, developers used to store serial numbers as string literals in their program code. This meant that an enterprising computer geek could easily defeat the intended protection scheme simply by searching for strings.

The fine tradition continues

Today, developers are more savvy about how they store sensitive information such as serial numbers and passwords. These things are usually well encrypted within the executable. Other less critical bits of information, however, often do not receive the same amount of care.

Unraveling the mysteries of DBCC

For example, in the last chapter, we told you about all sorts of undocumented commands for DBCC. How do you suppose we found those? Well, the story goes like this.

While writing the chapter on DBCC, we wondered if there were any undocumented features of the command. After all, it is one of the most powerful and useful tools in a good DBA's arsenal.

Normally, when faced with this question, we would open up the executable in question and look through it for strings that we didn't recognize. The problem is that DBCC isn't a standalone utility; it's a part of the basic SQL Server command set.

After scratching our heads for a couple of minutes (our heads were really itchy), we thought we'd open up the next best thing; the SQLSERVR.EXE executable.

Warning

Opening an executable up in an editor is a *very dangerous* proposition. If you inadvertently save over the old file, you are lost. We *do not* recommend this procedure for anyone who is the least bit faint of heart. We will not be responsible for any damage you may accidentally inflict upon your system as a result of trying these methods, so don't send us nasty e-mail!◀

The following is a section of the SQLSERVR.EXE executable file, as seen by MS Word:

```
monitor_startcurrent_versionconvert_34to42allow11loadcatalogcheckcheckcatalogcheck-
tablecheckidentcheckallocnewallocfix_alreport_alallocmapcheckdbdbrepairdbreindexd-
brecovermemusageshow_statisticsreindexlogdbtabledesprocbufresourcelockbuffermrulrug
ammonshowcontiggaminitshrinkdbuseroptionspagetraceontraceofftracestatustabpssindun-
dobhashextentcheckextentchainprtipageextentzapallocdumppglinkagefindnotfullextents-
bytesrebuildextentsextentdumpdbinfoshow_bucketsave_rebuild_logrebuild_logshowtextus
edextentsdelete_rowprint_bufsno_printbufcountdescountlocateindexpgshelpdelbuffwake-
upcapture_tdsaddextendedprocdropextendedprocupgradedbperfmonuserlicestatsproc-
cacheperflogsqlperftextalloctextalldevcontroldbcontrolinputbufferoutputbufferupdate
usageopentranpintableunpintablememstatsgetvalueadduserobjectdropuserobjectrowlockpr
obeIOStatssqlper60LRUStatssqlper60NETStatssqlper60RAStatssqlper60Input Buffer
```

We've put some important things in **bold** to emphasize a point. Notice the presence of both checktable and checkdb. We immediately recognized these as options to DBCC, yet we were unable to recall every having seen the keyword convert_34to42. More important, we noticed the presence of the keyword help!

Sure enough, with a little tinkering, we discovered that you can ask DBCC about any valid command by using the previously unknown command help.

Granted, it took us several days of fiddling and more than a few server restarts, but we finally mapped a bunch of these new commands. This is roughly how we got some of the more interesting material in the last chapter.

JUST ASK

Sometimes, discovering an undocumented feature is as simple as asking the right question. For example, if you go to a DOS prompt and run the bcp program with no arguments, you see the following output:

```
usage: C:\MSSQL\BINN\BCP.EXE dbtable {in | out} datafile
        [-m maxerrors] [-f formatfile] [-e errfile]
        [-F firstrow] [-L lastrow] [-b batchsize]
        [-n native type] [-c character type] [-q quoted identifier]
        [-t field terminator] [-r row terminator]
        [-i inputfile] [-o outfile] [-a packetsize]
        [-E explicit identity] [-U username] [-P password]
        [-S server] [-v version] [-T trusted connection]
```

This looks pretty normal, right? Wrong! The SQL Server manuals don't say anything about a -T trusted connection option. We looked!

This was a *huge* gain for us. For example, previously, when you needed to write a stored procedure that had to make a call to xp_cmdshell to do a bulk copy, you needed to encrypt the procedure because you were forced to hard code a valid user name and password. That means that any Joe Schmoe could run sp_helptext on your procedure and hack his (or her) way into a valid account. This requirement for encrypting the procedure made maintaining the code a nightmare.

Thankfully, you don't have to do that anymore. You can simply run the bcp operation with the -T parameter and get a trusted connection. Because the bcp operation is running on the same machine as the SQL Server service, this is a very reliable method. Sure, the method used to find this little gem isn't too sexy, but the result is sure useful!

Finding Undocumented Stored Procedures by Reading the System Tables

As you know, SQL Server stores the vast majority of its configuration and maintenance information in system tables. This is a great boon for you as a developer because it means that you can have complete control of your environment through the use of Transact SQL.

One of the interesting side effects of this architecture is that all objects must be registered in these tables. This includes objects not otherwise mentioned in the documentation.

This knowledge is especially helpful when it comes to stored procedures. Run the following query and compare the resulting list with the list of procedures that seem familiar to you:

```
Use master

select name
from sysobjects
where type in ('X','P')
order by name
```

This should generate the following list:

MS_sqlctrs_users	sp_a_count_bits_on	sp_abort_xact
sp_addalias	sp_addarticle	sp_addextendedproc
sp_addgroup	sp_addlanguage	sp_addlogin
sp_addmessage	sp_addpublication	sp_addpublisher
sp_addremotelogin	sp_addsegment	sp_addserver
sp_addsubscriber	sp_addsubscription	sp_addtype
sp_addumpdevice	sp_adduser	sp_altermessage
sp_articlecolumn	sp_articlefilter	sp_articletextcol
sp_articleview	sp_bindefault	sp_bindrule
sp_bindsession	sp_blockcnt	sp_certify_removable
sp_change_users_login	sp_changearticle	sp_changedbowner
sp_changegroup	sp_changepublication	sp_changesubscriber
sp_changesubscription	sp_changesubstatus	sp_check_objects
sp_check_removable	sp_checknames	sp_chklangparam
sp_coalesce_fragments	sp_column_privileges	sp_columns
sp_commit_xact	sp_commonkey	sp_configure
sp_create_distribution_tables	sp_create_removable	sp_cursor
sp_cursorclose	sp_cursorfetch	sp_cursoropen
sp_cursoroption	sp_databases	sp_datatype_info

(continued)

(continued)

sp_db_upgrade	sp_db_upgrade1	sp_db_upgrade2
sp_db_upgrade3	sp_dbinstall	sp_dboption
sp_dbremove	sp_ddopen	sp_defaultdb
sp_defaultlanguage	sp_depends	sp_devcreate
sp_devoption	sp_diskdefault	sp_distcounters
sp_dropalias	sp_droparticle	sp_dropdevice
sp_dropextendedproc	sp_dropgroup	sp_dropkey
sp_droplanguage	sp_droplogin	sp_dropmessage
sp_droppublication	sp_droppublisher	sp_dropremotelogin
sp_dropsegment	sp_dropserver	sp_dropsubscriber
sp_dropsubscription	sp_droptype	sp_dropuser
sp_dropwebtask	sp_dsninfo	sp_enumdsn
sp_enumfullsubscribers	sp_extendsegment	sp_fallback_activate_svr
sp_fallback_activate_svr_db	sp_fallback_deactivate_svr	sp_fallback_deactivate_svr_db
sp_fallback_enroll_svr_db	sp_fallback_help	sp_fallback_help_db_dev
sp_fallback_MS_enroll_db	sp_fallback_MS_enroll_dev	sp_fallback_MS_enroll_usg
sp_fallback_MS_sel_fb_svr	sp_fallback_MS_verify_ri	sp_fallback_permanent_svr
sp_fallback_upd_dev_drive	sp_fallback_withdraw_svr_db	sp_fixindex
sp_fkeys	sp_foreignkey	sp_get_volume_label
sp_getbindtoken	sp_GetMBCSCharLen	sp_hcchangesubstatus1
sp_hcchangesubstatus2	sp_help	sp_help_revdatabase
sp_helparticle	sp_helparticlecolumns	sp_helpconstraint
sp_helpdb	sp_helpdevice	sp_helpdistributor
sp_helpextendedproc	sp_helpgroup	sp_helpindex
sp_helpjoins	sp_helpkey	sp_helplanguage
sp_helplog	sp_helplogins	sp_helppublication
sp_helppublicationsync	sp_helpremotelogin	sp_helpreplicationdb
sp_helprotect	sp_helpsegment	sp_helpserver
sp_helpsort	sp_helpsql	sp_helpstartup
sp_helpsubscriberinfo	sp_helpsubscription	sp_helptext
sp_helpuser	sp_IsMBCSLeadByte	sp_lock
sp_lock2	sp_lockinfo	sp_logdevice
sp_lookup	sp_makestartup	sp_makewebtask
sp_markreport	sp_monitor	sp_MS_upd_sysobj_category
sp_MSdbuserprofile	sp_MSdependencies	sp_MSenumsubsystems
sp_MSfilterclause	sp_MSforeach_worker	sp_MSforeachdb
sp_MSforeachtable	sp_MSgetalertinfo	sp_MSgetexecinfo
sp_MShelpcolumns	sp_MShelpindex	sp_MShelptype
sp_MSindexspace	sp_MSkilldb	sp_MSloginmappings
sp_MSmatchkey	sp_MSobjectprivs	sp_MSsetalertinfo
sp_MSsetexecinfo	sp_MSsettopology	sp_MSSQLOLE_version
sp_MSSQLOLE65_version	sp_MSsubscriptions	sp_MStablechecks
sp_MStablekeys	sp_MStablerefs	sp_MStablespace
sp_MSuninstall_publishing	sp_MSuniquename	sp_namecrack

sp_namecrack2
sp_namecrack3
sp_OACreate
sp_OADestroy
sp_OAGetErrorInfo
sp_OAGetProperty
sp_OAMethod
sp_OASetProperty
sp_OAStop
sp_objcheck
sp_objectsegment
sp_password
sp_pkeys
sp_placeobject
sp_primarykey
sp_probe_xact
sp_processinfo
sp_processmail
sp_publishdb
sp_recompile
sp_remoteoption
sp_remove_xact
sp_rename
sp_renamedb
sp_replcmds
sp_replcounters
sp_repldone
sp_replflush
sp_replica
sp_replstatus
sp_repltrans
sp_runwebtask
sp_scan_xact
sp_schedulersignal
sp_sdidebug
sp_server_info
sp_serveroption
sp_setlangalias
sp_setnetname
sp_spaceused
sp_special_columns
sp_sproc_columns
sp_sqlexec
sp_sqlregister
sp_start_xact
sp_stat_xact
sp_statistics
sp_stored_procedures
sp_subscribe
sp_sysbackuphistory_limiter
sp_table_privileges
sp_tableoption
sp_tables
sp_tempdbspace
sp_textcolstatus
sp_unbindefault
sp_unbindrule
sp_unmakestartup
sp_unsubscribe
sp_user_counter1
sp_user_counter10
sp_user_counter2
sp_user_counter3
sp_user_counter4
sp_user_counter5
sp_user_counter6
sp_user_counter7
sp_user_counter8
sp_user_counter9
sp_userdefcounters
sp_validlang
sp_validname
sp_who
sp_who2
xp_availablemedia
xp_cmdshell
xp_deletemail
xp_dirtree
xp_dropwebtask
xp_dsninfo
xp_enumdsn
xp_enumerrorlogs
xp_enumgroups
xp_enumqueuedtasks
xp_eventlog
xp_findnextmsg
xp_fixeddrives
xp_getfiledetails
xp_getnetname
xp_grantlogin
xp_logevent
xp_loginconfig
xp_logininfo
xp_makewebtask
xp_msver
xp_perfend
xp_perfmonitor
xp_perfsample
xp_perfstart
xp_readerrorlog
xp_readmail
xp_regaddmultistring
xp_regdeletevalue
xp_regenumvalues
xp_regread
xp_regremovemultistring
xp_regwrite
xp_revokelogin
xp_runwebtask
xp_schedulersignal
xp_sendmail
xp_servicecontrol
xp_snmp_getstate
xp_snmp_raisetrap
xp_sprintf
xp_sqlinventory
xp_sqlregister
xp_sqltrace
xp_sscanf
xp_startmail
xp_stopmail
xp_subdirs
xp_unc_to_drive

There are 312 stored procedures in master alone, and a bunch of them aren't documented anywhere in the manuals. Generally speaking, there are three basic ways to learn how to use an undocumented stored procedure.

Naming Conventions

Microsoft names all its standard stored procedures with the *sp_* prefix and all its extended stored procedures with the *xp_* prefix. There is no rule that says you have to do it this way; it's just a very handy thing to have so that you know what kind of object you are looking at. For example, most of the custom stored procedures we have shown you start with the *usp_* prefix. This is to indicate that they are user-defined procedures.

Use the Source, Luke (with apologies to George Lucas)

The first thing you should notice about this list is that the majority of the procedures listed begin with the prefix *sp_*. This means that they are standard stored procedures. In other words, they are not extended stored procedures. This means that you should be able to read their source code by executing a call to sp_helptext. (We are, of course, assuming that the procedure source code is not encrypted.)

One of the procedures in the preceding long list of procedures is named sp_Msgetexecinfo. This procedure is not documented anywhere in either the online help or the SQL Server books. Suppose that you want to figure out what this code does. What do you do? It's a standard procedure, so you should first try to examine the source code:

```
create procedure sp_MSgetexecinfo
as
    /* Return all SQLExecutive info at one go, for performance reasons. */
    declare @AutoStart int
    declare @RestartSQLServer int
    declare @RestartSQLServerInterval int
    declare @LimitHistoryRows int
    declare @LimitHistoryRowsMax int
    declare @LimitHistoryRowsPerTaskMax int

    exec master.dbo.xp_regread 'HKEY_LOCAL_MACHINE',
'SYSTEM\CurrentControlSet\Services\SQLExecutive', 'Start', @param = @AutoStart OUT
    exec master.dbo.xp_regread 'HKEY_LOCAL_MACHINE',
'SOFTWARE\Microsoft\MSSQLServer\SQLExecutive', 'RestartSQLServer', @param =
@RestartSQLServer OUT
    exec master.dbo.xp_regread 'HKEY_LOCAL_MACHINE',
'SOFTWARE\Microsoft\MSSQLServer\SQLExecutive', 'RestartSQLServerInterval', @param =
@RestartSQLServerInterval OUT
    exec master.dbo.xp_regread 'HKEY_LOCAL_MACHINE',
'SOFTWARE\Microsoft\MSSQLServer\SQLExecutive', 'SyshistoryLimitRows', @param =
@LimitHistoryRows OUT
```

```
    exec master.dbo.xp_regread 'HKEY_LOCAL_MACHINE',
'SOFTWARE\Microsoft\MSSQLServer\SQLExecutive', 'SyshistoryMaxRows', @param =
@LimitHistoryRowsMax OUT
    exec master.dbo.xp_regread 'HKEY_LOCAL_MACHINE',
'SOFTWARE\Microsoft\MSSQLServer\SQLExecutive', 'TaskHistoryMaxRows', @param =
@LimitHistoryRowsPerTaskMax OUT

    /* Remember that for the Services, 2 == AutoStart, 3 == don't (don't ask me
why). */
    select
        AutoStart = case when (2 = @AutoStart) then 1 else 0 end,
        RestartSQLServer = @RestartSQLServer,
        RestartSQLServerInterval = @RestartSQLServerInterval,
        LimitHistoryRows = @LimitHistoryRows,
        LimitHistoryRowsMax = @LimitHistoryRowsMax,
        LimitHistoryRowsPerTaskMax = @LimitHistoryRowsPerTaskMax

GO
```

After a quick glance through the code, it's obvious that this procedure returns the settings for the SQLExecutive service. In fact, the first comment says as much!

```
/* Return all SQLExecutive info at one go, for performance reasons. */
```

Of course, not all procedures you examine will be this easy to figure out, but the point is still the same: Always start with the source!

Tip

There's an unexpected surprise in this procedure: It references an undocumented external procedure named xp_regread. This means that you can use the source code of this procedure to learn the correct syntax for this newly discovered external procedure.◄

Inferring syntax from code references

Although a great many undocumented stored procedures have the source code readily available for inspection, others do not. Specifically, external stored procedures have no available source code because they are merely wrappers for .dll function calls. Divining the correct syntax for these objects can be a little trickier.

One good place to start is with the source code you *do* have. As you saw in the last section, some available program code references these enigmatic procedures. This means that you can use the code you can see to infer the code you cannot.

For example, the sp_Msgetexecinfo procedure references the xp_regread code in the following way:

```
exec master.dbo.xp_regread 'HKEY_LOCAL_MACHINE', 'SOFTWARE\Microsoft\MSSQLServer
\SQLExecutive', 'RestartSQLServer', @param = @RestartSQLServer OUT
```

From this line of code, we can infer the following syntax for xp_regread:

```
Xp_regread @regTree, @regKey, @targetValue, @outputParm OUT
```

The following are the arguments for this procedure.

- @regTree: The specific registry tree to traverse (HKEY_CLASSES_ROOT, HKEY_CURRENT_USER, and so on).
- @regKey: The specific registry key to look for.
- @regValue: The specific registry value you want to be returned.
- @outputParm: The variable in which you want to store the value of @regValue.

Knowing that existing source code is a good facility for learning otherwise undocumented procedures, you can easily construct a stored procedure to show you all standard stored procedures that reference any external procedures. The following accomplishes this goal:

```
create procedure usp_findReferencedXPs @displayOrder int = 0 as

/* Get a rough list of the sp_'s and the xp_'s they reference */

select distinct o.name, convert(char(30),
SUBSTRING(c.text, PATINDEX('%xp[_]%', c.text), 20)) rawtext
into #tmpTable
from master..syscomments c, master..sysobjects o
where text like '%xp[_]%' and
    c.id = o.id
order by o.name

declare @CR char(1)
select @CR = CHAR(13)

/* clean up the list by removing anything that's not part of the xp_'s name */

update #tmpTable
set rawtext = SUBSTRING(rawtext, 1, CHARINDEX(' ', rawtext)-1)
    where CHARINDEX(' ', rawtext) > 0
```

```
update #tmpTable
set rawtext = SUBSTRING(rawtext, 1, CHARINDEX(@CR, rawtext)-1)
    where CHARINDEX(@CR, rawtext) > 0

update #tmpTable
set rawtext = SUBSTRING(rawtext, 1, CHARINDEX("'", rawtext)-1)
    where CHARINDEX("'", rawtext) > 0

/* If @displayOrder = 0, show the list sorted by sp_ name. Otherwise, show it
ordered by xp_ name */

if @displayOrder = 0
    select * from #tmpTable order by name
else
    select * from #tmpTable order by rawtext

drop table #tmpTable

go
```

The syntax for this procedure is as follows:

```
usp_findReferencedXps @displayOrder
```

The following are the parameters for this procedure.

@displayOrder: If 0, the output will be ordered by the referencing procedure (sp_). Otherwise, it will be ordered by the referenced procedure (xp_).

The results, therefore, of the code usp_findReferencedXPs 1 are shown in Table 27-1.

Table 27-1
Referenced External Stored Procedure in Master

Name	***Rawtext***
sp_certify_removable	xp_cmdshell
sp_certify_removable	xp_cmdshell
sp_dbinstall	xp_cmdshell
sp_dropdevice	xp_cmdshell
sp_processmail	xp_deletemail
sp_dropwebtask	xp_dropwebtask
sp_dsninfo	xp_dsninfo
sp_enumdsn	xp_enumdsn
sp_enumdsn	xp_enumdsn
sp_processmail	xp_findnextmsg

(continued)

Table 27-1 *(continued)*
Referenced External Stored Procedure in Master

Name	Rawtext
sp_addpublisher	xp_grantlogin
sp_addpublisher	xp_logininfo
sp_droppublisher	xp_logininfo
sp_makewebtask	xp_makewebtask
sp_makewebtask	xp_makewebtask
sp_processmail	xp_readmail
sp_Msenumsubsystems	xp_regenumvalues
sp_Msenumsubsystems	xp_regenumvalues
sp_helpdistributor	xp_regread
sp_helpdistributor	xp_regread
sp_Msgetalertinfo	xp_regread
sp_Msgetexecinfo	xp_regread
sp_MSuninstall_publishing	xp_regread
sp_certify_removable	xp_regread
sp_Mssetalertinfo	xp_regwrite
sp_Mssetexecinfo	xp_regwrite
sp_MSuninstall_publishing	xp_regwrite
sp_droppublisher	xp_revokelogin
sp_runwebtask	xp_runwebtask
sp_schedulersignal	xp_schedulersignal
sp_processmail	xp_sendmail
sp_sqlregister	xp_sqlregister

Let's say that you want to know the syntax of xp_grantlogin, for example. All you have to do is look in the source code for sp_addpublisher. From that, you should be able to decipher the intended parameters.

Inferring an unknown quantity

Unfortunately, using the preexisting source code as your guide will only get you so far. For example, the xp_sqltrace procedure isn't referenced in any of the existing source. To learn this procedures, you will have to experiment.

Sometimes, you get lucky and the code you are trying to figure out will give you hints. Xp_sqltrace is a good illustration of this. For instance, you might guess that the first parameter for this command is an integer, so you run the following code:

```
xp_sqltrace 1
```

and get the following error:

```
Msg 19024, Level 10, State 0
Error: Invalid @Function parameter, must be 'audit', 'control', 'remove', 'stop' or
'trace'.
```

Hmmm... It seems that the first parameter for this procedure is named @Function and needs to be either audit, control, remove, or trace.

Feeling encouraged by this response, you try something more daring:

```
Xp_sqltrace 'trace', ''
```

and get this:

```
Msg 19025, Level 10, State 0
Error: Invalid @EventFilter parameter type, expecting integer.
```

Ah ha! The second parameter is named @EventFilter and is an integer!

By using this process, you can eventually determine all the parameters for this procedure. Although xp_sqltrace is covered in the documentation, it provides a great example of this process.

Trial and error

Once again, however, luck will only help you so much. There are, unfortunately, not too many procedures that are as friendly as xp_sqltrace. For the rest of them, you are simply going to have to use trial and error.

For example, one of the items on your list is named xp_subdirs. It's probably safe to assume from the name that this code shows you the subdirectories for a given path. Perhaps the following will work

```
Xp_subdirs 'c:\mssql'
```

This returns the following:

```
subdirectory
--------------------------------
DATA
BINN
BIN
INSTALL
SYMBOLS
CHARSETS
LOG
```

(continued)

(continued)

```
REPLDATA
SQLOLE
SNMP
BACKUP

(11 row(s) affected)
```

That didn't seem too hard. What about relative paths?

```
Xp_subdirs '.'
```

yields the following:

```
subdirectory
--------------------------------------------------------------------
cache
CONFIG
dhcp
DRIVERS
LLS
LogFiles
OS2
RAS
REPL
SPOOL
viewers
wins

(12 row(s) affected)
```

OK, relative paths seem to work fine. How about UNC network paths?

```
Xp_subdirs '\\mwdkr00\cddrv\mssql'
```

gets us the following:

```
subdirectory
--------------------------------------------------------------------
BINN
INSTALL
SQLOLE
LOG

(4 row(s) affected)
```

We think you get the point. Of course, xp_subdirs was an easy example, but the technique is just as sound for other things.

SQL TRACE

Before SQL Server 6.5, trial, error, and inference were your only tools for learning the undocumented internals of the database. In its latest release, however, Microsoft has included a tool that enables system administrators to view *all* the SQL commands sent to a specific server. This tool is called SQL Trace.

Although the obvious intent of SQL Trace was to give DBAs the capability to see what their users are up to, it can also be used as a valuable resource for understanding the internals of SQL Server. In this section, we quickly cover some of the finer points of this application and show you several examples of its use.

The options

When using the SQL Trace tool, you have to set up a thing called a *filter*. A filter is just a set of parameters that define what it is you want to see. When setting up a filter, you are presented with the screen shown in Figure 27-1.

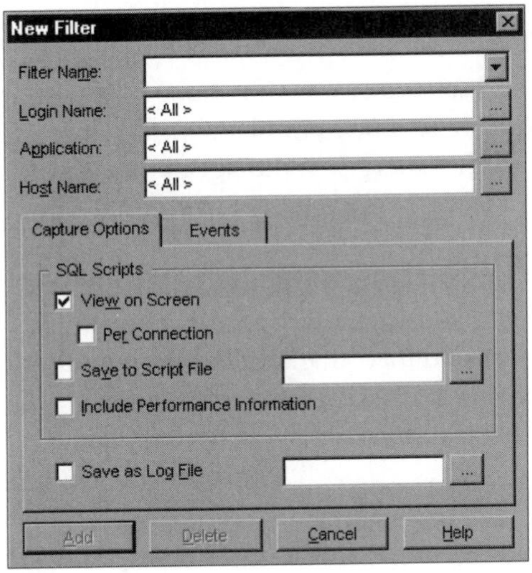

Figure 27-1:
You can set up a filter here.

The following sections discuss the parts of the screen shown in Figure 27-1.

More Than the Obvious

You can select from a list of known applications by clicking the button immediately to the right of this field. This does not mean, however, that you are restricted to trapping events just from those applications. You can enter any valid application name in this field. For example, in order to trap events from the SQL Web Assistant, you would enter **SQLOLE_1**.

Filter Name

This is the unique name you want to assign to your filter. It's a good idea to keep your names as descriptive as possible.

Login Name

In this box, you can enter any specific logins you want to watch. For example, if you enter **jschmoe;jsmith;fedorche**, you will only trap events for users jschmoe, jsmith, and fedorche. The default value of <All> means that events for all logins should be trapped.

Application

If you want to trap events that come from specific applications, you enter their names here. For example, if you want to trap only events that come from the SQL Enterprise Manager, you enter **MS SQLEW** in this field.

Host Name

In this field, you enter any specific host names you want to trap. For example, a value of dilbert;dogbert;catbert would only trap events from the hosts dilbert, dogbert, and catbert.

Capture Options

You also have some choices as to how you want your information to be captured. They are

- **View On Screen.** Clicking this option tells the tool to display all trace information in a trace screen.
- **Per Connection.** Selecting this option forces the tool to show the trace information for each connection in a separate trace window.

- **Save To Script File.** This box contains the name of a file in which you want the trace SQL written. This enables you to rerun the SQL at a later time. Be sure to review the contents of this file before executing it.
- **Include Performance Information.** If this option is selected, SQL Trace includes performance information in the trace output. This is helpful for debugging where performance lags are in your system code.
- **Save As Log File.** This box holds the name of a file in which you want to save ALL the trace contents. Unlike the script file, this file will include non-SQL code, such as performance information.

Events

Thankfully, you can also choose which events to trap.

- **Connections.** Select this option if you want to trap events when a new connection is established to the server.
- **SQL Statements.** Selecting this option causes SQL Trace to trap all SQL commands to the server.
- **SQL Filter.** If you have selected the SQL Statements option, you can filter what kinds of SQL you want to trap. For example, if you want to trap only UPDATE commands, then you would enter **UPDATE%** in this box.
- **RPC.** Select this option if you want to trap Remote Procedure Calls.
- **RPC Filter.** Like the SQL Filter option, the RPC Filter option allows you to trap for specific characters or patterns while trapping RPCs.
- **Attentions.** This option allows you to trap *attention* events. An attention event occurs when a client application interrupts a SQL Server command.
- **Disconnections.** This option specifies what SQL Trace should trap for when a client closes a connection.

Examples

In this section, we take you through some useful examples of how to use SQL Trace to find undocumented features of SQL Server.

Taking stock

Did you ever wonder what the SQL Enterprise Manager does behind the scenes when you view the list of databases on a server? We did. What we found was kind of interesting. Here's the output from SQL Trace:

```
– 5/3/96 13:01:06.10 SQL (ID=129, SPID=15, User=sa(HOME_NET\ROOT), App='MS SQLEW',
Host='MWDKR00'(fffd13d7) )
create table #SQLOLEDbUserProfile (dbid int NOT NULL PRIMARY KEY, profilebits int
NOT NULL)
go
– 5/3/96 13:01:06.100 SQL (ID=129, SPID=15, User=sa(HOME_NET\ROOT), App='MS SQLEW',
Host='MWDKR00'(fffd13d7) )
exec sp_MSdbuserprofile 'init'
go
– 5/3/96 13:01:06.770 SQL (ID=129, SPID=15, User=sa(HOME_NET\ROOT), App='MS SQLEW',
Host='MWDKR00'(fffd13d7) )
select o.name, o.version, o.crdate, suser_name(o.suid), o.dbid,floor(((select
sum(u.size) from master..sysusages u where u.dbid=o.dbid)*(2048.0/1024.0))/1024),
o.suid - suser_id(), o.status,spaceavail = 0,  LogOnSepDev = (select count(*) from
master..sysusages us where us.dbid = o.dbid and us.segmap = 4),  o.category, t.pro-
filebits from master..sysdatabases o, #SQLOLEDbUserProfile t where t.dbid =* o.dbid
and name like '%' order by o.name
go
– 5/3/96 13:01:07.270 SQL (ID=129, SPID=15, User=sa(HOME_NET\ROOT), App='MS SQLEW',
Host='MWDKR00'(fffd13d7) )
select name, status, category from master..sysdatabases
go
– 5/3/96 13:01:07.370 SQL (ID=129, SPID=15, User=sa(HOME_NET\ROOT), App='MS SQLEW',
Host='MWDKR00'(fffd13d7) )
exec sp_MSforeachdb 'use ? select dname = db_name(), username = user_name()'
go
```

The SQL Enterprise Manager seems to be doing five things here:

1. It creates a table named #SQLOLEDbUserProfile that holds a database id and an integer whose bits have a specific meaning.
2. It populates this new table with a call to the procedure sp_Msdbuserprofile.
3. It gets version and creation information about each database.
4. It determines the status of each database.
5. It figures out what user name the current login maps to in each database.

These steps yield some interesting results. For example, Step 5 makes a call to an undocumented procedure named sp_Msforeachdb. Apparently, you need to pass a SQL command to this procedure and substitute a question mark (?) for each place you want to use the given database name. For example, the following prints a list of the databases:

```
exec sp_Msforeachdb 'use ? select db_name() db_name'
```

This statement yields the following results:

```
dname         username
----------------------------- -----------------------------
master        dbo
dname         username
----------------------------- -----------------------------
model         dbo
dname         username
----------------------------- -----------------------------
msdb          dbo
dname         username
----------------------------- -----------------------------
pubs          dbo
dname         username
----------------------------- -----------------------------
tempdb        dbo
```

Scripting your tables

There are very few things in SQL Server that cannot be done with a simple call to a stored procedure. One of them is generating scripts for tables. We were curious just how the SQL Enterprise Manager does this, so we watched it with SQL Trace. What we discovered is that the it was making a call to an undocumented procedure named sp_Mshelpcolumns. This procedure returns information about the columns in a given table, which includes whether or not the column allows NULLS, whether it is an identity column, and so on.

After playing with this new procedure for a few minutes, we decided to write our own procedure to generate basic table scripts. The following is that code:

```
create procedure usp_basicTableScript @tableName varchar(255) as

/* Create table to hold column info */

create table #tableInfo (
        col_name varchar(30) NOT NULL,
        col_id tinyint NOT NULL,
        coltype varchar(255) NOT NULL,
        collen tinyint NOT NULL,
        col_prec tinyint NULL,
        col_scale tinyint NULL,
        col_basetype varchar(255) NULL,
        col_defname varchar(61)    NULL,
        col_rulname varchar(61) NULL,
```

(continued)

(continued)

```
        colnull bit NOT NULL,
        col_identity bit NOT NULL,
        col_flags int NULL,
        col_seed int NULL,
        col_increment int NULL,
        col_dridefname varchar(30) NULL,
        col_drideftext varchar(255) NULL
)

/* create table to hold final SQL statement */

create table #finalStatement (line varchar(255))

/* insert column info */

insert into #tableInfo
    exec sp_MShelpcolumns @tablename, @orderby = 'id'

insert into #finalStatement values ('create table ' + @tablename + '(')

/* generate SQL statement */

insert into #finalStatement
select '     ' + rtrim(col_name) + ' ' +
    rtrim(col_basetype) +
    case when PATINDEX('%char%',col_basetype) > 0 then
          "(" + rtrim(convert(char(3),collen)) + ")"
end +
    case when col_identity = 1 then 'IDENTITY' else '' end +
    case when colnull = 1 then 'NULL' else 'NOT NULL' end +
    ","

from #tableInfo

insert into #finalStatement values (')')

/* display the final SQL */

select * from #finalStatement

/* Clean up */

drop table #tableInfo
drop table #finalStatement

go
```

For example, the code:

```
exec usp_basicTableScript authors
```

yields the following result:

```
create table authors(
     au_id varchar(11) NOT NULL,
     au_lname varchar(40) NOT NULL,
     au_fname varchar(20) NOT NULL,
     phone char(12) NOT NULL,
     address varchar(40) NULL,
     city varchar(20) NULL,
     state char(2) NULL,
     zip char(5) NULL,
     contract bit NOT NULL,
)
```

As you can see, after you have the column information, the code becomes fairly straightforward. Clearly, this procedure isn't as robust as you might like. It doesn't address keys, rules, or defaults. We will leave that to you!

XP_SQLTRACE

As you may have guessed by now, the SQL Trace tool is just a nice GUI front end for an external stored procedure: xp_sqltrace. In this section, we will show you how to use this procedure in lieu of its GUI cousin.

The basic syntax for xp_sqltrace is as follows:

```
xp_sqltrace [[@Function = ] function] [, [ @EventFilter = ]
eventfilter]
[, [ @LangFilter = ] 'langfilter'] [, [ @RPCFilter = ] 'rpcfilter']
[, [ @UserFilter = ] userfilter] [, [ @AppFilter = ] appfilter] [, [
@HostFilter = ] hostfilter] [, [@BufSize = ] bufsize] [, [ @TimeOut
= ] timeout] [, [ @TraceId = ] traceid] [, [@FullText = ] fulltext]
[, [ @FullFilePath = ] 'outputfilename'] [, [ @IntegerEvents = ]
integerevents]
```

In the next few sections, we will discuss each element of this syntax.

@Function

This parameter specifies a string that describes what action xp_sqltrace performs. Following are the possible values for @Function:

- **Audit.** Logs all database activity requested by the specified filters to a file specified by @FullFilePath. Returns program control immediately. If @TraceId, @BufSize, or @TimeOut parameters are specified, they are ignored. If audit is used without any parameters, it generates a results set that displays the current audit settings for xp_sqltrace. Only one instance of audit can be executed at any time. A permanent connection is not necessary to execute an audit. For example, the system administrator can be connected, start the audit, and then disconnect. You can use audit in automatically started procedures.
- **Control.** Changes the settings for a running instance from a separate connection. You must run xp_sqltrace without parameters to obtain an @TraceId *before* starting a trace session. The @TraceId parameter is required.
- **Remove.** Unloads all event handlers. Stops all data from being sent to trace sessions until trace handlers are loaded again. Using Remove does not stop currently executing trace sessions. Starting or stopping a trace session also loads or unloads relevant handlers. You can use Remove to pause all trace sessions temporarily. No other parameters are required.
- **Stop.** Stops either a single trace session or all trace sessions for the current server. It is recommended that you execute xp_sqltrace stop, @traceid = <traceid> to stop a specific trace session. Using xp_sqltrace stop is useful if the server is under a heavy load and the system administrator must stop all trace activities.
- **Trace.** Captures all database activity requested by the specified filters and generates a log file or a results set. The @TraceId parameter has no effect.

@EventFilter

@Eventfilter specifies an integer that describes what server activity to monitor. To specify more than one @EventFilter value, add together the @EventFilter values. For example, @EventFilter = 31 means that xp_sqltrace should monitor CONNECT, DISCONNECT, POST_LANGUAGE, POST_RPC, and ATTENTION events. Following are the possible values for @EventFilter:

- **0.** PAUSE. Temporarily pauses the trace session. Must be the only @EventFilter specified.
- **1.** CONNECT. Traces CONNECT events to SQL Server.
- **2.** DISCONNECT. Traces DISCONNECT events from SQL Server.
- **4.** POST_LANGUAGE. Traces completed language events on SQL Server (for example, INSERT, SELECT).
- **8.** POST_RPC. Traces completed RPC events on SQL Server.
- **16.** ATTENTION. Traces ATTENTION events on SQL Server.
- **32.** PRE_LANGUAGE. Traces language batches immediately prior to execution. Not currently implemented.
- **64.** PRE_RPC. Traces RPC events immediately before execution. Not currently implemented.

@LangFilter

This parameter specifies what type of SQL statements to trap. Use the wildcard character (%) to indicate any sequence of characters. Delimit multiple filter strings with a semicolon (;) for the OR condition (%INSERT%;%SELECT%).

@RPCFilter

This parameter specifies which RPC calls to trap. Use the wildcard character (%) to indicate any sequence of characters. Delimit multiple filter strings with a semicolon (;) for the OR condition (%sp_cursors%;sp_run%).

@UserFilter

@UserFilter specifies the login name(s) of users for whom to monitor events. Delimit multiple filter strings with a semicolon (;) for the OR condition. Use the wildcard character (%) to indicate any sequence of characters. For example, specify Chan% as the login name to find login names Chan and Channing.

@AppFilter

This parameter specifies the application name(s) for which to monitor events. Delimit multiple filter strings with a semicolon (;) for the OR condition. Use the wildcard character (%) to indicate any sequence of characters. For example, specify the application name Acc% to find the Access application.

@HostFilter

This parameter specifies the host(s) for which to monitor events. Delimit multiple filter strings with a semicolon (;) for the OR condition. Use the wildcard character (%) to indicate any sequence of characters. For example, specify the host name air% to find the airedale host.

@BufSize

This parameter specifies the number of rows of data the server will buffer when the client is busy. The @BufSize parameter is of int datatype and can be a value 1 to 20,000. The default is 1,000.

@TimeOut

@TimeOut specifies the amount of time in seconds that the server will wait when the row buffer specified in @BufSize is full before terminating the trace session. The @TimeOut parameter is of int datatype and can be 1 to 10 seconds (the default is 5 seconds).

@TraceId

This parameter specifies the trace identification number used for the trace session. Each @TraceId value is static for a connection as long as you retain your current connection. The @TraceId parameter is of int datatype. You can find out your TraceId by executing xp_sqltrace with no parameters. You will get something like the following:

```
TraceId     Version
----------- ----------
1433872     6.50.201

(1 row(s) affected)
```

@FullText

This parameter specifies whether the language or RPC strings should be returned as varchar(255) (the default is 0) or as text (1). The @FullText parameter is of int datatype.

@FullFilePath

This parameter specifies the file to send the output to as a string (for example, 'C:\selects.txt'). This parameter uses the standard Microsoft SQL Trace log format for output.

@IntegerEvents

@IntegerEvents specifies whether the event column should be text (the default is 0) or integer (1). The @IntegerEvents parameter is of int datatype.

Example

Perhaps the easiest way to use xp_sqltrace is like this:

```
exec xp_sqltrace 'trace', 4
```

This starts a trace on all SQL calls. If you have started this from the SQL Enterprise Manager, your window should look something like the one shown in Figure 27-2.

To get this output to stop, you need to execute the folowing:

```
exec xp_sqltrace 'stop'
```

Uses

There is a bunch of really nice ways a system administrator can make use of this procedure. For example, you can use it to trap the actions of a particular user. Let's say that you suspect that user *jschmoe* is trying to hack into your system. You can run the following to get a file of all his activities:

```
Exec xp_sqltrace 'trace', @userfilter = 'jschmoe', @fullfilepah = 'joe.sql'
```

This creates a log file named joe.sql that will contain all actions undertaken by user *jschmoe*. When you want to review its contents, simply stop the trace and open the file. This is, of course, only one use for this code. There are hundreds more. It's really up to your needs and imagination.

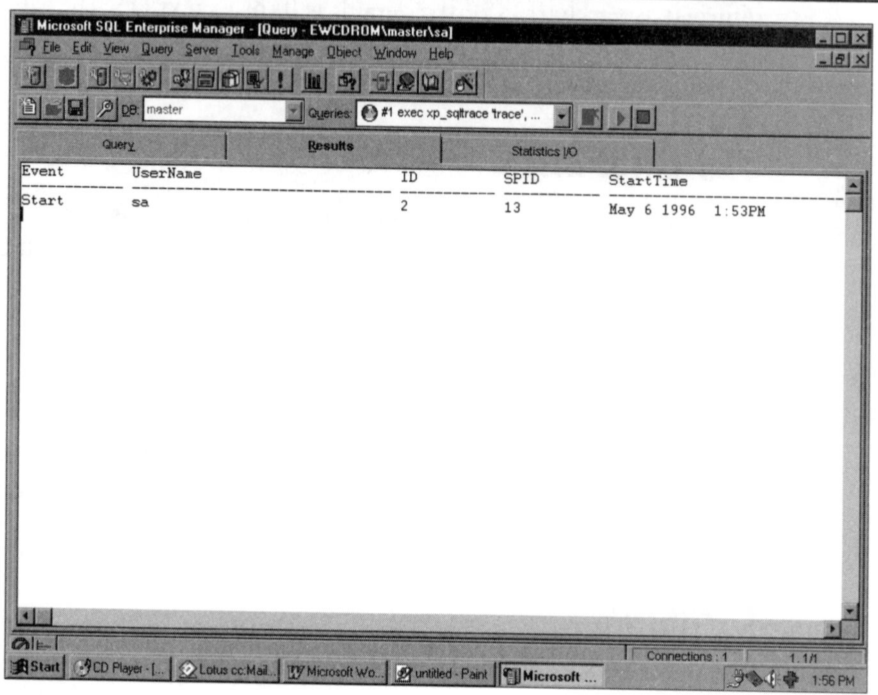

Figure 27-2:
The output from a typical call to xp_sqltrace.

Conclusion

Clearly, there are a number of ways for you to figure out things that the developers of SQL Server never intended for you to find out about. Oh, well, if they *really* wanted to hide these things, they shouldn't have made it so easy to find them!

Please be careful, though. Using things that the developers didn't document can lead to some unexpected surprises when you upgrade to your next version of the product. It also makes debugging code much more difficult. Our advice is this: If you are going to use these things in you production environment, document your methods thoroughly!

SUMMARY

Crawling around the dusty corners of SQL Server can be a fun and interesting experience, even if you never use what you find. If this chapter has been good for anything, we hope it has shown you that there's a lot more to SQL Server than what's in the documentation.

Whether you are searching through executables, sifting through system procedure code, or just plain guessing, we think that you will really enjoy the feeling of finding unexpected gems!

REVIEW QUESTIONS

Q: Will every string you find in an executable be useful?

A: Not a chance! A lot of what you will find will be debug code accidentally left in by the developers.

Q: Why isn't the -T option of bcp documented?

A: Our guess is that the documentation team just missed this one.

Q: If Microsoft didn't want users to know the internals of the undocumented system stored procedures, then why didn't they encrypt the source?

A: It's a *huge* pain to make changes to a procedure that's encrypted. You have to drop it and recreate it from scratch. When you consider all the procedures in master and msdb, it was probably time consuming even to consider this option.

Chapter

28

INDEXES AND QUERY OPTIMIZATION

What exactly happens in between sending a SQL statement to SQL Server and getting the output back in your application? Normally, you don't worry about that, unless the time interval exceeds a few seconds. When you have gotten up, gone to the soda machine, picked your caffeine source of choice, and come back, and the query is *still* running, you are definitely thinking about what SQL Server is doing. This chapter is all about the answer to that question and making it so that your queries run *much* faster.

The art of query optimization is what separates good database developers from mediocre database developers. By *queries*, we mean not just SELECT statements, but INSERT, UPDATE, and DELETE statements as well. Poorly optimized SQL will ruin the performance of an otherwise perfectly designed application. Well-optimized queries will make you and your users infinitely more productive.

As it turns out, *writing* about query optimization is quite a challenge, too, precisely because it seems to be more an art than a science. It would be easy for us to spend the next 300 pages talking about how SQL Server optimizes your SQL, the implication being that if you know how it works, you can make it work better. This approach misses the point, however. You might take the time to refine a query or two, but you can't get a whole system up and running if you spend an hour analyzing the best way to retrieve data for each and every query. The whole point of buying an RDBMS is to make it do that work. Therefore, we focus on the design principles you need to follow so that having an optimized database will simply be second nature to you.

What's in This Chapter

Our approach here will be first to discuss how SQL Server reads or writes data in response to query. With that in place, we can focus on the most critical element of query optimization: designing good indexes for SQL Server to use. The topics we cover in this chapter are

- How SQL Server stores and retrieves data from operating system files
- What the SQL Server optimizer does
- Why normalization aids query processing
- The principles you should follow in choosing indexes
- How to evaluate the indexes you already have

Reading or Writing Data in Response to a Query

Before we can discuss making queries run faster, we need to understand how they are running now. This involves understanding the following topics.

Pages

In earlier chapters, we discussed *devices*, which are the Windows NT files in which SQL Server stores your data. Now, we need to drill farther down. Each device is divided into 512K pieces called *allocation units*. (If you recall, database sizes are restricted to 512K increments — this is why.) Whereas a device can split among many databases, an allocation unit is used in its entirety for one specific database. Each allocation unit is further divided into 32 *extents*, which are 16K. An extent is dedicated to a specific object within the database. Finally, each extent is composed of eight 2K pages. A *page* is the smallest block of contiguous disk storage that SQL Server reads into memory as a unit. Therefore, the response to any SELECT statement boils down to a question of which pages SQL Server needs to read.

SQL Server uses a 2K page size, whereas Windows NT uses a 4K page size. Why? Microsoft started SQL Server from a partnership with Sybase, which predates Windows NT. Some RDBMSs do use a 4K page size; some even let you choose the page size. In SQL Server, it is fixed at 2K.◀

Pages have sequential numbers, from 0 on up. Each page in the database has a unique number, which is stored as an int. You might wonder if an int is enough to hold the maximum database size of 1TB = 2^{40} bytes, but because this means only 2^{29} pages, there is plenty of room in a 4-byte integer, which can range from 0 to 2^{32}. The page numbers are the foundation of the random access reads SQL Server has to do on the devices. Notice that the page numbers are *logical* numbers: they aren't actual pointers to memory locations, nor offsets in the file storage. SQL Server resolves page numbers into fetches from the cache or the disk.

There is no guarantee that the data for a table will be stored on pages with sequential numbers. The data pages of a table form a doubly linked list, so by looking at any given page you know what the "next" and "previous" pages are. You should wonder just what exactly "next" means in this context, because in the relational model, a table has no intrinsic order. The clustered index, if there is one, determines the order of the rows. If there is no clustered index, you can make no assumption about the ordering of the data or about what the next or previous pages will contain. In practice, you will find that the order in which the data is stored on the page is exactly the order in which you have inserted the data, if you have performed no UPDATEs or DELETEs.

Storing data on a page

The layout of a page is rather interesting and becomes very important as we discuss indexes and normalization. As you know, we have 2K, or 2,048 bytes, of space on each page. This is divided into a header, the data rows, and a footer. The header contains, among other things, such important information as the following:

- The number of the page
- The numbers of the next and previous pages
- The ID of the object that owns the page
- Information that SQL Server needs to write rows to the page

You can see the header of any page you want with the DBCC commands we covered in Chapter 26. The syntax is as follows:

```
DBCC TRACEON ( 3604 ) /* Directs the output to the client */
DBCC PAGE ( dbid, pageid, 0 ) /* The 0 means header only */
```

DBCC PAGE is of little help if you don't know which page you want, of course. We recommend you use the following command instead, but only on a *small* table:

```
DBCC TAB ( dbname, objectname, 0 ) /* Returns DBCC PAGE for all pages in the
objects */
```

For example, to see the employee table of pubs, you execute

```
DBCC TRACE ( 3604 )
DBCC TAB ( pubs, employee, 0 )
```

The first page header on our system is this:

```
DATABASE:4   OBJECT:752005710   PAGE:664 (0x298)

Page header for page 0xf9f800
pageno=664 nextpg=665 prevpg=0 objid=752005710 timestamp=000100000ce5
nextrno=41 level=0 indid=0  freeoff=1936 minlen=26
page status bits: 0x1
```

Data rows

Next after the header we have actual rows of data. SQL Server assigns a one-byte row number to each row on the page, starting with zero. For this reason, you can never have more than 256 rows on a single data page. The storage of the columns is complicated intensely by variable-length columns and columns that allow nulls (which are actually stored as variable-length columns). Table 28-1 indicates the layout of a SQL Server row.

Table 28-1
How SQL Server Stores a Row of Data

Length	*Contents*
1 byte	Number of variable-length columns in the row
1 byte	The row number
varies	All non-null, fixed length columns

Length	Contents
2 bytes	The total length of the row
varies	All the variable-length columns and columns that allow nulls
varies	Offset table of adjust bytes for rows that cross a 256 byte boundary
1 byte	The location of the offset table
1 byte each	The location of the variable-length and nullable columns

If a table does not allow nulls and has no variable-length columns, only the first three categories in Table 28-1 are needed. The total length of the row is a constant throughout the table, and the rest of the categories don't apply to such a table. SQL Server stores each row simply as one byte filled with a zero (no variable-length columns), one byte for the row number, and then the data. (The obvious question here is why bother storing a zero in every single row to indicate it has no variable-length columns? We don't know either.) As an example of a table with all fixed-width columns, look at sysconstraints. Its data will be laid out as shown in Table 28-2.

Table 28-2
How Sysconstraints Is Stored

Column	Datatype	Length	Position	Comments
		1	1	Number of variable-length fields
		1	2	The row number
constid	int	4	3	Data column
id	int	4	7	Data column
colid	tinyint	1	11	Data column
spare1	tinyint	1	12	Data column
status	int	4	13	Data column
actions	int	4	17	Data column
error	int	4	21	Data column

When a table has nulls, the picture is more complicated. How do you store a null? Suppose that you have an integer field that can be null. There is no value you can pick to indicate null because any number you choose to represent null is a valid integer. What should you do? One idea would be to store a little flag for a nullable column that indicates whether the column is null. One byte could store the flags for eight nullable columns. This would be a fine idea if we were considering nulls alone, but now consider the separate problem of variable-length columns.

The storage for fixed-width column works because you know exactly where the contents of a column will be, based on the sum of the widths of the previous columns, which you know before you look at the page. When column widths vary, you need some way to track where columns are on the data page. You could simply precede each column with a one-byte field indicating its width. In fact, this is exactly what BCP does when it uses native format. The problem, however, is that to find a given column, you are forced to scan past all the preceding columns. A better approach would be to store the relative location in which the column starts. This is essentially what SQL Server does. Now we are in a position to accommodate nulls easily: we will store the relative location of a column containing a null as zero, which indicates that the data are missing.

Offsets

We said that SQL Server stores row numbers within a page. How would you jump to, say, row number 5? That is what the footer of the page tells you. Starting at byte 2,048 and working backwards, SQL Server uses two bytes to store the absolute location on each page of each row number. You can view the contents of a page, including its offsets, with DBCC PAGE. The syntax is as follows:

```
DBCC PAGE ( dbid, pageno, 1 ) /* Prints page contents in a semi-readable form */
```

For example, for sysusers, we have this output from DBCC PAGE (4, 160, 1):

```
Page header for page 0xdf0000
pageno=160 nextpg=0 prevpg=0 objid=10 timestamp=0001 00000dc1
nextrno=3 level=0 indid=0  freeoff=86 minlen=8
page status bits: 0x1

Offset 32 -
00df0020:  0101feff 00000000 13007075 626c6963  ..........public
00df0030:  02100a                               ...

Offset 51 -
00df0033:  0102ffff 02000000 12006775 65737402  ..........guest.
00df0043:  0f0a                                 ..

Offset 69 -
00df0045:  02000100 01000000 11006462 6f030d0d  ..........dbo...
00df0055:  0a
```

```
OFFSET TABLE:
Row - Offset
2 (0x2) - 51 (0x33),   1 (0x1) - 32 (0x20),
The total number of data pages in this table is 1.
Table has 3 data rows.
0 (0x0) - 69 (0x45),
```

One word of warning: integers aren't stored or displayed the way you think they are. If you see 24e8aa0f in the hex dump, that corresponds to $24 \times 256^3 + 232 \times 256^2 + 100 \times 256^1 + 15$, right? Wrong! It is actually $24 + 232 \times 256^1 + 100 \times 256^2 + 15 \times 256^3$. The most significant byte is on the right. Be careful of this trap as you try to interpret hex dumps of pages.

Data retrieval

At this point, we know enough to implement the simplest of all data-retrieval methods: the table scan. A *table scan* is the reading of each and every data page of a table. When SQL Server does a table scan, it starts with the first page of a table (we'll say more about how to find that first page later), and from the nextpg value in that page, SQL Server knows which page to retrieve next, and so on, until SQL Server hits the page where nextpg = 0.

Cross-Reference

This will take awhile with a large table because the number of pages SQL Server has to read is the table size divided by 2K. Therefore, if your table is 1G, SQL Server has to read 524,288 pages. However, you will find that SQL Server often does choose to do a table scan because there are many times when a table scan is the most efficient way to retrieve data. This is especially true for reading small tables or for reading the outer-most table in a the nested iteration processing of a join. (We will talk more about when and why SQL Server chooses table scans in Chapter 29.) The key point about a table scan is that it bounds the worst-case scenario: in no case should SQL Server ever use a data-access method that entails reading more pages than a table scan would.◄

Faster data retrieval: indexes

We are now ready to talk about indexes. Let's start with how a nonclustered index works. When you define a nonclustered index on some combination of one or more columns, or keys, you are telling SQL Server you want rapid access to the table when you specify the value of these index keys. You don't want to wait for a table scan. SQL Server builds and maintains a lookup list for these index keys. For each key value, SQL Server will store the page and row numbers of the rows containing that value. These lookup lists are stored on separate pages called *index pages*.

The pages of an index are stored in tree-like levels. In fact, the method of indexing used in SQL Server is called *B-tree* (balanced-tree) indexing. The tree is arranged such that you can start at the top of the tree and quickly branch to find the data you want. The lowest level of an index is called the *leaf level*. At all levels of an index, the data are stored in index key order, and the pages are linked in index key order. For a nonclustered index, the leaf pages contain one entry per row in the table. Each entry contains the value of the index keys, the number of the actual data page the row is on, and the row number on that page. For example, sysobjects has a nonclustered index on name, uid. The leaf level of that index in master has entries like the following:

```
DF__spt_values, 1, 500, 10
helpsql, 1, 501, 7
MS_sqlctrs_users, 1, 555, 2
etc.
```

For this index, there are about 50 rows on each leaf page. Each of the text strings, 'DF__spt_values', 'helpsql', and 'MS_sqlctrs_users', are the names of objects in the master database and are entries in the sysobjects table. Remember that the index is on name and *uid*. The first line says, in effect, that "name = 'DF__spt_values', uid = 1, can be found on page 500, row 10."

The next level up from the leaf level has one entry for each leaf level page. On this level, the rows on a given page are the first rows from the leaf pages. The successively higher levels, if there are any, always have one row for each page on the lower level. For our non-clustered index on master..sysobjects, the first and only page of the next level up has entries for these keys:

```
DF__spt_values, 1
sp_create_removable, 1
sp_fallback_help, 1
sp_helpsort, 1
sp_replica, 1
spt_committab, 1
syssubscriptions, 1
```

In this example, 'DF__spt_values, 1' is the first row of leaf page one, 'sp_create_removable, 1' is the first row of leaf page two, ..., and 'syssubscriptions, 1' is the first row of the last leaf page. There are only seven entries because there are only seven leaf level pages, and so we only have one page at this level. By definition, the process stops when you get to the level where there is just one page, and this page is called the *root* page. To review, we have one root page with seven entries. Below it are seven leaf pages, each with about 50 or so rows. The leaf pages have one row for each row in the table, and we have about 350 rows in the sysobjects table.

Clustered indexes

As you know, a clustered index is the one index on a table that matches the physical ordering of rows on data pages. With a clustered index, the data pages are the leaf pages. This is a bit difficult to understand at first, but it makes sense when you think about it. Having a separate leaf level would be redundant because it would be recording things like this:

```
key1, page 1234, row 0
key2, page 1234, row 1
key3, page 1234, row 2
etc.
```

The page numbers would appear in their logical order; the row numbers would always be increasing within a page. This isn't telling us anything we don't already know, so it is a waste. Therefore, the first nonleaf/nondata page of a clustered index is just a list of the first key value from each data page, along with the page number. Note that there is no point in recording the row number because the first row on each page is always zero. The higher levels continue in this fashion until you get to the one root page.

Sysindexes

The sysindexes table has a row for each index on a table, and it also has a row for each table without a clustered index. Among the nifty pieces of information in sysindexes is the page number of the first page in an index and the page number of the root page. For a table with no clustered index, these fields list the first and last page of the table. We now know enough to implement data retrieval with an index. When SQL Server is using a non-clustered index to find a specific value specified for the key field(s), the steps SQL Server must follow are

1. Get the root page number from sysindexes.
2. Scan the root page to find the first and last pages on the next level down that contain the key value.

3. Scan that range of index pages to find the range on the next level until the leaf level is reached.
4. At the leaf level, scan the appropriate range of leaf-level pages, searching for the key value. Make a list of the data page numbers and row numbers for the matches.
5. Scan those data pages and return those rows.

At the very worst, SQL Server could end up scanning all the index pages and all the data pages. In this event, SQL Server has scanned more pages using the index than with a simple table scan. One of the things the SQL Optimizer has to watch out for is cases where the index will actually waste time.

Updating indexes

Clearly, every INSERT or DELETE will affect all the indexes defined on a table because the rows added or removed from the table must have references added or removed from the indexes. Most UPDATEs affect all indexes, too. An UPDATE on an indexed column clearly changes the index for that column. An UPDATE of a clustered index value changes row numbers and, therefore, changes all indexes. Furthermore, there are many times when SQL Server treats an UPDATE as a combination of DELETEs and INSERTs (these are called deferred UPDATEs), which again change all indexes.

At a minimum, the leaf-level index pages must change when you write to the data page, and the changes could go higher in the tree. This is a tradeoff you face with indexes: they speed up both reading *and* writing, but they can also slow your writing down. You know already how indexes speed up reading; the same applies to writing: SQL Server may be able to use an index to zero in on the pages it has to change quickly. However, INSERTs and UPDATEs that increase row size can pose a special problem: what happens when there is no more room on the page for the row you want to insert? SQL Server does what is called a page split, which is where indexes cause a performance hit. A *page split* is the process in which SQL Server takes one page and splits it into two pages, placing 50 percent of the data on each page. Now there is room for the new row.

For example, suppose that pageno 53267 (which has 42 rows), prevpg 53266, and nextpg 53268 need to be split. SQL Server will get a free page in an extent owned by the object. If the object has no free pages in any of its extents, SQL Server will allocate a new extent for the object. (If that fails, your database is full.) Let's say that SQL Server gets pageno 68901 to do the job. SQL Server will leave rows 0 – 21 on page 53267 and change its nextpg to 68901. Rows 22 – 41 will be put on pageno 68901, but there they will be renumbered to 0 – 21. Page 68901 will list prevpg as 53267 and nextpg as 53268. SQL Server then has to update page 53268 to reflect the fact that its prevpg is now 68901, not 52367. All the index pages that used to reference rows 22 – 41 of pageno 52367 are now wrong, so they have to be updated to reflect the new page number of 68901 and the new row numbers. Finally, SQL Server actually has to insert the row that caused all this work.

Clearly, page splits are a lot of work, and a lot of page splits slow down writes tremendously. Because most tables are written to, it is wise to leave some extra room on each page when you first load the data, rather than filling each page to the brim. That way, SQL Server can insert at least a few rows without having to split pages. How much extra room SQL Server leaves is called *free space*, and it is controlled by the FILLFACTOR. We will discuss this parameter under index optimization later in this chapter.

The SQL Optimizer

When you send a query to SQL Server, it uses an Optimizer so it can actually decide how to retrieve the data. There are three categories of decisions the Optimizer has to make:

- For each table in the query, whether to use a table scan, the clustered index, or which nonclustered index.
- The order in which to join tables, if more than one table is involved in the query.
- What temporary tables, if any, to create. SQL Server sometimes creates work tables to hold intermediary results, to facilitate sorting, or to reformat (create an index for) a table.

The second two decisions are strongly influenced by the first, so in a sense, index selection is the key to the whole ball of wax. The Optimizer makes a cost-based decision about which indexes, join orders, and temporary table to use. A *cost-based* decision is a choice derived by considering all possibilities, assigning an estimated cost (in terms of the number of page reads) to each, and then choosing the approach with the lowest estimated cost. Of course, when SQL Server is weighing the table scan option, the Optimizer doesn't have to estimate cost: the number of page reads is the number of pages in the table. When using an index, however, SQL Server has to guess how useful the index will really be. If you are searching for a given value, can SQL Server expect to find just 1 match or 1,000 or 100,000? SQL Server makes these estimates based on statistics it gathers on the indexes.

Here's the bombshell: SQL Server almost always chooses correctly. Let's make that point again. In the opinion of almost everyone we know and every book or article we have read, the SQL Server Optimizer almost always chooses the optimal path to retrieve the data for a given query. That being the case, you might wonder what the heck this chapter is about. Well, the problem boils down to "garbage in, garbage out." If SQL Server has 200 choices, all of them crummy, you can count on SQL Server's selecting the least lousy of the 200 crummy options you gave it. Your query will still run very slowly.

How often does this happen, that SQL Server is forced to pick the lesser of many evils? All the time. It is probably happening on all your SQL Servers right now. Therefore, read on, so you can give the Optimizer good choices.

A Plug for Normalization

We discussed the normal forms in Chapter 12 from the perspective of eliminating redundancy in data, which gives you a great advantage in maintaining your data integrity. What we didn't mention at the time is that normalization will also often *improve* your query performance. That's right, we said *improve*. No doubt you have heard all the objections that the 3NF is nice in theory, but doesn't hold up in practice. You have probably worked on projects where you made a pretty 3NF chart, dubbed it the "logical" model, tacked the chart to the wall to impress your boss and your clients, and forgot about the logical model altogether. You forged ahead to the "physical" model, which systematically undid all your normalization in the name of performance. Then, you actually started to create your database. ◀

If so, you made a mistake, the same mistake we used to make until we learned the right way. Sure, denormalization has its place, but only after you have verified by performance testing that your logical model performs too slowly. We ended up adding the normalization back into our production system to enhance performance as a last resort, and we felt rather silly when we saw things run more quickly. Here's why normalized databases often perform faster:

- You have lots more tables, which means lots more choices for the Optimizer to choose from in selecting an efficient query plan. (Compared to query execution time, the time it takes the optimizer to analyze all its options is trivial, so don't worry about that.)

- The several smaller tables of a normalized relationship are often smaller, in total, than the one large table they would be if you denormalized them. Therefore, table scans are faster.
- Updates are almost always faster in a normalized environment because you have eliminated the redundant information you would otherwise be updating in many places.
- You have fewer nulls in your columns, which often means the density of values is better for an index, making the index more useful.
- You have fewer columns in your tables, which reduces the number of indexes you need. This, in turn, boosts your INSERT, UPDATE, and DELETE performance.
- You need fewer locks for many operations.
- You can create indexes faster, and SQL Server can sort faster on tables with fewer columns.

Cross-Reference

Our recommendation: try out your fully normalized model. See whether it can support your performance requirements by going through the steps in this chapter and Chapter 29. Then use denormalization to fix your specific performance problems that cannot be solved any other way.◀

INDEXING

If we didn't make it clear just now, indexes are critical to the performance of your queries. You probably knew this already; the exciting question is *which* indexes to create. Will you index every column of every table? Certainly not. It will waste space like it's going out of style, and it will make the performance of writes (INSERT, UPDATE, and DELETE) crawl. No indexes is no good, either. Let's find the happy medium.

How to choose your indexes

The first step in index management is to create the indexes you need. If you have 5 major tables in your database and you know most of the queries that will be hitting those tables, you can probably guess what indexes to create. When you have 500 tables, it isn't so easy. We start with broad rules to get the database owner with hundreds of tables started, and then we focus on tweaking individual indexes.

Make sure that all your tables have at least one index

One way to guarantee that the optimizer will perform a table scan is to leave a table in your database with no index whatsoever. We have yet to encounter a circumstance where a table with no indexes is a valid strategy. (Refer to Chapter 12 for the reasons why each table needs a primary key, and hence an index.) To rout out these villains, we simply look for tables listed in sysobjects for which no index is listed in sysindexes, which means we must use not a NOT EXISTS query. The only catch is that sysindexes lists tables, too. Only when the column indid in sysindexes is in the range 1 - 250 does a row represent an index. Therefore, the query we want is

```
SELECT USER_NAME( uid ) + '.' + name
   FROM sysobjects o
   WHERE type = 'u'
      AND NOT EXISTS ( SELECT *
         FROM sysindexes
         WHERE id = o.id
            AND indid BETWEEN 1 AND 250 )
   ORDER BY 1
```

The first question you have to ask yourself is why these tables have no primary key. Hopefully, you can establish one. If not, consider redesigning the tables so that they can have a primary key. If that isn't feasible, at least put an index on the tables based on whatever column you suspect comes up most often in a WHERE clause. If you don't even have a guess at that, set up the SQL Trace utility to trap all SQL referencing these table names.

If you run the preceding query, you may get some surprises: tables that had indexes before, but don't now. Perhaps you dropped the index to do a BCP and forgot to put it back on. Consider making the query into a task that e-mails its results to you once a day.

Tables with no clustered index

The preceding standard — that all tables have an index, albeit any index — is pretty weak. After you have cleaned up that mess, you can go a lot further. For starters, locate all the tables with no clustered index. Clustered indexes are recorded in sysindexes with indid = 1, so all we have to do is restrict the range of indid in the subquery:

```
SELECT USER_NAME( uid ) +'.' +name
   FROM sysobjects o
   WHERE type = 'u'
      AND NOT EXISTS ( SELECT *
         FROM sysindexes
```

```
        WHERE id = o.id
          AND indid = 1 )
ORDER BY 1
```

Again, we have never seen a valid reason that a table should not have a clustered index. Let us assume for this discussion that the table does have some index, but you decided to make it nonclustered. From a querying standpoint, this is nonsense. A clustered index is always faster than a nonclustered index defined on the same columns because with the clustered index

- The leaf level and the data-page level are the same, which saves a step for SQL Server. This may save reading only one page when SQL Server is searching for a single row, but it may make a huge difference when SQL Server is searching for a range of values.
- The indexes of a clustered index don't have to store row numbers, which means that you need fewer index pages and maybe even fewer levels. This reduces the number of pages SQL Server must scan.

You might be thinking that having no clustered index will help your INSERT performance. In a table with no clustered index, all rows are inserted on the last page of the table, and SQL Server just adds new pages on the end as it needs them. In this case, a page split on an INSERT is impossible because you are never inserting in the middle of existing pages. This is the supposed performance gain. Because you do have a nonclustered index, however, every INSERT affects two pages: the last page of the table and the last page of your index. If you changed your index to a clustered index, you could often get by with INSERTs affecting just one page, the data page where the row is inserted. Another problem with the lack of a clustered index is that the last page becomes a "hot-spot": all INSERT activity is focused there. This is bad because no two people can ever INSERT data at the same time. Each person wanting to INSERT needs exclusive control of that last page. In our experience, it is better to set up a clustered index and try to minimize page splits with an appropriate FILLFACTOR.

Tables with no unique index

If you have already dealt with the tables with no index or no clustered index, the next focus of your ire should be tables with no unique index. This time the indid column of sysindexes doesn't help us. We have to use the status column; if the second bit of this integer is on, we have a unique index. Therefore, we search for tables not possessing such an index:

```
SELECT USER_NAME( uid ) +'.' +name
   FROM sysobjects o
   WHERE type = 'u'
      AND NOT EXISTS ( SELECT *
         FROM sysindexes
         WHERE id = o.id
            AND status & 2 != 0 )
   ORDER BY 1
```

These tables are also suspect, for a number of reasons:

- They don't have a primary key, which goes against the foundation of the relational model.
- It's not really clear how these tables should participate in joins. Almost all joins should involve the unique indexes of all but one table of the join. Tables with no unique index may lead to nonsensical query results.
- The Optimizer is losing one of its greatest assets. The Optimizer loves clustered indexes, but it also needs unique indexes to find data rapidly. With a unique index, the Optimizer knows that the search will return one row for one key value, which drastically limits the number of pages to be scanned.

For most tables, the unique index and the clustered index are the same. Not only is that okay, it is usually quite appropriate. After we get through this first salvo of index-sanity checks, we will revisit the issue of when to separate the clustered and unique indexes.

Tables with no primary key

The presence of a primary key per se isn't a requirement for good query performance, but we can't resist including it because checking for primary keys falls right in line with the rest of our discussion. The straightforward approach to checking for tables without primary keys is to search for tables in sysobjects without a corresponding primary key listed in the sysconstraints table. Finding out which entries in sysconstraints are primary keys is a bit tricky because Microsoft has a non-standard implementation of the status column in that table. (Yet another reason why you shouldn't violate the atomicity rule: different people will come up with different ideas about how to store compound information in a single column.) In sysconstraints, status = 1 means primary keys. This does *not*, for this table, mean that POWER(2,0) & status = 1 denotes a primary key. In this table, status values of 3 and 5 denote foreign keys and defaults, respectively. Worse yet, other information *is* stored by bit flags in higher order bits. The only way to find primary keys in sysconstraints is (status % 16) & 1 = 1. The query is

```
SELECT USER_NAME( uid ) +'.' +name
   FROM sysobjects o
   WHERE type = 'u'
      AND NOT EXISTS ( SELECT *
         FROM sysconstraints
         WHERE id = o.id
            AND (status % 16) & 1 != 0)
   ORDER BY 1
```

However, we can actually get by with a query more similar to the preceding ones because the eleventh bit of the status column in sysindexes denotes that the index is used to enforce a primary key:

```
SELECT USER_NAME( uid ) +'.' +name
   FROM sysobjects o
   WHERE type = 'u'
      AND NOT EXISTS ( SELECT *
         FROM sysindexes
         WHERE id = o.id
            AND status & POWER( 2, 11 ) != 0 )
   ORDER BY 1
```

All primary keys must have a unique index, so this is a special case of our previous query for unique indexes. For this reason, we only have to run two checks in our databases: the clustered index check and the primary key check. Every one of our tables has both. So far, you have, hopefully, established that each and every table has a clustered index.

Put indexes on foreign keys

If you have foreign keys defined in your database, they are prime candidates for indexes. For starters, SQL Server itself can use these indexes when enforcing the foreign key relationships on an UPDATE or DELETE to the table with the primary or unique key referenced by the foreign key. Furthermore, many joins between tables involve the foreign keys, and you want the Optimizer to have the option of using these indexes. Finally, even in a single-table query, users are often basing their search on a foreign key value because the foreign key represents something meaningful in the business model.

We assume that these will be non-unique, non-clustered indexes with the default FILLFACTOR. In that case, we can simplify the syntax of the CREATE INDEX statement to:

```
CREATE INDEX index_name ON table_name (column_name [, column_name]...)
```

The index name only has to be unique by table, so we can just use the same name as the foreign key constraint for which we created the index. All we need then to build the CREATE INDEX statements is the names of the columns in the foreign key. These columns are stored by their colid number in sysreferences; we use the COL_NAME function to convert the colids to names. Finally, we need to make sure that the indexes we are about to create do not duplicate existing indexes. This requires us to include NOT EXISTS clauses comparing what is in sysreferences to what is in sysindexes. Regrettably, sysindexes stores the colids of the index columns in varbinary(255) columns, which means we have to use the INDEX_COL function to extract the names. Combining all this into one query gives us:

```
SELECT 'CREATE INDEX ' + OBJECT_NAME( constid ), 'ON',
      OBJECT_NAME( fkeyid ), '( ' + COL_NAME( fkeyid, fkey1 )
      +CASE COL_NAME( fkeyid, fkey2 )
         WHEN null THEN ''
         ELSE ', ' + COL_NAME( fkeyid, fkey2 )
      END
      +CASE COL_NAME( fkeyid, fkey3 )
         WHEN null THEN ''
         ELSE ', ' + COL_NAME( fkeyid, fkey3 )
      END
      /* Repeat this pattern for fkey4, fkey5, fkey6, ... */
      /* This is the ugliness of querying a table not in 3NF. */
      +CASE COL_NAME( fkeyid, fkey16 )
         WHEN null THEN ''
         ELSE ', ' + COL_NAME( fkeyid, fkey16 )
      END
      +')'
   FROM sysreferences r
   WHERE NOT EXISTS ( SELECT *
      FROM sysindexes
      WHERE id = r.fkeyid
         AND INDEX_COL( OBJECT_NAME( id ), indid, 1 )
            = COL_NAME( r.fkeyid, r.fkey1 )
         AND INDEX_COL( OBJECT_NAME( id ), indid, 2 )
            = COL_NAME( r.fkeyid, r.fkey2 )
          /* Repeat this pattern for fkey3, fkey4, fkey5, ... */
         AND INDEX_COL( OBJECT_NAME( id ), indid, 16 )
            = COL_NAME( r.fkeyid, r.fkey16 ) )
```

In pubs sample database, this produces the following output:

```
CREATE INDEX NC__titles__pub_id__0E4E2B2E   ON titles      ( pub_id )
CREATE INDEX NC__titleauth__au_id__1312E04B ON titleauthor ( au_id )
```

```
CREATE INDEX NC__titleauth__title__14070484 ON titleauthor ( title_id )
CREATE INDEX NC__sales__stor_id__1AB40213   ON sales       ( stor_id )
CREATE INDEX NC__sales__title_id__1BA8264C  ON sales       ( title_id )
CREATE INDEX NC__roysched__title___1E8492F7 ON roysched    ( title_id )
CREATE INDEX NC__discounts__stor___2160FFA2 ON discounts   ( stor_id )
CREATE INDEX NC__pub_info__pub_id__2AEA69DC ON pub_info    ( pub_id )
CREATE INDEX NC__employee__job_id__30A34332 ON employee    ( job_id )
CREATE INDEX NC__employee__pub_id__337FAFDD ON employee    ( pub_id )
```

You should not just blindly run the output of this script because too many indexes slow down writes. Screen out indexes on columns that look fishy to you. If, however, you are working in a DSS database with plenty of extra disk space, index away! If you aren't sure which indexes are fishy, we will get to that soon.

Put indexes on columns matching your primary keys

If you have no foreign keys assigned in your database, the approach we described isn't worth much to you. Even in databases where the owner is meticulous about keeping foreign keys up to date, there may be denormalized tables where it is impossible or undesirable to create foreign keys. Yet many of these tables contain columns that should be indexed, precisely for the reasons we mentioned. In particular, if there is a table in your database that has a primary key on some column named foo, it is quite likely that foo represents something important to you and your users. Therefore, you will often be querying and joining other tables based on their foo column. This makes foo a prime candidate for indexing.

Make sure that column names are consistent

The strategy we are about to present assumes that you named columns consistently across tables. For example, if two different tables have a column named foo, it would be bad to call it foo in one place and foobar in another. This creates no end of chaos. Users and developers will forget which table calls the column which name. At best, this leads to a lot of cussing; at worst, it leads to bugs.

Conversely, it is also bad to overuse names. Overuse is where foo refers to some business attribute in one table, but in another table foo is something entirely different, so different that it doesn't make sense to join on the columns. This can lead to dirty, nasty bugs. Don't do it.

Arguing About Column Names

What is important to managers never ceases to amaze us. We had a boss once who didn't even know how to log in to SQL Server, but he knew what our data model was. He would get all bent out of shape about the column names. On some tables, he would insist a column be named one thing, but on another table something else. He said this was "to make it clear to the users." Every user we talked to said it created confusion, not clarity. The most compelling reason, however, to keep your columns named the same across tables is that it will be easier to identify and maintain potential foreign key candidates. If people don't know that author.au_id is the same thing as book.author_id, then they are going to have a heck of a time maintaining your data model!

If you are stuck with either situation, consider renaming some of your columns. Be very careful when you do it, though. If you designed your system well, your applications are referencing views and stored procedures, so you can change the names of underlying tables without recompiling applications. Even so, you have to remember to change all the following that may reference the old column name:

- Views
- Stored procedures
- Triggers
- CHECK constraints
- Rules

Creating the indexes

This is rather complex, but worthwhile. A table can have up to 16 columns in its primary key. Which columns compose the key is stored in a terribly denormalized format. We have to marry this up with the list of all columns for each specific table in the database. This is stored in a normalized format. Therefore, we first have to convert the list of primary keys into the proper 3NF. The table we need looks like this:

```
create table #primarykeys (
    id int,
    name sysname,
    col_order tinyint primary key (id, col_order) )
```

Next, we load this table from sysindexes. We can do this elegantly if we create table #n as follows:

```
create table #n ( n tinyint primary key )
```

Then, we fill it with the values 1, 2, . . ., 16. Here is a cheap way to do this:

```
insert #n select id from sysobjects where id < 17
```

Then, we can write this:

```
insert #primarykeys
select id, index_col(object_name(id),indid,n), n
    from sysindexes, #n
    where n <= 16
        and index_col(object_name(id),indid,n) <> null
        and power(2,11) & status != 0
```

Now we create a simple table to hold the object IDs of the tables for which we propose to create the foreign keys or indexes. Notice that we do not need to store the column names; they are in #primarykeys.

```
create table #newFK (
    fkeyid int,
    rkeyid int primary key ( fkeyid, rkeyid ) )
```

The scary step is populating this table. In English, our approach is this: find the distinct pairs of tables from syscolumns and #primarykeys that have at least one column name in common (so there might be a match on all names) have the property that for this pair there are no columns in the primary key table that aren't in syscolumns, too (so we know we have a match), and for which a foreign key doesn't already exist (which you can easily change to "an index doesn't exist"). In SQL, that translates to:

```
insert #newFK
select distinct c.id, k.id
    from syscolumns c, #primarykeys k, sysobjects o
    where c.name = k.name
        and c.id = o.id
        and o.type = 'u'
        and c.id <> k.id
        and not exists (select *
            from sysreferences r
            where c.id = r.fkeyid
                and k.id = r.rkeyid)
        and not exists (select *
            from #primarykeys k2
            where k2.id = k.id
```

(continued)

(continued)

```
and not exists (select *
    from syscolumns c2
    where c2.id = c.id
        and c2.name = k2.name ))
```

Now all that remains is to create new indexes. This is messy because we have to denormalize our structure to get the column names to appear in one row. We have to decide how many columns to include in each index. Though SQL Server lets you include up to 16 columns, we recommend you keep your indexes down to one or two columnns, except for primary and unique constraint indexes. Additional columns usually add size to and index without helping query performance much. We present the queries to index first one column and then the first two columns; the second query shows the general pattern for higher order indexes. Finally, we must remember to write this query so that it checks to make sure a similar index does not already exist

```
SELECT DISTINCT 'CREATE INDEX', INDEX_COL( OBJECT_NAME(id), indid, 1),
      'ON', OBJECT_NAME(fkeyid), '('
      + INDEX_COL( OBJECT_NAME(id), indid, 1)+')'
   FROM #newFK n, sysindexes i
   WHERE n.rkeyid = i.id
      AND POWER(2,11) & status != 0
      AND NOT EXISTS (SELECT *
         FROM sysindexes x
         WHERE n.fkeyid = id
            AND INDEX_COL(OBJECT_NAME(i.id), i.indid, 1)
               = INDEX_COL(OBJECT_NAME(x.id), x.indid, 1))
   ORDER BY 4, 2
```

If you run all of this (from 'create table #primarykeys…' to the query above) in the pubs sample database, the CREATE INDEX statements you get are

```
CREATE INDEX pub_id  ON employee  (pub_id)
CREATE INDEX pub_id  ON titles    (pub_id)
```

The more general form, for querying multiple columns, is

```
SELECT DISTINCT 'CREATE INDEX', SUBSTRING( INDEX_COL( OBJECT_NAME(id), indid, 1)
      +INDEX_COL( OBJECT_NAME(id), indid, 2), 1, 30),
      'ON', OBJECT_NAME(fkeyid), '('
      + INDEX_COL( OBJECT_NAME(id), indid, 1)
```

```
    + CASE INDEX_COL( OBJECT_NAME(id), indid, 2) WHEN null THEN '' ELSE ', '
    + INDEX_COL( OBJECT_NAME(id), indid, 2) END
    + ')'
  FROM #newFK n, sysindexes i
  WHERE n.rkeyid = i.id
    AND POWER(2,11) & status != 0
    AND NOT EXISTS (SELECT *
      FROM sysindexes x
      WHERE n.fkeyid = id
        AND INDEX_COL(OBJECT_NAME(i.id), i.indid, 1)
          = INDEX_COL(OBJECT_NAME(x.id), x.indid, 1)
        AND INDEX_COL(OBJECT_NAME(i.id), i.indid, 2)
          = INDEX_COL(OBJECT_NAME(x.id), x.indid, 2))
  ORDER BY 4, 2
```

The same type of query can be used to construct new foreign keys, instead of merely creating indexes. We simply change the literal strings in the query and expand the logic for all 16 possible key columns.

```
select char( 13 ) + 'ALTER TABLE', OBJECT_NAME( fkeyid ),
     'ADD FOREIGN KEY ('
     + INDEX_COL( OBJECT_NAME( id ), indid, 1 )
     + CASE INDEX_COL( OBJECT_NAME( id ), indid, 2 ) WHEN null THEN '' ELSE ', '
     + INDEX_COL( OBJECT_NAME( id ), indid, 2 ) END
     + CASE INDEX_COL( OBJECT_NAME( id ), indid, 3 ) WHEN null THEN '' ELSE ', '
     + INDEX_COL( OBJECT_NAME( id ), indid, 3 ) END
/* Repeat this pattern for 4, 5, 6, … */
     + CASE INDEX_COL( OBJECT_NAME( id ), indid, 16) WHEN null THEN '' ELSE ', '
     + INDEX_COL( OBJECT_NAME( id ), indid, 16) END
     + ') REFERENCES ' + OBJECT_NAME( id )
  from #newFK n, sysindexes i
  where n.rkeyid = i.id
    and power(2,11) & status != 0
```

In pubs, the final result is this:

```
ALTER TABLE publishers ADD FOREIGN KEY (pub_id ) REFERENCES pub_info
ALTER TABLE titles ADD FOREIGN KEY (pub_id ) REFERENCES pub_info
ALTER TABLE employee ADD FOREIGN KEY (pub_id ) REFERENCES pub_info
```

You would not actually want to create any of these foreign keys because all three of these tables already have a foreign key on pub_id referencing publishers. However, you might try creating the indexes. You can also try dropping various foreign keys in pubs and watching this SQL pick those keys back up.

Warning

We offer the preceding queries strictly as a tool to get started on foreign keys in your database or to check your DRI. Do not blindly make all these foreign keys. You risk linking up tables that should not be linked. You must review each new foreign key or index one by one.◀

Put indexes on columns used in joins and WHERE clauses

The preceding is probably a superset of all the possible indexes you might ever use in joins, and hopefully it covers a lot of the WHERE clauses, too. Try picking out indexes from the list that you think would be useful. Then, you can see whether you are right as you read the rest of this chapter.

How to evaluate your indexes

If your tables were read-only, you could create as many indexes as your disk space would allow and call it a day. In fact, this is a valid strategy for databases in a DSS server where disk space is not a constraint. However, this is a very bad idea for an OLTP server. Because SQL Server updates all indexes on the fly during INSERTs, UPDATEs, and DELETEs, your transaction-processing time increases with the number of indexes you create. If you insert or delete a row, you know for sure that SQL Server has to update the data page for this row and the leaf page of each nonclustered index. Therefore, in terms of page I/O, you would expect that the presence of one nonclustered index would double your transaction-processing time. If you have two nonclustered indexes, you expect the time will triple, and so forth. This is a rough estimate, but it isn't too far off. Our experience shows that one nonclustered index increases your processing time by around 50 percent; two indexes increase the processing by around 100 percent.

What about the impact of page splits on indexes? If a data page splits, SQL Server has to write to three data pages: the original page, the new page, and the successor page (to update its prevno). You also know that SQL Server has to change every index page that refers to data that was moved to the new page. To put this in more concrete terms, suppose you have a table where the row-storage size averages 128 characters, and therefore you have (2048 – 32) / 128 = 15.75 average rows per page. Let's say a data page with 16 rows splits. Eight of the rows will move to the new page. In the worst case, eight leaf pages of a nonclustered index might have to change. This is because the data on the data page are stored in the clustered index order, whereas the data on the leaf pages of the nonclustered index are in the order of the indexed column. For example, in a large table of employees clustered by last name, emp_id, suppose a page containing only rows with the last name 'Smith' splits. The new page created by the split might contain rows with the first names Andrew, David, Judith, Lia, Lynn, Mark, Ruth, and Suzanne. In an index on first names, these names could be eight different leaf pages. As the leaf pages change, so might higher level pages. One page split could force hundreds of pages to be rewritten on a table with a lot of indexes. This is why database owners try to avoid page splits.

Now we are in a bind. We have to have indexes for querying but indexes slow our updates. What should we do? First, consider these guidelines for tables that get a lot of write activity:

- Keep the indexes that are used in joins during updates or deletes. Although it is true that removing an index may almost double the speed of page writes, if SQL Server needed that index to determine *which* rows to update, your overall processing time could be 10,000 percent slower without it. Yes, that is *ten thousand* percent. Later in this chapter, we discuss how to see whether an index is being used; for right now, you can guess that an index is being used if you join on the first column of the index key during an update or delete.
- Consider dropping indexes not involved in the process of changing data. When we say "the process of changing data," we include not just the actual SQL needed for the writes, but any SQL used to retrieve data into an application so that a user can decide what to change.
- If you are using a table both for a lot of transaction processing and a lot of analysis, try to provide separate tables — and hopefully separate servers — for these two workloads. The transaction-processing table can then have fewer indexes.
- Remember that the first few indexes hurt the most on update performance. If you have just a clustered index, a write may affect one page. The first nonclustered index means two pages are affected by a change, or 100 percent more work. However, the next nonclustered index means three pages instead of two must change, and 3 versus 2 is 50 percent more work. The third nonclustered index is going to mean only 33 percent more work than before, and so on. The point is that when you have a table with a half dozen indexes, adding or deleting just one index will not affect you as much.
- Drop indexes with poor *selectivity.*

This last bullet leads to our next point in index management.

Index selectivity

Now that we have worked to create all these indexes, how do we know whether SQL Server will really use them? For example, suppose you work on the SQL Server development team, and you choose to index the type field in sysobjects. This seems to make sense on the surface of things; after all, you are almost always looking for an object of a specific type. The SQL Enterprise Manager is always querying sysobjects based on type to populate the lists in the "Manage" windows. Suppose we make such an index, and we submit this query to SQL Server:

```
SELECT *
   FROM sysobjects
   WHERE type = 'u'
   ORDER BY name, uid
```

Let's further suppose that sysobjects in your favorite database just happens to have 1,438 rows spread across 64 data pages, and that breakdown by type is as follows:

type	*rows*
C	33
D	133
F	224
K	253
P	264
S	18
TR	117
U	260
V	136

What would happen if SQL Server used the index on type? Well, type happens to be char(2), not null. At the leaf level of the index, we have 1 byte of overhead per row + 2 bytes for the type field + 4 bytes for the data page number + 2 bytes for the data = 9 bytes per row. We can get (2048 – 32) / 9 = 224 rows per page. We will need 1438 / 224 = 7 (rounding up) leaf pages and one root page for the index. This sounds efficient, so far. To use the index, we will read the root page, which will tell us that for type = 'u'; we have two leaf pages to read. The leaf pages will give us 260 pagenos, and we read each of those 260 pages. Total logical reads: 1 + 2 + 260 = 263. But wait a minute, you say. There are only 64 pages in the table. We should have used the leaf pages to get a distinct list of pagenos and then read only those. Perhaps, but that isn't how SQL Server does its estimates. Remember that there is overhead in creating and tracking a distinct list. In any case, you are right to notice that 263 is greater than 64, and SQL Server would notice, too. It would do a table scan for this query instead of using the index.

Distribution pages

Suppose that we change the WHERE clause to search for type = 'c'. Now what happens? We know there are only 33 rows, and in this case one leaf page, so the total number of logic reads is 1 + 1 + 33 = 35. This is better than the table scan. Will SQL Server use the index? Yes! How does SQL Server know that the index is worthwhile when type = 'c', but not when type = 'u'? It keeps a *distribution page* for the index. The distribution page contains statistics about the usefulness of the index, and it has a histogram of the values of the first column of an index, sort of like the previous table. SQL Server builds the histogram by sampling the leaf page index values at whatever step size is necessary for the histogram to fit on one data page. In the case of type, we have a 2 byte row number + 2 bytes for the type field = 4 bytes per histogram row. For a table of 1,438 rows, this permits a step size of 3, or 480 histogram rows. In the case of the query searching for type = 'c', SQL Server goes to the histogram and finds 11 entries for 'c'. Because the step size is 3, SQL Server predicts that roughly 33 rows will meet the search criteria, which happens to be exactly right. (Actually, SQL Server makes an adjustment for the fact that 'c' is at the start of the histogram, but let's not quibble about that.) When SQL Server hits case of type = 'u', there are 87 histogram entries, which leads to the estimate we gave previously: 263 reads. To see the distribution page for an index, you must first find the pageno of the distribution page from sysindexes, as follows:

```
SELECT distribution
   FROM sysindexes
   WHERE id = OBJECT_ID( 'your_table_name' )
      AND name = 'your_index_name'
```

Then, you can look at this page just like any other with DBCC. For example, suppose your dbid is 6, and the distribution page number is 13,656. You can see the distribution page with the following:

```
DBCC TRACEON( 3604 )
DBCC PAGE( 6, 13656, 1 )
```

However, a better way to look at the distribution page is to use DBCC SHOW_STATISTICS. This doesn't require you to find the distribution page number, and it prints information you don't see with the plain old DBCC PAGE. The syntax is as follows:

```
DBCC SHOW_STATISTICS( object_name, index_name )
```

The same thing is accessible to you from Manage⇨Indexes by selecting a table, an index, and clicking Distribution.

What should SQL Server do if the value you specify isn't one of the values listed in the histogram? In this case, SQL Server uses a value called *all density*. All density is an estimate, calculated by SQL Server, of the percentage of rows that it can expect to retrieve for a parameter value between histogram values. SQL Server factors the presence of duplicates into the all density factor. In the case of our table, the all density is 0.146417, and 1438 × 0.146417 = 211 rows. Therefore, SQL Server will decide not to pick this index for a value not in the histogram; a table scan would be more efficient.

The tricky question for SQL Server is what to do when the value we will be searching on isn't known when optimizing the query, for example:

```
select *
    from sysobjects
    where type = ( select max ( type ) from sysobjects )
```

To handle cases like this, SQL Server stores another estimate called simply *density*. Density is SQL Server's general estimate of what percentage of rows an index will retrieve without analyzing a specific parameter passed into a query.

Returning to our original example, of the nine possible values for type, you will see that only for two of them, 'c' and 's', will SQL Server use the index. Even then, 20 or 35 logical reads is not an enormous savings over 64 reads. Therefore, you will probably conclude that this index stinks, and not leave it on sysobjects. (Notice there is no such index in the real database catalog.)

What went wrong with the index on type, and how can we spot such questionable indexes at a glance? The problem is that too many rows have the same value of type, so a query based solely on type is often going to force SQL Server to read most of the data pages, whether it uses an index or not. This is obvious if you look at the fact that our sysobjects has 1,438 rows and only 9 values for type. The average number of rows per type is 160. As it turns out, *the ratio of the number of distinct values of an index key to the number of rows in a table is an excellent predictor of how useful the index is*. This ratio is so important that it has a special name, the *selectivity* of an index. When an index is unique, the ratio is one, which is perfect. With a unique index, SQL Server knows only one row will be returned, which limits the amount of pages to read to one more than the number of levels in the index. When a column has only one value throughout the table, the selectivity of an index on the column is the reciprocal of the number of rows, which is horrible. Such an index is completely worthless. In between these extremes, you must make a judgment call.

Though the selectivity is a good predictor of an index's value, SQL Server does not use the selectivity explicitly. In particular, neither the density nor the all density is computed by dividing the selectivity value by the row count, though you might think so at first. Only when an index is unique is it true that density = all density = selectivity/row count. When an index is not unique, the density and all density are adjusted to compensate for duplicate values.

Multicolumn indexes

Thus far, we have discussed only indexes defined on one column. SQL Server lets you create indexes on up to 16 columns. It is important to understand how SQL Server determines the usefulness of these indexes. First of all, SQL Server still only makes a histogram for the first column of the index. This is important because it means that the actual *values* you supply to the WHERE clause for the second, third, fourth, and so on columns of the index are not considered in the optimization. However, whether you supplied a value *does* matter, and SQL Server stores all density values for each depth of the index. What depth your query reaches depends on supplying parameters for successive columns of an index. For example, if a table has columns named A though Z with an index on columns A, B, and C, you can use the first level of the index by supplying values for (A), (A,B), or (A,B,C). If, however, your query simply supplies values for (A,C), this is no better than just supplying a value for A. Futhermore, if your query supplies values for only (B,C), the index can't be used. This is because the index stores and looks up key values in order in the index pages. If you just give values for (B,C), SQL Server has nowhere to start. The index is sorted first by A.

Frequently, you will be faced with choices about whether to index a column by itself or several columns in combination. The factors that will influence your decision are the following:

- Total index key length. The shorter the index key, the better. Shorter key length means more index rows per index page, which means fewer pages for SQL Server to scan in the index, which means the index is more useful.
- Poor selectivity of an outer column can negate the selectivity of an inner column. If the lead column in an index looks poor in the histogram, SQL Server might not use the index, even though the index will be effective because of an inner column. In a case like this, it is often better to index the column with good selectivity by itself.

Updating statistics

It should be clear by now that the statistics of an index are indispensable tools for SQL Server. Without the histogram and density values, SQL Server has to use "magic" numbers for an index, which are fixed numbers chosen by Microsoft to use for any random index. The magic numbers will never be the same as the true statistics for a table, and SQL Server will often choose less-than-optimal paths based on these fixed estimates. Now here's the scary part: SQL Server calculates statistics for an index when you create it, but SQL Server will never update the statistics until you tell it to. Never. Therefore, we present this important commandment:

After creating indexes, the most important thing you can do to optimize your queries is to keep your index statistics up to date. The command to update the statistics on a table or index is as follows:

```
UPDATE STATISTICS [[database.]owner.]table_name [index_name]
```

For example, to update the statistics of all indexes on the authors table in pubs do the following:

```
UPDATE STATISTICS pubs..authors
```

As you may have noticed, the DBCC SHOW_STATISTICS output tells you the last time the statistics for an index were updated. We recommend that you update all your statistics nightly, if you can afford the processing time. The best way to do this is to create a stored procedure that uses a cursor to update the statistics on all tables, and then make this procedure a task. There is an example of just such a procedure in the Transact-SQL Reference under UPDATE STATISTICS.

Getting rid of bad indexes

We now have enough knowledge to weed out bogus indexes — ones that aren't worth the performance hit on updates because they aren't going to be used by the Optimizer anyway.

Creating an Index on an Empty Table

One trap to watch out for is indexes that you create right after you create a table, while the table is still empty. When you create the indexes, SQL Server populates the statistics — which show nothing because your table is empty. After you load in the data, you have to remember to update the statistics. This is easy to forget, which is another reason that you should run nightly updates on statistics. Any primary key or unique constraint that you define with CREATE TABLE also has no statistics initially, but this is less of a concern. SQL Server will still use them because they are unique indexes.

Knock out duplicate indexes

Unfortunately, there is nothing to stop you from defining two indexes on a table with different names that have exactly the same columns. This is a complete waste of disk space and creates needless overhead on writes. Almost as bad are two indexes on the same table where the first column in each index is the same. It's difficult to imagine a situation where this would be appropriate. You might reason that if you are constantly querying your table based on either the values of columns X and Y or the values of columns X and Z, you should have an index on (X, Y) and an index on (X, Z). Although this might work, it would be worth trying simply three single-column indexes on X, Y, and Z. The performance might be better. The trouble with the two indexes on (X, Y) and (X, Z) is that they duplicate each other in keeping statistics on X.

The other situation in which you might be tempted to have two indexes, both starting with the same key column, is when you have some long primary or unique key. Suppose that you have a table with a 13-column primary key on columns A through M. This index might not be especially useful for querying, but it has to stay because it is enforcing your primary key. If many of your queries use A alone, you might want to index just column A separately. Your reasoning is that the index on A alone will be much smaller and, therefore, involve fewer index page scans. Good idea, but SQL Server doesn't take that fact into consideration. For the purposes of a query based on A alone, the two indexes are equally useful as far as SQL Server is concerned, and it will take the first one it finds.

You can find your superfluous indexes with this query:

```
dbcc traceon( 204 ) /* Turns off ANSI GROUP BY behavior */
go
select object_name(id) tname, name iname,
      index_col( object_name(id), indid, 1) iclname, status
   from sysindexes
   where indid < 251
   group by object_name(id), index_col( object_name(id), indid, 1)
   having count(*) > 1
   order by 1, 2
```

Dropping indexes with poor selectivity

Your next step is to hit indexes with poor selectivity. There are many ways to go about this. You can use the SQL Enterprise Manager's Manage⇨Indexes window to view the distribution of the indexes on each table. This becomes a bit tedious on large databases. You can compute the selectivity of each index yourself, or you can use DBCC to view the density of each index. The last approach is probably the best one because it gives you the most information and it doesn't entail a lot of computation, if your statistics are up to date. The only drawback to DBCC is that it doesn't readily lend itself to loading results into a table, which slows down your analysis considerably. As you review these statistics, you might ask yourself the following questions:

- Are there indexes on tables with heavy write activity? There isn't much harm in leaving a poor index on a table that doesn't get updated much anyway.
- Are your poor selectivity indexes likely to be used nonetheless? When you see an index that isn't very selective, it doesn't mean SQL Server never uses it. It means that *most* of the time SQL Server doesn't use it. Because SQL Server keeps a histogram of the first column of the index, however, it will be probably be smart enough to use the index when appropriate. If your queries are reaching for the less-duplicated values of the column, keep the index.
- Do you have some high selectivity indexes that are never likely to be used? A highly selective index on a column you will never query is worthless. A great example is an index on integers that represents dollars. You might use the index to search for a dollar amount above or below a certain threshold. If however, you don't often do much with the dollars other than sum them, you don't need this index.

Naming your indexes

We close our study of indexes with a few words on naming indexes. Unlike objects, index names need not be unique in a database, only unique within a table. We prefer to name indexes with a prefix showing what they are for. This is consistent with the fact that you already have indexes named 'PK__' and 'UQ__'. We would add 'FK__' for an index on a foreign key, 'CL__' for a clustered index that is not a primary key or unique constraint, and 'NC__' for a generic, nonclustered index that doesn't fit in the other categories. After the prefix, we list the column names of the index key. This naming convention is helpful for us because when we are looking at various output from SQL Server, such as SHOWPLAN output (see Chapter 29), we need to know at a glance what type of index we are dealing with and what columns are in the key. Putting the table name in the index name isn't worth much because in most output you will review, it is already clear to which table the index belongs. ◀

SUMMARY

SQL Server stores data on 2K pages that form a doubly linked list. The clustered index, if there is one, forces the rows to be stored in a specific order. Non-clustered indexes have leaf pages that contain one row for each row of the table. Traversing an index chain is much faster than traversing a linked list; hence, good indexes are critical to query performance. Too many indexes slow updates, however. The first step in index design is to make sure that each and every table has a clustered index and a unique index, which are often the same. Then, the issue becomes which nonkey columns to index. Foreign keys are an excellent start. After that, it is a judgment call, but with the queries in this book, you can get a head start.

REVIEW QUESTIONS

Q: Can you change the page size in SQL Server?

A: No, it is fixed at 2K.

Q: What is the minimum size of an object?

A: 16K, which is one extent.

Q: How many clustered indexes can a table have? Non-clustered?

A: One and 250.

Q: How much faster is a clustered index in retrieving a single row from a large table than a non-clustered one?

A: Not much faster at all, really. For the retrieval of a single row, the clustered index saves only one page read, which is insignificant.

Chapter

Query Plans and Optimizations 29

This chapter is round two in query optimization. The last chapter was all about how SQL Server stores and retrieves data and, using that knowledge, how to make good indexes. Ideally, after you have done that, the work is over. Unfortunately, this isn't the case. The other half of the battle is writing your SQL well. Then, everything should run fine, but there will still be problems, on either your end or SQL Server's. In that case, you have to roll up your sleeves and look at what SQL Server is doing internally.

What's in This Chapter

In this chapter, we guide you through a progression of optimization techniques, including:

- The pitfalls to avoid in writing queries
- How to decipher SHOWPLAN to figure out what SQL Server's plan is for executing a query
- Examining why SQL Server chose a particular plan, when you don't agree with the plan
- What to do when all the preceding steps have failed

Writing Good SQL

The mere fact that we have to talk about "good" SQL verses "bad" SQL is one of the leading criticisms you will hear about SQL. Part of the aim of the relational model is to insulate the programmer or user from trying to determine the optimal path to retrieving information. Therefore, the combination of the relational language and RDBMS products should be such that if there are several equivalent ways to formulate a question in the relational language, the RDBMS should always use the same optimal path no matter how the question is formulated. This certainly isn't the case with SQL and the current crop of RDBMS products, including SQL Server. Part of this may be because SQL allows too much freedom in query formulation in some places, while lacking certain basic constructs in other places. Much of what was missing is included in SQL-92, however; therefore, we have to lay the blame for the problem with RDBMS vendors. In any case, this won't get fixed any time soon, so you need to know what it means to write good SQL.

Using functions on columns

Cross-Reference

As you learned in the preceding chapter, you can be assured of a thorough analysis from SQL Server of which index to use when you write a query of the following form:

```
SELECT *
    FROM table_name
    WHERE index_column1 = some_value1
        AND index_column2 = some_value2
        AND index_column3 = some_value3
```

and so on.◀

This lets SQL Server use its histogram and its "all density" values. Regrettably, many queries do not fit this pattern, especially when doing DSS work. Often, some kind of analysis is being done, like whether or not the current monthly sales will lead to annual gross sales over some target value. This could be written in SQL as follows:

```
SELECT *
    FROM table_name
    WHERE monthly_sales * 12 > 1000000
```

Let's assume that this query runs on a table where there is an index on monthly_sales. If the selectivity of the index is good, you would expect SQL Server to use it, right? Well, unfortunately, SQL Server won't do that. Let's ask why:

> YOU: Why didn't you use the index?
>
> SQL SERVER: My only index is on monthly_sales. You didn't give me a value for that.
>
> YOU: Sure I did, "monthly_sales * 12 > 1000000."
>
> SQL SERVER: I don't have an index on "monthly_sales * 12," only an index on monthly_sales.
>
> YOU: Oh, give me a break. Just search for "monthly_sales > 1000000/12." It's the same thing.
>
> SQL SERVER: Huh?

The point is that, although it is immediately obvious to you that "monthly_sales * 12 > 1000000" is logically equivalent to "monthly_sales > 1000000/12," that requires an intelligence the Optimizer doesn't possess. You have to rewrite the WHERE clause yourself.

This example is a classic, and many of you probably already avoid pitfalls with numeric constants in your queries. However, the problem applies any time you modify a column in a WHERE clause. Following are the big problems you will encounter.

Using SUBSTRING and LIKE

SUBSTRING is generally a disaster for the SQL Server Optimizer, and LIKE isn't too far behind. (Strictly speaking, LIKE isn't a function, but it makes sense to discuss it here.) Of course, you can't give up using these functions, but you need to know what their impact is on index selection. Here's an easy rule to remember: SUBSTRING doesn't use indexes. That says it all. If the only search argument in your WHERE clause is using a SUBSTRING, SQL Server will do a table scan. (If there are other search arguments, SQL Server investigates which indexes might apply to them.) This means that a join on a SUBSTRING of columns from each table is a complete fiasco. For example, suppose that you use the first three characters of an object name to specify its type, and you try the following query to see if you are being consistent:

```
select distinct substring( a.name, 1, 3), a.name, a.type
    from sysobjects a
    join sysobjects b on substring( a.name, 1, 3 ) = substring( b.name, 1, 3 )
    where a.type != b.type
        and a.id > 50
        and b.id > 50
    order by 1, 2
```

This forces SQL Server to do a table scan on *both* tables. This query takes a while, and on a table of any appreciable size, a similarly constructed query would take *forever*.

The only way out of the double table scan in a case like this is to create a temporary table, as follows:

```
create table #no_substring_join (
    first3 char(3),
    name sysname,
    type char(2))
insert #no_substring_join
select substring( a.name, 1, 3), a.name, a.type
    from sysobjects a
    where a.id > 50
create clustered index CL__first3_type on #no_substring_join ( first3, type )
select distinct a.first3, a.name, a.type
    from #no_substring_join a
    join #no_substring_join b on a.first3 = b.first3
    where a.type != b.type
    order by 1, 2, 3
```

This example shows once again that RBDMS products are optimized around supporting the 3NF and using the first three characters to show the type violates atomicity.◀

The behavior of LIKE is a little bit better because SQL Server considers using an index if your search clause does not start with a wildcard. For example, SQL Server will evaluate the usefulness of an index in this query:

```
select *
    from authors
    where au_lname like 'sm%'
```

Notice that this search clause is equivalent to WHERE SUBSTRING (au_lname, 1, 2) = 'sm', which does not use an index. Even if the WHERE clause is something like 'sm%n%', SQL Server will still evaluate the effectiveness of the index. It merely checks the 'sm', and nothing else, for matches in the histogram.

Using the right system function

Most system functions come in pairs, such as DB_ID and DB_NAME. Be careful to put the function on the optimal side of the WHERE clause. For example, the following query forces a table scan and the use of a work table:

```
SELECT *
    FROM syscomments
    WHERE OBJECT_NAME(id) = 'my_procedure'
```

SQL Server has to take each row of syscomments, apply the OBJECT_NAME function, store the results in a work table, and then retrieve the correct rows from the worktable. This next query is logically equivalent:

```
SELECT *
    FROM syscomments
    WHERE id = OBJECT_NAME( 'my_procedure' )
```

However, it uses the clustered index of syscomments. This becomes all the more important when you are doing joins. For example, if you wanted to see the procedures in your database that depend directly on user tables (instead of views), you might write this query:

```
select distinct o1.name, o2.name
    from sysdepends d
    join sysobjects o1 on object_name(d.id) = o1.name
    join sysobjects o2 on object_name(d.depid) = o2.name
    where o1.type = 'p'
        and o2.type = 'u'
```

This couldn't be worse. You have forced SQL Server to create two intermediary tables for your two joins. The correct formulation is as follows:

```
select distinct o1.name, o2.name
    from sysdepends d
    join sysobjects o1 on d.id = o1.id
    join sysobjects o2 on depid = o2.id
    where o1.type = 'p'
        and o2.type = 'u'
```

Joining on the primary key

Most joins are performed over the primary key of all but one of the tables involved in the join. This is particularly true in data warehouses, which focus on a star join arrangement. You have one main table called the fact table, which consists of columns that are facts (sales figures, number of employees, and so on) and columns that are dimensions. The dimensions may be things such as fiscal years, geographic regions, store ID numbers, and so forth. You will need reports that pull information from the dimension tables, such as the store name. In this case, you may join the fact table with many dimension tables, but all these joins are on the primary keys of the dimension tables. There is only one table not joining on its primary key, the fact table.

Most runaway queries that need to be killed by the system administrator involve bad joins. Suppose that in the data warehouse, the stores table has a two-part key of region and store number, and you have arbitrarily designated 50 regions worldwide. Someone who isn't familiar with the data model might join with stores based on store number alone, thus accidentally retrieving 50 times the number of rows desired. Even worse is when the DSS database isn't designed around the data warehouse model, and one or more dimensions (it is usually the time dimension) is spread across many tables. This is the case when you have tables name Jan_Sales, Feb_Sales, . . . Dec_Sales, all with identical primary keys. This hinders analysis. Suppose that these sales tables have a five-part primary key and someone wants to compare the sum of the January and February Sales, summarized by the first two key fields. You will see people write queries like this:

```
select a.keycol1, a.keycol2, sum(a.sales), sum(b.sales)
   from Jan_Sales a
   join Feb_Sales b on a.keycol1 = b.keycol1 and a.keycol2 = b.keycol2
   group by a.keycol1, a.keycol2
```

This is totally nonsensical, but sometimes it is difficult to get users to understand why. They may be creating this query with an application that does the SQL for them, like MSQuery, which makes it even harder to explain to them why this is wrong.

The worst part is that a query like this one can take a good while to kill. The user will hit CANCEL and get no response. The user can shut the client machine down, and the query will still run. The system administrator can use the kill command, which should unconditionally interrupt the query, and yet SQL Server continues, apparently locked in some inner loop. The kill command will eventually work, but it can take a while. The only sure-fire way to stop this runaway query is to shut down SQL Server, which isn't really feasible in a production environment. One telltale sign that this is happening on your server is when all the processors are active, but the reads and writes are absolutely flat. This is because all the pages SQL Server needs are in the cache, and the processors are just churning though all the possible combinations of rows.

The preceding query runs in a timely fashion if you write it as follows:

```
select a.keycol1, a.keycol2, sum(a.sales), sum(b.sales)
   from Jan_Sales a
   join Feb_Sales b on a.keycol1 = b.keycol1
      and a.keycol2 = b.keycol2
      and a.keycol3 = b.keycol3
      and a.keycol4 = b.keycol4
      and a.keycol5 = b.koycol5
   group by a.keycol1, a.keycol2
```

This still isn't quite right, though, because the inner join may leave out rows from each of the two tables. You can switch to a full outer join, but the best approach performance-wise is to separate the query into temporary tables, as here:

```
create table #sum (
    keycol1 int,
    keycol2 int,
   month tinyint primary key (keycol1, keycol2, month),
    sales int)
insert #sum
select keycol1, keycol2, 1, sum(sales)
   from Jan_Sales
   group by keycol1, keycol2
union
select keycol1, keycol2, 2, sum(sales)
   from Feb_Sales
   group by keycol1, keycol2
select a.keycol1, a.keycol2, a.sales, b.sales
   from #sum a
   join #sum b on a.keycol1 = b.keycol1 and a.keycol2 = b.keycol2
   where a.month = 1
      and b.month = 2
```

GROUP BY and JOINS

One area where SQL Server tends to perform poorly is in some GROUP BY statements for tables that are being joined. To see why, you need to know that SQL Server always makes a worktable to process GROUP BY clauses.

A worktable is a temporary table SQL Server makes for itself. Worktables are generally used for the following reasons:

- To process a DISTINCT statement when a unique index couldn't do the job.
- To process an ORDER BY statement when the clustered index isn't returning rows in the desired order.
- To index a table that SQL Server has determined needs it.
- To hold intermediate results of joins.
- To process a GROUP BY statement.

Suppose that you have a table to which you want to apply vector aggregate functions, and after applying the aggregates you want to join the result with another table to pull in some columns of substantial total width, say, at least more than 100 characters. You could write this in two steps, but it is probably easier for you to write one single SQL statement:

```
SELECT (some columns from A), (some columns from B), SUM(whatever)
   FROM A
   JOIN B ON (The columns of A matching the primary key of B)
   GROUP BY (some columns from A), (some columns from B)
```

The problem with this construction is that the worktable has to perform the GROUP BY over a large number of columns, which is costly. The query runs more efficiently if you break it up:

```
SELECT (some columns from A), 'column_name' = SUM(whatever)
   INTO #C
   FROM A
   GROUP BY (some columns from A)
ALTER TABLE #C ADD CONSTRAINT PK__#C PRIMARY KEY (some colunms from A)
SELECT (some columns from #C), (some columns from B), 'column_name'
   FROM #C
   JOIN B ON (the columns of #C matching the primary key of B)
```

Too many tables in a JOIN

In theory, you can join up to 16 tables in a single query, but we don't recommend this if you want to see results some time this century. The general rule of thumb for SQL Server is to limit your join to not more than four tables. One of the reasons for this has to do with how SQL Server determines join orders. From the perspective of SQL, there is no such thing as an "order" to a join, but this is something SQL Server has to worry about. All joins are basically performed as nested iterations, much like nested loops in a programming language. The indexes let SQL Server pare down the number of retrievals it has to do on the various loops.

The order in which you list the tables has absolutely no bearing on how SQL Server will really join them; SQL Server decides for itself in which order to join them. The number of orders SQL Server has to consider is $n! = n \times (n\text{-}1) \times \ldots 1$, where n is the number of tables you want to join. For two tables, A and B, there are only two possibilities, A then B, or B then A. For three tables, you have 6 combinations; for four tables, you have 24. After that, it really takes off: 120, 720, 5,040, 40,320, 362,880,... . It isn't feasible for SQL Server to consider all these combinations, so it takes some shortcuts when you give it more than four tables to join.

The other reason for trying to limit your queries to joining not more than four tables is that the performance begins to drag. Suppose that you have a table in a normalized format listing numeric data for your organization, in this case, monthly sales. You might have a table that looks like this:

```
create table many_table_join (
   keycolumn int,
   month tinyint primary key ( keycolumn, month ),
    sales int)
```

This is the correct 3NF way of storing the data. However, the query to retrieve the data so that you see the months as column headings is the following:

```
select a12.keycolumn,
      a12.sales, a11.sales, a10.sales, a9.sales,
      a8.sales, a7.sales, a6.sales, a5.sales,
      a4.sales, a3.sales, a2.sales, a1.sales
    from many_table_join a12
    join many_table_join a11 on a12.keycolumn = a11.keycolumn
    join many_table_join a10 on a12.keycolumn = a10.keycolumn
    join many_table_join a9  on a12.keycolumn = a9.keycolumn
    join many_table_join a8  on a12.keycolumn = a8.keycolumn
    join many_table_join a7  on a12.keycolumn = a7.keycolumn
    join many_table_join a6  on a12.keycolumn = a6.keycolumn
    join many_table_join a5  on a12.keycolumn = a5.keycolumn
    join many_table_join a4  on a12.keycolumn = a4.keycolumn
    join many_table_join a3  on a12.keycolumn = a3.keycolumn
    join many_table_join a2  on a12.keycolumn = a2.keycolumn
    join many_table_join a1  on a12.keycolumn = a1.keycolumn
    where a12.month = 12
        and a11.month = 11
```

(continued)

(continued)

```
        and a10.month = 10
        and a9.month  = 9
        and a8.month  = 8
        and a7.month  = 7
        and a6.month  = 6
        and a5.month  = 5
        and a4.month  = 4
        and a3.month  = 3
        and a2.month  = 2
        and a1.month  = 1
    order by 1
```

If you think about it, this query really *ought* to run quickly. One scan of the table is all that is required. As you read the first row, you get the first keycolumn value for month 1. The next few rows are the sales for months 2, 3, and so on for that same keycolumn value. Then, you move on to the second key column value. Unfortunately, it isn't that obvious to SQL Server to do such a thing, and it doesn't possess the so-called "cross-tab" query you find in other applications, such as Microsoft Access. Therefore, you will be waiting a long, long time for this query to run.

The solutions to these kinds of problems generally lie in breaking the query into pieces. For example, simply chopping the preceding query in half, by first storing in a temp table the joins of January through June, and then storing the joins of July through December into another table, and joining the two temporary tables, is effective. However, in this special case, there is a trick to get timely results in one query:

```
create table pivot ( month tinyint primary key,
    p1 int, p2 int, p3 int, p4 int, p5 int, p6 int,
    p7 int, p8 int, p9 int, p10 int, p11 int, p12 int )
insert pivot values ( 1, 1, 0, 0, 0, 0, 0, 0, 0, 0, 0, 0, 0 )
insert pivot values ( 2, 0, 1, 0, 0, 0, 0, 0, 0, 0, 0, 0, 0 )
insert pivot values ( 3, 0, 0, 1, 0, 0, 0, 0, 0, 0, 0, 0, 0 )
insert pivot values ( 4, 0, 0, 0, 1, 0, 0, 0, 0, 0, 0, 0, 0 )
insert pivot values ( 5, 0, 0, 0, 0, 1, 0, 0, 0, 0, 0, 0, 0 )
insert pivot values ( 6, 0, 0, 0, 0, 0, 1, 0, 0, 0, 0, 0, 0 )
insert pivot values ( 7, 0, 0, 0, 0, 0, 0, 1, 0, 0, 0, 0, 0 )
insert pivot values ( 8, 0, 0, 0, 0, 0, 0, 0, 1, 0, 0, 0, 0 )
insert pivot values ( 9, 0, 0, 0, 0, 0, 0, 0, 0, 1, 0, 0, 0 )
insert pivot values (10, 0, 0, 0, 0, 0, 0, 0, 0, 0, 1, 0, 0 )
insert pivot values (11, 0, 0, 0, 0, 0, 0, 0, 0, 0, 0, 1, 0 )
insert pivot values (12, 0, 0, 0, 0, 0, 0, 0, 0, 0, 0, 0, 1 )
go
select keycolumn, sum( p1 * sales), sum( p2 * sales), sum( p3 * sales),
```

```
sum( p4 * sales), sum( p5 * sales), sum( p6 * sales),
sum( p7 * sales), sum( p8 * sales), sum( p9 * sales),
sum( p10* sales), sum( p11* sales), sum( p12 * sales)
from many_table_join m
join pivot p on m.month = p.month
group by keycolumn
order by 1
```

The trouble with NOT

Whereas SQL Server's index distribution page is quite helpful in searching for a particular value, the statistics won't give you much information on avoiding a value. Therefore, search arguments like this:

```
WHERE column_name != 'value'

WHERE column_name NOT LIKE 'search_string'

WHERE column_name like '[^x]%' /* X can be any character */
WHERE NOT ( column_name = 'value' )
```

All cannot be optimized. If you have some additional knowledge about the spread of values over which you are querying, use it to formulate the positive equivalents of the search clauses using NOT. For example, if you know a column has values 'A', 'I', 'O', 'E', 'U', instead of writing

```
WHERE column_name NOT IN ( 'A', 'I' )
```

write

```
WHERE column_name IN ( 'O', 'E', 'U' )
```

It is still quite possible that SQL Server will not use the index (because the index will cause more reads than the table scan), but at least you have given SQL Server a chance to use the index. With the NOT formulation there is no chance.

NOT IN versus NOT EXISTS

The preceding comments about using NOT do not apply to the NOT IN and NOT EXISTS constructions. Those usually can't be written any other way. However, how do you choose between them? For example, if you are comparing two tables that should have the same primary values, either you can write

```
select *
   from A
   where not exists ( select *
      from B
      where A.primarykey = B.primarykey )
```

or you can write

```
select *
   from A
   where primarykey not in ( select *
      from B
      where A.primarykey = B.primarykey )
```

Which is better? Fortunately, the answer with SQL Server 6.5 is neither: SQL Server converts the second query to the first form. By the way, if you don't have an index on the inner table on the column(s) on which you are joining, you can be assured that your query will take a while. In this case, SQL Server is going to make a temporary table and index it for you.

This OR that

The concept of OR is very important in query optimization because it means that there are at least two different ways that rows from the table can make their way into the result set. The basic idea for dealing with an 'OR' clause is this:

1. Treat the search arguments on either side of the OR clause as separate queries and optimize them.
2. If any of the component queries require a table scan, the query on the whole will be solved with a table scan. This is because, by definition, a table scan means accessing each individual page. If SQL Server has to read all the pages anyway, it would be pointless to use an index to resolve any other search criteria.
3. If all the OR clauses are covered by the same index, look at the cost of using the index to access all values in the range from the minimum to the maximum search arguments.
4. If the total estimated I/O of resolving the individual component queries is more than a table scan, do a table scan instead. Otherwise, use the indexes.

The biggest thing for you as a user to do is to realize when you are using an OR clause. Not only does the keyword OR invoke SQL Server's OR clause processing, but so do these constructions:

```
WHERE column_name in ( 'value1', 'value2', … , 'valueN' )
```

This is equivalent to the following:

```
WHERE column_name = 'value1' OR column_name = 'value2' OR …
```

Another item that is equivalent to an OR is

```
WHERE column_name LIKE '[ae]%'
```

This, of course, is

```
WHERE column_name LIKE 'a%' OR column_name like 'e%'
```

Analyzing SHOWPLAN

At this point, we have discussed what indexes to set up on your tables and how to write SQL that the optimizer can use effectively. Ideally, that should be all that you need. Invariably, however, you will still be staring at a spinning globe in the Query Window from time to time. Often, you can spot at a glance what the problem is. Sometimes you can't. This section is about what to do when you just don't understand what is taking so darn long.

When a query seems to be taking longer than you believe it should, your first step is to see just how SQL Server is executing your query. After that, you can dissect why.

The graphical SHOWPLAN

If you were a SQL Server customer before SQL Server 6.5, you know that the Enterprise Manager of SQL Server 6.0 and the Object Manager of SQL Server 4.2 included a graphical display of which indexes SQL Server was using to resolve queries. This was a wonderfully handy feature of the product. At a glance you could find trouble spots in either a single SQL statement or an enormous batch of statements. The utility was even nice enough to display in red the table scans. If you still have your copy of the SQL Server 6.0 tools you are in luck, because...

This is gone in SQL Server 6.5. Have a nice day!

What Next?

The loss of the graphical SHOWPLAN forms an alarming trend. In the SQL Server 6.0 release, Microsoft eliminated the graphical interface to BCP, to the frustration of many users. We hope the next release of the product will reverse this trend and include graphical BCP and SHOWPLAN. Isn't the whole point of Windows that GUIs make people more productive?

Why? Only Microsoft knows. Perhaps they couldn't update the feature fast enough to accommodate the new SQL extensions such as the ANSI-compliant joins. In any case, you are stuck with the hard-to-read text output we discuss next. The only advantage to the text output is that it was always more accurate and more informative than the graphical plan.

The text SHOWPLAN

In order for you to see how SQL Server is actually executing your queries, you can turn to a very complete, if not verbose, set of comments. From the Query Options Window, check the Show Query Plan box. From this point on, until you clear the flag, you will see a description of how each and every command you send to SQL Server is executed. The SHOWPLAN is even robust enough that it tells how each individual statement inside a stored procedure is executing. For example, here is the SHOWPLAN for the query we discussed earlier:

```
select o1.name, o2.name
    from sysdepends d
    join sysobjects o1 on d.id = o1.id
    join sysobjects o2 on depid = o2.id
    where o1.type = 'p'
        and o2.type = 'u'

STEP 1
The type of query is SELECT
FROM TABLE
sysobjects o1
Nested iteration
Table Scan
FROM TABLE
sysdepends d
Nested iteration
Using Clustered Index
FROM TABLE
```

```
sysobjects o2
Nested iteration
Using Clustered Index
```

With some experience, you can see at a glance what is happening with your query. After you read the following sections, you will be able to decipher the output above and even more complex feedback from SQL Server. Our focus will be on quickly locating the trouble spots.

Determining the access methods for each table

The first thing to do is to find each of your tables and figure out how they are being accessed. What you are looking for are groups of three lines like this:

```
FROM TABLE [alias]
<table name>
Nested iteration
```

The very next line will say one of these three things. (The three possibilities, "Using Clustered Index," "Index : <Index Name>", and "Table Scan" correspond to the green, yellow, and red colors you used to see in the graphical SHOWPLAN if you had SQL Server 6.0.):

```
Using Clustered Index
Index : <Index Name>
Table Scan
```

In the preceding query, sysobjects is being table scanned once and accessed once via its clustered index; sysdepends is being accessed via its clustered index.

You want to see lots of "Using Clustered Index" and "Index : <Index Name>". You don't want to see more than one "Table Scan" on the tables involved in your query, but sometimes one table scan is unavoidable. In the case of a lot of joins, including the preceding one, one of the tables is going to have to be scanned, the table in the outer loop of the nested iterations. Because SQL Server has to iterate through all the values of some table for the join, you expect a table scan. If you are seeing a nonclustered index being used, you know which one. You should also expect a table scan on very small tables because SQL Server can scan the table as fast as it can scan the index. Go ahead and leave the index on the table, though, just in case the table gets bigger.

If you felt an index should have been used and it wasn't, keep reading. That is our next topic after we finish how to read SHOWPLAN.

Nested table scans are bad

Consider this query:

```
select *
    from firsttable a
    join secondtable b on a.id = b.id
    join thirdtable c on c.id = c.id
    order by a.id
```

Though it is syntactically correct, there is a subtle flaw in this query. Can you spot it? The third join says 'c.id = c.id' instead of something like 'a.id = c.id'. Since 'c.id = c.id' is always true, this query returns the Cartesian product of thirdtable with the join of firsttable and secondtable. If the tables are even 1,000 rows or so, your result set is a million rows! Furthermore, SQL Server has to sort the results before returning them, so you-know-what will freeze over before you get the results. If you write a query like this and look at its SHOWPLAN, you will see something like this:

```
STEP 1
The type of query is SELECT
FROM TABLE
firsttable a
Nested iteration
Table Scan
FROM TABLE
secondtable b
Nested iteration
Using Clustered Index
FROM TABLE
thirdtable c
Nested iteration
Table Scan
```

Look carefully and notice that both firsttable and thirdtable are being table scanned. This is always wrong, unless the tables are trivially small, your are doing a FULL OUTER JOIN, or you really intended the query to return a Cartesian product. (Elsewhere we discuss worktables. Table scans are okay for them. It is only when two tables *from your query* are being table scanned that you should get excited.)

Multiple listing of a table

Sometimes, you will see this kind of output:

```
select *
    from yourtable
    where cl_ind_col = 'value' or nc_ind_col = 'value'

STEP 1
The type of query is SELECT
FROM TABLE
yourtable
Nested iteration
Using Clustered Index
FROM TABLE
yourtable
Nested iteration
Index : yourindex
FROM TABLE
yourtable
Nested iteration
Using Dynamic Index
```

This is a bit confusing. Is SQL Server using the clustered index, or is it using the nonclustered index 'yourindex', or it is using a 'Dynamic Index'? The answer is yes. Because this is a query with an OR clause, SQL Server is using two different indexes to find which rows it wants and then a Dynamic Index (one SQL Server builds on the fly) to retrieve the rows. The reason for the Dynamic Index is to avoid duplicate rows.

Other tables listed

Having found your own tables, you may notice there are some tables listed that aren't yours, as in this example:

```
select somecolumn, count(*) row_count
    from yourtable
    group by somecolumn
    having count(*) > 100
    order by count(*) desc

STEP 1
The type of query is SELECT (into a worktable)
GROUP BY
Vector Aggregate
FROM TABLE
yourtable
Nested iteration
```

(continued)

(continued)

```
Table Scan
TO TABLE
Worktable 1
STEP 2
The type of query is INSERT
The update mode is direct
Vector Aggregate
Worktable created for ORDER BY
FROM TABLE
Worktable 1
Nested iteration
Table Scan
TO TABLE
Worktable 2
STEP 3
The type of query is SELECT
This step involves sorting
FROM TABLE
Worktable 2
Using GETSORTED Table Scan
```

In this query, we have two other tables in addition to yourtable: Worktable 1 and Worktable 2. These are temporary tables that SQL Server needs to process your query. In this case, the GROUP BY requires a worktable, and the ORDER BY requires another worktable.

STEP

This example also introduces the idea of steps. You may have noticed that each of the previous SHOWPLANs had "STEP 1" at the top. This one has several steps, which happens with worktables.

Reformatting SHOWPLAN

Let's look at SHOWPLAN for the query we said was poorly written:

```
select o1.name, o2.name
    from sysdepends d
    join sysobjects o1 on object_name(d.id) = o1.name
    join sysobjects o2 on object_name(d.depid) = o2.name
    where o1.type = 'p'
        and o2.type = 'u'
```

```
STEP 1
The type of query is INSERT
The update mode is direct
Worktable created for REFORMATTING
FROM TABLE
sysdepends
Nested iteration
Table Scan
TO TABLE
Worktable 1
STEP 2
The type of query is INSERT
The update mode is direct
Worktable created for REFORMATTING
FROM TABLE
Worktable 1
Nested iteration
Table Scan
FROM TABLE
sysobjects
Nested iteration
Index : ncsysobjects
TO TABLE
Worktable 2
STEP 3
The type of query is SELECT
FROM TABLE
Worktable 2
Nested iteration
Table Scan
FROM TABLE
sysobjects o2
Nested iteration
Index : ncsysobjects
```

The big red flag here is the phrase "Worktable created for REFORMATTING." You never want to see this phrase unless you are doing a FULL OUTER JOIN, and when you do see it, you want to correct it by indexing tables, updating statistics, or rewriting the query. REFORMATTING means that SQL Server had to do a join on two tables and found no indexes to use on the join. Rather than forge ahead with a table scan nested within a table scan — which we said was really bad — SQL Server is going to copy one of your tables into a worktable, index it, and then proceed. Our experience shows that REFORMATTING rarely works well. The performance is invariably miserable. Furthermore, every time you run this query, you have to pay this time penalty, whereas if you create the necessary indexes, you will never have to wait again.

To figure out which tables are not joining well in your query, look at the first FROM TABLE and TO TABLE lines after the REFORMATTING. The FROM TABLE is sysdepends, and the TO TABLE is Worktable 1. This tells you that sysdepends isn't joining well with something. Look for the FROM TABLE line for Worktable 1, and see what other table(s) are selected from in that step. In this case, it is sysobjects, so you know your join between sysobjects and sysdepends can't find any good index to use.

FULL OUTER JOINs

We just finished saying that REFORMATTING is the kiss of death, but there is one case when it is not only acceptable but mandatory: a FULL OUTER JOIN. Recall that a FULL OUTER JOIN means that in addition to the normal INNER JOIN results, the query must include rows from the first table with no matches in the second table, and include rows from the second table with no matches from the first. The whole idea of a FULL OUTER JOIN doesn't fit into the nested iteration paradigm of query processing, so SQL Server makes it fit with a worktable. For example:

```
select l.id, r.id, l.name, r.name, l.type, r.type
    from lefttable l
    full outer join righttable r on l.id = r.id

STEP 1
The type of query is INSERT
The update mode is direct
Worktable created for REFORMATTING
FROM TABLE
lefttable
Nested iteration
Table Scan
TO TABLE
Worktable 1
STEP 2
The type of query is SELECT
FROM TABLE
righttable b
Nested iteration
Table Scan
FULL OUTER JOIN : nested iteration
  FROM TABLE
  Worktable 1
  Nested iteration
  Using Clustered Index
```

You will notice that both lefttable and righttable are being table scanned. That has to happen in a FULL OUTER JOIN because SQL Server must check each row of both tables to see if there is a match in the other table. This tells you at least two things:

- For a FULL OUTER JOIN, it doesn't matter what indexes, if any, you have on your tables. They aren't going to be used in the FULL OUTER JOIN process.
- The performance of a FULL OUTER JOIN isn't going to be very stellar.

If you don't see the REFORMATTING clause, something went wrong. For example, suppose you want to rerun the preceding query but only where the IDs of both lefttable and righttable are greater than some value, say 1,500,000,000. Your first (and incorrect) attempt at revising the query might be as follows:

```
select l.id, r.id, l.name, r.name, l.type, r.type
    from lefttable l
    full outer join righttable r on l.id = r.id
    where a.id > 1500000000
        and b.id > 1500000000
```

If you run a query like this, you will find what SQL Server seemed to forget about the FULL OUTER JOIN part: only matching IDs are in the output. Here's the SHOWPLAN:

```
STEP 1
The type of query is SELECT
FROM TABLE
lefttable l
Nested iteration
Using Clustered Index
FROM TABLE
righttable r
Nested iteration
Using Clustered Index
```

FULL OUTER JOIN isn't even mentioned! What went wrong? It has to do with the subtle behavior of nulls. The constraint a.id > 1500000000 prohibits a.id from being null, which reduces the query to a RIGHT OUTER JOIN. Likewise, b.id > 1500000000 restricts the query to a LEFT OUTER JOIN, so we are left with an INNER JOIN. The correct way to write the query is as follows:

```
select l.id, r.id, l.name, r.name, l.type, r.type
    from lefttable l
    full outer join righttable r on l.id = r.id
    where (l.id > 1500000000 or l.id = null)
        and (r.id > 1500000000 or r.id = null)
```

NOT EXISTS SHOWPLAN

When you have a query that uses a NOT EXISTS clause, as follows:

```
select *
    from yourtable a
    where not exists ( select *
            from innertable
            where a.id = id )
        and a.id > 2000010156

STEP 1
The type of query is SELECT
FROM TABLE
yourtable a
Nested iteration
Using Clustered Index
NOT EXISTS : nested iteration
  FROM TABLE
  innertable
  Nested iteration
  Using Clustered Index
```

SHOWPLAN prefaces "nested iteration" with "NOT EXISTS :" and indents the text. In this case, you absolutely do *not* want to see a table scan on the inner (indented) table, unless you know it is a trivially small table.

Nulls are Tricky

Here's a fun one: suppose you have a row in your table where id = null. Will that row return in a join with another table on a.id = b.id? No, not even when b.id is null. But what if we change the join to say NOT (a.id = b.id), or a.id != b.id? Now will the row with the null be in the result set? No! An expression with a null is always false.

Why Use FULL OUTER JOINS?

By the way, we don't find the need for FULL OUTER JOINs in our applications. In fact, we believe the need for a FULL OUTER JOIN may indicate poor database structure. We covered this rationale in more depth in Chapter 11.

CONSTRAINT SHOWPLAN

When you have foreign keys set up in your database, and we highly recommend that you do, you might wonder about the performance of INSERTs, UPDATEs, and DELETEs. In Chapter 28, we advised you to set up indexes on your foreign key columns. Are they being used? You can easily see by showing the plan for a change without actually executing it. Suppose that table2 has a foreign key on the id column referencing table1 and that table2 has an index on the id column. The SHOWPLAN for:

```
DELETE table1 WHERE name = 'value'
```

might look like the following:

```
STEP 1
The type of query is DELETE
The update mode is deferred
FROM TABLE
table1
Nested iteration
Index : name
FROM TABLE
table2
CONSTRAINT : nested iteration
Index : FK__table2__id
TO TABLE
table1
```

This is ever so slightly different from other SHOWPLANs because instead of saying

```
FROM TABLE
table2
Nested iteration
```

it says "CONSTRAINT : nested iteration" on the third line. No matter, the next line gives us the access method, and it is using our index.

Other SHOWPLANs

There are other words you might see in SHOWPLANs, such as "LEFT OUTER JOIN", "SUBQUERY", "WITH CHECK OPTION," and so on. However, these keywords are just telling you want kind of query is running, which is usually obvious already. The main ideas are the same: figure out what indexes are being used, look for table scans, and look for REFORMATTING.

Using DBCC to See Why a Plan Was Selected

At this stage, you have indexed your tables, you have written your SQL well, you have found out which indexes SQL Server is and isn't using, and you still aren't satisfied with the performance you are getting. There is probably an index you think SQL Server should use, and you can't for your life imagine why SQL Server isn't picking it. Let's find out what SQL Server is thinking as it formulates its plan for your query.

Our approach here is to turn on a bunch of trace flags, as follows:

- **302:** Prints information about index selection. Remember this flag if you remember only one.
- **310:** Prints information about join order.
- **325:** Prints information about using indexes to process order by clauses. We won't use this much.
- **326:** More information about sorts.
- **330:** Prints information about the ANSI joins.
- **3604:** Directs the output of all the flags to the client.

We might as well tell you up front: this is tedious work. It will take you several minutes to analyze a single query — when you are good at it. For a handful of key queries, it is worth it, but you could never do this every day. That is why we focused on the broad-brush approaches earlier.

We start off slowly:

```
DBCC TRACEON( 3604, 302 )
```

After you put these flags on, you are subjected to a blizzard of output. Consider the simplest case. You have a table called 'yourtable', with a primary key on id. If this query doesn't use that index, something is really wrong. Remember that if you are at the trace flag level, you have already run the SHOWPLAN, so you *know* which index is getting used. We will omit the SHOWPLAN output here and just tell you what it said. The following query does use the unique clustered index, of course:

```
select *
    from yourtable
    where id = 341223413
```

You can run the query with no execute and still see the Optimizer's analysis:

```
*******************************
Leaving q_init_sclause() for table 'yourtable' (varno 0).
The table has 1288 rows and 57 pages.
Cheapest index is index 0, costing 57 pages per scan.

*******************************
Entering q_score_index() for table 'yourtable' (varno 0).
The table has 1288 rows and 57 pages.
Scoring the search clause:
AND (!:0xde548a)  (andstat:0xa)
  EQ (L:0xde5476)  (rsltype:0x38 rsllen:4 rslprec:10 rslscale:0
  opstat:0x0)
    VAR (L:0xde551e)  (varname:id varno:0 colid:2 coltype(0x38):INT4
    colen:4 coloff:2 colprec:10 colscale:0 vartypeid:7 varnext:de54c2
    varusecnt:2 varstat:0x1 varlevel:0 varsubq:0)
    INT4 (R:0xde545c)  (left:0xde5464 len:4 maxlen:4 prec:9 scale:0
    value:341223413)

Unique clustered index found—return rows 1 pages 2
Cheapest index is index 1, costing 2 pages and generating 1 rows per
scan.
Search argument selectivity is 0.000776.
*******************************
```

We know. What a mess! First of all, the "leaving q_init_sclause()" will always be in the output, even if your query is just:

```
select *
    from yourtable
```

Therefore, ignore it and jump to the next section with "Entering q_score_index()". These sections always start with 'AND' and then some indentation. The first piece of real information is the 'EQ' on the line below. SQL Server has found that your WHERE clause contains an equality. You might also see GE, GT, LE, and LT here for >=, >, <, and <=, respectively. What you will not see is NE because <> does not use an index.

Below the EQ you see all the stuff you already know about your column and your search value. The column is an int, the value you are looking for is 341223413.

The second piece of exciting information is this line:

```
Unique clustered index found—return rows 1 pages 2
```

That's about it for this query. You used '=' and SQL Server has a UCI, so it's happy. Now let's try the following:

```
select *
    from yourtable
    where id < 341223413

Leaving q_init_sclause() for table 'yourtable' (varno 0).
The table has 1288 rows and 57 pages.
Cheapest index is index 0, costing 57 pages per scan.

*******************************
Entering q_score_index() for table 'yourtable' (varno 0).
The table has 1288 rows and 57 pages.
Scoring the search clause:
AND (!:0xde548a)  (andstat:0xa)
  LT (L:0xde5476)  (rsltype:0x38 rsllen:4 rslprec:10 rslscale:0
  opstat:0x0)
    VAR (L:0xde551e)  (varname:id varno:0 colid:2 coltype(0x38):INT4
    colen:4 coloff:2 colprec:10 colscale:0 vartypeid:7 varnext:de54c2
    varusecnt:2 varstat:0x1 varlevel:0 varsubq:0)
    INT4 (R:0xde545c)  (left:0xde5464 len:4 maxlen:4 prec:9 scale:0
    value:341223413)

Scoring clause for index 1
Relop bits are: 0x80,0x20,0x1
Qualifying stat page; pgno: 12665 steps: 321
Search value: INT4 value:341223413
No steps for search value—qualpage for LT search value finds
value between steps 60 and 61—use betweenSC
Estimate: indid 1, selectivity 1.880853e-001, rows 242 pages 9
Cheapest index is index 1, costing 9 pages and generating 242 rows
per scan.
Search argument selectivity is 0.188085.
```

This query also uses the clustered index. Once again, we jump to the indentation after the first "AND" to locate our LT and our value. Then, the real fun starts at the word "scoring". In some cases, like an equality search clause where a unique index is available, SQL Server automatically uses the index. No further analysis in necessary because the number of page reads will be exactly the number of levels in the index. In other cases, such as this one, SQL Server must estimate the number of page reads and compute a cost. One by one, the next few lines tell us:

```
Scoring clause for index 1
```

We are going to evaluate index 1 (the clustered index). If other indexes applied, we would evaluate them, too. Let's move on.

```
Relop bits are: 0x80,0x20,0x1
```

Ignore this line about "Relop bits."

```
Qualifying stat page; pgno: 12665 steps: 321
```

The distribution page is page number 12,665, and it has 321 steps in its histogram:

```
Search value: INT4 value:341223413
```

You knew that already.

```
No steps for search value-qualpage for LT search value finds
value between steps 60 and 61-use betweenSC
Estimate: indid 1, selectivity 1.880853e-001, rows 242 pages 9
```

When SQL Server bounces your value up against the histogram, it draws distinctions between matches and nonmatches and adjusts the selectivity accordingly. For example, if you just happened to hit the histogram value, you would see something like this:

```
Match found on statistics page
matchstep: 61
numsteps : 1
equal to a single row in middle of page-use midsingleSC
Estimate: indid 1, selectivity 1.896430e-001, rows 244 pages 9
```

Based on the selectivity, SQL Server estimates that it will scan 9 pages, which is better than 57, for a table scan. Your index gets used.

Now suppose we flip the inequality to >. The query analyzer makes this determination:

```
No steps for search value-qualpage for LT search value finds
value between steps 60 and 61-use betweenSC
Estimate: indid 1, selectivity 8.111383e-001, rows 1044 pages 32
Cheapest index is index 1, costing 32 pages and generating 1044 rows
per scan.
```

Thirty-two pages is still less than 57, so we stick with the index.

The magic statistics

One thing you don't want to see in the output is this:

```
No statistics page—use magicSC
Estimate: indid 1, selectivity 3.300000e-001, rows 425 pages 14
```

Remember that in the preceding example SQL Server gave you the page number of the statistics page? Here, SQL Server is telling you that you have *no* statistics page. It's probably because you created the index before you loaded the table, and you failed to update the statistics! In this case, SQL Server uses certain fixed selectivities, and they aren't too good. For GT and LT it is 33 percent.

Compound search clauses

We make our example progressively more difficult as we go along. What should happen with the following query?

```
select *
    from yourtable
    where name like 'xy%'
```

Here's SQL Server's reply:

```
Entering q_score_index() for table 'yourtable' (varno 0).
The table has 1288 rows and 57 pages.
Scoring the search clause:
AND (!:0xd64edc)  (andstat:0xa)
  LT (L:0xd64ec8)  (rsltype:0x2f rsllen:255 rslprec:30 rslscale:0
  opstat:0x0)
    VAR (L:0xde54f8)  (varname:name varno:0 colid:1
    coltype(0x27):VARCHAR colen:30 coloff:-1 colprec:30 colscale:0
    vartypeid:18 varusecnt:4 varstat:0x1 varlevel:0 varsubq:0)
    VARCHAR (R:0xd64eae)  (left:0xd64eb6 len:3 maxlen:3 value:'sQ ')
  AND (R:0xd64ee8)  (andstat:0xa)
    GE (L:0xd64e9a)  (rsltype:0x2f rsllen:255 rslprec:30 rslscale:0
    opstat:0x0)
      VAR (L:0xde54f8)  (varname:name varno:0 colid:1
      coltype(0x27):VARCHAR colen:30 coloff:-1 colprec:30 colscale:0
      vartypeid:18 varusecnt:4 varstat:0x1 varlevel:0 varsubq:0)
      VARCHAR (R:0xd64e80)  (left:0xd64e88 len:3 maxlen:3 value:'sp '
      )
```

```
Scoring clause for index 2
Relop bits are: 0x80,0x8,0x4,0x1
Scoring SARG interval, upper bound.
Qualifying stat page; pgno: 12808 steps: 52
Search value: VARCHAR value:'sQ '
No steps for search value—qualpage for LT search value finds
value between steps 47 and 48—use betweenSC
Scoring SARG interval, lower bound.
Qualifying stat page; pgno: 12808 steps: 52
Search value: VARCHAR value:'sp '
No steps for search value—qualpage for LT search value finds
value between steps 39 and 40—use betweenSC
Net selectivity of interval: 1.546226e-001
Estimate: indid 2, selectivity 1.546226e-001, rows 199 pages 206
Cheapest index is index 0, costing 57 pages and generating 199 rows
per scan.
Search argument selectivity is 0.154623.
```

Your first question should be, "What's that second AND doing in there?" SQL Server broke your query into LT and GT pieces. It will then figure out the selectivity of the interval. In this case, the index was going to cost 206 page reads, so a table scan of 57 pages is faster.

As a final example, we consider the following:

```
select *
   from yourtable
   where id in (1162346346,162346346,9090890803)
```

The output you get on this is as follows:

```
*******************************
Leaving q_init_sclause() for table 'yourtable' (varno 0).
The table has 1288 rows and 57 pages.
Cheapest index is index 0, costing 57 pages per scan.

*******************************
Entering q_score_index() for table 'yourtable' (varno 0).
The table has 1288 rows and 57 pages.
Scoring the search clause:

TREE IS NULL

q_new_orsarg built new SARGs:
AND (!:0xdddfbe)  (andstat:0x0)
  LE (L:0xdddfaa)  (rsltype:0x0 rsllen:0 opstat:0x20)
    VAR (L:0xde5646)  (varname:id left:de54e6 right:de545c varno:0
    colid:2 coltype(0x38):INT4 colen:4 coloff:2 colprec:10 colscale:0
```

(continued)

(continued)

```
    vartypeid:7 varnext:de55ea varusecnt:6 varstat:0xcd varlevel:0
    varsubq:0)
    INT4 (R:0xde545c)  (left:0xde5464 len:4 maxlen:4 prec:10 scale:0
    value:1162346346)
  AND (R:0xdddf9e)  (andstat:0x0)
    GE (L:0xdddf8a)  (rsltype:0x0 rsllen:0 opstat:0x20)
      VAR (L:0xde5646)  (varname:id left:de54e6 right:de545c varno:0
      colid:2 coltype(0x38):INT4 colen:4 coloff:2 colprec:10
      colscale:0 vartypeid:7 varnext:de55ea varusecnt:6 varstat:0xcd
      varlevel:0 varsubq:0)
      INT4 (R:0xde54e6)  (left:0xde54ee len:0 maxlen:6 prec:10
      scale:0 value:NULL)

<remainer omitted for brevity>
```

Focus your attention on the line "q_new_orsarg built new SARGs:". SQL Server is saying that it rearranged your search argument to a LE and a GE during optimization.

Forcing an Index

If you are still sure you are right, you can force SQL Server to use the index you believe to be the correct one. Don't expect much success. We never force the query plan because we find that the performance statistics show SQL Server's choices are better. The syntax for forcing the query plan is the following:

```
SELECT select_list
   FROM table_name ( INDEX = index_name | index_id )
   WHERE …
```

Other Issues

Hopefully, at this point you have wrestled your performance problems to the ground. The next time you have a query that doesn't work, you won't sit and wonder why. However, before you start looking at indexes and SHOWPLANs and trace flags and such, your very first instinct should be to run sp_who. In case you aren't familiar with sp_who, it is a simple procedure anyone can run that lists who is logged in and whether or not they are active:

```
spid   status     loginame     hostname   blk   dbname     cmd
------ ---------- ------------ ---------- ----- ---------- ----------------
1      sleeping   sa                      0     master     MIRROR HANDLER
2      sleeping   sa                      0     master     LAZY WRITER
3      sleeping   sa                      0     master     CHECKPOINT SLEEP
4      sleeping   sa                      0     master     RA MANAGER
10     sleeping   sa           DOGBERT    0     master     AWAITING COMMAND
11     sleeping   sa           DILBERT    0     Fedorchek  AWAITING COMMAND
12     runnable   sa           DILBERT    0     Fedorchek  SELECT
```

You will always see at least one spid id with an active status: the connection you used to run the sp_who. If you have a query running in another window, look for it under your host name. Its status should be runnable, too. Now look in the blk column. If the number is anything other than zero, someone has a lock on an object you need. The other thing to check is just how many spid's are active. A few very large queries can crush the performance for everyone else.

Summary

When you write queries, you have to be careful not to use calculated columns in queries if you can avoid it, and you have to know when to use your own temporary tables. You can see how SQL Server executes your queries with SHOWPLAN. On single-table queries, you can easily see which index, if any, SQL Server is using. When looking at SHOWPLAN for joins, keep an eagle eye out for cases when there are multiple table scans of REFORMATTING worktables. Trace flags enable you to see the actual decision-making process SQL Server uses to arrive at a query plan. When you think you have better information than SQL Server about how to execute a query, you can override the Optimizer.

Review Questions

Q: When is a temporary table advisable in breaking up a query?

A: When you are trying to join on substrings, you are trying to join too many tables, or you are using GROUP BY on joins.

Q: What's wrong with using a calculated columns in a query?

A: The Optimizer can't figure out which index to use.

Q: What is the biggest thing to remember in joining tables?

A: The joins should involve the primary keys of all but one central table. If not, your query probably doesn't make sense, and SQL Server will take forever to execute it anyway.

Q: How do you access the graphic showplan in SQL Server 6.5?

A: Go find yourself a copy of the SQL Server 6.0 or 4.2 Query Analyzer. Don't expect to see any graphs for ANSI joins.

Q: What are reasons SQL Server will table scan a table in a single-table query?

A: The table might be only a couple of pages, you might have given SQL Server a query it can't optimize, or SQL Server correctly determined that a table scan really is the best approach.

Q: When is it okay to see two table scans in a join?

A: When one of the tables is really small or you are doing a FULL OUTER JOIN.

Part

IX

SQL Server and the World Wide Web

Easily the hottest new thing to come along in the last few years has been the World Wide Web. Everyone is in a mad scramble to provide tools for users to access their data through Web browsers like Microsoft's Internet Explorer and Netscape's Navigator. In this part, we will show you several methods by which you can dynamically publish your data on the Web. We certainly do not cover every possible product you can use — that would easily fill another book. Hmmm...

Instead, we cover how to do these things with little more than SQL Server itself — and you thought we were kidding when we called SQL Server the "Swiss Army Knife" of DBMS's!

Chapter

The Server Push Model

30

If databases are the key technology for the central storage of information, the Internet and corporate intranets are the key technologies for the rapid distribution of that data. It was only a matter of time until someone invented a way to marry the two technologies.

In this chapter, we explore the sever push model and how it can be implemented in SQL Server 6.5. We also cover the SQL Web Assistant (SQLWA), but only so far as it implements this paradigm.

Because this is a *SECRETS* book, we don't talk much about the actual tool interface. Instead, we focus on what it does behind the scenes. In our opinion, the SQLWA interface is so simple to use, it doesn't merit any serious discussion in this text. We will, however, talk about what it is doing behind the scenes. In order to appreciate this chapter fully, however, we suggest that you take five minutes and run through the tool to get a sense of what it enables you to do.

What's in This Chapter

In this chapter, you will learn how to make your server publish data on the Web. Specifically, we will cover the following.

- How to create HTML pages from stored data
- How to generate new Web pages automatically when data changes
- How to write your own stored procedure to create custom Web pages that are far beyond what the SQLWA allows you to do

The Information Tug of War

Basically, there are two models for data publishing on the Web: the server push model and the client pull model.

The server push model is where the information store (in this case, a SQL Server database) dictates what the information server can publish. For example, if you create a trigger on a table that recreates a Web page every time the data has changed, you are using the *push* model.

With SQL Server 6.5, Microsoft has included a tool called the SQLWA. This application affords the user a quick-and-dirty way of creating an HTML document from data stored in a given database. More importantly, this tool is an easy front end for you to set up a basic server push model.

An Overview of the Entire Process

The SQLWA uses three stored procedures to create dynamic HTML documents: sp_makewebtask, sp_runwebtask, and sp_dropwebtask.

In the next few sections, we will talk about these procedures and how they are used by the SQLWA.

sp_makewebtask

This procedure creates a task that will eventually create an HTML document. The syntax for it is

```
sp_makewebtask {@outputfile = 'outputfile', @query = 'query'}[,
[@fixedfont fixedfont,] [@bold bold,] [@italic italic,] [@colheaders
colheaders,] [@lastupdated lastupdated,] [@HTMLHeader HTMLHeader,]
[@username username,] [@dbname dbname,] [@templatefile
'templatefile',] [@webpagetitle 'webpagetitle',] [@resultstitle
'resultstitle',] [[@URL = 'URL', @reftext = 'reftext'] |
[@table_urls table_urls, @url_query 'url_query',]] [@whentype
```

```
whentype,] [@targetdate targetdate,] [@targettime targettime,]
[@dayflags dayflags,] [@numunits numunits,] [@unittype unittype,]
[@maketask maketask,] [@rowcnt rowcnt,] [@tabborder = tabborder,]
[@singlerow = singlerow,] [@blobfmt = blobfmt,] [@procname =
 procname]]
```

The following sections describe the parameters in this syntax.

@outputfile

This parameter specifies the location of the generated HTML file. This parameter is required and must be unique for each task created.

@query

This parameter specifies the query to be run. This parameter is required.

@fixedfont

This parameter specifies that the query results be displayed in a fixed font (1) or a proportional font (0). Fixed font (1) is the default.

@bold

@bold specifies that the query results be displayed in a bold font (1) or nonbold font (0). Nonbold (0) is the default.

@italic

This parameter specifies that the query results be displayed in an italic font (1) or nonitalic font (0). Nonitalic (0) is the default.

@colheaders

This parameter specifies that the query results be displayed with column headers (1) or no column headers (0). Column headers (1) is the default.

@lastupdated

@lastupdated specifies whether the generated HTML output displays a Last Updated: timestamp indicating the last updated date and time (1) or no timestamp (0). Timestamp (1) is the default.

@HTMLHeader

This parameter specifies the HTML formatting code for displaying the text contained in the @resultstitle variable. These values are as follows:

Value	*HTML Formatting Code*
1	H1
2	H2
3	H3
4	H4
5	H5
6	H6

@username

@username specifies the username for executing the query. The default is dbo.

@dbname

This parameter specifies the database name on which to run the query. If a database name is not given, @dbname defaults to the current database.

@templatefile

@templatefile specifies the path of the template file used to generate the HTML document. The template file contains information about formatting characteristics for HTML documents and contains the tag <%insert_data_here%>, which indicates the position to add the query results in an HTML table. There are no spaces between the less than sign (<) and the *i* of *insert* and between the *e* of *here* and the greater than sign (>).

@webpagetitle

This parameter specifies the title of the HTML document. The default is Microsoft SQL Server Web Assistant.

@resultstitle

This parameter specifies the title displayed above the query results in the HTML document. The default title is Query Results.

@url

@URL specifies a hyperlink to another Web page. The hyperlink is placed after the query results and at the end of the HTML document.

@reftext

This parameter specifies the hyperlink that describes to what Web page or document the hyperlink should take the user. The hyperlink text describes the destination and the hyperlink address comes from the URL in the @URL parameter.

@table_urls

This parameter specifies whether hyperlinks will be included on the HTML document and whether the hyperlinks will come from a SELECT statement executed on a SQL Server machine. A value of 0 (the default) indicates that no hyperlinks from SQL Server should be generated on the HTML document from SQL Server, and 1 indicates that hyperlinks should be created from @URL and @reftext.

@url_query

This parameter specifies the SELECT statement to create the URL and its hyperlink text.

@whentype

@whentype specifies when to run the task that creates the HTML document. Valid values for this parameter are the following:

- **1.** Create page now. The Web task will be created, executed immediately, and deleted immediately after execution. This is the default.
- **2.** Create page later. The stored procedure for creating the Web page will be created immediately, but execution of the Web task is deferred until the date and time specified by @targetdate and @targettime (optional). If no @targettime is specified, the Web task will be executed at 12:00 a.m. @targetdate is required when using @whentype. This Web task will be deleted automatically after the targeted time and date have passed.

- 3. Create page every *n* day(s) of the week. The Web page will be created on day(s) specified in @dayflags and at the time specified by @targettime (optional), beginning with the date in @targetdate. If no @targettime value is specified, the default is 12:00 a.m. The @targetdate parameter is required when using @whentype. The day(s) of the week are specified in the @dayflags parameter. More than one day of the week can be specified with the @dayflags parameter. Web tasks created with @whentype = 3 will not be deleted automatically and continue to run on the specified day(s) of the week until the user deletes them by using sp_dropwebtask.
- 4. Create page every *n* hours, days, or weeks. The Web page is created every *n* time period beginning with the date and time specified in @targetdate and @targettime (optional). If no @targettime is specified, the Web task will be executed at 12:00 a.m. The @targetdate parameter is required in this case. The task will run automatically every *n* hours, days, or weeks as specified by the @numunits and @unittype parameters. The tasks will run until the user deletes them by using sp_dropwebtask.
- 5. Create page upon request. The procedure is created without automatic scheduling. The user creates a Web page by running sp_runwebtask and deletes it only by using sp_dropwebtask.
- 6. Create page now and later. The Web page is created immediately and recreated according to @whentype = 2.
- 7. Create page now and every *n* day(s) of the week. The Web page is created immediately and recreated according to @whentype = 3, except no @targetdate is required.
- 8. Create page now and periodically thereafter. The Web page is created immediately and recreated according to @whentype = 4, except no @targetdate is required.
- 9. Create page now and upon request. The Web page is created immediately and recreated according to @whentype = 5. The task must be deleted manually.

@targetdate

@targetdate specifies the date the page should be built. The format is YYYYMMDD. In cases where the @whentype parameter is greater than 3 and this parameter is left unspecified, the current date will be used. For @whentype=2 (later), 3 (dayofweek), 4 (periodic), and 6 (now and later), the @targetdate parameter is required.

@targettime

This parameter specifies the time the HTML document should be created. If this parameter is needed but not supplied, it will default to 12:00 a.m.

@dayflags

This parameter specifies on what days to update the page. The following values are the codes for each day:

Value	***Day of the Week***
1	Sunday
2	Monday
4	Tuesday
8	Wednesday
16	Thursday
32	Friday
64	Saturday

In order to specify more than one day, simply add values together. For example, to run the task on Tuesday and Friday, specify a value of 36.

@numunits

This parameter specifies how often to update the Web page. Values range from 1 to 255. This parameter is used only when @whentype = 4 (periodic) or @whentype = 8 (now and later). For example, if @whentype = 4, @numunits = 6, and @unittype = 1 (hours), the specified Web page will be updated every six hours.

@unittype

@unittype specifies how often the Web page should be updated for @numunits = 4 (periodic) or @whentype = 8 (now and later). Use 1 (hours), 2 (days), and 3 (weeks).

@procname

This parameter specifies the procedure name for the Web task. If the procedure name is system-generated by running sp_makewebtask, the name begins with *Web_*. If it is user-specified, the procedure name must meet the conditions for valid procedure names and the procedure name must be unique.

@maketask

@maketask specifies whether the stored procedure should create and build the Web task or create the stored procedure for execution later. The default is to build the task (1).

@rowcnt

This parameter specifies a maximum number of rows to return from the query to the HTML document. The default (0) shows all rows.

@tabborder

This parameter specifies whether a border should be drawn around the results table (1, the default) or no border should be drawn around the results table (0).

@singlerow

This parameter specifies whether the results are to be displayed as one row per page. If @singlerow is 0 (the default), all results appear on the same page and in the same table. With a value of 1, @singlerow causes a new HTML page to be generated for every qualifying row in the results set. Successive HTML pages are generated with a number in the filename. For example, if web.html is specified as the output filename by using @singlerow = 1, additional pages are called web1.html, web2.html, and so on.

@blobfmt

@blobfmt specifies whether fields of *text* or *image* datatypes should be embedded in the results page (NULL, the default) or whether these fields should be saved onto another page and linked through a URL to the main Web page.

sp_runwebtask

Assuming for the moment that you have used sp_makewebtask to create an HTML creation task that wasn't executed automatically, you will probably want to run the task. To do this, you use the sp_runwebtask procedure. The syntax for this procedure is as follows:

```
sp_runwebtask {@procname = procname@= | @outputfile = outputfile@}
```

These paramters are covered in the following sections.

@outputfile

This parameter specifies the name of the Web task to run.

@procname

This parameter specifies the name of the Web task procedure to run. The named procedure defines the query for the Web task.

sp_dropwebtask

After you have created and executed your Web task, you will eventually want to delete it. To do this, you use the sp_dropwebtask procedure. The syntax for this is as follows:

```
sp_dropwebtask {@procname = procname@= | @outputfile = outputfile@}
```

The following sections cover these parameters.

@outputfile

@outputfile specifies the name of the Web task to delete.

@procname

This parameter specifies the name of the Web task procedure to delete. The named procedure defines the query for the Web task.

EXAMPLES

Now that you have learned what procedures the SQLWA uses to do its business, it's time to go over some examples.

Creating a one-time page

Perhaps the most common and simplest example is the creation of a one-time page. Let's say that you want to create a simple page that has all the data from the pubs..authors table. Let's also say that you want the resulting file to be c:\webroot\webwizard.htm. The code for that would be the following:

```
exec sp_makewebtask
    @outputfile = 'c:\webroot\webwizard.htm',
    @query = 'select * from authors'
```

Scheduling page creation

Another nice feature of the SQLWA is the capability to have a page created at a specific time or date. Suppose that we want to create the same Web page every 12 hours, starting on 06/05/1996 at 01:15 a.m. The code for this example would be as follows:

```
sp_makewebtask
@outputfile = 'c:\webroot\webwizard.htm',
@query = 'SELECT * from authors',
@dbname = 'PUBS',
@whentype = 4,
@unittype = 1,
@numunits = 12,
@targetdate = 19960605,
@targettime = 011500
```

Triggering page creation

Probably the most useful thing the SQLWA can do is set up your tables so that a given Web page is created whenever a change is made to a given table. Basically, what it's doing is creating a trigger (for update, insert, and delete) that sets up a Web creation task to run one minute later. At first, this confused us. What's the point of going through all the rigmarole of creating a task for future execution? Why not simply execute a call to sp_makewebtask for an immediate creation of a page? For example, to trigger a new Web page whenever the pubs..authors table changed, we figure we could create a trigger on the table with the following code:

```
exec sp_makewebtask
   @outputfile = 'c:\webroot\webwizard.htm',
   @query = 'select * from authors'
```

A funny thing happened, though, when we went to test this code. The process ran forever! After a few minutes of confusion, we figured out why. The trigger is locking the table. Because of this, the call to sp_makewebtask has to wait for the trigger to complete. The trigger, however, needs to wait for the sp_makewebtask call to complete, so we have a circular dependency. Voilà! A deadlock has occurred.

A better way

After thinking about this process for a while, we decided that there's a better way to do this. We created a new task named authors_html_page, which simply runs the following code:

```
exec sp_makewebtask
    @outputfile = 'c:\webroot\webwizard.htm',
    @query = 'select * from authors'
```

We were, of course, sure to set the task to be run on demand and not scheduled. Then we created a trigger on the pubs..authors table that has the following code:

```
exec sp_runtask 5
```

In this example, *5* is the task number of the task we created earlier (fill in your own task number here.) As it happens, one of the nice features of the sp_runtask procedure is that it will return when the process has been started. In other words, it doesn't wait for the task to complete before it exits. This means that the trigger can finish, release the table lock, and let the waiting task create the Web page.

Why is this better than the Microsoft approach? First, we think that this approach is simpler. Second, and most important, the HTML is created as soon as the trigger is done. There isn't the one-minute lag that the other method has.

Opening the Black Box

After learning the nuts and bolts behind the SQLWA, we were anxious to see the stored procedure code that actually generates the HTML code. In order to view it, we decided to run the SQLWA and tell it to create Web pages when the pubs..publishers changed. Then, we reasoned, we would track down the stored procedure from the resulting task. As it turns out, our efforts were foiled. The resulting procedure code was encrypted! UGH!

This fact really got us interested. Why bother encrypting the procedure? In order to solve this riddle, we decided to create our own Web page stored procedure.

Three Cheers for Bulk Copy!

The procedure we are about to show you would not have been possible without the bcp utility. We used it for a wide range of critical things such as pivoting tables and inserting HTML code between columns. Remember back in Chapter 16 how we told you that the capability to run bcp from an xp_cmdshell call was an important tool that you would come to use often? Well, here's a perfect example!

A quick HTML primer

For the most part, we are going to assume that you know nothing about HTML code or how it's used. That's OK, we will bring you up to speed here. HTML stands for *Hypertext Markup Language*. Basically, it is a set of embedded tags that tell a normal Web browser (Netscape, Mosaic, and so forth) how to display text and images.

In general, text is formatted in blocks, which are defined by beginning and ending tags. For example, the begin tag for bold is <B> and the end tag is </B>. So, a valid line of HTML code to print the string "Hello World!" in bold would be

```
<B>Hello World</B>
```

The following is a list of some common tags and their meanings:

HTML Tag	Meaning
<BODY>, </BODY>	Begin/end body section
<CENTER>, </CENTER>	Begin/end centered text
<H1>, </H1>	Heading 1
<H2>, </H2>	Heading 2
<H3>, </H3>	Heading 3
<H4>, </H4>	Heading 4
<H5>, </H5>	Heading 5
<H6>, </H6>	Heading 6
<HR>	Draw a horizontal line
<HTML>, </HTML>	Begin/end HTML section
<P>	Begin new paragraph
<TABLE>, </TABLE>	Begin/end table
<TD>, </TD>	Begin/end table cell
<TR>, </TR>	Begin/end table row

Here's a quick example of some simple HTML. The following code prints a simple table:

```
<HTML>

<HEAD>
<TITLE>My Document</TITLE>
</HEAD>

<BODY>

<HR>
<H1><CENTER>This is my heading</CENTER></H1>
<HR>

<P>
This is an example of a simple table
<P>

<TABLE BORDER="1">
<TR><TD>A</TD><TD>B</TD></TR>
<TR><TD>C</TD><TD>D</TD></TR>
</TABLE>

<P>

</BODY>
</HTML>
```

When you view this code in a browser, it looks like Figure 30-1.

USP_MAKEWEBPAGEWITHTABLE

Now that you have a very basic familiarity with HTML, it's time to learn how to write your own procedure to produce Web documents. First, we show you the procedure we wrote and its syntax. The name of the procedure we wound up writing is usp_makeWebPageWithTable. Its syntax is as follows:

```
usp_makeWebPageWithTable {@sqlQuery = valid_SQL | @preFile =
header_file | @outputfile = final_document | @colheadings =
include_column_headings? | title = table_title }
```

@sqlQuery (required)

This parameter specifies the SQL you want to use to generate the result set data. There are two important restrictions on this item:

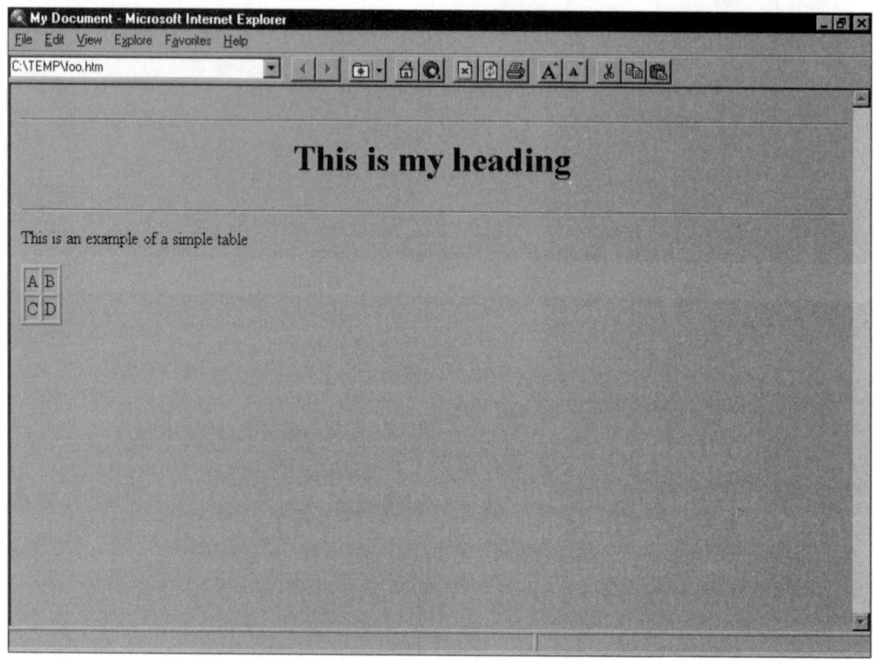

Figure 30-1:
The browser's view of the HTML code.

- The query must be fewer than 256 characters long.
- The SQL must be valid for a CREATE VIEW statement.

For example, the following SQL would yield a one-column table with the full name of each author:

```
Select au_fname + ' ' + au_lname 'Author Full Name'
from pubs..authors
```

We purposefully wrote this procedure with the SET QUOTED_IDENTIFIER option set to On. We did this so that you can use meaningful names for your columns.◀

@prefile (optional)

The parameter holds the name of a valid HTML file that you want to prepend to your final page. For example, let's say that you have a standard header that you like to put on all your Web pages and that the code for it is in the file c:\webroot\header.htm. By setting the @prefile parameter to this string, this header will appear above your data.

@postfile (optional)

This parameter holds the name of a valid HTML file that you want to append to the end of your final page. Suppose that you have a standard footer that you like to put on all your Web pages and that the code for it is in the file c:\webroot\footer.htm. By setting the @prefile parameter to this string, this header will appear after your data.

@outputfile (required)

This variable holds the name of the resulting HTML file you want to create.

@colheadings (optional, defaults to 1)

This parameter specifies whether you want column headings to appear in your final data. The default value of 1 means that column headings will appear.

@title (optional)

This parameter enables you to specify any HTML code that you want to appear directly over the data table. Let's say that you are creating a page that shows all the data from the pubs..authors table and that you want the text "Data From Pubs..Authors" to appear centered directly above it in bold. You pass the following string in for the @title parameter:

```
"<B><CENTER>Data From Pubs..Authors</CENTER></B>"
```

A brief example

This following code produces a simple page that shows the names and book titles for the authors in the pubs database:

```
declare @sqlText varchar(255)

select @sqlText =
    "select au_fname + ' ' + au_lname 'Author Name', title 'Book Title'
    from authors a, titles t, titleauthor ta
    where a.au_id = ta.au_id and
        t.title_id = ta.title_id"

exec tempdb..usp_makeWebPageWithTable
    @sqlQuery = @sqlText,
    @outputfile = 'c:\webroot\results.htm',
    @title = "<H3><CENTER>Author Data</CENTER></H3>"
```

The page looks like the one shown in Figure 30-2.

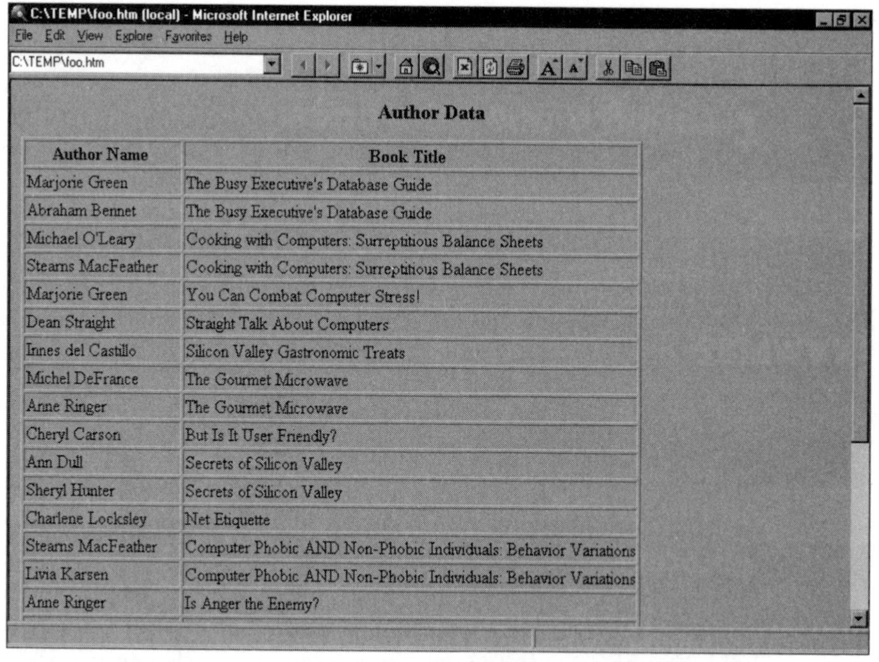

Author Name	Book Title
Marjorie Green	The Busy Executive's Database Guide
Abraham Bennet	The Busy Executive's Database Guide
Michael O'Leary	Cooking with Computers: Surreptitious Balance Sheets
Stearns MacFeather	Cooking with Computers: Surreptitious Balance Sheets
Marjorie Green	You Can Combat Computer Stress!
Dean Straight	Straight Talk About Computers
Innes del Castillo	Silicon Valley Gastronomic Treats
Michel DeFrance	The Gourmet Microwave
Anne Ringer	The Gourmet Microwave
Cheryl Carson	But Is It User Friendly?
Ann Dull	Secrets of Silicon Valley
Sheryl Hunter	Secrets of Silicon Valley
Charlene Locksley	Net Etiquette
Stearns MacFeather	Computer Phobic AND Non-Phobic Individuals: Behavior Variations
Livia Karsen	Computer Phobic AND Non-Phobic Individuals: Behavior Variations
Anne Ringer	Is Anger the Enemy?

Figure 30-2:
The results of the results.htm file.

How it all works

When you get right down to it, the usp_makeWebPageWithTable procedure is actually very simple. Basically, it goes through the following steps:

1. It creates a final temporary table that will contain all the data for the output file.
2. It bulk copies in any header file information you specify.
3. Next, it creates a view from the SQL you supply and bulk copies out the data from the view with the appropriate HTML table tag information.
4. Finally, it bulk copies back in the formatted data, inserts it into the destination table, appends any footer file, and creates the output file.

The complete code listing for this procedure is as follows:

```
create procedure usp_makeWebPageWithTable
    @sqlQuery varchar(255),
    @preFile varchar(255) =NULL,
    @postFile varchar(255) =NULL,
    @outputfile varchar(255),
    @colheadings int = 1,
    @title varchar(255) =NULL as

SET QUOTED_IDENTIFIER ON

-
- This is the table where the final HTML will go.
-

create table tempWeb (webline varchar(255) null)

declare @sTmp varchar(255)

-
- If a header file was specified, bcp it into tempWeb.
-

if @preFile <> NULL
begin
    select @sTmp = 'bcp tempdb..tempWeb in ' + @preFile + ' /c -T'
    exec master..xp_cmdshell @sTmp
    insert into tempWeb values('<P>')
end

-
- If a title was specified, insert it into the final output.
-

if @title <> NULL
```

(continued)

(continued)

```
    insert into tempWeb values('<TT> ' + @title + ' </TT>')

-
- Create a view from the incoming query.
-

execute ('create view vTmp as ' + @sqlQuery)

/*********************************
 This code handles the formatting
of the resulting data set into an
HTML table.
**********************************/

create table tempTable (col1 varchar(255))

-
- If the user wants column headings, create them.
-

if (@colheadings = 1)
begin

    insert into tempTable values ('<TR>')

    insert into tempTable
        select '<TD><CENTER><B> ' + name + ' </B></CENTER></TD>'
        from syscolumns
        where id = object_id('vTmp')
        order by colid


    insert into tempTable values ('</TR>')
end

-
- Use bcp to insert the table HTML code in between the columns
-

select @sTmp = 'bcp tempdb..vTmp out foo.txt -c -t"</TD><TD>" -r"</TD></TR>\t\t" -
T'

exec master..xp_cmdshell @sTmp

select @sTmp = 'bcp tempdb..tempTable in foo.txt /c -r"\t\t" -T'
exec master..xp_cmdshell @sTmp

update tempTable set col1 = '<TR><TD>' + col1 where col1 NOT LIKE '<%'
```

```
-
- Insert the final formatted data into a temp table
- along with a few other need HTML tags.
-

insert into tempWeb values ('<TABLE BORDER = "1">')
insert into tempWeb
    select * from tempTable
insert into tempWeb values ('</TABLE>')

drop table tempTable

/**********************
 End of data / table
processing stage.
**********************/

-
- If a footer file was specified,
- copy it into the final code.
-

if @postFile <> NULL
begin
    insert into tempWeb values('<P>')
    select @sTmp = 'bcp tempdb..tempWeb in ' + @postFile + ' -c -T'
    exec master..xp_cmdshell @sTmp
end

-
- Delete any miscellaneous ending tags.
-

delete from tempWeb where webline = '</BODY>'
delete from tempWeb where webline = '</HTML>'

-
- Append the appropriate end tags
-

insert into tempWeb values ('</BODY>')
insert into tempWeb values ('</HTML>')

-
- Create the final output file and
- drop the rest of the temp objects.
-
```

(continued)

(continued)

```
select @sTmp = "bcp tempdb..tempWeb out " + @outputfile + " -c -T"
exec master..xp_cmdshell @sTmp

drop view vTmp
drop table tempWeb

SET QUOTED_IDENTIFIER OFF

go
```

Who needs the cavalry when you have bcp?

This procedure really demonstrates the amazing versatility of the bcp utility. Consider the section of code where the result data is being placed in an HTML table. We used bcp to insert the appropriate formatting code in between the column data:

```
select @sTmp = 'bcp tempdb..vTmp out foo.txt -c -t"</TD><TD>" -r"</TD></TR>\t\t" -
T'

exec master..xp_cmdshell @sTmp
```

For example, let's say that a row of data was

```
Rensin,Dave,Computer Geek
```

This use of bcp would create the following line:

```
Rensin</TD><TD>Dave</TD><TD>Computer Geek</TD></TR>
```

By issuing a simple UPDATE statement, this code is easily changed to a valid line of HTML:

```
<TR><TD>Rensin</TD><TD>Dave</TD><TD>Computer Geek</TD></TR>
```

We don't believe there is any other way to do this other than to use bcp.

Practical examples and other oddments

This next section goes over a few interesting points about the usp_makeWebPageWithTable procedure.

Multiple tables on one page

Being able to create a Web page with a table of data is nice. Sometimes, however, you will want to create pages that have multiple data sets on them. You can easily do this by chaining together calls to usp_makeWebPageWithTable. Suppose that you want to create a page that holds data from both the authors and titles tables and that you also have standard header and footer pages that you want to attach. You can do this by letting the output from one procedure call be the input for the next procedure call. The following code shows you how to do this:

```
exec tempdb..usp_makeWebPageWithTable
    @sqlQuery = 'select * from authors',
    @preFile = 'c:\webroot\header.htm',
    @outputfile = 'c:\webroot\results.htm',
    @colheadings = 1,
    @title = "<H3><CENTER>Authors Table</CENTER></H3><HR>"

exec tempdb..usp_makeWebPageWithTable
    @sqlQuery = 'select title, notes from titles',
    @preFile = 'c:\webroot\results.htm',
    @postFile = 'c:\webroot\footer.htm',
    @outputfile = 'c:\webroot\results.htm',
    @colheadings = 1,
    @title = "<HR><H3><CENTER>Avilable Books</CENTER></H3><HR>"
```

The important thing here is that the first procedure call creates a file named results.htm, which the second procedure uses as its header information. By chaining subsequent calls together, you can create a page of any size with any number of data sets.

Installing usp_makeWebPageWithTable

To install the usp_makeWebPageWithTable procedure correctly, you have to install it in the model database. At this point, you may be wondering why you need to install it in the model database if all the references in the code are to tempdb. The answer is that each time you stop and start your server, the objects in tempdb are dropped. In order for the procedure to be available after a server restart, it must be installed in model. This is because when a server restarts, it makes an exact copy of model in tempdb. In other words, you will install the procedure in model, but execute it from tempdb.

The actual output

The last thing we want to show you in this chapter is the actual HTML code that this procedure generates. Let's say that you execute the following code:

```
exec tempdb..usp_makeWebPageWithTable
    @sqlQuery = 'SELECT au_lname FROM pubs..authors',
    @outputfile = 'c:\webroot\results.htm',
    @colheadings = 1,
    @title = "<H3><CENTER>Authors Table</CENTER></H3><HR>"
```

The resulting file, results.htm, contains the following lines of HTML information:

```
<TT> <H3><CENTER>Authors Table</CENTER></H3><HR> </TT>
<TABLE BORDER = "1">
<TR>
<TD><CENTER><B> au_lname </B></CENTER></TD>
</TR>
<TR><TD>White</TD></TR>
<TR><TD>Green</TD></TR>
<TR><TD>Carson</TD></TR>
<TR><TD>O'Leary</TD></TR>
<TR><TD>Straight</TD></TR>
<TR><TD>Smith</TD></TR>
<TR><TD>Bennet</TD></TR>
<TR><TD>Dull</TD></TR>
<TR><TD>Gringlesby</TD></TR>
<TR><TD>Locksley</TD></TR>
<TR><TD>Greene</TD></TR>
<TR><TD>Blotchet-Halls</TD></TR>
<TR><TD>Yokomoto</TD></TR>
<TR><TD>del Castillo</TD></TR>
<TR><TD>DeFrance</TD></TR>
<TR><TD>Stringer</TD></TR>
<TR><TD>MacFeather</TD></TR>
<TR><TD>Karsen</TD></TR>
<TR><TD>Panteley</TD></TR>
<TR><TD>Hunter</TD></TR>
<TR><TD>McBadden</TD></TR>
<TR><TD>Ringer</TD></TR>
<TR><TD>Ringer</TD></TR>
</TABLE>
</BODY>
</HTML>
```

As you can see, we've taken a lot of liberties with how we formatted the HTML code. It's not very pleasant to the human eye. Fortunately, the browsers we tested didn't have any problems.

Conclusion

It seems that just as the world was finally becoming accustomed to client-server computing, the Internet (more specifically, the World Wide Web) has turned the entire notion on its ear. As corporate intranets become more popular for group interaction, the demands on you as a DBA will increase. A good interface between your SQL Server databases and your company's intranet will become a critical tool in your arsenal of data distribution and maintenance.

Summary

Whoever coined the phrase "Change is the only constant" sure knew what he was talking about. Every time the computing world gets comfortable with a new paradigm, some group of enterprising folks come up with a new way to do things better. Just as people became comfortable with mainframe computing, client-server came along and shook things up. Now, our notions of what constitutes an enterprise database solution are being assaulted from all corners by this relative newcomer known as "the Web."

In this chapter, you took your first steps to using this new phenomenon to your advantage. You learned the basics of the server push model and how it can affect your ability to distribute data throughout an enterprise. In the next chapter, you learn the more complicated *client pull* model and how it can empower your users without draining your resources.

Review Questions

Q: What are the three procedures that the SQL Web Assistant uses?

A: The SQL Web Assistant uses three stored procedures to create dynamic HTML documents: sp_makewebtask, sp_runwebtask, and sp_dropwebtask.

Q: How would you create a one-time page ?

A: Let's say that you want to create a one-time page that will run now and create the file c:\webroot\webwizard.htm. Let's also say that the query will retrieve all the records from pubs..authors. The following is the SQL command:

```
exec sp_makewebtask
    @outputfile = 'c:\webroot\webwizard.htm',
    @query = 'select * from authors'
```

Q: How do you run an operation from a trigger that would normally cause a deadlock?

A: Put the offending code in a task and use sp_runtask. Because this procedure returns when the task starts, the trigger finishes and then the task finishes.

Q: Why did we write usp_makeWebTaskWithTable ?

A: We didn't like having to create dynamic tasks and encrypted stored procedures for the otherwise-simple task of generating an HTML page.

Chapter

The Client Pull Model

31

In the last chapter, you learned one of the two models for publishing data on the Internet: the push model. In this chapter, you learn the other: the pull model. As you might guess, the client pull model of data publishing is where the client application determines what data the server publishes. In truth, it's probably the more difficult model to implement and is also the most in demand.

What's in This Chapter

In the last chapter, we showed you how to enable your server to publish its data dynamically. In this chapter, we will show you how to enable you server to respond to specific client requests. Specifically, you will learn

- How to set your HTML pages to access dynamic data
- The structure and purpose of .IDC files
- The structure and purpose of .HTX files
- How to put it all together

What You Need and How to Get It

To use the information in this chapter effectively, you need the following items:

- A copy of SQL Server. You had better have this already!
- A copy of **The Microsoft Internet Information Server (MS IIS).**
- A copy of **Microsoft Front Page or some other HTML editor.** (A standard ASCII editor will do fine.)

About the tools

The Microsoft Internet Information Server is a full-featured Web server that runs under Windows NT. As we sit and write this book, you can get a copy of this program for free from the Microsoft Web site (http://www.microsoft.com).

The Microsoft Internet Information Server

As we said before, the MS IIS is a full-featured Web server that enables you to publish your own content on the World Wide Web. Because this is not a text on the MS IIS, we assume the following:

- You have gotten and successfully installed the MS IIS on a server.
- You have the authority to create files on that same server.

The Microsoft Internet Database Connector

At the heart of this chapter is a thing called the Microsoft Internet Database Connector (IDC). The IDC is a .DLL that enables the IIS to talk to a SQL Server machine through the ODBC. Actually, this is done with a single file named httpodbc.dll. If you have this file, you have the IDC.

The basic model

The basic model looks like this:

1. Your Web browser requests information from the IIS.
2. The IIS, in turn, sends the appropriate request to the IDC.
3. The IDC then gets the data from the SQL Server machine and passes it back to the IIS.
4. You see the requested data or any errors that may have occurred.

Creating the ODBC DSN

Before you can connect your database and your Web server, you must create an ODBC system Data Source Name (DSN) profile. This profile identifies how you will connect to your data.

Let's assume that you want to connect to the pubs database on the server DOGBERT and that you want to name the profile Connect to Dogbert. This section walks you through the process.

The first thing to remember is that this DSN must be created on the machine that is running the IIS. This is *very* important!

To create the DSN, go to the control panel on the IIS machine and select the ODBC32 applet. The screen shown in Figure 31-1 appears.

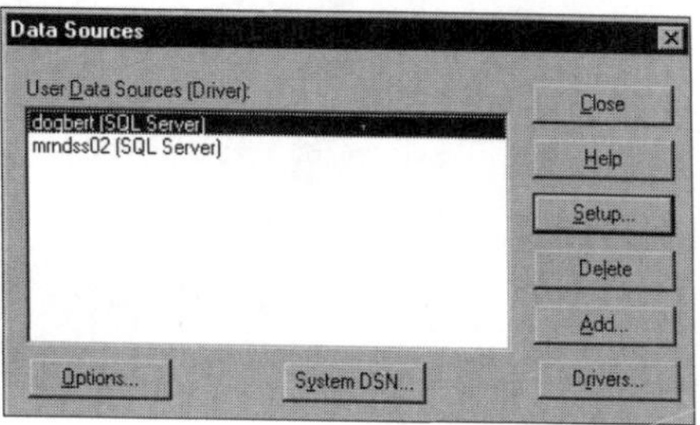

Figure 31-1:
Click the System DSN button.

There is no need for you to fill in any of the information here, so click the System DSN button and select Add. Figure 31-2 appears.

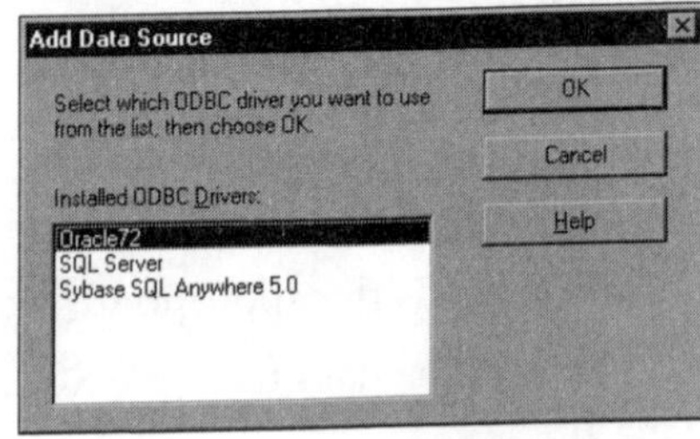

Figure 31-2:
Select what type of driver to use.

This is a list of all the installed 32-bit ODBC drivers on this machine. Choose the one that fits the server to which you are connecting. Because this example will connect you to a SQL Server machine, select the item named SQL Server and click OK. When the window appears, click the Options button. You will see the screen depicted in Figure 31-3.

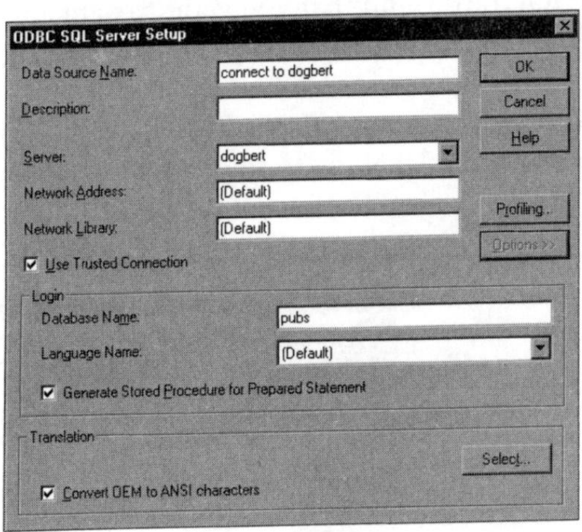

Figure 31-3:
Complete your DSN options here.

In this window, fill out the necessary information. In this example, the Data Source Name is Connect to Dogbert, the Server is DOGBERT, and the Database Name is pubs. If your machines can connect via a trusted connection, then you will want to check the Use Trusted Connection box.

When you are finished, click OK and negotiate your way out of the open screens.

Each With a Small Part

As we mentioned earlier, there are really three basic pieces to getting the IDC to work: an HTML page, an IDC file, and an HTX file. Don't worry; we'll cover the .HTX file in a second.

Basically, it works like this. Your users enter the needed data on the HTML page and then click some action item (a link, button, and so on). The page then launches the IDC file. The IDC file contains information about what DSN to connect with, what SQL to execute, and what HTX file to use for output. The HTX file is basically an HTML file that has a few extra things in it to tell the IIS where to the insert the returned data.

The HTML page

When you create a form that accepts input, you can then define that form to have an action. In other words, you can define your form to *do* something with that input. Typically, the form will launch a Common Gateway Interface (CGI) program.

Note

The Common Gateway Interface (CGI) architecture is a standard way for HTML forms to do some action. In this chapter, the CGI scripts are your .IDC files.◀

The <FORM> tag

In the HTML language, you can specify part of a page as a *form*. A form is just a designation that means that the specific section will do something at some special time. For example, you can have a page run a CGI script when the user clicks a submit button.

The <FORM> tag begins a form area and the </FORM> tag ends it. To specify which action a form should take, use the following syntax:

```
<FORM action = "<some action>" method="POST|GET">
```

In this case, <some action> will be something like mypage.idc. The choices between POST and GET simply refer to how the CGI script is to read the information you pass to it. All .IDC files must be POSTed. An example will help clear things up.

Let's say that you have a simple page named simple.htm and you want that page to launch the CGI script simple.idc. All you have to do is add the following line to your HTML code:

```
<form action = "simple.idc" method = "POST">
```

It's not important now to know what simple.idc does, just that it does something with your data.

Entering your data with <textarea> and <input>

In order to send information to a CGI script, your users first have to enter it. In this section, we briefly go over some code to do this.

The first thing you probably will want to define is a region on your page where your users can type some information. Although you can do this a number of ways, our favorite is with the <textarea> tag. This tag specifies a user input region and has the basic syntax of:

```
<textarea name="somename" rows=## cols=##>
```

For example, if you want to define a region or input named userinput that is 100 characters wide and 4 rows tall, you enter the following code:

```
<textarea name="userinput" rows=4 cols=100>
```

Finally, you need to add a control that signals your form to perform its action. Again, there are a bunch of ways to do this. The most common, though, is through the use of a submit button. This control type is simply a command button that executes the named action of the form on which it sits. Its most common syntax is this:

```
<input type=submit name="somename" value="somecaptiontext">
```

For example, let's say you want a button on your screen that says `GO!` and is named goButton. The code for that is the following:

```
<input type=submit name="goButton" value="GO!">
```

An easy example

Let's say that you want to create a form that accepts a SQL command from the user and then passes it to a CGI script. An example of that HTML code is as follows:

```
<html>
<body>
<form action="simple.idc" method="POST">

<center>
```

```
Enter SQL query to process<p>

<textarea name="userinput" rows=4 cols=100></textarea><p>

<input type=submit name="doSQL" value="Run This SQL!">

</center>

</form>
</body>
</html>
```

The resulting page looks like the one shown in Figure 31-4.

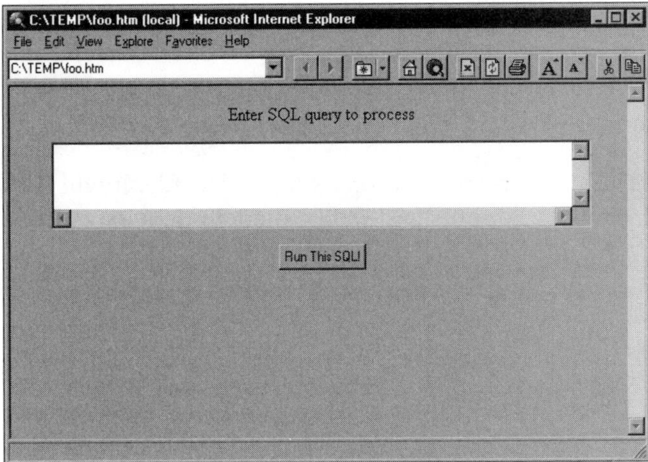

Figure 31-4:
A browser-eye view of your page.

Again, if you are using an authoring tool such as Frontpage, you never have to worry about this code because the tool takes care of it for you. For the purposes of this chapter, though, we thought we at least ought to go over it.

The IDC file

The Internet Database Connector (IDC) file is the real workhorse of this setup. It is where you define the actions to be taken with your user input.

The very basics of an IDC file

There are only three required fields in an IDC file. They are as follows:

Field	*Description*
Datasource	The name that corresponds to the System DSN name you created earlier by using the ODBC Administrator or the tool provided with the samples.
Template	The name of the HTML extension file that formats the data returned from this query. By convention, these files use the extension .htx.
SQLStatement	The SQL statement to execute. The SQL statement can contain parameter values, which must be enclosed with percent characters (%) from the client. The SQLStatement can occupy multiple lines in the Internet Database Connector file. Following the SQLStatement field, each subsequent line beginning with a plus sign (+) is considered part of the SQLStatement field.

A simple IDC file

Here's an example of a very simple IDC file. It will simply get all the records from pubs..authors and return them to the template file named simple.htx. Again, it is not important right now to understand how the HTX file works, just that it displays your records:

```
Datasource: Web SQL
Template: simple.htx
SQLStatement:
+select * from pubs..authors
```

Passing parameters from your form

As you can probably guess, an IDC file as simple as the one in the previous example has only marginal use. It doesn't really allow for dynamic data and, therefore, is not very helpful in the client pull model. Thankfully, you can also pass parameters to an IDC file. In fact, you don't really have to do anything particularly special to accomplish this.

Remember in the last section when you created an input control named userinput? As it turns out, you can reference the contents of that control in your IDC file. All you have to do is use the text %userinput%. When the IDC sees the name of a valid data control surrounded by percent signs (%), it goes back to the calling HTML page and gets the data in those controls. This means that you can make your IDC files a lot more dynamic by referencing user inputted data, for example:

```
Datasource: Web SQL
Template: simple.htx
SQLStatement:
+select * from pubs..authors where au_lname = %userinput%
```

With the simple addition of the %userinput% parameter, your users can query the authors table for all authors with a certain last name.

Tip

There are some limits to what you can use in an IDC file. Most importantly, you cannot use a percent sign (%) anywhere in your SQL statement because the MS IDC will attempt to interpret it as the beginning of a parameter name.◀

Optional elements of an IDC file

As you may have suspected, there are a bunch of optional things you can have in an IDC file as well. Here are some of them.

Field	***Description***
Expires	The number of seconds to wait before refreshing a cached output page. If a subsequent request is identical, the cached page will be returned without ever accessing the database. The Expires field is useful when you want to force a re-query of the database after a certain period of time. Httpodbc.dll does not cache output pages. It caches them only when the Expires field is used.
MaxFieldSize	The maximum buffer space allocated by httpodbc.dll per field. Any characters beyond this will be truncated. The parameter applies only to fields returned from the database that exceed 8192 bytes. The default value is 8192 bytes.
MaxRecords	The maximum number of records that httpodbc.dll will return from any one query. The MaxRecords value is not set by default, meaning that a query can return up to 4 billion records. Set this value to limit the records returned.
Password	The password that corresponds to the username. If the password is null, this field can be left out.
RequiredParameters	The parameter names, if any, that httpodbc.dll will ensure are passed from the client; otherwise, it will return an error. Parameter names are separated by a comma.
Username	A valid user name for the data source name supplied in the Datasource field. *Note:* If you use Microsoft SQL Server with the integrated security option, the username and password fields in the .idc file are ignored.

If you are not using a trusted connection for your DSN, you *must* specify the Username and Password fields.◀

The HTX file

An HTX file is a normal HTML file that the IDC scans for certain important tags. These tags tell it where to insert the data returned from the query in the IDC file.

<%column name%>

Assume for the moment that you have an IDC file that has the following SQL statement:

```
select au_lname from pubs..authors
```

Obviously, you know that you are going to get the column au_lname back as your result set. To reference a specific column name in an HTX file, simply enclose it in brackets (<>) and percent signs (%), for example:

```
Author last name is <%au_lname%>
```

We know what you're thinking. No, you do not specifically have to name your columns in the SQL in order to reference them in your HTX file. For example, if you have the following SQL statement in your IDC

```
select * from pubs..authors
```

you can still reference <%au_lname%> in your HTX file because au_lname is a column that is going to be returned.

<%idc.parameters>

You can also reference any parameters passed to your IDC file from your HTX file. In the previous section, you built an HTML file that had a control named userinput. Because all controls are passed as parameters to their IDC file, you can reference the control userinput via the convention <%idc.userinput%>. This literally means "the parameter named userinput that was passed to the calling IDC file."

<%begindetail%><%enddetail%>

Another set of very important tags is <%begindetail%> and <%enddetail%>. These tags define the detail band of your output page. Any HTML code or text that occurs between these tags will be repeated for each row of output, for example:

```
<%begindetail%>
Author last name = <%au_lname%>
<%enddetail%>
```

This code will produce output similar to the following:

```
Author last name = Fedorchek
Author last name = Rensin
Author last name = Smith
```

Example: Transact SQL online help

In this first example, we build a Web page with which users can get online Transact-SQL (TSQL) help. This page will contain a list box of a large number of SQL commands. When users click the Show Help button, they will see a page with the reference help for the selected command.

How it works

The crux of this system is in the use of the sp_helpsql stored procedure. This procedure returns reference help for a given TSQL command.

The HTML file

The following is the code for the HTML file named sqlhelp.htm. It is followed by a screen capture of what the page looks like when browsed (see Figure 31-5).

```
<html>
<body background="clouds.gif">
<form action="sqlhelp.idc" method="POST">
<center>
<h1>Transact SQL On-Line Help</h1>
<p>
```

(continued)

(continued)

```
<select name="sqlcommand" size=1>
<option>ALTER DATABASE</option>
<option>ALTER TABLE</option>
<option>BEGIN DISTRIBUTED TRANSACTION</option>
<option>BEGIN TRANSACTION</option>
<option>BEGIN...END</option>
<option>CASE</option>
<option>CHECKPOINT</option>
<option>CLOSE</option>
<option>COMMENTS</option>
<option>COMMIT TRANSACTION</option>
<option>CONTROL OF FLOW</option>
<option>CREATE DATABASE</option>
<option>CREATE DEFAULT</option>
<option>CREATE INDEX</option>
<option>CREATE PROCEDURE</option>
<option>CREATE RULE</option>
<option>CREATE SCHEMA</option>
<option>CREATE TABLE</option>
<option>CREATE TRIGGER</option>
<option>CREATE VIEW</option>
<option>CURSORS</option>
<option>DATATYPES</option>
<option>DBCC</option>
<option>DEALLOCATE</option>
<option>DECLARE CURSOR</option>
<option>DECLARE</option>
<option>DELETE</option>
<option>DISK INIT</option>
<option>DISK MIRROR</option>
<option>DISK REFIT</option>
<option>DISK REINIT</option>
<option>DISK REMIRROR</option>
<option>DISK RESIZE</option>
<option>DISK UNMIRROR</option>
<option>DROP DATABASE</option>
<option>DROP DEFAULT</option>
<option>DROP INDEX</option>
<option>DROP PROCEDURE</option>
<option>DROP RULE</option>
<option>DROP TABLE</option>
<option>DROP TRIGGER</option>
<option>DROP VIEW</option>
<option>DUMP</option>
```

```
<option>EXECUTE</option>
<option>EXPRESSION</option>
<option>FETCH</option>
<option>FUNCTIONS</option>
<option>GOTO...LABEL</option>
<option>GRANT</option>
<option>IF...ELSE</option>
<option>INSERT</option>
<option>KILL</option>
<option>LOAD</option>
<option>OPEN</option>
<option>OPERATORS</option>
<option>PRINT</option>
<option>RAISERROR</option>
<option>READTEXT</option>
<option>RECONFIGURE</option>
<option>RETURN</option>
<option>REVOKE</option>
<option>ROLLBACK TRANSACTION</option>
<option>SAVE TRANSACTION</option>
<option>SELECT</option>
<option>SET</option>
<option>SETUSER</option>
<option>SHUTDOWN</option>
<option>TRANSACTIONS</option>
<option>TRUNCATE TABLE</option>
<option>UNION</option>
<option>UPDATE STATISTICS</option>
<option>UPDATE</option>
<option>UPDATETEXT</option>
<option>USE</option>
<option>VARIABLES</option>
<option>WAITFOR</option>
<option>WHILE</option>
<option>WILDCARDS</option>
<option>WRITETEXT</option>
</select>

<p>
<input type=submit name="doSQL" value="Show Help">

</center>
</form>
</body>
</html>
```

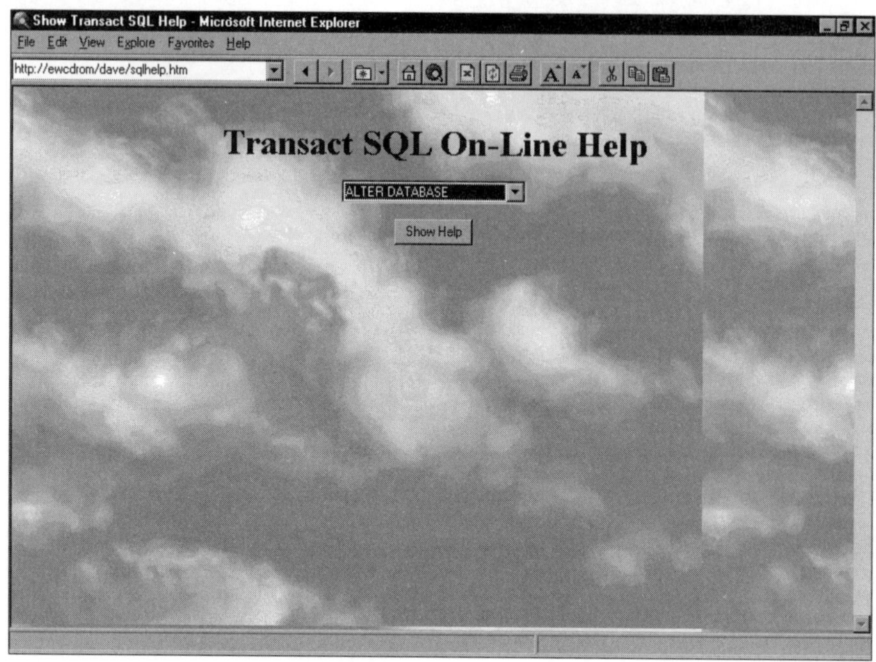

Figure 31-5:
How the SQL help page looks in a browser.

The IDC file

The most important part of this example is the IDC file. It's not very complicated, yet it is quite powerful. Here's the entire code listing:

```
Datasource: Web SQL
Template: sqlhelp.htx
SQLStatement:
+master..sp_helpsql '%sqlcommand%'
```

All this code does is pass the value contained in the sqlcommand list box control. We told you it was simple!

The HTX file

Finally, here's the code for the HTX file (sqlhelp.htx):

```
<HTML>
<body background="clouds.gif">
```

```
<H1><%idc.sqlcommand%></H1>

<%begindetail%>
<P>
<%Transact-SQL Syntax Help%>
<%enddetail%>

</BODY>
</HTML>
```

There are only a couple of things that need to be pointed out here.

First, notice how we make use of the <%idc.parameter%> syntax to reference the value of the sqlcommand control.

Second, notice the name of the field we are referencing. It's *Transact-SQL Syntax Help*. The reason we had to use that is because that's the name of the column that sp_helpsql returns. This is interesting because it shows that you can reference column names that would normally require a quoted identifier. In our opinion, this is pretty handy!

Truly Dynamic Data: Ad-Hoc Queries

You didn't think we'd end this chapter without talking about how to code ad-hoc queries, did you? Actually, this section fits very nicely with the material from the last chapter.

How to

We have seen a number of ways proposed to enable users to enter ad-hoc queries from a Web page. All of them involved one IDC creating another IDC file which, in turn, loads the data. We think that this is unnecessary and wasteful.

Cross-Reference

Our solution is simply this: have your IDC file call the usp_makeWebPageWithTable procedure outlined in the preceding chapter.◀

The HTML file

The basic HTML file in this example will enable a user to enter a title for the query and then the SQL query itself. The code for this and a picture of what it looks like follow (see Figure 31-6):

```
<html>
<body>
<form action="adhoc.idc" method="POST">

<p>
Enter Query Title:
<p>
<input type=text size=75 maxlength=256 name="qtitle" value="Query Results">
<p>
Enter SQL query:
<p>
(Note: This SQL must be valid for a CREATE VIEW statement.)
<p>
<textarea name="sqlcommand" rows=4 cols=50></textarea>
<p>
<input type=submit name="doSQL" value="Run This SQL!">

</form>
</body>
</html>
```

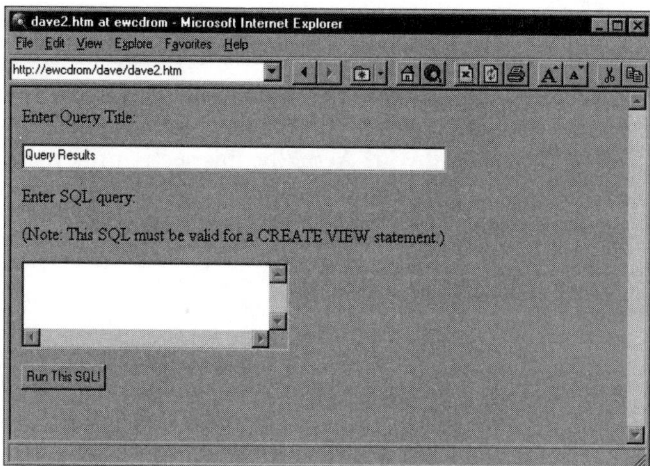

Figure 31-6:
The ad-hoc query screen.

Once again, this code is very simple. The only thing you have to keep track of are the names of the two user input controls, which are the following:

- **qtitle.** This is the text field into which the user enters the query title text.
- **sqlcommand.** This is the multiline edit control into which the user enters the ad hoc query.

The IDC file

The IDC file for this page has one interesting feature: it references a page that doesn't exist yet. You'll understand why in a moment. First, here's the code:

```
Datasource: Web SQL
Template: adhoc.htm
SQLStatement:
+tempdb..usp_makeWebPageWithTable @sqlquery = '%sqlcommand%',
+@outputfile = 'c:\inetsrv\wwwroot\dave\adhoc.htm',
+@title = '%qtitle%'
```

The template file referenced here is adhoc.htm. This is the file being created by usp_makeWebPageWithTable. Because HTX files are simply normal HTML files with some extra tags, we can get away with this.

Conclusion

The client pull model for data publishing is a very fascinating topic with many practical applications. Because this is not a text on HTML authoring or Web publishing, we didn't cover 99 percent of what's possible with these techniques. We will leave that up to you. The important thing to remember is that the combination of the Internet Information Server and SQL Server gives you a powerful set of tools to publish your data for millions of people.

Summary

Back in the early days of the Web, most sites were content with the server push model of publishing. As time went on and the client needs grew, this paradigm gave way to the current model of client pull.

In this chapter, you learned how to integrate your SQL Server data with the Microsoft Internet Information Server in order to publish your data on the Web or an intranet.

Do not, however, think that this material is, by any means, a comprehensive reference on the subject. To the contrary, we specifically chose a very narrow scope in order to illustrate our points more fully. There are, in fact, many different CGI implementations out there, and we suggest that you pick up a couple of books dedicated to the subject.

Review Questions

Q: What's the basic control flow in this particular client pull model?

A: The base HTML document calls the IDC file, which, in turn, accesses the database and returns rows to the template (HTX) file.

Q: What are the minimum items required in an IDC file?

A: The required fields are the following:

Field	***Description***
Datasource	The name that corresponds to the System DSN name you created earlier by using the ODBC Administrator or the tool provided with the samples.
Template	The name of the HTML extension file that formats the data returned from this query. By convention, these files use the extension .htx.
SQLStatement	The SQL statement to execute. The SQL statement can contain parameter values, which must be enclosed with percent characters (%) from the client. The SQLStatement can occupy multiple lines in the Internet Database Connector file. Following the SQLStatement field, each subsequent line beginning with a plus sign (+) is considered part of the SQLStatement field.

Q: Should you configure a standard ODBC profile, a system DSN, or both for MS IDC access?

A: Only the system DSN is needed.

Q: Did the authors have a lot of fun writing this chapter?

A: You betcha!

Schema-Independent Web Interfaces for RDBMS

The paper in this appendix presents a set of theories for creating platform-independent interfaces between the Web and any RDBMS. It is intended to show that the data-access tools do not have to be proprietary in nature, and they can be generalized to any data schema. Although some of the specific concepts mentioned may be foreign to you, we think that you will gain a better understanding of the issues involved in linking the Web to your data. We would like to extend our deepest thanks to Ron Lee and Sergey Petrov for allowing us to include their paper in this text. We hope you enjoy it as much as we did.

In order to preserve the intellectual integrity of this work, we have not altered this paper. You will read it *exactly* as it was written. Consequently, you may notice certain formatting choices that differ with the other text in this book. This is intentional.◀

A Dynamic, Schema-Independent Web Interface for a Relational Database

R.W. Lee and S. Petrov
Computer Science & Mathematics Division, Intelligent Systems Section
Oak Ridge National Laboratory

Abstract

Supporting use of the World Wide Web as a platform for application interface development, a general method for building dynamic HTML using data from external servers was derived, and an object-based development paradigm for Web interfaces was established. Further, the specific case of interfacing a relational database management system is addressed with a framework for schema-independent interfaces to databases. As an example, these techniques were applied to the National Sourcing Database.

Keywords: database navigation, dynamic HTML, object-based development, relational database, schema-independence

1. Introduction

The next step in the progression of the World Wide Web is its use as a platform for application interface development. In this mode, client browsers handle graphics user interface (GUI) presentation and interaction, and common gateway interface (CGI) processes on the server generate HTML forms and pages [1]. If this HTML depends upon results of computation or data manipulation, it must be generated dynamically.

Systematic techniques and methods for generating *dynamic HTML* in a robust and repeatable manner are needed. Further, Web interface applications must be managed and controlled like any development effort. Software engineering goals (modifiability, efficiency, reliability, and understandability) must be met by applying principles such as abstraction, information hiding, modularity, and localization [2].

Section 2 describes how these problems are addressed. First is a general method for building dynamic HTML. Second is an object-based development paradigm in which HTML forms and pages are encapsulated with methods operating on them. Issues fundamental to common gateway interface (CGI) processes interacting with external servers are also discussed.

Database applications introduce a further problem: interfaces typically "hard-code" relationships between classes of objects (i.e., items of information). Consequently, the addition or removal of classes or their relationships critically impacts the entire application.

In Section 3, the problem is addressed with a meta-data approach for making database interfaces schema-independent. Not only are data object contents retrieved at run time, classes and their relationships are determined on-the-fly as well.

Section 4 presents the application of the methods and techniques in developing the National Sourcing Database (NSDB). NSDB is an integration of five separately maintained data sources with information on textile industry manufacturers and their products. Its goal is to make sourcing and supply information available to users in the textile industry.

2. Web Application Interfaces

Web application interfaces are implemented with CGI processes generating dynamic HTML. In order to make development of such interfaces more efficient and productive, a general method for building dynamic HTML and a paradigm for system development are needed.

2.1 Building Dynamic HTML

2.1.1 Server Data Flow

In Web interfaces, all data manipulation and computation occurs at the server. Data flow through the Web server for a CGI process is well known. Depicted in Figure 1, it begins with a connection request from the client browser, often the result of an HTML form submission. Identified in the uniform resource locator (URL) [3] is the CGI process to be spawned by the server to handle the connection. The CGI process parses the query string, which may contain form input values.

At this point, data flow is dependent upon the application. Other processes may be spawned to fulfill computational and data manipulation tasks, and other servers may be accessed. Some process, possibly the form handler itself, must send the response to the client browser. The response is typically HTML but could be of any legal MIME type and subtype [4,5].

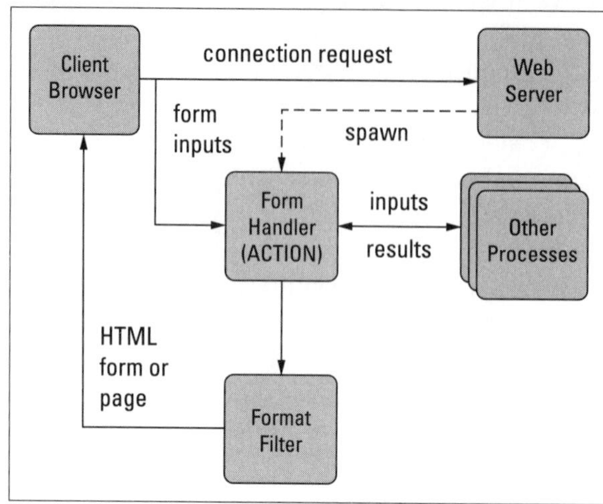

Figure 1:
Web server data flow.

2.1.2 Algorithm

From the data flow, a simple yet practical algorithm for producing dynamic HTML emerges. It consists of four processing steps:

1. Parse the query string for form inputs, if there are any.
2. Using form inputs, perform data manipulation and computation to produce results.
3. Use results to generate HTML.
4. Package and return results to the client.

In the last step, a proper HTTP response, simple or full, must be built as specified in the standard [6]. With most Web servers, the mechanics of sending the response to the client are as simple as writing to standard output, since the CGI process is spawned with the accepted socket duplicated as standard input and output. The Bourne shell script below, accessible as, builds a proper full response:

```
#!/bin/sh -a

cat <<END
HTTP/1.0 200 OK
Content-type: text/html
```

```
<head>
<title>Example1</title>
</head>
<body>
<h2>Example 1</h2>
<hr>
<p>You are <strong>$REMOTE_HOST ($REMOTE_ADDR)</strong>,
and I am <strong>`hostname`.epm.ornl.gov</strong>.
<p>Right now, it is <em>`date`</em>
</body>
END
```

2.1.3 HTML Templates

When generating an HTML response to the client which depends upon some processing result, there are basically two alternatives. First, the CGI process or one of its child processes can build the HTML from scratch. Second, templates containing HTML extended with variable names can be processed to replace variables with results from external computation. Generally, templates are more efficient if most of the HTML to be generated is not process dependent.

For example, suppose the '@' character at the beginning of a word identifies it as a variable. Substitution is easily accomplished using `perl` or the UNIX `sed` utility. The following illustrates the simple concept:

```
<select name="Class" size="5">@SelectList</select>

        —— after substitution ——

<select name="Class" size="5"><option>Apparel Product Categories
<option>Apparel Product
<option>Companies
</select>
```

2.1.4 CGI Process Issues

There are implementation issues common to all applications of dynamic HTML:

- development tools for CGI process implementation
- CGI process interactions
- interaction with other servers in general
- specifics of interaction with a relational database management system (RDBMS)

Many considerations go into the choice of development tools, including platform considerations, requirements volatility, and the need for development structure. With UNIX as the development platform, `perl` was chosen for its power, flexibility, and run-time binding at the cost of strong semantic error checking.

CGI interactions are the foundation for dynamic HTML applications. In many systems, such as database interfaces, interaction with an external server can be considered "kernel" functionality. Thus, code supporting such interactions should be easily shared and invoked by all CGI processes comprising the application. Functions can be implemented as subroutines in a `perl` package installed in the run-time library directory.

2.1.4.1 Obtaining Input Values

Every CGI process must parse the contents of the query string or data block and unescape spaces and control characters, as per the URL specification [3]. Values for form inputs passed by name are referenced in CGI processes. Similarly, when invoking processes expecting query strings, the information to be passed must be escaped. In the implementation, subroutines (`CgiEscape()` and `CgiUnescape()`) accept strings as parameters and return escaped and unescaped versions, respectively.

In addition, the `perl` package contains a `ParseInput()` subroutine, which expects an entire query string or data block. It splits the passed string into name-value pairs delimited with the ampersand ('&') character and processes each pair in turn. The name and value are obtained by splitting the pair on the equals ('=') delimiter, and both sides are unescaped with `CgiUnescape()`. Values are stored in two ways:

- As scalar variables in the top level scope
- In an associative array returned as the value of the subroutine

Two special cases must be handled. First, names can appear more than once in a query string (e.g., multiple select lists). For both scalar variables and associative arrays, subsequent values are appended with a delimiter so they can be split later into an array. Second, when inputs of type image are clicked on an HTML form, the resulting query string contains entries for the position of the mouse click. The names are built by appending `.x` and `.y` to the input item's name. Dots cannot appear in `perl` variable names, so `.x` and `.y` are substituted with _x and _y, respectively, in scalar variable names.

2.1.4.2 Interaction with Other Servers

Here the term "server" refers to any other process with which a CGI process must communicate in order to process its input data. The requirements for this communication are very specific to the server itself. However, there are two basic mechanisms for accomplishing the interaction: a call level interface (CLI) library and a command-line client utility. The nature of the implementation environment plays a key role in the choice between mechanisms. Command interpreters, like `perl` may be difficult or impossible to extend with calls to a 3GL library, and implementors may be forced to build a command utility if one doesn't exist. Data can be exchanged between processes using pipes, temporary files, or more sophisticated means (e.g., shared memory). On the other hand, function calls and/or class instantiations may be more productive in a 3GL environment.

2.1.4.3 Interaction with an RDBMS

There are issues specific to RDBMS's. Whereas CLI's for various RDBMS's can differ greatly, command line utilities differ mostly in input and output format. For example, Oracle, Informix, and Sybase utilities `sqlplus`, `isql`, and `isql`, respectively, all take SQL as input and produce results as rows of columns. Thus, use of command line utilities increases portability across RDBMS's. If portability is not an issue, RDBMS-specific tools, such as Web/Genera, may prove optimal [7]. The implementation uses Sybase `isql` to access a database under Microsoft SQL Server.

Query text is passed to a command utility via standard input or a file, and results are returned with some formatting via standard output or a result file. The output includes a line with column names and lines containing column values for each result row. If results are parsed into columns, values in a row can be associated with the column name by position.

Queries either return a list of object names or detail about one or more objects. In the first case, we need only filter out the column names and any other erroneous lines in the output. For details, we extract the column name line and all result row lines. The perl package includes filter subroutines, `ListIsql()` and `CaptureIsql()`, to handle the two cases, respectively, and return an array of lines. A third subroutine, `BuildValues()`, is passed the array returned by `CaptureIsql()` and returns values in an associative array indexed by row number and column name.

2.2 Development Paradigm

Given a model for data flow through the server and a simple algorithm for generating dynamic HTML, a development paradigm must be chosen. Considering the mapping between data and problem space preferable to a functional mapping, as described by Booch, an object-based approach is chosen [2]. There are two classes from which objects are derived:

- form: contains one or more HTML forms
- page: contains no HTML forms

The form class contains a single attribute, template HTML, and methods for building the form and responding to submissions. Much simpler is the page class, having only a build method. An object is instantiated when the attributes and methods are implemented. (Since methods are specific to objects, they are virtual in C++ terminology).

With an implementation environment consisting of `perl` and the UNIX (Bourne shell) command line, one instantiates forms by building template HTML files and `perl` method scripts. For example, form objects are implemented with the following files:

- Form.html.h: template HTML file
- Form.Build: build method
- Form.DoPost: method for handling "post" submissions

Page objects have only the `Build` method. Of course, derived classes may add methods as needed.

Adherence to this paradigm of encapsulation of data with methods for all form and page objects is one way in which engineering principles are applied. Further, the system is built on the form and object abstractions which comprise the problem space. Information hiding occurs in that other objects which must interact with a particular object via its methods need know none of its implementation details. Functions to be performed have been modularized into loosely coupled, highly cohesive object methods. All the code associated with an object is localized in its method(s). Finally, there is uniformity in the implementation of each object and page. This results in a modifiable, efficient, robust, and understandable system.

The method and paradigm described above apply to Web interfaces in general. For the special case of interfaces to databases, the impact on the interface of database design is critical. The problem is addressed in Section 3.

3. Making the Interface Independent of the Database

Like any software, a Web interface to a relational database is a compromise between universality and complexity (i.e., to build and to use). For example, the GSDB interface offers only a choice between retrieving data by an accession number or via a SQL query, the latter requiring knowledge of SQL and the very complicated structure of GSDB for ad hoc queries [8]. This reference doesn't represent the field and is chosen here just because it is not in [9] or in [10]. A universal interface approach implemented in [7] is based on a tree-like representation of objects with cross references made on the top of a relational Sybase database. The representation is similar to that in [11] and is indeed a very convenient and flexible way of structuring data. It is popular now not only among biologists but is used in other areas as well. In order to use Web/Genera, at least one user must create a special schema file [7]. The problem addressed here is logically simpler. Special conditions, described below, are imposed on the database, making it compatible with the schema-independent interface. Allowed object structures are much simpler than those in the ACEDB scheme. As a trade-off, a user can know nothing about a database structure to browse it.

Dynamic form generation gives an alternative to this approach: an interface can be made as a forms generator accessing a database server (in this case, Sybase) and browsing a relational database storing any kind of data. In order to make it work, database schema should satisfy certain conditions allowing navigation of all databases using meta-data stored in the database and available to the form generator. Here these conditions and a logic of navigation are described with examples.

3.1 Database Schema Requirements

As described above, the interface depends rather on the set of stored procedures providing access to objects than on a particular database schema. Still, it complies with a definite "browsing logic" which is supposed to be supported by these stored procedures. In order to be able to generate these procedures in the regular (ideally, automatic) way, we need to choose a model of data semantics representation. A very simple model is described below.

We assume that the database stores objects belonging to classes **C1,...,Ck** and relationships between them. In order to browse it with the schema-independent interface, we need to represent these classes and relationships in a particular way.

Let T be the set of database tables. We suppose that tables and classes are related as follows:

> For each class **Ci**, there is a unique table considered as *a master table* for the class. One of attributes of this table is a *unique id* for class objects.
>
> Each table in the database stores *master* and/or *detail* information for at least one class.
>
> No table can be a master table for several classes.

Thus, classes **C1,...,Ck** define a cover of the set **T**. Each element of the cover contains just one special element (*master table*), and all special elements are different. The relationships between classes are represented as in the Entity Relationship Model by common detail tables (though schema satisfying all requirements above do not necessarily comply with ER model definition).

In the database implementation, these links are usual references from a foreign to unique primary key. The referential integrity is supported by the set of triggers performing standard actions for every key in a table:

Primary Key Actions

insert	No action
update	Update the value in all possible detail tables
delete	Delete all detail rows

Foreign Key Actions

insert	Only if referencing row exists; add the table name to the '_links_' field in the referencing table if it is not there already
update	Can be changed only by update of the referencing table
delete	Strike out detail table name from '_links_' field in the referencing table if there are no other details for the same referencing row

Referential integrity is supported by the set of triggers generated from permanent templates for each table. Templates are compatible with Sybase and MS SQL Server SQL.

A database schema corresponds to a graph **G = <T, F>** where nodes from **T** correspond to tables, the set of edges **F** corresponds to functional links between tables: *primary key <== foreign key*, directed from master to detail. By the definition, the graph has no (directed) cycles. Classes **C1,...,Ck** correspond to the subset **TM** of **T**. The set **TM** contains all nodes with no entering edges, but not each node in **TM** has this property: a table can serve as a master table for one class and as a detail table for another.

The graph **G** is connected. If this is not true, there is no logical reason to put all data in one database.

Each class **Ci** corresponds to a connected subgraph of G, as shown in Figure 2.

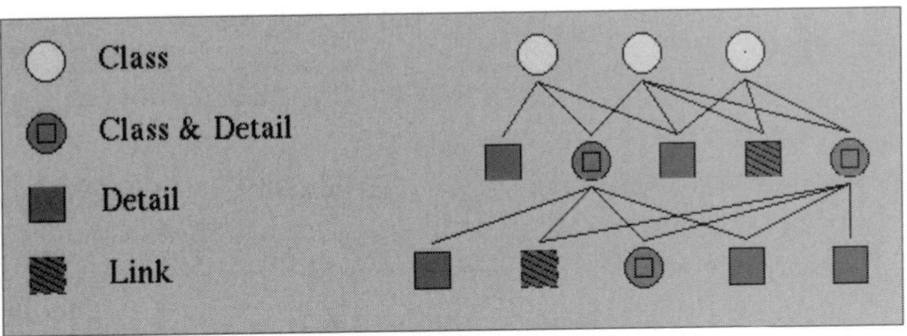

Figure 2:
Database Navigation Graph.

The same results can be achieved if instead of the set of tables above we consider a set of views defined by pre-written stored procedures. The set should satisfy exactly the same requirements.

An example of a database built according to the assumptions above, described in Section 4, may be considered evidence that the requirements above still allow enough design flexibility.

For navigational purposes, the graph **G** is represented in a database as meta-data tables. Their structure, described below, is independent of the subject area of the target database. We omit here some implementation-dependent details like naming convention.

3.2 Meta-Data Representation

Two tables are added to the database to contain meta-data: `MetaClass` and `MetaRelation`. They are created with the following SQL:

```
create table MetaClass
(
name                    varchar(32)     not null,
description             varchar(64)     not null,
list_proc               varchar(64)     not null,
detail_proc             varchar(64)     not null
)

create table MetaRelation
(
```

(continued)

(continued)

```
from_class          varchar(32)     not null,
to_class            varchar(32)     not null,
description         varchar(64)     not null,
list_proc           varchar(64)     null,
detail_proc         varchar(64)     not null
)
```

Each `MetaClass` row represents a class of information which can be used as a starting point for navigating the database. Classes of information need not correspond to actual tables or even views in the database, for the stored procedures which list object names and retrieve object details hide the specifics of the database. Whereas the `list_proc` is passed a string used for matching object names, the `detail_proc` expects a full object name, for which it returns detail information rows.

`MetaRelation` rows represent a relationship between two logical classes. The reference class is `from_class`, and the related class is `to_class`. List and detail procedures function as with `MetaClass` but take different parameters. For `list_proc`, the single parameter is the name of an object in `from_class`. All matching object names in the `to_class` are listed. Parameters for `detail_proc` are names of objects in `from_class` and `to_class`, respectively.

In addition, each referencing table contains the field `_links_`. For every row, `_links_` holds names of detail tables referenced by the row id. The field is used to minimize the number of joins and to avoid global identification of objects throughout the database.

3.3 Navigation

For a user, interaction with a database (session) consists of a set of searches. Each search starts with an object class and step by step reveals details about a chosen list of objects. These details are data stored in *detail* tables and data on related objects. At each step, the user controls lists of objects and chooses data displayed or reported.

The interface "unfolds" the graph **G** of a database (for example, ones shown on the Figure 2 or Figure 3) into the set of browsing traces. Each trace is a tree composed from the set of paths from the same root corresponding to one of the nodes from **TM**. A tree reveals all possible details on object(s) from the class corresponding to its root. The interface supports only steps down a tree path. The "back" option of any WWW browser allows a user to return to a node and explore another branch of the tree.

At any step, the interface holds a limited amount of information on previous searches and may be considered as an automata browsing the graph

G. The graph is an external object for the automata, and, therefore, the interface doesn't depend on a particular database schema. At any state, the interface retrieves information about its current position on the graph from meta-tables described above and displays it to the user.

The state of the interface is determined by (1) the list of current objects and (2) a referenced object. After the user chooses the "direction" (i.e, next table), a query is sent to the database server. The query is a request to select data from the chosen table by ids of objects in the list and by the id of the referenced object. If the referenced object is *NULL* or its id is not present in the table, it is not used. If the chosen table is the *master table* of another class, the highlighted item of the current list becomes the referenced object and its id is used to query the table. Therefore, for a user, data on chosen objects of this class look like additional information on the root object.

A step is a jump "down" or a jump "up" on the graph G (see Figure 3). A jump down reveals more details on the chosen list of objects, and a jump up finds objects related to the one highlighted on the previous step. A user has the option to nullify the referenced object and start another tree.

3.4 Report and Display Formatting

A mechanism for representing the format for data display is needed. We want it to be general, applicable to any results, and easily defined. In order to avoid a complicated report definition, we group attributes into sections. These groupings are conveniently specified in SQL column aliases. Detail procedures alias each returned column with a canonical `"group.attribute label"` form. (The alias format depends upon rules imposed by the specific SQL processor. SQL Server and Sybase accept this format.) Regardless of the order of the columns in the results, attribute groups are easily determined. Listed below are portions of SQL a detail stored procedure. Again, stored procedures hide all database details from the interface.

```
select
  "General.Company Name" = co.name,
  "General.Company Id" = co.vendor_id,
  "General.Last Update" = co.last_update,
  "General.Address 1" = co.address1,
  "General.Address 2" = co.address2,
  "General.City" = co.city,
  "General.State" = co.state,
  "General.Zip" = co.zip,
  "General.Country" = co.country,
  "General.County" = co.county,
```

(continued)

(continued)

```
"General.Phone" = co.phone,
"General.Fax" = co.fax,
"General.President" = co.president,
"General.Date Founded" = co.date_founded,
...
"Contact.Name" = co.data_contact,
...
"Parent Company.Name" = co.parent_company,
...
"Profile.Annual Sales" = co.annual_sales,
...
"Production.Product Id" = ap.product_id,
...
```

Section 4 presents an overview of an example application of the techniques described in Sections 2 and 3.

4. National Sourcing Database and Interface Prototype

NSDB is an integration of data from various sources on textile industry manufacturers and suppliers and their products. NSDB's design embraces all source databases, with complete redefinition of objects for some of them. Several source databases are still under design, so the NSDB schema was made as flexible as possible to make incorporation of future changes local. A simple semantic model fits well with the relatively simple subject area. Currently, NSDB holds about 100 Megabytes of data.

Usual reasons lead to the choice of the Web as the NSDB interface (e.g., easy on-line access, no client software, etc). Because the NSDB itself is under permanent modification, it was necessary to construct a framework making the interface independent of a particular database.

As usual, implementation of the database and the interface is a compromise between simple and clear logic and software and hardware limitations. The most important reason for the compromise is performance. For example, much better performance can be reached with precompiled stored procedures than with SQL generated on-the-fly. We consider the case when stored procedures can be automatically (or semi-automatically) generated for any database from a set of templates as a reasonable compromise between "true schema independence" and performance.

4.1. National Sourcing Database

The NSDB schema is shown Figure 3. It consists of *master* and *detail* tables as described above. For display purposes, we distinguish more table types:

:master-detail:: a table which serves as a master for one class and as detail for others (e.g., `Produce`).

detail-link:: a table which contains no data except ids from several object classes and is used to represent a relationship between them (e.g., `CompanyAddress`).

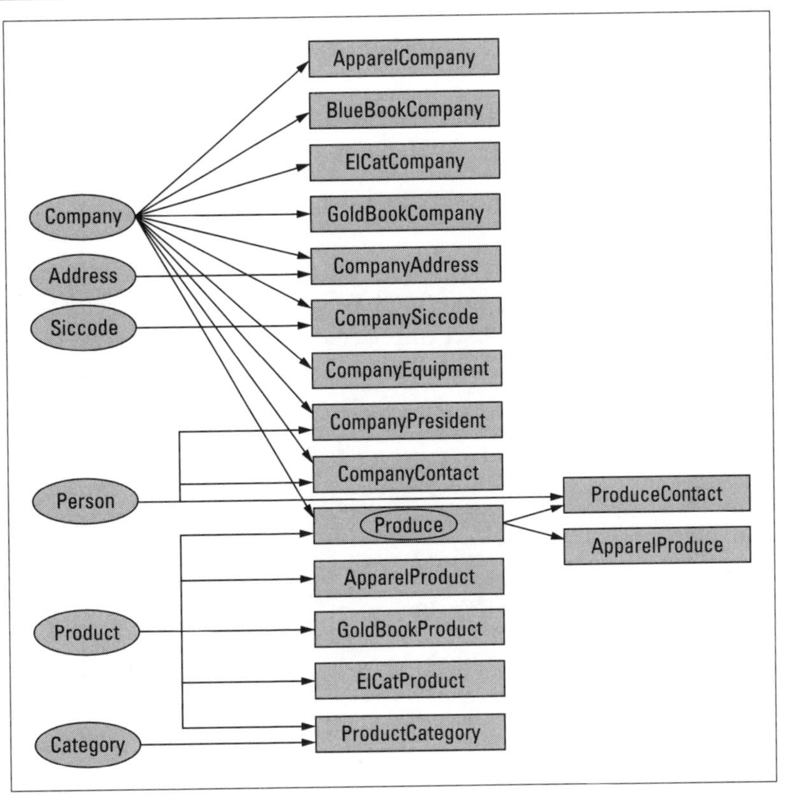

Figure 3:
NSDB Schema.

The database uses a mixed categorization of data: some of them are categorized by type and some by origination. This is the result of integration which is still under development. In general, a master table stores features common for all types and sources, and each particular type requires its own detail table. Detail tables are also used for classification of objects, which makes displayed lists shorter and more easily handled. The similarity between the graphs of Figures 2 and 3 is clearly evident.

4.2 The Interface

Using the method for generation of dynamic HTML, a development paradigm, and framework for schema-independent database navigation described above, a prototype NSDB interface was developed. A brief overview of the interface is presented to demonstrate its simplicity.

Four form and page objects comprise it:

- starting points form
- object list form
- relation list form
- detail report

Figure 4 illustrates the possible navigation paths through the interface objects. The navigation tree has leaves only when the database contains no related objects for a set of selected objects. All the data and information necessary to navigate the database is obtained dynamically.

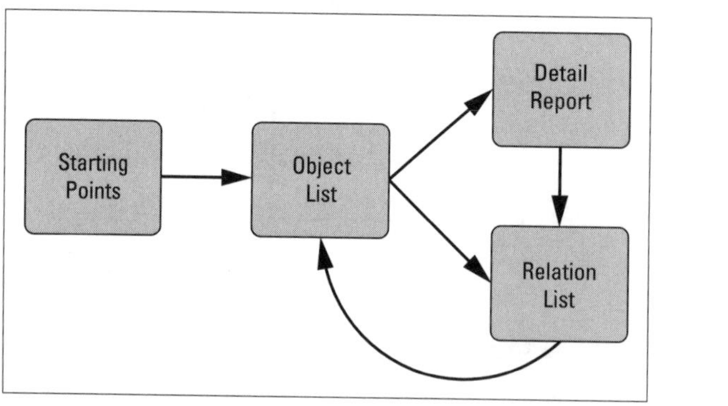

Figure 4:
Interface navigation paths.

4.2.1 Form Methods

Each form object has `Build` and `DoPost` methods. `StartingPoints.Build` queries `MetaClass` to get a list of class descriptions, which are presented to the user for selection, but the build methods for Object List and Relation

List are passed a set of objects to display. `DoPost` methods query `MetaRelation` or execute a list or detail stored procedure and invoke the build method for the next object. Figure 5 shows the Object List form.

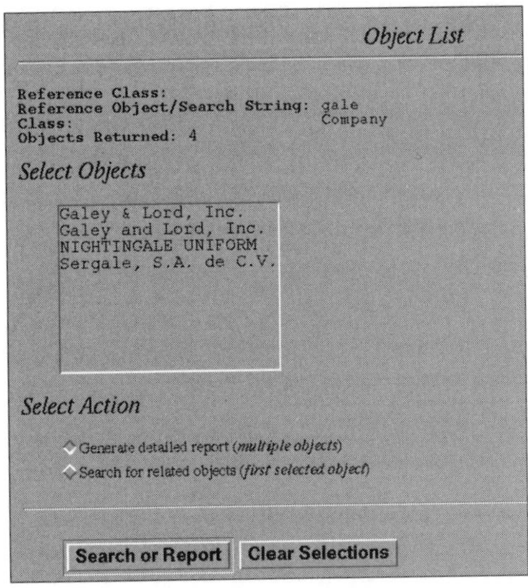

Figure 5:
Object list form.

4.2.2 Detail Reports

The Detail Report build method is passed the set of selected object names. It builds a hierarchical report by iterating over the objects then each row or record retrieved for an object. Records are displayed by the sections or attribute groups specified in the column aliases. Figure 6 illustrates a section in a report, which can be compared to the SQL listed above.

```
[Contact] [General] [Production] [Profile] [Parent Company] [Record Top]

Company Name: HICE SEWING
  Company Id: A161
 Last Update: 19940630
   Address 1: 14630 SECTION LINE ROAD
   Address 2:
        City: ELKMONT
       State: AL
         Zip: 35620-
     Country:
      County: LIMESTONE
       Phone: 205-232-0140
         Fax: 232-0140
   President: MARCHEL HICE
Date Founded: 1989
```

Figure 6:
Report page section.

Within the report, each object begins with a header, as shown in Figure 7. A hyperlinked button, labeled "Related Information", references a URL with a query string specifying the object name and class. The CGI process named in the URL is a special report method which invokes the Relation List form build method. In this way, database navigation can proceed from a detail report.

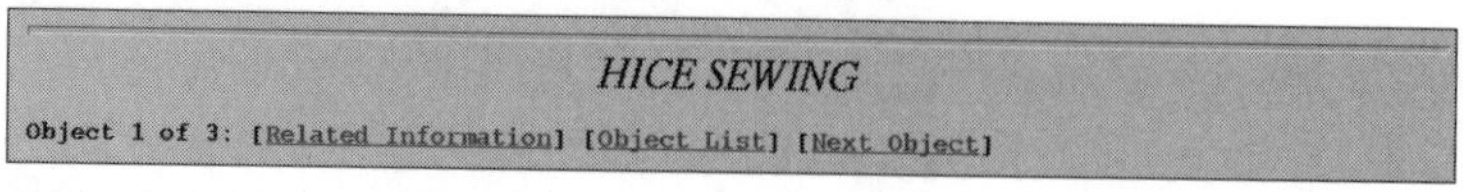

HICE SEWING

Object 1 of 3: [Related Information] [Object List] [Next Object]

Figure 7:
Report object header.

Heretofore, the development and implementation methods have received all the focus for the interface. Much work is needed to enhance its usability and improve its aesthetic appeal.

5. Conclusions

Approximately 1300 lines of `perl` source, including comments, were used to implement the interface and library package. This demonstrates the effectiveness of the method for building dynamic HTML and the compactness of the object-based development paradigm.

Interface performance of course depends upon the speed of Internet connection. However, the additional meta-data queries imposed by the schema-independent approach on a 100-Megabyte database do not adversely affect performance. With an Ethernet connection at the client node, HTML forms are loaded within a few seconds.

The system will continue to be enhanced to meet changing requirements and idealistic goals. However, current copies of the HTML templates and `perl` method scripts and library packages are available from ftp://arthur.emp.ornl.gov/pub/nsdb.

References

1. "CGI: Common Gateway Interface." http://hoohoo.ncsa.vivc.edu/cgi/intro.html.
2. Booch, G., "Object Oriented Design With Applications." Benjamin/Cummings, California, 1991.

3. Berners-Lee, T., L. Masinter, M. McCahill, "Uniform Resource Locators (URL)." RFC 1738, Internet Engineering Task Force, December 20, 1994.

4. Borenstein, N., N. Freed, "MIME (Multipurpose Internet Mail Extensions) Part One: Mechanisms for Specifying and Describing the Format of Internet Message Bodies." RFC 1521, Internet Engineering Task Force, September 23, 1993.

5. Moore, K., "MIME (Multipurpose Internet Mail Extensions) Part Two: Message Header Extensions for Non-ASCII Text." RFC 1522, Internet Engineering Task Force, September 23, 1993.

6. Berners-Lee, T., R.T. Fielding, H. Frystyk Nielsen, "Hypertext Transfer Protocol." Internet Engineering Task Force Working Draft, March 8, 1995.

7. "About Web/Genera." WWW page, http://gdbdoc.gdb.org/letovsky/genera/genera.html.

8. "GSDB: Home Page." WWW page, http://www.ncgr.org/gsdb/.

9. "Web-Database Gateways." WWW page, http://gdbdoc.gdb.org/letovsky/genera/dbgw.tml.

10. "Overview - OracleGate." WWW page, http://www.w3.org/hypertext/WWW/RDBGate/Overview.html.

11. "ACDEDB Documentation." WWW page, http://probe.nalusda.gov:8000/acedocs/index.html.

GLOSSARY

alert

A specified response to a SQL Server error. Alerts enable the system administrator to specify in advance responses to specific events.

alias

A database user name that is mapped to more than one SQL Server login. The primary use of aliases is to allow several SQL Server logins all to assume the identity of the database owner within one database. A secondary use is to let several users assume the identity of a given object owner.

ANSI

American National Standards Institute.

ANSI Standard Join

The SQL Commands CROSS JOIN, FULL OUTER JOIN, INNER JOIN, JOIN, LEFT OUTER JOIN, and RIGHT OUTER JOIN for joining tables in a query. Prior to SQL Server 6.5, the only way to join tables was to include the join criteria in the WHERE clause. The operators *= and =* allowed SQL Server to provide the functionality of all but the FULL OUTER JOIN. Now SQL Server supports both, but in the future, SQL Server may support only ANSI Standard Joins.

article
The basic unit of replication. An article is defined for a specific table.

batch
A string of SQL statements separated by the GO command. Some commands, such as CREATE TRIGGER, must be the first command in a batch.

Cartesian products
A join of two tables where there are no restrictions on the join. This is implemented with a CROSS JOIN in SQL Server 6.5. Every row in the first table is paired with every row in the second table, so the number of rows in the Cartesian product is the product of the number of rows in the individual tables.

cascading delete
Deleting rows in foreign key tables when you delete a row in a primary key table. This must be implemented with triggers in SQL Server. The ANSI-92 standard specifies SQL commands for cascading deletes, but SQL Server does not support those commands.

clustered index
An index that specifies the storage order of a table. A table can have only one clustered index.

database device
An operating system file that holds database data. SQL Server uses disk space in fixed chunks created by the system administrator. Many databases can reside on one device, and one database can span many devices.

database owner
A SQL Server login assigned to *uid* 1 within a database. The database owner has full privileges inside the database. There can be only one owner of a database. By default, the owner of each database is the creator, unless the system administrator changes the owner with sp_changedbowner. Within the database the database owner is recognized by the user name dbo. Other logins can be allowed to act as the database owner by aliasing them to the dbo.

deadlock
The stalemate that occurs when two processes have each locked on a resource while each is trying to acquire a lock on the other's resource. SQL Server detects this situation and kills one process so that the other can go forward.

Declarative Referential Integrity (DRI)

The SQL Server capability to check the integrity of data based on constraints that are part of table definitions. This was new in SQL Server 6.0; before that, referential integrity was enforced with triggers.

device

See *database device* or *dump device*.

drop

Destroy a SQL Server object. The word *drop* is used in database parlance to differentiate it from the word delete, which means to remove all data while leaving the structure intact.

dump device

A place for storing backups, which may be either a tape or an operating system file.

error log

The file to which SQL Server writes all error information. You can view this file from the SQL Enterprise Manager or from a text editor.

Extended Stored Procedures

An interface to Dynamic Link Libraries (DLL) from within SQL Server. Extended Stored Procedures give Transact-SQL access to functions outside of normal SQL scope, such as local e-mail or registry editing.

foreign key

A constraint defined on a table, which specifies that a set of columns in the table must draw its values from the primary key of another table. A foreign key is enforced on all DELETE, INSERT, and UPDATE commands unless temporarily suspended.

format file

A text file used by the BCP program to determine the input/output format for columns. The format file specifies information such as column order, storage type, prefix length, storage length, and delimiter. BCP enables you to create a format file interactively if you do not have one prepared.

group

A collection of SQL Server users used for administering privileges. Groups are defined within a database. Every user is a member of the group public; you can't remove users from public. Users can also be a member of one other group. You can grant and revoke privileges from groups, which spares you from having to grant privileges user by user.

guest

A special user that can be added to a database. When added to a database, guest does not appear in sysusers. If a user attempts to access a database, SQL Server looks for a match in sysusers. If a match exists, the user may access the database. If not, the user is denied access to the database unless the database has the guest user account.

identity property

A property of a numeric or integer column that instructs SQL Server to generate values automatically for the column. A table can have only one identity column. The table owner specifies a start and increment value for the identity. By default, a user cannot insert values for the identity column, but the user may override this feature. Because a user can insert values for the identity, SQL Server can't guarantee that the identity column will be unique. You can guarantee this with a primary key or unique constraint.

index

A set of pointers to database pages and rows that are ordered by a set of key values. Indexes can tremendously speed up access to tables for certain queries.

integrated security

A login validation method in which SQL Server uses trusted connections to allow or disallow access to SQL Server. To access SQL Server, a user must log into a Windows NT domain over a trusted connection. When the user attempts to access a SQL Server, the login and password string are ignored; the user is only granted access if the system administrator sets up access with the SQL Security Manager. It is not necessary to have individual logins for each SQL Server user under integrated security.

lock

A restriction on access to data in tables. Locks allow SQL Server to prevent two users from updating the same information at the same time and to prevent one user from seeing data while another user is changing the data.

login

A unique 30-character identifier of a SQL Server user. Logins must be unique within a SQL Server. Users' logins may or may not be the same as their Windows NT logins. The first character of a login must be a letter or the symbols # or _.

mixed security

A login validation method that combines integrated and standard security. When the login is blank or identical to the network login, SQL Server will use integrated security if a trusted connection exists. Otherwise, the login method is standard.

NULL

The absence of a value. When a column contains a null, it is not blank and it is not zero. NULL indicates that the data is either missing or inapplicable for this row. Columns in the primary key cannot allow NULLs. Foreign key columns can contain NULLs; the foreign key does not apply when the column is null. NULLs produce some bizzare behavior in search clauses because an expression involving NULL is always false. For example, if @test = null, then

```
WHERE column1 = @test
```

is always false, even when column1 is null. Even more confusing,

```
WHERE column1 <> @test
```

is always false, too. You can find a null value by explicitly writing the word **NULL**, as in the following:

```
WHERE column1 = null
```

object

One of several database components. Objects include constraints (check, default, foreign key, primary key, and unique), rules, stored procedures, tables, triggers, and views. Object definitions are stored in sysobjects.

page

The smallest unit of storage in SQL Server that is read from the disk into memory as a contiguous block. A page in SQL Server is always 2K. Data for tables is stored on data pages, which form a doubly linked list.

primary key

A constraint defined on a table, which specifies a set of columns that uniquely identify each row. SQL Server automatically creates a unique index to enforce a primary key. In the relational model, a primary key must also have a the property that no subset of the primary key columns is still a primary key.

publication

A publication is an administrative group of articles. A server can subscribe to an entire publication at once, rather than having to subscribe one article at a time.

quoted identifiers

Names for objects that can include all characters, such as spaces, colons, and so on. By specifying SET QUOTED_IDENTIFIER ON, you can use object names of this type.

recovery

The rolling back of incomplete transactions when a server restarts. SQL Server writes all transactions to the log and records when they are complete. If there is an unexpected shutdown of SQL Server (such as from a power failure), incomplete transactions may be in the log.

replication

An SQL Server process for maintaining loose consistency between two SQL Servers. Replication can be either snapshot (transferring a complete replacement of a table) or log-based (transferring transactions from the log).

security mode

The method SQL Server uses to validate login requests. The security mode is either integrated, mixed, or standard.

standard security

A login validation method in which SQL Server grants access to logins independent of the network. Each user must have a valid SQL Server login and password.

stored procedure

A set of precompiled SQL statements. Good stored procedure use is an integral part of three-tiered application design: it allows encoding business logic on the server instead of in the client application. Stored procedures run more quickly than dynamic SQL because they are precompiled.

table

A database object that stores data in rows and columns. A table is actual physical storage in the database, in contrast to a view. The number of columns in a table is fixed, unless the table owner uses ALTER TABLE to add columns. The number of rows varies.

task

A scheduled command that SQL Server will execute. A task command can be up to 255 characters of Transact-SQL. Because a task can call a stored procedure, there is almost no limit to what tasks can do. Tasks can be scheduled to run one time only, at scheduled times, on alerts, or at start-up.

trace flags

Parameters for controlling SQL Server behavior. Trace flags are turned on and off with the DBCC command. They usually control some kind of non-ANSI Standard behavior or trigger additional output a user would not normally want. Trace flags can be set for individual connections or an entire server.

Transact-SQL

Microsoft's particular brand of SQL. Though roughly compatible with the ANSI-92 standard for SQL, many ANSI-92 commands are not available in SQL Server. On the other hand, there is much in Transact-SQL that extends the ANSI standard.

trigger

A special stored procedure, defined for a specific table, that fires when a change is made to the table. There are at most three triggers for a table, one each for DELETE, INSERT, and UPDATE. Triggers can roll back the change to a table, so they are most useful in implementing custom business logic.

trusted connection

An authenticated connection between a client and a server. Only specific network protocols support trusted connections. Named Pipes and multiprotocols do; TCP/IP does not.

user

A login within a database. SQL Server logins must be explicitly added to databases with sp_adduser; otherwise, they cannot access the database unless the database has the guest user. Within a database, a user is recognized by his or her user name, which may or may not be the same as the login name.

view

A virtual table. A view is created with the CREATE VIEW command and consists of a SELECT statement without COMPUTE, ORDER BY, or UNION. A view behaves very much like a table. Views have rows and columns and can be referenced in SQL, just as a table can. Views cannot always be updated, however, and views do not correspond to physical storage in the database.

wildcard

A special character used with the LIKE keyword. The symbol _ denotes any single character, and the symbol % denotes any string of zero or more characters. The symbols [] delimit a list or range of characters. For example, LIKE '[list]%' means the first letter must be *l*, *i*, *s*, or *t*.

INDEX

B

C

D

(continued)

(continued)

N

O

P

Q

R

(continued)

T

(continued)

IDG BOOKS WORLDWIDE, INC. END-USER LICENSE AGREEMENT

Read This. You should carefully read these terms and conditions before opening the software packet(s) included with this book ("Book"). This is a license agreement ("Agreement") between you and IDG Books Worldwide, Inc. ("IDGB"). By opening the accompanying software packet(s), you acknowledge that you have read and accept the following terms and conditions. If you do not agree and do not want to be bound by such terms and conditions, promptly return the Book and the unopened software packet(s) to the place you obtained them for a full refund.

1. License Grant. IDGB grants to you (either an individual or entity) a nonexclusive license to use one copy of the enclosed software program(s) (collectively, the "Software") solely for your own personal or business purposes on a single computer (whether a standard computer or a workstation component of a multiuser network). The Software is in use on a computer when it is loaded into temporary memory (i.e., RAM) or installed into permanent memory (e.g., hard disk, CD-ROM, or other storage device). IDGB reserves all rights not expressly granted herein.

2. Ownership. IDGB is the owner of all right, title, and interest, including copyright, in and to the compilation of the Software recorded on the disk(s)/CD-ROM. Copyright to the individual programs on the disk(s)/CD-ROM is owned by the author or other authorized copyright owner of each program. Ownership of the Software and all proprietary rights relating thereto remain with IDGB and its licensors.

3. Restrictions on Use and Transfer.

   (a) You may only (i) make one copy of the Software for backup or archival purposes or (ii) transfer the Software to a single hard disk, provided that you keep the original for backup or archival purposes. You may not (i) rent or lease the Software, (ii) copy or reproduce the Software through a LAN or other network system or through any computer subscriber system or bulletin-board system, or (iii) modify, adapt, or create derivative works based on the Software.

   (b) You may not reverse engineer, decompile, or disassemble the Software. You may transfer the Software and user documentation on a permanent basis, provided that the transferee agrees to accept the terms and conditions of this Agreement and you retain no copies. If the Software is an update or has been updated, any transfer must include the most recent update and all prior versions.

4. Restrictions on Use of Individual Programs. You must follow the individual requirements and restrictions detailed for each individual program on the last page of this Book. These limitations are contained in the individual license agreements recorded on the disk(s)/CD-ROM. These restrictions may include a requirement that after using the program for the period of time specified in its text, the user must pay a registration fee or discontinue use. By opening the Software packet(s), you will be agreeing to abide by the licenses and restrictions for these individual programs. None of the material on this disk(s) or listed in this Book may ever be distributed, in original or modified form, for commercial purposes.

5. Limited Warranty.

   (a) IDGB warrants that the Software and disk(s)/CD-ROM are free from defects in materials and workmanship under normal use for a period of sixty (60) days from the date of purchase of this Book. If IDGB receives notification within the warranty period of defects in materials or workmanship, IDGB will replace the defective disk(s)/CD-ROM.

   (b) IDGB AND THE AUTHORS OF THE BOOK DISCLAIM ALL OTHER WARRANTIES, EXPRESS OR IMPLIED, INCLUDING WITHOUT LIMITATION IMPLIED WARRANTIES OF MERCHANTABILITY AND FITNESS FOR A PARTICULAR PURPOSE, WITH RESPECT TO THE SOFTWARE, THE PROGRAMS, THE SOURCE CODE CONTAINED THEREIN, AND/OR THE TECHNIQUES DESCRIBED IN THIS BOOK. IDGB DOES NOT WARRANT THAT THE FUNCTIONS CONTAINED IN THE SOFTWARE WILL MEET YOUR REQUIREMENTS OR THAT THE OPERATION OF THE SOFTWARE WILL BE ERROR FREE.

   (c) This limited warranty gives you specific legal rights, and you may have other rights which vary from jurisdiction to jurisdiction.

6. Remedies.

(a) IDGB's entire liability and your exclusive remedy for defects in materials and workmanship shall be limited to replacement of the Software, which may be returned to IDGB with a copy of your receipt at the following address: Disk Fulfillment Department, Attn: SQL Server 6.5 SECRETS, IDG Books Worldwide, Inc., 7260 Shadeland Station, Suite 100, Indianapolis, IN 46256, or call 1-800-762-2974. Please allow 3-4 weeks for delivery. This Limited Warranty is void if failure of the Software has resulted from accident, abuse, or misapplication. Any replacement Software will be warranted for the remainder of the original warranty period or thirty (30) days, whichever is longer.

(b) In no event shall IDGB or the author be liable for any damages whatsoever (including without limitation damages for loss of business profits, business interruption, loss of business information, or any other pecuniary loss) arising out of the use of or inability to use the Book or the Software, even if IDGB has been advised of the possibility of such damages.

(c) Because some jurisdictions do not allow the exclusion or limitation of liability for consequential or incidental damages, the above limitation or exclusion may not apply to you.

7. **U.S. Government Restricted Rights.** Use, duplication, or disclosure of the Software by the U.S. Government is subject to restrictions stated in paragraph (c) (1) (ii) of the Rights in Technical Data and Computer Software clause of DFARS 252.227-7013, and in subparagraphs (a) through (d) of the Commercial Computer—Restricted Rights clause at FAR 52.227-19, and in similar clauses in the NASA FAR supplement, when applicable.

8. General. This Agreement constitutes the entire understanding of the parties, and revokes and supersedes all prior agreements, oral or written, between them and may not be modified or amended except in a writing signed by both parties hereto which specifically refers to this Agreement. This Agreement shall take precedence over any other documents that may be in conflict herewith. If any one or more provisions contained in this Agreement are held by any court or tribunal to be invalid, illegal or otherwise unenforceable, each and every other provision shall remain in full force and effect.

THE COMPANION CD-ROM

The companion CD-ROM to this book contains several things that we think you will find useful.

SQL!

Throughout this book, we have shown you a lot of SQL. You will be able to find most of it here. All you need to do is go to the `\SQL\`*`<chapter_no>`* directory. For example, if you want to find a certain stored procedure from Chapter 30, it will be in `\SQL\30`.

WEB FORMS EXPRESS

Web Forms Express (WFE) is a shareware WWW server that has the unique ability to link to OLE 2.0 server applications. Although it is certainly no replacement for the Microsoft Internet Information Server or Netscape's Commerce Server, WFE can nicely augment any Web setup you have by giving access to OLE controls and applications.

We have included it on this CD-ROM to give you an idea of the kinds of ways you can integrate your database information and the World Wide Web. To install WFE, simply go to the `\Web Forms Express` directory on the CD and run `setup.exe`.

WFE *must* be run in either Windows 95 or Windows NT.◀

SQL-PROGRAMMER

SQL Programmer is a GUI administration tool for MS SQL Server. Although much of its functionality duplicates that of the SQL Enterprise Manager, some nice features make it worth looking at:

- SQL-Programmer will run in Windows 3.1. Because the SQL Enterprise Manager will not, this is a *big* plus.
- SQL-Programmer allows you to run reports on your objects. We found this to be very helpful, especially when it came time to document certain things.

To install SQL-Programmer, go to the `\sqlprog` and run `install.exe`.

You need to have both the `w3dblib.dll` and `dbnmp3.dll` files in your path. If you don't, you can find them on your SQL Server CD-ROM in `\client\win16`.◀